Criminal Law

Criminal Law

Katheryn Russell-Brown
University of Florida, Levin College of Law

Angela J. Davis
American University Washington College of Law

Los Angeles | London | New Delhi
Singapore | Washington DC | Boston

Los Angeles | London | New Delhi
Singapore | Washington DC | Boston

FOR INFORMATION:

SAGE Publications, Inc.
2455 Teller Road
Thousand Oaks, California 91320
E-mail: order@sagepub.com

SAGE Publications Ltd.
1 Oliver's Yard
55 City Road
London EC1Y 1SP
United Kingdom

SAGE Publications India Pvt. Ltd.
B 1/I 1 Mohan Cooperative Industrial Area
Mathura Road, New Delhi 110 044
India

SAGE Publications Asia-Pacific Pte. Ltd.
3 Church Street
#10-04 Samsung Hub
Singapore 049483

Printed in the United States of America

Cataloging-in-publication data is available for this title from the Library of Congress.

ISBN 978-1-4129-7789-0

Acquisitions Editor: Jerry Westby
Editorial Assistant: Laura Kirkhuff
Associate Editor: Jessica Miller
Associate Digital Content Editor: Nick Pachelli
Production Editor: Kelly DeRosa
Copy Editor: Renee Willers
Typesetter: C&M Digitals (P) Ltd.
Proofreader: Alison Syring
Indexer: Will Ragsdale
Cover Designer: Gail Buschman
Marketing Manager: Terra Schultz

This book is printed on acid-free paper.

SUSTAINABLE FORESTRY INITIATIVE
Certified Chain of Custody
Promoting Sustainable Forestry
www.sfiprogram.org
SFI-01268

SFI label applies to text stock

15 16 17 18 19 10 9 8 7 6 5 4 3 2 1

Brief Contents

Detailed Contents

©iStockphoto.com/uschools

Chapter 1: Introduction and Overview of Criminal Law   1

©iStockphoto.com/Merkuri2

Chapter 2: Constitutional Limitations on Criminal Laws   26

http:// commons.wikimedia.org/wiki/
File:John_Bryson_official_portrait.jpg

Chapter 3: The Elements of a Crime   52

Mitsu Yasukawa/The Star-Ledger

Chapter 4: Incomplete Crimes   76

Photo provided by Frank W. Abagnale and Associates

http://commons.wikimedia.org/wiki/File:Deface_Walls,_Loiter.jpg

REUTERS/Pat Little

Detroit News/PSG

Chapter 8: Criminal Homicide   188

©iStockphoto.com/jcenteno89

Chapter 9: Justification Defenses   218

Courtesy the Ronald Reagan Library

REUTERS/Chip East

Chapter 11: Punishment and Sentencing 270

Smallbones

Chapter 12: State-Involved Crimes 300

Preface

This textbook was born of need. A perusal of the existing criminal law textbooks establishes that each one is strong in its presentation and analysis of criminal law. However, few move beyond the law and decisions in court cases to delve into the sociological and criminological aspects of criminal law. As a consequence, most of these textbooks do not integrate issues of race, gender, and socioeconomic status with their discussion of criminal law. It is important and necessary to provide students with a real-world understanding of how the law works, its truth, and its consequences. Many students will go on to become lawyers or correctional officers or hold other careers within the justice system.

Each chapter includes four core elements. Each chapter begins with a discussion of a contemporary legal case or an excerpt from an article that addresses issues raised within the chapter. Second, each chapter includes a list of objectives. These objectives provide students with an introduction to the material that is covered in the chapter and highlights the information they should know by the conclusion of the chapter. Third, an Issue Spotter follows each chapter's detailed discussion of the substantive material. These are hypothetical cases, which in some instances are based on actual court cases. As already noted, the Issue Spotter gives students an opportunity to apply the legal rules and principles they learned about in the chapter. Fourth, the chapter concludes with a list of key words and cases that provide an end-of-the chapter review of the material. The list will also provide page cites so students may quickly locate the material.

Our plan from the beginning was to expose students studying criminal law to the laws, cases, data, and research that explain how criminal law and the justice system operate today. Our desire is that this book deepens not only students' understanding of criminal law, but also their interest in the workings of our system of criminal laws. We use the following four features to achieve this goal:

Chapter Organization

We were mindful as we organized the chapters to present the material in the order that cases proceed through the justice system. The introductory chapter and a discussion of the underlying constitutional issues are followed by a chapter on the elements of crime. We then present chapters on various crimes, followed by chapters on defenses to crimes. These chapters are followed by a look at the types of punishment and the rationales for sentencing. The final chapter addresses important issues and offenses not always covered in criminal law textbooks—crimes carried out against the state and crimes committed by state officials.

Use of Hypotheticals

We include a significant number of hypotheticals in the book. Our goal is to provide students with an opportunity to test their learning of case law and statutory law as they move through the book. The hypothetical scenarios are designed to illuminate and enhance student learning. They also serve as preparation for the Issue Spotters at the conclusion of each chapter.

Race, Gender, and Class Research

Throughout the text we incorporate a wide range of material that will aid student learning and broaden their understanding of criminal law. For instance, we include official criminal justice statistics, excerpts from law review articles, tables, charts, and photographs. Our objective is to contextualize criminal law within a sociological framework, with the goal of having students become familiar with how criminal law and the justice system impact the real world. To this end, we highlight cases and issues that involve race, gender, and socio-economic status.

Issue Spotters

We use exercises at the end of each chapter that provide students with an opportunity for a meaningful and comprehensive review of the chapter material. The Issue Spotters are hypothetical scenarios that are sometimes based on actual cases. The exercises require students to identify relevant legal issues posed by the scenarios and in some instances to take the perspective of a prosecutor, defense attorney, or legal researcher. The Issue Spotters offer a challenging and unique way for students to integrate the case material before moving onto the next chapter.

Acknowledgments

We express our deep gratitude for the work of SAGE Editor Jerry Westby, who is responsible for nurturing this project from a small seed to full bloom. He remained committed, excited, and constructively critical throughout. We also thank the associate editors we worked with at various points during the publication process—Jessica Miller, Terri Accomazzo, and Megan Kratti. We also appreciate the work of the copyeditor, Renee Willers.

Professor Russell-Brown extends thanks to the University of Florida, Levin College of Law, for its support of this project. The superb work of four University of Florida law students helped to shape and ground the research for this book: Warren Rhea, Christopher Shand, Sasha Lohn-McDermott, and Tiana Beaudouin. Professor Davis thanks Dean Claudio Grossman of American University Washington College of Law for his support. She also thanks Amber Bennett, Daniel Harawa, Dominic Jones, Joey Kavanagh, Erica McKinney, and LaNita McWilliams for their great research assistance.

We also thank the peer reviewers for their insights, recommendations, and wit:

Eric Bellone, Suffolk University

Richard Colangelo Jr., Norwalk Community College

Mark A. Jones, Palm Beach State College

Barry Langford, Columbia College

Robert W. Lockwood, Portland State University

Tim Robicheaux, The Pennsylvania State University

Vidisha Barua Worley, University of North Texas at Dallas

About the Authors

Katheryn Russell-Brown is the Chesterfield Smith Professor of Law and Director of the Center for the Study of Race and Race Relations at the University of Florida, Levin College of Law. Professor Russell-Brown received her undergraduate degree from the University of California, Berkeley; her law degree from the University of California, Hastings; and her PhD in criminology from the University of Maryland.

Prior to joining the University of Florida law faculty in 2003, Professor Russell-Brown taught Criminal Law in the Criminology & Criminal Justice department at the University of Maryland, College Park, for eleven years. She has been a visiting law professor at American University and the City University of New York (CUNY). She has been a lecturer at Howard University, and her first teaching position was at Alabama State University.

Professor Russell-Brown teaches, researches, and writes on issues of race and crime and the sociology of law. Her article, "The Constitutionality of Jury Override in Alabama Death Penalty Cases," was cited in the U.S. Supreme Court case, *Harris v. Alabama* (1995). In 2009, Professor Russell-Brown was awarded a Soros Justice Advocacy Fellowship. Her project focused on ways to integrate criminal justice issues into the elementary education curriculum.

Professor Russell-Brown's books include *The Color of Crime,* New York University Press (2009), *Protecting Our Own: Race, Crime and African Americans,* Rowman and Littlefield (2006), and *Underground Codes: Race, Crime, and Related Fires,* New York University Press (2004). She is also the author of a children's book, *Little Melba and Her Big Trombone,* Lee & Low (2014).

Angela J. Davis is a Professor of Law at the American University Washington College of Law where she teaches Criminal Law, Criminal Procedure, and Criminal Defense: Theory and Practice. Professor Davis has been a Visiting Professor at George Washington University Law School and Georgetown University Law Center. She has served on the adjunct faculty at George Washington, Georgetown, and Harvard Law Schools. Professor Davis is the author of *Arbitrary Justice: The Power of the American Prosecutor* (Oxford University Press, 2007), the coeditor of *Trial Stories* (with Professor Michael E. Tigar) (Foundation Press, 2007), and a coauthor of the sixth edition of *Basic Criminal Procedure* (with Professors Stephen Saltzburg and Daniel Capra; Thomson West 2012). Professor Davis' other publications include articles and book chapters on prosecutorial discretion and racism in the criminal justice system.

Professor Davis received the American University Faculty Award for Outstanding Teaching in a Full-Time Appointment in 2002, the American University Faculty Award for Outstanding Scholarship in 2009, and the Washington College of Law's Pauline Ruyle Moore award for scholarly contribution in the area of public law in 2000 and 2009. Professor Davis' book *Arbitrary Justice* won the Association of American Publishers 2007 Professional and Scholarly Publishing Division Award for Excellence in the Law and Legal Studies Division. She was awarded a Soros Senior Justice Fellowship in 2004. Professor Davis is a graduate of Howard University and Harvard Law School. She serves on the Board of Trustees of the Sentencing Project and the Southern Center for Human Rights. Professor Davis served as the Executive Director of the National Rainbow Coalition from 1994 to 1995. From 1991 to 1994, she was the Director of the Public Defender Service for the District of Columbia (PDS). She also served as the Deputy Director from 1988 to 1991 and as a staff attorney at PDS from 1982 to 1988, representing indigent juveniles and adults charged with crimes. Professor Davis is a former law clerk of the Honorable Theodore R. Newman of the District of Columbia Court of Appeals.

SAGE was founded in 1965 by Sara Miller McCune to support the dissemination of usable knowledge by publishing innovative and high-quality research and teaching content. Today, we publish more than 750 journals, including those of more than 300 learned societies, more than 800 new books per year, and a growing range of library products including archives, data, case studies, reports, conference highlights, and video. SAGE remains majority-owned by our founder, and after Sara's lifetime will become owned by a charitable trust that secures our continued independence.

Los Angeles | London | Washington DC | New Delhi | Singapore | Boston

Chapter 1

Whatever views one holds about the penal law, no one will question its importance in society. This is the law on which men place their ultimate reliance for protection against all the deepest injuries human conduct can inflict on individuals and institutions. By the same token, penal law governs the strongest force that we permit official agencies to bring to bear on individuals. Its promise as an instrument of safety is matched only by its power to destroy. If penal law is weak or ineffective, basic human interests are in jeopardy. If it is harsh or arbitrary in its impact, it works a gross injustice on those caught within its toils. The law that carries such responsibilities should surely be as rational and just as law can be. Nowhere in the entire legal field is more at stake for the community or for the individual.

Herbert Wechsler *"The Challenge of a Model Penal Code"* (1952)

The above comment paints a dynamic picture of our system of criminal laws in the United States. We each play a role: as victims, as offenders, as jury members, as voters, as responsible neighbors when we report crime, and as concerned community members when we protest criminal laws we believe to be unfair. Acknowledging the complexity and importance of our system of criminal laws is an ideal starting point for this first chapter. This chapter reviews definitions of crime, the sources of criminal law, and the organization of the justice system. By establishing a clear framework for understanding the criminal justice system, this discussion sets the stage for the remaining chapters. This book examines the constitutional limits on defining criminal activity, the elements of a crime, the elements of specific offenses (including incomplete crimes, property crimes, public order crimes, homicide, rape, and state-involved crimes), defenses to crimes, punishment, and sentencing.

Authority of Law statue at right entrance to the U.S. Supreme Court building in Washington, DC.

Introduction and Overview of Criminal Law

Learning Objectives

After reading and studying this chapter, you should be able to

➤ Discuss the difference between criminal and moral wrongdoing

➤ Understand the distinction between *mala in se* and *mala prohibita* offenses

➤ List three sources of criminal law

➤ Explain the differences between common law and statutory law

➤ List two goals of the Model Penal Code

➤ Differentiate between a crime and a tort

➤ Know the distinction between federal and state legislation

➤ State the four types of correctional supervision

➤ Identify the elements of a case brief

Introduction

This chapter provides an overview of the structure and processes of the American criminal justice system. This material is divided into five sections. Part 1 reviews a broad range of foundational issues related to criminal law. It introduces and explains the important concepts, terms, and definitions of criminal law. Part 2 reviews the sources of American criminal law. Our criminal law comes from a wide range of sources, from timeworn common law to modern legislation. Part 3 examines who is in the criminal justice system and looks at the number of people who are in the U.S. correctional system. Part 4 reviews the three-part structure of the criminal justice system, police, courts, and corrections. This section reviews the main decision points along the criminal justice system continuum—from arrest to arraignment to trial to sentencing and punishment. It also includes an overview of the federal and state court systems that handle criminal cases. The final part examines how all the structures of the justice system come together in a court case. It concludes with a detailed discussion on the elements of a case brief.

This first chapter should be used as a reference guide for the remaining chapters. The foundational terms, concepts, procedures, and structures related to criminal law are all included here. Students are encouraged to review this material as necessary.

Criminal Law Terms and Concepts ●———————————

Approximately one-half of all violent crime is not reported to the police.

Bureau of Justice Statistics, 2012[1]

Defining Crime

A criminal act may be the result of an affirmative act or a negative act. An affirmative act refers to an action that someone engages in, such as punching another person in the nose. Purchasing a penknife to puncture someone's tires or hacking into someone's computer would also constitute an affirmative act.

In contrast, a negative act refers to *in*action, or to an action that someone fails to take. In general, a person cannot be held criminally liable for failing to act. However, if a person has a legal duty to act, they can be held responsible for a failure to meet that responsibility. For example, parents have a legal duty to provide for the health, safety, and welfare of their children. If a father does not provide food for his children while they are in his care and they starve to death, he may be held criminally liable for their deaths. Likewise, a motorist who is involved in a traffic accident that causes injury to his passenger has a legal duty to call the police. If a driver hits a pedestrian walking across the street, the driver is required to stop and seek assistance. If she fails to do so, she may face punishment. In addition to an act or a failure to act, a crime requires that the action or inaction violate an existing law. Based on this discussion we can now consider a working definition of crime:

> An act or omission punishable by the state or federal government through the enforcement of its criminal law.

The definition of crime and the definition of wrongdoing are not the same. "Crimes" refer to actions and inactions that society deems both wrong *and* punishable. Thus, an act is only a crime if the law says it is. We might consider a particular action to be wrong: a teacher who does not grade fairly; a girlfriend who is unfaithful; or neighbors who do not mow their lawn. However wrong these actions may be, they are not crimes. An action constitutes a crime only if a legislative body—for example, a municipality, a state legislature, or Congress—has passed a law stating that it is a crime. Even after an act is defined as criminal, in order for it to be punishable, it must be brought to the attention of law enforcement.

Each year, U.S. law enforcement agencies receive millions of crime reports. As noted at the beginning of this section, more than one-half of all offenses are never reported to crime enforcement agencies. Legally speaking, these offenses do not exist. Unreported incidents are sometimes referred to as the "dark figure" of crime. There are many reasons that crime victims and witnesses may be reluctant to report crimes. One is fear of retaliation by the offender. Another is that the victim may be unaware that he has been the victim of a crime—for instance if he does not know that his checks or valuables were stolen from his home. It is also possible that a victim may be too embarrassed to go to the police to report a crime. An example of this is a person who fell prey to a Ponzi scheme and lost her retirement savings.

Crime and Morality

Making certain actions criminal reflects a value judgment by our society that an action or series of actions are wrong and should be punished. However, sometimes there is a gap between what is wrong and what is punished under the law. Consider the following scenario, drawn from a classic law school hypothetical:

> Janet is an excellent swimmer. She is enjoying winter break from college at the beach, soaking up some sun. She is reading her favorite blogs, updating her Facebook page, and painting her nails.
>
> As Janet basks in the sun, she sees Ambrosia who appears to be about three years old. Janet is playing in the water, approximately twenty-five feet from Janet. Janet does not see anyone else on the beach besides Ambrosia.
>
> Janet notices that Ambrosia is gasping for air. Ambrosia screams, "Help!" Janet watches. Janet does not want to get her hair or nails wet so she makes no attempt to rescue the sinking toddler. With a little effort, Janet could have saved Ambrosia. Instead, Janet uses her smartphone to take notes! She records how many times Ambrosia's head bobs up and down, how many times she yells for help, and her final gasp for air. Ambrosia drowns.

Is Janet criminally responsible for Ambrosia's death? Applying the definition of "crime," is there an affirmative act or an omission? In this instance, Janet failed to act to save Ambrosia. Should the law *require* people to act in some circumstances? Many of us would agree that Janet's failure to at least attempt to save Ambrosia is morally wrong. However, the law does not punish every moral wrong. In order to hold Janet criminally accountable for Ambrosia's death, she must have a legal duty to act. For instance, if Janet had been Ambrosia's babysitter, she would have had an affirmative duty to assist a child left in her care. The above scenario highlights the fact that in some instances an action that is considered wrong may not be considered criminal. Figure 1.1 below illustrates the relationship between criminal wrongs and moral wrongs.

Figure 1.1 Relationship Between Criminal and Moral Wrongs

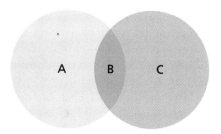

As indicated, there are three possible relationships between moral wrongs and criminal wrongs. In some instances, there is no intersection between actions that are deemed morally wrong and actions that are deemed criminally wrong. For instance, actions such as rudeness or greed can be considered moral wrongs but are not against the law. These are represented as the section "A" in Figure 1.1. In some instances, there is overlap between moral wrongs and criminal wrongs. The dark shaded section of the chart labeled "B" represents this overlap. In these instances, the criminal law is a reflection of society's moral sentiments. Some criminal wrongs are not moral wrongs. Examples of this include *mala prohibita* offenses. This is represented as section "C" on the chart.

Let's look more closely at these distinctions. The differences between these groups of wrongs may be understood by considering the distinction between mala in se offenses and mala prohibita offenses. Offenses that society considers to be inherently wrong and morally unacceptable are known as mala in se crimes. Mala in se, a Latin phrase, refers to crimes such as murder, rape, and theft. These contrast with mala prohibita offenses, which are actions that are considered wrong because they violate the law, not because they are morally wrong. Examples of mala prohibita offenses include laws that require automobile drivers to wear seat belts, laws that impose seasonal restrictions, such as months and time of day that one can hunt deer, and laws that prohibit carrying a concealed weapon. Figure 1.2 lists examples of mala in se and mala prohibita offenses.

Figure 1.2 Mala In Se Versus Mala Prohibita Offenses

Mala In Se	Mala Prohibita
• Theft	• Hunting restrictions
• Murder	• Seat belt laws
• Kidnapping	• Building without a permit
• Arson	• Littering
• Mayhem	• Prohibited alcohol purchases
• Rape	• Draft evasion

"Victimless" Crimes

There is another group of actions that does not fall neatly into either mala in se or mala prohibita categories. These are sometimes referred to as "victimless" crimes. One example is adultery, which many people view as morally objectionable. Some people believe it is wrong for a married person to have sexual relations with a person other than his spouse. However, in the majority of states, adultery is no longer unlawful. In centuries past, adultery was a felony—an offense that could result in not only a lifetime of community shame for the adulterer, but also jail, exile, and sometimes death. The view of adultery as a felonious act is symbolized by Hester Prynne, the protagonist in Nathanial Hawthorne's book, *The Scarlet Letter*. Following an adulterous affair, Prynne was forced to wear a red "A" on her clothing as a mark of her indiscretion. Today, a handful of states have laws against adultery. For instance, in Minnesota it is a misdemeanor for a married woman to have sexual intercourse with a man other than her husband.[2] (See Chapter 6 for further discussion of offenses against public decency.)

The issues of victimless crime, morality, and definitions of crime overlap. The following three scenarios explore these intersections in more detail:

- Yago is a twenty-one-year-old college junior. Before each of his midterm exams and final exams, he smokes three marijuana cigarettes to relax. He buys the drugs from another student in his dormitory on campus. Yago is a straight "A" student.

- Millicent is a college professor. She teaches large introductory courses at a top-ten community college. She has a ritual for the first day of each semester—she smokes crystal methamphetamine. The drug makes her feel upbeat, and she always gives a great first lecture.
- Anthony is a twenty-four-year-old student. Anthony attended college for one year but had to drop out because he could not afford the tuition. To make money, he works as a prostitute. His clients, whom he meets on the street or through referrals, pay to have sex with him. Anthony hates sex work but is doing it until he saves enough money to return to school.

Some legal commentators argue that each of the above instances involves a "victimless" crime. According to this view, if all the people involved are consenting adults, then there is no crime and no victim. In these instances, one's private actions should not subject to governmental scrutiny or regulation. Law professors Norval Morris and Gordon Hawkins strongly support this viewpoint:

> When the criminal law invades the spheres of private morality and social welfare, it exceeds its proper limits at the cost of neglecting its primary tasks. This unwarranted extension is expensive, ineffective, and criminogenic . . . [M]an has an inalienable right to go to hell in his own fashion . . . The criminal law is an inefficient instrument for imposing the good life on others.[3]

By this logic, Yago, Millilcent, and Anthony may be involved in morally questionable activity. However, because it is by choice, because they are adults, and because they are not forcing their behavior on anyone else, there should be no criminal sanction. In fact, each one of them has chosen to engage in the criminal activity to achieve a greater personal good. Those opposed to punishing actions like the ones described in the above scenarios, argue that when the law reaches too far into the personal lives of citizens, it loses its legitimacy and its likelihood of deterring crime. Enforcement, as Morris and Hawkins argue, is a waste of taxpayer dollars and encourages underground markets to develop. By this rationale, the violence associated with drug trafficking would end if marijuana, heroin, and cocaine were made legal. Further, social service agencies, not the criminal justice system, are best able to handle issues of drug addiction, mental illness, and structural unemployment.

There are legal commentators who reject the idea of victimless crime. They argue that whenever people are engaged in antisocial behavior, there is a victim, regardless of consent. Whether the activity takes place in public or private, there is a social cost when people engage in illicit activity. Dallin Oaks, the former president of Brigham Young University, argues that it is not always possible to identify the victims:

> In some so-called victimless crimes, all society is the victim . . . one person cannot rationally contend that what he does to or with himself is of no concern to anyone but himself. Each person steers his ship of life through a very narrow passage. The wreckage of one person in that passage becomes a serious navigational hazard for many others.[4]

In the case of Yago, his illegal use of marijuana is the end point of a violent underground international drug market enterprise. For Millicent, using crystal methamphetamine could cause her to have an accident while driving, lead to addiction, or bring about other negative consequences that could impact her family, friends, employers, or strangers. Anthony's prostitution involves a range of potential harms, including rape, assault, and the spread of sexually-transmitted diseases. Drug use, addiction, and sexually-transmitted diseases place enormous burdens on social service agencies. Oaks and others observe that individual choices have social and economic consequences and should be subject to public regulation and criminal sanction.

The punishments for many victimless crimes remain controversial, particularly for offenses involving low-level drug possession. Research indicates that harsh punishments for nonviolent crimes have detrimental social costs (see Jeremy Travis's essay, "Invisible Punishments," in Chapter 11). The criminal law's changing response to these questions reflects a shift in social attitudes and resource allocation within the justice system.

This section has addressed how crime is defined and how it is distinct from moral wrongdoing. The next section examines the sources of American criminal law. As discussed, criminal law is drawn from a wide range of sources, including the U.S. Constitution, common law, and federal, state, and local legislation.

Sources of Criminal Law ●━━━━━━━━━━━━━━━━

American criminal law is drawn from a broad range of historical and contemporary sources. These sources include English common law created by judges, the U.S. Constitution, administrative regulations, executive orders, and federal, state, and municipal legislation. This broad foundation highlights the fact that American criminal law comes from each of the three branches of government—legislative, judicial, and executive. This section provides an overview of the origins of criminal law and how each source links to today's criminal justice system.

Common Law

The common law refers to the legal rules applied by English judges in the absence of written laws. Judges imposed laws that reflected the customs and moral codes of the community. By the turn of the seventeenth century, English judges drew heavily from the common law. When North American colonizers brought common law with them from England in the 1600s, there was a solid body of common law in what became the United States. Common law is sometimes referred to as "judge-made" law because a judge, rather than a legislative body, makes the law. When judges were presented with cases involving harm that had no existing legal remedy, they had to determine what law should apply in a particular case. *Commonwealth v. Mochan* (1955)[5] offers a recent example of judge-made law.

In this 1955 Pennsylvania case, the defendant was charged and convicted of "immoral practices and conduct." During a one-month period, Mochan telephoned the victim numerous times and referred to her as lewd and immoral. He used obscene language to describe sex acts he would commit against the victim, a married woman. At trial, the defendant argued that he could not be convicted of a crime because there was no written or common law rule that outlawed his actions. The court disagreed and stated that the common law can be used to punish acts that directly harm the public. The court determined that Mochan's actions had injured public morality and could be punished as a misdemeanor offense.

Today most states have abolished common law crimes and replaced them with statutory crimes that have been enacted by state legislatures. There are several reasons for this. First is the constitutional prohibition against ex-post facto laws. A person cannot be charged with violating a law that did not exist at the time of his actions, an issue raised by the defendant in the *Mochan* case (see further discussion of this case, later in the chapter). A second reason for is that the common law does not promote uniform laws across the states. Judge-made laws may be responsive to local community beliefs, but they do not necessarily reflect national attitudes or broad public consensus. Further, under a common law system, legal outcomes are less predictable as different judges in different counties and states reach different legal conclusions. However, as noted, a handful of states still recognize common law crimes. For instance, the Maryland state courts have consistently held that some common law crimes (such as indecent exposure) are punishable as common law offenses.

Federal Legislation

The federal government operates with its own body of rules, separate from those of individual states. Whether an offense is a federal violation depends upon several factors, such as the location of the offense (whether it was on federal property) and the status of the victim and offender (whether the victim or offender is a federal employee). The U.S. Capitol building in Washington, DC, sits on federal property, and offenses that take place on its grounds, including its airspace, can trigger federal law. Federal legislation applies to federal employees, federal property, and federal lands. Approximately one-third of U.S. lands, which total more than 650 million acres, is owned by the federal government. This includes national parks, forests, wildlife refuges, military facilities, and American Indian reservations. Punishment may be greater for crimes that take place on federal property.

State Legislation

Each state and the District of Columbia has a criminal code. State legislation passed by state legislative bodies identifies various crimes, punishments, and procedures for handling unlawful actions that take place within a state's jurisdiction. Most criminal cases are prosecuted under state laws. Most of the criminal cases that make nightly news headlines involve a violation of state law.

Consider the following scenario:

> Jewell steals Anjuane's prized copy of Harper Lee's book *To Kill a Mockingbird*. Jewell removes the valuable book from Anjuane's library while visiting her home. It is a first edition copy, signed by the author and is valued at $20,000. Both Jewell and Anjuane live in Florida.

Under Florida law, a person can be convicted of grand theft if she intentionally and unlawfully takes another person's property to prevent her from using it or takes it for her own personal use. Under the law, it is second degree grand theft if the stolen property is worth between $20,000 and $100,000.[6] If the state is able to prove each element of the crime, Jewell can be found guilty of grand theft and will face up to fifteen years in prison. In addition to the value of the stolen property, the location of the crime matters. For instance, if Jewell had stolen the book from the Library of Congress, which sits on federal property, she would have been charged under a federal theft statute (and faced harsher punishment).

Municipal Ordinances

All municipalities, including towns, cities, counties, and boroughs, are empowered to enact laws that punish low-level, non-felony offenses. Municipal ordinances cover a broad range of actions that protect the general welfare and maintain public health and safety. For instance, zoning and building regulations detail land use restrictions, while fire and safety ordinances outline the rules for commercial and residential properties. Other examples include ordinances that impose leash laws and regulate parking and snow removal.

In some cases, municipal ordinances regulate city services to reduce costs and ensure public access. For instance, in Anchorage, Alaska, residents may be fined for making excessive calls to the police. If the police are called to a home more than eight times in one year, the property owner may face a maximum fine of $500.[7] City ordinances may also regulate the actions of residents. A Los Angeles ordinance, for example, restricts the use of gas-powered leaf blowers. It is unlawful to use them within five hundred feet of a residence. This ordinance was enacted to address environmental concerns that leaf blowers increase the presence of airborne particles, which could cause problems for people with upper respiratory ailments. A one hundred dollar fine may be imposed for violation of the ordinance.[8] When a state law and a municipal ordinance punish the same offense, the state law is the final authority.

Executive Orders

The executive order is a type of federal law that can only be enacted by a sitting U.S. president. Executive orders require neither the consent of Congress nor a vote by the people. In some instances, executive orders are largely symbolic and do not alter the status quo. In other cases, executive orders reflect a president's attempt to make or change the law. Some commentators argue that executive orders violate the separation of powers doctrine because they allow the executive branch to carry out legislative functions. The U.S. Congress may overturn an executive order by a two-thirds vote. A president may reverse the executive orders of former presidents.

In 1789, President George Washington issued the first executive order. It was a proclamation to recognize the first national day of Thanksgiving. In 1863, President Abraham Lincoln signed the Emancipation Proclamation. This executive order initiated freedom for Black slaves in select territories. Another significant executive order is the one signed by President Franklin Roosevelt, following Japan's 1941 attack on Pearl Harbor, Hawaii. More than two thousand people died in the air assault. In 1942, Roosevelt's response was to issue an executive order that authorized the internment of Japanese American citizens and Japanese citizens:

> . . . I hereby authorize and direct the Secretary of War, and the Military Commanders . . . to prescribe military areas in such places and of such extent as he or the appropriate Military Commander may determine, from which any or all persons may be excluded, and with respect to which, the right of any persons to enter, remain in, or leave shall be subject to

whatever restriction the Secretary of War or the appropriate Military Commander may impose in his discretion.[9]

This executive action mandated the removal of more than one hundred thousand Japanese American citizens and Japanese nationals to internment camps across America's West Coast, including California, Oregon, and Washington. The language of the presidential order did not explicitly reference race.

However, it was clear which racial groups were subject to removal. For instance, the above flyer provides "Instructions to All Persons of Japanese Ancestry," which includes "all Japanese persons, both alien and national." Executive Order 9066 was upheld by the U.S. Supreme Court in *Korematsu v. United States* (1944).[10] An executive order was also used to arrest and intern some Italian and German residents.

U.S. presidents continue to utilize the executive order. In 2012, President Barack Obama signed an executive order to impose sanctions against Iran. The order punishes individuals or companies that help the Iranian government develop or transport oil. More than eleven thousand executive orders have been signed into law by U.S. presidents (President Roosevelt leads the list with over 3,500). Governors also have the authority to pass executive orders at the state level.

World War II U.S. Army poster detailing evacuation and interment orders for people of Japanese ancestry.

Collection of Oakland Museum of California.

Federal and State Constitutions

The U.S. Constitution and each of the fifty state constitutions are also sources of criminal law. The federal Constitution outlines the foundational protections and guarantees of American criminal law. It references a few specific criminal offenses, including treason, bribery, breach of the peace, and "other high crimes and misdemeanors." Treason is the only explicit crime defined within the U.S. Constitution (see Chapter 12 for a detailed discussion of treason). The Bill of Rights place boundaries on the actions that state legislatures may criminalize (see Chapter 2). In contrast to the U.S. Constitution, state constitutions detail criminal offenses, underscore constitutional rights guaranteed by the federal constitution, and add additional protections. For instance some state constitutions include specific language to protect citizens' "right of privacy."

Treaties and Other International Conventions

In some instances, agreements between nations provide for criminal sanctions if the contract is broken. Countries sometimes enter into two-way treaties to reach an agreement on how they will handle potential criminal matters. Mutual legal assistance treaties (MLATs) offer an example. The United States has MLAT treaties with different countries, including Argentina, the Bahamas, Canada, Italy, the Netherlands, Panama, South Korea, Switzerland, Thailand, and Turkey. Countries may also agree to have particular kinds of disputes resolved by an international court. These disagreements may be resolved by courts such as the International Court of Justice (ICJ) and the International Criminal Court (ICC). The ICJ, the judicial arm of the United Nations, hears cases and writes advisory opinions. The ICC is designed to identify and punish war crimes, genocide, and crimes against humanity. The United States is a party to the ICJ but is not a party to the treaty that established the ICC.

In *Bond v. United States* (2014),[11] the U.S. Supreme Court was asked to determine whether an international treaty can apply to domestic actions. The case involved Carol Anne Bond, who learned that her best friend had become pregnant by her husband. In response, Bond smeared lethal chemicals on several surfaces, including the pregnant woman's mailbox, car, and doorknob. Bond was convicted of violating the Chemical Weapons Convention and sentenced to six years behind bars. The convention prohibits the use of chemical weapons. On appeal to the Supreme Court, Bond challenged her sentence and argued that her crime was an "ordinary" poisoning case and should be handled by state law. The Court held unanimously that the federal law did not apply to Bond's crime. Chief Justice John Roberts noted that the law that she was charged with violating focused on acts of war and terrorism, not simple assaults.

Administrative Regulations

Federal agencies are authorized by Congress to regulate a wide range of activities. These agencies adopt administrative regulations, which have the same force as statutory law. Some federal agencies, such as the Environmental Protection Agency (EPA), have regulations that impose criminal sanctions for regulatory violations. For instance, under the Clean Air Act, the owner of a construction company who is found guilty of unlawful asbestos removal could receive a prison term for violating EPA regulations. Other agencies with administrative regulations and criminal sanctions include the Equal Employment Opportunity Commission (EEOC), the Occupational Safety and Health Administration (OSHA), and the Food and Drug Administration (FDA).

Model Penal Code

In 1962, the American Law Institute (ALI) published the Model Penal Code (MPC). ALI members—judges, lawyers, and legal scholars—gathered to fix the widespread inconsistencies and disproportionate sanctions in state criminal laws. The Illinois state code that was in effect in 1961 provides an example of this problem. Different sections of the Illinois code listed different punishments for the same offenses. For instance, while one section stated there was a $200 fine for "contributing to delinquency," another imposed a $1,000 fine for the same offense. An example of disproportionate sentencing under the code was the punishment for stealing a horse. The minimum punishment for stealing a horse was three years in prison, while the minimum punishment for stealing a car was one year. Such widespread variations in punishment were problematic since they could result in unfair punishment and undercut public faith in the judicial system.

Criminal law in the United States is codified in fifty-two criminal codes. This includes the federal criminal code, the fifty state codes, and the criminal code of the District of Columbia. The MPC provides state legislatures with a template for drafting their criminal laws. Following the initial publication of the MPC, most states revised their criminal codes. This overhaul of state criminal laws led to greater uniformity across the states. Today the MPC continues to have a significant effect on the drafting and interpretation of criminal law by American courts. Additionally, judges frequently cite sections of the MPC in their judicial opinions. This is particularly notable given that the MPC is not legally binding on states. While non-binding, it has been suggested that the MPC comes close to operating as an American criminal code.[12]

As this discussion makes clear, the origins of U.S. criminal law are broad. In some instances, an individual may be responsible for deciding and making the law in a particular case. Common law and executive orders are examples of lawmaking by individuals. In other instances, groups of people write and adopt criminal laws. The U.S. Constitution and the fifty state constitutions are examples of lawmaking by groups. Laws passed by federal, state, and local legislatures are another example. Finally, in the case of treaties, countries voluntarily unite to establish rules for resolving conflicts.

Classifications, Distinctions, and Limitations in Criminal Law

Felony Versus Misdemeanor

In the hierarchy of crimes, a felony offense is more serious than a misdemeanor offense. A felony conviction may subject an offender to more than one year behind bars. A felony conviction may also result in a fine. Additional sanctions may attach to a felony conviction, such as disenfranchisement—loss of the right to vote (see Chapter 11 for a more detailed discussion of punishment). A person who is charged with a felony is entitled to a jury trial. A misdemeanor conviction may result in a jail sentence of up to one year or a fine. For a misdemeanor charge, a jury trial is only guaranteed if the punishment would result in more than six months behind bars. Both the federal and state systems distinguish between felonies and misdemeanors. Many state statutes also include a third tier of criminal offending, known as infractions. Infractions are petty offenses that are subject to fines but do not result in jail time. Examples include littering, jaywalking, and disturbing the peace.

Crime Versus Tort

A criminal action differs from a tort action. A tort is a civil action. Civil actions are brought in civil courts, which hear noncriminal cases. Examples of civil actions include a homeowner suing a construction company for failure to complete the work on a house, a driver filing a lawsuit against the owner of a vehicle who ran a red light and crashed into his car, and a patient suing a surgeon after she discovers that a surgical sponge was not removed from her abdomen following a medical procedure.

There are three key distinctions between a crime and a tort. First, the goal of a criminal case is to get a conviction and impose a sentence against the offender. However, with a tort action, the goal is to force someone to pay money damages for causing harm. Second, in a criminal action, the party who brings the case to court is a municipality, state, or the federal government. In a civil action, the suit is brought by an individual person, groups of individuals, or by the government. Third, the burden of proof is higher in a criminal case than in a civil action. In a criminal case, the prosecution is required to prove its case "beyond a reasonable doubt." By comparison, the burden of proof for the plaintiff in a civil case is by a "preponderance of the evidence." It is much harder to find someone liable in a criminal case because the defendant may face incarceration, a loss of physical freedom, or even death. These are not risks typically faced by a defendant in a civil action.

In some instances, a single incident can result in both criminal and civil charges. For example, in 1995 O.J. Simpson was tried and acquitted of two counts of murder. The following year, in a separate action (in a different court, with a different judge, and jury), he was sued by the parents of one of the murder victims. Simpson was found liable for wrongful death and a civil judgment was entered against him for thirty-three million dollars. As noted above, the burden of proof in a criminal case is much higher (beyond a reasonable doubt) than the one in a civil case (by a preponderance of the evidence). As noted, it is easier to find someone guilty in a civil action than in a criminal one.

The September 11, 2001, terrorist attacks are another example of how criminal and civil actions may arise from a single incident. Criminal charges were filed against members of Al Qaeda who were suspected of planning the strikes. Numerous civil actions were filed as result of the September 11 attacks. For instance, victims' family members filed tort claims against various corporations and agencies, including United Airlines and New York's Port Authority for pain and suffering, economic loss, and medical costs. Also, in 2010, thousands of Ground Zero rescue and maintenance workers reached a $675.5 million settlement against New York City for health-related injuries.

Capital Offenses Versus Non-Capital Offenses

Some offenses are considered so horrible that they may be punished by state-sanctioned death. These are capital offenses. The term "capital" refers to a method of execution practiced centuries ago—the severing of one's head with the guillotine. A capital offense is a type of aggravated murder. Examples of crimes that may trigger a death sentence include killing an on-duty law enforcement officer, killing two or more people, killing someone during a burglary, or killing someone for pecuniary gain. Capital cases are rare. Less than 1 percent of all homicide cases are charged as death penalty cases. Thirty-two states, the U.S. military, and the federal government permit the death penalty for the society's most heinous crimes. In 2013, there were approximately 3,100 people on death row in the United States. For more detailed discussions of capital punishment, see Chapters 8 and 11.

Ex-Post Facto Laws

Article 1 of the U.S. Constitution prohibits ex-post facto laws. Ex-post facto laws punish conduct that was *not* unlawful at the time the "crime" was committed. Written laws give us notice that certain actions violate the law. In fact, the Constitution requires that our laws be made public, not kept secret. Accordingly, a person can only be punished for actions that were criminal *prior* to the time of his action. Imagine the harm that would occur if people faced criminal punishment for actions that were not known to be criminal at the time of their actions. It would make deterrence—one of the stated purposes of punishment (see Chapter 11)—impossible to achieve. We cannot deter people from committing crimes that are nonexistent. We would question the law's fairness if someone could be charged with wrongdoing when she had no reasonable way of knowing her actions were against the law. Further, studies show that people are less likely to respect and obey the law if they think it is arbitrary and unfair.

To determine whether a law is ex-post facto, the courts examine two factors. First, they consider whether the law is retrospective (applies to events that occurred before its enactment) and second, whether it would disadvantage the offender. The U.S. Supreme Court's decision in *Lynce v. Mathis* (1977)[13] offers a case discussion of ex-post facto laws. In 1986, Kenneth Lynce was convicted of attempted murder and sentenced to twenty-two years in prison. While serving time, he earned credit for good behavior, which reduced his sentence. Beginning in 1982, in response to the problem of overcrowded prisons, Florida passed legislation that allowed some prisoners to receive an early release. In 1992, Lynce, who had accumulated good time credits, was released from prison. However, later that year, Florida decided to cancel the early release credit system. Lynce was rearrested and returned to prison. The Supreme Court held that Florida could not cancel early release credits for prisoners. They agreed with Lynce's argument that the new law violated the ex-post facto clause of the U.S. Constitution.[14]

This section reviews and discusses key material about the criminal justice system. Keep this discussion in mind as we continue to develop the framework for understanding the detailed working of the justice system. The next part of this chapter examines the people *in* the justice system—those under its control. This is followed by an outline of the key stages of the justice system.

Crime and People in the Criminal Justice System ●━━━━━━━━━━

In 2012, U.S. law enforcement officers made over twelve million arrests. Less than 5 percent were for violent crimes, such as murder, rape, robbery, and aggravated assault. Approximately 12 percent were for property offenses, such as burglary, theft, and arson. The overwhelming majority of arrests were made for low-level, nonviolent crimes.

As Figure 1.3 indicates, there are millions of people in the American correctional system. There are four ways someone can be under the supervision of the criminal justice system. Correctional supervision includes prison, jail, probation, and parole. In 2012, the Department of Justice estimated that there were approximately seven million people under correctional supervision in the United States. The majority were on probation (57 percent), followed by those serving prison sentences (21 percent), those on parole (12 percent), and those in jail (11 percent).[15]

Department of Justice statistics show that one of every thirty-three adults is in the correctional system. The millions of people tethered to the justice system result in a huge societal cost. The Vera Institute estimates that it costs American taxpayers approximately $31,286 per year to incarcerate one person.[16] A look at the racial breakdown of those in state and federal prisons show some noteworthy racial trends. More than 38 percent of the people incarcerated in the United States are African Americans. Whites make up approximately 34 percent of the incarcerated population, and Hispanics constitute over 20 percent. The next section examines the of the criminal justice system process—from arrest to sentencing—and an overview of the court system.

Figure 1.3 U.S. Total Population in Prison, Jail, Probation, Parole, 2012

Prison	1,571,013
Jail	744,524
Probation	3,942,800
Parole	851,200
Total	7,109,537

Source: Department of Justice

Notes: "Prisoners in 2012" DOJ, Dec. 2011; "Jail Inmates at Midyear 2012-Statistical Tables" DOJ May 2013; and "Correctional Population in the United States, 2012" DOJ Dec. 2013.

The Structure of the Criminal Justice System

The Criminal Justice System Process

http://www.cartoonstock.com/cartoonview.asp?catref=dcrn983

The American criminal justice system is both mammoth and complex. It is made up of three main parts: police, courts, and corrections (Figure 1.4). As the cartoon illustrates, people who enter the justice system face a daunting legal maze. An attorney is an important "user's guide" and can help an alleged or convicted offender navigate his way through the system—from criminal charges to post conviction. A person who has been charged with a crime is typically represented by either a private attorney or a public defender. In *Gideon v. Wainwright* (1963),[17] the Supreme Court held that the state must provide legal counsel to criminal defendants who cannot afford to hire their own attorneys. This section provides a structural overview for understanding the justice system. First, there is a discussion of the main parts of the justice system. Second, there is a discussion of how to prepare a case brief. Given that case law is the central focus of this material, we will also look at the organization of the American court system.

Figure 1.4 **Police, Courts, and Corrections**

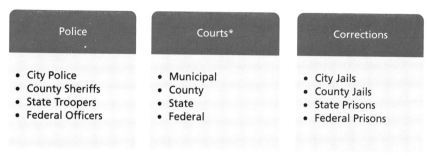

Police	Courts*	Corrections
• City Police • County Sheriffs • State Troopers • Federal Officers	• Municipal • County • State • Federal	• City Jails • County Jails • State Prisons • Federal Prisons

* For more detail, see Figure 1.5 on pages 16-17.

The criminal justice system typically begins with an arrest by a police officer (in some cases it begins with a grand jury investigation). The next part is the court system, which is followed by the corrections system. Each year, the number of reported crimes is much larger than the number of arrests. Further, the number of arrests is much larger than the number of cases that end in criminal punishment. This explains why the criminal justice system is commonly referred to as a funnel. Figure 1.5 is a streamlined snapshot of the key components of the criminal justice system process.

Arrest

The arrest of a suspected offender signals the starting point of the criminal justice system. Depending upon the location of the offense, an arrest may be made by local, state, or federal law enforcement officials. In some instances, there may be what is called a "citizen's arrest." When a non-law enforcement officer witnesses a crime, she may detain the suspect until a law enforcement officer arrives on the scene.

Formal Charging Process

At this stage, an alleged offender is officially charged with violating a specific section or sections of the criminal code under local, state, or federal law. The criminal charge is sometimes referred to as an "information," a formal criminal charge brought by the prosecutor. If the charge is a felony, it may also come in the form of a grand jury indictment, which is a criminal charge brought by a special jury.

Arraignment

After a person is charged with a specific crime, he is taken to court to stand before a judge. At this court appearance, the judge reads the charges to the accused and asks him to enter a plea. Most defendants enter a plea of "not guilty" at this early stage of the process. The judge often makes the bail decision at the arraignment hearing. The judge decides whether the person should remain free until his case is resolved, whether to impose a bond fee, or whether to detain the suspect. A defendant is detained when he cannot afford to pay bail, is deemed a danger to the community, or is determined to be a flight risk—someone unlikely to show up for his trial.

Guilty Plea

There is usually a status hearing at a later stage of the process during which the defendant informs the court whether he intends to go to trial or enter a guilty

Figure 1.5 The Criminal Justice System, Streamlined View

plea. The prosecutor may offer the defendant the option of pleading guilty to a lesser offense in exchange for his agreement to give up his right to a trial—a process known as "plea bargaining." If the person pleads guilty, the judge may determine the punishment at that time or at a sentencing hearing scheduled at a later date. If the person pleads not guilty, the judge sets a date for trial. Approximately 95 percent of all cases, federal and state, result in a guilty plea. In some states, a person accused of a crime may enter a plea of *nolo contendere* or "no contest"—he neither admits nor denies the offense. A person who pleads nolo contendere faces the same penalties as person who pleads guilty.

Jury Selection and Trial

A criminal case may be decided by either a jury or a judge. A person who faces a crime that could be punished with a sentence of six months or more behind bars is entitled to a jury trial. During the selection process, potential jurors are asked questions by the judge, the prosecutor, and the defense attorney. Based on their responses, they may be excused or selected as members of the jury. The names of eligible jurors are typically drawn from a state's list of registered voters or licensed drivers. After the prosecution presents its case, the defense may present evidence that refutes the charges but is not required to do so. After hearing all the evidence, the judge or jury either finds the defendant guilty or acquits him. When a jury cannot agree on a verdict, the judge declares a mistrial, which generally means that the court will retry the case from the beginning.

Sentencing

Following a guilty verdict, the judge imposes a sentence. State and federal codes establish the sentencing range for each crime. The more serious the crime, the greater the criminal sanction. For instance, rape and murder are punished more severely than lower-level crimes, such as theft and assault. The length of an offender's prison sentence and the amount of restitution an offender is required to pay will vary according to the seriousness of an offense. (See Chapter 11 for a detailed discussion of sentencing.)

Appeals

Following a conviction, a defendant may file an appeal. By initiating the appeals process, the defendant is asking a higher court to review his case to determine whether there were procedural or constitutional errors. If the appeals court agrees with the defendant, it will overturn his conviction. However, if the appeals court agrees with the trial court, it will uphold the conviction.

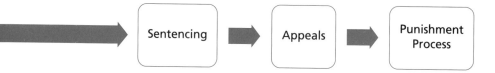

Punishment

The punishment phase of the justice system typically begins after the defendant is sentenced. Most defendants begin serving their time while their cases are being appealed. In some instances, judges will allow a defendant to remain free until his appeal is resolved. In cases where the defendant is detained before trial and ultimately found guilty, he will receive credit for the time he has already served behind bars. (See Chapter 11 for a detailed discussion of punishment.)

The U.S. Court System

U.S. courts have a heavy caseload of criminal cases. In 2010 alone, there were more than twenty million criminal cases brought in state courts. In 2012, more than one hundred and fifty thousand cases involving criminal matters were received by the U.S. Attorneys' office.[18] In the United States, there are two separate court systems that adjudicate criminal cases: the federal court system and the state court system. The U.S. Supreme Court, the "highest court in the land," sits at the top of both court systems, making it the court of last resort. Figure 1.6 provides a sketch of the two court systems. Cases begin in the lower courts and sometimes make their way farther up the court ladder. A typical state criminal case that goes to trial begins in the state's lower criminal court or trial court. These are sometimes referred to as district courts. At the federal level, cases start in U.S. magistrate or U.S. district court. This "district court" language can be confusing since both state and federal lower courts may be referred to as district courts. When reading a case, it is best to initially determine whether the case is in state or federal court. When lower federal courts issue conflicting decisions on a legal issue, the Supreme Court often decides to accept an appeal involving that issue to resolve the conflict and determine the law. In any given year, the Supreme Court hears fewer than one hundred cases—a tiny fraction when compared with the hundreds of thousands of criminal cases handled by U.S. courts each year.

In the federal system there is an additional tier of courts, including bankruptcy courts and courts of special jurisdiction (e.g., Military Court, Tax Court, and the Court of Appeals for the Armed Forces).

Case Briefing

Court cases are used throughout this textbook to illustrate how criminal law is applied and interpreted by the courts. With few exceptions, the case excerpts are decisions by appeals courts—courts that review the decisions of lower courts. The "State Courts of

Figure 1.6 **Federal and State Courts**

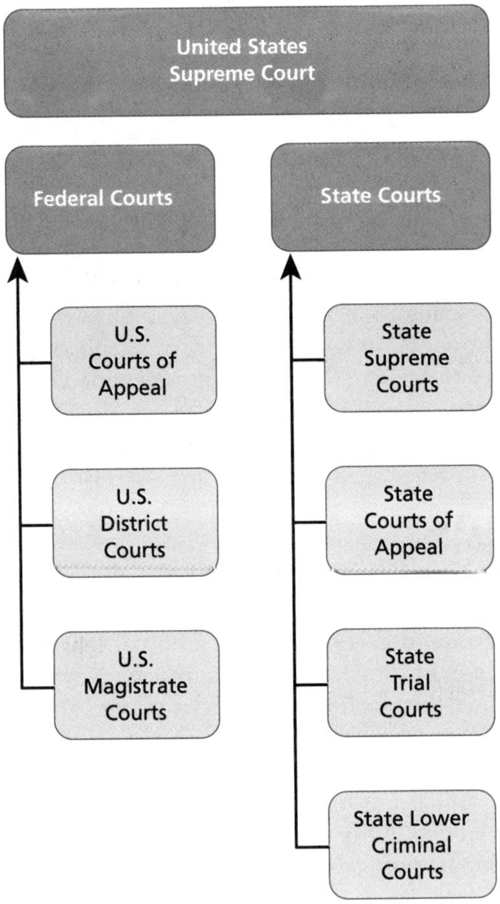

```
                    ┌─────────────────────────┐
                    │     United States       │
                    │     Supreme Court       │
                    └─────────────────────────┘

        ┌──────────────────┐         ┌──────────────────┐
        │  Federal Courts  │         │   State Courts   │
        └──────────────────┘         └──────────────────┘

          ┌──────────────┐             ┌──────────────┐
          │    U.S.      │             │    State     │
          │  Courts of   │             │   Supreme    │
          │   Appeal     │             │    Courts     │
          └──────────────┘             └──────────────┘

          ┌──────────────┐             ┌──────────────┐
          │    U.S.      │             │    State     │
          │  District    │             │  Courts of   │
          │   Courts     │             │    Appeal    │
          └──────────────┘             └──────────────┘

          ┌──────────────┐             ┌──────────────┐
          │    U.S.      │             │    State     │
          │ Magistrate   │             │    Trial     │
          │   Courts     │             │    Courts     │
          └──────────────┘             └──────────────┘

                                       ┌──────────────┐
                                       │ State Lower  │
                                       │  Criminal    │
                                       │   Courts     │
                                       └──────────────┘
```

Appeals" in Figure 1.6 above are examples of lower courts. These courts are "lower" than the U.S. Supreme Court and the State Supreme Courts. Most of the case excerpts are from either State Supreme Courts or State Courts of Appeal. Federal cases are also highlighted in this textbook, including numerous decisions by the U.S. Supreme Court. Reading and understanding court opinions takes practice. The first step is learning *how* to read the cases.

In this section, we will identify and define the key components of a court opinion. Following this, we will locate these parts in an actual judicial opinion. The case summary process is known as "briefing a case." The written summary is a "case brief." For a case brief, there are six main parts to focus on:

- *Citation*: The name of the case and the case citation, including the court and the year of the decision.
- *Prior Proceedings*: If the case is now before an appeals court, the prior proceedings are an overview of the legal decisions reached by the lower courts. In other words, the prior proceedings state what happened in court *before* the

current court's decision, such as the crime the defendant was convicted of committing, the statute she violated, and the sentence she received.

- *Facts*: The facts refer to the specific details of the case that led to the filing of criminal charges against the defendant. For instance, if there was an altercation between the defendant and the victim, the facts section would include the who, when, where, how, what, and why of the incident.
- *Issue*: The issue is a statement of the legal question(s) that the court is asked to address in the specific case. Generally speaking, the court is being asked to answer a question by the appellant—the side that lost in the court that previously heard the case. An issue may involve a question about the interpretation of a constitutional right, whether the trial court provided the proper instructions of law to the jury, or whether three was sufficient evidence to support the conviction.
- *Holding*: The holding is a statement of the court's decision. It is the court's answer to the issues and questions posed by the appealing party. The court's "disposition," the directive from the court, may also be included in this section. Examples of case dispositions include "Affirmed" or "Reversed and remanded." This language usually appears at the end of a case.
- *Rationale*: The rationale is an explanation of the court's reason for reaching its decision. The court's reasoning may include a range of factors, including prior case law (precedent) or public policy. Judicial opinions typically offer more than one rationale for their decisions.

When a case is appealed from a lower court to a higher court, the appeal may be heard by a court with more than one judge. For instance, the U.S. Supreme Court has nine justices, and in many cases, the justices who do not agree with the majority write separate dissenting opinions. Judges do not always agree on what the proper legal resolution should be in a case. This means that in some cases, there is a majority opinion, followed by either a "concurring" opinion or a "dissenting" opinion. A judge may write a concurring opinion when she agrees with the decision of the majority but for different reasons. For reasons of space, this textbook does not include concurring and dissenting opinions. If you are interested in reading concurring and dissenting opinions in a particular case, use the citation information to look up the full opinion.

- *Concurring Opinion*: The opinion of a judge (or judges) who agrees with the decision of the judges who are in the majority, but for different legal reasons.
- *Dissenting Opinion*: The opinion of one or more of the judges who disagrees with the legal decision and findings of the judges in the majority. Sometimes important facts that were not discussed in the majority opinion are discussed in a dissenting or concurring opinion.

There are nine justices on the U.S. Supreme Court. One of the justices in the majority is assigned to write the court's opinion in a case. In some instances, an opinion is written by the Court and is not authored by an individual Justice (these are known as "per curiam" decisions).

Next, we turn to the case of *State v. Woll* (1983). As you read through the court opinion, underline and highlight the sections that address the key parts of a case brief (detailed above). Following the decision, review the sample brief.

State v. Woll (1983)

668 P.2d 610
Court of Appeals of Washington

PETRIE, J. Plaintiff, the State of Washington, appeals an order dismissing "all charges against and prosecution" of defendant, Robert H. Woll . . . Woll [was convicted] by jury verdict of the crime of first degree theft . . .

The State's appeal raises [the] question [of] whether . . . theft under RCW 9A.56.020(1)(c) requires proof of an intent by the accused to deprive the owner permanently of the property.

On February 1, 1979, defendant Woll deposited $448 in his checking account at the Aberdeen Branch of the Seattle-First National Bank (Sea-First). The bank mistakenly credited Woll's account with $4,448. The defendant discovered this error when he received his next bank statement several days later. Woll testified that he contacted a person, whose name and title he did not obtain, at Sea-First about the mistake and was told to "keep it in limbo until the error has been found." For the next 3 months, Sea-First continued erroneously to credit Woll's account. Then, on April 18, 1979, Woll closed the Sea-First account by cashing a check in the amount of $4,223.93 and depositing the proceeds in an interest-bearing account in another bank. Although Woll denied that he had any "intention to deprive Sea-First of the money" and denied that he had any "intent to permanently take the money," he subsequently spent it all within 2 months.

The Federal Reserve Board detected the bank's mistake on February 21, 1980, and notified Sea-First of its error. The bank then demanded reimbursement from Woll. Because Woll did not timely repay Sea-First, the bank reported the matter to the prosecuting attorney who then initiated these criminal proceedings. On June 11, 1980, Woll was charged with having committed first degree theft "on or about April 18, 1979," by appropriating lost or misdelivered property under RCW 9A.56.020(1)(c). Three days before trial, Woll repaid the bank from the proceeds of a second mortgage he placed on his house . . .

We turn, then, to the central issue of whether theft by the appropriation of lost or misdelivered property requires proof of the intent to deprive the owner permanently of the property . . .

The wrongful withholding of property delivered by mistake, with knowledge of the mistake acquired *subsequent to the receipt,* may be punishable by statute under the name of larceny, but it is an offense distinct from common law larceny [R. Perkins, *Criminal Law* 254 n. 76 (2d ed. 1969)].

Thus, the common law of larceny required proof that the defendant's intent to steal concurred with his mistaken *receipt*

of the property,[7] whereas, under RCW 9A.56.020(1)(c) the "intent to deprive" must exist at the time of the appropriation. In the case at bench, Woll was charged with having committed the crime on or about April 18, 1979. Thus, under the charge and under the trial court's instruction, the prosecution had to prove defendant's intent on the date he transferred the funds—not the date or dates on which he subsequently spent the money. Under Washington law, "[t]he gravamen of the offense is the appropriation of the property *after having received it."* (Italics ours.) *State v. Heyes,* 44 Wn.2d at 588.

We are persuaded that in order to prove a charge of theft under the statutory offense of appropriation of misdelivered property, the quality of the intent required is the same as that required under the statutory offense of embezzlement. Embezzlement, also, was not larceny at common law. Washington courts have, accordingly, declined to read into the crime of embezzlement the common law requisite for larceny (the intent to deprive permanently). Embezzlement requires proof only of the intent to deprive, and the crime is completed when the accused fraudulently misappropriates the property . . .

Therefore, we reject the defendant's contention that theft by the appropriation of misdelivered property incorporates the intent to commit common law larceny. We hold that this crime requires proof of the intent merely to deprive, at any time, the property appropriated and not necessarily coincidental with the wrongful receipt, precisely as the jury was instructed.

Therefore, we reverse the trial court's order granting a new trial as well as the order dismissing the information. The jury's verdict is reinstated, and the cause is remanded for imposition of sentence.

PETRICH, C.J., and WORSWICK, J., concur.

Sample Case Brief

Prior Proceedings

I. Trial Court: Jury found defendant guilty of first degree theft under Washington state statute.

II. Trial Court: After the guilty verdict, the judge dismissed the charge against Woll and granted a new trial.

III. Court of Appeals (current case)

Facts

- February 1, 1979, Robert Woll, the defendant (D) deposited $448 into his checking account at the Seattle-First National Bank (Sea-First). The bank made an error and credited him with $4,448 (!)
- D discovered the bank's error some days later when he received his bank statement. D testified that he contacted someone at the bank who told him to "keep it in limbo." The extra $4,000 remained in D's account for three months.
- April 18, 1979, D closed his Sea-First bank account. He then deposited the money into a checking account at another bank. Over the next two months, D spent the entire amount.
- February 21, 1980, the Federal Reserve Board discovered the error and notified Sea-First. Sea-First demanded repayment by D. When D did not repay in a timely manner, the bank contacted the prosecutor. Criminal charges were initiated against D. D said he had no intent to permanently take the money.
- June 11, 1980, D was charged with first degree theft under state code, "by appropriating lost or misdelivered property" [RCW 9A.56.020(1)(c)]. D made repayment prior to trial.

Issue

Does a conviction for first degree theft require that D intend to deprive the bank of the money (misdelivered property) at the time he received it?

Holding

No, D can be convicted of larceny/theft if there was intent to deprive so long as D intended to deprive the owner of the property at some point after he received it.
The court upholds D's conviction for larceny.

Rationale

- Intent for theft can be established when D forms intent to deprive the owner *subsequent to the receipt* of the property. Intent does not have to be formed at the time D receives the property.
- The intent required to establish theft is the same as the intent required for the crime of embezzlement.
- There is a difference between the intent required for larceny and the intent required for common law larceny. There is a higher standard for common law larceny. This case involves theft only.

Concurring Opinion

- Judges Petrich and Worswick concur (no separate opinion).

The case brief has several purposes and benefits. It provides a short, one-page summary of the case. It is also useful for students as a learning tool during class lectures. When a case is reviewed in class, write notes and comments on the brief and make any necessary additions and corrections. Case briefs are also useful during preparation for midterms and final exams. Briefs allow for quick reviews and comparisons between court cases.

Writing case briefs is a skill that improves with repetition. Initially, it may be a challenge to determine the facts, issue, holding, and rationale. It will also be a challenge to confine the brief to one page. The more cases you read and discuss in class, the easier it will be to determine which facts matter the most and should be included in the case brief. With practice, it will become easier to spot the issue in a case, understand the holding, and identify a court's reasoning for its decision.

Concluding Note

This chapter has provided an overview and roadmap of criminal law and criminal justice issues that will be covered in detail in this textbook. Now test yourself on the material we have covered in this chapter. Good luck with the Issue Spotter exercise for this chapter. The exercise requires that you review and apply the case brief material discussed in this chapter.

IssueSpotter

Read the court case below and prepare a case brief. Use the case brief structure outlined above (prior proceedings, facts, issue, holding, rationale, concurring, and dissenting opinions). Be sure to include each of the elements of a case brief.

People of New York v. Sirico (2011)
Court of Appeals of New York
17 N.Y. 3d 744

Memorandum.

The order of the Appellate Division should be affirmed. Following a jury trial, defendant was convicted of murder in the second degree (Penal Law § 125.25 [1] [intentional murder]). The charges arose after defendant, an experienced archery hunter, shot an arrow from his compound bow towards his neighbor's yard, fatally striking the victim. On appeal, defendant principally contends that he was entitled to an intoxication charge (see Penal Law § 15.25). That section provides, in its entirety:

Intoxication is not, as such, a defense to a criminal charge; but in any prosecution for an offense, evidence of intoxication of the defendant may be offered by the defendant whenever it is relevant to negative an element of the crime charged.

An intoxication charge is warranted if, viewing the evidence in the light most favorable to the defendant, "there is sufficient evidence of intoxication in the record for a reasonable person to entertain a doubt as to the element of intent on that basis" (People v. Perry, 61 NY2d 849, 850 [1984]; see also People v. Farnsworth, 65 NY2d 734, 735 [1985]). A defendant may establish entitlement to such a charge "if the record contains evidence of the recent use of intoxicants of such nature or quantity to support the inference that their ingestion was sufficient to affect defendant's ability to form the necessary criminal intent" (People v. Rodriguez, 76 NY2d 918, 920 [1990]). Although a "relatively low threshold" exists to demonstrate entitlement to an intoxication charge, bare assertions by a defendant concerning his intoxication, standing alone, are insufficient (People v. Gaines, 83 NY2d 925, 927 [1994]).

Here, there is insufficient evidence to support an inference that defendant was so intoxicated as to be unable to form the requisite criminal intent. Indeed, the uncontradicted record evidence, including defendant's own account, supports the conclusion that his overall behavior on the day of the incident was purposeful. Accordingly, defendant was not entitled to an intoxication charge.

We have reviewed defendant's remaining contentions and find them to be without merit.

Jones, J. (dissenting). It is uncontroverted that defendant, on the day of the criminal incident, consumed two large glasses (approximately 12 to 15 ounces each) of Southern Comfort whiskey and ingested a Xanax pill. Shortly thereafter, he threatened friends and neighbors with a bow and arrow, fired an arrow into the side of a truck, and then fatally shot the victim—actions that call into question defendant's state of mind. Thus, given this record evidence and the "relatively low threshold" a defendant is required to meet for entitlement to a jury charge of intoxication, I respectfully dissent and would reverse the Appellate Division.

People v. Perry (61 NY2d 849, 850 [1984]) established that "[a] charge on intoxication should be given if there is sufficient evidence of intoxication in the record for a reasonable person to entertain a doubt as to the element of intent on that basis." . . . [T]here must be objective evidence in the record, "such as the number of drinks, the period of time during which they were consumed, the lapse of time between consumption and the event at issue, whether [the defendant] consumed alcohol on an empty stomach, whether his [or her] drinks were high in alcoholic content, and the specific impact of the alcohol upon his [or her] behavior or mental state" (People v. Gaines, 83 NY2d 925, 927).

The record evidence in this case satisfies the rule of Perry and Gaines and may serve to negate the mens rea element of intent for murder in the second degree (see Penal Law §§ 15.25, 125.25 [1]). Thus, it was error for the trial court to deny defendant's request for a charge of intoxication.

The People contend that defendant's testimony establishes that an issue with the mechanism of his prosthetic leg, and not intoxication, precipitated the fatal firing of the bow and arrow. However, it should be emphasized that in determining whether a theory of defense should be charged, a defendant is entitled to the "most favorable view of the record," and a trial court is obligated to charge a theory of defense where it is supported by a reasonable view of the trial evidence . . . Here, contrary testimony should not preclude the charge of intoxication where there is a reasonable view of the record evidence that would support such an instruction . . .

A trial court simply cannot forgo its obligation to properly charge a theory of defense when there is record support. Ultimately, whether a jury credits or discredits the testimony of defendant in rendering its factual determinations is a matter beyond our purview. But before reaching its final decision, the trier of fact should be presented with all relevant instructions, as supported by the record, for its due consideration.

. . . .

Order affirmed in a memorandum.

Key Terms and Cases ●━━━━━━━━━━━━━━━━━

Administrative regulations 6

Capital offense 12

Case brief 14

Common law 1

Crime 2

Executive order 6

Ex-post facto law 7

Federal legislation 7

Felony 4

Mala in se 4

Mala prohibita 4

Misdemeanor 4

Model Penal Code (MPC) 10

Municipal ordinances 8

People of New York v. Sirico 22

State legislation 7

State v. Woll 19

Tort 11

Treaties 9

U.S. Constitution 9

U.S. Supreme Court 13

Victimless crime 5

Notes ●━━━━━━━━━━━━━━━━━

1. Jennifer Truman and Michael Planty, "Criminal Victimization, 2011," NCJ 239437 (Washington, DC: U.S. Department of Justice, 2012).

2. Minn. Stat. 2011 §609.36(1).

3. Norval Morris and Gordon Hawkins, *The Honest Politician's Guide to Crime Control* (Chicago: University of Chicago Press, 1970) 2.

4. Dallin H. Oaks, *The Popular Myth of the Victimless Crime*, Commissioner's Lecture Series. (Provo, UT: Brigham Young University Press, 1974) 5–13.

5. *Commonwealth v. Mochan*, 177 Pa. Super. 454 (Pa. Super. Ct. 1955).

6. Fla. Stat. §812.014.

7. Anchorage, Alaska, AO No. 2009-71, "An Ordinance Repealing and Re-Enacting Anchorage Municipal Code Chapter 8.80 Regarding Fees for Excessive Police Responses," http://www.muni.org/Departments/Assembly/legislation/2009%20Ordinances/ao2009-071.pdf

8. Official City of Los Angeles Municipal Code, https://law.resource.org/pub/us/code/city/ca/Los Angeles/Municipal/chapter11.pdf

9. Executive Order No. 9066, February 19, 1942.

10. *Korematsu v. United States*, 323 U.S. 214 (1944).

11. *Bond v. United States*, 564 U.S. _____ (2014).

12. Paul H. Robinson and Mark Dubber, "The American Model Penal Code: A Brief Overview," *New Criminal Law Review* 10, no. 3 (2007): 319–341.

13. *Lynce v. Mathis*, 519 U.S. 443 (1997).

14. In some cases, the Supreme Court has upheld what would otherwise be an ex-post facto law. For instance, where there is a great benefit to society in imposing an additional punishment, a law may not be construed as ex-post facto. In *Smith v. Doe*, 538 U.S. 84 (2003), the Supreme Court held that convicted sex offenders can be required to register (and this information can be posted on the Internet).

15. U.S. Department of Justice, "Correctional Populations in the United States, 2012," Table 2, *BJS Bulletin*, December 2013, NCJ 243936, http://www.bjs.gov/content/pub/pdf/cpus12.pdf

16. Christian Henrichson and Ruth Delaney, *The Price of Prisons: What Incarceration Costs Taxpayers* (New York: Vera Institute of Justice, 2012).

17. *Gideon v. Wainwright,* 372 U.S. 335 (1963).

18. *United States Attorneys' Annual Statistical Report, Fiscal Year 2012* (2013) p. 6, http://www.justice.gov/usao/reading_room/reports/asr2012/12statrpt.pdf

Chapter 2

The Occupy Wall Street protests (OWS) began in 2011 in New York City's Liberty Square. People gathered in the financial district to bring attention to the increasing disparity between society's richest members and everyone else—referred to as the "99 percent vs. the 1 percent." On October 15, 2011, there were protests in over one hundred other cities, including Oakland, Portland, and Washington, DC. It is estimated that more than seventy thousand people gathered across the country to participate in OWS protests. There were even larger protests outside of the United States, including Europe. In Rome, Barcelona, and Madrid, there were gatherings of more than two hundred thousand people each.

Occupy Wall Street demonstrations resulted in numerous arrests. Some protesters were arrested for breach of the peace. In some places, including Zuccotti Park in New York, hundreds of protestors camped out on public grounds and refused to move. These encampments led to clashes between demonstrators and the police. Some cities attempted to have the protestors forcibly removed.

The Occupy Wall Street protests raise some of the issues that will be addressed in this chapter, including the First Amendment rights to freedom of speech and freedom of assembly. We will consider the legal boundaries of public speech and how far the government can reach to punish speech—popular and unpopular. Further, we will discuss how the law handles speech that some members find offensive. Is the best response *more* speech, limitations on the offensive speech, or an outright ban? More broadly, this chapter addresses the constitutional limits placed on states and the federal government in defining what activity is criminal.

Occupy Los Angeles protesters at city hall in 2011. Freedom of speech and freedom of assembly are rights protected by the U.S. Constitution.

Constitutional Limitations on Criminal Laws

Learning Objectives

After reading and studying this chapter, you should be able to

➤ Cite the constitutional guarantees protected by the Bill of Rights

➤ Identify the circumstances when the criminal law may infringe upon individual rights

➤ Define symbolic speech and provide examples of constitutionally protected symbolic speech

➤ State the test for obscenity

➤ Provide the definition of fighting words

➤ Explain freedom of assembly

➤ Discuss the right to free exercise of religion

➤ Summarize the right to bear arms

➤ Explain the prohibition against cruel and unusual punishment

➤ Differentiate between the due process clause and the equal protection clause

➤ Know the constitutional sources for the right to privacy

Introduction

State legislatures use their broad authority to enact criminal laws. These powers come with limitations. As a general rule, state laws may not encroach upon individual rights guaranteed by the Bill of Rights—the first ten amendments of the U.S. Constitution. A state law, for instance, may criminalize certain forms of language so long as it does not interfere with free speech guarantees protected by the First Amendment. A state may punish the crime of robbery. However, it may not impose a penalty so disproportionate to the crime (e.g., the death penalty) that it violates the Eighth Amendment's protection against cruel and unusual punishment. A state may make it unlawful for people to engage in certain types of activities (e.g., gambling). However, the state may not have a law that punishes one racial group more harshly than others for engaging in the activity. To do so would violate the equal protection clause of the Fourteenth Amendment. Courts strike down laws when they are found to interfere with constitutionally protected rights. By themselves, the constitutional protections in the Bill of Rights only apply to federal laws. However, the language of the Fourteenth Amendment requires that states also protect most of these rights. This is another way of saying that the Bill of Rights is made binding on the states through the Fourteenth Amendment. This is known as the doctrine of incorporation.

This chapter details protections under several constitutional amendments, including the First, Second, Fifth, Eighth, and Fourteenth, by examining their guarantees and legal boundaries. The discussion also includes a review of the right to privacy, which is drawn from several constitutional amendments. This discussion does not detail the Fourth and Sixth Amendment protections, because those are typically discussed as part of a criminal procedure course. We will examine how far states and the federal government can legislate to limit these rights. The cases illustrate how the Supreme Court balances the rights of the individual against the interests of the state or federal government.

First Amendment ●─────────────────────────

Congress shall make no law respecting an establishment of religion, or prohibiting the free exercise thereof; or abridging the freedom of speech, or of the press; or the right of the people peaceably to assemble, and to petition the Government for a redress of grievances.

United States Constitution, First Amendment

The First Amendment includes protections and guarantees that exist at the heart of democracy. Five rights are promised in its forty-five words: free speech, freedom of religion, freedom of press, freedom of assembly, and the right to petition the state for redress of grievances. In this section, we highlight three of these, freedom of speech, freedom of assembly, and freedom of religion (the free exercise clause).

Freedom of Speech

To suppress free speech is a double wrong. It violates the rights of the hearer as well as those of the speaker.

Frederick Douglass, A Plea for Free Speech in Boston *(1860)*

The right to speak freely is the bedrock of a democratic society. When speech is protected, it encourages people to talk and exchange ideas with each other—ideas that are popular as well as ideas that are incendiary. When free speech is not protected, for instance in totalitarian and militaristic societies, public speech may be censored by the government. In the United States, the right to free speech is both beloved and reviled. When we agree with what someone has said, we support and encourage more of the same kind of speech. When we disagree and believe that someone's speech has gone too far, we may want to ban the speech. In his comment above, Frederick Douglass, former slave and abolitionist, argues that society risks harm when it places barriers around speech. This section looks at how courts have determined which speech is constitutionally acceptable. The cases establish that the right to free speech is upheld even when the speech is unpopular and even when it is directed against the government. According to John Roberts, Chief Justice of the U.S. Supreme Court:

Speech is powerful. It can stir people to action, move them to tears of both joy and sorrow, and . . . inflict great pain . . . We cannot react to that pain by punishing the speaker. As a nation we have chosen a different course—to protect even hurtful speech on public issues to ensure that we do not stifle public debate.[1]

The First Amendment prevents the government from restricting expression based on its ideas, subject matter, message, or content. The bottom line is that freedom of speech and expression are constitutionally protected to encourage people to speak freely—without fear of punishment. The give and take of ideas in public makes it possible to have a social atmosphere of awareness, tolerance, and respect for different opinions—the makings of a vibrant democracy. However, the guarantee of free speech also comes with social costs. We will not always approve of what others say in their exercise of free speech. At some point each of us will likely encounter individuals or groups who engage in speech that deeply offend our sensibilities.

The next two Supreme Court cases, *Brandenburg v. Ohio* (1969) and *Cohen v. California* (1971), involve public language that many people would find offensive. The *Brandenburg* case involves words used by members of the Ku Klux Klan (KKK). The KKK, the oldest White supremacist organization in America, took shape after the Civil War. According to the Southern Poverty Law Center, in 2011 there were more than seven hundred active White supremacist organizations in the United States. The *Cohen* case involves language that some people would consider highly offensive, especially since it took place on government property. Together, these cases highlight the Constitution's broad protection of unpopular speech.

Brandenburg v. Ohio (1969)
U.S. Supreme Court
395 U.S. 444

PER CURIAM. The appellant [Clarence Brandenburg], a leader of a Ku Klux Klan group, was convicted under the Ohio Criminal Syndicalism statute for:

> [A]dvocat(ing) * * * the duty, necessity, or propriety * of crime, sabotage, violence, or unlawful methods of terrorism as a means of accomplishing industrial or political reform' [and for] voluntarily assembl(ing) with any society, group, or assemblage of persons formed to teach or advocate the doctrines of criminal syndicalism. Ohio Rev. Code Ann. §2923.13[. . .]

The appellant [Brandenburg] challenged the constitutionality of the criminal syndicalism statute under the First and Fourteenth Amendments to the United States Constitution, but the intermediate appellate court of Ohio affirmed his conviction without opinion. The Supreme Court of Ohio dismissed his appeal . . . Appeal was taken to this Court, and we noted probable jurisdiction . . . We reverse.

The record shows that a man, identified at trial as the appellant, telephoned an announcer-reporter on the staff of a Cincinnati television station and invited him to come to a Ku Klux Klan "rally" to be held at a farm in Hamilton County. With the cooperation of the organizers, the reporter and a cameraman attended the meeting and filmed the events. Portions of the films were later broadcast on the local station and on a national network.

The prosecution's case rested on the films and on testimony identifying the appellant as the person who communicated with the reporter and who spoke at the rally. The State also introduced into evidence several articles appearing in the film, including a pistol, a rifle, a shotgun, ammunition, a Bible, and a red hood worn by the speaker in the films.

One film showed 12 hooded figures, some of whom carried firearms. They were gathered around a large wooden cross, which they burned. [. . .] Most of the words uttered during the scene were incomprehensible when the film was projected, but scattered phrases could be understood that were derogatory of Negroes and, in one instance, of Jews. Another scene on the same film showed the appellant, in Klan regalia, making a speech. The speech, in full, was as follows:

(Continued)

(Continued)

This is an organizers' meeting. We have had quite a few members here today which are-we have hundreds, hundreds of members throughout the State of Ohio. I can quote from a newspaper clipping from the Columbus, Ohio Dispatch, five weeks ago Sunday morning. The Klan has more members in the State of Ohio than does any other organization. We're not a revengent organization, but if our President, our Congress, our Supreme Court, continues to suppress the white, Caucasian race, it's possible that there might have to be some revengeance taken.

We are marching on Congress July the Fourth, four hundred thousand strong. From there we are dividing into two groups, one group to march on St. Augustine, Florida, the other group to march into Mississippi. Thank you.

The second film showed six hooded figures one of whom, later identified as the appellant, repeated a speech very similar to that recorded on the first film. The reference to the possibility of "revengeance" was omitted, and one sentence was added: "Personally, I believe the nigger should be returned to Africa, the Jew returned to Israel." Though some of the figures in the films carried weapons, the speaker did not.

[Later Court] decisions have fashioned the principle that the constitutional guarantees of free speech and free press do not permit a State to forbid or proscribe advocacy of the use of force of law violation except where such advocacy is directed to inciting or producing imminent lawless action and is likely to incite or produce such action. As we said in *Noto v. United States,* 367 U.S. 290, 297 (1961),

The mere abstract teaching . . . of the moral propriety or even moral necessity for a resort to force and violence is not the same as preparing a group for violent action and steeling it to such action.

A statute which fails to draw this distinction impermissibly intrudes upon the freedoms guaranteed by the First and Fourteenth Amendments. It sweeps within its condemnation speech which our Constitution has immunized from government control . . .

Measured by this test, [Ohio's] Act cannot be sustained. The Act punishes persons who "advocate or teach the duty, necessity, or propriety" of violence "as a means of accomplishing industrial or political reform"; or who publish or circulate or display any book or paper containing such advocacy; or who "justify" the commission of violent acts "with intent to exemplify, spread or advocate the propriety of the doctrines of criminal syndicalism"; or who "voluntarily assemble" with a group formed "to teach or advocate the doctrines of criminal syndicalism." Neither the indictment nor the trial judge's instructions to the jury in any way refined the statute's bald definition of the crime in terms of mere advocacy not distinguished from incitement to imminent lawless action.

Accordingly, we are here confronted with a statute which, by its own words and as applied, purports to punish mere advocacy and to forbid, on pain of criminal punishment, assembly with others merely to advocate the described type of action. Such a statute falls within the condemnation of the First and Fourteenth Amendments. [. . .]

Reversed.

Questions

1. What is the issue in the case?

2. Are there any facts indicating that Mr. Brandenburg was involved in more than "mere advocacy"?

3. Assume that the Ohio Criminal Syndicalism statute made it unlawful to "advocate or encourage" the use of terrorism. Would the Court have reached a different conclusion in the case? Why or why not?

Clarence Brandenburg challenged the Ohio law and argued that it violated the First *and* Fourteenth Amendments. He included the Fourteenth Amendment because he argued that Ohio, by passing the Criminal Syndicalism Act, had violated his First Amendment rights. As you read *Cohen v. California* (1971), compare and contrast it with the *Brandenburg* decision. Consider the speaker's message and the intended audience for his speech.

Cohen v. California (1971)

U.S. Supreme Court
403 U.S. 15

Mr. Justice HARLAN delivered the opinion of the Court.

This case may seem at first blush too inconsequential to find its way into our books, but the issue it presents is of no small constitutional significance.

Appellant Paul Robert Cohen was convicted in the Los Angeles Municipal Court of . . . "maliciously and willfully disturb(ing) the peace or quiet of any neighborhood or person . . . by . . . offensive conduct . . . " He was given 30 days' imprisonment . . . :

On April 26, 1968, the defendant was observed in the Los Angeles County Courthouse [. . .] wearing a jacket bearing the words "Fuck the Draft" which were plainly visible. There were women and children present in the corridor. The defendant was arrested. The defendant testified that he wore the jacket knowing that the words were on the jacket as a means of informing the public of the depth of his feelings against the Vietnam War and the draft.

The defendant did not engage in, nor threaten to engage in, nor did anyone as the result of his conduct in fact commit or threaten to commit any act of violence. The defendant did not make any loud or unusual noise, nor was there any evidence that he uttered any sound prior to his arrest . . .

In affirming the conviction, the Court of Appeal held that "offensive conduct" means "behavior which has a tendency to provoke *others* to acts of violence or to in turn disturb the peace," and that the State had proved this element . . . The California Supreme Court declined review by a divided vote. We now reverse . . .

In order to lay hands on the precise issue which this case involves, it is useful first to canvass various matters which this record does *not* represent.

The conviction quite clearly rests upon the asserted offensiveness of the words Cohen used to convey his message to the public. The only "conduct" which the State sought to punish is the fact of communication. Thus, we deal here with a conviction resting solely upon "speech" . . . Further, the State certainly lacks power to punish Cohen for the underlying content of the message the inscription conveyed. At least so long as there is no showing of an intent to incite disobedience to or disruption of the draft, Cohen could not, consistently with the First and Fourteenth Amendments, be punished for asserting the evident position on the inutility or immorality of the draft his jacket reflected. [. . .]

Appellant's conviction, then, rests squarely upon his exercise of the "freedom of speech" protected from arbitrary governmental interference by the Constitution, and can be justified, if at all, only as a valid regulation of the manner in which he exercised that freedom, not as a permissible prohibition on the substantive message it conveys. This does not end the inquiry, of course, for the First and Fourteenth Amendments have never been thought to give absolute protection to every individual to speak whenever or wherever he pleases, or to use any form of address in any circumstances that he chooses. In this vein, too, however, we think it important to note that several issues typically associated with such problems are not presented here.

In the first place, Cohen was tried under a statute applicable throughout the entire State. Any attempt to support this conviction on the ground that the statute seeks to preserve an appropriately decorous atmosphere in the courthouse where Cohen was arrested must fail in the absence of any language in the statute that would have put appellant on notice that certain kinds of otherwise permissible speech or conduct would nevertheless, under California law, not be tolerated in certain places . . . No fair reading of the phrase "offensive conduct" can be said sufficiently to inform the ordinary person that distinctions between certain locations are thereby created.

In the second place, as it comes to us, this . . . is not, for example, an obscenity case. Whatever else may be necessary to give rise to the States' broader power to prohibit obscene expression, such expression must be, in some significant way, erotic . . . It cannot plausibly be maintained that this vulgar allusion to the Selective Service System would conjure up such psychic stimulation in anyone likely to be confronted with Cohen's crudely defaced jacket.

This Court has also held that the States are free to ban the simple use, without a demonstration of additional justifying circumstances, of so-called "fighting words," those personally abusive epithets which, when addressed to the ordinary citizen, are, as a matter of common knowledge,

(Continued)

(Continued)

inherently likely to provoke violent reaction . . . While the four-letter word displayed by Cohen in relation to the draft is not uncommonly employed in a personally provocative fashion, in this instance it was clearly not "directed to the person of the hearer" . . . No individual actually or likely to be present could reasonably have regarded the words on appellant's jacket as a direct personal insult. Nor do we have here an instance of the exercise of the State's police power to prevent a speaker from intentionally provoking a given group to hostile reaction . . . There is, as noted above, no showing that anyone who saw Cohen was, in fact, violently aroused, or that appellant intended such a result.

Finally, in arguments before this Court, much has been made of the claim that Cohen's distasteful mode of expression was thrust upon unwilling or unsuspecting viewers, and that the State might therefore legitimately act as it did in order to protect the sensitive from otherwise unavoidable exposure to appellant's crude form of protest. Of course, the mere presumed presence of unwitting listeners or viewers does not serve automatically to justify curtailing all speech capable of giving offense . . . While this Court has recognized that government may properly act in many situations to prohibit intrusion into the privacy of the home of unwelcome views and ideas which cannot be totally banned from the public dialogue . . . we have at the same time consistently stressed that "we are often 'captives' outside the sanctuary of the home and subject to objectionable speech" . . . The ability of government, consonant with the Constitution, to shut off discourse solely to protect others from hearing it is, in other words, dependent upon a showing that substantial privacy interests are being invaded in an essentially intolerable manner. Any broader view of this authority would effectively empower a majority to silence dissidents simply as a matter of personal predilections.

In this regard, persons confronted with Cohen's jacket were in a quite different posture than, say, those subjected to the raucous emissions of sound trucks blaring outside their residences. Those in the Los Angeles courthouse could effectively avoid further bombardment of their sensibilities simply by averting their eyes. And, while it may be that one has a more substantial claim to a recognizable privacy interest when walking through a courthouse corridor than, for example, strolling through Central Park, surely it is nothing like the interest in being free from unwanted expression in the confines of one's own home. Given the subtlety and complexity of the factors involved, if Cohen's "speech" was otherwise entitled to constitutional protection, we do not think the fact that some unwilling "listeners" in a public building may have been briefly exposed to it can serve to justify this breach of

the peace conviction where, as here, there was no evidence that persons powerless to avoid appellant's conduct did in fact, object to it, and where that portion of the statute upon which Cohen's conviction rests evinces no concern, either on its face or as construed by the California courts, with the special plight of the captive auditor, but, instead, indiscriminately sweeps within its prohibitions all "offensive conduct" that disturbs "any neighborhood or person."

Against this background, the issue flushed by this case stands out in bold relief. It is whether California can excise, as "offensive conduct," one particular scurrilous epithet from the public discourse, either upon the theory . . . that its use is inherently likely to cause violent reaction or upon a more general assertion that the States, acting as guardians of public morality, may properly remove this offensive word from the public vocabulary.

The rationale of the California court is plainly untenable. At most, it reflects an "undifferentiated fear or apprehension of disturbance [which] is not enough to overcome the right to freedom of expression" . . . We have been shown no evidence that substantial numbers of citizens are standing ready to strike out physically at whoever may assault their sensibilities with execrations like that uttered by Cohen. There may be some persons about with such lawless and violent proclivities, but that is an insufficient base upon which to erect, consistently with constitutional values, a governmental power to force persons who wish to ventilate their dissident views into avoiding particular forms of expression. The argument amounts to little more than the self-defeating proposition that, to avoid physical censorship of one who has not sought to provoke such a response by a hypothetical coterie of the violent and lawless, the States may more appropriately effectuate that censorship themselves . . .

Admittedly, it is not so obvious that the First and Fourteenth Amendments must be taken to disable the States from punishing public utterance of this unseemly expletive in order to maintain what they regard as a suitable level of discourse within the body politic. We think, however, that examination and reflection will reveal the shortcomings of a contrary viewpoint.

. . .

The principle contended for by the State seems inherently boundless. How is one to distinguish this from any other offensive word? Surely the State has no right to cleanse public debate to the point where it is grammatically palatable to the most squeamish among us. Yet no readily ascertainable general principle exists for stopping short of that result were we to affirm the judgment below. For, while the particular four-letter word being litigated here is perhaps more distasteful than most others of its genre, it is nevertheless often true that one man's vulgarity is another's lyric. Indeed, we think it is largely because governmental officials cannot make principled distinctions in this area that the Constitution leaves matters of taste and style so largely to the individual.

. . .

The State may not, consistently with the First and Fourteenth Amendments, make the simple public display here involved of this single four-letter expletive a criminal offense. Because that is the only arguably sustainable rationale for the conviction here at issue, the judgment below must be reversed.

Reversed.

Questions

1. What is the issue in *Cohen v. California*?

2. What are two rationales used by the Supreme Court to explain its decision?

3. Assume you are a prosecutor for the state of California. Which facts would you use to prove that by wearing his jacket Mr. Cohen had disturbed the "peace or quiet of any neighborhood or person"?

In both *Brandenburg* and *Cohen,* the Supreme Court makes clear that constitutionality is not a popularity contest. Even if a majority of people believe that certain language is offensive, it may still receive constitutional protection. As the *Cohen* opinion states, "One man's vulgarity is another man's lyric." However, the Supreme Court also makes clear that some speech does not have constitutional protection. The Court considered the public's response to the words on the back of the defendant's jacket. They found no evidence that Mr. Cohen's coat had caused anyone to become violent.

Consider whether a change in the fact patterns of *Brandenburg* and *Cohen* would lead to a different legal outcome. Review the scenarios below:

As a protest against the war in Vietnam, some people publicly burned their draft cards.

- Assume that Mr. Brandenburg's first speech had been delivered at a rally held in front of a synagogue and the second speech was delivered in front of a Morehouse College, a Historically Black College or University (HBCU).
- Assume that Mr. Cohen had worn his jacket while he walked down the hallway of a Veteran's Memorial Hospital or while walking through Arlington National Cemetery.

If Mr. Brandenburg's speech had been given in front of a Jewish place of worship, it is likely that the Court would have been concerned that his words could cause a public disruption and possibly violence. Likewise, if his speech, which included racial slurs, had been held in front of a HBCU, the Court might have determined that the speech would create a disturbance of the peace. In these scenarios, Mr. Brandenburg is speaking in person to members of racial and religious groups who are hated by Klansmen. The Court could find that Mr. Brandenburg's speech is not protected under the First Amendment because his advocacy might lead to a violent public eruption, or what the Supreme Court refers to as "imminent lawless action."

In *Cohen,* the Court says that in deciding whether speech is protected under the First Amendment, it considers whether it might provoke a violent reaction. If Mr. Cohen had worn his jacket while walking through a veteran's hospital or cemetery for veterans, it appears much more likely that his jacket would incite people to violence. Veterans who are in the hospital, the staff who work with them, and loved ones who are visiting them would be more likely to respond angrily than random people walking through a courthouse. This is also true for people who are visiting loved ones at a cemetery for veterans. However, the Court could still uphold Mr. Cohen's speech as constitutional since his remarks target a government policy, not individuals (unlike Mr. Brandenburg's speech).

Symbolic Speech

Freedom of speech is not limited to spoken or written words. As early as 1931, the U.S. Supreme Court acknowledged that symbolic speech—a form of nonverbal communication—has constitutional protection.[2] In order to receive First Amendment protection, symbolic speech must be designed to communicate a message. The Supreme Court has upheld various forms of symbolic speech. Table 2.1 lists several examples.

Table 2.1 **Examples of Constitutionally Protected Symbolic Speech**

Activity	Case
Refusing to Salute the U.S. Flag	*W. VA. State Board of Ed. v. Barnette* (1943)
Sitting-in at a Library (to protest segregation)	*Brown v. Louisiana* (1966)
Burning a Draft Card	*U.S. v. O'Brien* (1968)
Burning the Flag	*Texas v. Johnson* (1989) *U.S. v. Eichman* (1990)
Wearing a Black Armband With Peace Symbol	*Tinker v. Des Moines* (1969)
Wearing a Military Uniform to Protest War	*Schacht v. U.S.* (1970)
Placing a Peace Sign on the Flag	*Spence v. Washington* (1974)
Picketing Outside of the Supreme Court	*U.S. v. Grace* (1983)
Burning a Cross	*R.A.V. v. St. Paul* (1992) *Virginia v. Black* (2003)

As Table 2.1 highlights, the high Court has given constitutional protection to many expressions of nonverbal communication. Notably many of these cases involve people who have used the American flag to express their discontent with U.S. laws, policies, or practices. For some people, making any physical alterations to the American flag—beyond a proper burial when the flag is tattered or has been torn—is sacrilegious. These sentiments have historical roots. Thomas Jefferson and James Madison, for instance, believed that the flag, as an emblem of national sovereignty, should be protected from defacement.[3] Next is a discussion of three well-known flag cases that involve symbolic speech.

In *Spence v. Washington* (1974),[4] a college student was arrested for altering a U.S. flag. Harold Spence, a community college student, hung his U.S. flag from the window of his apartment. Using removable tape, he placed a large peace symbol on both sides of his flag. It was 1970, and Mr. Spence, a Native American, said he displayed his flag to protest the U.S. invasion of Cambodia. He was also upset because six days earlier, four Kent State University students who were antiwar protesters had been killed by National Guardsman. After seeing the flag, three Seattle police officers went to Mr. Spence's door. He was arrested and charged with violating a Washington state law prohibiting the "improper" display of an American flag. The statute made it unlawful to place "any word, figure, mark, picture, design, drawing, or advertisement of any nature upon any flag" and display it in public.[5] Mr. Spence was sentenced to ten days in jail and a $75 fine.

At his trial Mr. Spence stated, "I felt that the flag stood for America and I wanted people to know that I thought America stood for peace." He was convicted of a misdemeanor and sentenced to jail. He argued that he used the flag and peace sign as symbolic communication and that his conviction violated his free speech rights. The case was appealed to the Supreme Court. The Court upheld Mr. Spence's speech as constitutional and said the flag carries different meanings for different people: "What is one man's comfort and inspiration is another's jest and scorn."

The case of *Texas v. Johnson* (1989)[6] centers on an incident that occurred during the 1984 Republican National Convention. Gregory Johnson took part in a protest rally and march that began outside the convention hall. When the protest ended in front of the Dallas City Hall building, Johnson used kerosene to set fire to an American flag. As it burned, dozens of protestors chanted, "America, the red, white, and blue, we spit on you." Following a conviction for flag desecration, Johnson was fined two thousand dollars and sentenced to one year in prison. On appeal, Johnson argued that his actions were protected speech under the First Amendment. The Supreme Court agreed and reversed Johnson's conviction. It held that flag burning is constitutionally protected symbolic speech.

In response to the *Johnson* decision, Congress passed the Flag Protection Act, which made it unlawful to deface an American flag. A year later, in *United States v. Eichman* (1990), the Flag Protection Act was challenged, and the Supreme Court struck it down. Noting that "desecration of the flag is deeply offensive to many," the Court repeated the language it used in *Johnson,* "[T]he Government may not prohibit the expression of an idea simply because society finds the idea itself offensive or disagreeable."[7] Concerns about flag burning have also spurred Congress to consider passing a constitutional amendment that would outlaw the desecration of a U.S. flag. However, proposed amendments have failed to win the required two-thirds majority vote of Congress.

The Limits of Free Speech

The right of free speech does not mean that you may say whatever you want whenever you want to whomever you want. There are legal limits. To determine whether a particular type of speech is constitutionally protected, the Supreme Court engages in a balancing act—weighing an individual's right to free expression against society's larger interests. We now consider three categories of speech that do not have constitutional protection. If the speech is obscene, if the words can be classified as "fighting words," or if the language causes a "clear and present danger," it may be prohibited.

In 2010, Black students at U.C. Berkeley held a silent campus vigil to protest a noose hanging at a U.C. San Diego library.

Obscenity. Obscenity is not protected by the U.S. Constitution. The Supreme Court took many twists and turns on its path to define obscene speech. At one point, each Supreme Court Justice was allowed to set his own benchmark for obscenity. In *Jacobellis v. Ohio* (1964), the manager of a movie theater was convicted of possessing obscene material after he showed the French film, *The Lovers.* The Supreme Court decided that the film was not obscene. In the decision, Justice Potter Stewart famously commented that while he did not know how to define obscenity, "I know it when I see it."[8] Over decades, the Court looked at several factors to determine whether something was obscene, including whether the material was "prurient" (lewd), whether the material violated community standards, whether the material had social value, and whether the material was offensive.

In 1973, after deciding a series of obscenity cases, the Supreme Court announced a new test for obscenity in *Miller v. California* (1973).[9] The defendant, Marvin Miller, sent mass mailings of unsolicited brochures to individuals and businesses. The brochures advertised sexually explicit illustrated books and films, with titles including, *Sex Orgies Illustrated* and *An Illustrated History of Pornography*. One of the unsolicited brochures arrived at a restaurant in Newport Beach, California. The envelope was opened by the manager and his mother, who later complained to the police. Miller was convicted of knowingly distributing obscene material, a misdemeanor. The case was appealed all the way to the Supreme Court. In a five to four decision, the Court outlined a three-part test for the fact finder (jury or judge) in an obscenity case:

1. Material, taken as a whole, appeals to prurient interest in sex and portrays sexual conduct in a patently offensive way, based upon contemporary (state) community standards;

2. Material that depicts or describes sexual conduct and is defined by the applicable state law; and

3. Material taken as a whole does not have serious literary, artistic, political, or scientific value.[10]

More than forty years later, the Supreme Court continues to use the *Miller* test to decide whether material is obscene and therefore, without constitutional protection.

While public displays of obscene material are not protected under the First Amendment, private displays may be constitutional. In *Stanley v. Georgia* (1969), the Supreme Court held that a person has a right to have obscene material in the privacy of his home.[11] State and federal agents went to the home of Robert Stanley to carry out a search warrant for illegal gambling. While looking through a bedroom dresser, an agent discovered three reels of 8mm film. The agents located a projector in Stanley's home and watched the films. One of the agents concluded that the films, which contained pornography, were obscene and removed them. Stanley was arrested and convicted under a Georgia law that punished "knowingly hav[ing] possession of obscene matter." He appealed his conviction to the Supreme Court, arguing that he had the right to keep obscene material in his house. In his majority opinion, Justice Thurgood Marshall stated, "[T]he States retain broad power to regulate obscenity; that power simply does not extend to mere possession by the individual in the privacy of his home."[12]

Pornography is no longer confined to magazines and movies. Technological advances have increased the spaces that display obscene material. For instance, the transmission of sexually explicit photographs via mobile phone—also known as *sexting*—has emerged as a controversial area of criminal prosecution. While sexting between consenting adults is generally protected speech under the First Amendment, other issues remain (see Chapter 7, "Rape and Other Violent Crimes," for a detailed discussion of sexting).

Fighting Words and Hate Speech. "Sticks and stones may break my bones but words will never hurt me" goes the popular children's adage. Fighting words and words that single out people because they are different force us to ask whether this maxim is true, and if so, whether the Constitution should protect harmful speech when it is directed at specific individuals.

Some speech is so inflammatory that it is considered an invitation to violence. "Fighting words," the Supreme Court held in *Chaplinsky v. New Hampshire* (1942), are words that "by their very utterance inflict injury or tend to incite an immediate breach of the peace."[13] These words involve language that is likely to provoke a person to a violent response. In the case, Mr. Chaplinsky, a Jehovah's Witness, referred to a local official as "a God Damned racketeer" and "Damned fascist." The Court held that fighting words, which were used in this case, are not protected by the Constitution. These words, "by their very utterance, inflict injury or tend to incite an immediate breach of the peace." The Court held that because fighting words have "slight social value," they are outweighed by the "social interest in order and morality." Thus, fighting words are not protected speech under the Constitution. However, if someone is hurling fighting words at you, you are not legally allowed to punch the person; fighting words do not excuse an assault.

Issues involving hate speech arise in various contexts. Sometimes the circumstances involve symbolic speech, such as when someone burns a cross. In other instances, the speech is accompanied by conduct. An example is someone who uses an ethnic slur while committing an assault. These instances raise the question of whether it should be a separate crime to use hate speech while committing a criminal offense. In *R.A.V. v. St. Paul* (1992),[14] the Supreme Court held that states can prohibit intentionally hateful communication (e.g., Whites had burned a cross on a Black family's lawn). However, the government cannot single out certain types of speech to punish over others. Speech prohibitions must be "content-neutral." In 1993, the Supreme Court decided *Wisconsin v. Mitchell* (1993),[15] a case involving a White youth who was targeted and assaulted by a group of Black youths. The defendant was convicted of aggravated battery and received an additional two-year sentence because the victim had been targeted because of his race. The Court held that it is constitutional for a state to impose a longer sentence against an offender for a racially motivated crime.

Hate speech is sometimes joined with hateful actions. Some commentators believe that some hate speech is so connected to action that it should be criminal. Law professor Mari Matsuda, for instance, argues that race-based hate speech, by itself, should be a crime. She describes her parents' warnings to her when she was little—a Japanese American child during a World War II:

> As a young child, I was told never to let anyone call me a J—P. My parents . . . told me this in the tone reserved for dead-serious warnings. Don't accept rides from strangers. Don't play with matches. Don't let anyone call you that name. In their tone they transmitted a message of danger, that the word was a dangerous one, tied to violence.[16]

Professor Matsuda argues that the failure to punish hate speech encourages violence against some members of society. In an effort to encourage civil discourse and discourage hateful speech, many colleges in the United States have adopted speech codes. However, many university speech codes have been successfully challenged as infringements upon free speech. As a result, the impact of campus speech codes is largely symbolic—as a statement of a particular university's goal to foster and maintain an open learning environment.

Imminent Lawless Action

In *Schenck v. United States* (1919),[17] the Supreme Court applied a "clear and present danger" test to determine whether speech could be prohibited. In *Schenck*, Justice Oliver Wendell Holmes famously observed that the right to free speech does not give a person the right to yell "fire" in a crowded theater when there is no fire. In contemporary terms, the right to free speech does not give someone the right to send out a "fire" message on Twitter or email (unless there is an actual fire). In 1969, the court amended the "clear and present danger" standard to "imminent lawless action" (discussed in *Brandenburg v. Ohio* [1969]; bold added). Speech that creates an immediate threat of violence or unrest is *not* constitutionally protected.

Time, Place, and Manner Restrictions. As the Supreme Court said in *Cohen v. California* (1971), even protected forms of speech may be regulated by the state. The government and its entities can decide when, where, and under what circumstances public speech is permissible. For instance, states, municipalities, counties, cities, parks, airports, and schools may impose rules for public gatherings (e.g., rallies); establish hours during which public protests can be held; and set the noise level for gatherings in public spaces. These are known as time, place, and manner restrictions.

Freedom of Assembly

The First Amendment protects "the right of the people peaceably to assemble." The next case, *Edwards v. South Carolina* (1963), demonstrates that this constitutional right was an important legal tool in the fight for racial equality during the 1960s civil rights movement. Without it, civil rights advocates could have been prevented from planning and participating in large group demonstrations, including marches such as the Selma to Montgomery marches and the 1963 March on Washington. Earlier protests, including the Montgomery bus boycott in 1955 and sit-ins throughout the South, showed the power of nonviolent public assembly. The right to assemble is often raised along with other First Amendment guarantees, such as freedom of speech and the right to petition the government.

Edwards v. South Carolina (1963)

U.S. Supreme Court
372 U.S. 229

MR. JUSTICE STEWART delivered the opinion of the Court. The petitioners, 187 in number, were convicted in a magistrate's court in Columbia, South Carolina, of the common-law crime of breach of the peace. Their convictions were ultimately affirmed by the South Carolina Supreme Court, 239 S. C. 339, 123 S. E. 2d 247. We granted certiorari . . . to consider the claim that these convictions cannot be squared with the Fourteenth Amendment of the United States Constitution.

There was no substantial conflict in the trial evidence. Late in the morning of March 2, 1961, the petitioners, high school and college students of the Negro race, met at the Zion Baptist Church in Columbia. From there, at about noon, they walked in separate groups of about 15 to the South Carolina State House grounds, an area of two city blocks open to the general public. Their purpose was "to submit a protest to the citizens of South Carolina, along with the Legislative Bodies of South Carolina, our feelings and our dissatisfaction with the present condition of discriminatory actions against Negroes, in general, and to let them know that we were dissatisfied and that we would like for the laws which prohibited Negro privileges in this State to be removed."

Already on the State House grounds when the petitioners arrived were 30 or more law enforcement officers, who had advance knowledge that the petitioners were coming. Each group of petitioners entered the grounds through a driveway and parking area known in the record as the "horseshoe." As they entered, they were told by the law enforcement officials that "they had a right, as a citizen, to go through the State House grounds, as any other citizen has, as long as they were peaceful." During the next half hour or 45 minutes, the petitioners, in the same small groups, walked single file or two abreast in an orderly way through the grounds, each group carrying placards bearing such messages as "I am proud to be a Negro" and "Down with segregation."

During this time a crowd of some 200 to 300 onlookers had collected in the horseshoe area and on the adjacent sidewalks. There was no evidence to suggest that these onlookers were anything but curious, and no evidence at all of any threatening remarks, hostile gestures, or offensive language on the part of any member of the crowd. The City Manager testified that he recognized some of the onlookers, whom he did not identify, as "possible trouble makers," but his subsequent testimony made clear that nobody among the crowd actually caused or threatened any trouble. There was no obstruction of pedestrian or vehicular traffic within the State House grounds. No vehicle was prevented from entering or leaving the horseshoe area. Although vehicular traffic at a nearby street intersection was slowed down somewhat, an officer was dispatched to keep traffic moving. There were a number of bystanders on the public sidewalks adjacent to the State House grounds, but they all moved on when asked to do so, and there was no impediment of pedestrian traffic. Police protection at the scene was at all times sufficient to meet any foreseeable possibility of disorder.

In the situation and under the circumstances thus described, the police authorities advised the petitioners that they would be arrested if they did not disperse within 15 minutes. Instead of dispersing, the petitioners engaged in what the City Manager described as "boisterous," "loud," and "flamboyant" conduct, which, as his later testimony made clear, consisted of listening to a "religious harangue" by one of their leaders, and loudly singing "The Star Spangled Banner" and other patriotic and religious songs, while stamping their feet and clapping their hands. After 15 minutes had passed, the police arrested the petitioners and marched them off to jail.

Upon this evidence the state trial court convicted the petitioners of breach of the peace, and imposed sentences ranging from a $10 fine or five days in jail, to a $100 fine or 30 days in jail. In affirming the judgments, the Supreme Court of South Carolina said that under the law of that State the offense of breach of the peace "is not susceptible of exact definition," but that the "general definition of the offense" is as follows:

> In general terms, a breach of the peace is a violation of public order, a disturbance of the public tranquility, by any act or conduct inciting to violence . . . , it includes any violation of any law enacted to preserve peace and good order. It may consist of an act of violence or an act likely to produce violence. It is not necessary that the peace be actually broken to lay the foundation for a prosecution for this offense. If what is done is unjustifiable and unlawful, tending with sufficient directness to break the peace, no more is required. Nor is actual personal violence an essential element in the offense. . . .
>
> By "peace," as used in the law in this connection, is meant the tranquility enjoyed by citizens of a municipality or community where good order reigns among its members, which is the natural right of all persons in political society. 239 S. C., at 343–344, 123 S. E. 2d, at 249.

The petitioners contend that there was a complete absence of any evidence of the commission of this offense, and that they were thus denied one of the most basic elements of due process of law . . . Whatever the merits of this contention, we need not pass upon it in the present case. The state courts have held that the petitioners' conduct constituted breach of the peace under state law, and we may accept their decision as binding upon us to that extent. But it nevertheless remains our duty in a case such as this to make an independent examination of the whole record . . . And it is clear to us that in arresting, convicting, and punishing the petitioners under the circumstances disclosed by this record, South Carolina infringed the petitioners' constitutionally protected rights of free speech, free assembly, and freedom to petition for redress of their grievances.

(Continued)

(Continued)

It has long been established that these First Amendment freedoms are protected by the Fourteenth Amendment from invasion by the States. . . . The circumstances in this case reflect an exercise of these basic constitutional rights in their most pristine and classic form. The petitioners felt aggrieved by laws of South Carolina which allegedly "prohibited Negro privileges in this State." They peaceably assembled at the site of the State Government and there peaceably expressed their grievances "to the citizens of South Carolina, along with the Legislative Bodies of South Carolina." Not until they were told by police officials that they must disperse on pain of arrest did they do more. Even then, they but sang patriotic and religious songs after one of their leaders had delivered a "religious harangue." There was no violence or threat of violence on their part, or on the part of any member of the crowd watching them. Police protection was "ample."

This, therefore, was a far cry from the situation in *Feiner v. New York*, 340 U.S. 315 , where two policemen were faced with a crowd which was "pushing, shoving and milling around," id., at 317, where at least one member of the crowd "threatened violence if the police did not act," id., at 317, where "the crowd was pressing closer around petitioner and the officer," id., at 318, and where "the speaker passes the bounds of argument or persuasion and undertakes incitement to riot." Id., at 321. And the record is barren of any evidence of "fighting words." See *Chaplinsky v. New Hampshire*, 315 U.S. 568.

We do not review in this case criminal convictions resulting from the evenhanded application of a precise and narrowly drawn regulatory statute evincing a legislative judgment that certain specific conduct be limited or proscribed. If, for example, the petitioners had been convicted upon evidence that they had violated a law regulating traffic, or had disobeyed a law reasonably limiting the periods during which the State House grounds were open to the public, this would be a different case. . . . These petitioners were convicted of an offense so generalized as to be, in the words of the South Carolina Supreme Court, "not susceptible of exact definition." And they were convicted upon evidence which showed no more than that the opinions which they were peaceably expressing were sufficiently opposed to the views of the majority of the community to attract a crowd and necessitate police protection.

The Fourteenth Amendment does not permit a State to make criminal the peaceful expression of unpopular views. "[A] function of free speech under our system of government is to invite dispute. It may indeed best serve its high purpose when it induces a condition of unrest, creates dissatisfaction with conditions as they are, or even stirs people to anger. Speech is often provocative and challenging. It may strike at prejudices and preconceptions and have profound unsettling effects as it presses for acceptance of an idea. That is why freedom of speech . . . is . . . protected against censorship or punishment, unless shown likely to produce a clear and present danger of a serious substantive evil that rises far above public inconvenience, annoyance, or unrest. . . . There is no room under our Constitution for a more restrictive view. For the alternative would lead to standardization of ideas either by legislatures, courts, or dominant political or community groups." *Terminiello v. Chicago*, 337 U.S. 1, 4-5. As in the *Terminiello* case, the courts of South Carolina have defined a criminal offense so as to permit conviction of the petitioners if their speech "stirred people to anger, invited public dispute, or brought about a condition of unrest. A conviction resting on any of those grounds may not stand." Id. at 5.

As Chief Justice Hughes wrote in *Stromberg v. California*, "The maintenance of the opportunity for free political discussion to the end that government may be responsive to the will of the people and that changes may be obtained by lawful means, an opportunity essential to the security of the Republic, is a fundamental principle of our constitutional system. A statute which upon its face, and as authoritatively construed, is so vague and indefinite as to permit the punishment of the fair use of this opportunity is repugnant to the guaranty of liberty contained in the Fourteenth Amendment. . . . " 283 U.S. 359, 369.

For these reasons we conclude that these criminal convictions cannot stand.

Reversed.

Questions

1. Which constitutional issues do the protesters raise in this case?

2. What rationales does the Supreme Court give for its decision? What does the Court have to say about the decision by the Supreme Court of South Carolina?

3. What if instead of peaceful and religious songs the protesters had sung anti-American chants, and in response, some onlookers had begun to fight and scream at the protesters? Would that have led to a different outcome in the case?

Free Exercise of Religion

Religion and the goals of religious freedom have played a central role in development of American jurisprudence. In the early 1600s, many people, including Pilgrims and Puritans, fled England. They left Europe on the Mayflower to escape religious persecution and to start a new life on another continent. They traveled across the Atlantic to the New World, to a land inhabited by Native Americans. Religion continued to be a flashpoint and led to political conflict, including the American Revolution. Scholars, politicians, and working people fought over the role of religion in government. On the topic of religious autonomy, Thomas Jefferson said it is "the most inalienable and sacred of all human rights."[18] James Madison stated that religion "must be left to the conviction and conscience of every man . . . This right is in its nature an unalienable right."[19] These core beliefs held by Jefferson and Madison, among others, are now enshrined in the First Amendment's protection of religious freedom. It protects an individual's right to worship and practice religion. It also protects a person's choice not to believe in God. The free exercise clause is broadly interpreted and subject to careful curtailment.

In a variety of cases, courts have determined that the right to the free exercise of religion outweighs the government's interest in promoting concerns related to public health and safety. For instance, members of the Amish religion cannot be forced to have their children attend school past the eighth grade.[20] Likewise, the Supreme Court upheld the practice of animal sacrifice for members of the Santeria religion.[21] *Wooley v. Maynard* (1977) offers another example of the free exercise clause at work.[22] The case involved a challenge to a New Hampshire law that required drivers to display the state motto on their vehicle license plates. George and Maxine Maynard, a married couple who were Jehovah's Witnesses, objected to the state motto, "Live Free or Die." They used tape to cover up the motto on the license plates for both of their cars. Within a five-week period, the Maynards were stopped three times by the police. The Maynards covered up the state motto because it conflicted with their religious, moral, and political beliefs. At trial, Mr. Maynard testified:

> I believe my government—Jehovah's Kingdom—offers everlasting life. It would be contrary to that belief to give up my life for the state, even if it meant bondage . . . [T]his slogan is directly at odds with my deeply held religious convictions.[23]

On appeal, the U.S. Supreme Court agreed that the covered up license plate was protected speech under the First Amendment. The freedom to exercise religion does not mean being forced to become a "mobile billboard" for the state.

Not all challenges brought under the free exercise clause have been successful. In these cases, courts have held that a person's religious practices must give way to health and public safety concerns. For instance, some courts have denied parents the right to refuse medical treatment for a sick child based on religious doctrine.

The New Hampshire state license plate motto, "Live Free or Die," was challenged in *Wooley v. Maynard* (1977).

Second Amendment ●━━━━━━━━━━━━━━━━━━━━━━━

A well regulated Militia, being necessary to the security of a free State, the right of the people to keep and bear Arms, shall not be infringed.

United States Constitution, Second Amendment

The Second Amendment is no shrinking violet when it comes to stirring public comment and stoking controversy. Second Amendment advocates interpret it as giving U.S. citizens an unfettered and unlimited right to bear arms. On the other side, gun control advocates interpret the amendment as granting a limited right to bear arms. In a duet of deeply divided cases, the Supreme Court has upheld the right of citizens to bear arms. In *District of Columbia v. Heller* (2008),[24] the Court heard an appeal in a case involving a Washington, DC, police officer. The officer, Dick Heller, sought a permit to keep a handgun in his private residence for protection. At the time of Heller's request, DC had a ban on handgun ownership. His request was denied, and he appealed the decision as a denial of his Second Amendment rights. In a five to four decision, the Court held that the Second Amendment's "right of the people to keep and bear arms" language protects the right of individuals to maintain firearms for lawful purposes. While the Court was clear as to the rights protected by the Second Amendment, it left unanswered a big question: Did the *Heller* ruling extend to all fifty states or was it limited to Washington, DC, and other federal enclaves? Two years later, in *McDonald v. Chicago* (2010),[25] the Court, in another five to four decision, responded: The Second Amendment applies to the states through the Fourteenth Amendment's due process clause. (See Chapter 9, "Justification Defenses," for a discussion of firearms and self-defense).

Fifth Amendment ●━━━━━━━━━━━━━━━━━━━━━━━

Due Process

The Constitution requires that laws provide the public with notice as to which activities are criminal. This is guaranteed by the due process clause. There are two due process clauses—one in the Fifth Amendment and another one in the Fourteenth Amendment. The Fifth Amendment guarantees due process for federal laws, and the Fourteenth Amendment, for state laws. In instances where a law is written in language that is too general and fails to give clear notice that certain actions are unlawful, it may be unconstitutional and struck down as "void for vagueness." Cases involving challenges to state law are discussed later in this chapter under the due process section of the Fourteenth Amendment.

Eighth Amendment ●━━━━━━━━━━━━━━━━━━━━━━━

Excessive bail shall not be required, nor excessive fines imposed, nor cruel and unusual punishments inflicted.

United States Constitution, Eighth Amendment

The brevity of the Eighth Amendment—sixteen words—belies its weight and promise. The prohibition against cruel and unusual punishment refers specifically to post-conviction punishments, not for instance, to a pretrial jail term. Most discussions of the Eighth Amendment are about capital punishment and whether and under which circumstances it is cruel and unusual. However, claims of cruel and unusual punishment extend beyond death penalty cases. In *Harmelin v. Michigan* (1991),[26] the defendant was convicted of possessing 672 grams of cocaine (approximately one and one-half pounds) and sentenced to a mandatory term of life imprisonment. He argued that the sentence violated the Eighth Amendment because it was "cruel and unusual" and "significantly disproportionate" to the crime. The U.S. Supreme Court held that as long as a sentence is not grossly disproportionate to the crime, it may be upheld, concluding that mandatory punishments may be cruel, but they are not unusual.

In *Graham v. Florida* (2010),[27] the Supreme Court was asked to determine whether it is constitutional to allow juveniles to be sentenced to life in prison for a crime that does not involve death. Terrance Graham, a repeat offender, who was seventeen years old at the time of his offense, received a life sentence after an armed robbery conviction. He argued that the punishment was grossly disproportionate to his crime and therefore, a violation of the Eighth Amendment. The Supreme Court agreed and held that a state cannot sentence a minor to life in prison for a non-homicide offense. Justice Anthony Kennedy observed that life sentences for juveniles (in non-homicide cases) had been "rejected the world over."[28] In 2010, when *Graham* was decided, there were 129 juvenile offenders in the United States who were serving life sentences for non-homicide crimes.[29] In a later case, the Supreme Court expanded this ruling to cases involving murder. (See Chapter 11, "Punishment and Sentencing," for discussion other issues raised by capital punishment).

Fourteenth Amendment

Equal Protection Clause

The Fourteenth Amendment was passed in 1868, just three years after the end of the U.S. Civil War. The equal protection clause was explicitly written to level the racial playing field. Congressional representative Thaddeus Stevens, one of the drafters of the Fourteenth Amendment, said that his goal in crafting the amendment was to establish that "no distinction would be tolerated in this purified Republic but what arose from merit and conduct."[30] Cases brought under the Fourteenth Amendment's equal protection clause represent a history-making group of Supreme Court decisions.[31] The Fourteenth Amendment mandates the "equal protection of the laws." Laws are required to treat people equally, unless the government can show that it has a "compelling state interest" to treat people differently. Equal protection clause challenges have been raised in a wide array of criminal law cases, including ones involving, racial desegregation in public spaces, interracial marriage, and capital punishment. A Florida law that made it unlawful for Blacks and Whites to live together is addressed in the next case.

McLaughlin v. Florida (1964)

U.S. Supreme Court
379 U.S. 184

Mr. Justice WHITE delivered the opinion of the Court. At issue in this case is the validity of a conviction under s 798.05 of the Florida statutes, F.S.A., providing that:

> Any negro man and White woman, or any White man and negro woman, who are not married to each other, who shall habitually live in and occupy in the nighttime the same room shall each be punished by imprisonment not exceeding twelve months, or by fine not exceeding five hundred dollars.

Because the section applies only to a White person and a Negro who commit the specified acts and because no couple other than one made up of a White and a Negro is subject to conviction upon proof of the elements comprising the offense it proscribes, we hold s 798.05 invalid as a denial of the equal protection of the laws guaranteed by the Fourteenth Amendment. . . .

It is readily apparent that s 798.05 treats the interracial couple made up of a White person and a Negro differently than it does any other couple. No couple other than a Negro and a White person can be convicted under s 798.05 and no other section proscribes the precise conduct banned by s 798.05. Florida makes no claim to the contrary in this Court. However, all whites and Negroes who engage in the forbidden conduct are covered by the section and each member of the interracial couple is subject to the same penalty. . . .

We deal here with a racial classification embodied in a criminal statute. In this context, where the power of the State weighs most heavily upon the individual or the group, we must be especially sensitive to the policies of the Equal Protection Clause which, as reflected in congressional enactments dating from 1870, were intended to secure "the full and equal benefit of all laws and proceedings for the security of persons and property" and to subject all persons "to like punishment, pains, penalties, taxes, licenses, and exactions of every kind, and to no other." R.S. s 1977, 42 U.S.C. s 1981 (1958 ed.). Our inquiry, therefore, is whether there clearly appears in the relevant materials some overriding statutory purpose requiring the proscription of the specified conduct when engaged in by a White person and a Negro, but not otherwise. Without such justification the racial classification contained in s 798.05 is reduced to an invidious discrimination forbidden by the Equal Protection Clause.

The Florida Supreme Court, relying upon *Pace v. Alabama*, supra, found no legal discrimination at all and gave no consideration to statutory purpose. The State in its brief in this Court, however, says that the legislative purpose of s 798.05, like the other sections of chapter 798, was to prevent breaches of the basic concepts of sexual decency; and we see no reason to quarrel with the State's characterization of this statute, dealing as it does with illicit extramarital and premarital promiscuity.

We find nothing in this suggested legislative purpose, however, which makes it essential to punish promiscuity of one racial group and not that of another. . . . That a general evil will be partially corrected may at times, and without more, serve to justify the limited application of a criminal law; but legislative discretion to employ the piecemeal approach stops short of permitting a State to narrow statutory coverage to focus on a racial group. Such classifications bear a far heavier burden of justification. 'When the law lays an unequal hand on those who have committed intrinsically the same quality of offense and sterilizes one and not the other, it has made as an invidious a discrimination as if it had selected a particular race or nationality for oppressive treatment. *Yick Wo v. Hopkins* (118 U.S. 356,); (State of Missouri ex rel.) *Gaines v. Canada*, 305 U.S. 337, 59 S.Ct. 232, 83 L.Ed. 208.' *Skinner v. Oklahoma* ex rel. Williamson, 316 U.S. 535, 541. . .

There is involved here an exercise of the state police power which trenches upon the constitutionally protected freedom from invidious official discrimination based on race. Such a law, even though enacted pursuant to a valid state interest, bears a heavy burden of justification, as we have said, and will be upheld only if it is necessary, and not merely rationally related, to the accomplishment of a permissible state policy. . . . Florida has offered no argument that the State's policy against interracial marriage cannot be as adequately served by the general, neutral, and existing ban on illicit behavior as by a provision such as s 798.05 which singles out the promiscuous interracial couple for special statutory treatment. In short, it has not been shown that s 798.05 is a necessary adjunct to the State's ban on interracial marriage. We accordingly invalidate s 798.05 without expressing any views about the State's prohibition of interracial marriage, and reverse these convictions.

Reversed.

Questions

1. What is the issue in the case?

2. What is the holding in *McLaughlin*? What is the two-part test that the Supreme Court uses to determine whether the Florida law is constitutional?

3. The Florida law was written to punish intimate relationships between Whites and Blacks (the Court notes that Florida had also outlawed marriages between Blacks and Whites). Assume the law had prohibited all mixed-race marriages. Under the Court's reasoning, would that have been constitutionally permissible?

A few years after the Supreme Court decided *McLaughlin v. Florida* (1964), it was asked to determine the constitutionality of laws that criminalized interracial marriage. The case was *Loving v. Virginia*,[32] and when the Court heard the case in 1967, sixteen states had antimiscegenation laws on the books. In 1958, Richard Loving, a White man, and Mildred Jeter, a Black woman, were married in Washington, DC. The newly wedded couple returned to Virginia, and they were charged with violating a Virginia law that banned Whites from marrying non-Whites. According to the statute:

It any White person intermarry with a colored person, or any colored person intermarry with a White person he shall be guilty of a felony and shall be punished by confinement in the penitentiary for not less than one nor more than five years.[33]

The Lovings pled guilty to violating the law and were each sentenced to a one-year prison term. The trial court judge offered to waive the sentences if the married couple would agree not to return to Virginia for at least twenty-five years. He stated:

Almighty God created the races white, black, yellow, malay and red, and he placed them on separate continents . . . The fact that he separated the races shows that he did not intend for the races to mix.[34]

The Lovings moved back to Washington, DC, and filed papers stating that their convictions should be set aside because the Virginia law violated the Fourteenth Amendment's equal protection clause. Following a series of legal proceedings, the Supreme Court agreed to hear the case. The Court determined that Virginia's antimiscegenation laws were unconstitutional holdovers from the era of slavery: "The fact that Virginia prohibits only interracial marriages involving white persons demonstrates that the racial classifications must stand on their own justifications, as measures designed to maintain White Supremacy."[35] Racial classifications in the law must be subjected to the "most rigid scrutiny" and must be necessary to accomplish a permissible state goal. The state of Virginia could not establish that it had a compelling reason for making interracial marriage illegal.

Due Process

Papachristou v. Jacksonville (1972)[36] is a memorable case that tackles the issue of due process. Several individuals were convicted of violating a Jacksonville, Florida, vagrancy ordinance. In one incident, a man was arrested when he arrived home early one morning and was charged with being a "common thief." Although he was not issued a speeding ticket, police officers said the man had been stopped because he had been speeding. In another incident, two men were arrested after driving to a friend's home. Police were in the friend's driveway, arresting another person. When the defendants began to back out of the driveway, the officers told them to stop and get out of the car. A police search of the car revealed no incriminating evidence. However, police arrested both men—one was charged with being a "common thief" based on his reputation, the other with "loitering." The defendants argued that the ordinance violated the due process clause because the language was too vague. Here is the text of the Jacksonville ordinance:

> Rogues and vagabonds, or dissolute persons who go about begging, common gamblers, persons who use juggling or unlawful games or plays, common drunkards, common night walkers, thieves, pilferers or pickpockets, traders in stolen property, lewd, wanton and lascivious persons, keepers of gambling places, common railers and brawlers, persons wandering or strolling around from place to place without any lawful purpose or object, habitual loafers, disorderly persons, persons neglecting all lawful business and habitually spending their time by frequenting houses of ill fame, gaming houses, or places where alcoholic beverages are sold or served, persons able to work but habitually living upon the earnings of their wives or minor children shall be deemed vagrants.[37]

The Court decided that the ordinance was unconstitutional. It stated that the law allowed for arbitrary and discriminatory enforcement and provided a "convenient tool" for singling out people who are members of unpopular groups.

Papachristou affirmed the Supreme Court's earlier decision in *Coates v. Cincinnati* (1971). Following his participation in a student antiwar demonstration, Dennis Coates was charged with violating a Cincinnati ordinance that made it unlawful for three or more people to gather on sidewalks, vacant lots, or street corners "in an annoying manner." The Court struck down the law as unconstitutionally vague, saying the ordinance made "a crime out of what under the Constitution cannot be a crime."[38]

The Supreme Court has consistently held that laws should be written to minimize unfair discretion on the part of police officers. The defendant in *Kolender v. Lawson* (1983) walked everywhere he went. Edward Lawson, a tall Black man who wore dreadlocks, enjoyed taking long nighttime walks in mostly White areas of San Diego, California. He was stopped by police fifteen times in twenty-two months. Lawson was convicted under a California law that allowed police to request "credible and reliable" identification from people who loiter. Lawson argued that the law was unconstitutionally vague. In its 1983 decision, the Supreme Court agreed with Lawson and struck down the state law.[39]

One of the key concerns with vague laws is that they may be used to punish members of socially marginal groups. For instance, a law that allows broad police discretion could be used to target members of disfavored groups, such as the homeless, or readily identifiable group members, such as racial, ethnic, or religious minorities. (See Chapter 6, "Public Order Crimes and Offenses Against Public Decency" for further discussion of vagrancy and other public order offenses).

Right to Privacy

The U.S. Constitution protects the right to privacy. Unlike the other constitutional guarantees discussed in this chapter, the right to privacy was not written into the wording of the Constitution. In fact, the word "privacy" is not explicitly referenced in the document. However, the right to privacy is a protected right that has evolved over the decades through Supreme Court decisions. The right to privacy is based on the idea that an individual should be allowed to make personal decisions without interference from the government. The right to privacy covers a broad range of areas, including contraception, family relations, adoption, sexual relations, and the private possession of obscene material. This protection has roots in several amendments, including the First, Fourth, Fifth, Ninth, and Fourteenth (see appendix for text of U.S. Constitution). Some legal scholars argue that because the right to privacy is not explicitly referenced in the Constitution, it should not receive constitutional protection.

One of the most controversial areas involving the right to privacy is a woman's right to terminate a pregnancy. This was the issue in *Roe v. Wade* (1973).[40] The Supreme Court concluded that during the first three months of pregnancy, women have the right to choose abortion, in consultation with a physician, without interference from the government. However, the state's authority to regulate and outlaw abortion increases as pregnancy advances. During the final three-month period of pregnancy (third trimester), states may ban abortion, except where it is necessary to protect the health or life of the woman. While upholding the main finding in *Roe v. Wade* (1973), later Supreme Court cases have upheld greater restrictions on a woman's decision to end a pregnancy—such as a twenty-four-hour waiting period, informed consent provisions, parental consent for minors, and a ban on late-stage abortions.

Laws punishing sodomy have also been challenged as violations of individual privacy rights. In *Bowers v. Hardwick* (1986),[41] the Supreme Court was asked to decide whether a Georgia law that punished sodomy was constitutional. After an officer saw Michael Hardwick engaged in consensual sodomy with another man, Hardwick was arrested and charged with violating a Georgia law that prohibited sodomy. Under the statute, "a person commits the offense of sodomy when he performs or submits to any sexual act involving the sex organs of one person and the mouth or anus of another."[42] Mr. Hardwick, a gay man, challenged the law as a violation of his fundamental constitutional rights. The Supreme Court rejected this argument and held there is no constitutional right for homosexuals to engage in sodomy.

Seventeen years later, the Supreme Court decided *Lawrence v. Texas* (2003).[43] After observing John Lawrence and Tyron Garner engaging in a sex act, Houston police charged the men with violating a state law that criminalized "deviate sexual intercourse."[44] Following their conviction, they appealed. After hearing the case, the Supreme Court held that private, consensual sodomy, between adults is constitutionally protected activity. This overruled the *Bowers* decision. The Court stated that the Constitution is to be interpreted through a contemporary lens:

> [The Founders] knew times can blind us to certain truths and later generations can see that laws once thought necessary and proper in fact serve only to oppress. As the Constitution endures, persons in every generation can invoke its principles in their own search for greater freedom.[45]

The Court also noted that there was little public support for *Bowers* within the national and international communities.

Table 2.2 "Bill of Rights, Summary Chart" below gives an overview of the constitutional protections, key terms and concepts, and cases discussed in this chapter. Use this to organize and review the material.

Table 2.2 **Bill of Rights, Summary Chart**

Amendment	Terms & Concepts	Key Cases
First Amendment		
Freedom of Speech	Symbolic speech, Obscenity, Fighting Words	*Brandenburg v. Ohio* *Cohen v. California* *Spence v. Washington* *Texas v. Johnson* *Chaplinsky v. New Hampshire* *Miller v. California* *Stanley v. Georgia*
Freedom of Assembly		*Edwards v. S. Carolina*
Freedom of Religion	Free Exercise of Religion	*Wooley v. Maynard*
Second Amendment	Right to Bear Arms	*D.C. v. Heller* *McDonald v. Chicago*
Eighth Amendment	Cruel & Unusual Punishment	*Harmelin v. Michigan* *Graham v. Florida*

Concluding Note

This chapter has provided an overview of the constitutional limits placed on states and the federal government in defining criminal activity. The First, Second, Fifth, Eighth, Fourteenth Amendments, and the right to privacy, set boundaries for criminal legislation. The constitutional protections discussed in this chapter lay the foundation for the cases and materials we will discuss in the coming pages. We will further analyze these issues and discuss their policy implications. Now test yourself on the material we have covered in this chapter. Good luck with the Issue Spotter exercise.

Issue Spotter

Read the hypothetical (based on an actual court case) and spot the issues discussed in this chapter.

The Funeral Protest[46]

Felicia Anson is cofounder and pastor at the Eastside Baptist Church in Kansas City, Missouri. Eastside congregation members steadfastly believe that God hates the United States because it tolerates homosexuality. Members believe it is an abomination against God to allow gay men and women to serve in the U.S. military. Eastside Baptist church members make their views known by picketing, frequently at military funerals. Over the years, they have picketed at more than one hundred military funerals.

Marine Lance Corporal Jeffrey Yu was killed in Iraq in the line of duty. Lance Corporal Yu's parents selected a non-denominational church in their hometown of Silver Spring, Maryland, for their son's memorial service. Through news reports, Anson learned details regarding Jeffrey Yu's funeral and arranged to travel to Maryland with six other members of Eastside Baptist.

At 1:00 p.m. on the day of the service, members of Eastside Baptist picketed across the street from the church on public property. They stood approximately one hundred feet from the church entrance. The picketers carried signs that read: "God Hates the USA/Thank God for 9/11," "Thank God for Dead Soldiers," "God Hates Fags," and "You're Going to Hell." The protesters did not have a permit to protest.

Members of Eastside Baptist raised their signs, sang hymns, and recited Bible verses as people arrived for the 2:30 p.m. memorial service. As they were driving by, many people screamed at the picketers, "Go home!" Some gave the picketers "the middle finger" (a derogatory gesture). One man was so enraged that he jumped out of his car and began to run over to where the picketers stood. He yelled, "You are a disgrace to mankind!" The man was held back by friends who then led him into the church.

After receiving numerous calls, Silver Spring police officers arrived and arrested Anson and the other members of Eastside Baptist Church. They were charged with the following:

- Violating a law that prohibits the "gathering of five or more persons in a public space in a disruptive or disorderly manner."

- Violating an ordinance that requires advance written permission from the city to hold a protest and that only permits protests between the hours of 9:00 a.m. and 3:00 p.m.

Following a jury trial, Pastor Felicia Anson is convicted on both counts. Assume that her appeal is heard by the U.S. Supreme Court. Answer the following questions:

1. Assume that you are Pastor Anson's attorney. Which arguments would you make to convince the court that the statutes are unconstitutional? Which cases would you use to support your arguments?

2. Assume you are an attorney for the state of Maryland. Which arguments would you make in support of the constitutionality of the statutes? Which cases would you use to support your arguments?

3. How do you think the Court would decide this case? What would be the rationale(s)?

Key Terms and Cases

Notes ●━━━━━━━━━━━━━━━━━

1. *Snyder v. Phelps*, 562 U.S. 1 (2011).

2. *Stromberg v. California*, 283 U.S. 359 (1931).

3. See generally, S. Rep., No. 105–298 (1998) (S.J. Res. 40 and H.J. Res. 54—Proposing an Amendment to the Constitution of the United States Authorizing Congress to Prohibit the Physical Desecration of the Flag of the United States 105th Congress, Mr. Hatch, Committee on the Judiciary, Report with Minority Views).

4. *Spence v. Washington*, 418 U.S. 405 (1974).

5. Wash. Rev. Code § 9.86.020(1) (2004).

6. *Texas v. Johnson*, 491 U.S. 397 (1989).

7. *United States v. Eichman*, 496 U.S. 310, 319 (1990).

8. *Jacobellis v. Ohio*, 378 U.S. 184, 197 (1964).

9. *Miller v. California*, 413 U.S. 15 (1973).

10. Id. at 24. The Court sent the case back to the lower court to have it decide the case in light of the new standard.

11. *Stanley v. Georgia*, 394 U.S. 557 (1969).

12. Ibid., 568.

13. *Chaplinsky v. New Hampshire*, 315 U.S. 568 (1942).

14. *R.A.V. v. St. Paul*, 505 U.S. 377 (1992).

15. *Wisconsin v. Mitchell*, 508 U.S. 476 (1993).

16. Mari Matsuda, "Public Response to Racist Speech: Considering the Victim's Story," in *Words that Wound*, ed. Mari Matsuda, Charles Lawrence, Richard Delgado, and Kimberle Williams Crenshaw (Boulder: Westview Press, 1993), 17–51.

17. *Schenck v. United States*, 249 U.S. 47 (1919).

18. E. Gregory Wallace, "Justifying Religious Freedom: The Western Tradition," *Penn State Law Review* 114 (2010): 485, 486.

19. Ibid.

20. *Wisconsin v. Yoder*, 341 U.S. 494 (1972).

21. *Church of the Lukumi Babalu Aye v. City of Hialeah*, 508 U.S. 520 (1993).

22. *Wooley v. Maynard*, 430 U.S. 705 (1977).

23. Ibid., 718, fn 2.

24. *District of Columbia v. Heller*, 554 U.S. 570 (2008).

25. *McDonald v. Chicago*, 561 U.S. 3025 (2010).

26. *Harmelin v. Michigan*, 501 U.S. 957 (1991).

27. *Graham v. Florida*, 560 U.S. ____ (2010).

28. Ibid., 2033.

29. The U.S. Supreme Court has expanded this ruling to cases involving murder. See, e.g., *Miller v. Alabama*, 132 S.Ct. 2455 (2012).

30. Congressional Globe 39ᵗh Cong. 1ˢᵗ Session 3148 (1866).

31. See generally, *Plessy v. Ferguson*, 163 U.S. 537 (1896); *Brown v. Board of Education*, 347 U.S. 483 (1954); *McCleskey v. Kemp*, 481 U.S. 279 (1987); and *Lawrence v. Texas*, 539 U.S. 558 (2003).

32. *Loving v. Virginia*, 388 U.S. 1 (1967).

33. VA Code § 20–59 (Repealed by Acts 1968, c. 318).

34. Loving, 3.

35. Ibid., 11.

36. *Papachristou v. Jacksonville*, 405 U.S. 156 (1972).

37. Jacksonville Ord. Code § 25–57.

38. *Coates v. Cincinnati*, 402 U.S. 611, 616 (1971).

39. *Kolender v. Lawson*, 461 U.S. 352 (1983).

40. *Roe v. Wade*, 410 U.S. 113 (1973).

41. *Bowers v. Hardwick*, 478 U.S. 186 (1986).

42. GA Code Ann. §16–6-2 (1984).

43. *Lawrence v. Texas*, 539 U.S. 558 (2003).

44. Tex. Penal Code Ann. § 21.06(a) (2003).

45. 539 U.S. at 578–579.

46. The hypothetical is based on the case of *Snyder v. Phelps*, 562 U.S. 48 (2011).

Chapter 3

Former Commerce Secretary John Bryson was driving his automobile in Los Angeles on June 9, 2012, when he crashed into a car. He got out of the car after the crash and exchanged information with the driver. As Mr. Bryson was leaving the scene, he crashed into the car again, but this time, he kept going. The driver of the other car and his two passengers decided that they should call 911 and follow him. Mr. Bryson drove less than two miles before hitting another car. When the police arrived on the scene, he was still behind the wheel, unconscious. Mr. Bryson was taken to the hospital where it was discovered that he had suffered a seizure. He was not charged with a crime even though the other cars were damaged and the passengers suffered minor injuries because he did not intentionally or even voluntarily crash into the cars.

Suppose Bryson had been aware that he had a condition that caused him to have seizures, and he had been advised not to drive because of the condition. His victims may sue him in civil court and win financial damages. But should Mr. Bryson also be charged with a crime?

This scenario raises some of the issues we will examine in this chapter.

Former Secretary of Commerce John Bryson.

http://commons.wikimedia.org/wiki
/File:John_Bryson_official_portrait.jpg

The Elements of a Crime

Learning Objectives

After reading and studying this chapter, you should be able to

➤ Identify and define the elements of a crime

➤ Know the five circumstances that create a legal duty to act

➤ Differentiate between a voluntary and an intentional act

➤ Know the difference between specific and general intent

➤ Define *actus reus* and *mens rea*

➤ Understand the four levels of culpability in Section 2.02 of the Model Penal Code

➤ Distinguish between "but for" and proximate causation

➤ Explain strict liability

Introduction

All crimes consist of a number of elements that the prosecution must prove beyond a reasonable doubt before a person may be convicted of a crime. For most crimes, these elements are as follows:

1. A voluntary act (actus reus)

2. A guilty state of mind (mens rea)

3. The concurrence of the act and the guilty state of mind

4. Causation, and

5. A resulting harm

In other words, while a person is performing an act of his own free will, he must have the state of mind required by the statute. The state must prove that some harm occurred and that the defendant's actions caused that harm. There are some exceptions to this general rule. For example, you will learn that there are some instances in which a person's *failure* to act makes him criminally liable.

Some crimes also require the proof of "attendant circumstances"—additional facts that must also exist at the time of the criminal act. For example, for the crime of statutory rape, which is sexual intercourse with an individual under the age of consent, the victim's age would be the attendant circumstances.

This chapter will define and discuss the elements of a crime, the circumstances under which a person may be charged with a crime for failing to act, the different states of mind that expose a person to criminal liability, and the circumstances under which a person may be criminally liable even when he has no guilty state of mind at all.

A Voluntary Act (Actus Reus) ●━━━━━━━━━━

Thoughts and Statuses

Most people agree that a person must actually *do* something harmful before he may be convicted of a crime. However, what if we knew for certain that an individual was about to commit a crime. Would we want to give the state the power to stop him?

In the science fiction movie *Minority Report*, the crime of murder is eliminated because the Justice Department's Pre-Crime Unit uses psychic beings who are able to see into the future and predict when murders will be committed. Police officers are given the power to arrest the potential murderers before they commit the crimes.

We do not punish individuals for thinking harmful thoughts. Of course our police officers do not have magical powers like the officers in *Minority Report* that enable them to read the minds of potential criminals. But even if they did, would it be a good idea to arrest and punish people for thinking about committing crimes? Sometimes people think about doing bad things but then change their minds and decide to obey the law. With the limited resources in our criminal justice system, do we really want to punish people who do no more than think bad thoughts—especially when they cause no harm? Many of us have thought bad thoughts but never acted upon them. Shouldn't people who refrain from acting upon their bad thoughts be rewarded for exercising self-control and obeying the law?

Suppose a person has a certain condition or status as a result of the commission of certain criminal acts. Should status crimes be criminalized? In the following case, the U.S. Supreme Court struck down a California law that made it a crime to be a drug addict.

Robinson v. California (1962)

U.S. Supreme Court

370 U.S. 660

A California statute makes it a criminal offense for a person to "be addicted to the use of narcotics." This appeal draws into question the constitutionality of that provision of the state law, as construed by the California courts in the present case.

The appellant was convicted after a jury trial in the Municipal Court of Los Angeles. The evidence against him was given by two Los Angeles police officers. Officer Brown testified that he had had occasion to examine the appellant's arms one evening on a street in Los Angeles some four months before the trial. The officer testified that at that time he had observed "scar tissue and discoloration on the inside" of the appellant's right arm, and "what appeared to be numerous needle marks and a scab which was approximately three inches below the crook of the

elbow" on the appellant's left arm. The officer also testified that the appellant under questioning had admitted to the occasional use of narcotics.

The trial judge instructed the jury that the statute made it a misdemeanor for a person 'either to use narcotics, or to be addicted to the use of narcotics * * *. That portion of the statute referring to the "use" of narcotics is based upon the "act" of using. That portion of the statute referring to 'addicted to the use' of narcotics is based upon a condition or status. They are not identical. * * * To be addicted to the use of narcotics is said to be a status or condition and not an act. It is a continuing offense and differs from most other offenses in the fact that (it) is chronic rather than acute; that it continues after it is complete and subjects the offender to arrest at any time before he reforms. The existence of such a chronic condition may be ascertained from a single examination, if the characteristic reactions of that condition be found present."

The judge further instructed the jury that the appellant could be convicted under a general verdict if the jury agreed either that he was of the "status" or had committed the "act" denounced by the statute. All that the People must show is either that the defendant did use a narcotic in Los Angeles County, or that while in the City of Los Angeles he was addicted to the use of narcotics

Under these instructions the jury returned a verdict finding the appellant "guilty of the offense charged.." . . . The broad power of a State to regulate the narcotic drugs traffic within its borders is not here in issue. . . . Such regulation, it can be assumed, could take a variety of valid forms. A State might impose criminal sanctions, for example, against the unauthorized manufacture, prescription, sale, purchase, or possession of narcotics within its borders. In the interest of discouraging the violation of such laws, or in the interest of the general health or welfare of its inhabitants, a State might establish a program of compulsory treatment for those addicted to narcotics. Such a program of treatment might require periods of involuntary confinement. And penal sanctions might be imposed for failure to comply with established compulsory treatment procedures. . . . Or a State might choose to attack the evils of narcotics traffic on broader fronts also—through public health education, for example, or by efforts to ameliorate the economic and social conditions under which those evils might be thought to flourish. In short, the range of valid choice which a State might make in this area is undoubtedly a wide one, and the wisdom of any particular choice within the allowable spectrum is not for us to decide. Upon that premise we turn to the California law in issue here.

It would be possible to construe the statute under which the appellant was convicted as one which is operative only upon proof of the actual use of narcotics within the State's jurisdiction. But the California courts have not so construed this law. Although there was evidence in the present case that the appellant had used narcotics in Los Angeles, the jury [was] instructed that they could convict him even if they disbelieved that evidence. The appellant could be convicted, they were told, if they found simply that the appellant's "status" or "chronic condition" was that of being "addicted to the use of narcotics." And it is impossible to know from the jury's verdict that the defendant was not convicted upon precisely such a finding.

This statute, therefore, is not one which punishes a person for the use of narcotics, for their purchase, sale or possession, or for antisocial or disorderly behavior resulting from their administration. It is not a law which even purports to provide or require medical treatment. Rather, we deal with a statute which makes the "status" of narcotic addiction a criminal offense, for which the offender may be prosecuted "at any time before he reforms." California has said that a person can be continuously guilty of this offense, whether or not he has ever used or possessed any narcotics within the State, and whether or not he has been guilty of any antisocial behavior there.

It is unlikely that any State at this moment in history would attempt to make it a criminal offense for a person to be mentally ill, or a leper, or to be afflicted with a venereal disease. A State might determine that the general health and welfare require that the victims of these and other human afflictions be dealt with by compulsory treatment, involving quarantine, confinement, or sequestration. But, in the light of contemporary human knowledge, a law which made a criminal offense of such a disease would doubtless be universally thought to be an infliction of cruel and unusual punishment in violation of the Eighth and Fourteenth Amendments.

We cannot but consider the statute before us as of the same category. In this Court counsel for the State recognized that narcotic addiction is an illness. Indeed, it is apparently an illness which may be contracted innocently or involuntarily. We hold that a state law which imprisons a person thus afflicted as a criminal, even though he has never touched any narcotic drug within the State or been guilty of any irregular behavior there, inflicts a cruel and unusual punishment in violation of the Fourteenth Amendment. To be sure, imprisonment for ninety days is not, in the abstract, a punishment which is either cruel or unusual. But the question cannot be considered in the abstract. Even one day in prison would be a cruel and unusual punishment for the "crime" of having a common cold.

Questions

1. The California statute makes it a crime "to use narcotics, or to be addicted to the use of narcotics." Which part of the statute does the Court find unconstitutional?

2. What is the rationale for the Court's holding?

3. The Court compares the statute to the criminalization of leprosy, mental illness, or the common cold. Are these fair comparisons? Why or why not?

The Voluntariness Requirement

The Supreme Court in *Robinson* made it clear that a person has to *do* something in order to be charged with a crime—there must be an act. But what if a person does an act involuntarily—because she is ill or otherwise has no control over her harmful acts? Should she still be held criminally liable? Commerce Secretary Bryson was not charged with a crime when he crashed into two cars, as described at the beginning of this chapter. However, some accidents involving involuntary acts are criminalized. Courts reached different results in the following two cases.

People v. Decina (1956)

N. Y. Court of Appeals
138 N.E. 2d 799

At about 3:30 p.m. on March 14, 1955, a bright, sunny day, defendant was driving, alone in his car, in a northerly direction on Delaware Avenue in the city of Buffalo. The portion of Delaware Avenue here involved is 60 feet wide. At a point south of an overhead viaduct of the Erie Railroad, defendant's car swerved to the left, across the center line in the street, so that it was completely in the south lane, traveling 35 to 40 miles per hour.

It then veered sharply to the right, crossing Delaware Avenue and mounting the easterly curb at a point beneath the viaduct and continued thereafter at a speed estimated to have been about 50 or 60 miles per hour or more. During this latter swerve, a pedestrian testified that he saw defendant's hand above his head; another witness said he saw defendant's left arm bent over the wheel, and his right hand extended towards the right door.

A group of six schoolgirls were walking north on the easterly sidewalk of Delaware Avenue, two in front and four slightly in the rear, when defendant's car struck them from behind. One of the girls escaped injury by jumping against the wall of the viaduct. The bodies of the children struck were propelled northward onto the street and the lawn in front of a coal company, located to the north of the Erie viaduct on Delaware Avenue. Three of the children, 6 to 12 years old, were found dead on arrival by the medical examiner, and a fourth child, 7 years old, died in a hospital two days later as a result of injuries sustained in the accident.

After striking the children, defendant's car continued on the easterly sidewalk, and then swerved back onto Delaware Avenue once more. It continued in a northerly direction, passing under a second viaduct before it again

veered to the right and remounted the easterly curb, striking and breaking a metal lamppost. With its horn blowing steadily apparently because defendant was "stopped over" the steering wheel the car proceeded on the sidewalk until if finally crashed through a 7 1/4-inch brick wall of a grocery store, injuring at least one customer and causing considerable property damage.

When the police arrived, defendant attempted to rise, staggered and appeared dazed and unsteady. When informed that he was under arrest, and would have to accompany the police to the station house, he resisted and, when he tried to get away, was handcuffed. The foregoing evidence was adduced by the People, and is virtually undisputed. [D]efendant did not take the stand nor did he produce any witnesses.

From the police station defendant was taken to the E. J. Meyer Memorial Hospital, a county institution, arriving at 5:30 P.M.

[A doctor] asked defendant how he felt and what had happened. Defendant, who still felt a little dizzy or blurry, said that as he was driving he noticed a jerking of his right hand, which warned him that he might develop a convulsion, and that as he tried to steer the car over to the curb he felt himself becoming unconscious, and he thought he had a convulsion. He was aware that children were in front of his car, but did not know whether he had struck them.

Defendant then proceeded to relate to Dr. Wechter his past medical history, namely, that at the age of 7 he was struck by an auto and suffered a marked loss of hearing. In 1946 he was treated in this same hospital for an illness during which he had some convulsions. Several burr holes were made in his skull and a brain abscess was drained. Following this operation defendant had no convulsions from 1946 through 1950. In 1950 he had four convulsions, caused by scar tissue on the brain. From 1950 to 1954 he experienced about 10 or 20 seizures a year, in which his right hand would jump although he remained fully conscious. In 1954, he had 4 or 5 generalized seizures with loss of consciousness, the last being in September, 1954, a few months before the accident. Thereafter he had more hospitalization, a spinal tap, consultation with a neurologist, and took medication daily to help prevent seizures.

On the basis of this medical history, Dr. Wechter made a diagnosis of Jacksonian epilepsy, and was of the opinion that defendant had a seizure at the time of the accident.

We turn first to the subject of defendant's cross appeal, namely, that his demurrer should have been sustained, since the indictment here does not charge a crime. The indictment states essentially that defendant, knowing "that he was subject to epileptic attacks or other disorder rendering him likely to lose consciousness for a considerable period of time," was culpably negligent "in that he consciously undertook to and did operate his Buick sedan on a public highway" (emphasis supplied) and "while so doing" suffered such an attack which caused said automobile "to travel at a fast and reckless rate of speed, jumping the curb and driving over the sidewalk" causing the death of 4 persons. In our opinion, this clearly states a violation of section 1053-a of the Penal Law. The statute does not require that a defendant must deliberately intend to kill a human being, for that would be murder. Nor does the statute require that he knowingly and consciously follow the precise path that leads to death and destruction. It is sufficient, we have said, when his conduct manifests a "disregard of the consequences which may ensue from the act, and indifference to the rights of others. No clearer definition, applicable to the hundreds of varying circumstances that may arise, can be given. Under a given state of facts, whether negligence is culpable is a question of judgment."

Assuming the truth of the indictment, as we must on a demurrer, this defendant knew he was subject to epileptic attacks and seizures that might strike at any time. He also knew that a moving motor vehicle uncontrolled on public highway is a highly dangerous instrumentality capable of unrestrained destruction. With this knowledge, and without anyone accompanying him, he deliberately took a chance by making a conscious choice of a course of action, in disregard of the consequences which he knew might follow from his conscious act, and which in this case did ensue. How can we say as a matter of law that this did not amount to culpable negligence within the meaning of section 1053-a?

To hold otherwise would be to say that a man may freely indulge himself in liquor in the same hope that it will not affect his driving, and if it later develops that ensuing intoxication causes dangerous and reckless driving resulting in death, his unconsciousness or involuntariness at that time would relieve him from prosecution under the statute. His awareness of a condition which he knows may produce such consequences as here, and his disregard of the consequences, renders him liable for culpable negligence, as the courts below have properly held. . . . To have a sudden sleeping spell, an unexpected heart or other disabling attack, without any prior knowledge or warning thereof, is an altogether different situation, . . . and there is simply no basis for comparing such cases with the flagrant disregard manifested here.

Questions

1. What was Mr. Decina's voluntary act?

2. The court acknowledged that Mr. Decina did not intentionally hit the schoolgirls but holds that he was negligent in driving his car. What facts support this holding?

3. How does the court compare Mr. Decina's behavior with that of a drunk driver?

Martin v. State (1944)[1] examines the voluntary act requirement in an entirely different context. Martin was in his home when police officers arrived, placed him under arrest, and drove him to a public highway. While on the highway, Mr. Martin allegedly committed the act of using loud and profane language while drunk. He was charged and convicted of "being drunk on a public highway" under the following statute:

Any person who, while intoxicated or drunk, appears in any public place where one or more persons are present, * * * and manifests a drunken condition by boisterous or indecent conduct, or loud and profane discourse, shall, on conviction, be fined, etc. Code 1940, Title 14, Section 120.[2]

Martin appealed his conviction. The Alabama Court of Appeals reversed his conviction, holding that Martin could not be convicted unless he voluntarily went to the highway in a drunken condition. Since the police officers "involuntarily and forcibly" carried him to the highway, there was no voluntary act, and his conviction could not stand.

How is this case different from *Decina*? Notice that both cases demonstrate the difference between "voluntary" and "intentional" acts. "Voluntariness" refers to a person's acts (actus reus) while "intent" describes his mental state (mens rea). Mr. Decina intended to get into his car and drive it, but he did not intend the physical movements during the seizure that caused him to hit and kill the children. Those movements were involuntary. Likewise, Mr. Martin intended to drink the alcohol that caused him to become intoxicated, but he did not intend to go onto the highway, nor did he voluntarily move his body to that location.

Consider the following hypothetical:

Rick and Bernie were bricklayers working at a construction site on the second floor of a building. Rick walked past Bernie just as he was about to position a brick on the wall and accidentally bumped his arm. The brick flew out of Bernie's hand and hit Kecia on the head as she was walking on the sidewalk below.

Would Bernie be charged with assaulting Kecia? Bernie neither intentionally nor voluntarily hit Kecia with the brick. Rick's accidental bumping of Bernie's arm caused the brick to fall and hit Kecia. There was no criminal act.

Omissions

Under certain circumstances, an individual's *failure to act* may be a crime. Peter is walking past the lake in the park when he sees a man on a small boat fall into the water. The man does not appear to know how to swim. Peter watches the man struggle and go under water for the third time. Does he have a duty to jump in and save him? Should Peter have a duty only if he knows how to swim? Does he have a duty to call for help? If the man drowns, may Peter be charged with homicide for his failure to save or at least assist the drowning man?

Most crimes punish individuals for committing acts that cause harm. Should the law impose a responsibility on individuals to act in order to prevent harm to others and punish them when they fail to act? Should it depend on the individual's relationship to the person who is in danger? Many people are hesitant to interfere in the affairs of individuals they do not know. For example, if a parent spanks her child in a public place, most people would not intervene unless it is a life-threatening situation. Even in situations involving a physical fight between two or more people, many individuals would choose to "mind their own business" for a variety of reasons. In the case of the parent spanking the child, most people—even those who feel strongly that children should not be hit—would believe that parents have the right and freedom to decide how to discipline their own children. In the case involving individuals fighting each other, some may wonder whether the people involved are just "horsing around" rather than actually fighting. Or perhaps they fear that they may be injured if they try to stop the fight. As for the drowning man, many people would not only fear drowning themselves but may be concerned that they might make the situation worse. But are there some situations where we should impose a duty to act? The following case is likely the most famous example of a tragic death that occurred as a result of the failure to act.

The Kitty Genovese Case

Kitty Genovese was twenty-eight years old when she was raped and murdered near her apartment in New York City. On March 13, 1964, Ms. Genovese drove home from her job as a manager at a bar. She parked her red Fiat near the Long Island Railroad and proceeded to walk toward her apartment in the Kew Gardens area of Queens. A man followed her from the parking lot and stabbed her in the back. He stabbed her repeatedly and sexually assaulted her as she screamed for help. A police investigation later revealed that numerous neighbors—as many as thirty-eight—heard her screams but did nothing. They did not intervene or even call the police.[3]

New York Daily News Archive/New York Daily News/Getty Images

Kitty Genovese

The Genovese case garnered national attention—not because of the gruesome details of the murder but because of the neighbors' failure to assist. Although some have questioned whether thirty-eight people really knew what was going on and failed to help, it is clear that many people heard a woman screaming for help and did nothing. Social scientists studied the case and labeled the phenomenon "the bystander effect." After doing a number of experiments, they concluded that the more people present, the less likely any of them will help a person in distress. According to the experiments, presumably everyone thought that someone else would come to the person's aid.[4]

It is very possible that Kitty Genovese's life would have been saved had just one person called the police and reported that someone was screaming for help. Few would expect a bystander to personally come to a stranger's rescue by confronting an assailant and attempting to fight him off. Such actions would likely cause even further harm, and no one would expect a person to endanger his own life in order to save the life of a total stranger. But what possible harm would come from the simple act of calling the police to report that someone was possibly in danger? Should society criminalize the failure to at least report dangerous situations that could result in the loss of life? It may have been difficult to determine who actually heard Kitty Genovese's cries for help, but law enforcement difficulties aside, should these omissions be criminalized?

A person may be held criminally liable for her failure to act only if she has a legal duty to do so. In *Jones v. United States* (1962), the court held that there are at least four circumstances that create a legal duty to act:

> One can be held criminally liable: first, where a statute imposes a duty to care for another; second, where one stands in a certain status relationship to another; third, where one has assumed a contractual duty to care for another; and fourth, where one has voluntarily assumed the care of another and so secluded the helpless person as to prevent others from rendering aid.[5] . . .

A fifth circumstance may also create a legal duty: when a person creates a risk of harm. For example, if a driver hits a pedestrian and injures him, he has a legal duty to call an ambulance or do whatever is necessary to make sure that the pedestrian receives medical treatment.

AP Photo/KABC TV

A Good Samaritan Law was passed in Nevada when a witness failed to report Sherrice Iverson's murder to the police. Should other states pass similar laws?

Statutes that impose a legal duty include laws that require individuals to file income tax returns or register firearms. If a person has a contractual duty to care for a disabled person, he may be held criminally liable if his failure to do so results in that person being harmed. A parent's legal duty to care for her child and a married couple's legal duty to care for each other come from those special status relationships. If a person assumes the care of a neighbor and the neighbor becomes ill and dies, that person is criminally liable for the death if he secludes the neighbor so that no one else is able to come to the neighbor's assistance. Finally, if a driver accidentally hits a pedestrian, the driver has a legal duty to get assistance for the pedestrian and may be criminally liable for any additional harm to the pedestrian as a result of the driver's failure to do so because she created the risk of harm.

The Case of David Cash

On May 25, 1997, twenty-year-old David Cash and his nineteen-year-old friend Jeremy Strohmeyer went to a casino in Las Vegas. In the early morning hours, Strohmeyer followed a seven-year-old girl named Sherrice Iverson into the women's restroom. David Cash came in later and found Strohmeyer struggling with the little girl in one of the restroom stalls. Cash walked out and went for a walk. He didn't report what he had seen to the security guards or to the police. In fact, he told no one. Less than an hour later, Strohmeyer told David Cash that he had molested the little girl and killed her. At around 5 a.m., Sherrice's body was found stuffed in the toilet in the women's restroom.

Strohmeyer eventually pled guilty to murder, kidnapping, and two counts of sexual assault. He was sentenced to four life terms without the possibility of parole. Cash, on the other hand, was not charged with anything because at that time, there was no legal duty to even report the horrible crimes Stromeyer had committed.

Cash's behavior received almost as much attention and condemnation as Strohmeyer's. In addition to his failure to report the crime, he later angered the public even more by saying that he felt sorrier for his friend Jeremy than for the little girl because he did not know her or her family.[6] Cash was a student at the University of California at Berkeley at the time, and there was a protest at the university with demands that he be expelled. The University Chancellor issued a statement informing the public that Cash had not broken any laws and would not be expelled, but added that he also was outraged by Cash's statements.[7]

Cash's failure to report the crime led to the passage of the Sherrice Iverson Bill in Nevada in 2000. The law makes it a crime to fail to notify the police upon witnessing the sexual assault of a child. Most states do not have laws that require members of the public to take action to assist others in peril. Minnesota is one state that does have such a law:

Minnesota's Good Samaritan Statute

1. **Duty to assist.** A person at the scene of an emergency who knows that another person is exposed to or has suffered grave physical harm shall, to the extent that the person can do so without danger or peril to self or others, give reasonable assistance to the exposed person. Reasonable assistance may include obtaining or attempting to obtain aid from law enforcement or medical personnel. A person who violates this subdivision is guilty of a petty misdemeanor.

The few states that have Good Samaritan laws make it clear that bystanders are not required to assist others if such assistance may cause harm to the "good Samaritan," to the person in need of help, or to anyone else. The Minnesota law emphasizes that the person in need of help must have been exposed to or have suffered "grave physical harm" and notes that calling the police or an ambulance will fulfill the bystander's responsibility under the law. Another section of Minnesota's law states that any person who provides such assistance will not be liable for civil damages as a result of his assistance unless he provides the assistance in a reckless manner.

Although Good Samaritan laws are rare in the United States, they are common in Europe and Canada. Like the laws in the United States, the Good Samaritan laws in Europe and Canada do not require bystanders to risk harm to themselves; they provide immunity from civil liability except in cases of gross negligence or recklessness; and they require little more than notifying law enforcement or medical personnel.

Guilty State of Mind (Mens Rea) ●━━━━━━━━━━

There is no crime if there is only an act (or a legal duty to act). The act or omission must be accompanied by a guilty state of mind. Although most people believe that an individual must have "criminal intent" to be guilty of a crime, there are a number of crimes that punish unintentional behavior. The drunk driver who accidentally hits another car, causing the death of the driver and passengers, may be charged with involuntary manslaughter or even second degree murder—even though he did not intend to kill anyone. The parents who fail to take their sick child to the doctor when the child is obviously very ill may be criminally liable for that child's death, even if they earnestly believed that the child would live, if their behavior was a gross deviation from the standard of care that a reasonable person would observe. Because the mental element of criminal behavior may involve unintentional as well as intentional behavior, it is often referred to as mens rea or "guilty mind."

Model Penal Code Section 2.02

Model Penal Code Section 2.02 sets forth four levels of mens rea, from the most serious to the least serious: purposely, knowingly, recklessly, and negligently. Most jurisdictions have adopted at least some if not all of the definitions of Section 2.02:

MPC § 2.02-General Requirements of Culpability

(1) Minimum Requirements of Culpability. Except as provided in Section 2.05, a person is not guilty of an offense unless he acted purposely, knowingly, recklessly, or negligently, as the law may require, with respect to each material element of the offense.

(2) Kinds of Culpability Defined.

(a) Purposely.

A person acts purposely with respect to a material element of an offense when:

(Continued)

(Continued)

(i) if the element involves the nature of his conduct or a result thereof, it is his conscious object to engage in conduct of that nature or to cause such a result; and

(ii) if the element involves the attendant circumstances, he is aware of the existence of such circumstances or he believes or hopes that they exist.

(b) Knowingly.

A person acts knowingly with respect to a material element of an offense when:

(i) if the element involves the nature of his conduct or the attendant circumstances, he is aware that his conduct is of that nature or that such circumstances exist; and

(ii) if the element involves a result of his conduct, he is aware that it is practically certain that his conduct will cause such a result.

(c) Recklessly.

A person acts recklessly with respect to a material element of an offense when he consciously disregards a substantial and unjustifiable risk that the material element exists or will result from his conduct. The risk must be of such a nature and degree that, considering the nature and purpose of the actor's conduct and the circumstances known to him, its disregard involves a gross deviation from the standard of conduct that a law-abiding person would observe in the actor's situation.

(d) Negligently.

A person acts negligently with respect to a material element of an offense when he should be aware of a substantial and unjustifiable risk that the material element exists or will result from his conduct. The risk must be of such a nature and degree that the actor's failure to perceive it, considering the nature and purpose of his conduct and the circumstances known to him, involves a gross deviation from the standard of care that a reasonable person would observe in the actor's situation.

Purposely and Knowingly

A person who acts purposely or knowingly engages in intentional behavior. These two levels of mens rea are very similar, but there is a fine distinction between the two. The person who acts purposely wants or hopes for a particular harmful result. That result is the "conscious object" of his behavior. The person who acts knowingly does not necessarily want or hope for a particular result, but is "practically certain" that his actions will cause that result.

Consider the following hypothetical:

John wants to kill Aaron. He makes a bomb to plant in Aaron's house. The bomb is powerful enough to destroy the house and all of its occupants. On the day that John plans to activate the bomb, he knows that Aaron's wife, Sarah, is in the house. Although Sarah is not the "conscious object" of his behavior and he does not want her to die, he is "practically certain" that she will die, yet he activates the bomb anyway.

What level of mens rea describes John's state of mind toward Aaron? Toward Sarah? Is there a meaningful difference between the two? These two levels of mens rea are so similar that some statutes use both "purposely" and "knowingly." For example, the Illinois battery statutes state, "A person commits battery if he *intentionally or knowingly* without legal justification and by any means, (1) causes bodily harm to an individual or (2) makes physical contact of an insulting or provoking nature with an individual" (italics added).[8]

Recklessly and Negligently

The lowest levels of mens rea—recklessly and negligently—are similar, but the distinction between the two is not as fine as the distinction between purposely and knowingly. Reckless and negligent behaviors are both unintentional, but a person who acts recklessly has some sense of awareness. The reckless person is aware of a substantial and unjustifiable risk that a particular result will occur, but she acts anyway. She consciously disregards that risk. The person who acts negligently is clueless—she has no level of awareness. She is *not* aware of the substantial and unjustifiable risk when she acts, but she *should have* been aware of that risk.

Consider the following hypotheticals:

Sam goes drinking with his buddies at the local bar. He has six beers and two shots of tequila. Sam is so drunk by the end of the evening that he is stumbling and slurring his words. His friends urge him to leave his car at the bar and ride with one of them. They tell him that if he drives, he is likely to injure himself or someone else, but Sam does not listen. He gets in his car and speeds off, driving about 70 miles per hour in a residential area. Sam runs a red light and hits a minivan, killing all the occupants of the car.

Sarah and Todd are Christian Scientists. Their five-year-old daughter Megan becomes very ill with a rare disease. They take the child to the doctor and are told that she will not live if she does not have a surgical procedure. Sarah and Todd refuse to allow the procedure because it is against their religious beliefs. They honestly believe that Megan will be cured if they continue to pray. Megan dies.

Was Sam's behavior reckless or negligent? There is a strong argument that Sam acted recklessly. Surely he was aware of the dangers of driving while intoxicated. Even if he was not, his friends told him that he would likely injure someone if he drove, yet he disregarded their advice.

Were Sarah and Todd reckless or negligent? Most likely they acted negligently. They were not aware of a substantial and unjustifiable risk that Megan would die. They honestly believed that prayer would cure her.

Many scholars believe that negligent behavior should not be punished in the criminal law. They believe that people who act negligently should be sued in civil court instead because it seems unfair to punish individuals who act without any awareness of the harm that they will cause. Although there are some crimes that punish negligent behavior, the mens rea for most crimes is either purposefully, knowingly, or recklessly. Often crimes that punish negligent behavior require "gross" negligence—a higher level of negligence than is required in civil cases.

General Versus Specific Intent Crimes

Some jurisdictions, generally those that do not follow the Model Penal Code, distinguish between general and specific intent crimes. General intent crimes are those which only require a mental state that pertains to the act that causes the harm of the criminal offense. For example, the crime of breaking and entering is a general intent crime because it only requires that the person intend to break and enter a particular building or structure. Specific intent crimes involve the general intent to do the act that causes the harm plus some additional special mental element. Common law burglary (which will be discussed in detail in Chapter 5) is a specific intent crime because it involves breaking and entering of the dwelling of another *with the intent to commit a felony therein* (italics added). If the actor does not have the additional intent to commit a felony while breaking and entering, he has not committed the crime of burglary. Other specific intent crimes include possession with the intent to distribute an illegal substance and driving under the influence of alcohol. Although there are other definitions of general and specific crimes, these definitions are the most common. The distinction is only important when considering whether the defendant may present certain defenses. For example, the defense of voluntary intoxication is only permitted for specific intent crimes.

Proving Intent

The state must prove each element of an offense beyond a reasonable doubt. If there are witnesses to the crime or a videotape, proving the actus reus may not be difficult. But how does the prosecution prove what is in the defendant's mind? In the absence of a confession to the required mens rea or the testimony of a mind reader, how does the state prove this element? The following case addresses this issue.

People v. Conley (1989)

Illinois Appellate Court

543 N.E. 2d 1138

The defendant was charged with aggravated battery in connection with a fight which occurred at a party on September 28, 1985, in unincorporated Orland Township. Approximately two hundred high school students attended the party and paid admission to drink unlimited beer. One of those students, Sean O'Connell, attended the party with several friends. At some point during the party, Sean's group was approached by a group of twenty boys who apparently thought that someone in Sean's group had said something derogatory. Sean's group denied making a statement and said they did not want any trouble. Shortly thereafter, Sean and his friends decided to leave and began walking toward their car which was parked a half block south of the party.

A group of people were walking toward the party from across the street when someone from that group shouted "there's those guys from the party." Someone emerged from that group and approached Sean who had been walking with his friend Marty Carroll ten to fifteen steps behind two other friends, Glen Mazurowski and

Dan Scurio. That individual demanded that Marty give him a can of beer from his six-pack. Marty refused, and the individual struck Sean in the face with a wine bottle causing Sean to fall to the ground. The offender attempted to hit Marty, but missed as Marty was able to duck. Sean had sustained broken upper and lower jaws and four broken bones in the area between the bridge of his nose and the lower left cheek. Sean lost one tooth and had root canal surgery to reposition ten teeth that had been damaged. Expert testimony revealed that Sean has a permanent condition called mucosal mouth and permanent partial numbness in one lip. The expert also testified that the life expectancy of the damaged teeth might be diminished by a third or a half.

The jury returned a guilty verdict for aggravated battery based on permanent disability . . . The defendant initially contends on appeal that the State failed to prove beyond a reasonable doubt that Sean O'Connell incurred a permanent disability. Section 12–4(a) of the Criminal Code of 1961 provides that: "[a] person who, in committing a battery, intentionally or knowingly causes great bodily harm, or permanent disability or disfigurement commits aggravated battery." (Ill.Rev.Stat. (1983) ch. 38, par. 12–4(a).) The defendant contends there must be some disabling effect for an aggravated battery conviction based on permanent disability. The defendant does not dispute that Sean lost a tooth or that surgery was required to repair damaged teeth. The defendant also does not dispute that Sean will have permanent partial numbness in one lip or suffer from a condition called mucosal mouth. The defendant maintains, however, that there is no evidence as to how these injuries are disabling because there was no testimony of any tasks that can no longer be performed as a result of these injuries. . . . It seems apparent that for an injury to be deemed disabling, all that must be shown is that the victim is no longer whole such that the injured bodily portion or part no longer serves the body in the same manner as it did before the injury. Applying this standard to the case at hand, the injuries Sean O'Connell suffered are sufficient to constitute a permanent disability. Sean will endure permanent partial numbness in one lip and mucosal mouth. He lost one tooth and there is also a chance he may lose some teeth before attaining the age of seventy.

The defendant further argues that the State failed to prove beyond a reasonable doubt that he intended to inflict any permanent disability. The thrust of defendant's argument is that under section 12–4(a), a person must intend to bring about the particular harm defined in the statute. The defendant asserts that while it may be inferred from his conduct that he intended to cause harm, it does not follow that he intended to cause permanent disability. The State contends it is not necessary that the defendant intended to bring about the particular injuries that resulted. The State maintains it met its burden by showing that the defendant intentionally struck Sean.

For proper resolution of this issue, it is best to return to the statutory language. Section 12–4(a) employs the terms "intentionally or knowingly" to describe the required mental state. The relevant statutes state:

> "4–4. Intent. A person intends, or acts intentionally or with intent, to accomplish a result or engage in conduct described by the statute defining the offense, when his conscious objective or purpose is to accomplish that result or engage in that conduct." (Ill.Rev.Stat.1987, ch. 38, par. 4–4.)

> "4–5. Knowledge. A person knows or acts knowingly or with knowledge of: (b) The result of his

conduct, described by the statute defining the offense, when he is consciously aware that such result is practically certain to be caused by his conduct." (Ill.Rev.Stat.1987, ch. 38, par. 4–5.)

Section 12–4(a) defines aggravated battery as the commission of a battery where the offender intentionally or knowingly causes great bodily harm, or permanent disability or disfigurement. Because the offense is defined in terms of result, the State has the burden of proving beyond a reasonable doubt that the defendant either had a "conscious objective" to achieve the harm defined, or that the defendant was "consciously aware" that the harm defined was "practically certain to be caused by his conduct." . . .

Although the State must establish the specific intent to bring about great bodily harm, or permanent disability or disfigurement under section 12–4(a), problems of proof are alleviated to the extent that the ordinary presumption that one intends the natural and probable consequences of his actions shifts the burden of production, though not persuasion, to the defendant. . . . If the defendant presents evidence contrary to the presumption, then the presumption ceases to have effect, and the trier of fact considers all the evidence and the natural inferences drawn therefrom. . . . . Intent can be inferred from the surrounding circumstances, the offender's words, the weapon used, and the force of the blow. . . . As the defendant's theory of the case was mistaken identity, there was no evidence introduced negating the presumption of intent. However, even if Conley had denied any intention to inflict permanent disability, the surrounding circumstances, the use of a bottle, the absence of warning and the force of the blow are facts from which the jury could reasonably infer the intent to cause permanent disability. Therefore, we find the evidence sufficient to support a finding of intent to cause permanent disability beyond a reasonable doubt.

The judgment of the circuit court is affirmed.

Questions

1. What issues did Mr. Conley raise on appeal?

2. What was the court's rationale in rejecting the appellant's arguments?

3. After reading *Conley*, what did you learn about how the state proves mens rea in a criminal case?

Concurrence and Causation ●────────────────

Concurrence

A criminal act occurs when there is a voluntary act (or omission) that causes the resulting harm, a guilty state of mind, and the concurrence of the two. Mary commits a burglary when she breaks and enters John's house with the intent to steal his expensive flat screen television set. If she breaks and enters the house with the intent of taking a nap on John's sofa, she is not guilty of burglary, even if she decides to steal the television set after she wakes up from her nap. She would be guilty of theft of the television and breaking and entering, but not of burglary.

One exception to the concurrence rule is the continuing trespass doctrine. This doctrine is often applied in cases involving theft of property, when the thief forms the intent to deprive his victim of his property after he takes the property. As you will learn in Chapter 5, a person commits the crime of theft only when he takes property with the intent to permanently deprive the victim of the property. So if Tom takes Jerry's bike without Jerry's permission, it is considered a wrongful or trespassory taking. But if at the time Tom takes the bike, he only intends to borrow it for thirty minutes and then return it, he has not committed the crime of theft. Suppose that after Tom takes the bike, he decides to keep it? In that case, there is no concurrence of the act and the guilty state of mind. However, the continuing trespass doctrine establishes that Tom is guilty of theft by attributing his subsequent decision to permanently deprive Jerry of the bike back to the time when he originally took the bike without permission.

Causation

Unlike concurrence, causation can sometimes be a complicated issue in criminal cases. There is no criminal liability if the act or omission of the accused did not cause the resulting harm. In some cases, causation is clear. Jim takes out his pistol and shoots Dan in the head. Dan falls and dies instantly. Jim clearly caused Dan's death. But suppose Jim shoots Dan in the head, and Dan is rushed to the hospital. Dan is rushed to the operating room where surgery is performed. He dies during the surgery. It is later discovered that the surgery was unsuccessful because of the surgeon's negligence. Did Jim or the negligent surgeon cause Dan's death?

There are two types of causation in the criminal law: actual or "but for" causation and proximate causation. The defendant may not be found guilty of the crime unless the prosecutor proves both types of causation beyond a reasonable doubt. If the resulting harm would not have occurred but for the actions of the defendant, then actual causation is proven. The defendant's act (or omission) must not only be the actual cause of the harm, but it must be the proximate or direct cause as well. Proximate causation is at issue when other acts or omissions that occur after the defendant's act or omission contribute to the resulting harm. In the example above, Jim and the surgeon may have caused Dan's death. The question is whether the defendant should be held criminally liable if some other intervening cause appears to have contributed to the resulting harm. Was Jim's act the proximate cause of death, or should the surgeon's negligent act relieve Jim of criminal liability? The following case illustrates the complexities of proximate causation.

People v. Kibbe (1974)

N. Y. Court of Appeals

321 N.E.2d 773

During the early evening the defendants were drinking in a Rochester tavern along with the victim, George Stafford. The bartender testified that Stafford was displaying and "flashing" one hundred dollar bills, was thoroughly intoxicated and was finally "shut off" because of his inebriated condition. At some time between 8:15 and 8:30 p.m., Stafford inquired if someone would give him a ride to Canandaigua, New York, and the defendants, who, according to their statements, had already decided to steal Stafford's money, agreed to drive him there in Kibbe's automobile. The three men left the bar and proceeded to another bar where Stafford was denied service due to his condition. The defendants and Stafford then walked across the street to a third bar where they were served, and each had another drink or two.

After they left the third bar, the three men entered Kibbe's automobile and began the trip toward Canandaigua. Krall drove the car while Kibbe demanded that Stafford turn over any money he had. In the course of an exchange, Kibbe slapped Stafford several times, took his money, then compelled him to lower his trousers and to take off his shoes to be certain that Stafford had given up all his money; and when they were satisfied that Stafford had no more money on his person, the defendants forced Stafford to exit the Kibbe vehicle.

As he was thrust from the car, Stafford fell onto the shoulder of the rural two-lane highway on which they had been traveling. His trousers were still down around his ankles, his shirt was rolled up towards his chest, he was shoeless and he had also been stripped of any outer clothing. Before the defendants pulled away, Kibbe placed Stafford's shoes and jacket on the shoulder of the highway. Although Stafford's eyeglasses were in the Kibbe vehicle, the defendants, either through inadvertence or perhaps by specific design, did not give them to Stafford before they drove away. It was some time between 9:30 and 9:40 p.m. when Kibbe and Krall abandoned Stafford on the side of the road. The temperature was near zero, and, although it was not snowing at the time, visibility was occasionally obscured by heavy winds which intermittently blew previously fallen snow into the air and across the highway; and there was snow on both sides of the road as a result of previous plowing operations. The structure nearest the

point where Stafford was forced from the defendants' car was a gasoline service station situated nearly one half of a mile away on the other side of the highway. There was no artificial illumination on this segment of the rural highway.

At approximately 10:00 p.m. Michael W. Blake, a college student, was operating his pickup truck in the northbound lane of the highway in question. Two cars, which were approaching from the opposite direction, flashed their headlights at Blake's vehicle. Immediately after he had passed the second car, Blake saw Stafford sitting in the road in the middle of the northbound lane with his hands up in the air. Blake stated that he was operating his truck at a speed of approximately 50 miles per hour, and that he "didn't have time to react" before his vehicle struck Stafford. After he brought his truck to a stop and returned to try to be of assistance to Stafford, Blake observed that the man's trousers were down around his ankles and his shirt was pulled up around his chest. A deputy sheriff called to the accident scene also confirmed the fact that the victim's trousers were around his ankles, and that Stafford was wearing no shoes or jacket.

At the trial, the Medical Examiner of Monroe County testified that death had occurred fairly rapidly from massive head injuries. In addition, he found proof of a high degree of intoxication with a .25%, by weight, of alcohol concentration in the blood.

For their acts, the defendants were convicted of murder, robbery in the second degree and grand larceny in the third degree. However, the defendants basically challenge only their convictions of murder, claiming that the People failed to establish beyond a reasonable doubt that their acts "caused the death of another," as required by the statute. . . . They contend that the actions of Blake, the driver of the pickup truck, constituted both an intervening and superseding cause which relieves them of criminal responsibility for Stafford's death.

We subscribe to the requirement that the defendants' actions must be a sufficiently direct cause of the ensuing death before there can be any imposition of criminal liability, and recognize, of course, that this standard is greater than that required to serve as a basis for tort liability. Applying these criteria to the defendants' actions, we conclude that their activities on the evening of December 30, 1970 were a sufficiently direct cause of the death of George Stafford so

(Continued)

(Continued)

as to warrant the imposition of criminal sanctions. In engaging in what may properly be described as a despicable course of action, Kibbe and Krall left a helplessly intoxicated man without his eyeglasses in a position from which, because of these attending circumstances, he could not extricate himself and whose condition was such that he could not even protect himself from the elements. The defendants do not dispute the fact that their conduct evinced a depraved indifference to human life which created a grave risk of death, but rather they argue that it was just as likely that Stafford would be miraculously rescued by a good samaritan. We cannot accept such an argument. There can be little doubt but that Stafford would have frozen to death in his state of undress had he remained on the shoulder of the road. The only alternative left to him was the highway, which in his condition, for one reason or another, clearly foreboded the probability of his resulting death.

Under the conditions surrounding Blake's operation of his truck (i.e., the fact that he had his low beams on as the two cars approached; that there was no artificial lighting on the highway; and that there was insufficient time in which to react to Stafford's presence in his lane), we do not think it may be said that any supervening wrongful act occurred to relieve the defendants from the directly foreseeable consequences of their actions. In short, we will not disturb the jury's determination that the prosecution proved beyond a reasonable doubt that their actions came clearly within the statute (Penal Law, s 125.25, subd. 2) and "cause(d) the death of another person."

The orders of the Appellate Division should be affirmed.

Questions

1. What issue did Mr. Kibbe raise on appeal?

2. What was the court's rationale for rejecting Kibbe's argument?

3. Did the defendants intend to kill Stafford? Did they act purposely, knowingly, recklessly, or negligently?

Strict Liability ●━━━━━

For some behaviors, criminal liability is imposed even if there is no guilty state of mind. Strict liability crimes only require that a person do a voluntary act. Persons guilty of these crimes do not act purposely, knowingly, recklessly, or negligently. They may have done something accidentally or made a mistake—even a reasonable one. Nonetheless, the criminal law holds them liable.

Some strict liability laws are called "regulatory" or "public welfare" laws because they are meant to assure public health and safety. For example, there are strict liability laws that prohibit the sale of alcohol to minors and punish manufacturers who sell adulterated or misbranded drugs. So if a bartender sells alcohol to a minor, she is guilty even if she honestly believes that the minor is an adult and even if any reasonable person would have shared that belief. Likewise, the manufacturer who sells contaminated drugs is guilty even if she had no idea that the drugs were contaminated and even if she took reasonable steps to assure the purity of drugs. The penalties for these regulatory strict liability crimes are almost always very minor—usually a fine.

There are a few strict liability crimes that carry stiff penalties, including prison time. Statutory rape, or sex with a minor child, is one such crime. Rape and other sex offenses will be discussed in detail in Chapter 7. You will learn that the crime of rape involves sexual intercourse by force or threat of force and without consent. Consent is usually a defense to rape of an adult, but it is not a defense to sex with a minor child. The fact that the child appeared to be an adult is no defense. Even if the mistake was a reasonable one under the circumstances, many jurisdictions will hold the defendant strictly liable. Some states permit a defense of reasonable mistake in these cases, particularly when there is not much of an age difference between the defendant and the alleged victim.

The purpose of strict liability crimes is the protection of the public, and in the case of statutory rape, the protection of young children. If the manufacturer knows that he will be held strictly liable for distributing adulterated drugs, he will be motivated to take particular care to assure that his products are safe and pure. Likewise, adults will make sure that the individuals with whom they have sex are over the age of consent, and bartenders will take similar precautions when serving alcoholic drinks.

The following case illustrates some of the problems inherent in strict liability offenses.

Garnett v. State (1993)

Maryland Court of Appeals

332 Md. 571

Maryland's "statutory rape" law prohibiting sexual intercourse with an underage person is codified in Maryland Code (1957, 1992 Repl.Vol.) Art. 27, § 463, which reads in full:[9]

"Second degree rape.

(a) *What constitutes.*—A person is guilty of rape in the second degree if the person engages in vaginal intercourse with another person:

(1) By force or threat of force against the will and without the consent of the other person; or

(2) Who is mentally defective, mentally incapacitated, or physically helpless, and the person performing the act knows or should reasonably know the other person is mentally defective, mentally incapacitated, or physically helpless; or

(3) Who is under 14 years of age and the person performing the act is at least four years older than the victim.

(b) *Penalty.*—Any person violating the provisions of this section is guilty of a felony and upon conviction is subject to imprisonment for a period of not more than 20 years."

Subsection (a)(3) represents the current version of a statutory provision dating back to the first comprehensive codification of the criminal law by the Legislature in 1809. Now we consider whether under the present statute, the State must prove that a defendant knew the complaining witness was younger than 14 and, in a related question, whether it was error at trial to exclude evidence that he had been told, and believed, that she was 16 years old.

Raymond Lennard Garnett is a young retarded man. At the time of the incident in question he was 20 years old. He has an I.Q. of 52. His guidance counselor from the

Montgomery County public school system, Cynthia Parker, described him as a mildly retarded person who read on the third-grade level, did arithmetic on the fifth-grade level, and interacted with others socially at school at the level of someone 11 or 12 years of age. Ms. Parker added that Raymond attended special education classes and for at least one period of time was educated at home when he was afraid to return to school due to his classmates' taunting. Because he could not understand the duties of the jobs given him, he failed to complete vocational assignments; he sometimes lost his way to work. As Raymond was unable to pass any of the State's functional tests required for graduation, he received only a certificate of attendance rather than a high-school diploma.

In November or December 1990, a friend introduced Raymond to Erica Frazier, then aged 13; the two subsequently talked occasionally by telephone. On February 28, 1991, Raymond, apparently wishing to call for a ride home, approached the girl's house at about nine o'clock in the evening. Erica opened her bedroom window, through which Raymond entered; he testified that "she just told me to get a ladder and climb up her window." The two talked, and later engaged in sexual intercourse. Raymond left at about 4:30 a.m. the following morning. On November 19, 1991, Erica gave birth to a baby, of which Raymond is the biological father.

Raymond was tried before the Circuit Court for Montgomery County (Miller, J.) on one count of second degree rape under § 463(a)(3) proscribing sexual intercourse between a person under 14 and another at least four years older than the complainant. At trial, the defense twice proffered evidence to the effect that Erica herself and her friends had previously told Raymond that she was 16 years old, and that he had acted with that belief. The trial court excluded such evidence as immaterial, explaining:

"Under 463, the only two requirements as relate to this case are that there was vaginal intercourse, [and]

(Continued)

(Continued)

that . . . Ms. Frazier was under 14 years of age and that . . . Mr. Garnett was at least four years older than she.

"In the Court's opinion, consent is no defense to this charge. The victim's representation as to her age and the defendant's belief, if it existed, that she was not under age, what amounts to what otherwise might be termed a good faith defense, is in fact no defense to what amount[s] to statutory rape.

"It is in the Court's opinion a strict liability offense."

The court found Raymond guilty. It sentenced him to a term of five years in prison, suspended the sentence and imposed five years of probation, and ordered that he pay restitution to Erica and the Frazier family. Raymond noted an appeal; we granted certiorari prior to intermediate appellate review by the Court of Special Appeals to consider the important issue presented in the case. . . . .

Section 463(a)(3) does not expressly set forth a requirement that the accused have acted with a criminal state of mind, or *mens rea*. The State insists that the statute, by design, defines a strict liability offense, and that its essential elements were met in the instant case when Raymond, age 20, engaged in vaginal intercourse with Erica, a girl under 14 and more than 4 years his junior. Raymond replies that the criminal law exists to assess and punish morally culpable behavior. He says such culpability was absent here. He asks us either to engraft onto subsection (a)(3) an implicit *mens rea* requirement, or to recognize an affirmative defense of reasonable mistake as to the complainant's age. Raymond argues that it is unjust, under the circumstances of this case which led him to think his conduct lawful, to brand him a felon and rapist.

Raymond asserts that the events of this case were inconsistent with the criminal sexual exploitation of a minor by an adult. As earlier observed, Raymond entered Erica's bedroom at the girl's invitation; she directed him to use a ladder to reach her window. They engaged voluntarily in sexual intercourse. They remained together in the room for more than seven hours before Raymond departed at dawn. With an I.Q. of 52, Raymond functioned at approximately the same level as the 13-year-old Erica; he was mentally an adolescent in an adult's body. Arguably, had Raymond's chronological age, 20, matched his socio-intellectual age, about 12, he and Erica would have fallen well within the four-year age difference obviating a violation of the statute, and Raymond would not have been charged with any crime at all.

To be sure, legislative bodies since the mid-19th century have created strict liability criminal offenses requiring no *mens rea*. Almost all such statutes responded to the demands of public health and welfare arising from the complexities of society after the Industrial Revolution. Typically misdemeanors involving only fines or other light penalties, these strict liability laws regulated food, milk, liquor, medicines and drugs, securities, motor vehicles and traffic, the labeling of goods for sale, and the like. . . . Statutory rape, carrying the stigma of felony as well as a potential sentence of 20 years in prison, contrasts markedly with the other strict liability regulatory offenses and their light penalties.

We think it sufficiently clear . . . that Maryland's second degree rape statute defines a strict liability offense that does not require the State to prove *mens rea;* it makes no allowance for a mistake-of-age defense. The plain language of § 463, viewed in its entirety, and the legislative history of its creation lead to this conclusion.

Section 463(a)(3) prohibiting sexual intercourse with underage persons makes no reference to the actor's knowledge, belief, or other state of mind. As we see it, this silence as to *mens rea* results from legislative design. First, subsection (a)(3) stands in stark contrast to the provision immediately before it, subsection (a)(2) prohibiting vaginal intercourse with incapacitated or helpless persons. In subsection (a)(2), the Legislature expressly provided as an element of the offense that "the person performing the act *knows or should reasonably know* the other person is mentally defective, mentally incapacitated, or physically helpless." Code, § 463(a)(2) (emphasis added). In drafting this subsection, the Legislature showed itself perfectly capable of recognizing and allowing for a defense that obviates criminal intent; if the defendant objectively did not understand that the sex partner was impaired, there is no crime. That it chose not to include similar language in subsection (a)(3) indicates that the Legislature aimed to make statutory rape with underage persons a more severe prohibition based on strict criminal liability.

Maryland's second degree rape statute is by nature a creature of legislation. Any new provision introducing an element of *mens rea,* or permitting a defense of reasonable mistake of age, with respect to the offense of sexual intercourse with a person less than 14, should properly result from an act of the Legislature itself, rather than judicial fiat. Until then, defendants in extraordinary cases, like Raymond, will rely upon the tempering discretion of the trial court at sentencing.

Questions

1. How does the court distinguish Maryland's statutory rape law from other strict liability crimes?

2. What is the court's rationale for affirming Mr. Garnett's conviction?

3. What does the court mean when it notes, "Defendants in extraordinary cases, like Raymond, will rely upon the tempering discretion of the trial court at sentencing"?

In the following excerpt from her article "Incomprehensible Crimes: Defendants With Mental Retardation Charged With Statutory Rape," Professor Elizabeth Nevins-Saunders proposes that the strict liability standard should not apply in statutory rape cases involving defendants who are mentally retarded:

"Incomprehensible Crimes: Defendants With Mental Retardation Charged With Statutory Rape" by Elizabeth Nevin-Saunders

There are at least three different options for dealing with defendants with mental retardation charged with statutory rape, and each addresses a different point in the legal process. First, judges and prosecutors could use their discretion to pursue the prosecution only of defendants who are truly morally culpable. Second, legislators could modify sentencing schemes applied to these defendants. Finally, judges or legislators could interpret or change the governing rule of statutory rape (or the elements of the crime) to require consideration of the effect of a defendant's mental retardation.

All three of these options have limitations, not the least of which is the determination of when a defendant is or should be considered mentally retarded. Each option, however, improves the current model of holding a defendant strictly liable—and often subject to significant penalties—regardless of his mental capacity and blameworthiness. I argue that the first two of these options are variations on the status quo and, by themselves, are insufficient responses to the issues raised in this Article. The third option, however—injecting a *mens rea* element into statutory rape for defendants with mental retardation—is an effective way to address the policy and constitutional concerns underlying the prosecution and sentencing of defendants with mental retardation for statutory rape. . . . In these cases, the government should have to prove that a defendant with mental retardation actually knew the complainant was underage and that her age meant she could not legally consent to sex. In essence, this burden merely requires the government to demonstrate that the assumptions underlying the strict liability standard are well founded. Significantly, if the prosecutor cannot make this case, the defendant may not necessarily be completely free, for the government could always seek supervision of the individual through civil commitment.

Change the Gatekeeping

One potential solution to the problems explored above is to rely on prosecutors and judges to use their discretion to prosecute only those defendants revealed to be truly culpable. In some ways, designating prosecutors and judges as gatekeepers makes sense. Yet in the final analysis, this "solution" is ineffective, in large part because there are too many incentives for these institutional actors not to act on behalf of this class of defendant.

Scholars widely acknowledge that prosecutors already exercise a gatekeeping function in virtually all criminal prosecutions. In their decision to charge a crime at all, or to treat it as a misdemeanor, felony, or case for diversion, prosecutors regularly exercise vast discretion. Further, at least in theory, the prosecutor's mission "is not that [he] shall win a case, but that justice shall be done. As such, he is in a peculiar and very definite sense the servant of the law, the twofold aim of which is that guilt shall not escape or innocence suffer." This mission, along with knowledge of the defendant, the factual allegations, and the victim, arguably places prosecutors in the best position to make a decision as to which defendants are most appropriate for prosecution. According to this logic, a case in which a person with mental retardation was not fully aware of the meaning and consequences of his actions would be highly unlikely to work its way through the justice system at all, as prosecutors would decline to prosecute either through dismissal of the case or diversion of the defendant. . . .

While there are no statistics concerning the number of defendants with mental retardation charged with (or convicted of) statutory rape, it is clear that such discretion is frequently not exercised.

Some skeptics, believing the population of people with mental retardation in the criminal justice system to be relatively insignificant, might argue that the numbers do not justify a full prosecutorial or judicial policy, particularly if the policy is limited to statutory rape cases. But without a formal policy change, a prosecutor has virtually no incentive to abandon a strict liability standard in these cases. As some commentators and courts have noted, the standard "affords both an efficient

(Continued)

(Continued)

and nearly guaranteed way to convict defendants." In a statutory rape case, a strict liability standard alleviates the prosecutor's burden to prove intent—often the most difficult element of a criminal case—as well as force or lack of consent. Of course, prosecutors, many of whom are elected, face political pressure to enhance their office's record of convictions and to prosecute crime vigorously. Nowhere is this more true than with regard to defendants alleged to have raped a child, where public pressure often compels an aggressive response.

Change the Sentencing Scheme

Altering the sentencing scheme as applied to defendants with mental retardation is another possible way for the criminal justice system to account for the fact that people with mental retardation who are convicted of statutory rape are likely to be different from defendants of average intelligence in ways that affect their individual moral culpability. As with the other alternatives, however, there are both advantages and disadvantages to seeking change through sentencing. While I recommend that sentencing adjustments be made in addition to modifications to the elements constituting the crime of statutory rape, even by themselves, sentencing tools could be used to improve outcomes for this class of defendants.

As with the gatekeeping solution, the danger is that the reliance on discretion—particularly unfettered discretion—does not guarantee that justice will be done. Indeed, there may be reason to fear that jurors, or even judges, will sentence more, rather than less, harshly because of the defendant's mental retardation if they have the option to do so. The difficulty is in ensuring that judges, juries, and litigants are appropriately trained to deal with people with mental retardation and that their discretion is cabined with guidelines that encourage or mandate—rather than merely permit—mitigation due to a defendant's mental retardation. For this to occur, there may well need to be some policy or legislative change through training, statutes, or administrative rules.

There are dangers to focusing exclusively on sentencing reform as a remedy because sentencing comes at the end of the criminal justice process. First, this means that a defendant will be subjected to a traumatic criminal justice process that he may have failed to fully understand. Second, while sentencing reform may ameliorate some of the concerns regarding the imposition of a strict liability standard on defendants with mental retardation, it does not address those concerns as directly as would a rule adding a subjective *mens rea* element to the crime of statutory rape.

Change the Rule

The best remedy for the problematic strict liability standard for statutory rape is to modify the liability rule for people with mental retardation who are accused of the offense. To accomplish such a change, courts or legislatures could (1) create a blanket, per se rule absolving all people with mental retardation of criminal responsibility for statutory rape (making them subject to prosecution only under "regular" rape laws) or (2) change the elements of the offense specifically for people with mental retardation. . . . The only meaningful way to address the difference in culpability of most people with mental retardation is to require prosecutors to prove that defendants exhibited a truly "guilty" mind.[10]

Questions

1. Professor Nevins-Saunders proposes that mentally retarded defendants should not be held strictly liable in cases involving statutory rape. Do you agree or disagree with her approach?

2. What are Professor Nevins-Saunders three suggestions for dealing with mentally retarded defendants in statutory rape cases?

3. Should statutory rape be a strict liability crime? Why or why not?

Concluding Note

Think of the elements of a crime as the parts or components that must all be present before any act may be called a crime. A person who is alleged to have committed a crime may not be convicted unless and until a prosecutor proves each one of these necessary components beyond a reasonable doubt. In the upcoming chapters, you will learn about different crimes—theft, robbery, rape, murder, and many more. You will apply what you have learned in this chapter as you learn the elements of each of these crimes. Now test yourself on the material we have covered in this chapter. Good luck with the Issue Spotter exercise.

IssueSpotter

Read the hypothetical and spot the issues discussed in this chapter.

Abandoned Baby

Donna Lewis was a single mother who lived in New Town with her daughters, sixteen-year-old Wanda and three-year-old Tina. Donna was an unemployed dancer and was on welfare. Wanda had been having problems in school and was suspended twice for fighting. Donna suspected that Wanda was using drugs and on one occasion found methamphetamine (also known as crystal meth) in Wanda's bedroom. Donna sought help for Wanda, but Wanda never attended the Narcotics Anonymous meetings at the local community center as she was instructed to do. On occasion, Donna left little Tina with Wanda for short periods of time while she went out job hunting.

One day, Donna got a call from her old friend Sharon Rogers who lived in Las Vegas. Sharon told Donna about an opening in a chorus line at the Starlight Hotel in Las Vegas. Sharon told Donna that she knew the manager and could practically guarantee that Donna would be hired. The only catch was that Donna had to come out to Las Vegas within twenty-four hours. Donna borrowed money for the plane ticket from a friend, packed her bags, and instructed Wanda to take care of Tina until she got back. Donna promised to call Wanda as soon as she got to Las Vegas and to send for Wanda and Tina as soon as she could get the money for their airfare.

Donna was hired shortly after her audition and moved in with her friend Sharon. She was so excited, she forgot to call Wanda. Donna had not left a phone number where she could be reached. Three days passed and Donna never called home. Wanda began to get angry. She was getting tired of taking care of Tina. The food in the apartment was running low, and Wanda didn't have much money.

Wanda's friend Robin came to visit four days after Donna left town and offered Wanda some crystal meth to cheer her up. The two of them smoked meth in the apartment for several hours. Totally under the influence of the drug, Wanda went to a party with Robin, leaving Tina alone in the apartment. She then went home with Robin where she stayed for the next three days, smoking meth and drinking vodka. Wanda never went back to the apartment, leaving Tina in her crib with no food or water.

On the third day after Wanda left, the landlord entered the apartment and found Tina dead in her crib. An autopsy report revealed that she died from dehydration and malnutrition. Neighbors told the police that they had heard little Tina crying for a long time several days before. They had not come to check on her because Tina always cried a lot, they assumed someone was home with her, and they couldn't have entered the apartment anyway since the door was locked.

The police located Wanda, and Donna returned home after hearing a news report about Tina's death. Both Wanda and Donna gave statements to the police consistent with the aforementioned facts. In addition, Donna told the police she did not call or send for Wanda and Tina because she had not saved enough money and believed that Wanda would take care of Tina.

In New Town, involuntary manslaughter is defined as follows:

A person is guilty of involuntary manslaughter when, as a direct result of the doing of an act in a reckless or grossly negligent manner, he causes the death of another person.

You are the prosecutor in New Town. You are considering charging Wanda and/or Donna with involuntary manslaughter.

1. What arguments would you make in support of charging Donna?

2. What arguments would you make in support of charging Wanda?

3. Use the cases and other materials in this chapter to support your arguments.

Key Terms and Cases

Actus reus   58

"But for" causation   66

Garnett v. State   69

Good Samaritan laws   61

Knowingly   61

Mens rea   58

Negligently   61

People v. Conley   64

People v. Decina   56

People v. Kibbe   67

Proximate causation   66

Purposely   61

Recklessly   61

Robinson v. California   54

Status crimes   54

Strict liability   68

Voluntary act   57

Notes

1. *Martin v. State*, 31 Ala. App. 334 (Ala. Crim. App. 1944).

2. Ibid., 335.

3. Martin Gansberg, "Thirty-Eight Who Saw Murder Didn't Call the Police," *New York Times*, March 27, 1964, http://www2.southeastern.edu/Academics/Faculty/scraig/gansberg.html

4. Rachel Manning, Mark Levin, and Alan Collins, "The Kitty Genovese Murder and the Social Psychology of Helping: The Parable of the 38 Witnesses," *American Psychologist* 62, no. 6 (2007): 555–562.

5. *Jones v. United States* 308 F.2d 307, 310 (D.C. Cir. 1962).

6. Cathy Booth, "The Bad Samaritan," *Time*, September 7, 1998, http://content.time.com/time/magazine/article/0,9171,989037,00.html

7. Ibid.

8. Ill.Rev.Stat.1983, ch. 38, par. 12–3(a).

9. Maryland's rape statute has since been revised. The term *statutory rape* is no longer used. See Md. Code, Com. Law §3–305.

10. Elizabeth Nevins Saunders, "Incomprehensible Crimes: Defendants with Mental Retardation Charged with Statutory Rape," *NYU Law Review* 85, no. 4 (2010): 1067.

Chapter 4

For several years, Isaac Rosenbaum, an Israeli citizen living in New York, worked with a group of people to locate kidney donors and recipients. He was the broker for the illegal organ sales. Rosenbaum was responsible for finding donor and recipient matches based on blood type. With the help of others, Rosenbaum found willing donors in Israel and arranged for their transportation to the United States. Rosenbaum also secured their housing arrangements. For his efforts, Rosenbaum received as much as $160,000 for each organ sale.[1] Rosenbaum pled guilty to being part of a conspiracy to sell human kidneys, and in 2012, he was sentenced to serve two and one half years in prison.

The Rosenbaum case and others like it, push us to consider how we define crime. Specifically, they present the question of whether a crime has to be completed to be punishable. In this case, Rosenbaum entered into an agreement with other people to engage in unlawful acts. He helped arrange organ donations that never took place because law enforcement was able to intervene. Incomplete offenses represent a unique category of crimes—ones that either did not happen or could not happen. This chapter explores the range of issues involving incomplete—sometimes referred to as "inchoate"—crimes.

Isaac Rosenbaum was sentenced to two and one-half years in prison for his role in an international underground market for buying and selling kidneys.

Incomplete Crimes

Learning Objectives

After reading and studying this chapter, you should be able to

➤ List the elements of attempt

➤ Differentiate between "mere preparation" and "substantial step"

➤ Provide examples of actus reus for attempt

➤ Know the elements of solicitation

➤ Define factual impossibility

➤ State the elements of conspiracy

➤ List two differences between attempt and conspiracy

➤ Explain why incomplete crimes are subject to criminal punishment

➤ Identify the defenses to conspiracy

➤ Define legal impossibility

➤ Explain the merger doctrine and when it applies

➤ Contrast stalking with threats

Introduction

Nightly news broadcasts and local newspapers sometimes include a segment on "stupid" criminals, such as the would-be burglar who thought she could break into a home using plastic tools, the man who called 911 and announced that he was going to smash his neighbor's car because she was playing loud music, or the almost-bank robber who emailed himself a detailed plan for a bank heist, but inadvertently sent the message to everyone in his address folder. If these would-be criminals had not done something "dumb," they might have successfully committed their planned crimes. The people involved in these incidents have three things in common. Each one intended to commit a crime, each one took steps to commit a crime, and in each instance, the would-be criminal was unable to complete the planned crime. May they still be charged with criminal wrongdoing? The law answers yes.

Consider the following hypotheticals:

- Police officers pull over Sayo while she is driving to work. She is pulled over for failing to use her turn signal. The police ask if they can conduct a search of her vehicle. Sayo says, "Sure." A search of her vehicle uncovers the following items: butane, a butane burner, piping, glue, fittings, and $1,200 cash. These are items commonly used to manufacture the drug hashish. However, police do not find marijuana, an essential ingredient for hashish. Sayo is arrested and charged with attempting to manufacture hashish.
- Moby is an HIV-positive man. His doctor explained to him the seriousness of the disease, how it is spread, and told him that using condoms reduces the risk of passing the virus to sexual partners. Over a two-year period, Moby engaged in unprotected sex with several women. When asked by various partners to wear a condom, he declined. One of these women, Lily, became infected with the virus that causes HIV. Moby was arrested and charged with attempted murder.
- Blue and Gretchen decide to burglarize the home of a college classmate, Eduardo. Eduardo has a valuable collection of B.B. King, Beatles, and Beastie Boys albums. Blue and Gretchen pick Thursday at 3:00 p.m. as the date and time for the burglary—when Eduardo will be in his anthropology class. On Thursday, they drive over to Eduardo's with their bag of burglars' tools. When they arrive at the house, ready to break in, they discover it has been demolished by

a wrecking ball. There is no house to burglarize. The police were tipped off and were waiting at Eduardo's house for Blue and Gretchen. The officers arrest the pair and charge them with attempted burglary.

These hypotheticals raise some of the thorny issues associated with incomplete crimes.[2] This chapter examines how courts determine whether a person has taken sufficient steps toward committing a crime to be convicted of attempting to commit the crime. The law also requires that courts consider whether a person intended to commit a crime. The actions of Blue and Gretchen in the above hypothetical come closest to showing people who had intent to commit a crime and took steps to carry out the crime. The items found in Sayo's car give some suggestion of criminal activity, but it is not clear what she intended to do with the drug paraphernalia (or even whether she knew the items were in the car). Moby engaged in risky behavior, but it is not certain that he intended to kill Lily. Keep these scenarios in mind as we continue the discussion of incomplete criminal offenses.

Some legal commentators argue that punishing incomplete offenses violates a cardinal rule of criminal law—in order to punish, there must be harm. If no completed criminal offense has taken place, there has been no harm. Therefore, no punishment should be imposed. The criminal law, however, does punish inchoate offenses. There are several rationales for sanctions against those who intend to commit crime but have not completed the planned offense. First, incomplete crimes pose a danger to society. Offenses such as attempt, solicitation, and conspiracy violate society's interest in security. Thus, they harm society even though they may not cause direct physical harm. Second, punishing incomplete crimes encourages law enforcement to intervene before crime happens. If the justice system did not criminalize incomplete crimes, law enforcement could prevent crimes, but the intended offenders would not be brought to justice. Third, punishing incomplete crimes has a deterrent effect. Potential offenders will be discouraged from planning a crime if they know that taking even small steps toward the commission of a crime could result in punishment. The punishment for an incomplete crime is typically less than the punishment for the intended crime.

This chapter highlights the three main incomplete offenses: attempt, solicitation, and conspiracy. Each was an offense at common law. Each shares a common thread—an offender who intends to carry out a criminal offense. Inchoate crimes do not happen by accident. They are the product of intentional actions taken by would-be offenders. The chapter concludes with a discussion of two additional incomplete offenses—threats and stalking. Each of the incomplete crimes examined in this chapter represents a discrete point along the line of criminal offenses.

Attempt ●━━━━━━━━━━━━━━━━━━━━━━━━━━━━━━━━━

Under early English common law, attempt was not punished as a crime. However, by the late 1700s and early 1800s, cases emerged that recognized attempt as an offense and imposed sanctions against unsuccessful offenders. In *Rex v. Scofield* (1784)[3] for instance, the court held that a defendant could be charged with attempting to burn down a house. Some years later in *Rex v. Higgins* (1801), the court stated that acts or attempts that harm a community may be subject to criminal indictment.[4]

Two elements are required for the crime of attempt. First, there must be a specific intent to commit a crime. Specific intent means that the offender not only intended to engage in the actions that caused the crime, but also intended to carry out a crime. Specific intent is required for attempt (and all other incomplete crimes). The offender must be on a purposeful course to commit a particular crime, such as burglary, robbery, assault, fraud, or identity theft. The offender's mindset is referred to as mens rea. Specific intent is the mens rea for attempt. Second, the offender must take some action—some steps—toward the target crime. The intended crime is the target offense. The offender's actions are referred to as actus reus. States differ as to the steps that are necessary to meet the actus reus requirement for attempt. In some states, an offender may do very little and still meet the actus reus requirement. In other states, the offense has to be all-but-completed before a person may be convicted of attempt. Given these diverse standards, we can conceptualize the action requirement as steps along a continuum, described in Figure 4.1.

To determine whether a person has engaged in conduct sufficient to convict them of attempt, courts examine the defendant's actions to see how close he came to the completed crime. As Figure 4.1 demonstrates, there are many steps that separate "no action" from the last act a person can take to commit a crime. On this continuum, a substantial step is where an offender's actions cross the legal threshold to possibly become an attempt crime. Conversely, if there is no action or the action amounts to mere preparation, this will be insufficient to prove an attempt crime. When a court finds mere preparation, it concludes that while the defendant took some action toward committing the crime, he did not do enough to be held criminally responsible.

People v. Paluch (1966)[5] addresses the distinction between actions that constitute mere preparation and those that amount to substantial steps toward a completed crime. In this case, a man went to a barbershop for a haircut. Michael Paluch opened the door, let the man enter, put on his smock, and pointed to a chair for the man to sit in. Paluch had his own barbers' tools, including clipping shears, razors, and combs.

Figure 4.1 Attempt "Action" Continuum

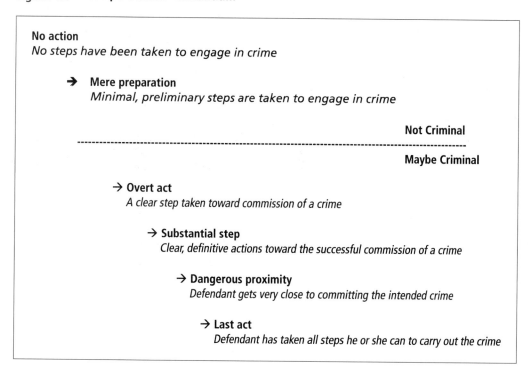

No action
No steps have been taken to engage in crime

➜ **Mere preparation**
Minimal, preliminary steps are taken to engage in crime

Not Criminal

Maybe Criminal

→ **Overt act**
A clear step taken toward commission of a crime

→ **Substantial step**
Clear, definitive actions toward the successful commission of a crime

→ **Dangerous proximity**
Defendant gets very close to committing the intended crime

→ **Last act**
Defendant has taken all steps he or she can to carry out the crime

When the customer asked if he had a license, Paluch pointed to a license on the wall. In fact, the license belonged to someone else. The customer worked for the barber's union. Paluch was charged with attempting to practice barbering without a license. He argued that his actions were mere preparation, since he had not begun to cut the man's hair. The court disagreed and held that Paluch had taken substantial steps toward practicing barbering without a license and found him guilty of attempt.

The dangerous proximity to success and last act tests for attempt impose a high benchmark for the prosecutor. The dangerous proximity test requires that the defendant's actions come very close to ensuring a successful crime. The last act test allows for criminal liability only when the defendant has done everything he can to make sure the crime takes place. Most states use the overt act or substantial step test, which is easier to establish than the last act or dangerous proximity to success.

The punishment for an attempt offense is based upon the punishment for the target offense. The target crime is the crime the offender planned to carry out. For instance, in the hypothetical involving Blue and Gretchen, their target crime was burglary. The more serious the target offense, the more serious the law treats the attempt to carry out the crime. For instance, the punishment for attempted murder is more severe than the punishment for attempted assault or attempted burglary (see the Vermont statute below). In most jurisdictions, if the target offense is a felony, the attempt to commit it will be a felony as well. For a handful of crimes, an attempt may carry the same punishment as the completed crime (e.g., attempt to commit murder or treason).

Next we compare and contrast how two states, Vermont and Connecticut, define attempt:

Vermont and Connecticut Attempt Statutes

Vermont Attempt Statute

a. A person who attempts to commit an offense and does an act toward the commission thereof, but by reason of being interrupted or prevented fails in the execution of the same, shall be punished as herein provided . . . If the offense attempted to be committed is murder, aggravated murder, kidnapping, arson causing death, aggravated sexual assault or sexual assault, a person shall be punished as the offense attempted to be committed is by law punishable.[6]

Connecticut Attempt Statute

a. A person is guilty of an attempt to commit a crime if, acting with the kind of mental state required for commission of the crime, he: (1) Intentionally engages in conduct which would constitute the crime if attendant circumstances were as he believes them to be; or (2) intentionally does or omits to do anything which, under the circumstances as he believes them to be, is an act or omission constituting a substantial step in a course of conduct planned to culminate in his commission of the crime.

b. Conduct shall not be held to constitute a substantial step . . . unless it is strongly corroborative of the actor's criminal purpose.[7]

In all fifty states and the District of Columbia, a conviction for attempt requires proof that the offender had the specific intent to commit the crime. However, Vermont and Connecticut differ in the evidence a prosecutor must present to establish the action requirement. Under Vermont law, attempt requires an affirmative act ("an act toward the commission"). By this language, a single act committed by the defendant could be enough for an attempt conviction in Vermont (in addition to specific intent). A single act, such as carrying burglars' tools or carrying the floor plans of a bank a person intends to rob could be sufficient to establish an act necessary for attempt. This is an easy standard to meet when compared with the action required under Connecticut law. Connecticut requires a substantial step. Thus, it may be easier to convict someone of attempt in Vermont than it is in Connecticut. The Connecticut statute lists examples of actions that meet the substantial step requirement. For instance, in the earlier hypothetical involving Sayo, her possession of drug paraphernalia would likely satisfy the action required under both Vermont and Connecticut law. This would also be true for the scenario involving Blue and Gretchen, who have chosen a date and time for the burglary, have the required tools, and have traveled to the victim's home.

It is noted that under Connecticut's attempt law both actions and inactions can be used to establish the action requirement [see (a) (2) on page 80]. The Connecticut law closely mirrors the Model Penal Code, which considers whether the offender purposely intended his actions. Under the Model Penal Code, an act or omission may establish a substantial step. In almost one-half of the states, the law allows a person to be convicted of attempt for a failure to act. However, very few attempt cases have been brought based on a failure to act. *State v. Smith* (2004)[8] offers a rare example. The defendant, Barbara Smith, appealed a conviction for attempted cruelty to the infirm. Smith provided at-home care for her eighty-three-year-old bedridden mother, Ms. Scott. Ms. Scott stayed on the living room couch for more than three months. During that time, Smith cleaned her mother only once. Family members made several unsuccessful attempts to clean Ms. Scott and get her to visit a doctor. In response to family members' attempts to provide physical assistance, Ms. Scott screamed, made verbal threats, and threatened them with a knife. For more than thirty days, she lay on the couch in her own urine and feces. When paramedics were called, they removed Ms. Scott from the home. She later died at a nursing home. The defendant's conviction was upheld on appeal. As to Smith's intent (mens rea), the court found that she knew or should have known that her mother required help.

We turn now to *People v. Rizzo* (1927), a classic case on the affirmative act requirement for attempt.

People v. Rizzo (1927)

Court of Appeals of New York

246 N.Y. 334

CRANE, J.

The police of the city of New York did excellent work in this case by preventing the commission of a serious crime. It is a great satisfaction to realize that we have such wide-awake guardians of our peace. Whether or not the steps which the defendant had taken up to the time of his arrest amounted to the commission of a crime, as defined by our law, is, however, another matter. He has been convicted of an attempt to commit the crime of robbery in the first degree, and sentenced to state's prison. There is no doubt that he had the intention to commit robbery, if he got the chance. An examination, however, of the facts is necessary to determine whether his acts were in preparation to commit the crime if the opportunity offered, or constituted a

(Continued)

(Continued)

crime in itself, known to our law as an attempt to commit robbery in the first degree.

Charles Rizzo, the defendant, appellant, with three others, Anthony J. Dorio, Thomas Milo, and John Thomasello, on January 14th planned to rob one Charles Rao of a pay roll valued at about $1,200 which he was to carry from the bank for the United Lathing Company. These defendants, two of whom had firearms, started out in an automobile, looking for Rao or the man who had the pay roll on that day. Rizzo claimed to be able to identify the man, and was to point him out to the others, who were to do the actual holding up. The four rode about in their car looking for Rao. They went to the bank from which he was supposed to get the money and to various buildings being constructed by the United Lathing Company. At last they came to One Hundred and Eightieth street and Morris Park avenue. By this time they were watched and followed by two police officers. As Rizzo jumped out of the car and ran into the building, all four were arrested. The defendant was taken out from the building in which he was hiding.

Neither Rao nor a man named Previti, who was also supposed to carry a pay roll, were at the place at the time of the arrest. The defendants had not found or seen the man they intended to rob. No person with a pay roll was at any of the places where they had stopped, and no one had been pointed out or identified by Rizzo. The four men intended to rob the pay roll man, whoever he was. They were looking for him, but they had not seen or discovered him up to the time they were arrested.

Does this constitute the crime of an attempt to commit robbery in the first degree? The Penal Law, § 2, prescribes: "An act, done with intent to commit a crime, and tending but failing to effect its commission, is an attempt to commit that crime." The word "tending" is very indefinite. It is perfectly evident that there will arise differences of opinion as to whether an act in a given case is one *tending* to commit a crime. "Tending" means to exert activity in a particular direction. Any act in preparation to commit a crime may be said to have a tendency towards its accomplishment. The procuring of the automobile, searching the streets looking for the desired victim, were in reality acts tending toward the commission of the proposed crime. The law, however, had recognized that many acts in the way of preparation are too remote to constitute the crime of attempt. The line has been drawn between those acts which are remote and those which are proximate and near to the consummation. The law must be practical, and therefore considers those acts only as tending to the commission of the crime which are so near to its accomplishment that in all reasonable

probability the crime itself would have been committed, but for timely interference.

The cases which have been before the courts express this idea in different language, but the idea remains the same. The act or acts must come or advance very near to the accomplishment of the intended crime. In *People v. Mills,* it was said: "Felonious intent alone is not enough, but there must be an overt act shown in order to establish even an attempt. An overt act is one done to carry out the intention, and it must be such as would naturally effect that result, unless prevented by some extraneous cause." In *Hyde v. U.S.* it was stated that the act amounts to an attempt when it is so near to the result that the danger of success is very great. "There must be dangerous proximity to success." Halsbury in his "Laws of England," says: "An act in order to be a criminal attempt must be immediately and not remotely connected with and directly tending to the commission of an offense." *Commonwealth v. Peaslee* refers to the acts constituting an attempt as coming *very near* to the accomplishment of the crime.

The method of committing or attempting crime varies in each case, so that the difficulty, if any, is not with this rule of law regarding an attempt, which is well understood, but with its application to the facts. As I have said before, minds differ over proximity and the nearness of the approach.

How shall we apply this rule of immediate nearness to this case? The defendants were looking for the pay roll man to rob him of his money. This is the charge in the indictment. Robbery is defined in section 2120 of the Penal Law as "the unlawful taking of personal property from the person or in the presence of another, against his will, by means of force, or violence, or fear of injury, immediate or future, to his person;" and it is made robbery in the first degree by section 2124 when committed by a person aided by accomplices actually present. To constitute the crime of robbery, the money must have been taken from Rao by means of force or violence, or through fear. The crime of attempt to commit robbery was committed, if these defendants did an act tending to the commission of this robbery.

Did the acts above described come dangerously near to the taking of Rao's property? Did the acts come so near the commission of robbery that there was reasonable likelihood of its accomplishment but for the interference? Rao was not found; the defendants were still looking for him; no attempt to rob him could be made, at least until he came in sight; he was not in the building at One Hundred and Eightieth street and Morris Park avenue. There was no man there with the pay roll for the United Lathing Company whom these defendants could rob. Apparently no money had been drawn from the bank for the pay roll by anybody at the time of the arrest. In a word, these defendants had planned to commit a crime, and were looking around the city for an opportunity to commit it, but the opportunity fortunately never came. Men would not be guilty of an attempt at burglary if they had planned to break into a building and were arrested while they were hunting about the streets for the building not knowing where it was.

Neither would a man be guilty of an attempt to commit murder if he armed himself and started out to find the person whom he had planned to kill but could not find him. So here these defendants were not guilty of an attempt to commit robbery in the first degree when they had not found or reached the presence of the person they intended to rob.

The judgment of conviction of this defendant, appellant, must be reversed, and a new trial ordered.

Questions

1. What is the issue in *People v. Rizzo*?

2. What test does the court apply to determine whether Mr. Rizzo is guilty of attempt? Refer to the attempt "action" continuum (Figure 4.1).

3. Based on the court's reasoning, would Mr. Rizzo and his cohorts have been found guilty if they had been parked in front of the United Lathing Company building when Rao or Previti left for the bank? What if they were parked there on a Sunday (when the bank was closed)?

Attempt Defenses

Abandonment

Abandonment, or renunciation, is one of the few defenses available to someone who has been charged with an incomplete criminal offense. A person has abandoned or renounced her crime when she decides to commit a crime, takes some steps toward its commission, but then changes her mind. To successfully establish that the crime has been abandoned, the defendant must have voluntarily taken steps to ensure that the planned crime would not happen. It does not count if the defendant "chickened out" or gave up her planned crime because she heard a police siren and thought the law enforcement officers were on her trail. If the defendant's actions establish that she no longer wanted to commit the crime, she may be able to avoid an attempt conviction. Why should we give would-be criminals an escape route? Society benefits when people decide not to commit crime. An abandonment defense encourages would-be offenders not to go through with their criminal actions. If the law did not allow renunciation as a defense, it would send the message that once you take certain steps toward a criminal outcome, you cannot, legally speaking, turn back. An abandonment defense rewards a person who changes his mind about committing a crime. The abandonment defense also promotes public safety by making crime less likely to happen.

Commonwealth v. McCloskey (1975)[9] offers an example of the abandonment defense. The defendant was charged with attempting to break out of prison. As part of his escape plan, McCloskey climbed a wall inside the prison. A silent alarm alerted prison security that someone was trying to escape. Correctional officials discovered a laundry bag filled with clothes and cut barbed wire. They were able to determine that the clothes belonged to

I hope you realize this is an "overt act" under the law of attempt.

I hope it's not just an attempt.

stus.com

Stu Rees

McCloskey. Several hours after the incident, the defendant voluntarily approached one of the guards and told him that he had planned to escape but changed his mind. The court upheld McCloskey's defense of abandonment because he had independently and voluntarily given up his plan to escape. If the abandonment is not voluntary or is based on a belief that law enforcement will discover the crime in the making, the defense of abandonment is not available. Despite McCloskey's success with an abandonment defense, most defendants fail.

Impossibility

The defense of impossibility addresses whether the law should allow someone to avoid criminal punishment if it was impossible to commit the planned crime. Should impossibility be recognized as a legal defense? Consider the following hypothetical:

> Judy plans to steal Linus's car, a Prius. Linus is her despicable neighbor. Judy is tired of paying high gas prices and wants an environmentally friendly vehicle. However, she cannot afford to buy a car. One night when Linus (accidently) left his keys in his apartment door, Judy steals them. The next day Judy goes to the parking garage looking for Linus's car. Unbeknownst to Judy, Linus left town the night before. He used his spare key.

Let us consider whether the law should punish Judy for attempted auto theft. More specifically, think about whether it makes sense to punish someone for attempt when it was impossible for him to commit the intended crime. Assume that in the above scenario Judy argues that she cannot be held criminally liable for auto theft because it was impossible for her to commit the crime since Linus's car was not in the parking garage. In fact, impossibility may be a defense to an attempt crime.

There are two types of impossibility defenses—factual and legal. The dividing line that separates them is not always clear. When an offender argues that he should not be found guilty of an incomplete crime because he has the defense of factual impossibility, the offender is saying that even though he was planning to commit a crime and took some steps toward it, he would not have been successful in completing the crime. Most states do not recognize factual impossibility as a defense to attempt crimes. The test for factual impossibility is whether a crime would have taken place if the facts were as the defendant believed them to be. If the crime would have been carried out if the circumstances were as the defendant believed them to be, then impossibility will not be a successful defense. Now we can apply this test to two of the previous hypothetical examples. Using the "if the facts were as the defendant believed them to be" test, in the hypothetical above, Judy would not be successful using a defense of factual impossibility. If the facts had been as she believed them to be and Linus's car was in the parking lot, Judy would have been able to steal the automobile. Likewise, in the hypothetical in the chapter introduction that involved Blue and Gretchen, if Eduardo's house had not been destroyed, the pair would have burglarized his home. The impossibility defense would not work for Blue and Gretchen.

State v. Dlugash (1977), a case with a memorable fact pattern, addresses the impossibility defense:

State v. Dlugash (1977)

Court of Appeals of New York

41 N.Y.2d 725

JASEN, J.

The 1967 revision of the Penal Law approached the impossibility defense to the inchoate crime of attempt in a novel fashion. The statute provides that, if a person engages in conduct which would otherwise constitute an attempt to commit a crime, "it is no defense to a prosecution for such attempt that the crime charged to have been attempted was, under the attendant circumstances, factually or legally impossible of commission, if such crime could have been committed had the attendant circumstances been as such person believed them to be." (Penal Law, § 110.10.) This appeal presents to us, for the first time, a case involving the application of the modern statute. We hold that, under the proof presented by the People at trial, defendant Melvin Dlugash may be held for attempted murder, though the target of the attempt may have already been slain, by the hand of another, when Dlugash made his felonious attempt.

On December 22, 1973, Michael Geller, 25 years old, was found shot to death in the bedroom of his Brooklyn apartment. The body, which had literally been riddled by bullets, was found lying faceup on the floor. An autopsy revealed that the victim had been shot in the face and head no less than seven times. Powder burns on the face indicated that the shots had been fired from within one foot of the victim. Four small caliber bullets were recovered from the victim's skull. The victim had also been critically wounded in the chest. One heavy caliber bullet passed through the left lung, penetrated the heart chamber, pierced the left ventricle of the heart upon entrance and again upon exit, and lodged in the victim's torso. A second bullet entered the left lung and passed through to the chest, but without reaching the heart area. Although the second bullet was damaged beyond identification, the bullet tracks indicated that these wounds were also inflicted by a bullet of heavy caliber. A tenth bullet, of unknown caliber, passed through the thumb of the victim's left hand. The autopsy report listed the cause of death as "[m]ultiple bullet wounds of head and chest with brain injury and massive bilateral hemothorax with penetration of [the] heart." Subsequent ballistics examination established that the four bullets recovered from the victim's head were .25 caliber bullets and that the heart-piercing bullet was of .38 caliber.

[During police questioning] Defendant stated that, on the night of December 21, 1973, he, Bush and Geller had been out drinking. Bush had been staying at Geller's apartment and, during the course of the evening, Geller several times demanded that Bush pay $100 towards the rent on the apartment. According to defendant, Bush rejected these demands, telling Geller that "you better shut up or you're going to get a bullet." All three returned to Geller's apartment at approximately midnight, took seats in the bedroom, and continued to drink until sometime between 3:00 and 3:30 in the morning. When Geller again pressed his demand for rent money, Bush drew his .38 caliber pistol, aimed it at Geller and fired three times. Geller fell to the floor. After the passage of a few minutes, perhaps two, perhaps as much as five, defendant walked over to the fallen Geller, drew his .25 caliber pistol, and fired approximately five shots in the victim's head and face. Defendant contended that, by the time he fired the shots, "it looked like Mike Geller was already dead." After the shots were fired, defendant and Bush walked to the apartment of a female acquaintance. Bush removed his shirt, wrapped the two guns and a knife in it, and left the apartment, telling Dlugash that he intended to dispose of the weapons. Bush returned 10 or 15 minutes later and stated that he had thrown the weapons down a sewer two or three blocks away.

After [Detective] Carrasquillo had taken the bulk of the statement, he asked the defendant why he would do such a thing. According to Carrasquillo, the defendant said, "gee, I really don't know." Carrasquillo repeated the question 10 minutes later, but received the same response. After a while, Carrasquillo asked the question for a third time and defendant replied, "Well, gee, I guess it must have been because I was afraid of Joe Bush."

At approximately 9:00 P.M., the defendant repeated the substance of his statement to an Assistant District Attorney. Defendant added that the time he shot at Geller, Geller was not moving and his eyes were closed. While he did not check for a pulse, defendant stated that Geller had not been doing anything to him at the time he shot because "Mike was dead."

Defendant was indicted by the Grand Jury of Kings County on a single count of murder in that, acting in concert with another person actually present, he intentionally caused the death of Michael Geller. At the trial, there were four principal prosecution witnesses: Detective Carrasquillo, the Assistant District Attorney who took the second admission, and two physicians from the office of the New York City

(Continued)

(Continued)

Chief Medical Examiner. For proof of defendant's culpability, the prosecution relied upon defendant's own admissions as related by the detective and the prosecutor. From the physicians, the prosecution sought to establish that Geller was still alive at the time defendant shot at him. Both physicians testified that each of the two chest wounds, for which defendant alleged Bush to be responsible, would have caused death without prompt medical attention. However, the victim would have remained alive until such time as his chest cavity became fully filled with blood. Depending on the circumstances, it might take 5 to 10 minutes for the chest cavity to fill. Neither prosecution witness could state, with medical certainty, that the victim was still alive when, perhaps five minutes after the initial chest wounds were inflicted, the defendant fired at the victim's head.

The defense produced but a single witness, the former Chief Medical Examiner of New York City. This expert stated that, in his view, Geller might have died of the chest wounds "very rapidly" since, in addition to the bleeding, a large bullet going through a lung and the heart would have other adverse medical effects. "Those wounds can be almost immediately or rapidly fatal or they may be delayed in there, in the time it would take for death to occur. But I would say that wounds like that which are described here as having gone through the lungs and the heart would be fatal wounds and in most cases they're rapidly fatal."

The jury found the defendant guilty of murder. The defendant then moved to set the verdict aside. He submitted an affidavit in which he contended that he "was absolutely, unequivocally and positively certain that Michael Geller was dead before [he] shot him." Further, the defendant averred that he was in fear for his life when he shot Geller. "This fear stemmed from the fact that Joseph Bush, the admitted killer of Geller, was holding a gun on me and telling me, in no uncertain terms, that if I didn't shoot the dead body I, too, would be killed." This motion was denied.

On appeal, the Appellate Division reversed the judgment of conviction on the law and dismissed the indictment. The court ruled that "the People failed to prove beyond a reasonable doubt that Geller had been alive at the time he was shot by defendant; defendant's conviction of murder thus cannot stand." Further, the court held that the judgment could not be modified to reflect a conviction for attempted murder because "the uncontradicted evidence is that the defendant, at the time he fired the five shots into the body of the decedent, believed him to be dead, and there is not a scintilla of evidence to contradict his assertion in that regard."

Preliminarily, we state our agreement with the Appellate Division that the evidence did not establish, beyond a reasonable doubt, that Geller was alive at the time defendant fired into his body. To sustain a homicide conviction, it must be established, beyond a reasonable doubt, that the defendant caused the death of another person. While the defendant admitted firing five shots at the victim approximately two to five minutes after Bush had fired three times, all three medical expert witnesses testified that they could not, with any degree of medical certainty, state whether the victim had been alive at the time the latter shots were fired by the defendant. Thus, the People failed to prove beyond a reasonable doubt that the victim had been alive at the time he was shot by the defendant. Whatever else it may be, it is not murder to shoot a dead body. Man dies but once.

Turning to the facts of the case before us, we believe that there is sufficient evidence in the record from which the jury could conclude that the defendant believed Geller to be alive at the time defendant fired shots into Geller's head. Defendant admitted firing five shots at a most vital part of the victim's anatomy from virtually point blank range. Although defendant contended that the victim had already been grievously wounded by another, from the defendant's admitted actions, the jury could conclude that the defendant's purpose and intention was to administer the coup de grace.

. . .

The jury convicted the defendant of murder. Necessarily, they found that defendant intended to kill a live human being. Subsumed within this finding is the conclusion that defendant acted in the belief that Geller was alive. Thus, there is no need for additional fact findings by a jury. Although it was not established beyond a reasonable doubt that Geller was, in fact, alive, such is no defense to attempted murder since a murder would have been committed "had the attendant circumstances been as [defendant] believed them to be." (Penal Law, § 110.10.) The jury necessarily found that defendant believed Geller to be alive when defendant shot at him. The Appellate Division erred in not modifying the judgment to reflect a conviction for the lesser included offense of attempted murder. An attempt to commit a murder is a lesser included offense of murder and the Appellate Division has the authority, where the trial evidence is not legally sufficient to establish the offense of which the defendant was convicted, to modify the judgment to one of conviction for a lesser included offense which is legally established by the evidence. Thus, the Appellate Division, by dismissing the indictment, failed to take the appropriate corrective action.

Questions

1. What crime was Mr. Dlugash convicted of by the jury?
2. What is the holding in the case?
3. Is there a compelling reason why a person should be convicted of attempted murder even when his intended victim is already dead?

The defense of legal impossibility arises in cases where a person has engaged in actions believed to be criminal when in fact they were not. One example is a person who bribes another person he thinks is a juror (to vote for acquittal) and the person is not on the jury. Another example is a person who believes he has purchased stolen goods, but the items were not stolen. This defense exposes a legal conflict between the goal of protecting the public's interest in safety (by avoiding the actions of criminals who plan crime) and the legal principle that a person can only be convicted of conduct specifically prohibited under the law.

Consider the following hypothetical:

In response to local complaints that people were unlawfully hunting and shooting deer, local game wardens created a deer decoy. The decoy was made of Styrofoam and wood, a deer hide covering, and a mounted deer head. The decoy was made to closely resemble the proportions of a live deer. The decoy was placed 80 feet from the road.

One night, Ollie and his buddy Frank went out looking to hunt deer. They drove slowly down the road, past the decoy. They turned the car around, drove slowly, and Ollie pulled out his gun, loaded it, and aimed it in the direction of the fake deer. One of Ollie's shots hits the decoy, knocking it down.

The wardens, who could not be seen from the road, watched the entire episode. After the decoy was shot, they surrounded the vehicle and arrested Ollie. He was later charged with attempting to take a wild deer out of season.

The question this fact pattern raises is whether a defense of legal impossibility would be successful. Ollie could argue that no crime took place because he did not shoot a live deer. Instead, Ollie says the shooting of the fake deer is not a crime and it did not cause harm. However, if the facts were as Ollie believed them to be, he would have killed a deer, in violation of the state law. Ollie had taken all of the steps he could to kill a deer. Legal impossibility will not work as a defense for Ollie. This hypothetical highlights the difficulty of distinguishing between factual and legal impossibility.[10]

Today, most jurisdictions have followed the lead of the Model Penal Code and abolished legal impossibility as a defense. It has been rejected as a defense through state statutes and case law. Therefore the general rule is that impossibility—factual or legal—is not a defense to an attempt crime. One reason that so many states have rejected legal impossibility is that it has become increasingly difficult to determine whether a set of facts raises an issue of legal or factual impossibility. A second reason is that states want to deter people from committing any crime. In the above hypothetical, although Ollie did not cause harm, his actions established that he intended to cause harm. If he could not be punished for shooting the decoy, he would benefit from his mistaken belief (that the deer was real). A conviction in his case sends a message to other would-be offenders that they will be punished for shooting deer, live or otherwise.

Atheer Labs designed 3-D glasses that operate as wearable computers. People who wear the glasses will be able to scan passersby and spot individual faces among a crowd of people. Facial recognition may then be used to scan criminal databases to see if there is a match (e.g., missing child or an outstanding warrant). Allan Yang, the company's founder, said the glasses will provide a new crime fighting tool: "In the optimal scenario," said Yang, "the police will be able to get an alert when they are patrolling the streets and they can prevent something from happening."[11]

Solicitation

Let's return again to the hypothetical used in the introduction with Blue and Gretchen. Consider these additional facts:

> Blue says to Gretchen, "I don't think it's fair that Eduardo has all that awesome music. He won't loan me any of his CDs or albums. I'm going to steal his prized album collection. If you help me, I'll pay you $342." Gretchen, a poor, starving student, responds "I'm in!"

If you ask another person to commit a crime with you or for you, you are guilty of criminal solicitation. To be liable for solicitation, you must intend to get another person to participate in a crime (mens rea) and you must ask or encourage another person to commit a crime (actus reus). Solicitation statutes use various terms to describe the actus reus element— for example, to ask, to encourage, to importune, to request, or to command. It is a crime to intentionally seek out other people to have them commit criminal offenses. In the above hypothetical, Blue has solicited Gretchen to participate in the burglary of Eduardo's home.

The offense of solicitation punishes activity that is considered harmful to society, but is not considered as harmful as an attempt offense. Asking another person to commit a crime may not involve an overt act, but may constitute the first step of what could become a criminal offense. The goal of laws that punish inchoate offenses, including solicitation, is to intervene at an early stage and prevent crimes. There is heightened concern with solicitation because it involves more than one criminal actor—if the person being solicited agrees. Some legal commentators believe that a crime is more likely to happen when more than one person is committed to carrying it out. Other commentators argue that because solicitation requires the involvement of at least two people, it poses a less serious threat to society than attempt, which only requires action by one person.

At common law, solicitation was a crime. Specifically, it was a misdemeanor to ask another person to commit a felony that involved a breach of the peace or obstruction of justice. Today, however, many states have general solicitation statutes. These laws classify solicitation as a separate criminal offense. Solicitation is sometimes referred to as a "double inchoate" offense (*see State v. Lee* [1991], below) or as "attempted conspiracy." This is because when someone asks another person to commit a crime and the person agrees, two incomplete crimes have occurred, solicitation *and* conspiracy.

The punishment for solicitation is usually lighter than the punishment for the planned target crime. It is usually punished at one or two degrees below the target offense. For instance, if the planned crime was a first degree felony, such as armed robbery, then the solicitation of an armed robbery would be punished as a second degree felony. In a number of states, there are separate laws that punish solicitation for murder or murder for hire. As noted, solicitation is typically a lower-level offense than attempt. However, some states place the punishment for solicitation on par with the punishment for attempt.

The Pennsylvania and Kansas criminal solicitation statutes appear below:

Pennsylvania and Kansas Solicitation Statutes

Pennsylvania Solicitation Statute

a. A person is guilty of solicitation to commit a crime if with the intent of promoting or facilitating its commission he commands, encourages or requests another person to engage in specific conduct which would constitute such crime or an attempt to commit such crime or which would establish his complicity in its commission or attempted commission.[12]

Kansas Solicitation Statute

a. Criminal solicitation is commanding, encouraging or requesting another person to commit a felony, attempt to commit a felony or aid and abet in the commission or attempted commission of a felony for the purpose of promoting or facilitating the felony.

b. It is immaterial under subsection (a) that the actor fails to communicate with the person solicited to commit a felony if the person's conduct was designed to effect a communication.[13]

The Pennsylvania and Kansas solicitation laws are representative of state solicitation statutes. Some provide more detail as to the various methods of solicitation. In a nod to the digital age, under Tennessee law, a solicitation may be "oral, written, or electronic."[14] Interpreted broadly, these statutes would punish a solicitation communicated in different ways, including American Sign Language or Morse code. While the core definition of criminal solicitation is the same for both Pennsylvania and Kansas, they differ in one key respect: whether the invitation to participate in a crime has to be received by the person it was intended to reach. The Kansas statute adheres to the language of the Model Penal Code (§ 5.02); the solicitation does *not* have to be received. The next case, *State v. Lee* (1991), which involves a solicitation letter written by an inmate, explores this issue.

State v. Lee (1991)

Court of Appeals of Oregon

804 P.2d 1208

DEITS, Judge. Defendant appeals his conviction for solicitation to commit robbery in the first degree. ORS 161.435. He argues that a letter that was not delivered can support, at most, a conviction for attempted solicitation. We agree.

In July, 1989, defendant, while in jail, wrote letters to an acquaintance who was in the Hillcrest Juvenile Center, outlining plans to rob a store and a residence. The letters were intercepted by Hillcrest personnel and never reached their intended recipient. The first intercepted letter stated:

> I wrote about two weeks ago. I guess you didn't get it. So, I'll tell you again. The job I got set up will get us some guns. On the other page is a picture of the place. And then I want to go to Washington. Okay.

The letter also described plans for robbing a store and burglarizing a residence. The other letter intercepted at Hillcrest also discussed plans for a "job." Defendant admitted that he wrote the letters.

Defendant first argues that there was insufficient evidence to convict him of solicitation. He contends that the evidence was insufficient for the court to find that he had the requisite "intent of causing another to engage in specific conduct constituting a crime." ORS 161.435(1). Defendant failed to move for a judgment of acquittal, and we decline to address the issue.

Defendant next contends that, because the letters were never received by the addressee, he did not commit the crime of solicitation, but only attempted solicitation. Solicitation is defined in ORS 161.435(1): "A person commits the crime of solicitation if with the intent of causing another to engage in specific conduct constituting a crime punishable as a felony or as a Class A misdemeanor or an attempt to commit such felony or Class A misdemeanor the person commands or solicits such other person to engage in that conduct."

The statute contains two elements: *mens rea* and *actus reus*. Defendant was found by the trial court to have the specified state of mind. He argues, however, that the *actus reus* proved by the state was insufficient to support a conviction, because the intercepted letters do not constitute a completed solicitation.

(Continued)

(Continued)

The statute provides that a person is guilty of solicitation if that person "commands or solicits" another to engage in criminal conduct constituting a felony or a Class A misdemeanor. However, the terms "command" or "solicit" are not defined in the statute, and it is unclear whether they include circumstances where a communication is not received. Our function is to construe the statute to carry out the legislature's intent. *See* ORS 174.020. The issue of an unreceived solicitation is not specifically discussed in the commentary to the statute. It is noted in the commentary, however, that the terms "request" and "encourage" were not included in the statute, because the drafters were concerned that such language might be "too open-ended." *Commentary to Oregon Criminal Code of 1971* 54, § 57 (1975 ed.).

It is also noted in the commentary that the word "solicits" was used "because it is an historic legal term that would carry with it the traditional limitations that are intended." *Commentary to Oregon Criminal Code of 1971* 54, § 57 (1975 ed). At common law, solicitation probably required that the communication be completed:

What if the solicitor's message never reaches the person intended to be solicitated, as where an intermediary fails to pass on the communication or the solicitor's letter is intercepted before it reaches the addressee? The act is nonetheless criminal, although it may be that the solicitor must be prosecuted for an attempt to solicit on such facts. 2 LeFave, *Substantive Criminal Law* 12, § 6.1 (1986).

Solicitation in the Oregon Penal Code was based, in part, on the Model Penal Code. *See Commentary to Oregon Criminal Code of 1971* 53, § 57 (1975 ed). Significantly, the legislature did not adopt the provision of the Model Penal Code that specifically provides that solicitation may be based on an incomplete communication.

We conclude that a completed communication is required to prove the crime of solicitation. Accordingly, defendant's conviction for solicitation was error. An attempt to solicit is necessarily included in the completed crime. Because the trial court found defendant guilty of acts constituting attempted solicitation, no new trial is required.

Questions

1. What is the issue in the case?

2. Why did the court hold that Mr. Lee should not have been convicted of solicitation?

3. How does the Oregon solicitation statute in the *Lee* case compare with the Pennsylvania and Kansas statutes discussed earlier?

The *Lee* decision is in line with the general rule that a completed solicitation requires that the recipient has received the request to participate in a crime. Now consider what happens when an offer to commit a crime is received not by an individual, but by a large group of people. Read the following hypothetical:

Professor Benny is a renowned psychology professor at a Midwestern college. He has been invited to give a lecture at a nearby college. Ninety-nine people attend Professor Benny's rousing talk, "Feelings and Finances."

At the close of his remarks, he informs the audience that the previous morning his girlfriend Desdemona jilted him and ran off with the dry cleaner. Professor Benny says Desdemona used him for his money and broke his heart into fifty-eight pieces.

With tears streaming down his cheeks, Professor Benny announces, "It's payback time! I'll give anyone in the audience $1,500 if you steal Desdemona's ATM card and bring it to me." He then writes Desdemona's first, middle, and last name on the white board, along with her home address. Professor Benny bows, thanks the crowd for its support and walks off the stage.

Has Professor Benny engaged in solicitation? The mens rea element is met because he intended to get someone in the audience to unlawfully take Desdemona's ATM card. Benny's offer of $1,500 to anyone who steals the bank card meets the actus reus requirement. The criminal law allows for the prosecution of a solicitation made to an individual or a group.

Solicitation Defenses

Abandonment

The defenses to solicitation mirror those available for attempt crimes. In addition to arguing that the prosecution has not established the elements of the crime (e.g., that facts do not establish that the defendant had the specific intent to encourage another person to commit a crime), a defendant charged with criminal solicitation could argue a defense of abandonment or renunciation. The Pennsylvania solicitation statute reviewed on page 88 provides:

> It is a defense that the actor, after soliciting another person to commit a crime, persuaded him not to do so or otherwise prevented the commission of the crime, under circumstances manifesting a complete and voluntary renunciation of his criminal intent.

The Pennsylvania law reflects the rule in many states. Abandonment may be a defense to solicitation when a defendant, who has encouraged someone to commit a crime, either persuades that person not to go through with it or alternatively, takes steps to prevent the crime (e.g., alerts law enforcement or the potential victim). Voluntariness is a key component of this defense. Some states also require that the abandonment is "complete," meaning that the offender does not plan to engage in the crime at a later date.

Impossibility

> Joe and Maxine meet for breakfast at their favorite diner. Maxine spends most of her time complaining about her Aunt Rhoda—"Rude Rhoda" she calls her. Joe responds to Maxine's comments by saying, "Why don't you knock off that mean lady. You should kill her once and for all." Maxine says, "No way, Joe!" She is appalled that Joe would encourage her to murder Rude Rhoda. That evening, Maxine goes to the authorities with an audiotape of her conversation with Joe. Neither Joe nor Maxine knew that Rude Rhoda had died of a heart attack two days earlier. Joe is later charged with soliciting the murder of Rude Rhoda.

This hypothetical raises the issue of whether Joe has a defense of factual impossibility. He could argue that there was no way he could successfully complete the crime. At the time of the solicitation, the intended victim was already dead. Joe's argument will be unsuccessful. Factual impossibility is typically rejected as a defense to criminal solicitation. What matters is the actor's (Joe's) mindset and actions, *not* whether the crime could be carried out. As discussed in the section on attempt defenses, the standard for the factual impossibility defense is if the facts had been as the defendant believed them to be, the defendant would have been able to commit the crime. In a typical solicitation case, the offender takes far fewer steps toward the target offense than an offender involved in a typical attempt case.

A defendant charged with solicitation might also raise a defense of legal impossibility. What happens when the would-be criminal's actions are not against the law? What if someone asks an undercover police officer (who is pretending to be a prostitute) to engage in a sexual act for pay? What if an adult entices a minor child to engage in a sexual act, but does not know that the "minor" is an undercover police officer? Both cases raise the issue of legal impossibility—whether the law should allow a defendant to argue that she should not be found guilty when her actions, even if completed, would not constitute a crime. State and federal courts widely reject this defense. This is particularly true in cases involving child sexual predators. As already noted, there is not always a bright line between factual and legal impossibility. This distinction matters in those states that recognize legal impossibility as a defense. Increasingly, however, states reject both factual impossibility and legal impossibility defenses.

Solicitation Versus Attempt

Generally speaking, solicitation is a less serious offense than attempt. A person may face charges of both solicitation and attempt to commit a particular crime. Under most state laws, however, a person can be convicted of either the solicitation *or* attempt to commit a crime (not both). The next section examines conspiracy, the most serious of the inchoate offenses.

Conspiracy ●━━━━━━━━━━━━━━━━━━

> For two or more to . . . combine together to commit . . . a breach of the criminal laws, is an offense of the gravest character.
>
> *Pinkerton v. U.S.*, U.S. Supreme Court (1941)

Conspiracy is serious business. A crime is more likely to happen if two or more people agree to carry it out. We need look no further than the national headlines to see criminal cases with conspiracies at their core: the Columbine High School murders; the September 11, 2001, terrorist attacks; Wall Street insider trading; the Enron financial scandal; and Bernard Madoff's multibillion-dollar Ponzi scheme.

Of the inchoate offenses, conspiracy is perhaps the most controversial. For many, it epitomizes the problem of the slippery slope. The legal proof required for conspiracy is minimal, the punishment can be harsh, and there is little proof that by themselves, conspiracies cause harm. It has been criticized as an offense that punishes "evil thoughts." Therefore, some commentators argue that conspiracy laws amount to legislative overreaching. Those on the other side of this debate believe that criminal conspiracies represent the first step on the path to commit crime. They believe that society is better served by having laws that punish people who take preliminary steps toward breaking the law. This supports the idea that early intervention would allow law enforcement to prevent crime. In making conspiracy a crime, the Model Penal Code notes that a crime has a greater likelihood of being carried out when two or more people have agreed to carry it out.

Conspiracy has a long legal history. The first conspiracy statute was enacted as early as 1285. As a common law offense, it required proof only of an agreement to commit a crime. Today, however, most jurisdictions also require an overt act in addition to an agreement. The punishment for conspiracy varies, but it is typically connected to the target crime of the conspiracy (e.g., murder or drug smuggling). In most instances, it is punished at one statutory rung below the target offense. In some jurisdictions, a conspiracy conviction may yield the same punishment as the crime at the center of a conspiracy. Notably, punishment for conspiracy varies under federal law. In some instances, the punishment is predetermined by statute (see the Federal Conspiracy statute below), and in others, the punishment is the same as the punishment for the crime targeted by the conspiracy. Under the Model Penal Code, a person convicted of conspiracy may be subject to punishment that equals the punishment for the planned crime.

Conspiracy is a specific intent offense. Criminal conspiracies, like attempt and solicitation offenses, do not happen by mistake. Unlike attempts or solicitations, conspiracies require an agreement between two or more people to engage in criminal activity (including an agreed upon offense). Most jurisdictions require that the co-conspirators take a step or some action toward carrying out the planned crime. Compare the following state and federal conspiracy statutes:

Wyoming and the Federal Conspiracy Statutes

Wyoming Conspiracy Statute[15]

A person is guilty of conspiracy to commit a crime if he agrees with one or more persons that they or one or more of them will commit a crime and one or more of them does an overt act to effect the objective of the agreement.

Federal Conspiracy Statute[16]

If two or more persons conspire either to commit any offense against the United States, or to defraud the United States, or any agency thereof in any manner or for any purpose, and one or more of such persons do any act to effect the object of the conspiracy, each shall be fined under this title or imprisoned not more than five years, or both.

Wyoming imposes an overt act requirement for conspiracy. In jurisdictions that follow the common law, an overt act is not required for a conspiracy conviction. At the federal level, there are dozens of conspiracy statutes. Under the above general conspiracy statute, a conviction requires both an agreement and any act. This is an easier standard to meet than the overt act standard under the Wyoming law. Notably under both statutes, if an individual conspirator commits an overt act in furtherance of the agreed upon crime, it can be used to establish the overt act requirement for the other members of the conspiracy. Legal scholars disagree as to whether an overt act should be an element of conspiracy. Some argue that if an overt act is not required, conspiracy laws are a thin line away from punishing thoughts and speech. We will revisit this issue later in the chapter (see *People v. Epton* [1967] on page 98).

Over time, the justice system has looked for ways to punish people who are involved in conspiracies that involve numerous people who do not know one another. If a conspirator can be held responsible for the actions of other members of the conspiracy, he faces greater criminal liability. To this end, there are various types of conspiracies that link large groups of people to a common criminal goal. Two examples are chain and wheel conspiracies. A chain conspiracy refers to a group of people who each have a role in carrying out actions that will lead to a larger criminal outcome. The members of a chain conspiracy do not necessary know one another but know (or should know) that there are other people involved in the conspiracy. An example of a chain conspiracy is a drug trafficking ring. For instance, one person makes arrangements to get the drugs, a second person divides the drugs into smaller packages, a third person determines who the drugs will be distributed to, a fourth person delivers the drugs, and a fifth person collects the money for the sale of the drugs. Chain conspiracies operate in a linear progression. If the prosecutor can establish that each participant was aware of the other participants, he may be able to establish a single conspiracy and convict each person for his participation. From a prosecutor's perspective, chain conspiracies are preferable to having to establish separate, smaller conspiracies, which would be subject to lesser penalties. In general, chain conspiracies are easier to prosecute than wheel conspiracies.

A wheel conspiracy has a key person at the center. This person, known as the "hub," has contact with the other members of the conspiracy—sometimes referred to as "spokes." Let us return to the opening scenario at the beginning of the chapter. Assume there was one person, Nelson, who was behind the scheme to sell organs. Nelson then enlists various people to carry out other parts of the plan. He asks Morris to find organ donors, Owen to find recipients, and Paolo to locate doctors who are willing to perform organ transplant surgeries. Nelson is the hub, or mastermind behind this conspiracy. If a prosecutor was able to establish that the spokes—Morris, Owen, and Paolo—were aware of one another's activities and agreed to join this larger group, he might be able to get a single-conspiracy conviction. In order to successfully prosecute members of a wheel conspiracy, each person must be aware of the other people who are involved.

Agreement and Specific Intent

A conspiracy agreement may be formal, such as an explicit, detailed verbal agreement between co-conspirators to hack credit card websites and steal Social Security card numbers. However, most conspiracies involve informal agreements—tacit, non-spoken alliances—to commit crime. We turn now to *State v. Smith* (1992) for a cautionary tale on what constitutes an agreement for conspiracy.

State v. Smith (1992)

Court of Appeals of Washington

828 P.2d 654

KENNEDY, J. Appellant Brian Smith appeals his conviction of conspiracy to deliver a controlled substance, lysergic acid diethylamide (LSD). Smith contends that the evidence was insufficient to support a finding that he conspired to deliver a controlled substance. We affirm.

On the evening of February 16, 1988, Corporal Corey Cook of the Snohomish Police Department, working undercover, agreed to purchase 50 doses of LSD from Bruce Erickson. They arranged to meet at a park and ride lot in the city of Snohomish.

On that same evening, Smith stopped by Erickson's residence in Everett. Erickson asked Smith for a ride to Snohomish, ostensibly to meet David Hensler. Smith agreed to give Erickson a ride as Smith also wanted to see Hensler. Hensler owed Smith $600 for rent and telephone bills. Smith and Erickson arrived at the Snohomish park and ride lot at 8:15 p.m., in Smith's Datsun pickup. Smith drove and Erickson was in the passenger seat.

Corporal Cook approached the passenger side and spoke to Erickson, asking Erickson if he had any LSD. Erickson produced a plastic bag containing LSD. Corporal Cook asked Smith if he had tried the LSD and if it was any good. Smith replied that "he was going to college at the time and he

couldn't afford to get messed up, but that his wife had taken some of it, and . . . 'it really [messed] her up.'" Corporal Cook testified that he took this to refer to a beneficial quality of LSD. Corporal Cook then agreed to purchase the LSD, handed the money to Erickson, and arrested both Smith and Erickson.

At the police station, Corporal Cook questioned Smith. Corporal Cook recorded the following statement in his police report:

> Smith told me that he was aware that Erickson was selling me acid at the Park and Ride and said that he was in Everett at the time and had to go to Snohomish anyway and that Erickson said that he needed a ride.

Smith was charged with conspiracy to deliver a controlled substance. Smith waived his right to a jury trial. At the bench trial, Corporal Cook testified that he interpreted Smith's statement that he recorded in the police report to mean that Smith was in Everett when he learned of the impending LSD sale.

At the close of the State's case, Smith moved to dismiss for lack of sufficient evidence. Smith argued that there was insufficient evidence from which the trier of fact could find all of the essential elements of conspiracy to deliver a controlled substance. The trial court denied the motion, finding that there was sufficient evidence of conspiracy because Smith agreed to assist Erickson in delivering LSD by giving Erickson a ride to Snohomish, knowing that Erickson's purpose was to sell LSD.

Smith then testified on his own behalf and stated that he had not known in advance of the sale that Erickson was going to sell LSD. Smith also denied telling Corporal Cook that his wife had used LSD.

At the conclusion of the bench trial, the court found Smith guilty of conspiracy to deliver a controlled substance because Smith "knew that Erickson's purpose was to go sell some LSD."

Smith appeals challenging the sufficiency of the evidence.

Smith argues that his conviction must be reversed because the evidence is insufficient to support a finding of conspiracy to deliver a controlled substance. Smith contends that the trial court failed to find beyond a reasonable doubt the essential elements of conspiracy, specifically an agreement to engage in the delivery of a controlled substance and the intent that a controlled substance be delivered.

When a conviction is attacked on the basis of insufficiency of evidence, the proper inquiry on review is, after viewing the evidence in the light most favorable to the State, "whether there was sufficient evidence to justify a rational trier of fact to find guilt beyond a reasonable doubt." *State v. Green,* 616 P.2d 628 (1980) (quoting *Jackson v. Virginia,* 443 U.S. 307 (1979)). Thus to affirm Smith's conviction for conspiracy to deliver a controlled substance, we must determine whether a rational trier of fact could have found beyond a reasonable doubt that Smith agreed with Erickson to deliver LSD to Corporal Cook and that Smith intended that LSD be delivered to Corporal Cook.

A formal agreement is not essential to the formation of a conspiracy. *State v. Casarez-Gastelum,* 738 P.2d 303 (1987). An agreement can be shown by a "concert of action, all the parties working together understandingly, with a single design for the accomplishment of a common purpose.'" *Casarez-Gastelum,* (quoting *Marino v. U. S.,* 91 F.2d 691, 694 (9th Cir. 1937)). Proof of a conspiracy may be established by overt acts and "much is left to the discretion of the trial court." *Casarez-Gastelum,* 48 Wn. App. at 116 (quoting *Marino v. U.S.,* supra).

Here the trial court found Smith guilty of violating RCW 69.50.407, conspiracy to deliver a controlled substance, which provides:

Any person who attempts or conspires to commit any offense defined in this chapter is punishable by imprisonment or fine or both which may not exceed the maximum punishment prescribed for the offense, the commission of which was the object of the attempt or conspiracy.

The trial court noted that, because conspiracy is not defined in the controlled substances act, it was applying the definition of conspiracy under the general conspiracy statute, RCW 9A.28.040(1), without the substantial step requirement. RCW 9A.28.040(1) provides:

A person is guilty of criminal conspiracy when, with intent that conduct constituting a crime be performed, he agrees with one or more persons to engage in or cause the performance of such conduct, and any one of them takes a substantial step in the pursuance of such agreement.

The court stated that it was omitting the substantial step requirement based on *State v. Hawthorne,* 737 P.2d 717 (1987), which held that substantial step is not an element of conspiracy under RCW 69.50.407. Thus, the court defined conspiracy as: "A person commits the crime of criminal conspiracy when, with the intent that conduct constituting a crime be performed, he or she agrees with one or more persons to engage in or causes the performance of such conduct."

The evidence, although conflicting in some respects, convinced the trier of fact that, although Smith's primary purpose in giving Erickson a lift to the park and ride lot was to meet with Hensler, who owed Smith $600, his secondary purpose was to assist Erickson in delivering LSD. As conceded by Smith in oral argument for this appeal, the presence of a primary, legal reason for the trip, does not in and of itself negate a secondary illegal reason. By agreeing to drive Erickson to Snohomish with prior knowledge that the purpose of Erickson's trip was to sell LSD, Smith agreed to engage in the delivery. That the trip also satisfied Smith's own primary purpose of meeting up with Hensler does not negate the agreement and concerted action.

Smith argues that the trial court confused "knowledge" of the sale with the "agreement and concerted action" requirement of conspiracy. We disagree. Here there was evidence not only of knowledge of Erickson's unlawful purpose, but an agreement to assist with the plan by providing the necessary transportation. The evidence was sufficient to prove an agreement. An agreement may be proved by overt acts. *See, Casarez-Gastelum.* Here there were two overt acts: first, that Smith drove Erickson to Snohomish knowing, according to Corporal Cook, Erickson's purpose for the trip; and second, that

(Continued)

(Continued)

Smith provided encouragement for the sale by assuring the officer of the potency of the drug.

We hold that there is sufficient evidence to convince a rational trier of fact beyond a reasonable doubt that Smith agreed to transport Erickson to Snohomish for the common purpose of delivering LSD.

The State also had to prove that Smith intended to deliver LSD to convict him of conspiracy to deliver a controlled substance.[2] See RCW 9A.28.040(1). In *Casarez-Gastelum,* the court held that once a conspiracy has been established, the State must prove beyond a reasonable doubt that the defendant had at least a "slight" connection with the conspiracy. 48 Wn. App. at 117. Evidence establishing a "slight" connection with the conspiracy must be of the quality which will reasonably support a conclusion that the particular defendant in question wilfully participated in the unlawful plan with the intent to further some object or purpose of the conspiracy. . . .

Intent is defined as action "with the objective or purpose to accomplish a result which constitutes a crime." RCW 9A.08.010(1)(a).

Smith argues that his conviction must be reversed because the trial court failed to find that he intended to deliver LSD. Smith contends that the trial court's finding that he had knowledge of Erickson's illegal purpose is insufficient to support a finding of intent. We disagree with Smith's interpretation of the trial court's findings.

Here, the trial court found that Smith's "primary purpose was to go and try to get his 600 bucks out of Hensler, but he knew that Erickson's purpose was to go to sell some LSD." Implicit in the trial court's finding is that Smith not only knew of Erickson's unlawful purpose, but that Smith agreed to assist with the plan by providing the necessary transportation to complete the sale and that Smith provided encouragement for the sale by assuring Corporal Cook that the LSD was potent. Such evidence is sufficient to show that Smith intended to assist Erickson in the delivery of LSD.

Accordingly, we affirm Smith's conviction.

Questions

1. What overt acts did Mr. Smith engage in?

2. What facts establish that Mr. Smith had specific intent?

3. Based on the court's reasoning, how would it have decided the case if Mr. Erickson had revealed his intention to make the LSD sale after he and Mr. Smith had already driven halfway to Snohomish County?

Overt Act

Evidence of something beyond an agreement—the overt act—is proof that the conspiracy is alive and operative. The overt act requirement allows for a window of time within which the agreement to commit crime might be abandoned. Between the time of the agreement but before an overt act is committed, potential co-conspirators could decide *not* to engage in a criminal enterprise. This window provides a safety zone for potential criminals, an exit door out of criminal charges. In conspiracy cases, the factfinder must find an overt act. Because the overt act does not have to be unlawful, this requirement is easy to meet. Notably, it is a much lower standard to meet than the substantial step requirement for attempt. An overt act that would be sufficient for a conspiracy charge might only establish mere preparation, which would be insufficient to prove attempt. In a case involving numerous overt acts, jurors have to find at least one (they may disagree as to which one).

Numerous, otherwise lawful actions could satisfy the overt act requirement for conspiracy. Examples include the following:

- making a phone call,
- purchasing or renting a getaway car for a robbery,
- mailing a letter,
- taking an automobile trip with co-conspirators, and
- attending a meeting to plan the crime.

In jurisdictions that do not require an overt act, the agreement itself is the actus reus. Under the general federal conspiracy statute, the actus reus can be established with proof that *one* of the co-conspirators committed an act that furthers the conspiracy.

Conspiracy Defenses

Abandonment

There are fewer avenues of escape for a person who has become part of a conspiracy than there are for someone who participates in other incomplete crimes. In order for a person to prove that she no longer is a member of a conspiracy and no longer wants to take part in the target crime, she has to prove that she took action to stop the crime from taking place. This is known as abandonment or renunciation. At common law, renunciation was not recognized as a defense to a conspiracy charge. Today a successful defense of renunciation requires that the defendant show that she did more than simply change her mind about committing a crime. Courts look to see whether the defendant made a serious attempt to prevent the planned crime. If the defendant notified each of his fellow co-conspirators of his plans to withdraw he might escape responsibility for the future acts of his former partners in crime. The Model Penal Code recognizes renunciation as a defense to a conspiracy charge, if the defendant takes action to prevent the crime. Under the Wyoming statute, referenced earlier, an offender who wishes to use renunciation as a defense must voluntarily withdraw from the planned crime and prevent the conspiracy from being successful. The Wyoming law is based on the Mode Penal Code.

Merger Doctrine ●━━━━━━━━━━━━━━━━━━━━━━━━━

The merger doctrine addresses which crimes an offender can be convicted of once the intended crime has been completed. For the crime of attempt, a defendant may be convicted of attempt *or* the completed crime, not both. For instance, if a defendant has been charged with burglary, a jury might find that the defendant was guilty of burglary or attempted burglary (which is a lesser included offense). He might be found not guilty. If the defendant is found guilty of burglary, he cannot also be found guilty of attempted burglary. This is the rule of merger—the attempt offense (attempted burglary) merges with the more serious completed crime (burglary). Another example of merger occurs with solicitation. Assume that Gina asks Wei to steal her geography teacher's grade book. Wei says yes to the solicitation. Now there is a conspiracy between Gina and Wei to commit theft. Both could be charged with conspiracy. Gina will not face a separate charge of solicitation.

Conspiracy is the exception to the doctrine of merger. For example, if Tyson and Marty decide to steal Social Security numbers from the computer files at the bank where they are managers, the pair could be convicted of both conspiracy to hack computers and computer hacking. The crime of conspiracy is considered too dangerous to let the offender avoid punishment after completion of the target crime.

Table 4.1 summarizes the elements, punishment, and merger rules for attempt, solicitation, and conspiracy.

Table 4.1 **Summary Table: Attempt, Solicitation, and Conspiracy**

	Elements	Punishment	Merger
ATTEMPT	1. Specific intent and 2. Overt act [beyond preparatory steps]	Depends on target crime –Usually punished less than or at one grade below target crime	D cannot be convicted of both attempt and target crime
SOLICITATION	1. Specific intent and 2. Encourages another to commit crime	Depends on target crime –Usually punished as fraction of target crime	†Merges with target crime †Merges with attempt and conspiracy
CONSPIRACY	1. Specific intent and 2. Overt Act†	May be same or less than punishment for target crime	†Does not merge with target crime †D can be convicted of conspiracy and attempt

† Required in some jurisdictions

Let's consider what happens when members of a group intentionally engage in speech that invites others to engage in criminal action. Can group members be penalized or is their speech constitutionally protected? The next case, *People v. Epton*, tackles this issue.

People v. Epton (1967)

Court of Appeals of New York

19 N.Y.2d 496

SCILEPPI, J. The defendant [William Epton] was convicted of conspiracy to commit a riot, conspiracy to commit advocacy of criminal anarchy, and advocacy of criminal anarchy. He argues, among other issues, that his two conspiracy convictions should not stand since they consisted of free speech under the First Amendment.

The defendant, a self-acknowledged Marxist and president of the Harlem "club" of the Progressive Labor Movement, a splinter communist club dedicated to violent revolution, was shown by the evidence on his trial to have been active in the Harlem community for many months prior to the 1964 riots. His activities . . . appear largely to have been limited to formation of a small cadre of followers . . . There is no evidence in the record that Epton or his party at any time had a substantial following in the community . . . [I]n the summer of 1964, following the killing of a 15-year-old African-American boy by an off-duty police lieutenant, tensions within the African-American communities in New York City heightened. Defendant seized upon this unrest by preaching his "gospel of revolution" in the streets and calling for organized resistance to the police. At one point, he addressed a group of 50 persons and called for violent action. According to defendant, "[We'll] begin

a campaign to organize a mass demonstration against the cops somewhere in this city . . . [The cops] declared war on us and we should declare war on them and every time they kill one of us damn it, we'll kill one of them and we should start thinking that way right now . . . because we had better stop talking about violence as a dirty word . . . "

When riots broke out in the city, defendant and his helpers continued their incendiary speeches. At one meeting, defendant urged participants to "organize to combat the police . . . including 'suckering' the officers off the main avenues into the side streets away from other policemen where they could be killed one by one."

According to the court, "[D]efendant's contention that his conviction for conspiracy to commit riot cannot stand because so much of the evidence against him consisted of speech, misrepresents the [substantial importance] of the conspiracy to riot charge. The [substantial importance of] the charge is that the defendant entered into an unlawful agreement with others to incite and instigate riot and committed certain overt acts in furtherance of this end . . . [S]peech in and of itself is not the object of a prosecution for conspiracy to incite riot . . . [A] conviction relying upon speech . . . as evidence of violation may be sustained only when the speech . . . created a 'clear and present danger' of attempting or accomplishing the prohibited crime . . . [T]he evidence adduced by the People [in this case] was more than sufficient to sustain a finding of 'clear and present danger' of riot . . . We have examined the other contentions raised by the defendant and have found them to be equally lacking in merit . . . [T]he judgment . . . affirming the defendant's conviction for the crimes of conspiracy to riot, conspiracy to commit the crime of advocacy of criminal anarchy and advocacy of criminal anarchy should be affirmed."

Questions

1. What argument does Mr. Epton make on appeal?

2. What is the holding in the case?

3. Assume that Mr. Epton had been a street preacher who had no identifiable followers. Do you think the court would have decided the case differently?

Other Incomplete Offenses

Scholars agreed that attempt, solicitation, and conspiracy are the major inchoate offenses. However, there is debate about whether other offenses fall under the umbrella of inchoate crimes. For instance, threats, aiding and abetting another in the commission of a crime, and stalking are incomplete crimes. Inchoate offenses are typically divided into two categories, complex and simple. Attempt, solicitation, and conspiracy are complex incomplete crimes. Complex inchoate offenses refer to crimes that involve actions that are not necessarily criminal by themselves—lawful acts such as purchasing a weapon, sitting in a vehicle outside of a bank, and walking into a bank. However, with complex inchoate offenses, the offender carries out his actions with an unlawful goal in mind—to commit the target crime (e.g., bank robbery). By contrast, simple inchoate crimes do not have a target offense. Also, the steps taken to carry out a simple inchoate offense are criminal.[17] In this section we examine two examples of simple inchoate offenses, threats and stalking.

Threats

Threats involve statements and actions that indicate an imminent offense against an individual or a group. In these instances, it does not matter whether the person making the threat is capable of carrying it out. The threat itself is a crime. In some cases, a threat, without any additional action, is sufficient for a criminal charge. An example of this is where threats are made against the president of the United States. The U.S. Code punishes "Threats Against the President and Successors to the Presidency":

> Whoever knowingly and willfully deposits for conveyance in the mail or for a delivery from any post office or by any letter carrier any letter, paper, writing, print, missive, or document containing any threat to take the life of, to kidnap, or to inflict bodily harm upon the President of the United States, the President-elect, the Vice President or other officer next in the order of succession to the office of President of the United States, or the Vice President-elect . . . shall be fined under this title or imprisoned not more than five years, or both.[18]

In 2012, Joaquin Serrapio Jr. pled guilty to threatening to harm or kill the president of the United States, in violation of above federal statute. Serrapio, a twenty-year-old student who attended Miami-Dade College, sent threats against President Obama on Facebook and Twitter. Obama was scheduled to visit Miami the same week. Here are three of Serrapio's messages, posted under the name "Jay Valor":

Jay Valor
@Jay_Valor

Secret service where u at! I threatened ur precious tyrant! Ull b sorry u didnt come lookong for me in a couple of hours ;) ⊓⊓

12:28 PM - 23 Feb 12 via Echofon · Embed this Tweet

← Reply ↻ Retweet ★ Favorite

Twitter

Jay Valor's February 23, 2012, Twitter message. How is attempt treated differently when it concerns threats against elite government officials?

February 21, 2012

Who wants to help me assassinate Obummer while hes at UM this week?

February 23, 2012

If anyone goes to [the University of Miami] to see Obama today, get ur phones out and record. Cause at any moment im gonna put a bullet through his head and u don't wanna miss that! Youtube![19]

During a search of Serrapio's bedroom, Secret Service agents discovered an Apple iPad showing the February 21, 2012, Facebook posting. Agents also found a sniper rifle-style Airsoft pellet gun and a handgun-style Airsoft pellet gun.[20] Serrapio said his goal was to get a reaction from supporters of President Barack Obama. Serrapio, who faced a maximum punishment of five years in prison, was sentenced to three years of probation, four months home confinement, and 250 hours of community service. The federal judge who imposed the sentence also required that Serrapio write a Facebook post on the broad impact of social media.[21]

A comparison of the elements of attempt with the elements needed to prove threats against high-ranking government officials reveals some differences. First, attempt and the majority of inchoate crimes require proof of specific intent—proof that the would-be offender intended to carry out a crime and took steps toward its commission. However, threats against elite government officials do not impose the same high standard for the mens rea requirement. Instead, one can be convicted when there is proof that someone intended to make threats, regardless of whether he intended to carry them out.

Second, for an attempt offense, some action on the part of the would-be offender is required. The actus reus may vary (e.g., "substantial step" or "dangerous proximity to success"). However, something more than a verbal or written statement is required for attempt. By contrast, a prosecution for threats under the U.S. Code does not require proof that the person engaged in an overt act. For instance, in the Serrapio case, there was no evidence that President Obama was in any danger from Serrapio. Nor was there evidence that Serrapio had made further moves to carry out the threats (e.g., that he purchased his weapons with the intent to use them against the President). The threat itself is a sufficient basis for the criminal charge.

Stalking

The crime of stalking has been defined as "a course of conduct directed at a specific person that would cause a reasonable person to fear."[22] After several stalking-related deaths, including the high-profile case of actress Rebecca Schafer, in 1990, California became the first state to pass anti-stalking legislation. In a 2012 report, the Justice Department estimates that each year there are approximately 3.3 million stalking victims.[23] The stalking cases that receive the most attention involve strangers. However, in most cases the victim knows her stalker, either as an acquaintance or intimate partner.

Today, all fifty states, the District of Columbia, and U.S. territories have passed laws against stalking. Here is an example:

Mississippi's Stalking Statute

Any person who purposefully engages in a course of conduct directed at a specific person, or who makes a credible threat, and who knows or should know that the conduct would cause a reasonable person to fear for his or her own safety, to fear for the safety of another person, or to fear damage or destruction of his or her property, is guilty of the crime of stalking.[24]

Under the Mississippi law, stalking is a misdemeanor offense punishable by one year in jail or a one thousand dollar fine (or a combination of both). Stalking behaviors take many forms, including unwanted phone calls, unsolicited letters or emails, waiting in places for the victim, leaving unwanted items or gifts for the victim, and spying on or following the victim.

As the number of communication mediums has increased, anti-stalking legislation has been extended to electronic communications, such as cyberstalking.[25]

Concluding Note

Incomplete crimes raise numerous legal issues. These issues include how they are defined, how they should be punished, and why they should be punished. This chapter's discussion of inchoate offenses provides both a foundation and a springboard for our continuing discussions of the elements of criminal offenses and the rationales for laws that punish criminal actions. As we continue our examination of American criminal law, we will revisit many of the issues raised in this chapter. Now test yourself on the material we have covered in this chapter. Good luck with the Issue Spotter exercise.

IssueSpotter

Read the hypothetical and spot the issues discussed in this chapter.

Liberate This

Kalani is the leader of the Take it Back Alliance (TBA). Members of this group of young Hawaiians believe that thousands of valuable historical Hawaiian artifacts are illegally housed in museums across the country. TBA claims that there are historical documents that prove the artifacts, including paintings, jewelry, clothing, pottery, and other cultural symbols, were stolen from indigenous Hawaiian lands.

TBA has 293 members and they have monthly meetings. At the meetings, members strategize about how to obtain and return the stolen property to its rightful owners (or their descendents). If owners or descendants cannot be found, the property is donated to a museum on one of the eight Hawaiian Islands.

Through their research, three TBA members, Malie, Akamu, and Ola, discover that a museum in Anaheim, California, has more than two dozen stolen Hawaiian artifacts. At the next TBA meeting, Malie, Akamu, and Ola announce their findings. Kalani asks the trio, "Are you willing to make good on the TBA promise to 'Liberate when possible!'?" Malie, Akamu, and Ola nod their heads "yes." Akamu says, "I'll purchase the plane tickets and rent

(Continued)

(Continued)

a car." Ola adds, "I found a map of the museum online and photos of all the stolen items."

The trio is excited about their plan to travel to the California museum and "liberate" as many artifacts as possible.

On the planned day, the three TBA members drive to the airport. On the way, they are stopped by Honolulu police officers. The police had received a tip that TBA members were on their way to California to burglarize a museum. Akamu, Ola, and Malie were not aware that over a month ago the Anaheim museum had been relocated to Washington, DC, more than 2,000 miles away.

Based on the above hypothetical, answer the following questions:

1. What charges are prosecutors likely to file and against whom?

2. Which facts support each of these charges? What is the likely outcome of each case?

3. Are there any defenses available? Will they be successful?

Key Terms and Cases

Notes

1. *U.S.A. v. Rosenbaum*, 2011 WL 5119688 (D.N.J.). Available at http://www.justice.gov/usao/nj/Press/files/pdffiles/2011/Rosenbaum,%20Levy%20Izhak%20Information.pdf

2. The first two are based on actual cases. See *People v. Luna*, 170 Cal.App.4th 535 (Jan. 15, 2009) and *State v. Hinkhouse*, 139 Or.App.446 (1996).

3. *Rex v. Scofield*, Cald. 397 (1784).

4. *Rex v. Higgins*, (1801) 2 East 5.

5. *People v. Paluch*, 78 Ill.App.2d 356 (Ill. App. Ct. 1966).

6. Vermont Stat. Ann.,13 § 9.

7. Conn. Gen. Stat. Ann. 952 § 53a-49.

8. *State v. Smith*, 870 S0.2d 618 (La. Ct. App. 2004).

9. *Commonwealth v. McCloskey*, 234 Pa.Super.577; 341 A.2d 500 (Pa. Sup. Ct. 1975).

10. This hypothetical is based on an actual case, *State v. Curtis*, 603 A.2d 356 (Vt. 1991).

11. Adan Salazar, "Facial Recognition Glasses to 'Stop Crime Before it Happens,'" *Infowars*, March 11, 2014, www.infowars.com; http://sanfrancisco.cbslocal.com/2014/02/04/bay-area-researcher-developing-facial-recognition-glasses-to-help-stop-crime

12. 18 Pennsylvania Cons. Stat. § 092(a).

13. Kansas Stat. Ann. § 21–3303.

14. Tenn. Code Ann.§ 39–12–102.

15. WY Stat. § 6–1-303 (1983).

16. 18 U.S.C. § 371.

17. See generally, Nick Zimmerman, "Attempted Stalking: An Attempt-To-Almost-Attempt-To-Act," *Northern Illinois University Law Review* 20 (2000): 219.

18. 18 U.S.C. §871.

19. Curt Anderson (2012) "Fla. Student Pleads guilty to Online Obama Threat," *Associated Press*, May 24, 2012.

20. *U.S.A. v. Serrapio*, No. 12–2244-GARBER, U.S. District Ct., Southern District of Florida (Criminal Complaint, 2012).

21. As a result of comments Serrapio made to his college newspaper following his sentence, the judge modified the conditions of his probation to include serving forty-five days in a halfway house and one year of home confinement. This enhanced sentence was upheld on appeal. *U.S.A. v. Serrapio*, No. 12–14897 (U.S. Ct. App.,11th Cir. 2014)

22. The National Center for Victims of Crime, "Stalking and the Law," http://www.ncvc.org/ncvc/main.aspx?dbName=DocumentViewer&DocumentID=32514

23. Shannon Catalano, "Stalking Victims in the United States-Revised" *Bureau of Justice Statistics*, September 2012, NCJ 224527.

24. Miss. Code Ann. § 97-3-107 (2010).

25. See, generally, Nicole Rodriguez Naeser, "The Oregon Court's Stalking Failure," *University of Toledo Law Review* 41 (2010): 703.

Chapter 5

Frank Abagnale, Jr. was one of the most infamous imposters in American history. He began committing crimes when he was a teenager, starting with shoplifting. Abagnale later went on to commit fraud with his father's credit card and later developed an elaborate, sophisticated operation of forging and writing bad checks. During the course of his life as a criminal, he successfully impersonated an airline pilot, a doctor, a lawyer, and a professor. When he was eventually caught, Abagnale served time in prisons in France, Sweden, and the United States. He was paroled at the age of twenty-six and worked for the Federal Bureau of Investigation (FBI) for over thirty years as an expert in document fraud, forgery, and embezzlement.[1] Abagnale now has his own consulting firm, Abagnale and Associates,[2] and lectures extensively on fraud prevention. The 2002 movie *Catch Me If You Can*, based on Abagnale's book of the same title, chronicles his extraordinary life.

Ex-forger and security expert Frank W. Abagnale, Jr. committed many of the theft and other property crimes discussed in this chapter.

Photo provided by Frank
W. Abagnale and Associates

Theft and Other Property Crimes

Learning Objectives

After reading and studying this chapter, you should be able to

➤ Define common law larceny

➤ Explain the difference between common law larceny and modern theft statutes

➤ Define embezzlement

➤ Differentiate between embezzlement and false pretenses

➤ List the elements of burglary

➤ Define arson

➤ Explain the difference between white collar and other crimes

➤ List examples of computer crime

Introduction

Many images come to mind when one thinks of the crime of theft. There is the common thief who may steal because he or she is broke, cannot find a job, or is just too lazy to work. Or perhaps one thinks of the noble thief—Robin Hood, who stole from the rich to give to the poor, or the poor man who steals a loaf of bread to feed his starving family. However, the crime of theft comes in many forms. Not everyone who steals is poor or in need. Bernard Madoff was already wealthy by most people's standards when he defrauded thousands of people of billions of dollars. People commit theft and other property crimes for a variety of reasons, including simple greed.

In the early English common law, the crime of theft was called larceny. However, there were other property crimes that were not covered by the definition of larceny, so lawmakers created the crimes of embezzlement and false pretenses. Although some states continue to follow the common law, many have created modern theft statutes that attempt to simplify the more complex common law definitions. In this chapter, we examine the common law and modern statutory property crimes of larceny, embezzlement, false pretenses, burglary, and arson. We also discuss white-collar crime, including computer crime and identity theft.

As Table 5.1 on page 106 illustrates, larceny/theft crimes are the most prevalent of all of the property crimes.

Larceny and Theft

Common Law Larceny

Common Law Larceny is defined as the

1. Trespassory taking

2. And carrying away

3. Of the personal property

4. Of another

5. With the intent to permanently deprive.

Table 5.1 **Property Victimization, by Type of Property Crime, 2003, 2011, and 2012**

Type of crime	Number			Rate[a]		
	2003	2011	2012	2003	2011	2012
Property crime[b]	19,792,450	17,063,150	19,622,980[†]	173.4	138.7	155.8[†]
Household burglary	3,648,670	3,613,840	3,674,540	32.0	29.4	29.9
Motor vehicle theft	1,032,470	628,220	633,740	9.0	5.1	5.0
Theft	15,111,310	12,821,090	15,224,700[†]	132.4	104.2	120.9[†]

Source. Bureau of Justice Statistics, National Crime Victimization Survey, 2003, 2011, and 2012.

Note: Total number of households was 114,136,930 in 2003; 123,038,570 in 2011; and 125,920,480 in 2012. See appendix table 5 for standard errors.

[a] Per 1,000 households.

[b] Includes households burglary, motor vehicle theft, and theft.

[†] Significant change from 2011 to 2012 at the 95% confidence level.

In the common law, each of these elements was applied very strictly. A trespassory taking simply means a wrongful taking, or put another way, taking without permission. So if John stole Paul's horse from Paul's barn, John would be guilty of larceny. But if Paul loaned John his horse and John did not bring it back, under common law, John would not be guilty of larceny and Paul would have to bring a civil action against John to reclaim his property.

Carrying away the property involves simply moving it, even a very slight distance. The carrying away element is called asportation. So if Kate takes a pair of gloves from the counter of a department store and puts them in her purse with the intent to steal them, she has fulfilled the carrying away element of larceny. She does not have to walk out of the store or even toward the door before the larceny is complete.

Under the common law, a person may only steal personal property that is in another person's possession. Land, crops, or minerals under the land are not personal property. If the personal property is co-owned by the defendant and someone else or if it is abandoned property, there is no larceny because it is not the property of another person. Likewise, if the property has no value (such as dead flowers or trash), there is no larceny.

Modern Theft Statutes

Although some states maintain the common law definition of larceny, many have enacted theft statutes that attempt to simplify and resolve some of the problems inherent in the common law definition of larceny. As illustrated by the following theft statutes, some states have expanded the definition of property to include services and real property. They also have eliminated the requirement that the thief have the intent to permanently deprive the victim of his or her property. These statutes include a broader range of crimes, including embezzlement and false pretenses. In the District of Columbia, all of the crimes are called "theft" while New York maintains the term "larceny."

District of Columbia's Theft Statute

§ 22–3211. Theft.

a) For the purpose of this section, the term "wrongfully obtains or uses" means: (1) taking or exercising control over property; (2) making an unauthorized use, disposition, or transfer of an interest in or possession of property; or (3) obtaining property by trick, false pretense, false token, tampering, or deception. The term "wrongfully obtains or uses" includes conduct previously known as larceny, larceny by trick, larceny by trust, embezzlement, and false pretenses.

b) A person commits the offense of theft if that person wrongfully obtains or uses the property of another with intent:

(1) To deprive the other of a right to the property or a benefit of the property; or

(2) To appropriate the property to his or her own use or to the use of a third person.

c) In cases in which the theft of property is in the form of services, proof that a person obtained services that he or she knew or had reason to believe were available to him or her only for compensation and that he or she departed from the place where the services were obtained knowing or having reason to believe that no payment had been made for the services rendered in circumstances where payment is ordinarily made immediately upon the rendering of the services or prior to departure from the place where the services are obtained, shall be prima facie evidence that the person had committed the offense of theft.[3]

New York's Larceny Statute

§ 155.05 Larceny; defined.

1. A person steals property and commits larceny when, with intent to deprive another of property or to appropriate the same to himself or to a third person, he wrongfully takes, obtains or withholds such property from an owner thereof.

2. Larceny includes a wrongful taking, obtaining or withholding of another's property, with the intent prescribed in subdivision one of this section, committed in any of the following ways:

(a) By conduct heretofore defined or known as common law larceny by trespassory taking, common law larceny by trick, embezzlement, or obtaining property by false pretenses;

(b) By acquiring lost property. . . .

(c) By committing the crime of issuing a bad check, as defined in section 190.05;

(d) By false promise. . . .

(e) By extortion.[4]

Consider the following hypotheticals:

- Maria went to a beauty salon in the District of Columbia to get her hair styled. While there, she decided to get a facial and a massage as well. After her treatments were completed, she sneaked out the back door of the salon without paying.

- Jay was walking through Central Park in New York City when he saw a wallet on a park bench. Jay opened the wallet and discovered eighty dollars in cash along with numerous credit cards and a driver's license with the name Keith J. Brown. Mr. Brown's address was on his driver's license. Jay put the cash in his pocket and took the wallet and credit cards home with the intent to keep them indefinitely.

Maria would be charged with theft in the District of Columbia. Section (C) of the District of Columbia statute includes the theft of services. Jay would be charged with larceny in New York as he "acquir[ed] lost property" pursuant to Section 2(b) of the New York statute that requires a person who finds lost property to take reasonable steps to return the property to its owner.

The following case illustrates how modern theft statutes criminalize behavior that would not be included in the common law definition of larceny.

People v. Davis (1998)

Supreme Court of California

965 P.2d 1165

We granted review to determine what crime is committed in the following circumstances: the defendant enters a store and picks up an item of merchandise displayed for sale, intending to claim that he owns it and to "return" it for cash or credit; he carries the item to a sales counter and asks the clerk for a "refund"; without the defendant's knowledge his conduct has been observed by a store security agent, who instructs the clerk to give him credit for the item; the clerk gives the defendant a credit voucher, and the agent detains him as he leaves the counter with the voucher; he is charged with theft of the item. In the case at bar the Court of Appeal held the defendant is guilty of theft by trespassory larceny. We agree, and therefore affirm the judgment of the Court of Appeal.

Defendant entered a Mervyn's department store carrying a Mervyn's shopping bag. As he entered he was placed under camera surveillance by store security agent Carol German. While German both watched and filmed, defendant went to the men's department and took a shirt displayed for sale from its hanger; he then carried the shirt through the shoe department and into the women's department on the other side of the store. There he placed the shirt on a sales counter and told cashier Heather Smith that he had "bought it for his father" but it didn't fit and he wanted to "return" it. Smith asked him if he had the receipt, but he said he did not because "it was a gift." Smith informed him that if the value of a returned item is more than $20 and there is no receipt, the store policy is not to make a cash refund but to issue a Mervyn's credit voucher. At that point Smith was interrupted by a telephone call

from German; German asked her if defendant was trying to "return" the shirt, and directed her to issue a credit voucher. Smith prepared the voucher and asked defendant to sign it; he did so, but used a false name. German detained him as he walked away from the counter with the voucher. Upon being questioned in the store security office, defendant gave a second false name and three different dates of birth; he also told German that he needed money to buy football cleats, asked her if they could "work something out," and offered to pay for the shirt.

Count 1 of the information charged defendant with the crime of petty theft with a prior theft-related conviction, a felony-misdemeanor . . . , alleging that defendant did "steal, take and carry away the personal property" of Mervyn's in violation of Penal Code section 484, subdivision (a). In a motion for judgment of acquittal filed after the People presented their case, defendant argued that on the facts shown he could be convicted of no more than an *attempt* to commit petty theft, and therefore sought dismissal of the petty theft charge. . . . The court denied the motion.

When the formerly distinct offenses of larceny, embezzlement, and obtaining property by false pretenses were consolidated in 1927 into the single crime of "theft" defined by Penal Code section 484, most of the procedural distinctions between those offenses were abolished. But their substantive distinctions were not: "The elements of the several types of theft included within section 484 have not been changed, however, and a judgment of conviction of theft, based on a general verdict of guilty, can be sustained only if the evidence discloses the elements of one of the consolidated offenses."

The elements of theft by larceny are well settled: the offense is committed by every person who (1) takes possession (2) of personal property (3) owned or possessed by another, (4) by means of trespass and (5) with intent to steal the property, and (6) carries the property away. . . . The act of taking personal property from the possession of another is always a trespass unless the owner consents to the taking freely and unconditionally or the taker has a legal right to take the property. . . . The intent to steal or *animus furandi* is the intent, without a good faith claim of right, to permanently deprive the owner of possession. . . . And if the taking has begun, the slightest movement of the property constitutes a carrying away or asportation.

Applying these rules to the facts of the case at bar, we have no doubt that defendant (1) took possession (2) of personal property, the shirt, (3) owned by Mervyn's and (4) moved it sufficiently to satisfy the asportation requirement. Defendant does not contend otherwise.

Defendant does contend, however, that the elements of trespass and intent to steal are lacking. He predicates his argument on a distinction that he draws by dividing his course of conduct into two distinct "acts." According to defendant, his first "act" was to take the shirt from the display rack and carry it to Smith's cash register. He contends that act lacked the element of intent to steal because he had no intent to permanently deprive Mervyn's *of the shirt;* he intended to have the shirt in his possession only long enough to exchange it for a "refund." His second "act," also according to defendant, was to misrepresent to Smith that he had bought the shirt at Mervyn's and to accept the credit voucher she issued. He contends that act lacked the element of trespass because the store, acting through its agent German, *consented* to the issuance of the voucher with full knowledge of how he came into possession of the shirt.

Defendant's argument misses the mark on two grounds: it focuses on the wrong issue of consent, and it views that issue in artificial isolation from the intertwined issue of intent to steal.

To begin with, the question is not whether Mervyn's consented to Smith's issuance of the voucher after defendant asked to "return" the shirt; rather, the question is whether Mervyn's consented to defendant's taking the shirt in the first instance. As the Court of Appeal correctly reasoned, a self-service store like Mervyn's impliedly consents to a customer's picking up and handling an item displayed for sale and carrying it from the display area to a sales counter with the intent of purchasing it; the store manifestly does not consent, however, to a customer's removing an item from a shelf or hanger if the customer's intent in taking possession of the item is to steal it.

In these circumstances the issue of consent—and therefore trespass—depends on the issue of intent to steal. We turn to that issue.

As noted earlier, the general rule is that the intent to steal required for conviction of larceny is an intent to deprive the owner *permanently* of possession of the property. . . . For example, we have said it would not be larceny for a youth to take and hide another's bicycle to "get even" for being teased, if he intends to return it the following day. . . . But the general rule is not inflexible: "The word 'permanently,' as used here is not to be taken literally." . . . Our research discloses three relevant categories of cases holding that the requisite intent to steal may be found even though the defendant's primary purpose in taking the property is not to deprive the owner permanently of possession: i.e., (1) when the defendant intends to "sell" the property back to its owner, (2) when the defendant intends to claim a reward for "finding" the property, and (3) when, as here, the defendant intends to return the property to its owner for a "refund."

Applying the foregoing reasoning to the facts of the case at bar, we conclude that defendant's intent to claim ownership of the shirt and to return it to Mervyn's only on condition that the store pay him a "refund" constitutes an intent to permanently deprive Mervyn's of the shirt within the meaning of the law of larceny, and hence an intent to "feloniously steal" that property within the meaning of Penal Code section 484, subdivision (a) (fn.1, *ante*). Because Mervyn's cannot be deemed to have consented to defendant's taking possession of the shirt with the intent to steal it, defendant's conduct also constituted a trespassory taking within the meaning of the law of larceny. It follows that the evidence supports the final two elements of the offense of theft by larceny, and the Court of Appeal was correct to affirm the judgment of conviction.

Questions

1. What are the two issues that Mr. Davis raises on appeal?

2. What is the court's rationale in affirming Mr. Davis' conviction?

3. Courts do not require that a shoplifter actually leave the store with the stolen property to fulfill the asportation requirement, but would not the state have a stronger case if the store detective waited until the suspect left the store? Are there reasons why a detective would want to arrest the suspect sooner rather than later?

Embezzlement ●────────────────────────

Common law embezzlement is defined as the

1. Fraudulent

2. Conversion or theft

3. Of property

4. By someone in lawful possession of the property.

For example, Joe the bank teller is lawfully in possession of the funds that he distributes from his window at the bank. In other words, he is allowed to keep the money in "his" drawer at "his" window at the bank, distribute it to and collect it from bank customers, and conduct other bank business with the money. However, the money is the property of the bank. So if he takes any of the cash and keeps it for his own use, he has committed the crime of embezzlement. This crime filled one of the gaps left open by common law larceny—namely the need to criminalize theft of property that was not in the possession of someone else. As illustrated in the District of Columbia and New York statutes earlier in this chapter, embezzlement is included in many modern statutes under the umbrella terms theft and larceny.

In the example above, the definition of possession is clear. However, as the following case illustrates, physically handling property is not the only way that a person may be in possession of it.

Batin v. State (2002)

Supreme Court of Nevada

38 P.3d 880

Appellant Marlon Javar Batin was convicted of three counts of embezzlement for stealing money from his employer, John Ascuaga's Nugget Hotel and Casino. On direct appeal, Batin contended that his conviction was not supported by sufficient evidence. Specifically, Batin contended that there was no evidence establishing the entrustment element of the crime of embezzlement. . . . Having considered the evidence presented in the light most favorable to the State, we now conclude that Batin did not commit embezzlement as a matter of law because there was no evidence presented of the entrustment element of that crime. Because we cannot sustain a conviction where there is no evidence of an essential element of the charged offense, we reverse the judgment of conviction.

In 1993, Batin moved to Sparks [Nevada] from the Philippines and began working as a dishwasher at the Nugget. After several years at the Nugget, Batin became a slot mechanic. Batin's job duties as a slot mechanic included fixing jammed coins and refilling the "hopper." Warren Reid Anderson, Batin's supervisor, explained that

the "hopper" is the part of the slot machine that pays coins back, and is separate from the "bill validator" component of the slot machine where the paper currency is kept. Anderson further testified that Batin had no duties with respect to the paper currency in the bill validator, except to safeguard the funds, and that the cash in the bill validator "wasn't to be touched." Likewise, Anderson testified that if a customer had a problem with a machine that required a cash refund "it would require supervisory backup in order to take any money out of a slot machine and pass it back to a customer." Batin also testified about his job duties as a slot mechanic. Like Anderson, Batin testified that he was prohibited from handling the paper currency inside the bill validator.

As a slot mechanic, Batin was given an "SDS" card that was used to both access the inside of the slot machine and identify him as the employee that was opening the slot machine door. The computerized SDS system is physically connected to each slot machine and counts the paper currency placed into each machine's bill validator. The

SDS actually records the different denominations of bills and runs numerous reports concerning the currency. The SDS also registers every time that the slot machine door is opened or closed. If the power is turned off to a particular slot machine, the SDS system will only record the opening and closing of the door; it cannot track what happens inside the machine.

Lori Barrington, soft count supervisor, explained that after the money is counted by SDS, it is then counted three more times by a minimum of three Nugget employees. Barrington further testified that there was not much variance between the amount of money SDS recorded that the casino was supposed to have and the amount of money the casino actually had. In fact, out of 1100 slot machines, there were perhaps three errors per month totaling approximately $100.00 in variance.

In March and early June 1999, however, there were larger discrepancies discovered between the amount of money that the SDS recorded had been put into the slot machines and the amount of money the slot machine actually contained. Kathleen Plambeck, the Nugget's Internal Auditor, testified to several shortages from four different slot machines, totaling approximately $40,000.00.

In reviewing the SDS reports, Plambeck testified that she found a pattern of conduct. Namely, prior to the time that a shortage had been detected on a slot machine, Batin inserted his SDS card into the slot machine, opened the door, turned off the power, and thereafter closed the door on the machine. Plambeck found this pattern of conduct unusual because it was not necessary to turn off the slot machine for most repairs, and no one other than Batin had been turning off the power on the slot machines with the shortages. Batin testified at trial, however, that he turned off the power on the slot machines so that he would not be electrocuted and that he had always turned off the power prior to working on the slot machines.

James Carlisle, an agent with the Nevada Gaming Control Board, investigated Batin and discovered that he gambled regularly at three local casinos, and that he lost tens of thousands of dollars. When Carlisle questioned Batin about how he was able to afford to gamble such large sums of money, Batin could not or did not answer. At trial, however, Batin testified that he was able to afford to gamble large sums of money because he won often.

Although Batin adamantly denied taking the money, Batin was arrested and charged with three counts of embezzlement. The information alleged that Batin had been entrusted with money by his employer and converted the money for a purpose other than that for which it was entrusted. After a jury trial, Batin was convicted of all three counts of embezzlement.

Batin contends that his convictions for embezzlement should be reversed because there was insufficient evidence of an essential element of the crime. We agree.

In the instant case, the State charged Batin with embezzlement and, consequently, at trial, had the burden of proving every element of that crime beyond a reasonable doubt. To prove that a defendant committed the crime of embezzlement, the State must demonstrate beyond a reasonable doubt that the defendant was a *"person with whom any money, property or effects ha[d] been deposited or entrusted,"* and that the defendant "use[d] or appropriate[d] the money, property, or effects . . . in any manner or for any other purpose than that for which [it was] deposited or entrusted."

The key distinguishing element of the crime of embezzlement is the element of entrustment. In order to be guilty of embezzlement, a defendant must have been entrusted with lawful possession of the property prior to its conversion. For purposes of proving embezzlement, the lawful possession need not be actual; rather, the State may show that a defendant had constructive possession of the property converted. This court has defined constructive possession as "both the power and the intention at a given time to exercise dominion or control over a thing, either directly or through another person or persons." In proving constructive possession, a showing that a defendant was given mere access to the property converted is insufficient. Often, an individual is entrusted with access to a particular place or thing without being given dominion and control over the property therein. This is particularly true in instances, like the present one, where the individual is expressly told that he is not allowed to touch the property in the place to which access is granted.

In the instant case, the record reveals that Batin was not entrusted with lawful possession, constructive or otherwise, of the currency he allegedly took from the bill validators. In fact, both Batin and his supervisor testified that Batin had no job duties whatsoever involving this currency and that it "wasn't to be touched." Further, Batin had absolutely no power to exercise control over this currency, as Batin was required to contact his supervisor for any job task involving possession of the currency inside the bill validator, such as a cash refund to a customer. Because the aforementioned testimony was not contradicted at trial, we conclude that there was insufficient evidence of an essential element of embezzlement, as Batin was never entrusted with actual or constructive possession of the currency taken.

(Continued)

(Continued)

Our dissenting colleagues conclude that there was sufficient evidence of constructive possession because Batin had access to the inside of the slot machine where the bill validator was located and, occasionally, observed non-employee slot repairmen work on the slot machine. As previously discussed, however, constructive possession requires a showing that the accused was entrusted with control over property. We cannot say that an individual exercises control over property when he is prohibited from touching it.

In light of the foregoing, we are compelled to reverse Batin's conviction. The State failed to prove the entrustment element of the crime of embezzlement beyond a reasonable doubt, and we cannot sustain a conviction where the record is devoid of an essential element of a charged offense. To do otherwise, would imperil our system of justice by undermining the presumption that those charged with crimes are innocent until proven guilty beyond a reasonable doubt.

Questions

1. What was the basis of Mr. Batin's appeal?
2. What was the court's rationale in reversing Mr. Batin's conviction?
3. What is the difference between actual and constructive possession?

False Pretenses

Common law false pretenses is defined as the

1. False representation
2. Of a material past or present fact
3. Which the person making the representation knows to be false
4. Made with the intent to defraud a person into passing title to property to the wrongdoer.

A person who obtains both possession and title to property by making false representations is guilty of false pretenses. The false representation must be about a material (i.e., important) present or past fact. For example, Jean has a rhinestone ring but tells Henry that it is a two carat diamond ring. She agrees to give Henry the ring in exchange for his three-year-old red Corvette. Henry agrees and passes title to the car to Jean in exchange for the ring. Jean is guilty of false pretenses. The crime of false pretenses filled another gap in the criminal law that was not covered by the crime of larceny. Like embezzlement, false pretenses is included in many modern theft and larceny statutes.

The following case is an example of theft by false pretenses.

People v. Whight (1995)

California Court of Appeal (3rd District)

43 Cal.Rptr.2d 163

Defendant Theodore Whight discovered that the automated teller machine (ATM) card connected to his defunct checking account could still be used to obtain cash at four local Safeway stores. For several weeks he availed himself freely of this happenstance to obtain thousands of dollars.

This led to his conviction by a jury of four counts of fraudulent use of an access card or "ATM" theft (Pen. Code, § 484g; undesignated references are to this code) and four counts of grand theft by false pretenses (§§ 484, subd. (a), 487, 532).

We consider two questions in the published portion of this opinion. The first is whether Safeway relied upon defendant's misrepresentations within the meaning of the crime of grand theft by false pretenses. Defendant was able to obtain large amounts of cash from the Safeway stores because the computer verification system was not working properly. Defendant contends that the only misrepresentation he made was that his ATM was valid and Safeway did not rely on this but rather upon the computer authorization. For the reasons which follow, we reject the claim.

Defendant opened a regular checking account at Tri Counties Bank (the bank) in Chico in January 1991. He was issued an ATM card which bore no expiration date. This card did not offer any overdraft protection and could be used only with the checking account. Thereafter, monthly statements for his checking account were sent to defendant by the bank at his post office box. Defendant originally deposited $3,750.99 into his checking account. By June 1991, defendant's account was overdrawn by $6.17. In accordance with the bank's normal practice, defendant was mailed a letter stating that his account was over-drawn, that his bank statement and canceled checks would be held at the bank and if no deposits were made to cover the shortage, the account would be closed. . . . On July 10, 1991, no deposit having been made, the bank closed the account because of the negative balance. From the bank's viewpoint, when defendant's checking account was closed, his ATM card was simultaneously canceled and revoked.

Despite the cancellation by the bank, defendant continued to use his ATM card, mainly at local Safeway markets. Safeway allows customers to make purchases and receive cash back by using ATM cards. Safeway's practice was to verify the cards through the use of a computer system operated by Wells Fargo Bank (Wells Fargo). Wells Fargo would report a code to Safeway which approved or disapproved of the proposed transaction. In some cases Wells Fargo would not be able to link up with the customer's bank or otherwise verify the card. If this lasted for more than about thirty seconds, Wells Fargo would report a "stand in" code to Safeway. Upon receipt of this code, Safeway would approve the transaction.

It appears that there was an error in the Wells Fargo computer, which repeatedly failed to notify Safeway that defendant's ATM card was invalid. In March and April 1992, defendant was able to use his ATM card at four different Safeway markets in Butte County. He would purchase a small item, then use his ATM card to pay for the item and to receive cash back, usually $200 at a time, often more than once a day. He received a total of over $19,000. During that time his ATM card was rejected at two other (non-Safeway) markets.

Defendant . . . contends his convictions for grand theft by false pretense must be reversed because "Safeway relied on the code issued by Wells Fargo, rather than [defendant's] presentation of his ATM card, in approving [defendant's] request for money." This leaky contention cannot hold water.

Theft by false pretenses is committed by "[e]very person who knowingly and designedly, by any false or fraudulent representation or pretense, defrauds any other person of money, labor, or property, whether real or personal. . . . "

"To support a conviction of theft for obtaining property by false pretenses, it must be shown: (1) that the defendant made a false pretense or representation, (2) that the representation was made with intent to defraud the owner of his property, and (3) that the owner was in fact defrauded in that he parted with his property in reliance upon the representation." . . . We are here concerned with causation or reliance.

The representation need not be in the form of an oral or written statement; it may also consist of conduct. "The false pretense may consist in any act, word, symbol, or token calculated and intended to deceive. It may be either express or implied from words or conduct." . . . Thus, when defendant proffered his ATM card he impliedly represented, falsely, that it was valid. . . . Reliance on a false representation may be, and in some cases must be, inferred from the evidence. . . . However, if the evidence establishes that the victim did not rely on the false pretense, a conviction cannot stand. Defendant maintains that because the Safeway employees did not merely hand him cash upon presentation of the card, but instead verified the card through the computer system, Safeway did not actually rely on his implied representation and therefore he did not commit the crime of theft by false pretenses. In short, he urges there was no substantial evidence of the reliance element of the crime.

It is true that "[f]or false pretenses it is necessary that the swindler's misrepresentation *cause* the victim to pass title to his property or money to the swindler. Looking at the matter from the point of view of the victim, the same thought may be expressed thus: for false pretenses it is required that the victim pass title to his property *in reliance upon* the swindler's misrepresentation." . . . Thus, "[e]ven though a false representation is made and property obtained by the person making the representation, no prosecution will lie where the complainant parted with his property to the accused from some cause other than such false representation since to constitute this offense the representation must have been a material element in proximately causing the complainant to part with his

(Continued)

(Continued)

property and without which he would not have done so." . . . Consequently, "[i]f the owner did not rely on the false pretense in parting with his property, then a conviction cannot be sustained." . . .

But it is settled, as the Attorney General points out, that the false pretense need not be the sole reason for the victim to part with his money or property. "The false pretense or representation must have materially influenced the owner to part with his property, but the false pretense need not be the sole inducing cause." . . .

Defendant claims that Safeway relied upon the computer authorization rather than upon his implicit representation that his card was valid. Whether Safeway relied exclusively on the computer authorization would ordinarily pose a factual question to be resolved by the jury under proper instructions. . . . But in this case the record conclusively established that Safeway did not rely upon any computer authorization from Wells Fargo.

The ATM terminals in the Safeway stores were connected to a computer system operated by Wells Fargo. When a customer uses his ATM card in the ATM terminal at a checkstand in a Safeway store by swiping it through the terminal, the magnetic stripe on the back of the card is read. This information is then sent by modem via telephone lines to computers at Wells Fargo. These computers then pass the information to a banking network. As a banking supervisor for Safeway described it, the information "goes from that network to the card holder's bank for an authorization. If the money's in the account, the bank approves it, comes back in through the network, through our bank and back to the store." For the most part, the system generates a code either approving or disapproving the transaction. If approved, the transaction is consummated. On the other hand, if the transaction is denied, the screen at checkstand states, "transaction declined" and sale and/or request for cash would be refused.

In addition to codes for approval and disapproval, the system generates what are called "stand-in" codes. Two types of "stand-in" codes were described by the banking supervisor. "First one being if any place along that network, that phone path that I have described may be down, the phone line may not be operational at any given point in time. That's one type. The other type where Safeway will stand in is if we don't get that authorization or that response through the system in a reasonable amount of time, then we will stand in for that transaction." Safeway would then automatically resubmit the transaction at a later time for approval. Thus, a "stand-in" code meant that either Safeway could not make connection with the Wells Fargo Bank computers or Wells Fargo could not make connection with the bank it sought approval from. In short, a "stand-in" code simply tells the Safeway store that there

has been no response to its request for authorization. In these circumstances, as a Safeway accountant explained it, Safeway "management has elected to take stand-in. They will do it after approximately 25 to 30 seconds. If the card is a card from an approved bank, from a bank that Safeway deals with, we will accept the card in stand-in, management made that decision, and then the system will keep trying to connect to the bank and then get the approval for the card and get the money from the person's account, but after 25 or 30 seconds, we will take the card and give the person the money for it rather than holding the customer up and making them stand there and wait." This corporate decision was reiterated by Safeway's banking supervisor. "Again, it's for customer service. We feel that just because our system may not be available at a given point in time or that we don't get a response within a few seconds, that we will ultimately get an authorization and approval for those transactions, so we take the risk on stand-in transactions."

As it turned out, there was a glitch in Wells Fargo's system concerning defendant's account. Rather than transmitting a code declining the transaction because defendant's account had been closed, Wells Fargo kept returning a code to Safeway indicating that there was no response. This, in turn, caused Safeway to treat each transaction as a "stand-in" without a verification or approval from the computer banking system. Given these facts, it can hardly be said that Safeway relied upon the Well Fargo's computer system instead of defendant's representation that his card was valid. Even assuming that the use of a computer verification system can be described as an investigation, the computer system in fact never approved defendant's transactions. As a result, Safeway had nothing to rely upon except defendant's implicit representation that his ATM card was valid. It elected to take the risk and to rely solely on defendant's representation. On this record, the element of reliance or causation was indisputably established.

. . . [T]he judgment is affirmed. The cause is remanded to the trial court with directions to resentence defendant in light of this disposition.

Questions

1. What was the basis of Mr. Whight's argument that he was not guilty of false pretenses?

2. What was the court's rationale in rejecting that argument?

3. The court made it clear that the false representation may consist of conduct rather than an oral or written statement. What conduct by Mr. Whight satisfied this requirement?

Burglary ●━━━━━━━━━━━━━━━━━━━━━━━━━━━━

Common law burglary is defined as the

1. Breaking and

2. Entering

3. Of the dwelling of another

4. In the nighttime

5. With the intent to commit a felony therein.

As with most common law crimes, these elements had very specific definitions that were strictly applied. If someone broke into a house in the daytime, for example, the crime was not considered burglary. Modern burglary statutes follow the trend of modern theft statutes—they include a broader range of conduct and often include different levels of burglary depending on the seriousness of the offense. Modern burglary statutes do not require that the crime be committed in the nighttime and generally grade the offense—classifying different types of burglaries as first, second, third, and even fourth degree burglary, with first degree burglary being the most serious. The seriousness of the offense is defined in a variety of ways. Some states consider a burglary of a home that is occupied by people as the most serious (first degree) and a burglary of an unoccupied home to be less serious (second degree). Others define the seriousness of the offense according to the type of structure. For example, under Maryland law, breaking and entering a home with the intent to commit a theft, crime of violence, or arson is more serious (first degree) than breaking and entering a store with the intent to commit any of those crimes (second degree). In Maryland, third degree burglary is the breaking and entering of the home of another with the intent to commit any other crime (including misdemeanors). Fourth degree burglary includes breaking and entering a home or store, regardless of intent, or possession of burglar's tools with the intent to use them to commit burglary. A person found lurking around outside a home in possession of burglar's tools might be charged with fourth degree burglary.

The terms "breaking" and "entering" have been defined broadly. Breaking does not necessarily involve destroying property. If a burglar breaks a lock and goes in to a house, there is clearly a "breaking." However, even if he just opens a closed door and walks in, there has been a "breaking." If he walks in an open door, there has not been a breaking. He may have committed some other crime (trespassing, perhaps), but not burglary. Similarly, any time a burglar walks in the front door, crawls through a window, or otherwise physically goes into the house, she has "entered" for purposes of the law of burglary. However, even if the burglar uses a tool to gain access to the inside of the house and commit a felony, she has "entered" under most burglary statutes.

Consider the following hypotheticals:

- Bob comes to the door dressed as a repairman and tells Mary that he works for the gas and electric company and that he needs to check her home for a possible gas leak. Mary believes him, lets him in, and he attacks her.
- Suppose Bob looks through the open bedroom window of Mary's house and sees a mink jacket hanging on the back of a chair near the window. He extends his crowbar through the window and uses it to lift the jacket from the back of the chair. Bob carefully pulls the jacket through the window and leaves with it.

Has Bob committed a burglary in either hypothetical? In most jurisdictions, both scenarios constitute burglary. Bob's use of trickery to gain entrance in the first hypothetical is considered a constructive breaking, and the use of the crowbar in the second hypothetical is constructive entering.

Can a person burglarize his or her own dwelling? What does it mean to burglarize the dwelling of another? Is ownership or residency the deciding factor? The following case, with a shocking fact pattern, addresses these issues.

Jewell v. State (1996)

Indiana Court of Appeals

672 N.E.2d 417

Barry L. Jewell broke into his estranged wife's house, beat her lover in the head with a board until he was unconscious, amputated the lover's penis with a knife, and fed the severed penis to the dog. Jewell appeals his convictions, after a jury trial, of Burglary with a deadly weapon resulting in serious bodily injury, a class A felony, and Battery resulting in serious bodily injury, a class C felony. Jewell was sentenced to an aggregate term of 48 years imprisonment. . . .

This is a direct appeal after the retrial ordered in *Jewell v. State*, 624 N.E.2d 38 (Ind. 1993). The facts in the light most favorable to the verdict reveal that, in 1989, Bridget Fisher, who later married Jewell and changed her name to Bridget Jewell, purchased a home on contract in her maiden name from her relatives. Bridget and Jewell lived in the house together on and off before and after they married in 1990. Jewell helped fix the house up, and therefore, had some "sweat equity" in the house.

Jewell and Bridget experienced marital difficulties and dissolution proceedings were initiated. Jewell moved out of the house and Bridget changed the locks so that Jewell could not reenter. At a preliminary hearing in the dissolution proceedings, Bridget's attorney informed Jewell that Bridget wanted a divorce and wanted Jewell to stop coming by the house. Jewell moved into a friend's house, agreeing to pay him $100.00 per month in rent and to split the utility expenses.

Bridget resumed a romantic relationship with her former boyfriend, Chris Jones. Jewell told a friend that he wanted to get Jones in a dark place, hit him over the head with a 2x4 (a board), and cut his "dick" off. Jewell confronted Jones at his place of employment and threatened to kill him if he were to continue to see Bridget. Jewell was observed on numerous occasions watching Bridget's house. Jewell used a shortwave radio to intercept and listen to the phone conversations on Bridget's cordless phone.

At approximately 4:00 a.m. on the morning of June 13, 1991, Jewell gained entry to Bridget's house through the kitchen window after having removed a window screen. Bridget and Jones were inside sleeping. Jewell struck Jones over the head with a 2x4 until he was unconscious, amputated Jones' penis with a knife, and fed the severed penis to the dog. Bridget awoke and witnessed the attack, but she thought she was having a bad dream and went back to sleep. Bridget described the intruder as the same size and build as Jewell and as wearing a dark ski mask similar to one she had given Jewell. She observed the assailant hit Jones on the head with a board, and stab him in the lower part of his body.

A bloody 2x4 was found at the scene. The sheets on the bed where Bridget and Jones had been sleeping were covered in blood. Bridget discovered that one of her kitchen knives was missing. However, the police did not preserve the sheets or take blood samples and permitted Bridget to dispose of the sheets. A police officer involved explained that the possibility that any of the blood at the crime scene could have come from anyone other than Jones had not been considered.

Jones' severed penis was never found and he underwent reconstructive surgery. His physicians fashioned him a new penis made from tissue and bone taken from his leg. Jones experienced complications and the result was not entirely satisfactory.

At the crime scene, Bridget gave a statement to police in which she identified Jewell as the assailant. Later that morning, however, she waffled on the certainty of her identification, explaining that the assailant had worn a mask and that she had thought that she had been having a dream. However, in the written statement she gave later that morning, she repeatedly stated that she was certain that Jewell had been the assailant.

The police visited the house where Jewell had been staying at approximately 6:00 that morning. One roommate stated that Jewell had not been home when the roommate went to bed at 1:30 a.m. Another roommate stated that he saw Jewell asleep on the couch at 5:30 a.m. The police observed that the hood of Jewell's car was warm and there was no dew on the car, in contrast to the other car parked there. The police told Jewell that they were investigating a complaint that Jones had been hit on the head at Bridget's house. Jewell denied involvement and stated that he had been out cruising around with his buddies the night before. Jewell later told his roommate that the police had accused him of hitting Jones with a board. (The police had not mentioned that Jones had been hit with a board.) Later that day, Jewell went to a house where he had been working. There, he again stated that the police had been at his house investigating a report that a man had been hit on the head with a board.

Jewell admitted to a good friend of his that he had committed the crime. Jewell asked the friend to lie to the police and tell them that he and Jewell had been out drinking beer and riding around the night of the attack. Initially, this friend corroborated Jewell's false alibi with the police, but later recanted and told police that Jewell had told him that he had committed the crime and had enlisted his aid to falsely corroborate his alibi.

The police obtained an arrest warrant and arrested Jewell. At the jail, a detective enlisted the aid of an inmate to collect evidence against Jewell. The detective told the inmate that someone was going to be put in his cell, and that the inmate should report anything he learned from this person. The inmate had not been given any information about the instant crime, and had been instructed not to question Jewell, but only to report what he heard. The inmate overheard Jewell's conversation with another inmate in which Jewell stated that he had committed the crime and described it in detail. In this conversation, Jewell mentioned that there were rubber gloves in a coat pocket. Jewell threatened the inmate not to tell the police what he had heard. The police obtained and executed a search warrant upon the house where Jewell had been staying and found the rubber gloves in the coat pocket. The inmate who reported Jewell's conversation received a favorable disposition of the charges against him.

Jewell attacks the sufficiency of evidence supporting his conviction of Burglary, which is defined as:

A person who breaks and enters the building or structure *of another person,* with intent to commit a felony in it, commits burglary.

Ind.Code 35–43–2-1 (Emphasis added). Jewell argues he was improperly convicted of breaking into his own house.

The Burglary statute's requirement that the dwelling be that "of another person" is satisfied if the evidence demonstrates that the entry was unauthorized. . . . In *Ellyson,* we held a husband was properly convicted of burglary for breaking into the house in which he and his estranged wife had lived previously with the intent of raping his wife. We noted that dissolution proceedings had been initiated and that wife alone controlled access to the home. . . . We upheld the husband's burglary conviction even though he may have had a right to possession of the house co-equal with his wife at the time of the breaking and entering. . . .

In the present case, Bridget had purchased the house in her own name before the marriage. When she and Jewell experienced marital difficulties, Jewell moved out and Bridget changed the locks to prevent Jewell from reentering the house. Bridget alone controlled access to the house. Jewell entered the house at 4:00 a.m. through the kitchen window after having removed the screen. The evidence supports the conclusion that the entry was unauthorized; and, therefore, we find no error.

Next, Jewell argues there was insufficient evidence that he had entered the house with the intent to commit a felony battery therein. That a burglary defendant entered the structure with the intent to commit the felony charged therein is a matter that the jury can infer from the surrounding circumstances. . . . Although the fact of breaking and entering is not itself sufficient to prove the entry was made with the intent to commit the felony, such intent may be inferred from the subsequent conduct of the defendant inside the premises. . . .

In the present case, before the date of the crime, Jewell had expressed his intention to get Jones in a dark place, hit him with a 2x4, and cut off his penis. Jewell did precisely that after breaking into his estranged wife's house. The jury could properly infer that Jewell broke into the house with the intent to commit the felony battery therein as charged. Therefore, we find no error.

Questions

1. What issues did Jewell raise on appeal?

2. What was the court's rationale in affirming Jewell's convictions?

3. Do you think that Jewell should have been considered a co-owner because of the "sweat equity" he put into the house? Does your answer depend upon whether they were divorced rather than separated?

Burglars may use social media to determine which homes will be unoccupied.

A Facebook Burglary?

On March 20, 2010, Keri McMullen and Kurt Pendleton of New Albany, Indiana, went to see a band play in nearby Louisville, Kentucky. Before they left, McMullen posted a Facebook status message that stated, "Heading to the Hill with Kurt . . . to see Fire Department."[5] At approximately 8:42 p.m., two men entered and burglarized their home, stealing over ten thousand dollars worth of electronics, jewelry, and other valuables. Fortunately for Ms. McMullen, she had recently installed a surveillance system that captured the entire burglary on tape. After viewing the images on the tape, she recognized one of the burglars as one of her Facebook friends—a man who had grown up across the street from her but whom she had not seen in over twenty years. McMullen believed that the message she posted on Facebook alerted the burglars to the fact that no one would be home that evening.[6]

Arson

Common law arson is defined as

1. The intentional burning
2. Of the dwelling
3. Of another.

The burning element of common law arson required that there be some charring of the structure of the home. Smoke damage or burning of the furniture or draperies did not constitute arson, nor did the burning of a structure that was not someone's home. Likewise, with common law a person could not commit arson on his or her own home.

Modern arson statutes cover a much broader category of behaviors, and as with other modern statutory property crimes, categorize arson offenses according to the seriousness of the behavior. For example, some statutes classify the burning of a home (or dwelling) as first degree arson and the burning of commercial or other types of buildings as second degree. Another factor that determines the seriousness of the offense is whether the building was occupied at the time of the act. The following excerpt from Florida's arson statute provides an example:

Florida's Arson Statute

(1) Any person who willfully and unlawfully, or while in the commission of any felony, by fire or explosion, damages or causes to be damaged:

(a) Any dwelling, whether occupied or not, or its contents;

(b) Any structure, or contents thereof, where persons are normally present, such as: jails, prisons, or detention centers; hospitals, nursing homes, or other health care facilities; department stores, office buildings, business establishments, churches, or educational institutions during normal hours of occupancy; or other similar structures; or

(c) Any other structure that he or she knew or had reasonable grounds to believe was occupied by a human being, is guilty of arson in the first degree, which constitutes a felony of the first degree. . . .

(2) Any person who willfully and unlawfully, or while in the commission of any felony, by fire or explosion, damages or causes to be damaged any structure, whether the property of himself or herself or another, under any circumstances not referred to in subsection (1), is guilty of arson in the second degree, which constitutes a felony of the second degree. . . .

Consider the following hypothetical:

Jason worked at a department store in Tallahassee, Florida. His supervisor fired him for regularly coming to work late. Jason was very angry with his supervisor. He made a Molotov cocktail (a homemade firebomb made with a glass bottle, gasoline, and a kerosene-soaked rag as a wick) and drove to the store at midnight after the store was closed. Jason lit the wick and threw the Molotov cocktail through the window of the store causing a massive fire that destroyed most of the building.

Would Jason be charged with first or second degree arson? According to the Florida statute, if the fire is in a structure "where persons are normally present," the defendant would be charged with first degree arson. People are normally present in a department store, but not at midnight. Unless the prosecutor could show that there were persons normally present in the store at midnight, Jason might be convicted of second degree arson.

Neither common law nor statutory arson requires that the burning be done for any particular purpose, as long as it is intentional. Serial arsonists often suffer from serious mental problems and burn buildings and other structures for various psychological reasons. However, some arsons are committed for profit. For example, some arsonists burn homes or other buildings to collect the insurance money, as illustrated in the following case.

U.S. v. Thompson (2008)

U. S. Court of Appeals, 7th Circuit

523 F.3d 806

At one time, Marc Thompson owned a seat on the Chicago Board of Trade and earned over $1 million a year. He is now in prison after a jury found him guilty of setting his house on fire in an attempt to collect on an insurance policy. In an even more disturbing finding, the district court concluded that he deliberately killed his own mother in the fire while trying to make it appear that she had committed suicide. We find that sufficient evidence supported the jury's conclusion that Thompson set the fire, so we affirm his convictions. We also find no error in the district court's conclusion that Thompson committed premeditated murder. . . .

For a time, Marc Thompson seemed to have it all. He held an undergraduate degree from Berkeley and had performed graduate work at Stanford. He became a successful broker. He at one point made over $1 million a year. He lived in a home overlooking Lake Michigan with his wife and three children. After an expensive divorce, however, his finances began to fall apart. He lost his biggest client and then his job, and he began to borrow money from business associates and friends, often in large amounts. Several loaned him over $100,000.

On September 15, 2000, Thompson filed an insurance claim for about $50,000, alleging that burglars broke into his home on Paulina Avenue in Chicago and stole a computer and other belongings. Chubb Insurance Company promptly paid the claim. In June of the next year, Thompson moved his then eighty-nine-year-old mother, Carmen Thompson, from California to live with him in Chicago. He arranged for her home to be sold, placed the proceeds into her bank account, and then spent the majority of the proceeds. In December of 2001, Thompson raised his Chubb homeowner's insurance policy from $275,000 to $350,000.

The next year, Thompson told his housekeeper that his mother had said she wanted to burn the house down. Then, on August 8, 2002, Thompson brought his mother to the hospital after she sustained a burn injury on her shoulder. He first told caregivers that she had fallen on the stove after he had left the room. Later that night, though, he told hospital employees that she was injured after he left her alone in the house. The hospital treated and released Carmen, but not before calling an elder abuse hotline, and Thompson brought her back to his home.

(Continued)

(Continued)

Three days later, Thompson's house caught fire. Neighbors saw Thompson and two of his sons leave their home around 7:00 p.m. that evening. Thompson told investigators that he left the house around 6:15 p.m., made one stop, and then went to see a 7:05 p.m. movie with his children at a theater located at 600 N. Michigan Avenue in Chicago. Travel time would have been about fifteen minutes from the house directly to the theater. The parties stipulated at trial that Thompson's youngest son remembered arriving at the movie theater about 8 minutes and 30 seconds into the movie, making arrival time (after accounting for previews) into the theater 7:29:30 p.m.

Back near Thompson's home, neighbors saw smoke coming from the house at about 7:10 p.m. and called 911. Firefighters quickly extinguished the fire but found Thompson's mother in the basement, dead of smoke inhalation, about four feet from the fire's origin. The area underneath her body was untouched by the fire. Chicago Police Department detectives subsequently questioned Thompson, and he told them his mother sometimes acted in a psychotic manner, was taking medications, had previously burned herself, and had talked about committing suicide in the past. The detectives quickly ended their investigation, and the Cook County Medical Examiner declared Carmen's death a suicide.

At the time, however, the police and Medical Examiner were unaware of the neighbors' observations regarding the night of the fire, Thompson's financial condition, the fact that steep stairs led to the basement, and that Carmen had physical disabilities limiting her mobility. In addition, analysis showed that at the time of her death, Carmen had alcohol, Nordiazepam (from the Valium family), and Risperdal, an anti-psychotic drug, in her system. Valium had been prescribed to Thompson but not to his mother, and Thompson had obtained the Risperdal prescription for his mother from a physician who had not examined her. Also, a codicil to Carmen's will dated August 4, 2002—a week before the fire—stated she did not want an autopsy performed in the event of her death and also that she wished to be cremated immediately, noting in bold that this marked a change from her most recent will.

Fire Marshal Carmelita Wiley-Earls led the Chicago Fire Department's investigation into the fire's cause. She arrived while firefighters were still extinguishing the blaze and spent six hours on the scene. She ultimately concluded that the fire had been caused by the ignition of a flammable liquid that had been poured or splashed in the basement of the house.

Thompson called his insurance company the night of the fire. (He telephoned his sister the following morning to inform her of their mother's death.) His claims for content loss totaled $756,766, but his policy only provided for "replacement value"—the amount it would take to replace the contents and to replace the damaged house. Because the house was not a total loss and could be repaired, the insurance company would only pay a reduced amount. As a result, Thompson chose to sell the property, and the insurance company ultimately paid $269,000 for damage to the house. Thompson also claimed that property had been stolen from his fire-damaged house, and the insurance company paid over $350,000 for lost and stolen items.

Four days after the fire, Thompson opened a bank account in Chicago. In November and December of 2002, he transferred $400,000 from that account to one in the Netherland Antilles held in the name of Toscana Consulting Services, Ltd., a shell company he had set up in 2000 to hide money from his ex-wife. He filed for bankruptcy in May of 2003. At trial, he admitted that he had committed bankruptcy fraud when he made false statements on his bankruptcy application and used his offshore account to conceal assets from creditors.

A jury rendered a verdict of guilty against Thompson on all nineteen counts with which he had been charged, including wire fraud, use of fire to commit a felony, bankruptcy fraud, and money laundering. . . . The resulting sentence was 190 years' imprisonment. . . .

Thompson's argument focuses on the testimony of the government's fire cause and origin expert, Carmelita Wiley-Earls from the Chicago Fire Department. Wiley-Earls concluded that the fire at Thompson's home was incendiary in origin, fueled by a liquid that had been poured or splashed in the home's basement and then ignited with an unknown open flame. Thompson maintains that Wiley-Earls's testimony was so conclusory that it did not provide enough support for a rational jury to find beyond a reasonable doubt that the fire was caused by arson.

Wiley-Earls ultimately concluded that a flammable liquid poured or splashed in the area of origin, ignited with an open flame, caused the fire. She had eliminated all natural causes. Firefighters and Wiley-Earls had both smelled a flammable liquid at the scene. And the uniform burning on the baseboard indicated to her that an ignitable liquid had been used.

Thompson's primary defense at trial was that his mother had burned down the home, and negative test results would not have supported that theory. Moreover, "arson, like most other crimes, may be proved by the use of circumstantial evidence." . . . And we will reverse a jury's verdict on a sufficiency of the evidence challenge "only if no rational trier of fact could have found him guilty of the charges beyond a reasonable doubt." . . . In this case, as we detailed, there was more than sufficient evidence for a rational jury to find that Marc Thompson caused the fire at his home on August 11, 2002. We will not disturb the jury's verdict. . . .

Questions

1. Mr. Thompson argued that there was insufficient evidence to convict him of arson. What was the evidence in support of his conviction?

2. What was the court's rationale for rejecting the defendant's argument?

3. Arson is a general intent crime. The defendant need not burn the dwelling for any particular reason or with any additional intent, as with larceny, burglary, or the other common law property crimes. Should arson be a specific intent crime? Why or why not?

Table 5.2 summarizes the common law property crimes.

Table 5.2 **Overview of Common Law Property Crimes**[7]

Crime	Elements	Example
Larceny (petty/grand theft, stealing)	1. Trespassory taking (without consent) 2. carrying away (asportation) 3. personal property 4. of another 5. with the intent to permanently deprive owner of possession.	"When I was not looking, you took possession of my property and planned to keep it and never give it back to me."
Embezzlement	1. The fraudulent conversion (taking) 2. of the property 3. of another 5. while the person is still in possession of the property.	"I am a bank teller and I deposit some of the cash that I receive from a customer to my personal account for my own use."
False Pretenses (con man, scam artist, cheating victim)	1. Using deceit to obtain possession and title 2. carrying away (asportation) 3. personal property 4. of another 5. with the intent to permanently deprive owner of possession.	"We had a deal; I gave you my diamond ring in exchange for a new TV set, but the TV you gave me was a hollow shell with a brick inside."
Burglary	1. Breaking and entering 2. the home of another (or commercial building, burglary II) 3. with the intent to commit a felony therein (i.e., larceny, kidnapping, rape, arson).	"You broke the lock on my front door, came into bedroom while I was sleeping, and tried to rape me."
Arson	1. The intentional burning 2. of the dwelling 3. of another.	"You tossed a Molotov cocktail through the window of my house causing it to burn to the ground."

Source: Professor Cynthia E. Jones, American University Washington College of Law.

White-Collar Crime

The term "white-collar crime" includes a broad range of property crimes, including embezzlement, fraud, computer crimes, and identity theft. These crimes are distinguished from "blue-collar crimes" based on the people who commit them and the type of harm they cause. White-collar crimes generally are not violent crimes and do not cause physical harm to its victims, unlike blue-collar crimes such as murder, rape, robbery, and assault. However, the harm caused by white-collar criminals can be massive in terms of its scope, and the lives of large numbers of people may be affected, as in the Bernie Madoff case discussed below.

According to the FBI website, white-collar crime is "lying, cheating, and stealing. That's white-collar crime in a nutshell. The term—reportedly coined in 1939—is now synonymous with the full range of frauds committed by business and government professionals."[8] White-collar crimes listed on the FBI website include a wide range of crimes, many involving fraud.[9] The list includes:

Asset Forfeiture/Money Laundering

Bankruptcy Fraud

Corporate Fraud

Financial Institution Fraud & Failures

Health Care Fraud

Insurance Fraud

Mortgage Fraud

Identity Theft

Disaster/Hurricane Katrina Fraud

Internet Fraud

E-scams & Warnings

Public Corruption/Government Fraud

Adoption Scams

Housing Stealing

Illegal Pharmacies

Jury Duty Scams

Social Security Card Fraud

Staged Auto Accidents

Sports Memorabilia Fraud

Timeshare Fraud

Work at Home Scams

One of the most infamous white-collar crimes in recent history was the massive Ponzi scheme carried out by Bernard Madoff. Madoff committed numerous white-collar crimes that involved various forms of fraud and theft. His criminal behavior ruined the lives of thousands of people and destroyed many businesses and organizations.

Bernard Madoff's Ponzi Scheme

Madoff was the founder, sole member, and principal of Bernard L. Madoff Investment Securities LLC (BLMIS). BLMIS was a market maker Wall Street business that was registered with the Securities and Exchange Commission (SEC). Thousands of individuals and organizations invested in Madoff's firm, and he reaped massive profits. In 2009, he reported a net worth of almost $126 million, not including the value of his business interest in the firm. Madoff owned a yacht, expensive art, and homes and property in Manhattan, Palm Beach, Montauk, and France.

On December 10, 2008, Madoff confessed to his two sons Mark and Andrew that he had been operating a giant Ponzi scheme. He had been paying artificial returns to his investors using money entrusted to him by other investors.[10] During the course of the Ponzi scheme, Madoff stole billions of dollars from thousands of individuals and companies who invested money with his firm.[11] Madoff's victims included banks, charitable trusts and foundations, universities, pension funds, and individual investors, many of whom were robbed of their life savings.[12]

Bernard Madoff pled guilty to eleven federal felonies and was sentenced to 150 years in prison.

Madoff's sons reported Madoff to the FBI soon after he confessed to them. He was arrested and charged with a number of federal offenses, including securities fraud, investment advisor fraud, mail fraud, wire fraud, money laundering, international money laundering, false statements, perjury, and theft. Madoff ultimately pled guilty to all charges and was sentenced to 150 years in prison.[13]

Computer Crimes

Almost everyone relies on computers to conduct a range of professional and personal tasks. Email is the primary means of communication at most workplaces, and very few people do not have personal email addresses to communicate with family and friends. From browsing the Internet to playing computer games or paying bills and purchasing merchandise, it is fair to say that most individuals use computers in some way, and many do so on a daily basis.

Not surprisingly, the increased use of computers has resulted in their use for criminal activity. The term "computer crimes" has been used to describe a wide range of criminal activity that includes using a computer to commit a crime or stealing from or destroying computer hardware or software. The crimes that fall in this category are all classified as white-collar crimes. Most states have separate statutes that criminalize the use of a computer to commit other crimes and crimes that target computers. Individuals who commit these crimes are usually charged with the computer crime along with other crimes. For example, computers may be used to access bank accounts, locate credit card information, distribute or view pornography, or lure individuals to a location to harm them. Individuals may also infect computers with viruses or hack into computers to alter or damage data in the computer system.

The North Carolina computer crimes statute penalizes a wide range of criminal activity committed with or directed at a computer, including accessing and damaging computers. The following excerpt from the statute sets forth additional acts that may be characterized as computer crimes. Note that the North Carolina statute includes cyberbullying, which is technically a crime against persons rather than a property crime. As with other types of computer crimes, individuals who engage in cyberbullying are usually charged with the computer crime and additional crimes such as assault and/or harassment.

AP Photo/ Kathy Willens

North Carolina's Computer Crime Statute

§ 144–58. Computer trespass

(a) Except as otherwise made unlawful by this Article, it shall be unlawful for any person to use a computer or computer network without authority and with the intent to do any of the following:

(1) Temporarily or permanently remove, halt, or otherwise disable any computer data, computer programs, or computer software from a computer or computer network.

(2) Cause a computer to malfunction, regardless of how long the malfunction persists.

(3) Alter or erase any computer data, computer programs, or computer software.

(4) Cause physical injury to the property of another.

(5) Make or cause to be made an unauthorized copy, in any form, including, but not limited to, any printed or electronic form of computer data, computer programs, or computer software residing in, communicated by, or produced by a computer or computer network.

§ 144–58.1. Cyberbullying

(a) Except as otherwise made unlawful by this Article, it shall be unlawful for any person to use a computer or computer network to do any of the following:

(1) With the intent to intimidate or torment a minor:

a. Build a fake profile or Web site;

b. Pose as a minor in:

1. An Internet chat room;

2. An electronic mail message; or

3. An instant message;

c. Follow a minor online or into an Internet chat room; or

d. Post or encourage others to post on the Internet private, personal, or sexual information pertaining to a minor.

(2) With the intent to intimidate or torment a minor or the minor's parent or guardian:

a. Post a real or doctored image of a minor on the Internet;

b. Access, alter, or erase any computer network, computer data, computer program, or computer software, including breaking into a password protected account or stealing or otherwise accessing passwords; or

c. Use a computer system for repeated, continuing, or sustained electronic communications, including electronic mail or other transmissions, to a minor.

The federal government also penalizes criminal activity committed with a computer or that causes harm to computer data. The Computer Fraud and Abuse Act,[14] criminalizes a range of activity, from hacking to using a computer to obtain National Security information. The CAN-SPAM Act,[15] provides for prosecution of individuals who send large amounts of spam (commercial emails). There are also a number of federal laws that punish the use of a computer to commit fraud and other related activity.

Consider the following hypotheticals:

- Josh was a senior at Brookside High School. One week before graduation, he learned that he had failed a history course that was required for graduation. Josh was not good at history, but he was a computer genius. Determined to graduate, he hacked into the school's computer system, found the program with his transcript, and changed his history grade from an "F" to a "B."
- Cindy was a junior at Brookside High School. She ran for class president but lost the election to Brenda, whom she disliked immensely. Cindy was furious. Cindy followed Brenda into the restroom and secretly took an embarrassing photo of her while she was using the toilet. Cindy posted the photo of Brenda on Facebook.

Assume that Brookside High School is in North Carolina. Josh would most likely be charged with computer trespass and Cindy with cyberbullying. Can you identify the sections of the statute that Josh and Cindy violated?

Identity Theft

Identity theft (sometimes called identity fraud) is the term that is used to describe the crime of obtaining another person's name, social security number, or other identifying information for purposes of committing fraud, theft, or some other criminal behavior. There are many different forms of identity theft and it is often committed in conjunction with other crimes such as credit card fraud and various computer crimes. Identity thieves often use computers to obtain identifying information of other individuals, but there are many other ways to obtain this information.

Paper shredders have become almost as common as trash cans in many American homes as a result of one of the most popular forms of identity theft. Sometimes called dumpster diving, one form of identity theft involves retrieving discarded mail from trashcans. Most households receive numerous solicitations from credit card companies. These mailings sometimes include pre-approved credit cards that can be activated and used by the thief. Likewise, bank statements, bills, and other mail with identifying information may be stolen and used to get access to these accounts. For that reason, consumers are advised to shred all documents that contain their name, address, and especially other identifying information such as bank account and credit card numbers.

Other forms of identity theft consist of using fraud or false pretenses to obtain identifying information over the phone or through email; listening as an individual provides his or her social security number or other identifying information to a bank teller, store clerk, or other individual; or looking over an individual's shoulder as he or she types in his or her PIN number at an ATM machine. A person's identity may even be stolen by a server in a restaurant. For that reason, some restaurants now require servers to bring the credit card machine to the customer's table so that the customer may swipe his or her own credit card without giving it to the server.

There is a federal identity theft statute and identity theft statutes in all fifty states and the District of Columbia. Individuals charged under these laws are also often charged with other related crimes such as credit card fraud, wire fraud, and false pretenses, depending upon the facts of the case. The following brief excerpt from Maryland's identity theft statute illustrates how one state attempted to criminalize and punish some forms of identity theft. The penalties range from eighteen months to fifteen years, depending on particular acts and the value of the property.

Maryland's Identity Fraud Statute

§ 8–301 Identity fraud.

(b) Prohibited—Obtaining personal identifying information without consent.—A person may not knowingly, willfully, and with fraudulent intent possess, obtain, or help another to possess or obtain any personal identifying information of an individual, without the consent of the individual, in order to use, sell, or transfer the information to get a benefit, credit, good, service, or other thing of value in the name of the individual

(c) Prohibited—Assuming identity of another.—A person may not knowingly and willfully assume the identity of another:

(1) to avoid identification, apprehension, or prosecution for a crime; or

(2) with fraudulent intent to:

(i) get a benefit, credit, good, service, or other thing of value; or

(ii) avoid the payment of debt or other legal obligation.

Consider the following very different cases involving identity theft:

The Albert Gonzalez Case

Albert Gonzalez was the mastermind of one of the largest identity theft cases in U.S. history. In 2008, when Mr. Gonzalez was twenty-seven years old, he and ten other people from five countries were charged with stealing forty-one million credit and debit card numbers from a number of companies, including Barnes & Noble, BJ's Wholesale Club, Boston Market, Forever 21, OfficeMax, Sports Authority, and the TJX Companies.[16] He was later charged with stealing an additional 130 million credit card numbers from other companies, including the Heartland Payment Systems and the retail chains 7-Eleven and Hannaford Brothers.[17]

Federal charges were brought against Gonzalez in New York, Massachusetts, and New Jersey. He accepted a plea bargain in which he pled guilty to all 19 counts of the Massachusetts case (which involved the TJ Maxx company) in exchange for the government's agreement to dismiss the other charges against him. In March 2010, Gonzalez was sentenced to two twenty-year prison terms, to be served concurrently.[18]

Gonzalez was introduced to computers at an early age. His parents bought him his first computer when he was just eight years old. By the time he was nine, he was removing computer viruses from computers. Gonzalez attended South Miami High School where he was described as a "computer nerd." During his senior year, he hacked into the computer system of the government of India but was never charged with a crime.

The Wendy Brown Case

Although identity theft is primarily used to commit theft, as the following unusual case illustrates, identity thieves may be motivated by other goals.

Wendy Brown was thirty-three years old when she decided to steal her fifteen-year-old daughter's identity. Ms. Brown enrolled in Ashwaubenon High School in the little town of Ashwaubenon, Wisconsin, using her daughter's name and other personal information while her daughter was living with her grandmother in Nevada. Ms. Brown tried out for the cheerleading squad, was given a cheerleader locker, and even attended a pool party and a class with other students. She was ultimately caught when she did not show up for school.

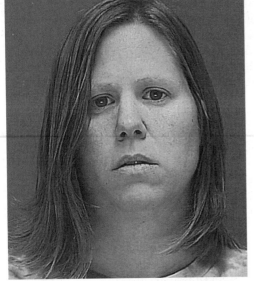

As seen in the case of Wendy Brown, the motivations for crime vary widely.

According to court documents, Ms. Brown stated that "she wanted to get her high school degree and be a cheerleader because she had no childhood and was trying to regain a part of her life she missed."[19] Ms. Brown had a history of committing various types of fraud throughout her adult life. She was found not guilty due to mental impairment and committed to three years in a psychiatric unit.

Concluding Note

When most people think of property crimes, they think of stealing—taking the property of someone else without permission. But as this chapter demonstrates, there are many different types of property crimes, ranging from basic theft to computer hacking. All of the crimes involve taking or destroying property without permission. All crimes cause harm, and although there is usually a distinction between crimes against property and crimes against persons, there is often overlap between the two. For example, in Chapter 7 you will learn about the crime of robbery, which involves assaulting a person while stealing from him or her. And as the *Thompson* case illustrates, the crime of arson can certainly cause physical harm or even death. Although most other property crimes generally do not cause physical harm to human beings in the same way that violent crimes such as assault and rape do, people who lose their property may certainly experience great harm. Property crimes are generally considered to be less serious than crimes against persons, but what about the victim of identity theft who spends years trying to restore his or her credit? Or the thousands of victims who lost their life savings as a result of Bernie Madoff's numerous crimes? Think about these cases as you discuss the crimes against persons in Chapters 7 and 8. Now test yourself on the material we have covered in this chapter. Good luck with the Issue Spotter exercise.

Issue Spotter

Read the hypothetical and spot the issues discussed in this chapter.

The VMA Thief

Kareem Kanard was widely criticized for his "performance" at the Video Music Awards. He had grabbed the microphone from Tammy Taylor, the winner of the Best Female Video, and proclaimed that his friend Nikki had made "the best video of all time!" Even the president of the United States proclaimed him a "jackass" for his behavior.

Kareem was at a party at a friend's house a few nights after the awards ceremony. After having a few drinks, he decided to steal the award from Tammy's house and deliver it to Nikki. Kareem left the party and spotted a snazzy sports car parked in front of the house with the keys in the ignition. He jumped in the car and drove to Tammy's house. When Kareem arrived, he walked up to the front door and rang the doorbell several times. When there was no answer,

Kareem remembered that he had heard that Tammy kept a spare key under a statue by her pool. He found the key, unlocked the door, and walked in. The award was on the table in the living room. Kareem took the award, locked the door, returned the key to its hiding place, and got back in the car. He drove to Nikki's house and placed the award on her front lawn.

Kareem then drove back to the party, parked the car in front of the house, and went back inside. He immediately began talking about his "prank" and bragged about how he had delivered the Best Female Video award to its rightful owner. Someone at the party made an anonymous call to the police and reported that Kareem had stolen Tammy's award. When Tammy returned home that night and discovered that her award was missing, she called the police also. Kareem was arrested later that night.

1. You are a prosecutor considering charges against Kareem. What charge or charges would you bring?

2. What are the strengths and weaknesses of the charge or charges?

Key Terms and Cases

Notes

1. "Frank Abagnale Jr.," *Bio* (2014), http://www.biography.com/people/frank-abagnale-20657 335?page=2

2. *Frank Abagnale Jr.* (2014), http://www.abagnale.com/index2.asp

3. D.C. Code § 22–3211.

4. N.Y. Penal Law § 155.05 (McKinney).

5. "Facebook "friend" Victimized," CNN.com Video (Mar. 26, 2010), http://www.cnn.com/video/?/video/crime/2010/03/26/am.facebook.burglary.cnn

6. "Facebook "Friend" Suspected in Burglary," CBSNEWS.com Video (Mar. 25, 2010), http://www.cbsnews.com/stories/2010/03/25/earlyshow/main6331796.shtml

7. Chart from Professor Cynthia E. Jones, American University Washington College of Law (modified) (on file with author).

8. Federal Bureau of Investigation, "White-Collar Crime," The FBI Federal Bureau of Investigation, http://www.fbi.gov/about-us/investigate/white_collar, accessed July 12, 2011.

9. Ibid.

10. Binyamin Appelbaum, David S. Hilzenrath, and Amit R. Paley, "All Just One Big Lie," *Washington Post*, December 13, 2008, http://www.washingtonpost.com/wp-dyn/content/article/2008/12/12/AR2008121203970.html?hpid=topnews

11. Ibid.

12. "Madoff's Victims," *Wall Street Journal*, March 6, 2009, http://s.wsj.net/public/resources/documents/st_madoff_victims_20081215.html

13. Sent. Tr. June 29, 2009, http://www.justice.gov/usao/nys/madoff/20090629sentencingtranscriptcorrected.pdf

14. 18 U.S.C. § 1030

15. 18 U.S.C. § 1307

16. Reuters, "Man Accused of Stealing Stores' Data Pleads Guilty," *New York Times*, August 28, 2009, http://www.nytimes.com/2009/08/29/technology/29hacker.html

17. Ibid.

18. U.S. Department of Justice, "Leader of Hacking Ring Sentenced for Massive Identity Thefts From Payment Processor and U.S. Retail Networks," Department of Justice, March 26, 2010, http://www.justice.gov/usao/nj/Press/files/pdffiles/2010/dojgonzalez0326rel.pdf

19. Associated Press, "Mom, That's My Cheerleading Outfit! WisconsinWoman Steals Daughter's Identity to Join Pom PomSquad," *Daily News*, http://www.nydailynews.com/news/world/mom-cheerleading-outfit-wisconsin-woman-steals-daughter-identity-join-pom-pom-squad-article-1.325255, accessed September 28, 2014.

Chapter 6

At the community level, disorder and crime are usually inextricably linked, in a kind of developmental sequence . . . If a window in a building is broken and left unrepaired, all the rest of the windows will soon be broken. This is as true in nice neighborhoods as in rundown ones.

"Untended" behavior also leads to the breakdown of community controls. A stable neighborhood of families who care for their homes, mind each other's children, and confidently frown on unwanted intruders can change, in a few years or even a few months, to an inhospitable and frightening jungle. A piece of property is abandoned, weeds grow up, a window is smashed. Adults stop scolding rowdy children; the children, emboldened, become more rowdy. Families move out, unattached adults move in. Teenagers gather in front of the corner store. The merchant asks them to move; they refuse. Fights occur. Litter accumulates. People start drinking in front of the grocery; in time, an inebriate slumps to the sidewalk and is allowed to sleep it off. Pedestrians are approached by panhandlers.[1]

The above theory, known as "broken windows," predicts that serious crime will decrease if police target low-level offenses, such as vandalism and **vagrancy**. Supporters claim it explains how some neighborhoods become hot spots for crime, while opponents note that there is little empirical support for the theory. Further, studies indicate this approach encourages police to target poor people and minorities for arrest. The broken windows theory was initially attractive to law enforcement agencies and criminologists. However, because there has not been solid and consistent evidence that it works, the theory has been widely debunked.[2] The above excerpt highlights some of the core issues tackled in this chapter, including how public order crimes and crimes against public decency are defined and treated under the law.

Graffiti and vandalized signs and buildings can be indicators of disorder and crime. How do you think the law should respond to such activities?

© John Steedman

Public Order Crimes and Offenses Against Public Decency

Learning Objectives

After reading and studying this chapter, you should be able to

➤ Define public order offenses

➤ List four public order offenses

➤ Identify the rationale for the punishment of public order offenses

➤ State two arguments against the punishment of public order offenses

➤ Define offenses against public decency

➤ List three public decency offenses

➤ Identify the rationale for the punishment of public decency offenses

➤ State two arguments against the punishment of public decency offenses

➤ Assess whether public order offenses and public decency offenses are different from other types of criminal offenses

Introduction

This chapter is divided into two parts. The first section addresses public order offenses. These are actions that are made criminal because it is believed that they unreasonably intrude into and endanger our public spaces. The second section focuses on offenses against public decency. These are actions that some people believe are harmful to our moral values and our social fabric, even when the actions involve consenting adults. While these two offense categories—public order and public decency—are distinct, they have some common features. First, both types of offenses are typically misdemeanors (there are some important exceptions to this general rule that we will discuss). Second, both types of offenses generate sharp debate as to whether they should be subject to criminal punishment. With regard to public order offenses and victimless crimes, some people believe the government should do all that it can to punish offenders (see the Chapter 1 discussion on victimless crimes). Others argue that living with public order offenses and victimless crimes is the part of the price we pay for living in a diverse society. Further, they argue that the government should not punish actions between consenting adults. Third, crimes against public order and offenses against morality raise constitutional issues, which may involve the First Amendment, the due process clause, or the equal protection clause (see Chapter 2 for a more detailed discussion of the link between constitutional issues and criminal law). Although both state and federal laws punish public order offenses and crimes against decency, the focus of this chapter is on state laws.

Public Order Crimes ●━━━━━━━━━━━━━━━━━━━━━━━━━━━

Defining Terms, Background, and Concepts

Public order offenses refer to a loosely connected group of actions that occur in public and cause disruption. Generally speaking, public order crimes are low-level offenses. Historically, actions classified as offenses against the public order were not viewed as serious criminal incidents. Today some offenses that fall under the public order heading are considered serious crimes, such as offenses involving weapons. In the latest report by the Bureau of Justice Statistics, there were a reported 1.4 million prisoners who were serving time in state prison, approximately 10 percent (142,500) of whom had been convicted of a public order offense. This category includes drunk driving and violations of weapon laws. It also includes commercialized vice, such as prostitution, morals offenses (e.g., bigamy), and liquor law violations.[3] Figure 6.1 provides a visual image of arrests for public order offenses:

Figure 6.1 Public Order Arrests in America, 2010

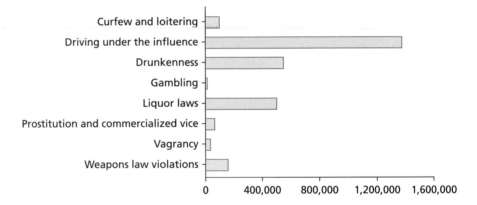

Source: U.S. Department of Justice.

The above table includes both public order crimes and offenses against public decency (the latter are discussed in more detail in the next section). Also, the alcohol-related public order crimes (e.g., driving under the influence, drunkenness, and liquor law violations) have the highest rate of arrests. One rationale for this is that of the public order and public decency, those that involve alcohol have the greatest potential for causing harm to uninvolved third parties. Overall, arrests for public order offenses make up less than 10 percent of all annual arrests.

With this background in mind, we are ready to examine the definition and application of public order offense laws. The next section reviews vagrancy, loitering, homelessness, alcohol offenses, weapon offenses, and animal abuse. These public order crimes are analyzed through statutes, hypotheticals, and court cases. Sometimes there is an overlap among public order offenses. For instance, a law that punishes loitering will likely punish activities engaged in by the homeless. The discussion includes an examination of how public order offenses are defined, how they are punished, and how punishment is rationalized.

Vagrancy and Loitering

Across the country, states, counties, and cities pass legislation to regulate who can do what in public places. At common law, vagrancy laws were designed to sanction actions that upset the public peace and tranquility. Vagrancy statutes punish a person's movement from one place to another. A 1965 Jacksonville, Florida, ordinance offers a notably detailed example. Among other things, it was unlawful for people to wander or stroll around "from place to place without any lawful purpose or object."[4] (See Chapter 2 for a more detailed discussion of vagrancy statutes.) This ordinance and others like it were holdovers from early English law. Historically, vagrancy laws were passed to stabilize local economies by discouraging workers from moving from one town to another. They were also designed to punish the non-working poor, those most likely to be idle in public.[5] Laws that sanction loitering typically focus on stationary activity, such as standing around. Over time, these laws have come to include a broad range of undesirable public acts, such as gang activity, homelessness, and prostitution, discussed in this chapter. Laws that punish loitering are controversial because they can result in arbitrary and racially discriminatory enforcement by police officers.

Now let us consider how an anti-loitering statute would apply to various fact patterns. Review the Florida law and apply it to the three hypothetical scenarios that follow.

Florida's Anti-Loitering Statute

It is unlawful for any person to loiter or prowl in a place, at a time or in a manner not usual for law-abiding individuals, under circumstances that warrant a justifiable and reasonable alarm or immediate concern for the safety of persons or property in the vicinity.[6]

1. Bethany, Renee, and Liza gather outside their favorite mall each day after attending their college classes. The three young women discuss homework and share stories. They always dress in the latest fashions. When they get together, they talk and laugh loudly and sometimes use curse words.

2. Efron, Yancy, and Mr. Fernando meet each afternoon. The men, all in their 60s, gather on a park bench. The three men like to talk, share stories, and laugh. Their clothes are tattered, and the men smell bad. Sometimes the men holler at one another and use curse words. The three men are homeless.

3. Zeus, Apocalypse, and Dru get together each day after college classes. They meet in front of Stop and Shop—their favorite convenience store. The young men like to discuss their classes, share stories, and laugh. They wear sagging, baggy pants. Their speech is loud and includes lots of curse words. They do not smile at passersby.

The Florida anti-loitering law draws directly from the Model Penal Code (MPC), which provides guidance to states in drafting criminal laws. The MPC provision defines loitering and identifies circumstances that would indicate "reasonable alarm" (§ 250.6). These factors include whether the person flees after seeing a police officer, refuses to identify himself, or attempts to hide an object. The MPC advises that an officer should give the person under suspicion an opportunity to provide identification before making an arrest.

The next step is to analyze how each group of people might be treated under Florida law. Are any of the three groups likely to face a loitering charge? For the first group, it is unlikely that the actions of the three young women would result in an arrest. There is no indication that their behavior would create a "reasonable alarm." Further, their location, a mall, is a place where people are expected to gather. The young women's activity does not create a security threat. The second group does not appear to pose harm. The men's location, a park, is also an expected place for people to gather. Their actions do not appear likely to cause an immediate safety concern. Except for differences in their gender, age, and economic background, the men are engaged in activity similar to the first group of young women. In the third group, the young men congregate outside a store. They appear to be having fun and are not engaging in activity that would cause reasonable alarm.

The above scenarios have core similarities—a group of people standing outside who are engaged in a loud conversation. However, it is likely that each gathering would provoke a different response from the public. In turn, this might impact the response of law enforcement—whether they treat the conduct as loitering and arrest the group.

These scenarios highlight the interplay between the law, sociology, and the criminal justice system. A broad range of factors, legal and extralegal, may impact the likelihood that a particular person will face criminal charges. Factors include the type of offense, location of the crime, and the offender's age, gender, race, and socioeconomic status. In general, police officers have wide latitude in deciding whether to arrest someone for committing a public order crime. Social science research indicates that members of socially marginalized groups, such as racial minorities and the poor, are more likely to be arrested than members of other groups.

This means that although they are engaged in similar activities, the homeless men in the second scenario are more likely to face arrest than the young women in the first fact pattern. Many people have disdain for or fear of the homeless. For some observers, the three older men sitting on the bench might be interpreted as behavior "not usual for law-abiding individuals." Their loud, sometimes profane conversations might be viewed as cause for reasonable alarm. As to the third hypothetical, consider whether the race of the young men and the location of the store would impact the likelihood the young men would be arrested for loitering. Would it matter whether Zeus, Apocalypse, and Dru were all Latino, White, American Indian, Asian American, or African American, or a mixed-race group?

Chicago v. Morales

With the above discussion in mind, now consider an actual case involving an anti-loitering law that was passed to target the activities of a specific group. In 1992, the Chicago city council passed an antigang ordinance. The Gang Congregation Ordinance made it unlawful for gang members to loiter with one another or other people on a public sidewalk. The ordinance was specifically designed to reduce gang activity in Chicago. It was passed by the city council with support from the community.[7]

Under the ordinance, it was unlawful to stay in a place with no obvious purpose. Violators could be subject to six months in jail, a five hundred dollar fine, and one hundred twenty hours of community service. Over a three-year period, police arrested more than 42,000 people for violating the ordinance. The defendants, young men who had been charged with violating the ordinance, argued that its language was too vague and violated the Fourteenth Amendment's due process clause. The case made its way to the U.S. Supreme Court after the ordinance was struck down as unconstitutional by the Illinois Supreme Court. The Supreme Court affirmed the Illinois Supreme Court decision, finding that the Chicago ordinance was unconstitutionally vague and failed to meet due process clause standards. Justice John Paul Stevens, who wrote the majority opinion, said the law gave "too much discretion to the police and too little notice to citizens who wish to use the public streets."[8]

Floyd v. New York

This 2013 case also raised a challenge under the Fourteenth Amendment. However, this time the claim was that the equal protection clause had been violated. David Floyd and eleven other people, Black and Hispanic, brought federal charges against the New York Police Department (NYPD), alleging that its Stop and Frisk policy resulted in racial profiling—intentional discrimination based upon race.[9] Each person had been stopped at least once by the NYPD. Under the policy, between 2004 and 2012, NYPD officers conducted more than 4.4 million stops. Over 80 percent involved Blacks or Hispanics. A review of the stops showed that while Blacks were much more likely to be stopped and detained by the police, Whites, when stopped, were much more likely to be found with a weapon or contraband. The NYPD argued that the policy targeted Blacks and Hispanics because of their disproportionately high rates of offending and said that the policy had been effective in reducing crime. After evaluating the opposing arguments, massive evidence, and statistical analysis, Judge Shira Scheindlin determined that the NYPD policy, as carried out by law enforcement, was unconstitutional.[10] The judge observed that there is a distinction between effectiveness and constitutionality and stated "The Equal Protection Clause does not permit the police to target a racially defined group as a whole because of the misdeeds of some of its members."[11] In a 2014 settlement with the NYPD, the City of New York agreed to implement the court-ordered reforms.

The *Morales* and *Floyd* cases highlight some of the issues raised by "quality of life" or crime control ordinances and practices. As referenced in the excerpt that opens this chapter, the public presence of some members of society—urban youth, the poor, and the inebriated, for instance—sometimes makes other members of society fearful for their safety. Just how far can state legislation go to protect the public without infringing on personal freedoms, such as the freedom to congregate with friends on a public street? The *Morales* case, the Florida loitering ordinance, and our examination of how the Florida statute might apply in three diverse instances, all underscore the importance of ensuring that laws protect the public, but that they do not unfairly target members of unpopular groups.

Homelessness

Sister, can you spare a dime?

Anonymous quote

The nature of homelessness makes it difficult to compile accurate statistics. Different reporting agencies report different numbers. The U.S. Department of Housing and Urban Development (HUD) found that in 2013 there were approximately

©iStockphoto.com/AvailableLight

Do anti-loitering laws punish homelessness?

610,000 homeless people in the United States.[12] Sixty-two percent of these were individuals on their own, and 38 percent were part of a family household. It is estimated that one in forty-five children is homeless. This adds up to more than one million homeless children in the United States.[13]

The homeless population is concentrated in a handful of states. Five states hold one-half of America's homeless people: California (22 percent), New York (13 percent), Florida (8 percent), Texas (5 percent) and Massachusetts (3 percent).[14] According to HUD estimates, approximately 40 percent of homeless men are veterans. Many agencies that advocate on behalf of homeless people state that the problem is much larger than indicated by official statistics. Many homeless people do not live in shelters, and many homeless people do not report their homeless status because they fear they will face further economic penalty or shame. The 2013 report by the National Alliance to End Homelessness states that while most homeless people were living in emergency shelters or transitional housing, almost 40 percent of the homeless population was "unsheltered"— living on the street, in cars, on campgrounds, in abandoned buildings, and other spaces not intended for habitation.[15]

As the homeless population has swelled and become more visible, cities and municipalities have passed legislation that limits or bans activities engaged in by the homeless. Among other things, these laws restrict where the homeless can gather and how and whether they can engage in panhandling. Anti-homeless laws have proliferated as a solution to combat the public disorder associated with the homeless population. The next case, *State v. Boehler* (2011), highlights the tension between the activities of the homeless and the reach of the criminal law.

State v. Boehler (2011)

Court of Appeals of Arizona

262 P.3d 637

JOHNSEN, Judge. In this case we invalidate on First Amendment grounds a section of a Phoenix ordinance that bans panhandlers and other solicitors from orally asking passersby for cash after dark. We hold the measure is unconstitutional because it is not narrowly tailored to serve legitimate government interests. Accordingly, we reverse the convictions of three men cited for violating the ordinance by asking passersby for money after an evening baseball game in downtown Phoenix.

After receiving complaints about downtown panhandling, Phoenix police undertook an undercover program to enforce Phoenix City Code ("P.C.C.") section 23–7(B)(4), which makes it unlawful to vocally "solicit any money or other thing of value, or to solicit the sale of goods or services" after dark in a public area. P.C.C. § 23–7(B)(4) (2003). Timothy Boehler was sitting on a downtown sidewalk as undercover officers walked by after an Arizona Diamondbacks game, and he asked the officers if they could spare some change. Not far away, Frank Simpson approached two undercover officers on the street. He said to the officers, "I'm homeless, on the streets. Can you spare some change?" A short while later, officers walked past Clyde Davis, who was sitting on stairs leading to a public garage. Davis asked one of the officers, "Can you help me out? Can you spare some change?" None of the defendants followed, accosted or shouted at any passersby; there were no reports that any of them behaved aggressively or even impolitely.

The three defendants were convicted in municipal court of violating P.C.C. § 23–7(B)(4). They timely appealed to the superior court, challenging the constitutionality of the ordinance. Their cases were consolidated, and the superior court affirmed the convictions . . .

The defendants argue that on its face, the measure under which they were convicted is unconstitutionally overbroad, an issue we review de novo . . .

The first step in determining whether a law is impermissibly overbroad is to construe it. . . . In 1996, the Phoenix city council adopted Ordinance No. G–3954, amending P.C.C. § 23–7, to address what the council viewed as "the increase in aggressive solicitations throughout the city," which it found had "become extremely disturbing and disruptive to residents and businesses, and has contributed not only to the loss of access to and enjoyment of public places, but also to an enhanced sense of fear, intimidation and disorder." Phoenix, Ordinance No.G–3954 (Sept. 4, 1996). According to the city council, "aggressive solicitation usually includes approaching or following pedestrians, repetitive soliciting despite refusals, the use of abusive or profane language to cause fear and intimidation, unwanted physical contact, or the intentional obstruction of pedestrian traffic." Ordinance No.G–3954.

As enacted in 1996, the ordinance banned soliciting "in an aggressive manner in a public area." P.C.C. § 23–7(B)(1) (1996). It defined "solicit" as to request an immediate donation or exchange of money or other thing of value from another person, regardless of the solicitor's purpose or intended use of the money or other thing of value. The solicitation may be by spoken, written, or printed word, or by any other means of communication. Soliciting does not include requesting or accepting payment of the fare on a public transportation vehicle by the operator of the vehicle.

. . .

[A]s amended in 2003, the ordinance sweeps widely in several respects. It bans any vocal request in any public area after dark for an "immediate" donation, "regardless of the solicitor's purpose or intended use of the money." P.C.C. § 23–7(A)(6). Likewise prohibited is any vocal request made after dark for an "exchange of money or other thing of value." Id.

The ordinance's application in any "public area" undoubtedly implicates locations that are public forums, meaning "places which by long tradition or by government fiat have been devoted to assembly and debate." *Perry Educ. Ass'n v. Perry Local Educators' Ass'n*, 460 U.S. 37, 45, 103 S.Ct. 948, 74 L.Ed.2d 794 (1983). . . . When government seeks to regulate speech in a public forum based on the content of the speech, it "must show that its regulation is necessary to serve a compelling state interest and that it is narrowly drawn to achieve that end." *Perry*, 460 U.S. at 45. Even a content-neutral regulation of speech in a public forum may survive constitutional scrutiny only if it is "narrowly tailored to serve a significant government interest, and leave[s] open ample alternative channels of communication." Id.

. . .

As amended in 2003, the ordinance distinguishes between a vocal "solicitation" and other vocal speech. For example, a person standing on a street corner at 8 p.m. asking for cash contributions to a candidate's campaign could be cited for violating the ordinance, while one urging passersby to come to a rally to hear the same candidate speak would avoid citation. A person violates the ordinance by asking passersby after dark to donate change to a church fund for the poor; on the other hand, the ordinance does not apply to a sidewalk proselytizer— as long as he refrains from orally requesting donations. But the amended ordinance does not ban all solicitation. It permits written requests for in-hand donations after dark—under the ordinance, one may ask for spare change by silently holding a sign seeking donations. And, subject to other constraints, the ordinance allows oral requests for in-hand donations during daylight and imposes no time-of-day restrictions on oral requests for donations by mail.

. . .

. . . [E]ven if we assume the prohibition added to the Phoenix ordinance in 2003 is content-neutral, it cannot survive constitutional scrutiny. Under the First Amendment, the government may impose a content-neutral restriction on protected speech in a public forum only if the regulation is "narrowly tailored to serve a significant government interest, and leave[s] open ample alternative channels of communication." *Perry*, 460 U.S. at 45. We conclude the provision under which the defendants were cited fails that test because it is not narrowly tailored to serve a significant government interest.

An ordinance is narrowly tailored if it "promotes a substantial government interest that would be achieved less effectively absent the regulation" without burdening "substantially more speech than is necessary to further the government's legitimate interests." *Ward v. Rock Against Racism*, 491 U.S. 781, 799. . . . "Government may not regulate expression in such a manner that a substantial portion of the burden on speech does not serve to advance its goals." Id.

The State contends the 2003 amendment to the ordinance is designed to "shield citizens from the fear, intimidation, abusive language, or crime that sometimes accompany solicitation." It further argues that dangers associated with solicitation are "heightened at night, when darkness provides a cover for harassing or criminal conduct." . . .

(Continued)

(Continued)

The City of Phoenix of course has a significant interest in promoting safety in its public areas after dark. . . . The 2003 amendment to the solicitation ordinance, however, is not narrowly drawn to achieve that purpose.

. . . The 2003 amendment . . . bars any cash solicitation spoken after dark in any public area without regard to whether it is made in an abusive, aggressive or intimidating manner. It would prohibit both a cheery shout by a Salvation Army volunteer asking for holiday change and a quiet offer of a box of Girl Scout cookies by a shy pre-teen if either were uttered on a street corner after dark. See P.C.C. § 23–7(B)(4).

For this reason, the 2003 amendment is not "narrowly tailored" to advance the City's interest in sparing citizens from abusive, threatening or harassing acts by panhandlers or other solicitors at night. The pre–2003 ordinance already prohibited all manner of solicitation conducted in an offensive, aggressive or abusive manner; the 2003 amendment broadens the existing prohibition to apply regardless of whether a vocal solicitation is abusive, threatening or harassing. . . .

The State argues the prohibition added by the 2003 amendment is justified because vocal solicitations made in the dark of night are more likely to cause passersby to be fearful and intimidated. The 2003 amendment, however, does not distinguish between solicitations that occur in dark alleyways and solicitations that take place in lighted buildings or well-lit street corners. See P.C.C. § 23–7(A)(5), (B)(4).

Moreover, the ban cannot be justified by general concerns about the effect that even peaceful, non-aggressive requests for donations may have on passersby at night. Our constitution does not permit government to restrict speech in a public forum merely because the speech may make listeners uncomfortable. . . .

The State urges us to follow the Seventh Circuit's decision in *Gresham*, in which that court upheld a ban on vocal panhandling after dark because the prohibition applied in places "where [soliciting] is considered especially unwanted or bothersome" or where "people most likely would feel a heightened sense of fear or alarm, or might wish especially to be left alone." 225 F.3d at 906; see also *Smith*, 177 F.3d at 956–57 (total ban on panhandling on beach was permissible means of serving government interest in "safe, pleasant environment and eliminating nuisance activity on the beach"). We conclude that other portions of the Phoenix ordinance adequately address fearsome or alarming solicitations; as for the 2003 amendment, the First Amendment does not allow the City to restrict speech in a public forum merely because listeners might prefer not to hear a message that may annoy them or make them uneasy. . . .

In sum, the burden that P.C.C. § 23–7(B)(4) imposes on protected speech is not narrowly tailored to further the City's legitimate purpose. Because the defendants therefore were convicted in violation of the First Amendment to the United States Constitution, their convictions cannot stand.

. . .

For the reasons stated, we hold subsection (B)(4) of P.C.C. § 23–7, which prohibits certain vocal solicitations in any public area between sunset and sunrise, is unconstitutionally overbroad. We therefore reverse the defendants' convictions.

Questions

1. What are the prior proceedings in the case?

2. The court focuses on whether the ordinance was "narrowly tailored." What does this mean and how does the court evaluate this?

3. Assume that the defendants used gestures rather than words to ask for money. For example, what if they had rubbed their fingers together and pulled out the lining of their pants pockets in front of the officers? Do you think that activity would have been permissible or prohibited under the ordinance?

Alcohol Offenses

Alcohol-related offenses, such as driving under the influence, public drunkenness, violating open container laws, and the sale of alcohol to minors, are all public order offenses. Some are classified as misdemeanors while others are labeled as felonies. As a group, these laws respond to social concerns about the impact of alcohol on public behavior. In this section we examine laws that punish drunk driving, public drunkenness, and the sale of alcohol to minors.

Drunk Driving

Laws that punish someone for driving a vehicle while drunk have various names, such as driving under the influence (DUI), driving while intoxicated, driving while impaired (DWI), and operating while impaired (OWI), among others. States typically use a broad definition of vehicle. It may include automobiles, trucks, motorcycles, all-terrain vehicles, watercraft, and aircraft. In all fifty states and the District of Columbia, it is unlawful to operate a vehicle while under the influence of alcohol (or other drugs). Federal, state, and local laws vary as to the level of alcohol required to trigger criminal punishment. The general threshold for drunk driving is a driver with a blood alcohol level of .08 percent or higher. The punishment for drunk driving increases based upon the amount of alcohol found in the driver's bloodstream—the higher the blood alcohol level, the greater the sanction. In Florida, for instance, a person with a blood alcohol level of .10 percent who is convicted of drunk driving faces a maximum jail sentence of six months and a fine from five hundred to one thousand dollars. However, a person with a blood alcohol level of .15 percent who is convicted of drunk driving faces a maximum jail term of nine months and a fine between one and two thousand dollars.[16] In some cases, a person may be subject to an arrest and a fine for driving while impaired (not intoxicated). For instance, a person who is found to have a blood alcohol level of .02 may be convicted of driving while impaired—substantially lower than the amount necessary for a DUI conviction.

Public Drunkenness

In *Powell v. Texas* (1968),[17] the U.S. Supreme Court upheld state laws that punish public drunkenness. The defendant, Leroy Powell, was convicted under a Texas statute that made it unlawful to be drunk in a public place. He argued that he had chronic alcoholism, a disease, and that the conviction violated the Eighth Amendment's prohibition against cruel and unusual punishment. The court rejected the defendant's arguments and upheld the conviction and fine. The Supreme Court stated that the scientific findings were inconclusive as to whether alcoholism is a recognized disease. Today many jurisdictions make it unlawful to appear drunk in public. Here is an example from the Mississippi criminal code:

Mississippi's Profanity or Public Drunkenness Statute

If any person shall profanely swear or curse, or use vulgar and indecent language, or be drunk in any public place, in the presence of two (2) or more persons, he shall, on conviction thereof, be fined not more than one hundred dollars ($100.00) or be imprisoned in the county jail not more than thirty (30) days or both.[18]

Some states take a very different approach to handling public drunkenness. They treat public intoxication as a medical issue rather than a criminal justice problem. They reject the idea of using the criminal law to punish drinking or being drunk. This approach grew out of the recommendations from the Uniform Alcoholism and Intoxication Treatment Act, which concluded that states should decriminalize alcohol abuse.[19] States that adopt a medical model do sanction drunk driving—an action that endangers the lives of others beyond the drinker. Here is an example from South Dakota law:

South Dakota's Protective Custody of Intoxicated or Incapacitated Person Statute

Any person who appears to be intoxicated or incapacitated by the effects of alcohol or drugs and is clearly dangerous to the health and safety of himself or herself or others may be taken into protective custody by law enforcement authorities, acting with probable cause . . . If emergency commitment is not appropriate . . . the person may be detained as a patient in protective custody until no longer intoxicated or up to forty-eight hours after admission.[20]

As indicated, the Mississippi and South Dakota laws reveal a difference in approach to public intoxication. Under the Mississippi law, the emphasis is on removing the drunken person from a public place. By contrast, South Dakota law focuses on both the harm a drunken person could cause others and on how to prevent an intoxicated person from causing herself harm.

Sale of Alcohol to Minors

In 1984, Congress passed the National Minimum Drinking Age Act. The act required states to adopt twenty-one as the legal age for alcohol purchase and possession. States are motivated to comply with the federal law—or face loss of federal funds for highways. All fifty states are in compliance, and each one has its own laws regarding the sale of alcohol to minors. The sale of alcohol to a minor can result in stiff fines for the business and in some cases, criminal penalties for the individual employee who made the sale. In Ohio, for instance, the sale of intoxicating liquor to a minor is punishable by up to six months in jail and a fine. However, in some states, a store employee is not responsible if a minor uses false identification to represent himself as being old enough to purchase alcohol. In South Dakota, for instance, a person under the age of twenty-one who uses fake identification to purchase alcohol faces a fine, a jail sentence, and a suspension of driving privileges.[21]

While the laws are uniform on the prohibition against alcohol for minors, some commentators point to the paradox of eighteen year olds being eligible to fight in wars and vote, but not being old enough to legally drink. Medical research, however, has found that alcohol consumption has a particularly harmful impact on brain development in young people. Alcohol use may cause impaired memory, impede rational thinking, increase learning difficulties, and increase later risk of developing mental health problems.

Gun-Related Offenses

The nature of the violent act has changed from the fist, stick, and knife to the gun.

Geoffrey Canada (1995)

Gun-related violence is a staple of the nightly news. Guns are often at the center of mass killings, such as the massacres at the Newtown, Connecticut, elementary school where children were beginning their school day; the Aurora, Colorado, theater where it was opening night for the latest Batman movie; the Oak Creek, Wisconsin, Sikh Temple where people were worshipping; and the Tucson, Arizona, Safeway store where Congresswoman Gabrielle Giffords was holding a public meeting. At the same time, gun violence, such as gang-related crime and domestic violence, continue to plague communities across the country, particularly large cities. In 2011, there were over eleven thousand fatal firearm incidents and four hundred thousand nonfatal firearm incidents in the United States. Today, the percentage of U.S. homes with guns is approximately 34 percent. This is a steep decline from the 1970s and 1980s when it reached a high of 50 percent of U.S. households.[22]

Surveys indicate that the majority of Americans support the right to gun ownership and do not favor increased restrictions on gun ownership. In *McDonald v. Chicago* (2010),[23] the Supreme Court upheld the constitutionality of gun ownership. The Court struck down an ordinance that made it unlawful for residents to have handguns in their homes. The law banning firearms was designed to protect residents from loss of life or property. The Court held that there is a constitutional right to gun ownership under the Second Amendment. The *McDonald* decision extends the Court's earlier decision in *District of Columbia v. Heller* (2008) to all fifty states (see Chapter 2 for a more detailed discussion of the *Heller* decision and the Second Amendment).

Concealed Weapons

The question of whether citizens can carry concealed weapons is a major issue. Approximately eight million Americans have concealed carry permits. Today all fifty states permit residents to apply for a license to carry a concealed weapon—for example, a handgun, a tear gas gun, or an electronic device—in public.[24]

Stand Your Ground Laws

The relationship between concealed weapons laws and self-defense laws such as Florida's stand your ground law came under intense scrutiny following the killing of Trayvon Martin in 2012. Martin, a sixteen-year-old African American youth, was returning to his father's home from a convenience store when he was followed by George Zimmerman, a twenty-eight-year-old Hispanic man. Zimmerman, the president of the Neighborhood Watch Association, believed Martin was "up to no good" and continued to follow him, even though he was instructed not to by the 911 operator. Zimmerman, following an encounter with Martin, shot and killed him. Immediately following Martin's death, Zimmerman was taken into custody, questioned, and released. He was not charged until forty-six days later, following a groundswell of public interest in the case, rallies around the country, and newspaper editorials.[25] At trial, the jury acquitted Zimmerman of second degree murder charges in Martin's death. At the time of the killing, Zimmerman had a permit to carry a concealed weapon (for more detail on the Zimmerman case, see Chapter 9).The case raised numerous social, political, and criminological issues, including racial profiling, stand your ground legislation, interracial crime, gun violence, and the criminalized images of young, Black men.

Another Florida case made international headlines in 2014. This case involved a shooting death at a movie theater. Curtis Reeves, a seventy-one-year old a retired sheriff's deputy, became agitated when another movie patron, Chad Oulson, seated in the row in front of him, began to text during the previews. After the two exchanged words, Reeves left the theater and returned a short time later. He again insisted that Oulson stop texting on his phone. At one point, Oulson began to throw popcorn at Reeves. Reeves pulled out his pistol and shot Oulson in the chest, killing him. Reeves, who had a Florida license to carry a concealed weapon, told authorities that he felt threatened after being hit with an unknown object (a bag of popcorn). He was charged with second degree murder. Reeves' attempt to claim a stand your ground defense was rejected by the state attorney's office.

Guns on Campus

In recent years, there has been a spate of incidents involving mass shootings at schools. Many have taken place at a college or university. In a 2010 report, the Federal Bureau of Investigation (FBI) found that between 2005 and 2008 there were almost three hundred campus incidents that resulted in death, and the majority of these cases involved the use of a firearm.[26] Another report found that in 2013 there were twenty-seven shootings on or near college campuses. The list includes shootings at the Massachusetts Institute of Technology, University of Maryland, Santa Monica College, New River Community College, Howard University, and Elizabeth City State University.[27] In response, politicians and organizations have called for firearm-free zones around institutions of higher learning.

The actions of Florida Carry, a gun rights group, have brought this debate to a head in Florida. The group has sued several universities in the state, arguing that university regulations prohibiting firearms on campus violate the Second Amendment. A Florida appeals court agreed that a state cannot make it unlawful for students to keep a loaded gun in their vehicles parked on campus. Those who support increasing firearms regulations argue that more guns on college campuses will lead to more gun-related violence. At some point, the courts will determine whether dormitory rooms are entitled to the same protection as homes under the Second Amendment. (See Chapter 2 for a more detailed discussion of the Second Amendment).

Control and Protection of Animals

As early as the mid-1640s, legal protections were extended to animals. One of these laws prevented "tirrany or crueltie [sic]" towards animals.[28] In the late 1700s, Jeremy Bentham, an English lawyer and philosopher, was among the first scholars to address the legal treatment of animals. He made a compelling case that animals deserve legal protection. In a noted passage, Bentham observed, "The question is not, 'Can they reason?' Nor, 'Can they talk?' But 'Can they suffer?'"[29] In 1866, the American Society for the Prevention of Cruelty to Animals (ASPCA) was founded in the United States. The organization works to pass legislation to protect animals from abuse. Today a variety of federal and state laws regulate the treatment of domestic and wild animals. These laws punish a range of offenses, including less serious ones such as leash laws and more serious offenses such as cruelty or abandonment of animals.

Leash Laws

Not so long ago, it was common to see dogs, with or without collars, trotting about on public streets, sometimes alone and sometimes with other dogs. Dog owners let them go outside to "do their business" and return home when done.

However, concerns for public safety increased as more cases involving dog attacks received publicity and as pit bulls became more popular as domestic pets. There was also rising concern that free-roaming animals could themselves be harmed. They could be hit by a car, for example, or they could cause a driver to have an accident while trying to avoid a collision with the animal. The public and legal response to these concerns was to increase regulations. Today, leash laws, which impose requirements on animal owners, are common in states, counties, and municipalities. Tennessee, for instance, makes it a misdemeanor offense for a dog to go "uncontrolled by the owner upon a highway, public road, street or any other place open to the public generally."[30] The rise in the number of dog parks is another response to laws that require pet owners to take more responsibility for their animals in public spaces.

Animal Cruelty

There is no official database that tracks incidents of animal abuse. Thus, the number of annual incidents is unknown. Across the fifty states, the District of Columbia, and U.S. territories, animal cruelty is a criminal offense. Based on the harm, animal cruelty may be punished as a misdemeanor or as a felony offense when the harm is particularly malicious. Notably, many incidents of animal cruelty (maiming and killing) are committed in conjunction with acts of domestic violence. Under some state criminal codes, these acts are accorded felony status. Animal cruelty laws also punish both overexertion and neglect. Below is an excerpt from the District of Columbia code:

District of Columbia's Animal Cruelty Code

Whoever knowingly overdrives, overloads . . . overworks, tortures, torments, deprives of necessary sustenance, cruelly chains, cruelly beats or mutilates, any animal, or knowingly causes or procures any animal to be so overdriven . . . and whoever, having the charge or custody of any animal . . . knowingly inflicts unnecessary cruelty . . . or unnecessarily fails to provide the same with proper food, drink, air, light, space, veterinary care, shelter, or protection from the weather, shall for every such offense be punished by imprisonment in jail not exceeding 180 days, or by fine not exceeding $250, or by both.[31]

In addition to the penalties stated above, a court may require that someone convicted of animal cruelty obtain psychological counseling, forfeit their rights to own or possess animals, or to repay any costs incurred for the care of the harmed animal. Animal cruelty may be punished under criminal laws or civil laws.

The Model Penal Code (MPC) is widely relied upon as a resource and template for state criminal codes. However, the MPC has not revised its cruelty to animals section since its initial publication in 1962. While many states follow the MPC guidelines and treat animal abuse as a public order misdemeanor, others as noted above classify animal abuse as a serious criminal offense.[32] The animal abuse case involving professional football player Michael Vick is an example. This case, which attracted international attention, is highlighted below.

Blueag9

Michael Vick, NFL quarterback

Dogfighting: The Case of Michael Vick

In 2006, NFL star-player Michael Vick was indicted on charges that he sponsored a dogfighting business, Bad Newz Kennels. This highly publicized case brought out animal rights advocates and those who believed Vick was being used as a scapegoat. Vick pled guilty to a felony charge of underwriting a dogfighting ring. The ring resulted in the deaths of at least six dogs. In 2007, he was sentenced to twenty-three months in federal prison and suspended indefinitely from the NFL. After serving his sentence, Vick was released by the Atlanta Falcons and later hired by the Philadelphia Eagles and the New York Jets.

The next case, *Commonwealth of Pennsylvania v. Craven* (2003), raises old and new issues. As a society, how far should our laws go to discourage activity involving animal cruelty? Should people who witness animal cruelty face criminal liability?

Commonwealth of Pennsylvania v. Craven (2003)

Supreme Court of Pennsylvania

572 Pa. 431

Justice NIGRO. The issue before the Court in this consolidated appeal is whether the trial court properly determined that 18 Pa.C.S. § 5511(h.1)(6), which criminalizes an individual's attendance at an animal fight "as a spectator," is unconstitutionally vague and overbroad. As we conclude that the statute is constitutionally sound, we reverse.

On June 26, 1999, two Pittsburgh police officers, Officer Nicholas Uva and Officer Eric Churilla, were on routine patrol in the Ferrywood section of Pittsburgh when they noticed three men standing near a sport utility vehicle with the tailgate open. As they neared the vehicle, the officers could see a dog crate that appeared to be full of blood. The officers approached the three men, later identified as Appellee Erik Craven, Appellee Otis Townsend, and William Tench, to see if there was an injured dog to which they could offer any assistance. Tench told the officers that his dog had broken loose and fought with another dog. The officers then heard whimpering sounds from a nearby garage and asked Tench if he owned the garage. Tench responded that the garage was owned by

his cousin, but that his cousin had given him permission to use it. Officer Uva then asked Tench if he could conduct a search and Tench consented. At that point, three more men, later identified as Marvin Howard, John Moran, and Phillip Worthy, emerged from the garage and joined Craven, Townsend, and Tench.

Officer Uva entered the garage and traced the whimpering to another dog crate, in which he found a pit bull terrier bleeding from lacerations and bite wounds. Officer Uva also noticed equipment commonly used to train dogs for fighting. After making these observations, Officer Uva exited the garage and asked Tench where he could find the other dog from the fight. Tench said that the dog was in another vehicle parked directly in front of the sports utility vehicle. Upon looking into the second vehicle, Officer Uva found another pit bull terrier covered by a towel. The dog was lethargic and its breathing was labored.

The officers then asked the men for identification before they seized both vehicles, finding a video camera and two videotapes. One videotape contained two recorded dogfights and the other videotape contained commercials/endorsements for dogs that participated in such fights. Appellees Craven and Townsend were clearly seen on the videotapes during the dogfights, standing above the fighting ring with their arms crossed, watching the fight. N.T., 8/12/99, at 38–42 (identifying Townsend and Craven as spectators at dogfights). See also Videotape of Dogfights, Exhibit B, Motions Hearing, 3/9/2000. Based on their attendance at the dogfight, Appellees were charged with one count of cruelty to animals and one count of criminal conspiracy.

Although the Commonwealth stipulated that there was no evidence that Appellees paid a fee to view the dogfights, it nonetheless contended that Appellees were guilty under subsection six of the animal cruelty statute, which provides, in relevant part:

> Animal fighting-A person commits a felony of the third degree if he: pays for admission to an animal fight or attends an animal fight as a spectator.

18 Pa.C.S. § 5511(h.1)(6). Craven filed a petition for a writ of habeas corpus, asserting that Subsection 5511(h.1)(6) is unconstitutionally vague and overbroad. The trial court agreed, finding that Subsection 5511(h.1)(6) fails to place ordinary individuals on notice as to what conduct violates that part of the statute. According to the trial court, Subsection 5511(h.1)(6) imposes criminal liability upon an individual merely for being present at the scene of an animal fight and by doing so, the subsection "seeks to eliminate a mens rea requirement for culpability and to impose strict liability" for mere presence at the scene of such a fight. Trial Ct. Op. at 9. We disagree.

A statute is presumed constitutional and will not be declared unconstitutional unless it "clearly, palpably and plainly" violates the Constitution. *Commonwealth v. Barud*, 545 Pa. 297, 681 A.2d 162, 165 (1996) (quoting *Commonwealth v. Mikulan*, 504 Pa. 244, 470 A.2d 1339, 1340 (1983)). All doubts are therefore to be resolved in favor of a finding of constitutionality. *Commonwealth v. Hendrickson*, 555 Pa. 277, 724 A.2d 315, 317 (1999). A statute will only be found to be void for vagueness if it fails to define unlawful conduct with sufficient definiteness so that ordinary people understand what conduct is prohibited. Id. at 319 . . . At the same time, a statute will only be deemed to be overbroad if it punishes a substantial amount of constitutionally protected conduct. Id. at 317–18.

Here, the trial court concluded that Subsection 5511(h.1)(6) was unconstitutional because it criminalizes one's mere presence at an animal fight. The statute, however, does no such thing. Rather, under its plain language, the statute only criminalizes attendance at an animal fight "as a spectator." 18 Pa.C.S. § 5511(h.1)(6). Webster's Dictionary defines "spectator" as "one that looks on or beholds; [especially] one witnessing an exhibition (as a sports event)." Webster's Third New International Dictionary Unabridged 2188 (1993). "Presence," on the other hand, is defined as "the state or being in one place and not elsewhere[;] the fact of being in company, attendance, or association." Id. at 1793. The two are clearly distinct. A spectator does more than a person who is merely present at a particular place by happenstance, since a spectator, by definition, makes a conscious choice to view and witness an exhibition. Thus, contrary to the trial court's finding, Subsection 5511(h.1)(6), like all of the other subsections in Section 5511(h.1) of the animal cruelty statute, does "indicate a conscious and knowing activity by the individual committing [the] crime." Trial Ct. Op. at 10. We therefore conclude that Subsection 5511(h.1)(6) is neither unconstitutionally vague nor overbroad as it does not, as the trial court found, impose strict liability on a person merely for being present at a dogfight. Rather, it criminalizes a person's conscious decision to attend an illegal animal fight as a spectator and by doing so, puts individuals on sufficient notice as to what conduct is proscribed.

The Michigan Court of Appeals reached a similar conclusion in *People v. Cumper*, 83 Mich.App. 490, 268 N.W.2d 696 (1978), where the defendants were charged with violating Michigan's animal cruelty statute, which makes it illegal to, inter alia, "be present as a spectator" at a dogfight. In rejecting the defendants' claim that this part of the statute was unconstitutionally vague and overbroad, the court explained:

It is apparent that the statute does not punish the witnessing of a dogfight per se. It punishes attendance as a spectator at an event legitimately prohibited by law. It is neither vague nor overbroad. The accused had fair notice of the conduct proscribed. Id. at 698.

As we likewise hold that Subsection 5511(h.1)(6) of Pennsylvania's animal cruelty statute is not unconstitutionally vague or overbroad, we reverse the trial court's order finding otherwise and remand the matter for proceedings consistent with this opinion.

(Continued)

(Continued)

Questions

1. Which constitutional issue(s) are raised in the case?

2. How does the court determine whether Mr. Craven was a spectator or someone who was present at a dogfight?

3. Review the Pennsylvania statute and determine how each person would be classified—as either a "spectator" or as someone who was "present" at a dogfight:

   a. A person selling hotdogs at a dogfight.

   b. A person standing over the boxing ring with his arms crossed and eyes closed.

   c. A person who is sitting ringside at a dogfight and is sending text messages.

Crimes Against Public Decency ●━━━━━━━━━━━━━━━

There is a tie that binds public order offenses and crimes against public decency. It is the idea that activity in our public spaces and in our private lives should reflect our social and moral beliefs and promote safety and security. However, the actions that constitute public order crimes differ from the actions that constitute crimes against public decency. The key distinction is that crimes against decency usually take place away from public view, unlike public order offenses.

For many people, hackles are raised at the idea that the criminal law punishes activity engaged in by consenting adults. Some people argue that public decency offenses such as prostitution, adultery, and sodomy are examples of government overreaching—the government going outside the scope of what it should punish. For centuries, legal philosophers have debated how far the law should be reach to punish offenses involving morality. British Judge Patrick Devlin observed, "[S]ociety cannot ignore the morality of the individual any more than it can his loyalty."[33] A contrary view was highlighted by the 1957 Wolfenden Report.[34] It concluded that "there must remain a realm of private morality and immorality which is, in brief and crude terms, not the law's business."[35]

This section highlights several public decency offenses. It includes a look at how each one is defined and the elements of the crime.

"Victimless" Crimes

Sodomy, fornication, adultery, bigamy, and nudity are among the offenses classified as victimless crimes. These offenses against public decency are sometimes called victimless because they involve the actions of consenting adults. The label is rejected by those who argue that if there is a crime, there is a victim. Many of the offenses that fall under crimes against public decency involve sexual acts.

Sodomy

Antisodomy laws reserve particular types of sexual conduct for criminal sanction. These laws have typically been enforced against gay couples. *Bowers v. Hardwick* (1986)[36] involved a challenge to a Georgia statute that outlawed anal and oral sex in private between consenting adults. Michael Hardwick and another man were charged with violating the law after they were observed engaging in anal sex in Mr. Hardwick's bedroom. On appeal, the U.S. Supreme Court upheld the conviction and stated that there is no constitutional right to engage in sodomy. Seventeen years later, the Supreme Court reversed course and struck down an antisodomy law as unconstitutional. *Lawrence v. Texas* (2003)[37] involved a challenge to a Texas law that prohibited "deviate sexual intercourse" between members of the same sex. In a six to three decision, the Court held that sex between consenting adult males is protected under the Fourteenth Amendment's due process clause.

Fornication

Over the centuries, laws have been enacted to permit, regulate, or prohibit sexual relationships between consenting adults based on their relationship status. For instance, there are laws that criminalize (and hence discourage) sex between unmarried people. Although they are largely unenforceable, these laws still remain on the books in some states. For instance, in *Martin v. Ziherl*,[38] a 2005 case, a defendant challenged a Virginia law that made it a misdemeanor for an unmarried person to have sexual intercourse with another person.[39] Under the law, which had not been enforced in over two hundred years, violators could be fined up to $250. The Virginia Supreme Court invalidated the statute after the U.S. Supreme Court's *Lawrence v. Texas* (2003) decision.

John Lawrence and Tyron Garner. The Texas sodomy law that they were convicted of violating was overturned by the U.S. Supreme Court.

AP Photo/DAVID J. PHILLIP

Adultery

Laws prohibiting sex outside of marriage date back to the days of the Old Testament. Laws against adultery punished women, who were men's chattel, for adulterating, or poisoning a husband's bloodline by having another man's child. Though public attitudes toward a spouse who has sex outside of her marriage are more liberal than in the past, many state and local laws do not reflect these changes. Today in almost one-half of all states, adultery is a crime, typically a misdemeanor. Under Maryland law, for example, adultery is a misdemeanor offense, subject to a ten dollar fine.[40] In a handful of states—Idaho, Massachusetts, Michigan, Oklahoma, and Wisconsin— adultery is a felony. Under Oklahoma law, a person found guilty of committing adultery may be fined five hundred dollars and sentenced up to five years in prison.[41] West Virginia's bigamy statute allows for a five-year maximum sentence. Adultery is socially condemned, but is rarely prosecuted as a criminal offense. Here is the Idaho legislation, notable for its sweeping language:

Idaho's Adultery Statute

A married man who has sexual intercourse with a woman not his wife, an unmarried man who has sexual intercourse with a married woman, a married woman who has sexual intercourse with a man not her husband, and an unmarried woman who has sexual intercourse with a married man, shall be guilty of adultery, and shall be punished by a fine of not less than $100, or by imprisonment in the county jail for not less than three months, or by imprisonment in the state penitentiary for a period not exceeding three years, or in the county jail for a period not exceeding one year, or by fine not exceeding $1,000.[42]

The Idaho law punishes married people who engage in sex outside of their marriage, as well as unmarried people who engage in sex with married people. It treats the actions of men and women equally, sanctioning the behavior whether it is engaged in by a married man or by a married woman. It also punishes both an unmarried woman who sleeps with a married man and an unmarried man who sleeps with a married woman. However, the statute does not punish someone who is married and engages in same sex intercourse outside of marriage.

Bigamy and Polygamy

All states prohibit someone from being married to more than one person at one time. Bigamy and polygamy are classified as public order offenses. These laws have been challenged on religious grounds. As early as 1878, the U.S. Supreme Court ruled that states can outlaw polygamy, marriage to more than one person, without infringing upon religious freedom.[43] This issue resurfaced in 2012 when the Sister Wives, a group of four women, challenged Utah's bigamy law. Kody Brown and the women are fundamentalist Mormons. One of the women is legally married to Brown. The other women live under the same roof and also refer to themselves as wives of Brown. Utah law makes it unlawful for someone to attempt to marry or cohabit with an already married person. In 2013, a judge struck down parts of the Utah law after determining that they violated the First Amendment's protection of religious freedom (see Chapter 2). The court also decided that Utah may outlaw multiple marriages.

Nudity and Public Indecency

Public nudity straddles the line between being an offense against morality and being a public order offense. Unlike sodomy, adultery, fornication, and bigamy, public nudity takes place beyond the private sphere. It is also an offense that most people agree should be unlawful. How far should the law reach to punish public indecency? The next case, *Whatley v. State* (1999), asks the court to define "public place."

Whatley v. State (1999)

Court of Appeals of Indiana

No.36A05–9806-CR-307

When a motor carrier inspector found Craig E. Whatley completely nude in the cab of his semi-trailer truck he was arrested for and ultimately found guilty of public indecency as a Class A misdemeanor. He now appeals raising three issues for our review which we consolidate into two and rephrase as follows: (1) is the cab of a semi-trailer truck a public place within the meaning of the public indecency statute, and (2) was the evidence sufficient to sustain the conviction.

We affirm.

Whatley is an independent operator who owns a semi-trailer truck equipped with a sleeping berth. On September

11, 1997, Whatley was driving his semi northbound on Interstate 65 when he pulled into a weigh station east of Seymour, Indiana. A state police motor carrier inspector approached the semi to check whether the driver was wearing a seat belt or in possession of a radar detector, firearms, or drugs. The inspector asked Whatley to open the door to his cab. He did so and the inspector observed that Whatley was completely nude. . When asked why he was nude, Whatley replied that he was in too big a hurry to get dressed. The inspector shut down the scales, called for backup assistance, and redirected traffic. Ultimately Whatley was arrested for and charged with public indecency. After a bench trial he was found guilty as charged. This appeal followed.

Ind.Code § 35–45–4-1(a) provides in pertinent part: "[a] person who knowingly or intentionally, in a public place: (1) engages in sexual intercourse; (2) engages in deviate sexual conduct; (3) appears in a state of nudity; or (4) fondles the person's genitals or the genitals of another person; commits public indecency, a Class A misdemeanor." Characterizing his truck as a "home on wheels" Whatley argues that he was not in a public place within the meaning of the statute. In *Long* [*v. State*, 666 N.E.2d 1258 (Ind. Ct.App. 1996)], a case involving public indecency, we held "a public place is any place where members of the public are free to go without restraint." Id. at 1261. According to Whatley his semi was not a public place because "'members of the public' did not enter and exit or congregate within the cabin of his rig." Brief of Appellant at 8.

"Public place" is defined neither by the public indecency statute nor by the public intoxication statute. However on numerous occasions in the context of public intoxication we have defined public place consistent with the definition in Long . . .

We acknowledge that one's vehicle may indeed be a "home on wheels" and thus under some circumstances riding in the buff presents no violation of law. . . . However, we have no hesitation concluding that a person driving a semi-trailer truck on this state's highways is in a public place, that is, a place where members of the public are free to go without restraint. Whatley's argument on this point fails.

Whatley next contends the evidence was insufficient to sustain his conviction. Whatley concedes that he "appeare[d] in a state of nudity." He argues however that he was observed only because of the inspector's command to open his cab door. Whatley also argues that he did not knowingly

or intentionally commit a violation of law; rather he merely showed a lapse of good judgment. Our standard of review is well settled. When reviewing a claim of insufficient evidence we do not reweigh evidence or judge witness credibility. *Nield v. State*, 677 N.E.2d 79, 81 (Ind.Ct.App.1997). Rather, we consider only the evidence favorable to the verdict and any reasonable inferences to be drawn therefrom. Id. Contrary to Whatley's assertion it is not the observation of his nudity that the statute proscribes. Rather the prohibition is against Whatley's appearance in a public place in a state of nudity. The observation is simply evidence of that which occurred. As for Whatley's second claim, the law presumes that a person intends the consequences of his act. *Austin v. State*, 425 N.E.2d 736, 738 (Ind.Ct.App.1981). Further, whether conduct is "knowingly" and "intentionally" performed may be inferred from the voluntary commission of the prohibited act as well as from the surrounding circumstances. *Carty v. State*, 421 N.E.2d 1151, 1155 (Ind.Ct.App.1981). In this case the evidence of record is sufficient to show that Whatley knowingly and intentionally appeared in a public place in a state of nudity.

Judgment affirmed.

Questions

1. What is the issue in this case?

2. What is the court's rationale for upholding the state law?

3. The court states that in some instances it would be lawful for a person to ride naked in his "home on wheels." What if Mr. Whatley had been nude in his truck parked in his driveway? What about in his truck parked on a busy street? Should the time of day matter?

The *Whatley* case addresses the issue of public versus private nudity. Some cities and counties have been forced to address a more direct issue: Should people be allowed to walk around without clothing? It is commonplace for cities and counties to ban public nudity. Some city ordinances focus on general nudity in public places. A 2013 decision by the San Francisco Board of Supervisors provides an interesting case in point.

Nudists were riding subways and buses without pants. Some nudists spent time lounging in city plazas. Businesses complained that nudists were harming business, especially for stores considered "family friendly." In a close vote, the Board of Supervisors passed an ordinance that banned nudity in public. Although ordinances are a step below misdemeanors in terms of punishment, the Board of Supervisors' vote sent

Naked people walk in downtown San Francisco before the city passed a ban on public nudity.

a clear message about nudity. The law prohibits nudity on the streets, on sidewalks, in transit stations, and in vehicles. A first offense can result in a hundred dollar fine. The ordinance does not apply to children under the age of five and parade participants who have a permit.

Cities have adopted ordinances to address specific types of indecent exposure, such as sexually explicit nudity—epitomized by the *Girls Gone Wild* videos. In response to public displays of nudity during spring break, an annual ritual for thousands of college students, some cities have sought, with mixed results, to ban bare breasts.

Prostitution and Pandering

Sometimes referred to as the "world's oldest profession," prostitution—the selling of sexual services—has had a varied history. Over the centuries, it has been treated as a socially acceptable fact of life, as constituting a high moral offense that contributes to the decline in the social fabric, and as a crime with no victims. In contemporary times, prostitution has come under further scrutiny as the public has become more aware of the prevalence of human sexual trafficking and the high percentage of children forced into the sex trade. As a consequence, prostitution is increasingly considered a serious crime and not simply an offense against morality.[44] With the exception of certain counties in Nevada, states punish people who engage in sex for pay, both the sellers and buyers. Other key players in the sex trade are people who pander, bribe, or force others to sell sexual services. These actions—pimping—are criminal. Next we discuss the case *People v. Zambia* (2011), an example of how the Supreme Court of California analyzes the state's pandering law.

People v. Zambia (2011)

Supreme Court of California

51 Cal. 4th 965

Defendant Jomo Zambia was convicted of pandering in violation of Penal Code section 266i, subdivision (a)(2), which defines pandering as encouraging "another person to become" a prostitute. Here, the target of defendant's encouragement was an undercover police officer. He contends that section 266i, subdivision (a)(2) does not apply when the target is already a prostitute or an undercover police officer acting as one. The trial and appellate court rejected this argument. We affirm.

On June 8, 2007, Officer Erika Cruz was working undercover as a street prostitute in Los Angeles. Defendant drove past her, looked in her direction, made a U-turn, and stopped about 15 feet across the street from her.

Defendant lowered his window and told Cruz to get into his truck. When Cruz asked why, defendant said he was a pimp. The officer told him to back up so they could talk. As he did so, Cruz called Officer Paschal, her "security officer" to report that she was possibly "working a pimp."

Standing by the defendant's open passenger-side window, Officer Cruz saw cell phones on the truck's center console. Defendant again told her to get in the truck, repeating that he was a pimp. Cruz asked what defendant meant. He said that he would "take care of [her]" and asked how much money she had in her possession. Hearing that she had $400, defendant said if she gave the money to him, he would provide her with housing and clothing.

Officer Cruz hesitated, telling defendant she was not comfortable. Defendant told her he was a legitimate businessman, showed her a business card, and said he would not "strong-arm" her, which Cruz understood to mean to take her money by force. Cruz testified that defendant used an aggressive tone of voice and demeanor. She characterized him as acting like a [type of pimp] who uses "verbal threats and violence to get their way and to scare prostitutes into working for them." Cruz asked defendant if she could continue to work the same neighborhood. Defendant told her she could and that he would "just take care of [her]."

At this point, Officer Cruz alerted her backup unit. Defendant was arrested and charged with one count of pandering. (§ 266i, subd. (a)(2).)

In addition to Officer Cruz's testimony summarized above, Officer Paschal testified that pimps commonly provide condoms to their prostitutes, and use multiple cell phones to contact them. When she arrested defendant, Paschal found cell phones, condoms, and a business card on the truck's console . . .

Defendant did not testify. His mother testified that he lived at her home and worked in her family-owned janitorial business. Defendant would usually work between 6:00 p.m. and 12:30 a.m. He carried one working mobile phone, but also had a broken one in his car, along with a third that he had borrowed from a friend. She explained that defendant was clumsy and often broke his phones. She recognized two of the three phones found in defendant's vehicle as well as defendant's business card from the family business.

Defendant's fiancée testified that his work hours varied, but that he would often return to his jobsite to pick up equipment in the early morning. She recognized the three cell phones found in defendant's truck, and had no reason to believe defendant was a pimp.

Defendant was convicted by jury and sentenced to four years in prison. The Court of Appeal affirmed.

. . .

At issue here is the proper construction of section 266i, subdivision (a)(2), which provides in pertinent part that any person who "[b]y promises, threats, violence, or by any device or scheme, causes, induces, persuades, or encourages another person to become a prostitute" is guilty of pandering.

"In construing any statute, we first look to its language. [Citation.] 'Words used in a statute . . . should be given the meaning they bear in ordinary use. [Citations].

. . .

Defendant argues that section 266i, subdivision (a)(2)'s phrase "to become a prostitute" does not include encouraging a person who is already a prostitute, or is

posing as one. The People argue that the better view is that "to become a prostitute" means to "engage in any future acts of prostitution," regardless of the victim's status at the time of a defendant's encouragement.

With a single exception, an unbroken line of cases, beginning with *People v. Bradshaw* (1973) 31 Cal.App.3d 421 (*Bradshaw*), has rejected defendant's argument . . .

. . . .

The interpretation urged by defendant could also lead to mischievous and potentially absurd results. (See *City of Poway v. City of San Diego, supra,* 229 Cal.App.3d at p. 858.) Trial court and appellate inquiry might be required to tease out just who might qualify as an "active prostitute." Would the defense be available only if the pimp's overture was made while his target was actually engaged in soliciting? Would people qualify as active prostitutes only if that was their sole occupation, or would occasional resort to prostitution be sufficient? Would it make a difference if the prostitute also had legitimate employment? Would a hiatus of weeks or months transform an "active prostitute" into a former or inactive one? There is nothing in the legislative history or decades of case law that even remotely suggests an intent to raise these esoteric inquiries.

The language of the pandering statute describes current conduct on the part of the defendant: inducing and encouraging. That current conduct is aimed at producing subsequent conduct by the target: that the target thereafter engage in acts of prostitution following a defendant's inducement or encouragement. To encourage an established prostitute to change her business relationship necessarily implies that a defendant intends a victim "to become a prostitute" in the future regardless of her current status. We also think it safe to say that someone who encourages another to become a prostitute is seldom giving disinterested advice about a possible career path . . .

It is also significant that section 266i has been amended six times since *Bradshaw* was decided in 1973, without any attempt by the Legislature to alter the interpretation set out above. "When a statute has been construed by the courts, and the Legislature thereafter reenacts that statute without changing the interpretation put on that statute by the courts, the Legislature is presumed to have been aware of, and acquiesced in, the courts' construction of that statute." (*People v. Bouzas* (1991) 53 Cal.3d 467, 475.) . . .

. . .

Considering subdivision (a)(2) in the context of the other provisions of the statute reveals that the intent and purpose behind section 266i, subdivision (a)(2) is to prohibit a person from encouraging a prostitute to work under his

(Continued)

(Continued)

aegis or that of someone else, regardless whether the target being solicited is already a working prostitute.

. . .

Defendant's reasoning rests on the flawed "assumption that the Legislature was concerned only with actual, rather than potential, harm." (*Patton, supra,* 63 Cal.App.3d at p. 218.) "[T]he relevant social policy question is the potential for harm which defendant's conduct reveals. A substantial potential for social harm is revealed even by the act of encouraging an established prostitute to alter her business relations. Such conduct indicates a present willingness to actively promote the social evil of prostitution." (*Ibid.*) As noted, the Legislature intended section 266i to "cover all the various ramifications of the social evil of pandering and include them all in the definition of the crime, with a view of effectively combating the evil sought to be condemned." (*Hashimoto, supra,* 54 Cal.App.3d at p. 866, quoting *People v. Montgomery, supra,* 47 Cal.App.2d at p. 24.)

. . .

We clarify here that pandering is a specific intent crime. Its commission requires that a defendant intends to persuade or otherwise influence the target "to become a prostitute" as that phrase has been interpreted here. This construction of section 266i, subdivision (a)(2) effectuates the purpose and intent of the pandering statute, which is to criminalize the *knowing and purposeful* conduct of any person seeking to encourage "another person" to work with the panderer or another pimp in plying the prostitution trade. The long-standing and broader construction of the phrase "encourages another person *to become a prostitute*" places the focus on the defendant's unlawful actions and intent, rather than making the targeted victim's character or occupation the determinative factors for conviction.

. . .

Accordingly we conclude that the proscribed activity of encouraging someone "to become a prostitute," as set forth in section 266i, subdivision (a)(2), includes encouragement of someone who is already an active prostitute, or undercover police officer. . . .

We also reject defendant's contention that there was insufficient evidence that he encouraged anyone to become a prostitute. Officer Cruz testified that defendant offered his services as a pimp by telling her he would provide her with protection, housing, and clothing if she turned her earnings over to him. Defendant twice identified himself as a pimp, assured Officer Cruz that she could continue to work in the same area, and promised that he would "take care of [her]." The evidence was sufficient and supports the judgment.

The Court of Appeal's judgment is affirmed. Corrigan, J.

We concur: Cantil-Sakauye, C.J., Baxter, J., Chin, J., Bamattre-Manoukian, J.

Questions

1. The defendant argues that he cannot be convicted of pandering because he did not encourage another person to "become a prostitute." Which facts support his position?

2. According to the court, what harm or potential harm was caused by Mr. Zambia's actions?

3. Mr. Zambia was convicted of soliciting prostitution, an inchoate crime. It turns out that the person he solicited was an undercover police officer. Should the defense have argued factual impossibility? Would it have been a successful defense? (Hint: Review Chapter 4: "Incomplete Crimes.")

Drugs: A Look at Marijuana

Marijuana is a drug with a massive and loyal public following. It has inspired grass roots activism. Books have been written, magazines have been created, websites have been developed, and organizations have been founded to support legalization of the drug. It has also inspired songs, including Rick James's 1978 classic, "Mary Jane." "Mary Jane" is a colloquial term for marijuana. In this double entendre musical tribute, James sings about Mary Jane as if she were a beloved girlfriend. From late-night TV hosts and comedians, to stoner movies, marijuana is portrayed as the "funny" drug, the one that causes people to feel lightheaded, at peace with the world, and hungry. The issue of legalization has moved from the margins to the mainstream. A 2013 Gallup Poll found that 58 percent of Americans believe that marijuana should be legalized. Those who support legalization or **decriminalization** point out that marijuana does not cause harm or provoke violence. Many who support decriminalization note that alcohol, a dangerous and much more potent drug, is legal. In a 2014 interview, President Barack Obama echoed this sentiment when he stated that marijuana is less harmful than alcohol "in terms of its impact on the individual consumer."[45] Those who oppose legalization or decriminalization argue that it is a gateway drug, one that will cause some users to experiment with more potent and addictive drugs. There is no clear support for this hypothesis. In fact, some research findings indicate that alcohol, not marijuana, is a gateway drug.[46]

Marijuana has long been a source of controversy, consistently stirring public debate about the national drug policy. In the early 1900s, when increased quantities of marijuana arrived in the United States, the relatively unknown drug was viewed with loathing and suspicion. Some public officials stated that the drug would corrupt the young and pure. By the 1920s, "reefer madness" was in full swing and a social panic was born. The 1936 movie by the same name dramatized the evils of marijuana. Newspaper headlines warned of the dangers of reefer. There were public warnings about the dangers of marijuana and the dangerous people who were reportedly using or pedaling the drug—Mexicans, Blacks, and jazz musicians. In 1937, the Marihuana Tax Act was passed by Congress. The legislation prohibited the sale and distribution of marijuana. Violators faced a maximum fine of two thousand dollars and five years in prison. The law was propelled by Harry Anslinger, the first commissioner of the Federal Bureau of Narcotics. In 1969, the act was declared unconstitutional by the Supreme Court.

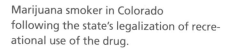

Poster for 1936 movie, *Reefer Madness.*

Today marijuana use is widespread, and those who favor decriminalization continue to push for legislation or ballot initiatives that would make the drug available under certain circumstances (e.g., medical marijuana) or reduce the criminal penalties for those who are found with the drug. In 2012, Colorado voters passed Amendment 64, which legalized recreational marijuana use. The ballot initiative made it legal for anyone age twenty-one or older to purchase and grow the drug (with some limits). The legislation allows a person to be in possession of up to one ounce of marijuana outside of his or her home. It is still unlawful to use the drug in public and drive while under its influence. This initiative amended the Colorado Constitution. As we discussed in Chapter 1, state constitutions are a source of criminal law. Washington also has passed legislation allowing for the recreational marijuana use. Approximately one-half of the states have passed bills legalizing the use of medical marijuana. In 1996, California was the first state to permit the use of medical cannabis. The other states passed similar legislation within the last few years.

Marijuana smoker in Colorado following the state's legalization of recreational use of the drug.

Notably, marijuana use is still illegal under federal law. Under federal law it remains a Schedule I drug. It is on the list of drugs that are considered to be the most dangerous—along with heroin, LSD, ecstasy, and peyote. In 2014, the Department of Justice indicated that it would not take action against states that permit recreational marijuana use.

Concluding Note

Public order crimes and offenses against public decency are often overlooked in discussions of criminal law. However, these offenses act as a barometer of our concerns about safety, morality, and punishment. Thus, the issues discussed in this chapter are an important part of the larger criminal law matrix. Good luck with the Issue Spotter exercise.

IssueSpotter

The below hypothetical is based on an actual case. Read it and spot the issues discussed in this chapter.

Disorderly Words?[47]

In March 2009, Boston police officers received a call that there were people on Wallace Street who might be in possession of marijuana. When the four officers arrived, they found a young woman with three young men standing on the curb in front of a house. The officers stated their intention to search the young men.

One of the men, Scott Winthrop, objected and shouted, "Fuck this man. I haven't been smoking anything." Officer Blake informed Winthrop that if he continued to curse, he would be arrested for disturbing the public order.

Mr. Winthrop threw his hands in the air and shouted, "Man, leave me the fuck alone. I'm not bothering anybody. You are!"

Passersby began to gather, and neighbors could be seen peering out from their windows.

Officer Blake searched Mr. Winthrop and found no drugs. After the search was completed, Winthrop said, "I told you, you wouldn't find shit. You men in blue are just harassin' us." During the entire incident, the three other officers stood in close proximity to Officer Blake.

Mr. Winthrop was arrested for violating a section of the city's "Public Order Act." The act, below, gives police broad authority to maintain peace and public order:

It is a violation of a the city code for a person to use threatening, abusive or insulting words or engage in disorderly behavior, in public, within hearing or sight of a person who is likely to experience harassment, alarm, or distress.

The maximum fine for violation of this section is two hundred dollars.

Mr. Winthrop is charged with violating the "harassment, alarm, and distress" section of the act.

You are the judge.

1. What criminal law issues are raised by the above fact pattern?

2. Which facts support the claim that Mr. Winthrop violated the Public Order Act?

3. Which facts support the defense that Mr. Winthrop did not violate the act? If you were Mr. Winthrop's attorney, what other issues would you would ask the court to consider?

4. What is your holding in the case? Give two rationales for your decision.

Key Terms and Cases

Notes ●━━━━━━━━━━━━━━━━━━━━━━━━━━━

1. George Kelling and James Q. Wilson, "Broken Windows: The Police and Neighborhood Safety," *The Atlantic*, March 1, 1982.

2. Bernard Harcourt and Jens Ludwig, "Broken Windows: New Evidence from New York City and a Five-City Social Experiment," *University of Chicago Law Review* (2006): 291.

3. E. Ann Carson and William J. Sabol, "Prisoners in 2011," Table 9, NCJ 239808 (Washington, DC: Bureau of Justice Statistics, 2012).

4. Jacksonville, Fla. Ord. Code §26–57 (1965).

5. See Robert Ellickson, "Controlling Chronic Misconduct in City Spaces: Of Panhandlers, Skid Rows, and Public-Space Zoning," *Yale Law J.* 105 (1996): 1165, 1210.

6. Florida Stat. § 856.021 (2012).

7. *Chicago v. Morales*, 527 U.S. 41 (1999).

8. Ibid. at 64.

9. U.S. District Court, Southern District of New York, Case 1:08-cv-01034-SAS-HBP (08 Civ. 1034).

10. "The Stop, Questions and Frisk Data," NYPD, The City of New York, http://www.nyc.gov/html/nypd/html/analysis_and_planning/stop_question_and_frisk_report.shtml

    Seizure of Weapons or Other Contraband by Suspect Race, 2010–2012

Stops	% Gun Seizure	% Weapon Seizure	% Contraband	
White	148,283	.07	1.94	2.37
Black	843,684	.16	1.06	1.79
Hispanic	520,171	.09	1.25	1.73

11. *Floyd v. New York*, 959 F. Supp. 2d 540 (S.D.N.Y. 2013), Judge Scheindlin's Opinion and Order p. 15. See also Benjamin Weiser and Joseph Goldstein, "Mayor Says New York City Will Settle Suits on Stop-and-Frisk Tactics," *New York Times*, January 30, 2014, http://www.nytimes.com/2014/01/31/nyregion/de-blasio-stop-and-frisk.html?hpw&rref=nyregion&_r=0

12. Jason Kravitz, "HUD Reports Slight Decline in Homelessness in 2012," HUD 12-191 (Washington, DC: U.S. Department of Housing and Urban Development, 2012), http://portal.hud.gov/hudportal/HUD?src=/press/press_releases_media_advisories/2012/HUDNo.12-191

13. See Ellen L. Bassuk, Christina Murphy, Natalie Thompson Coupe, Rachael R. Kenney, and Corey Anne Beach, "America's Youngest Outcasts 2010" (Needham, MA: The National Center on Family Homelessness, 2011), http://www.homelesschildrenamerica.org/media/NCFH_AmericaOutcast2010_web_032812.pdf

14. Meghan Henry, Alvaro Cortes, and Sean Morris, "The 2013 Annual Homeless Assessment Report (AHAR) to Congress" (Washington, DC: U.S. Department of Housing and Urban Development, 2014), https://www.onecpd.info/resources/documents/ahar-2013-part1.pdf

15. National Alliance to End Homelessness, "The State of Homelessness in America 2013" (Washington, DC: Author, 2013), http://www.endhomelessness.org/library/entry/the-state-of-homelessness-2013

16. FL Stat, XXIII § 316.193 (2012).

17. *Powell v. Texas*, 392 U.S. 514 (1968).

18. Mississippi Code § 97–29–47 (2013).

19. National Conference of Commissioners on Uniform State Laws, Uniform Alcoholism and Intoxication Treatment Act approved and recommended for enactment in all the states at annual conference meeting at Vail, Colorado, August 21–28, 1971, http://www.law.upenn.edu/bll/archives/ulc/fnact99/1970s/uaita71.pdf

20. South Dakota, § 34–20A-55 (1985).

21. South Dakota, CL § 35–9-7 (2012).

22. Lydia Saad, "Self-Reported Gun Ownership in U.S. Is Highest Since 1993: Majority of Men, Republicans, and Southerners Report Having a Gun in Their Households," Gallup Politics, October 26, 2011, http://www.gallup.com/poll/150353/self-reported-gun-ownership-highest-1993.aspx

23. *McDonald v. Chicago*, 561 U.S. 3025 (2010).

24. Jack Nicas and Ashby Jones, "Permits Soar to Allow More Concealed Guns," *Wall Street Journal*, July 4, 2013.

25. Charles Blow, "The Curious Case of Trayvon Martin," *The New York Times*, March 16, 2012.

26. Diana A. Drysdale, William Modzeleski, and Andre B. Simons, "Campus Attacks Targeted Violence Affecting Institutions of Higher Education," (Washington, DC: U.S. Secret Service, U.S. Department of Education, Federal Bureau of Investigation, 2010).

27. Tyler Kingkade, "There Were More Than Two Dozen Reported Shootings At College Campuses In 2013," January 13, 2014, http://www.huffingtonpost.com/2014/01/13/shootings-college-campuses-2013_n_4577404.html

28. Nathaniel Ward, *Body of Liberties* (1641), 92.

29. Jeremy Bentham, *Introduction to the Principles of Morals and Legislation* (1823; repr. New York: Hafner Publisher Company, 1948), Ch. 17, 236.

30. Tennessee Stat. § 44–8-408 (b).

31. D.C. Code § 22–1001.

32. See generally, Nicole Pakiz, "Why the ALI Should Redraft the Animal-Cruelty Provision of the Model Penal Code," Selected Works of Nicole Pakiz, 2012, http://works.bepress.com/nicole_pakiz/1

33. Patrick Devlin, *The Enforcement of Morals* (Oxford: Oxford University Press, 1965) 1.

34. "The Report of the Committee on Homosexual Offences and Prostitution" is generally referred to as the "Wolfenden Report" (the committee was chaired by Sir John Wolfenden). Findings were based upon a 1950s report on homosexuality and prostitution in Great Britain.

35. S. Kadish, "The Crisis of Overcriminalization" *American Criminal Law Quarterly* 7 (1968): 17, 19.

36. *Bowers v. Hardwick*, 478 U.S. 186 (1986).

37. *Lawrence v. Texas*, 539 U.S. 558 (2003).

38. *Martin v. Ziherl*, 607 S.E.2d 367 (Va. 2005).

39. Virginia Code § 18.2–344.

40. Maryland Code.41 § 10–501 (Repealed by Acts 1988, c.6 § 1, eff. Feb. 18, 1988).

41. Oklahoma, O.S. § Title 21–872.

42. Idaho Code, I.C. § 18–6601.

43. *Reynolds v. U.S.*, 98 U.S. (8 Otto.) 145 (1878).

44. See, e.g., Department of Justice, Human Trafficking Prosecution Unit, http://www.justice.gov/crt/about/crm/htpu.php

45. David Remnick, "Going the Distance: On and Off the Road with Barack Obama," *The New Yorker Magazine,* January 27, 2014.

46. Amir Khan, "Alcohol, Not Marijuana A Gateway Drug," *International Science Times,* July 11, 2012, http://www.isciencetimes.com/articles/3400/20120711/alcohol-marijuana-gateway-drug.htm

47. This hypothetical is based upon an English case, *Harvey v. Director of Public Prosecutions* (2011) EWHC Crim B1, Queen's Bench.

Chapter 7

Jerry Sandusky was a famous coach for the award-winning Pennsylvania State football team for thirty years before he retired in 1999. Sandusky's retirement came on the heels of an allegation that he had sexually assaulted a young boy he met through his activities with a charity he founded in 1977 called The Second Mile. Although no criminal charges were brought at that time, Sandusky was eventually charged in 2011 in a fifty-two-count indictment, including numerous sex offenses against minor boys and related charges. He was convicted of forty-eight of the charges and was sentenced to thirty to sixty years in prison. The Sandusky case shocked the nation and brought to light some of the issues we will discuss in this chapter, including the fact that there are many different types of sexual assault and many reasons why victims frequently do not report these crimes to the police.

Jerry Sandusky in 2012 after he was convicted of numerous sexual assault offenses against minors

Rape and Other Violent Crimes

Learning Objectives

After reading and studying this chapter, you should be able to

➤ Explain the difference between common law rape and modern sexual assault statutes

➤ Distinguish between force and lack of consent

➤ Define statutory rape

➤ Define sexting

➤ Explain the purpose of rape shield laws

➤ List the elements of common law robbery

➤ Distinguish between common law assault and battery and modern assault statutes

Introduction

Murder is considered to be the most serious criminal offense, but many view rape and sexual assault as equally serious and harmful. Rape is such a violent and harmful crime that it was once punishable by death.[1] It remains an offense that may be punished by life in prison in all fifty states. Rape, kidnapping, robbery, assault, battery, and other serious crimes against persons are generally punished at a higher level than most property crimes because of the physical (and sometimes psychological) harm that they cause to human beings. In this chapter, we will examine these crimes and how they have been defined and prosecuted over the years.

Rape and Other Sexual Assaults

A strong case can be made that the crime of rape causes greater harm to its victims than any crime except homicide. It is sometimes difficult to prove because of the unique nature of the elements of the crime. As with all other crimes, the prosecutor must prove that the defendant did an act with a guilty state of mind—intentionally performing a forcible sexual act on the victim. However, unlike most other crimes, the prosecutor must also prove that the victim did not consent to the act. No other violent crime has such a requirement. The victim of a homicide, robbery, assault, or battery cannot legally consent to the acts that cause them harm. But it is the lack of consent in rape cases that constitutes at least part of the injury caused by this crime. This element of the crime is easiest to prove in stranger rape cases that involve a clear and obvious use of force. However, in so-called date rape cases where the defendant and complainant know each other and may have had consensual sexual contact in the past, proving lack of consent and even force or threat of force may be more difficult.

Under the common law, rape was defined as follows:

1. Unlawful sexual intercourse (or carnal knowledge)

2. Of a female

3. With force or the threat of force

4. And without consent.

This definition limited rape to a crime committed by a man against a woman, and the term "unlawful sexual intercourse" meant that the woman was not his wife. Any sexual intercourse between a husband and wife, whether or not it was forceful or consensual, was not considered rape under the common law. Although some jurisdictions maintain this antiquated definition, most have reformed their rape statutes to make them gender neutral and to include many different types of criminal sexual acts. Some jurisdictions have abandoned the term rape, instead describing these crimes as sexual assault or sexual abuse. Some also have followed the modern trend of grading the crime as first, second, and third degree sexual assault or abuse, depending upon the particular acts of the defendant. The following excerpts from the Alabama and District of Columbia statutes illustrate the range of rape and sexual assault statutes.

Alabama and District of Columbia Rape Statutes

Alabama Rape Statute

13A—6—61 Rape; first degree.

a. A person commits the crime of rape in the first degree if:

1. He or she engages in sexual intercourse with a member of the opposite sex by forcible compulsion; or

2. He or she engages in sexual intercourse with a member of the opposite sex who is incapable of consent by reason of being physically helpless or mentally incapacitated; or

3. He or she, being 16 years or older, engages in sexual intercourse with a member of the opposite sex who is less than 12 years old. . . .

13A—6—62 Rape; second degree.

b. A person commits the crime of rape in the second degree if:

4. Being 16 years old or older, he or she engages in sexual intercourse with a member of the opposite sex less than 16 and more than 12 years old; provided, however, the actor is at least two years older than the member of the opposite sex.

5. He or she engages in sexual intercourse with a member of the opposite sex who is incapable of consent by reason of being mentally defective.

District of Columbia Rape Statute

§ 22–3002. First degree sexual abuse.

a. A person shall be imprisoned for any term of years or for life, and in addition, may be fined in an amount not to exceed $250,000, if that person engages in or causes another person to engage in or submit to a sexual act in the following manner:

1. By using force against that other person;

2. By threatening or placing that other person in reasonable fear that any person will be subjected to death, bodily injury, or kidnapping;

3. After rendering that other person unconscious; or

4. After administering to that other person by force or threat of force, or without the knowledge or permission of that other person, a drug,

intoxicant, or other similar substance that substantially impairs the ability of that other person to appraise or control his or her conduct.

§ 22–3003. Second degree sexual abuse.

A person shall be imprisoned for not more than 20 years and may be fined in an amount not to exceed $200,000, if that person engages in or causes another person to engage in or submit to a sexual act in the following manner:

(1). By threatening or placing that other person in reasonable fear (other than by threatening or

placing that other person in reasonable fear that any person will be subjected to death, bodily injury, or kidnapping); or

(2). Where the person knows or has reason to know that the other person is:

(A). Incapable of appraising the nature of the conduct;

(B). Incapable of declining participation in that sexual act; or Incapable of communicating unwillingness to engage in that sexual act.

The Alabama and District of Columbia statutes illustrate the range of rape and sexual assault laws. The Alabama law abandons much of the antiquated language of the common law definition in that it is gender neutral and recognizes marital rape. It includes statutory rape (discussed later in this chapter) and different degrees of the offense. The District of Columbia statute, which also includes third and fourth degree sexual abuse, represents the modern trend of abandoning the term rape. Sexual abuse and sexual assault are the preferred terms in most modern statutes. The District of Columbia law is also more precise and punishes a wide range of sexual offenses against children in separate sections of the statute.

Statistics on Rape and Sexual Assault

Statistics on the crime of rape are inherently unreliable because rape and sexual assault are among the most underreported crimes despite the harm and trauma to its victims. Many rape victims are hesitant to report the crime because the judicial process forces them to relive the traumatic incident over and over with the police, the hospital personnel, the grand jury, the prosecutor, and most significantly, during the public trial. If the complainant knows his or her assailant, there is always the possibility that the defendant will present a consent defense. If the jury finds that the complainant consented to sex, the defendant will be found not guilty. In these cases, the defense attorney usually aggressively cross-examines the complainant at trial. For all of these reasons, many sexual assault victims decline to report these crimes to the police.

Table 7.1 on page 162, from the U.S. Department of Justice, Bureau of Justice Statistics undoubtedly does not reflect the true number of rapes and other sexual assaults in 2008.

As Table 7.2 on page 162 demonstrates, the majority of rape and sexual assault victims are female.

The Force Requirement

To prove rape or most forms of first degree sexual assault, prosecutors must prove force or threat of force by the accused as well as lack of consent by the victim. These terms have distinct meanings. Lack of consent is easy to prove in cases where the accused uses clear obvious force. If he or she strikes or otherwise assaults the victim,

Table 7.1 **Victimizations by Type of Crime**

Type of Crime	Number of Victimizations	Percent of All Victimizations	Rate per 1,000 Persons or Households
All Crimes	21,312,400	100	
Personal Crimes	4,993,220	23.4	19.8
Rape/Sexual Assault	203,830	1.0	0.8
Rape/Attempted Rape	123,010	0.6	0.5
Rape	52,470	0.2	0.2
Attempted Rape	70,540	0.3	0.3
Sexual Assault	80,810	0.4	0.3

Source: U.S. Department of Justice, Bureau of Justice Statistics.[2]

Table 7.2 **Number of Victimizations and Victimization Rates for Persons Age 12 or Older, by Type of Crime and Sex of Victims**

Type of Crime	Male Victims		Female Victims	
	Number	Rate	Number	Rate
Rape/Sexual Assault	39,590	0.3	164,240	1.3
Rape/Attempted Rape	37,910	0.3	85,100	0.7
Rape	6,010*	0.0*	46,460	0.4
Attempted Rape	31,900*	0.3*	38,640	0.3
Sexual Assault	1,680*	0.0*	79,140	0.6

Source: U.S. Department of Justice, Bureau of Justice Statistics.[3]
*Estimate is based on ten or fewer sample cases.
Rate per 1,000 persons or households.

with or without a weapon, there is obviously both force and lack of consent. But in cases where there is no strong evidence of obvious force, the prosecutor may have an easier time proving lack of consent than force or threat of force. For example, if the alleged victim testifies that he or she said "No" or told the accused to stop, such testimony may prove lack of consent but does not necessarily prove force or threat of force. The *Berkowitz* case on page 163 illustrates this issue.

Sexual Assault Policies on College Campuses

Sexual assaults are crimes that may be prosecuted by the state, whether or not they occur on college campuses. In addition to the criminal laws, most college campuses have implemented policies on rape and sexual assault, which are distributed to all students. Violation of these policies may subject students to a disciplinary process within the university. Many colleges conduct seminars and other informational sessions to educate students about sexual assault and misconduct. Ironically, the victim in the *Berkowitz* case had attended such a seminar.

Commonwealth v. Berkowitz (1992)

Superior Court of Pennsylvania

609 A.2d 1338

In the spring of 1988, appellant and the victim were both college sophomores at East Stroudsburg State University, ages twenty and nineteen years old, respectively. They had mutual friends and acquaintances. On April nineteenth of that year, the victim went to appellant's dormitory room. What transpired in that dorm room between appellant and the victim thereafter is the subject of the instant appeal.

During a one day jury trial held on September 14, 1988, the victim gave the following account during direct examination by the Commonwealth. At roughly 2:00 on the afternoon of April 19, 1988, after attending two morning classes, the victim returned to her dormitory room. There, she drank a martini to "loosen up a little bit" before going to meet her boyfriend, with whom she had argued the night before. Roughly ten minutes later she walked to her boyfriend's dormitory lounge to meet him. He had not yet arrived.

Having nothing else to do while she waited for her boyfriend, the victim walked up to appellant's room to look for Earl Hassel, appellant's roommate. She knocked on the door several times but received no answer. She therefore wrote a note to Mr. Hassel, which read, "Hi Earl, I'm drunk. That's not why I came to see you. I haven't seen you in a while. I'll talk to you later, [victim's name]." She did so, although she had not felt any intoxicating effects from the martini, "for a laugh."

After the victim had knocked again, she tried the knob on the appellant's door. Finding it open, she walked in. She saw someone lying on the bed with a pillow over his head, whom she thought to be Earl Hassel. After lifting the pillow from his head, she realized it was appellant. She asked appellant which dresser was his roommate's. He told her, and the victim left the note.

Before the victim could leave appellant's room, however, appellant asked her to stay and "hang out for a while." She complied because she "had time to kill" and because she didn't really know appellant and wanted to give him "a fair chance." *Id.* Appellant asked her to give him a back rub but she declined, explaining that she did not "trust" him. *Id.* Appellant then asked her to have a seat on his bed. Instead, she found a seat on the floor, and conversed for a while about a mutual friend. No physical contact between the two had, to this point, taken place.

On cross-examination, the victim testified that during this conversation she had explained she was having problems with her boyfriend.

Thereafter, however, appellant moved off the bed and down on the floor, and "kind of pushed [the victim] back with his body. It wasn't a shove, it was just kind of a leaning-type of thing." Next appellant "straddled" and started kissing the victim. The victim responded by saying, "Look, I gotta go. I'm going to meet [my boyfriend]." Then appellant lifted up her shirt and bra and began fondling her. The victim then said "no."

After roughly thirty seconds of kissing and fondling, appellant "undid his pants and he kind of moved his body up a little bit." The victim was still saying "no" but "really couldn't move because [appellant] was shifting at [her] body so he was over [her]." Appellant then tried to put his penis in her mouth. The victim did not physically resist, but rather continued to verbally protest, saying "No, I gotta go, let me go," in a "scolding" manner.

Ten or fifteen more seconds passed before the two rose to their feet. Appellant disregarded the victim's continual complaints that she "had to go," and instead walked two feet away to the door and locked it so that no one from the outside could enter.

The victim testified that she realized at the time that the lock was not of a type that could lock people inside the room.

Then, in the victim's words, "[appellant] put me down on the bed. It was kind of like—he didn't throw me on the bed. It's hard to explain. It was kind of like a push but no. . . . " She did not bounce off the bed. "It wasn't slow like a romantic kind of thing, but it wasn't a fast shove either. It was kind of in the middle."

Once the victim was on the bed, appellant began "straddling" her again while he undid the knot in her sweatpants. *Id.* He then removed her sweatpants and underwear from one of her legs. The victim did not physically resist in any way while on the bed because appellant was on top of her, and she "couldn't like go anywhere." She did not scream out at anytime because, "[i]t was like a dream was happening or something."

Appellant then used one of his hands to "guide" his penis into her vagina. At that point, after appellant was inside her, the victim began saying "no, no to him softly in a moaning kind of way . . . because it was just so scary." After about thirty seconds, appellant pulled out his penis and ejaculated onto the victim's stomach.

(Continued)

(Continued)

Immediately thereafter, appellant got off the victim and said, "Wow, I guess we just got carried away." To this the victim retorted, "No, we didn't get carried away, you got carried away." The victim then quickly dressed, grabbed her school books and raced downstairs to her boyfriend who was by then waiting for her in the lounge.

Once there, the victim began crying. Her boyfriend and she went up to his dorm room where, after watching the victim clean off appellant's semen from her stomach, he called the police.

Defense counsel's cross-examination elicited more details regarding the contact between appellant and the victim before the incident in question. The victim testified that roughly two weeks prior to the incident, she had attended a school seminar entitled, "Does 'no' sometimes means 'yes'?" Among other things, the lecturer at this seminar had discussed the average length and circumference of human penises. After the seminar, the victim and several of her friends had discussed the subject matter of the seminar over a speaker-telephone with appellant and his roommate Earl Hassel. The victim testified that during that telephone conversation, she had asked appellant the size of his penis. According to the victim, appellant responded by suggesting that the victim "come over and find out." She declined.

When questioned further regarding her communications with appellant prior to the April 19, 1988 incident, the victim testified that on two other occasions, she had stopped by appellant's room while intoxicated. During one of those times, she had laid down on his bed. When asked whether she had asked appellant again at that time what his penis size was, the victim testified that she did not remember.

Appellant took the stand in his own defense and offered an account of the incident and the events leading up to it which differed only as to the consent involved. According to appellant, the victim had begun communication with him after the school seminar by asking him of the size of his penis and of whether he would show it to her. Appellant had suspected that the victim wanted to pursue a sexual relationship with him because she had stopped by his room twice after the phone call while intoxicated, laying down on his bed with her legs spread and again asking to see his penis. He believed that his suspicions were confirmed when she initiated the April 19, 1988 encounter by stopping by his room (again after drinking), and waking him up.

Appellant testified that, on the day in question, he did initiate the first physical contact, but added that the victim warmly responded to his advances by passionately returning his kisses. He conceded that she was continually "whispering . . . no's," but claimed that she did so while "amorously . . . passionately" moaning. In effect, he took such protests to be thinly veiled acts of encouragement. When asked why he locked the door, he explained that "that's not something you want somebody to just walk in on you [doing."]

According to appellant, the two then laid down on the bed, the victim helped him take her clothing off, and he entered her. He agreed that the victim continued to say "no" while on the bed, but carefully qualified his agreement, explaining that the statements were "moaned passionately." According to appellant, when he saw a "blank look on her face," he immediately withdrew and asked "is anything wrong, is something the matter, is anything wrong." He ejaculated on her stomach thereafter because he could no longer "control" himself. Appellant testified that after this, the victim "saw that it was over and then she made her move. She gets right off the bed . . . she just swings her legs over and then she puts her clothes back on." Then, in wholly corroborating an aspect of the victim's account, he testified that he remarked, "Well, I guess we got carried away," to which she rebuked, "No, we didn't get carried, you got carried away."

After hearing both accounts, the jury convicted appellant of rape and indecent assault. . . . Appellant was then sentenced to serve a term of imprisonment of one to four years for rape and a concurrent term of six to twelve months for indecent assault.

In Pennsylvania, the crime of rape is defined by statute as follows:

A person commits a felony of the first degree when he engages in sexual intercourse with another person not his spouse:

1. by forcible compulsion;

2. by threat of forcible compulsion that would prevent resistance by a person of reasonable resolution;

3. who is unconscious; or

4. who is so mentally deranged or deficient that such person is incapable of consent.

"[F]orcible compulsion" as used in section 3121(1) includes not only physical force or violence but also moral, psychological or intellectual force used to compel a person to engage in sexual intercourse against that person's will.

. . . [A]ppellant urges that the victim's testimony itself precludes a finding of "forcible compulsion." Appellant essentially argues that the indisputable lack of physical injuries and physical resistance proves that the evidence was insufficient to establish rape.

In beginning our review of these arguments, it is clear that any reliance on the victim's absence of physical injuries or physical resistance is misplaced. Although it is true that the instant victim testified that she was not "physically hurt in any fashion," and that it was "possible that [she] took no physical action to discourage [appellant]," such facts are insignificant in a sufficiency determination. As our Supreme Court has made clear, "'rape . . . is defined, not in terms of the physical injury to the victim, but in terms of the effect it has on the victim's volition.'" . . .

. . . [B]oth the victim and appellant testified that throughout the encounter, the victim repeatedly and continually said "no." Unfortunately for the Commonwealth, under the existing statutes, this evidence alone cannot suffice to support a finding of "forcible compulsion."

If the legislature had intended to define rape, a felony of the first degree, as non-consensual intercourse, it could have done so. It did not do this. It defined rape as sexual intercourse by "forcible compulsion." . . . If the legislature means what it said, then where as here no evidence was adduced by the Commonwealth which established either that mental coercion, or a threat, or force inherently inconsistent with consensual intercourse was used to complete the act of intercourse, the evidence is insufficient to support a rape conviction. Accordingly, we hold that the trial court erred in determining that the evidence adduced by the Commonwealth was sufficient to convict appellant of rape.

Questions

1. What issue does Mr. Berkowitz raise on appeal?

2. What is the court's holding and rationale?

3. The court notes that force includes "not only physical force or violence but also moral, psychological or intellectual force used to compel a person to engage in sexual intercourse against that person's will." Can you provide examples of moral, psychological, and intellectual force?

Sexual assault policies vary from college to college and define sexual assault in different ways. The following excerpt is from a brochure distributed at the University of Minnesota called "Consent is Sexy":[4]

WHAT IS CONSENT?

Consent is informed, freely and actively given, and mutually understood.

WHEN IS THERE LACK OF CONSENT?

If physical force, coercion, intimidation, and/or threats are used, there is no consent. If the victim/survivor is mentally or physically incapacitated or impaired so that the victim/survivor cannot understand the fact, nature, or extent of the sexual situation, and the condition was or would be known to a reasonable person, there is no consent. This includes conditions due to alcohol or drug consumption, or being asleep or unconscious.
   University of Minnesota Policy 2.6.3

- Consenting to kissing, hugging, touching, etc. DOES NOT mean there is consent for sex or further sexual activity.
- Thinking your partner "owes" you sex is not consent.
- The absence of "NO" does not mean "YES." Silence, hesitation, or passivity does not mean "yes."
- Pressuring out a "yes" is not consent.
- Trickery, manipulation, intimidation, or threats against your partner is not consent

WHEN SHOULD I ASK FOR CONSENT?

Before you act. It's the responsibility of the person initiating a sexual act to obtain clear consent. Whenever you're unsure if consent has been given or to know if your partner is comfortable, ASK. Check-in throughout. But remember, giving consent ahead of time DOES NOT waive a person's right to change their mind or say no later.

(Continued)

(Continued)

WILL ASKING FOR CONSENT RUIN THE MOOD?

Nope. Asking is HOT. The mood is ruined when someone feels uncomfortable, un-safe, or pushed beyond their limits.

HOW DO I ASK FOR CONSENT?

"MAY I . . . ?"

"ARE YOU OKAY IF . . . ?"

"WOULD YOU LIKE TO . . . ?"

GIVING CONSENT.

Partners should communicate how they're feeling throughout sexual activity. Giving consent doesn't have to be verbal, but that's the clearest way.

WHAT ABOUT ALCOHOL & CONSENT?

Alcohol complicates sexual activity. Expectations, assumptions, as well as interpretations can be greatly altered because alcohol impairs decision-making.

By law and University policy, a person who is incapacitated is unable to give consent. Regardless of who was drinking or how much was consumed, the responsibility for any sexual assault falls on the shoulders of the person who chooses to assault. It is NEVER the victim's fault. It's best to engage in sexual activity when you and your partner are sober. This ensures both of you will be able to understand what's happening and you'll greatly reduce the risk of harm.

GAUGING CONSENT

RED: SIGNS YOU SHOULD STOP

- You're too intoxicated to gauge or give consent.
- Your partner is asleep or passed out.
- You hope your partner will say nothing and go with the flow.
- You intend to have sex by any means possible.

YELLOW: SIGNS YOU SHOULD PAUSE & ASK

- You're not sure what your partner wants.
- You're getting mixed signals.
- You haven't talked about how far to go.
- You assume that you'll do the same thing as last time.
- Your partner stops, hesitates, or is not responsive.

GREEN: KEEP COMMUNICATING

- Everyone's come to a mutual decision about how far to go.
- Everyone clearly expresses their comfort with the situation.
- You both feel comfortable and safe stopping at any time.
- Everyone's turned on!

Source: The Univeristy of Minnesota

Consider the following excerpt from the Sexual Assault Policy at Occidental College in California:[5]

Sexual assault—Attempted or actual sexual contact performed without the active, verbal consent of another individual.

Consent—A verbal agreement and positive physical cooperation in the course of physical intimacy so long as both parties are acting freely and voluntarily. A verbal "no," even if it may sound indecisive or insincere, constitutes a lack of consent. The absence of a verbal "no" does not mean "yes." Lack of protest does not imply consent.

The Occidental policy appears to require students to have a verbal agreement before engaging in any kind of sexual activity. The Minnesota brochure gives very specific instructions on how two individuals should engage with each other sexually. Both policies raise interesting questions about whether sexual activity should be policed this closely in the interest of preventing sexual misconduct.

Consider the following hypothetical:

Mary and John are college students who have been dating for a while. They decide to go out to dinner. After dinner, they go back to Mary's dorm room where they begin to kiss and fondle each other, and they ultimately have sex. John did not specifically ask Mary if she consented to having sex, but she did not ask him to stop nor did she say "no" at any time. In fact, no words were spoken between them, and Mary actively participated in the act.

Did John and Mary violate Minnesota's sexual assault policy? The policy states that "it's the responsibility of the person initiating a sexual act to obtain clear consent." Since no words were spoken between them, the policy arguably was violated. If neither John nor Mary is sure which one of them "initiated the act," it is not clear which one of them violated the policy. Perhaps both did. How about Occidental's policy? It appears to require a verbal agreement. Should John be required to say, "Mary do you consent to have sex with me?" and wait for Mary to say, "Yes, John, I agree to have sex with you?" How can these policies be enforced?

White House Response to Sexual Assault on College Campuses

In January 2014, President Barack Obama's Administration joined forces with the Office of the Vice-President and the White House Council on Women and Girls to create the White House Task Force to Protect Students from Sexual Assault.[6] A major goal of the task force is to find best practices for schools to implement that will prevent sexual assaults, promote reporting of sexual violence, and create safe learning environments for all students.

The task force will work with the Justice Department to urge schools to do surveys on their campuses to determine the extent of the problem. It also will work with participating colleges to engage men as allies and encourage them to step in and speak up when they see that someone is in trouble. Additional plans include the launch of a comprehensive online technical assistance project for campus officials and the development of trauma-informed training materials for campus health staff. The Justice Department will release a solicitation for a pilot sex offender treatment program targeting perpetrators, and schools will be encouraged to create Memorandums of Understanding with local law enforcement to create a united front against sexual assaults on college campuses.

Two days after the task force released its report, the Department of Education released the names of fifty-five colleges currently under investigation for alleged mishandling of sexual assault allegations.[7] Some critics argue that the report of the task force goes too far in embracing a criminal justice model and that colleges are not the proper venues for the adjudication of sexual assault allegations.[8]

Gender, Race, and the Crime of Rape

Sexism and the Law of Rape

"Rape" by Susan Estrich[9]

Eleven years ago, a man held an ice pick to my throat and said: "Push over, shut up, or I'll kill you." I did what he said, but I couldn't stop crying. A hundred years later, I jumped out of my car as he drove away.

I ended up in the back seat of a police car. I told the two officers I had been raped by a man who came up to the car door as I was getting out in my own parking lot (and trying to balance two bags of groceries and kick the car door open). He took the car, too.

They asked me if he was a crow. That was their first question. A crow, I learned that day, meant to them someone who is Black.

They asked me if I knew him. That was their second question. They believed me when I said I didn't. Because, as one of them put it, how would a nice (White) girl like me know a crow?

Now they were on my side. They asked me if he took any money. He did; but while I remember virtually every detail of that day and night, I can't remember how much. But I remember their answer. He did take money; that made it an armed robbery. Much better than a rape. They got right on the radio with that.

We went to the police station first, not the hospital, so I could repeat my story (and then what did he do?) to four more policemen. When we got there, I borrowed a dime to call my father. They all liked that.

By the time we went to the hospital, they were really on my team. I could've been one of their kids. Now

there was something they'd better tell me. Did I realize what prosecuting a rape complaint was all about? They tried to tell me that "the law" was against me. But they didn't explain exactly how. And I didn't understand why. I believed in "the law," not knowing what it was.

Late that night, I sat in the Police Headquarters looking at mug shots. I was the one who insisted on going back that night. My memory was fresh. I was ready. They had four or five to "really show" me; being "really shown" a mug shot means exactly what defense attorneys are afraid it means. But it wasn't any one of them. After that, they couldn't help me very much. One shot looked close until my father realized that the man had been the right age ten years before. It was late. I didn't have a great description of identifying marks, or the like: No one had ever told me that if you're raped, you should not shut your eyes and cry for fear that this really is happening. You should keep your eyes open focusing on this man who is raping you so you can identify him when you survive. After an hour of looking, I left the police station. They told me they'd be back in touch. They weren't.

A clerk called me one day to tell me that my car had been found minus tires and I should come sign a release and have it towed—no small matter if you don't have a car to get there and are slightly afraid of your shadow. The women from the rape crisis center called me every day, then every other day, then every week. The police detectives never called at all.

I learned, much later, that I had "really" been raped. Unlike, say, the woman who claimed she'd been raped by a man she actually knew, and was with voluntarily. Unlike, say, women who are "asking for it," and get what they deserve. I would listen as seemingly intelligent people explained these distinctions to me, and marvel; later I read about them in books, court opinions, and empirical studies. It is bad enough to be a "real" rape victim.How terrible to be—what to call it—a "not real" rape victim.

To examine rape within the criminal law tradition is to expose fully the sexism of the law. Much that is striking about the crime of rape—and revealing of the sexism of the system—emerges only when rape is examined relative to other crimes, which the feminist literature by and large does not do. For example, rape is most assuredly not the only crime in which consent is a defense; but it is the only crime that has required the victim to resist physically in order to establish nonconsent. Nor is rape the only crime where prior relationship is taken into account by prosecutors in screening cases; yet we have not asked whether considering prior relationship in rape cases is different, and less justifiable, than considering it in cases of assault.

Sexism in the law of rape is no matter of mere historical interest; it endures, even where some of the most blatant testaments to that sexism have disappeared. Corroboration requirements unique to rape may have been repealed, but they continue to be enforced as a matter of practice in many jurisdictions. The victim of rape may not be required to resist to the utmost as a matter of statutory law in any jurisdiction, but the definitions accorded to force and consent may render "reasonable" resistance both a practical and a legal necessity. In the law of rape, supposedly dead horses continue to run.

The study of rape as an illustration of sexism in the criminal law also raises broader questions about the way conceptions of gender and the different backgrounds and perspectives of men and women should be encompassed within the criminal law. In one of his most celebrated essays, Oliver Wendell Holmes explained that the law does not exist to tell the good man what to do, but to tell the bad man what not to do. Holmes was interested in the distinction between the good and bad man; I cannot help noticing that both are men. Most of the time, a criminal law that reflects male views and male standards imposes its judgment on men who have injured other men. It is "boys' rules" applied to a boys'

fight. In rape, the male standard defines a crime committed against women, and male standards are used not only to judge men, but also to judge the conduct of women victims. Moreover, because the crime involves sex itself, the law of rape inevitably treads on the explosive ground of sex roles, of male aggression and female passivity, of our understandings of sexuality—areas where differences between a male and a female perspective may be most pronounced.

At one end of the spectrum is the "real" rape, what I will call the traditional rape: A stranger puts a gun to the head of his victim, threatens to kill her or beats her, and then engages in intercourse. In that case, the law-judges, statutes, prosecutors and all-generally acknowledge that a serious crime has been committed. But most cases deviate in one or many respects from this clear picture, making interpretation far more complex. Where less force is used or no other physical injury is inflicted, where threats are inarticulate, where the two know each other, where the setting is not an alley but a bedroom, where the initial contact was not a kidnapping but a date, where the woman says no but does not fight, the understanding is different. In such cases, the law, as reflected in the opinions of the courts, the interpretation, if not the words, of the statutes, and the decisions of those within the criminal justice system, often tell us that no crime has taken place and that fault, if any is to be recognized, belongs with the woman. In concluding that such acts—what I call, for lack of a better title, "non-traditional" rapes—are not criminal, and worse, that the woman must bear any guilt, the law has reflected, legitimized, and enforced a view of sex and women which celebrates male aggressiveness and punishes female passivity. And that vision, while under attack in recent years, continues to be a dominant force in our society and in the law of rape.

Questions

1. What does Professor Estrich mean when she says, "It is 'boys' rules applied to a boys' fight"?

2. According to Professor Estrich, is the common law definition of rape a sexist rule of law? Why or why not?

3. Should "traditional" and "nontraditional" rapes be punished at the same level? Why or why not?

Rape Shield Laws. **Rape shield laws** limit the defendant's ability to introduce evidence of the complainant's prior sexual conduct. Prior to the enactment of these laws, defense attorneys would cross-examine the complainant or introduce evidence of a victim's prior sexual history in cases involving a consent defense. The purpose of this evidence and cross-examination was to try to paint a picture of the complainant as a promiscuous person with a propensity to consent to sexual intercourse. The ability of defense attorneys to expose the private sexual history of rape complainants in public courtrooms discouraged them from reporting assaults to the police.

In the 1970s, states began to pass rape shield laws to protect the privacy of rape victims. Legislators reached the conclusion that it was neither fair nor logical for jurors to conclude that because a woman consented to sex in the past, she is likely to consent in the future. Rape shield laws prohibit defense attorneys from cross-examining about, or introducing evidence of, the victim's prior sexual history. There are a few exceptions, which vary from state to state. The most common are (1) when the victim previously had consensual sex with the defendant, (2) to prove that someone other than the defendant was the source of physical evidence, or (3) when the judge determines evidence to be relevant and admissible in the interest of justice.

All fifty states and the District of Columbia have enacted some form of a rape shield law. The following excerpt from Michigan's rape shield law provides an example:

Michigan's Rape Shield Statute

750.520j. Admissibility of evidence of victim's sexual conduct[10]

Sec. 520j. (1) Evidence of specific instances of the victim's sexual conduct, opinion evidence of the victim's sexual conduct, and reputation evidence of the victim's sexual conduct shall not be admitted . . . unless and only to the extent that the judge finds that the following proposed evidence is material to a fact at issue in the case and that its inflammatory or prejudicial nature does not outweigh its probative value:

(a) Evidence of the victim's past sexual conduct with the actor.

(b) Evidence of specific instances of sexual activity showing the source or origin of semen, pregnancy, or disease.

Consider the following hypothetical:

Tom was charged with the rape of Sara. He claimed that there was no rape because Sara consented to having sex with him. During the trial, the defense attorney attempted to cross-examine Sara on whether she had sex with another man, Harry, on their first date. The defense attorney also attempted to introduce evidence that she had consensual sex with Tom in the past.

Would Michigan's rape shield law allow the cross-examination about prior sexual contact with Harry? The law clearly prohibits evidence of the victim's prior sexual conduct, so this evidence likely would be excluded. How about the evidence of sex with Tom? Evidence that Sara had sex with Tom might be admitted under Sec. 520j(1)(a) depending on the facts of the case. For example, the judge might allow

Tom to present evidence that Sara did not claim that he raped her after he and Sara had the same type of sexual interaction in the past. This evidence would be relevant to the reasonableness of his belief that she consented in the present case.

Race and the Prosecution of Rape Cases

"Rape As A Badge of Slavery: The Legal History of, and Remedies For, Prosecutorial Race-of-Victim Charging Disparities" by Jeffry J. Pokorak[11]

For most of this nation's history, raping a Black woman was simply not a crime. First, laws prevented the prosecution of any offender for the rape of a slave woman. At the same time, the rape of a White woman by a Black man was treated with especial violence. The Thirteenth and Fourteenth Amendments were proposed and ratified as vehicles to ensure the equal protection of the laws. After their enactment, although the de jure prohibition on prosecuting the rape of Black women ended, de facto barriers to prosecution remained.

Perhaps in no other aspect of capital punishment was the effect of race more obvious than in sentencing for the crime of rape. Severe punishments for Black men accused of even planning to rape a White woman were widely used to restrict interactions between master and slave. In 1816, Georgia required the death penalty for a Black man who raped or attempted to rape a White woman while reducing the minimum penalty from seven to two years and taking out the "hard labor" requirement for a White man convicted of the same crime. The result was that the pre-Civil War statutory system not only reinforced the institution of slavery but perpetuated a gendered racist narrative that survived the war and informs our conceptions of prosecutable rape to this day.

While the Thirteenth and Fourteenth Amendments to the United States Constitution ended the de jure prohibition on prosecuting the rapists of Black women, antebellum prejudices and practices kept the prosecution of rape of a Black woman a rare, if extant, occurrence. Although the prosecution rates for rape of a Black woman have increased, there is still an identifiable pattern in prosecution in which White women victims are overvalued and women of color who are raped are undervalued. This means that Black women are less likely to have their cases prosecuted and perpetrators of sexual assaults on Black women will more likely escape punishment.

Questions

1. Why do you think sexual assaults on Black women are prosecuted and punished less than similar assaults on White women?

2. Do you think police or prosecutors intentionally discriminate against Black victims of sexual assault?

3. Might there be unintentional or unconscious bias against Black victims? Why or why not?

The Scottsboro Boys. The case of the Scottsboro Boys is another well-known case that epitomizes how the criminal law was used to brutally punish Black men who were suspected of "violating" the purity of White women—even when there was very little evidence to support the suspicions. On March 25, 1931, nine young Black men between the ages of thirteen and nineteen were illegally riding on a freight train between Chattanooga and Memphis. A group of White young men and women were also "hoboing" on the train at the same time. The Black boys eventually got into a fight with the White boys and threw them off the train. The White boys reported the incident to local authorities, and a posse of about fifty

The Scottsboro Boys in Jefferson County Jail Birmingham, Alabama, 1931.

CSU Archives/Everett Collection

White men armed with guns and other weapons stopped the train in Paint Rock, Alabama, captured the Black boys, and sent them to a jail in Scottsboro, Alabama. The vigilantes noticed that there were two White women dressed in overalls on the train as well. One of the women—Ruby Bates—either on her own or in response to a question, said the Black boys had raped her. This accusation led to a lynch mob of one hundred vigilantes surrounding the Scottsboro jail. The governor called in the National Guard to protect the jail, and the Scottsboro boys were tried for the rape of Ruby Bates and Victoria Price.

The Scottsboro boys were indicted, tried, convicted, and sentenced to death within ten days of their arrival in Scottsboro (one of the nine defendants' trials ended in a mistrial). Within one year of the trial, Victoria Price confessed that there had been no rape and eventually worked to help free the Scottsboro boys. Despite Ms. Price's recantation, the cases proceeded. The Scottsboro cases were appealed to the Supreme Court twice, and twice the Court reversed their convictions in two major cases upholding the right to counsel in death penalty cases and the prohibition against excluding African Americans from juries.[12] Charges were dropped against four of the Scottsboro Boys in 1937. The other five were convicted of rape and spent many years in prison, despite Victoria Price's admission that the crime never occurred.

Emmett Till. American history is filled with examples of Black men being beaten, lynched, or otherwise brutally murdered based on unproven accusations that they raped White women or behaved in some other sexually inappropriate way toward White women. The lynching of Emmett Till is one of the most well known of these incidents. Emmett Till was a fourteen-year-old boy who was brutally murdered for allegedly whistling at a White woman in Money, Mississippi, in 1955. Two White men beat him, gouged out his eye, and threw his body in the river. Emmett Till's killers were acquitted by an all-White jury.[13]

Two Cases of Rape

The Central Park Jogger Case

In 1989, five Black boys under the age of sixteen were charged with raping a twenty-three-year-old White woman in Central Park in New York City. After hours of interrogation by multiple police officers, the boys eventually confessed. Soon after the confessions, however, the boys denied that they had committed the crime and claimed that they confessed as a result of intimidation and coercion by the police officers. All five were convicted and sentenced to prison. In 2002, their convictions were vacated on the request of the prosecutor after DNA evidence proved that a man named Matias Reyes committed the crime. Reyes was also convicted of murder and four other rapes that occurred after the Central Park assault. Many have referred to the Central Park jogger case as a modern day "Scottsboro Boys" case.[14] The young men filed a lawsuit against the city claiming false arrest and malicious prosecution. The case eventually settled in 2014 with the city agreeing to pay forty million dollars—an average of one million dollars for each year of imprisonment.[15]

The Duke Lacrosse Players' Case

In 2006, the Duke lacrosse team held a party at the home of the team captains. Some of the members called an escort service and requested two White strippers, but the service instead sent two African American strippers. The women ultimately left after an argument with some of the team members. The women later reported that after they left the house and walked to their car, one member of the team came out to their car, apologized, and asked them to return. When they came back in, they were separated. It was during this time that one of the women claimed she was raped. After the women left the house, the alleged victim reported to police that several White males had raped her at the party earlier that evening.[16]

The prosecutor, Mike Nifong, ultimately charged three of the team players—Reade Seligmann, Collin Finnerty, and David Evans—with rape and related charges. The defendants were represented by a team of lawyers who discovered that the prosecutor withheld evidence that the prosecutor was legally required to turn over to the defense. The evidence was a forensic report revealing that the DNA of several other men had been found in the complainant's body. No DNA from any of the defendants had been found in or on the complainant. The prosecutor also failed to inform the defense attorneys that the complainant had made several contradictory statements that

Former Duke lacrosse players David Evans, Collin Finnerty, and Reade Seligmann at a press conference addressing the dismissal of the charges against them.

cast serious doubt on her credibility. The cases against the defendants were dismissed in April 2007, and the prosecutor was disbarred for his misconduct.

Questions

1. Is it fair to compare the Central Park jogger case with the Scottsboro Boys cases? Why or why not?

2. What are the differences and similarities between the Central Park jogger case and the Duke lacrosse players' case?

3. Do you think that race or class played a role in the outcome of the Duke lacrosse players' case?

Statutory Rape and Other Sex Offenses Against Minors

Statutory rape is the common law term used to describe the crime of an adult having sex with a minor under the age of consent. Although most state penal codes do not use the term statutory rape, the act is a crime in every state. Statutory rape is one of the few strict liability crimes in the criminal law. Even if the accused does not have the mens rea, or guilty state of mind, he or she may be guilty of the offense. For example, if the accused honestly believes that the minor is an adult and the jury agrees that it was reasonable for the accused to have such a mistaken belief, he or she is still guilty of statutory rape. The age of consent varies from state to state, and the crime is often punished in varying degrees depending on the difference in age between the adult and the child. For example, if an eighteen-year-old young man has sex with his sixteen-year-old girlfriend, the act could be statutory rape in a jurisdiction where the age of consent is eighteen. For that reason, many states have laws that require a significant age difference between the accused and the victim.

Until recently, Georgia was one state that did not distinguish between the act of an older man or woman raping a child and a teenager having sex with another teenager under the age of consent. The Genarlow Wilson case illustrates how such laws can have unintended consequences.

Genarlow Wilson

"The Legal Profession's Failure to Discipline Unethical Prosecutors" by Angela J. Davis[17]

Genarlow Wilson was seventeen years old when he decided, along with some of his teenage friends, to rent a hotel room. The young men invited their girlfriends, and the group drank alcohol, smoked marijuana, and performed various sexual acts at the hotel. They also videotaped themselves engaging in this behavior. One of the girls called her mother after she woke up the following morning and reported that she had been raped. Her mother called the police who searched the room and found the videotape. The police arrested the boys and the prosecutor charged them with several sex offenses, including rape. All of the boys except Wilson accepted a plea offer with a five-year prison sentence and the requirement that they register as sex offenders.

Wilson went to trial and the jury acquitted him of rape, but found him guilty of aggravated child molestation. At the time of the trial, this offense included having oral sex with a child under the age of sixteen—even if the child is fifteen, the "offender" is her seventeen-year-old boyfriend, and the behavior is totally consensual. The videotape clearly demonstrated that Wilson participated in this behavior with a girl who also willingly participated in the act. Several jurors were outraged and upset when they later found out that the penalty for this offense was ten mandatory years in prison with no possibility of parole.

After Wilson had been incarcerated for some time, his story slowly caught the attention of the media. Prior to his arrest, Wilson was a college bound high school athlete on the honor roll with no prior criminal record. A ten year mandatory prison sentence and registration as a sex offender for having consensual sex with another teenager seemed harsh to just about everyone. There were rallies led by civil rights leaders and many stories in the national press. Former President Carter spoke out in support of Wilson's release, as did then-presidential candidate Barack Obama. The Georgia state legislature eventually changed the law to make Wilson's behavior a misdemeanor, but it did not make the law retroactive. A judge ordered Wilson's release, finding the sentence to be "cruel and unusual punishment," but the state attorney general Thurbert Baker appealed the judge's decision. Finally, on October 26, 2007, after Wilson spent over two years in adult prison, the Georgia Supreme Court freed him in a 4–3 decision in which the court found the sentence to be in violation of the Eighth Amendment's prohibition against cruel and unusual punishment.

Most legislators passed these laws to protect children from sexual abuse by adults, not to punish teenagers who have sex. Although most of these cases involve grown men preying on children of either gender, there have been some cases of adult women seducing and having sex with minor boys. These cases often involve teachers having sex with their students. One of the most unusual of these cases involved a teacher named Mary Kay Letourneau.

Two Cases of Statutory Rape

Mary Kay Letourneau

Mary Kay Letourneau was married, had four children, and was working as a teacher at Shorewood Elementary School in Seattle, Washington,[18] when she began to take a particular interest in one of her students, twelve-year-old Vili Fualaau. During the 1995 academic year, Letourneau formed a close relationship with Fualaau and began to spend a significant amount of time with him, sometimes at her home with her family and sometimes alone. She eventually began to have sex with him, and in late 1996, became pregnant with his child.[19]

Letourneau was arrested and charged with statutory rape in 1997, the same year she gave birth to a baby girl. Letourneau's lawyer worked out a deal with the prosecutor in which Letourneau agreed to plead guilty to statutory rape, take prescribed psychiatric medication, serve three months in jail, participate in a sex offender treatment program after her release, and stay away from Fualaau. She was released in January 1998, and just one month later, she was found having sex with Fualaau in a car. The judge sentenced Letourneau to seven and one-half years in prison. After she returned to prison, she discovered that she was pregnant with her second child with Fualaau.[20]

Letourneau was released from prison in 2004. By then, she was forty-two and Fualaau twenty-three. A judge lifted the order prohibiting Letourneau from having contact with Fualaau. The two were married in 2005 and now live together with their children just outside of Seattle in King County, Washington.[21]

Roman Polanski

The famous actor and director Roman Polanski was arrested in 1977 for the sexual assault of thirteen-year-old Samantha Gailey (now Samantha Geimer). Polanski, who was forty-four years old at the time, was taking photographs of young girls for *Vogue* Magazine at the home of actor Jack Nicholson when he met Geimer. When Geimer later testified before a grand jury, she said that Polanski had given her champagne and drugs (Quaaludes) before raping her.[22] Polanski was indicted on six felony counts, including rape by use of drugs, child molesting, and sodomy.[23]

Polanski pled guilty to unlawful sexual intercourse and was sent to the Chino state prison for a ninety-day

Former elementary school teacher Mary Kay Letourneau and her former student Vili Fualaau at their beach front home in 2006, in Normandy Park, Washington.

psychiatric evaluation. He was released after only forty-two days, and the judge received a psychiatric report recommending that he not serve jail time.[24] However, Polanski heard that the judge planned to renege on the plea bargain and sentence him to prison. In February 1978, he fled to France where there was no risk of extradition to the United States. Polanski lived in France as a fugitive for over thirty years, only travelling to countries that would not likely extradite him to the United States.[25]

In September 2009, while en route to accept a lifetime achievement award at the Zurich Film Festival, Polanski was taken into custody in Zurich, Switzerland, at the request of U.S. authorities.[26] On January 22, 2010, Judge Peter Espinoza rejected a request that Polanski be sentenced without returning to the United States and ruled that Polanski must be extradited to the United States in order to be present for sentencing on all six felony counts.[27] On July 12, 2010, the Swiss authorities announced that they would not extradite Polanski, and he remains a free man as long as he does not return to the United States.[28]

When Polanski was arrested in Switzerland, many filmmakers, actors, and other celebrities in the United States came to his defense, arguing that he had suffered enough. Even Ms. Geimer came to Polanski's defense,

(Continued)

(Continued)

stating that she was hurt more by the media, prosecutor, and judge than by Polanski.[29]

Questions

1. Mary Kay Letourneau and Roman Polanski were both vilified in the court of public opinion, but Polanski received much more support than Letourneau, even though there was an even greater age difference between Polanski and his victim. Although Polanski was never sentenced, the psychiatrist who examined him recommended that he not be sentenced to jail time while Letourneau received a substantial prison sentence. Why do you think they were treated so differently?

2. Polanski is now seventy-nine years old. His supporters argue that no purpose would be served by punishing him at his advanced age. Do you agree?

3. Does it matter that his victim, now forty-nine years old, does not support his extradition and prosecution?

Sexting

Sending text messages on mobile telephones has become one of the most popular means of electronic communication—especially among young people. Many teens and young adults prefer texting over email or even talking on the phone. Most mobile phones also have the ability to send photographs. When individuals send text messages containing nude photographs, sexually explicit messages, or other sexual content, they may be subject to prosecution.

The modern term for sending sexually explicit text messages is sexting. Several legislators have introduced bills to make sexting a crime, but in the meantime, some prosecutors have brought misdemeanor obscenity charges or more serious child pornography charges against alleged offenders.[30] In some cases, persons convicted of sexting are required to register as sex offenders. Because many of these cases involve consensual communications between teens, there has been considerable opposition to these prosecutions.

In *Miller v. Mitchell* (2010),[31] the court held that parents could seek an order blocking the prosecution of their children on child pornography charges for appearing in photographs found on their classmates' cell phones.[32] The decision is limited to the girls who appeared in the photos, not those who possessed or transmitted the photographs. The American Civil Liberties Union represented the parents in the case and has been challenging other sexting prosecutions around the country.[33]

Race, DNA, and Wrongful Convictions

The Scottsboro and Central Park jogger cases provide historical and modern day examples of wrongful convictions in rape cases. There have been many other rape cases where the defendant was wrongfully convicted, and no phenomenon has brought the prevalence of these injustices to light more than the use of DNA testing. There have been a total of 316 DNA post-conviction exonerations in the history of the United States through 2013,[34] and of those, over 80 percent have included rape convictions.[35]

The overwhelming majority of rape exonerations have been in cases involving Black defendants and White victims. In 2002, 58 percent of all prisoners serving time for rape were White, 29 percent were Black, and 13 percent were Latino.[36] However, for rape exonerations, just the opposite was true: 64 percent were Black, 28 percent were White, and 7 percent were Latino.[37] These statistics suggest that Black men are disproportionately falsely accused of rape. The race of the victim was noted in 75 percent of these cases, and in each of these cases, the victim was White. These statistics are even more startling when one considers that most rapes occur between people of the same race. Well under 10 percent of all rapes involve a Black defendant and White victim.

The case of Ronald Cotton is one of the most well-known cases involving a wrongful rape conviction. Mr. Cotton is Black, and the alleged victim is White.

Ronald Cotton

In July 1984, a man broke into Jennifer Thompson's apartment, held a knife to her throat, and raped her. He then went to Elizabeth Watson's apartment and raped her at knifepoint. Thompson told the police that she had studied the man's face and helped them create a composite sketch of her assailant. Watson did not remember her assailant's face but described him as an African American man in his twenties and noted that he carried a flashlight. The police put together a photo spread that included young men who they believed resembled the composite sketch. A mug shot of Ronald Cotton from a previous juvenile arrest was included. Thompson picked Cotton's photo, but Watson was unable to identify anyone.[38]

Ronald Cotton was convicted of raping Thompson later that year, but the North Carolina Supreme Court overturned his first conviction because the judge did not allow the jury to hear evidence that Watson had picked another man from a lineup and identified him as the rapist. After Cotton's conviction was reversed, Watson changed her mind and identified Cotton as her rapist. The prosecutor then charged Cotton with the second rape. Before the second trial began, a man named Bobby Poole who was in prison for similar crimes told another inmate that he had committed the rapes. However, the trial judge refused to allow the jury to hear about this evidence at the second trial, and Mr. Cotton was convicted of both rapes. He was sentenced to life plus fifty-four years for the crimes.[39]

In 1994, Mr. Cotton's new lawyer requested that DNA testing be done to prove that Mr. Cotton was innocent. The forensic samples from Thompson were too deteriorated to test, but the samples from Watson conclusively matched the DNA of Bobby Poole—the man who previously confessed to the rapes. Poole again confessed to both rapes.[40] The district attorney dismissed all charges, and on June 30, 1995, Cotton was released from prison. In July 1995, the governor of North Carolina officially pardoned Mr. Cotton, and he was given $110,000 compensation from the state. Mr. Cotton had served ten and one-half years of his sentence.[41]

Thompson met Cotton after he was released, and they became friends. They began to do speaking engagements together on the unreliability of eyewitness

Jennifer Thompson and Ronald Cotton in Greensboro, North Carolina, September 14, 2000.

identification. They eventually co-authored a book about the case—*Picking Cotton: Our Memoir of Injustice and Redemption*. Ms. Thompson is now an advocate for criminal justice reform and a member of the North Carolina Actual Innocence Commission.

Robbery

Robbery is defined as follows:

1. The trespassory taking, and

2. Carrying away

3. Of the personal property of another

4. With the intent to permanently deprive the owner

5. By force or threat of force.

Simply put, it is often defined as a larceny and an **assault**:

Larceny + Assault = Robbery

Although sometimes described as a property crime because it involves taking property, the assaultive part of the crime makes robbery a violent crime. It is described as such by the Department of Justice Bureau of Justice Statistics.

Consider the following scenarios:

- John points a gun at Joe and demands that he give him all of his money. Joe immediately reaches into his pocket and gives John his wallet. John leaves and never returns.
- John runs by Mary, suddenly grabs her purse from her shoulder, and runs away.

In the first scenario, John clearly has robbed Joe by taking his property using the threat of force. Likewise, if John walks over to Joe and says, "Give me all your money or I will break your arm!" and Joe gives up his wallet, John has robbed Joe by using the threat of force, assuming John has the apparent capacity to carry out the threat.

The second scenario is the type of robbery about which there is some disagreement—the so-called robbery purse snatch. The majority view is that such thefts are robberies.Grabbing a purse (or other object) from an individual involves force, however slight. Such robberies are to be distinguished from pickpocket thefts. If John sneaks up behind Joe and slides his wallet out of his back pocket without Joe's knowledge, no robbery has occurred because there has been no force. However, if John tries to slide the wallet out, but it gets stuck, and he has to pull it out with force (even a slight amount), John is a robber. The minority view of robbery purse snatches is that they are thefts unless a significant amount of force is used.

Consider the following two cases:

State v. Curley (1997)

New Mexico Court of Appeals

939 P.2d 1103

The prosecution arose out of a purse snatching. The evidence was that the victim was walking out of a mall with her daughter when Defendant grabbed her purse and ran away. The victim described the incident as follow: "I had my purse on my left side . . . and I felt kind of a shove of my left shoulder where I had my purse strap with my thumb through it and I kind of leaned—was pushed—toward my daughter, and this person came and just grabbed the strap of my purse and continued to run." The victim used the words "grab" or "pull" to describe the actual taking of the purse and "shove" or "push" to describe what Defendant did as he grabbed or "pulled [the purse] from her arm and hand." However, there was also evidence that the victim's thumb was not through the strap of the purse, but was rather on the bottom of the purse. The purse strap was not broken, and the victim did not testify that she struggled with Defendant for the purse in any way or that any part of her body offered any resistance or even moved when the purse was pulled from her arm and hand. Defendant presented evidence that he was drunk and did not remember the incident at all.

Robbery is theft by the use or threatened use of force or violence. Because the words "or violence" refer to the unwarranted exercise of force and do not substantively state an alternative means of committing the offense . . . we refer simply to "force" in this opinion. The force must be the lever by which the property is taken. . . . Although we have cases saying in dictum that even a slight amount of force, such as jostling the victim or snatching away the property, is sufficient, . . . we also have cases in which a taking of property from the person of a victim has been held not to be robbery, *see State v. Sanchez* . . . (wallet taken from victim's pocket while victim was aware that the defendant was taking the wallet).

Defendant contends that such evidence exists in that the jury could have found that Defendant's shoving of the victim was part of his drunkenness, and then the purse was taken without force sufficient to constitute robbery. We agree. We are persuaded by an analysis of our own cases, as well as cases from other jurisdictions, that the applicable rule in this case is as follows: when property is attached to the person or clothing of a victim so as to cause resistance, any taking is a robbery, and not larceny, because the lever that causes the victim to part with the property is the force that is applied to break that resistance; however, when no more force is used than would be necessary to remove property from a person who does not resist, then the offense is larceny, and not robbery.

Commonwealth v. Zangari (1997)

Massachusetts Court of Appeals

677 N.E.2d 702

About 7:30 P.M., June 10, 1994, two elderly women, Nancy Colantonio and Vera Croston, returned in Croston's 1981 Chevrolet Citation automobile to their home at 36 Webster Street, Haverhill. Croston, upon entering the driveway, located by the side of the stairs leading to the porch and front door, stopped the car to let Colantonio out. Colantonio walked up the stairs. She felt someone snatch her purse from under her arm. She was stunned. Turning, she saw the back of a man running down Webster Street in the direction of Summer Street. She said she couldn't believe what she was seeing.

While Colantonio was making her way, before the purse snatch, Croston was easing the car up the rest of the short driveway and locking the car. Standing at the back of the car and looking over it, Croston saw a man walking diagonally across Webster Street toward the house. She saw him full face, then lost sight of him until she saw his back as he fled down Webster Street.

Cheryl Klley, tending her flower garden on the opposite side of Webster Street, saw a man run up the stairs, snatch Colantonio's purse, run down the stairs and turn and run down Webster Street. Kiley had a side view of the man.

(Continued)

(Continued)

Upon testimony to the foregoing effect and further identification evidence from selections of photographs, Zangari was tried to a jury in Superior Court and found guilty of violating G.L. c. 265, § 19(a), unarmed robbery from a person over the age of sixty-five. (Colantonio was eighty-six at the time.)

On the present appeal from the judgment of conviction, Zangari contends that the trial judge erred when he denied motions for a required finding of not guilty because, says Zangari, the force the thief applied in snatching the purse was, as matter of law, insufficient to satisfy the "force and violence" denounced in the statute. Zangari intimates that he could have been found guilty of larceny from the person, G.L. c. 266, § 25 (a) where force is not made part of the offense.

Zangari is complaining that the force applied to Colantonio was no more or little more than that used by a pickpocket who is chargeable only with larceny; hence some substantial force should be required to convict of armed robbery. The point of our leading case of *Commonwealth v. Jones* . . . as observed in *Commonwealth v. Davis* . . .

was that "where the snatching or sudden taking of property from a victim is sufficient to produce awareness, there is sufficient evidence of force to permit a finding of robbery."

In pickpocketing, which is accomplished by sleight of hand, such evidence is lacking. The difference accounts for the perceived greater severity of the offense of unarmed robbery in contrast with larceny.

Judgment affirmed.

Questions

1. Which interpretation of the common law definition of robbery is best—the Curley view or the Zangari view?

2. Were Mr. Curley's actions less violent or forceful than Mr. Zangari's?

3. Were these cases decided differently because of the difference in the facts or because of the courts' interpretation of the law?

Kidnapping ●

Common law kidnapping is defined as follows:

1. The forcible

2. Abduction

3. And carrying away

4. Of a person.

At common law, the additional element of carrying the person from one country to another was an essential part of the definition of kidnapping, but most modern statutes have eliminated this element.

The Model Penal Code (MPC) defines kidnapping as follows:

A person is guilty of kidnapping if he unlawfully removes another from his place of residence or business, or a substantial distance from the vicinity where he is found, or if he unlawfully confines another for a substantial period in a place of isolation, with any of the following purposes:

(a) to hold for ransom or reward, or as a shield or hostage; or

(b) to facilitate commission of any felony or flight thereafter; or

(c) to inflict bodily injury on or to terrorize the victim or another; or

(d) to interfere with the performance of any governmental or political function.[42]

When most people think of kidnapping, they think of an individual being held for ransom money. The criminal takes the individual away and agrees to return him or her only if he or she is paid a certain amount of money. Although some states require intent to seek ransom money as an essential element of the offense, some do not, as the following excerpts from the Pennsylvania and California statutes illustrate:

Pennsylvania and California Kidnapping Statutes

Pennsylvania Kidnapping Statute

18 Pa.C.S. § 2901 (2010) § 2901. Kidnapping

a. OFFENSE DEFINED.—A person is guilty of kidnapping if he unlawfully removes another a substantial distance under the circumstances from the place where he is found, or if he unlawfully confines another for a substantial period in a place of isolation, with any of the following intentions:

1. To hold for ransom or reward, or as a shield or hostage.

2. To facilitate commission of any felony or flight thereafter.

3. To inflict bodily injury on or to terrorize the victim or another. . . .

California Kidnapping Statute

Cal Pen Code § 207 (2011) § 207. Kidnapping defined

a. Every person who forcibly, or by any other means of instilling fear, steals or takes, or holds, detains, or arrests any person in this state, and carries the person into another country, state, or county, or into another part of the same county, is guilty of kidnapping.

b. Every person, who for the purpose of committing any act defined in Section 288, hires, persuades, entices, decoys, or seduces by false promises, misrepresentations, or the like, any child under the age of 14 years to go out of this country, state, or county, or into another part of the same county, is guilty of kidnapping. . . . .

Kidnapping usually involves taking a person away against his or her will, but some statutes include a definition of kidnapping that involves simply holding and confining a person against their will, even if they are not taken away. All definitions require that the person be taken or held against his or her will, which usually involves the use of force. Some statutes, such as the California statute, specifically use the word "forcibly," while others, such as Pennsylvania, do not. Whenever force is a required element, as with robbery, difficult questions about how much force is necessary arise, especially when the defendant is charged with both kidnapping and robbery. The following case illustrates this problem.

State v. Beatty (1998)

Supreme Court of North Carolina

347 N.C. 555

Defendant was convicted of kidnapping, robbery with dangerous weapon, and other offenses following jury trial in the Superior Court, Mecklenburg County, Steelman, J., and he appealed. The Court of Appeals found no error, and defendant appealed again. The Supreme Court, Whichard, J., held that: (1) kidnapping statute as interpreted in *Fulcher* precludes conviction when only evidence of restraint is that which is inherent and inevitable feature of another felony; (2) binding one victim's wrists and kicking his back twice was enough additional restraint to satisfy restraint element of kidnapping; but (3) threatening another victim with gun was not.

Affirmed in part, reversed in part, and remanded.

On 23 May 1994 a Mecklenburg County grand jury indicted defendant Edward Ronald Beatty for robbery with a dangerous weapon, assault with a deadly weapon with intent to kill inflicting serious injury, felonious breaking and entering, safecracking, first-degree kidnapping, two counts of second-degree kidnapping, and possession of a firearm by a convicted felon.

The jury found defendant guilty as charged. . . . The trial court arrested judgment on the conviction for first-degree kidnapping and sentenced defendant to imprisonment of thirty years for the robbery with a dangerous weapon, ten years for felonious assault, ten years for entering, and fifteen years for each of the second-degree kidnappings, all sentences to be served consecutively.

Defendant appealed to the Court of Appeals asserting, *inter alia,* that his kidnapping convictions should be vacated because there was insufficient evidence of restraint separate and apart from that inherent in the crime of robbery with a dangerous weapon to support those convictions. The Court of Appeals majority disagreed. Judge Wynn dissented in part on the ground that "the restraint in this case was an inherent and inevitable feature of the commission of the armed robbery" and thus could not support a conviction for second-degree kidnapping. Defendant appeals based upon Judge Wynn's dissent. For reasons that follow, we affirm with regard to defendant's conviction for the second-degree kidnapping of victim Koufaloitis, and we reverse with regard to defendant's conviction for the second-degree kidnapping of victim Poulos.

The State's evidence tended to show that on 19 March 1994 defendant met a group of men at a party. They decided to rob South 21, a drive-in restaurant in Charlotte,

North Carolina. When they approached the restaurant, the owner, Nicholas Copsis, stood just outside near an open door. The robbers approached this door, put a gun to Copsis' head, and told him to go inside and open the safe.

Once inside, the robbers saw restaurant employees Hristos Poulos and Tom Koufaloitis. Poulos was on his knees washing the floor at the front, and Koufaloitis stood three to four feet from the safe cleaning the floor in the back. One robber put a gun to Poulos' head and stood beside him during the robbery. An unarmed robber put duct tape around Koufaloitis' wrists and told him to lie on the floor.

Copsis did not open the safe on his first attempt. One robber said, "Let's go. We're taking too long. Hurry up." Another shot Copsis twice in the legs. Copsis then opened the safe. The robbers took more than $2,000 and fled. The robbery took approximately three to four minutes.

Defendant contends that his convictions for second-degree kidnapping must be vacated because the State presented insufficient evidence of restraint separate from that inherent in the robbery. He asserts that such evidence is necessary to satisfy the requirements of N.C.G.S. § 14–39, the kidnapping statute, as interpreted by this Court in *State v. Fulcher,* . . . .

N.C.G.S. § 14–39(a) provides in pertinent part that a person is guilty of kidnapping if he or she shall unlawfully confine, restrain, or remove from one place to another, any other person 16 years of age or over without the consent of such person . . . if such confinement, restraint or removal is for the purpose of:

. . .

(2) Facilitating the commission of any felony or facilitating flight of any person following the commission of a felony. . . . N.C.G.S. § 14–39(a) (1993) (amended 1994). In *Fulcher* this Court recognized that certain felonies, such as robbery with a dangerous weapon, cannot be committed without some restraint of the victim; and it held that "restraint, which is an inherent, inevitable feature of such other felony," could not form the basis of a kidnapping conviction. . . . The Court stated that the legislature did not intend N.C.G.S. § 14–39 "to permit the conviction and punishment of the defendant for both crimes." *Id.* The Court further noted that "[t]o hold otherwise would violate the constitutional prohibition against double jeopardy." *Id.*

As noted, under N.C.G.S. § 14–39 as construed and applied in *Fulcher,* a person cannot be convicted of kidnapping when the only evidence of restraint is that "which is an inherent, inevitable feature" of another felony such as armed robbery.... "The key question . . . is whether the kidnapping charge is supported by evidence from which a jury could reasonably find that the necessary restraint for kidnapping 'exposed [the victim] to greater danger than that inherent in the armed robbery itself.'"(quoting *Irwin*. . .) Here, the robbers, including defendant, restrained two victims, Koufaloitis and Poulos, and defendant was convicted of one count of second-degree kidnapping for each restraint. We address each in turn.

The evidence of defendant's restraint of victim Koufaloitis supports a finding that the robbers, including defendant, put duct tape around the victim's wrists, forced him to lie on the floor, and kicked him in the back twice. Because the binding and kicking were not inherent, inevitable parts of the robbery, these forms of restraint "exposed [the victim to a] greater danger than that inherent in the armed robbery itself." See also *Pigott* (holding that when the defendant bound the victim's hands and feet, he exposed the victim to a greater danger than that inherent in the armed robbery and therefore upholding the defendant's kidnapping conviction); *Fulcher* (holding that binding of victims' hands was *not* an inherent and inevitable feature of rape and therefore upholding the defendant's kidnapping convictions based upon that restraint). When defendant bound this victim's wrists and kicked him in the back, he increased the victim's helplessness and vulnerability beyond what was necessary to enable him and his comrades to rob the restaurant. Such actions constituted sufficient additional restraint to satisfy the restraint element of kidnapping under N.C.G.S. § 14–39, and the Court of Appeals properly found no error in defendant's conviction for the second-degree kidnapping of victim Koufaloitis. . . .

With regard to victim Poulos, the evidence shows only that one of the robbers approached the victim, pointed a gun at him, and stood guarding him during the robbery. The victim did not move during the robbery, and the robbers did not injure him in any way. In order to commit a robbery with a dangerous weapon under N.C.G.S. § 14–87(a), defendant had to possess, use, or threaten to use a firearm while taking personal property from a place of business where persons were in attendance. The only evidence of restraint of this victim was the threatened use of a firearm. This restraint is an essential element of robbery with a dangerous weapon under N.C.G.S. § 14–87, and defendant's use of this restraint exposed the victim to no greater danger than that required to complete the robbery with a dangerous weapon. We thus hold that threatening victim Poulos with a gun was an inherent, inevitable feature of the robbery and is insufficient to support a conviction for kidnapping under N.C.G.S. § 14–39. The Court of Appeals therefore erred in finding no error in defendant's conviction for the second-degree kidnapping of victim Poulos.

For the reasons stated, we affirm the Court of Appeals with regard to defendant's conviction for the second-degree kidnapping of victim Koufaloitis, and we reverse the Court of Appeals with regard to defendant's conviction for the second-degree kidnapping of victim Poulos. . . .

Questions

1. What was the basis of defendant Beatty's appeal?

2. Why did the court affirm the kidnapping conviction with regard to Mr. Koufaloitis and reverse the conviction for the kidnapping of Mr. Poulos?

3. The court noted that the binding and kicking of Mr. Koufaloitis were not "inherent, inevitable parts of the robbery." What does the court mean by this statement? Are "binding and kicking" considered "force" for purposes of the offense of robbery?

Assault and Battery

In the common law, the crimes of assault and battery were two separate crimes. An assault was an attempt to commit a battery, and a battery was any unlawful or unwanted touching. If Dave took a swing at Buster and missed, he committed an assault. If his fist made contact, he committed a battery. Batteries included any unwanted touching, even if there was no injury or force.

Many modern statutes have merged these two offenses into one and refer to them both as assaults. As with many other crimes, there are various degrees of assault, depending on the harm caused by the act. More serious assaults are referred to as "aggravated assaults" or first degree assaults, while less serious forms of this crime are called "simple assaults" or second degree assaults. Most of these statutes punish assaults whether they are committed intentionally, recklessly, or negligently.

Consider the MPC's definition of assault:

Section 211.1 Assault

1. Simple Assault. A person is guilty of assault if he:

   a. Attempts to cause or purposely, knowingly or recklessly causes bodily injury to another; or

   b. Negligently causes bodily injury to another with a deadly weapon; or

   c. Attempts by physical menace to put another in fear of imminent serious bodily injury.

2. Aggravated Assault. A person is guilty of aggravated assault if he:

   a. Attempts to cause serious bodily injury to another, or causes such injury purposely, knowingly or recklessly under circumstances manifesting extreme indifference to the value of human life; or

   b. Attempts to cause or purposely or knowingly causes bodily injury to another with a deadly weapon.

Many states follow the MPC's classification of assault as either simple or aggravated. Maryland is a state that classifies assaults in terms of degrees. An assault that involves serious physical injury or that is committed with a firearm is considered first degree assault. A minor assault that does not cause serious injury is a second degree assault.

Consider the following hypotheticals:

- Claudio and Juan are in a bar watching Chile and Mexico compete in the World Cup Soccer Tournament. Claudio's team is Chile, and Juan is rooting for Mexico. The two men begin to argue over the referee's decision to penalize one of the Chilean players. Claudio attacks Juan, breaking his nose and causing numerous internal injuries. Juan is hospitalized for a week.
- Robert is driving to work. Because he is late, he begins to speed, driving forty miles per hour in a thirty mile per hour residential neighborhood. Robert decides to call his boss on his cell phone while driving. When Robert looks at his phone to enter the phone number, he hits Mark who was walking in the crosswalk. Luckily, Mark was not seriously injured.

Since Claudio caused serious bodily injury to Juan, he would be charged with aggravated assault under the MPC and first degree assault under the Maryland statute. Robert did not intentionally hit Mark. His behavior was either negligent or reckless, and he did not seriously injure Mark. Robert would likely be charged with simple assault under the MPC and second degree assault under the Maryland statute.

Concluding Note

Rape, other sexual assaults, robbery, kidnapping, assault, and battery all have a common theme—they are violent crimes that cause serious physical and even psychological harm to their victims. Some of these offenses have elements in common. For example, the element of force is required for rape, robbery, and kidnapping and is inherent in the offenses of assault and battery. Others, such as statutory rape, may have no element of force but are nonetheless dangerous crimes that cause serious harm. Rape, some other forms of sexual assault, and kidnapping are considered to be so violent and harmful that they are punished as much and sometimes even more than many forms of criminal homicide, as you will learn in the Chapter 8 and in Chapter 11.Now test yourself on the material we have covered in this chapter. Good luck with the Issue Spotter exercise.

IssueSpotter

Read the hypothetical and spot the issues discussed in this chapter.

Talk Show Rivals

Bob Olsen was a conservative television talk show host. He hated liberals and particularly hated Kevin Davis, who hosted a liberal television talk show. The two men constantly competed for television ratings. Bob heard that Kevin had a copy of a very unflattering video recording of Bob at Bob's fiftieth birthday party and that Kevin planned to show the video on his television show. Bob was half-dressed in the video, drunk, and singing out of tune. Bob was determined to retrieve the video.

Bob drove to Kevin's television studio. He went into the building, walked into Kevin's office, and confronted Kevin about the video. Kevin denied knowing anything about a video. Bob started yelling at Kevin and demanded that he give him the video. Kevin stood up. Bob, who was much bigger, towered over Kevin. Bob said in a loud voice,

"I'm going to ask you one more time. Give me that video!" Kevin opened his desk drawer, took out the video, and handed it to Bob. Bob then took out a gun, pointed it at Kevin, and ordered him to come with him. While holding the gun on Kevin, Bob led Kevin to his car, ordered him to sit in the passenger seat, and drove Kevin to his house.

When they arrived at Bob's home, Bob ordered Keith into the house, bound his hands behind his back with duct tape, tied his feet together with rope, and ordered him to sit on the floor in the living room. Bob then called Keith's studio and asked to speak to the producer. Bob, disguising his voice, informed the producer that they would never see Kevin again unless they left one million dollars in a suitcase behind a building near the studio by midnight.

The producer called the police who were able to locate Bob in a short period of time using cell phone GPS technology. Bob surrendered to the police immediately.

1. What charges should be brought against Bob?

2. What are the strengths and weaknesses of the state's case?

Key Terms and Cases ●━━━━━━━━━━━━━━

Notes●━━━━━━━━━━━━━━━━━━━━━━━━━━━━━━━━━━━

1. See *Coker v. Georgia*, 433 U.S. 584 (1977) (holding that it is unconstitutional to execute a person found guilty of the rape of an adult woman); see also Kennedy v. Louisiana, 554 U.S. 407 (2008) (abolishing the death penalty for the rape of a child).

2. U.S. Department of Justice, Bureau of Justice Statistics, "Criminal Victimization In the United States, 2008 Statistical Tables," Table 91, NCJ 227669 (Washington, DC: Author, 2010), http://www.bjs.gov/content/pub/pdf/cvus08.pdf (Providing number, percent distribution, and rate of victimizations by type of crime.)

3. See U.S. Department of Justice, Bureau of Justice Statistics, "Criminal Victimization in the United States, 2008 Statistical Tables," Table 2, NCJ 227669 (Washington, DC: Author, 2010), http://www.bjs.gov/content/pub/pdf/cvus08.pdf (Providing number of victimizations and victimization rates for persons 12 or older.)

4. University of Minnesota, *Got Consent? Consent is Sexy* (2012), http://www1.umn.edu/aurora/pdf/2012%20Consent%20Brochure.pdf

5. Occidental College, *Sexual Assault Policy* (2010), http://www.oxy.edu/sexual-assault-resources-support/policies-procedures

6. White House Task Force to Protect Students from Sexual Assault, *Not Alone: The First Report of the White House Task Force to Protect Students from Sexual Assault* (Washington, DC: Author, 2014), http://www.whitehouse.gov/sites/default/files/docs/report_0.pdf

7. Nick Anderson, "55 Colleges Under Title IX Probe for Handling of Sexual Violence and Harassment Claims," *Washington Post*, May 1, 2014, http://www.washingtonpost.com/local/education/federal-government-releases-list-of-55-colleges-universities-under-title-ix-investigations-over-handling-of-sexual-violence/2014/05/01/e0a74810-d13b-11e3-937f-d3026234b51c_story.html

8. Angus Johnston, "Colleges Respond to White House Report on College Sexual Assault," *Rh Reality Check*, May 6, 2014, http://rhrealitycheck.org/article/2014/05/06/advocates-respond-white-house-report-college-sexual-assault/

9. Susan Estrich, "Rape," *Yale Law Journal* 95 (1986): 1087.

10. Mich. Comp. Laws Ann. § 750.520j (West).

11. Jeffrey J. Pokorak, "Rape As A Badge of Slavery: The Legal History of, and Remedies For, Prosecutorial Race-of-Victim Charging Disparities," *Nevada Law Journal* 7 (2006): 1.

12. See *Powell v. Alabama*, 287 U.S. 45, 73 (1932); see also Norris v. Alabama, 294 U.S. 587, 589 (1935).

13. Andrew D. Leipold, "Symposium on Race and Criminal Law: Objective Tests and Subjective Bias: Some Problems of Discriminatory Intent in the Criminal Law," *Chicago Kent Law Review* 73, no.83 (1998):559, 579.

14. See N. Jeremi Duru, "The Central Park Five, the Scottsboro Boys, and the Myth of the Bestial Black Man," *Cardozo Law Review* 25 (2004): 1315, 1315–18; see also Elizabeth Jensen, "Ken Burns, the Voice of the Wilderness," *New York Times*, September 10, 2009, http://www.nytimes.com/2009/09/13/arts/television/13jens.html

15. Benjamin Weiser, "5 Exonerated in Central Park Jogger Case Agree to Settle Suit for $40 Million," *New York Times*, June 19, 2014, http://www.nytimes.com/2014/06/20/nyregion/5-exonerated-in-central-park-jogger-case-are-to-settle-suit-for-40-million.html?_r=1

16. Angela J. Davis, "The Legal Profession's Failure to Discipline Unethical Prosecutors," *Hofstra Law Review* 36 (2007): 275, 297.

17. Id at 303.

18. Denise Noe, "A Boy and His Teacher," *Mary Kay Letourneau: The Romance That Was A Crime, Crime Library*, http://www.crimelibrary.com/criminal_mind/psychology/marykay_letourneau/5.html

19. Ibid.

20. Ibid.

21. Denise Noe, "Happy Ever After?" *Mary Kay Letourneau: The Romance That Was A Crime*, Crime Library, http://www.crimelibrary.com/criminal_mind/psychology/marykay_letourneau/12.html

22. Jonathan Romney, "Roman Polanski: The Truth About his Notorious Sex Crime," *The Independent*, Oct. 5, 2008, http://www.independent.co.uk/news/people/profiles/roman-polanski-the-truth-about-his-notorious-sex-crime-949106.html

23. Associated Press, "Judge: Roman Polanski Must Return to U.S.," MSNBC.COM, January 22, 2010, http://www.msnbc.msn.com/id/35020812/ns/entertainment-celebrities

24. Romney, supra n. 18.

25. Jura Koncius, "A Roman in Paris," *Washington Post*, February 3, 1978, http://www.vachss.com/mission/roman_polanski.html

26. Paul Verschuur and Edvard Pettersson, "Polanski Arrested in Switzerland on 1978 U.S. Warrant," *Bloomberg*, September 28, 2009, http://www.bloomberg.com/apps/news?pid=20601088&sid=acnp0zi_Edgw

27. Associated Press, supra n. 19.

28. Nick Cumming-Bruce and Michael Cieply, "Swiss Reject U.S. Request to Extradite Polanski," *New York Times*, July 12, 2010, http://www.nytimes.com/2010/07/13/movies/13polanski.html?pagewanted=1&_r=1&src=mv

29. "Exclusive: Polanski Victim Blames Media," ABCNews. com, March 10, 2011, http://abcnews.go.com/GMA/video/exclusive-roman-polanski-victim-blames-media-13103307

30. "Five Va. Teens Charged With Felonies in Sexting Case," *The Roanoke Times*, May 20, 2010, http://hamptonroads.com/2010/05/five-va-teens-charged-felonies-sexting-case

31. See *Miller v. Mitchell,* 598 F.3d 139 (3d Cir. 2010).

32. Tamar Lewin, "Court Says Parents Can Block 'Sexting' Cases," *New York Times*, March 17, 2010, http://www.nytimes.com/2010/03/18/education/18sext.html

33. Martha Neil, "'Sexting' Cases Put Pa. Prosecutor on ACLU's Litigation List," *ABA Journal*, Mar. 25, 2009, http://www.abajournal.com/news/article/sexting_cases_put_prosecutor_on_aclus_litigation_list/; see also "'Sexting' Case to Take Center Stage at 3rd Circuit," *Sentencing Law and Policy*, January 15, 2010, http://sentencing.typepad.com/sentencing_law_and_policy/2010/01/sexting-case-to-take-center-stage-at-3rd-circuit.html

34. Innocence Project, "DNA Exoneree Case Profiles," http://www.innocenceproject.org/know/

35. Barry Scheck and Peter Neufeld, "250 Exonerated, Too Many Wrongfully Convicted," Benjamin N. Cardozo School of Law, Yeshiva University (2010), http://www.innocenceproject.org/docs/InnocenceProject_250.pdf

36. Samuel R. Gross et al., "Symposium: Innocence in Capital Sentencing: Exonerations in the United States 1989 Through 2003," *Journal of Criminal Law & Criminology* 95 (2005): 523, 547.

37. Ibid.

38. Scot Abrahamson and Will Robinson, "Ronald Cotton: A Decade Behind Bars for a Rape He Didn't Commit," Northwestern Law, Center on Wrongful Convictions (2009), http://www.law.northwestern.edu/legalclinic/wrongfulconvictions

39. Innocence Project, "Ronald Cotton," http://www.innocenceproject.org/Content/72.php

40. Ibid.

41. Ibid.

42. Model Penal Code § 212.1 (2001).

Chapter 8

Dr. Jack Kevorkian was a medical pathologist who became famous for promoting physician-assisted suicide for terminally ill patients who wanted to end their lives. He participated in about 130 assisted suicides during his lifetime.[1] Dr. Kevorkian was prosecuted four times for violating Michigan's law banning assisted suicide. He was acquitted in the first three trials, and the fourth case was dismissed after the judge declared a mistrial. Finally, in 1998, Dr. Kevorkian was charged with first degree murder in the death of Thomas Youk. In the previous cases, Dr. Kevorkian had simply provided the lethal medications and assisted the patients who gave themselves the drugs using an apparatus he made (pictured below). In Mr. Youk's case, Dr. Kevorkian actually administered the lethal injection himself. He videotaped the procedure and sent the tape to CBS's *60 Minutes*, which broadcasted the video on November 22, 1988. Dr. Kevorkian was convicted of second degree murder and delivery of a controlled substance and was sentenced to ten to twenty-five years in prison. He was released on June 1, 2007, after promising that he would not perform another assisted suicide. Dr. Kevorkian died on June 3, 2011.

When most people think of murder, they think of a dangerous, violent person who acts with the intent of causing the ultimate harm to another human being. In this chapter, you will learn, as Dr. Kevorkian's case illustrates, that there are many different forms of criminal homicide. Some are intentional, malicious acts while others are unintentional and caused by reckless or even negligent behavior.

Dr. Jack Kevorkian with his "suicide machine."

Criminal Homicide

Introduction ●──────────────────────────────

In our society, we value human life above all. When a human life is lost, regardless of the reason, it is seen as the ultimate tragedy. We mourn the loss of life and seek answers—not only how did the person die, but why? If someone dies at the hands of another human being, there is a great desire to blame and punish that person, even if the perpetrator acted unintentionally. Not surprisingly, the wrongful killing of another human being is viewed as the most serious crime. With very limited exceptions, it is the only crime for which an individual may receive the death penalty.

In 1980, the homicide rate reached an all-time high of 10.2 homicides per 100,000 people. In 1991, the rate was 9.8 per 100,000 but declined sharply between 1992 and 2000. By 2007, the homicide rate was 5.6 per 100,000,[2] and by 2011, it had declined to 4.7 homicides per 100,000 persons, the lowest level since 1963.[3] The overwhelming majority of murder victims and offenders are young men (between the ages of 18 and 35), and a disproportionate percentage of victims and offenders are Black.[4] Young adults between the ages of 18 and 24 have the highest offending rate in each racial and gender group.[5] From 2002 to 2011, the average homicide rate for males was 3.6 times higher than the rate for females, and the average homicide rate for Blacks was 6.3 times higher than the rate for Whites.[6]

This chapter will discuss the different forms of homicide and explain how judges and juries make the fine distinctions between the various degrees of murder. As the cases will illustrate, much depends upon the facts of the particular case and the strength of the evidence presented.

Definitions ●──────────────────────────────

Homicide is the killing of a human being by another person. Although this chapter will discuss criminal homicide, not all homicides are crimes. Some are considered to be justifiable under the law. For example, as will be discussed in Chapter 9, a person who kills another in self-defense is not guilty of any form of homicide. When a soldier kills an enemy during wartime, the killing is authorized by law, as are the deaths that occur as a result of lethal injections administered in jurisdictions that permit the death penalty.

Learning Objectives

After reading and studying this chapter, you should be able to

➤ Explain the difference between murder and manslaughter

➤ Provide the elements of intentional and unintentional first degree murder, second degree murder, and manslaughter

➤ Know the difference between premeditation and deliberation

➤ Explain provocation and "heat of passion"

➤ Define the "year and a day" rule

➤ Explain the felony murder rule

➤ Provide the rationale for the felony murder rule

➤ Explain the two-part trial process for capital cases

➤ Define and list aggravating and mitigating circumstances in capital cases

➤ List the limitations on the death penalty

➤ Explain judicial override

A term as simple as "killing" has been the subject of litigation and legislation over the years. A person is considered dead if either the heart has stopped beating or the brain no longer functions. Most jurisdictions have adopted the Uniform Determination of Death Act (UDDA), which states, "[A]n individual who has sustained either (1) irreversible cessation of circulatory or respiratory functions, or (2) irreversible cessation of all functions, including the brain stem, is dead. A determination of death must be made in accordance with accepted medical standards."[7]

The year and a day rule was an old English rule that was recognized in common law. According to this rule, an individual could not be held criminally liable for causing the death of an individual who died more than a year and a day after the act. For example, suppose John shot Dave on January 1, 2001, and Dave suffered catastrophic injuries that caused him to go into a coma. If Dave did not die until January 15, 2002, under the year and a day rule, John would not be criminally liable for his death. The primary justification for the rule was the difficulty proving the cause of death after such a long period of time. This rule has been abolished in many jurisdictions, primarily because advances in medical science have caused individuals to live much longer, even after potentially fatal injuries. These same medical advances also permit doctors to accurately pinpoint the cause of death, even after an extended period of time. Should an individual who would otherwise be criminally responsible for taking a human life escape liability because of medical advances? To avoid this outcome, some states have extended the time period to three years and a day while others have eliminated time periods altogether.

The definition of human being also varies from state to state. Most adopt some version of the Model Penal Code (MPC) definition: human being means a person who has been born and is alive.[8] Some states have expanded the definition of murder to include fetuses in cases where a pregnant woman is killed, and her unborn child also dies. California is one such state. California's Penal Code Section 187-A defines murder as "the unlawful killing of a human being, or a fetus, with malice aforethought." On Christmas Eve in 2002, Scott Peterson reported that his pregnant wife Laci was missing from their home in Modesto, California. Almost four months later, a couple discovered the decomposing but well-preserved body of a male fetus on the San Francisco shore north of Berkeley. A day later, Laci Peterson's decapitated and badly mutilated body was discovered on the same shore about a mile from where the fetus' body was found. Scott Peterson was charged with the murders of both his wife and unborn son. He was convicted of both counts and sentenced to death.

Homicide is the most serious of all crimes. However, some forms of homicide are considered to be more dangerous than others. Murder and manslaughter are the two broad categories of criminal homicide. Murder is the most serious type of homicide and is usually punished more severely than manslaughter.

At common law, murder was defined as the killing of a human being with malice aforethought. The root of the word malice is from the Latin "mal," which means "bad" or "evil." However, "malice aforethought" is a legal term that has a number of different definitions. Malice can manifest itself in many ways, in both intentional and unintentional forms of murder, and is the element that distinguishes murder from manslaughter. Manslaughter is defined as the unlawful killing of a human being without malice. As with murder, there are intentional and unintentional forms of manslaughter.

Most states have laws that distinguish different types of murder by categorizing them into degrees, with first degree murder as the most serious form. Some states also classify manslaughter into different degrees, although most simply differentiate between voluntary and involuntary manslaughter. There are intentional and unintentional forms of murder and manslaughter. When a prosecutor decides to charge a suspect with homicide, he or she must first decide whether it is an intentional or unintentional killing. The prosecutor must then decide which charge or charges to bring, depending on the level of homicide he or she is able to prove beyond a reasonable doubt. If there is a trial, after the case is presented to the jury, the judge instructs the jury on the law, including the elements of the crime or crimes that the government must have proven beyond a reasonable doubt.

Sometimes, the judge instructs the jury on what are called lesser included offenses—less serious charges that the jury may consider if it decides that the defendant is not guilty of the more serious charges. So, for example, if the defendant is alleged to have committed first degree premeditated murder, and the jury finds him or her not guilty, it may then go on to consider whether the defendant is guilty of the lesser included offense of second degree murder. If there was also evidence of voluntary manslaughter, the judge may instruct the jury on that lesser included offense as well, if there is evidence that would support the charge. Similarly, if the killing was unintentional, the prosecutor might charge the defendant with second degree unintentional murder (sometimes called depraved heart murder), but the judge might also instruct the jury on the lesser included offense of involuntary manslaughter, if there is sufficient evidence to support such a charge.

Table 8.1 illustrates the different levels of homicide in a typical homicide statute.

Table 8.1 **Types of Homicide**

	INTENTIONAL	UNINTENTIONAL
1st DEGREE MURDER	PREMEDITATED	FELONY MURDER (INTENT NOT REQUIRED)
2nd DEGREE MURDER	INITENT TO KILL OR SERIOUSLY INJURE	DEPRAVED HEART MURDER (EXTREME RECKLESSNESS)
MANSLAUGHTER	VOLUNTARY (HEAT OF PASSION/ADEQUATE PROVOCATION)	INVOLUNTARY (GROSS NEGLIGENCE OR ORDINARY RECKLESSNESS)

The definitions for the various forms of murder and manslaughter vary greatly from state to state. For example, in California, murder is the killing of a person or a fetus (other than a legal abortion).[9] If someone kills a woman who is pregnant and the fetus also dies, that person might be charged with two counts of murder. About half the states have similar fetal homicide statutes. Some states include vehicular manslaughter as a form of homicide, in addition to involuntary manslaughter. Other states simply classify vehicular manslaughter as involuntary manslaughter. States also differ in how they characterize homicide. Some, such as California, simply distinguish murder from manslaughter. Others, such as Pennsylvania, not only distinguish murder from manslaughter, but establish different degrees of murder, with first degree as the most serious form (as in Table 8.1 above).

Intentional Killings

First Degree Premeditated Murder

Most states consider an intentional killing with premeditation and deliberation as the most serious form of homicide. In states that classify murder in various degrees, this form is considered first degree murder. Premeditated murder is certainly intentional, but it involves much more than the simple intent to kill. The person who commits this form of murder not only intends to cause the death of his or her victim, but also thinks about the killing in advance, turns the idea over in his or her head, and makes a conscious choice to kill.

Consider the following hypotheticals:

- Mary discovers that her husband John has been having an affair for many years. She decides to kill him. She does research for about a week to try to figure out the easiest way to kill John. Mary finally decides that poisoning John would be the most efficient, least detectable way to kill him. After deciding on a poison, Mary goes to the hardware store to purchase it. She returns home, mixes the poison in a dish she prepared for John's supper, and serves it to him. He dies almost instantly.
- Joe goes to a bar to have a drink after work. While sitting at the bar, he gets into an argument with Tom. As the two men drink, the argument escalates, and they begin to fight. The bartender separates the two men and asks them both to leave. Each man walks to his car, but instead of leaving, Joe immediately retrieves his pistol from the glove compartment of his car, calmly walks over to Tom's car, and shoots him, killing him instantly.

Both killings involved premeditation and deliberation although, Joe premeditated and deliberated for a much shorter period of time.

The terms "premeditation" and "deliberation" have very distinct meanings. Premeditation involves thinking about the killing in advance. Premeditation can occur long before the killing and can last for some time, as in the case of Mary planning her husband's murder for a week before killing him. It may also occur moments before the killing for a short period of time, as with Joe killing Tom shortly after a fight. An individual like Mary who plans a murder well in advance presents a clear case of premeditation. However, premeditation has been found in cases like Joe's, where the defendant has been involved in a fight, cools off, and decides to kill his adversary moments later.

Deliberation involves making a decision after reflection, or turning the idea over in one's mind. When a person deliberates, he or she weighs the options and makes a choice. Premeditation is thinking about the killing; deliberation is choosing to do it. As with premeditation, deliberation can take place in a short period of time. So in the case of Mary and Joe, at some point after thinking about killing their victims (premeditation), they made a choice to do it (deliberation).

First degree premeditated murder is committed by an individual who acts in a cool, calm, collected manner—hence the phrase "in cold blood." Should a killer who acts calmly after thought and deliberation be considered more dangerous than someone who is angry and who kills in the heat of passion? Does this make sense? How does a jury decide whether there is sufficient evidence of premeditation and deliberation? Consider these issues in the following case.

State v. Thompson (2003)

Arizona Supreme Court
202 Ariz. 471

Defendant Larry Thompson challenges the constitutionality of Arizona's first degree murder statute. . . . He argues that the definition of premeditation, which provides that "[p]roof of actual reflection is not required," eliminates any meaningful distinction between first and second degree murder and renders the first degree murder statute unconstitutionally vague. . . . We accepted review to consider the constitutionality of the statute and to clarify both the meaning of premeditation and the State's burden of proof.

On May 17, 1999, Thompson shot and killed his wife, Roberta Palma. Several days before the shooting, Palma had filed for divorce, and Thompson had discovered that she was seeing someone else. Just a week before the shooting, Thompson moved out of the couple's home. As he did so, Thompson threatened Palma that, "[i]f you divorce me, I will kill you."

Thompson returned to the couple's neighborhood the morning of May 17. He was seen walking on the sidewalk near the home and his car was spotted in a nearby alley. Two witnesses reported that a man dragged a woman by the hair from the front porch into the home. That same morning, police received and recorded a 9-1-1 call from the house. The tape recorded a woman's screams and four gunshots. The four gunshots span nearly twenty-seven seconds. Nine seconds elapse between the first shot and the third, and there is an eighteen-second delay between the third shot and the fourth.

Police arrived shortly after the call and found Palma dead from gunshot wounds. An autopsy of her body revealed several fresh abrasions, five non-contact gunshot wounds, and one contact gunshot wound.

At trial, Thompson did not deny killing his wife, but claimed that he did so in the heat of passion, making the killing manslaughter or, at most, second degree murder. During closing arguments, Thompson's counsel argued that the crime had occurred in the heat of passion and that Thompson had "simply snapped."

In her closing arguments, the prosecutor argued that the evidence that Thompson premeditated the murder was "overwhelming." She emphasized the timing of the shots and the delay between them. The prosecutor also reminded the jury of Thompson's threat, made a week before the murder, to kill his wife. The prosecutor then argued that Thompson need not actually have reflected, but only had the time to reflect: "But the main point to remember about premeditation is that premeditation is time to permit reflection. The instruction also tells you that actual reflection is not necessary, [only] the time to permit reflection." Nonetheless, the prosecutor referred to circumstantial evidence suggesting that Thompson actually had reflected, but then told the jury it need only decide that Thompson had the time to reflect, not that he actually had reflected.

After closing arguments, the judge instructed the jury regarding premeditation as follows:

> "Premeditation" means that the defendant acts with either the intention or the knowledge that he will kill another human being, when such intention or knowledge precedes the killing by any length of time to permit reflection. Proof of actual reflection is not required, but an act is not done with premeditation if it is the instant effect of a sudden quarrel or heat of passion.

The jury found Thompson guilty of first degree murder and the judge sentenced him to life in prison without the possibility of parole. Thompson appealed, arguing that the definition of premeditation, particularly the clause stating that "[p]roof of actual reflection is not required,"

(Continued)

(Continued)

unconstitutionally relieved the State of the burden of proving the element of premeditation.

The statute at issue, Arizona's first degree murder statute, provides that "[a] person commits first degree murder if . . . [i]ntending or knowing that the person's conduct will cause death, the person causes the death of another *with* premeditation." . . . Thompson challenges the constitutionality of the statute, arguing that it renders first degree murder indistinguishable from second degree murder. A person commits second degree murder in Arizona "if *without* premeditation . . . [s]uch person intentionally causes the death of another person." . . . Thus, for the purposes of this appeal, first and second degree murder are indistinguishable except that first degree murder requires premeditation.

According to the definition adopted by the legislature,

"[p]remeditation" means that the defendant acts with either the intention or the knowledge that he will kill another human being, when such intention or knowledge precedes the killing by any length of time to permit reflection. *Proof of actual reflection is not required,* but an act is not done with premeditation if it is the instant effect of a sudden quarrel or heat of passion.

The question before us is whether this definition of premeditation abolishes the requirement of actual reflection altogether, whether it eliminates the requirement of direct proof of actual reflection, or whether it substitutes for the necessary proof of actual reflection the mere passage of enough time to permit reflection. The State asserts the third interpretation, that the legislature intended to relieve the State of the burden of proving a defendant's hidden thought processes, and that this definition of premeditation establishes that the passage of time may serve as a proxy for reflection. The court of appeals agreed with this interpretation.

Thompson maintains that reducing premeditation to the mere passage of time renders the statute vague and unenforceable because courts have held that actual reflection can occur as quickly as "successive thoughts of the mind." . . . Thus, he argues and the court of appeals agreed, the difference between first and second degree murder has been eliminated.

We have not, until this case, had the opportunity to address the confusion surrounding the issue of premeditation. . . . Thompson urges us to overturn his conviction on the ground that the statute is unconstitutionally vague. The State, on the other hand, argues that the statute is constitutional and that the current definition of premeditation meaningfully distinguishes between first and second degree murder.

We conclude, as did the court of appeals, that if the only difference between first and second degree murder is the mere passage of time, and that length of time can be "as instantaneous as successive thoughts of the mind," then there is no meaningful distinction between first and second degree murder. Such an interpretation would relieve the state of its burden to prove actual reflection and would render the first degree murder statute impermissibly vague and therefore unconstitutional under the United States and Arizona Constitutions.

Our decision today distinguishes the *element* of premeditation from the *evidence* that might establish that element. Although the mere passage of time suggests that a defendant premeditated—and the state might be able to convince a jury to make that inference—the passage of time is not, in and of itself, premeditation. To allow the state to establish the element of premeditation by merely proving that sufficient time passed to permit reflection would be to essentially relieve the state of its burden to establish the sole element that distinguishes between first and second degree murder.

In the case before us, the jury was instructed that "proof of actual reflection is not required." We hold that, without further clarification, this instruction was erroneous. The State also argued that it did not have to prove actual reflection, but had to prove only that enough time had elapsed to allow reflection. This, too, was in error. However, the jury was not instructed that actual reflection can occur as instantaneously as successive thoughts of the mind. Moreover, the State presented overwhelming evidence that Thompson actually reflected on his decision to kill his wife, including evidence of threats to kill her a week before the murder, the time that elapsed between each gunshot, and the victim's screams as recorded on the 9-1-1 tape between each gunshot. We conclude beyond a reasonable doubt that the flawed jury instruction and the State's reliance on that instruction did not affect the jury's verdict, and we will not overturn Thompson's conviction and sentence.

As we have interpreted it, we find the definition of premeditation in Arizona's first degree murder statute, A.R.S. § 13–1105(A)(1), constitutional. We vacate the opinion of the court of appeals, but affirm Thompson's conviction and sentence for first degree murder.

Questions

1. What evidence in this case supports the jury's finding that Thompson's actions were premeditated?

2. Why did the court hold that the jury instruction was erroneous?

3. Was the court's holding correct? Why or why not?

Second Degree Intentional Murder—Intent to Kill or Seriously Injure

An individual who premeditates and deliberates definitely intends to kill. However, it is possible for a person to intend to kill without premeditating or deliberating. The line between premeditation on the one hand and simple intent to kill on the other is often a thin one. Jurors sometimes return verdicts of second degree intentional murder in cases where the evidence of premeditation is weak or where jurors cannot agree on this issue. Some argue that juries compromise on a verdict of second degree murder when all twelve of them cannot agree that there was premeditation and deliberation.

This level of intentional murder may be charged when there is evidence that the defendant intended to either kill the victim or seriously injure him. For example, if a defendant shoots or stabs an individual in the chest, and the person later dies, the defendant might testify that she did not intend to kill the victim, only seriously injure him. If the jury believes this testimony, it could reach a not guilty verdict, even though the defendant's actions directly caused the victim's death. Thus, most homicide statutes provide for criminal liability for second degree murder in cases where the defendant intended to seriously injure the defendant, and death resulted. If an individual injures another with a deadly weapon in a vital area of the body, the jury may infer that the defendant intended the natural and probable consequences of her actions—namely death.

In the following case, the defendant was convicted of first degree premeditated murder and appealed his conviction. He argued that there was insufficient evidence of premeditation. The appellate court agreed, holding that the evidence only proved second degree murder.

State v. Bingham (1986)

Supreme Court of Washington

105 Wash.2d 820

In this case, we review the sufficiency of the evidence of the premeditation element in an aggravated first degree murder conviction. The Court of Appeals found the evidence insufficient and reversed and remanded for resentencing for second degree murder.... We affirm the Court of Appeals decision.

On February 18, 1982, the raped and strangled body of Leslie Cook, a retarded adult, was found in a pasture in Sequim. Cook was last seen alive on February 15, 1982, with respondent Charles Dean Bingham. The Clallam County Prosecutor, by amended information, charged Bingham with aggravated first degree (premeditated) murder, rape being the aggravating circumstance. The prosecutor also notified Bingham that the State would seek the death penalty.

The evidence presented at trial showed that on February 15, Cook and Bingham got off a bus together in Sequim about 6 p.m. There was no evidence that they knew each other before this time. They visited a grocery store and two residences. Cook was last seen at the residence of Wayne Humphrey and Enid Pratt where Bingham asked for a ride back to Port Angeles. When he was told no, Bingham said they would hitchhike. They left together heading toward the infrequently traveled Old Olympic Highway. None of the witnesses who saw the two heard any argument or observed any physical contact between them. Three days later, Cook's body was found in a field about a 1/4 mile from the Humphrey-Pratt residence.

At trial, King County Medical Examiner Reay described the results of the autopsy he performed on Cook's body. The cause of death was "asphyxiation through manual strangulation," accomplished by applying continuous pressure to the windpipe for approximately 3 to 5 minutes. . . . Cook had a

(Continued)

bruise on her upper lip, more likely caused by a hand being pressed over her mouth than by a violent blow. Tears were found in Cook's vaginal wall and anal ring. Spermatozoa was present. These injuries were inflicted antemortem. Also, there was a bite mark on each of Cook's breasts. Reay testified that these occurred perimortem or postmortem.

The prosecutor's theory, as revealed in both his opening statement and closing argument, was that Bingham wanted to have sex with Cook and that he had to kill her in order to do so. The prosecutor hypothesized that Bingham had started the act while Cook was alive, and that he put his hand over her mouth and then strangled her in order to complete the act. The prosecutor also told the jury that the murder would be premeditated if Bingham had formed the intent to kill when he began to strangle Cook, and thought about that intent for the 3 to 5 minutes it took her to die.

The court instructed the jury on aggravated first degree murder and on the lesser included offenses of first and second degree murder and first degree manslaughter. The court also gave Bingham's proposed instruction on voluntary intoxication.

The jury found Bingham guilty of aggravated first degree murder.

We must determine whether evidence of premeditation was sufficiently demonstrated in order for the issue to go to the jury and in order to sustain a finding of premeditated killing.

Bingham was charged with first degree murder pursuant to RCW 9A.32.030(1)(a), which requires for conviction "a premeditated intent to cause the death of another." The element of premeditation distinguishes first and second degree murder. . . . Section (1)(a) of the second degree murder statute, RCW 9A.32.050, requires for conviction "intent to cause the death of another person but without premeditation."

The only statutory elaboration on the meaning of premeditation is found in RCW 9A.32.020(1), which states that premeditation "must involve more than a moment in point of time." Washington case law further defines premeditation as "the mental process of thinking beforehand, deliberation, reflection, weighing or reasoning for a period of time, however short." (Footnote omitted.) . . . We recently approved an instruction which defined premeditation as "the deliberate formation of and reflection upon the intent to take a human life." . . .

Premeditation may be shown by direct or circumstantial evidence. Circumstantial evidence can be used where the inferences drawn by the jury are reasonable and the evidence supporting the jury's verdict is substantial. . . . In this case, the State presented no direct evidence. The issue thus becomes whether sufficient circumstantial evidence of premeditation was presented. Bingham was not charged with felony-murder.

To show premeditation, the State relied on the pathologist's testimony that manual strangulation takes 3 to 5 minutes. The State argues this time is an appreciable amount of time in which Bingham could have deliberated. Bingham argues that time alone is not enough and that other indicators of premeditation must be shown.

We agree with the Court of Appeals majority that to allow a finding of premeditation only because the act takes an appreciable amount of time obliterates the distinction between first and second degree murder. Having the opportunity to deliberate is not evidence the defendant did deliberate, which is necessary for a finding of premeditation. Otherwise, any form of killing which took more than a moment could result in a finding of premeditation, without some additional evidence showing reflection. Holding a hand over someone's mouth or windpipe does not necessarily reflect a decision to kill the person, but possibly only to quiet her or him. Furthermore, here a question of the ability to deliberate or reflect while engaged in sexual activity exists.

Here, *no* evidence was presented of deliberation or reflection before or during the strangulation, only the strangulation. The opportunity to deliberate is not sufficient.

Exercising our responsibility, we find manual strangulation alone is insufficient evidence to support a finding of premeditation. We affirm the Court of Appeals decision.

Questions

1. What was the evidence in support of premeditation?

2. What was the court's rationale in holding that there was insufficient evidence of premeditation?

3. Why do you think the *Thompson* court found sufficient evidence of premeditation while the *Bingham* court did not?

Commonwealth of Virginia v. George W. Huguely

The George Huguely case illustrates how prosecutors sometimes have difficulty proving premeditation in first degree murder cases. Huguely and Yeardley Love were varsity lacrosse players at the University of Virginia at the time of her death in

May 2010. They had a very volatile, on-again, off-again relationship. Huguely had a history of drinking and was previously charged with underage drinking and public drunkenness. Their relationship was frequently violent; there were allegations that Huguely had placed Love in a chokehold at one point, and Love was seen hitting Huguely with her purse on another occasion. After one of their breakups, Love slept with a lacrosse player from a rival team, and Huguely sent her an email stating that he should have killed her after finding out about the incident.[10]

On the evening of May 3, 2010, Huguely went to Love's apartment after drinking a large quantity of alcohol. He attacked Love after kicking in her bedroom door. There were no witnesses to the killing, so it was unclear exactly how and under what circumstances Huguely killed Love, but it was undisputed that he left her bleeding, face down in a pillow on her bed. Her roommate found her later that night and called the police at 2:15 a.m. Love's body was bloody and bruised. Later when the police interrogated Huguely, he stated that he and Love had "wrestled" in her bedroom and seemed shocked when the police informed him that she was dead. He insisted that he never intended to kill her.[11]

Huguely was charged with first degree premeditated murder, felony murder, robbery, burglary, entering a house with intent to commit a felony, and grand larceny. The felony murder, robbery, burglary, and grand larceny charges were based on the fact that Huguely took Love's laptop computer when he left her apartment. Felony murder (which will be discussed in detail later in this chapter) occurs when someone dies during the course of the commission of a dangerous felony. The jury ultimately convicted Huguely of second degree murder and grand larceny.

George Huguely was convicted of the second degree murder of Yeardley Love.

Abemarle-Charlottesville Regional Jail, Virginia

After the trial, two of the jurors discussed the jury deliberations and explained how they reached their verdicts:

> "Most of us were in agreement about what really happened," said Ian Glomski, an assistant professor at the University of Virginia School of Medicine. The arguments, he said, were about how to apply the law to the case.[12]
>
> "We all agreed that the murder wasn't premeditated," said Serena Gruia, a graphic designer and the jury's forewoman. She added that first-degree murder was eliminated from the discussion fairly quickly."[13] The jurors rejected both forms of first degree murder—premeditated murder and felony murder. Most of their deliberations were about whether the killing was with malice (second degree murder) or in the "heat of passion" (voluntary manslaughter):
>
> "If it's heat of passion, it can't be second-degree murder," Gruia said, adding that jurors spent about two hours discussing malice. "It was a really long debate," Glomski agreed.[14]

The jury's quick dismissal of the first degree premeditated murder charge in the Huguely case demonstrates how difficult it can be for the prosecutor to prove premeditation in cases where there is not clear, direct evidence that the defendant thought about the killing ahead of time. When the defendant hires a hit man to do the killing or otherwise plans the murder well ahead of time, premeditation is much easier to prove. However, in cases like *Thompson, Bingham,* and *Huguely,* the prosecution must argue that premeditation can be inferred from the circumstantial evidence in the case. In *Bingham* and *Huguely,* there was not sufficient circumstantial evidence to sustain a first degree murder conviction.

The *Huguely* case also gives us a window into the process that jurors must go through as they consider the different levels of homicide. In cases where they are considering not only first degree murder but also the lesser included offenses of second degree murder and manslaughter, they start with the most serious offense, and if that charge is eliminated, they move on to the next charge, as the *Huguely* jurors did. Ultimately, they decided that Huguely acted maliciously and not with the heat of passion required for voluntary manslaughter, discussed in the next section.

Voluntary Manslaughter

In distinguishing intentional murder from voluntary manslaughter, it may be helpful to think about cold-blooded versus hot-blooded killings. If a first degree premeditated and deliberated murder is committed after calm reflection in cold blood, a voluntary manslaughter is committed by a hot-blooded killer in the heat of passion. Most jurisdictions recognize two types of manslaughter—heat of passion and imperfect self-defense. The heat of passion type of voluntary manslaughter is the killing of a human being in the heat of passion caused by adequate provocation. The imperfect self-defense type occurs when an individual uses excessive force to defend him or herself or acts in an unreasonable belief that deadly force was necessary under the circumstances. The imperfect self-defense type of voluntary manslaughter is discussed in more detail in Chapter 9.

Manslaughter (voluntary or involuntary) is a killing without malice. The theory is that the person who kills in the heat of passion is less culpable than a murderer because the decedent did something to provoke the killer into losing his or her self-control. Thus, a killing that would otherwise be murder is reduced to manslaughter because of mitigating factors. The early common law only recognized specific types of behaviors as constituting adequate provocation sufficient to reduce murder to manslaughter, including an aggravated assault or battery, mutual combat, or a man catching his wife in the act of sexual intercourse with another man. Whether there was adequate provocation was considered a question of law, and jurors had no discretion to decide whether facts that fell outside of these limited categories were sufficient to constitute adequate provocation. The modern trend, however, is to permit jurors to decide on a case-by-case basis whether the person who was killed did something to provoke the killer and whether that provocation was adequate to reduce the charge of murder to manslaughter.

One limitation recognized in most jurisdictions is that mere words are never sufficient to reduce a killing to manslaughter, although there are some exceptions to this rule. In other words, if John kills Paul because Paul called him a nasty name, John will be guilty of either first or second degree murder, not manslaughter. However, some courts distinguish between insulting words and informational words. Informational words are words, which if heard by the defendant, would constitute the adequate provocation that would reduce a murder to a manslaughter. For example, if Paul said to John, "Your wife is an ugly, fat pig!" and John then killed Paul, John would likely be convicted of some form of murder. On the other hand, if Paul said, "John, I just had sex with your wife!" and John then killed Paul, Paul's informational words might be sufficient to reduce a murder charge to manslaughter.

In reaching a verdict of manslaughter, a jury must find not only that the person acted in the heat of passion, but also that it was reasonable for the person to have acted in the heat of passion under the circumstances. A person who kills because he or she is more angry or passionate than the reasonable person would be under the circumstances may be guilty of murder rather than manslaughter. In other words, it is both a subjective and an objective test—was the person acting in the heat of passion, and would a reasonable person have acted similarly under the circumstances?

The following case provides one example of circumstances that most states recognize as adequate provocation to reduce a murder charge to manslaughter. There is a four-part test that is invoked for voluntary manslaughter:

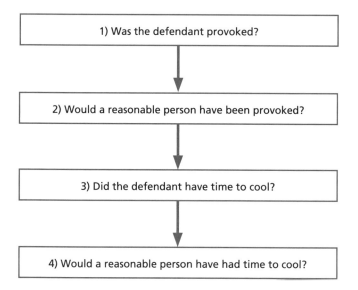

1) Was the defendant provoked?
↓
2) Would a reasonable person have been provoked?
↓
3) Did the defendant have time to cool?
↓
4) Would a reasonable person have had time to cool?

To return a verdict of voluntary manslaughter, the jury must answer yes to all four of these questions.

State v. Knoten (2001)

Supreme Court of South Carolina
347 S.C. 296

Appellant was convicted of two counts of murder, two counts of kidnapping, and one count of first degree criminal sexual conduct in connection with the deaths of thirty-year-old Kimberly Brown ("Kim") and three-year-old Layah Brazil ("Layah"). He received consecutive sentences of life without the possibility of parole for the murder offenses and a consecutive sentence of thirty years for criminal sexual conduct. On appeal, he alleges the trial court erred in refusing to instruct the jury on voluntary manslaughter in connection with Kim's homicide. . . .

Around noon on Tuesday, November 18, 1997, Cora Brown, Kim's mother, went to her daughter's apartment after receiving no answer to phone calls placed to the apartment and after learning from Kim's employer that Kim had not arrived for work. She found the door to the apartment unlocked, and entered to find blood on the floor, but no sign of Kim, or Layah. Mrs. Brown immediately called the Richland County Sheriff's Department and reported her daughter missing.

The Sheriff's Department began investigating the case as a missing persons incident. After investigators found Appellant's name in Kim's address book, police contacted him on Tuesday night. Appellant told police that he had been at Kim's apartment between 9 and 10 p.m. on Monday evening.

Wednesday morning, police contacted Appellant at work and asked if he would come to the sheriff's office to speak with investigators. Appellant agreed to do so, and arrived at the office around 11:00 a.m. He again told police he had seen Kim and Layah at Kim's apartment Monday evening, and that he had arrived around 9 p.m. and

(Continued)

(Continued)

remained for an hour. He stated that when he left Kim's apartment, he went to a co-worker's home and spent the night. When police contacted this co-worker, he provided Appellant with an alibi. Later, the co-worker told investigators that Appellant had not been at his home on the night of the disappearance, but that Appellant had asked him to tell police otherwise.

The investigating officer asked for and received permission to search Appellant's car. Upon inspecting the trunk of vehicle, he discovered what appeared to be blood. Thereafter, police resumed questioning Appellant regarding Kim's and Layah's disappearance.

Over the course of the next two days, Appellant gave a number of inconsistent statements to police, each more inculpatory than the last. In the first signed statement, taken between 8:30 and 9:30 p.m. Wednesday evening, Appellant claimed he left Kim's house on Monday evening between 10 and 10:30, that he got in his car, drove away from the apartment complex, and then blacked out. He woke up the next morning at the Rosewood boat ramp and went to work. He said he did not know if he had killed Kim or Layah.

In his second signed statement, given around 1 a.m. Thursday morning, Appellant stated that he and Kim had consensual sex that Monday evening, and afterwards, Kim became agitated. She armed herself with a knife and threatened him. She cut him on the leg and chased him out of the apartment. Appellant, nude in the parking lot, retrieved a foot-long steel bar from the trunk of his car. He reentered the apartment. Kim cut him again, and he hit her over the head with the metal bar. Kim collapsed from the blow. He wrapped her body in a blanket and put her in the trunk of his car. He returned to the apartment, cleaned up, and napped for two hours. He awoke at 5:00 a.m. (now Tuesday morning), got Layah out of bed, and told the child they were going to look for Kim. He drove to a boat landing on Sumter Highway where he disposed of Kim's body. He left Layah at the landing, and went to work.

Appellant gave his final written statement around 11 a.m. Thursday. In that statement he admitted raping Kim. He further admitted pushing Layah into the river. Otherwise, the third statement is largely consistent with the second statement.

Did the trial court err in refusing Appellant's request to instruct the jury on the crime of voluntary manslaughter in the death of Kimberly Brown?

The law to be charged must be determined from the evidence presented at trial. . . . In determining whether the evidence requires a charge of voluntary manslaughter, the Court views the facts in a light most favorable to the defendant. . . . "To warrant a court's eliminating the offense of manslaughter, it should very clearly appear that

there is no evidence whatsoever tending to reduce the crime from murder to manslaughter." . . .

Manslaughter is defined as "the unlawful killing of another without malice." S.C.Code Ann. § 16–3–50 (Supp.2000); . . .

Voluntary manslaughter is the unlawful killing of a human being in sudden heat of passion upon sufficient legal provocation. Heat of passion alone will not suffice to reduce murder to voluntary manslaughter. Both heat of passion and sufficient legal provocation must be present at the time of the killing. The sudden heat of passion, upon sufficient legal provocation, which mitigates a felonious killing to manslaughter, while it need not dethrone reason entirely, or shut out knowledge and volition, must be such as would naturally disturb the sway of reason, and render the mind of an ordinary person incapable of cool reflection, and produce what, according to human experience, may be called an uncontrollable impulse to do violence. . . .

Even when a person's passion has been sufficiently aroused by a legally adequate provocation, if at the time of the killing those passions had cooled or a sufficiently reasonable time had elapsed so that the passions of the ordinary reasonable person would have cooled, the killing would be murder and not manslaughter. . . .

Viewing the evidence in the light most favorable to Appellant, a charge of voluntary manslaughter was warranted here. The State introduced all three of Appellant's written statements at trial. The second statement was as follows:

Q: Can you provide additional information about Kim and Layah?

A: I went over to Kim's about 9:00 p.m. We were talking. Layah was awake. Kim was cooking chicken and corn. Kim fed the baby in the kitchen. Kim and I did not eat. She put the baby to bed. Kim and I went upstairs. We had sex in her bed. I did not use a condom.

Q: What next?

A: We got up and started washing up. We started talking. I don't know what I said wrong or what happened to her. She got a knife from the kitchen and came back up the stairs. She started threatening me. She chased me down the stairs. I ran out the front door. I did not have on any clothes. She did not have on any clothes. I thought she was kidding. She cut me on the right leg. I went to my car and got a bar. It is about a foot long and silver. It's made out of steel. I pulled the latch in the car and the trunk opened. I got the bar from the trunk. We were in the house near the front door. Kim cut me with the knife then. I hit her with the bar across the head. She feel [sic] and hit the floor. She was crawling the stairs and she collapsed. I rolled her up in a blanket while she was on the stairs. I put her in the trunk. I went back in and tried to clean up. I went to sleep on the floor in the living room. I woke up around 5:00 a.m. I think I feel [sic] asleep around 3:00 a.m. When I woke up, I got Layah out of bed. I washed my hands. Layah walked downstairs and got into the front passenger seat of the car. I told her that we were going to try and find her mom. I was talking about Kim. I drove out and turned onto Sumter Hwy [sic]. I drove until I saw a sign that said "landing." It was to the right of Sumter Highway. I went down to the end by the water. I backed the car up. I took her out. I dragged Kim a few feet. I covered her with a big blanket. I went around and got Layah out of the car. I left her beside the car. I told her I would be back.

The State argues two grounds for affirming the trial court's refusal to charge voluntary manslaughter: first, it contends that the above evidence indicates, as a matter of law, that sufficient "cooling off" time elapsed while Appellant was retrieving the pipe such that he could not have been acting in the heat of passion when he killed Kim; additionally, the State contends that because Appellant recanted the confession at trial, he was not entitled to a charge on voluntary manslaughter.

Appellant argues that because Kim cut him before he struck her with the pipe, the trial court should have instructed the jury on voluntary manslaughter. We agree. Twice in the above statement, Appellant claims Kim cut him. After the first cut, he was chased out of the apartment,

went to his car, and got the metal pipe. He reentered the apartment, and killed Kim after she cut him again.

Were a jury to believe the facts as represented in Appellant's second statement, he and Kim were . . . in a heated encounter and she had twice cut him with a knife when he struck her with the pipe. It follows that a charge on voluntary manslaughter was required.

. . . There can be little argument that an unprovoked knife attack constitutes sufficient legal provocation to warrant the requested charge. Furthermore, . . . there is no evidence that a significant period of time elapsed between the alleged knife attack and Appellant's striking the fatal blows. Appellant claims he was chased from the apartment by the knife-wielding victim. It was a cold November evening and he was naked. He opened the trunk of his car with the trunk latch and retrieved the pipe. He then reentered the apartment. Kim cut him again, and he responded to the attack by hitting her with the pipe. Viewing this evidence in the light most favorable to Appellant, as we must, there is simply no evidence that, as a matter of law, Appellant had sufficient time to cool.

Because a jury instruction on voluntary manslaughter was required based on the evidence presented at trial, we REVERSE Appellant's conviction for the murder of Kim Brown. . . .

Questions

1. What did the state argue in support of its claim that the jury should not have considered a voluntary manslaughter charge?

2. What was the court's rationale for rejecting the state's argument?

3. In your opinion, was the court's ruling correct? Why or why not?

The Kenneth Peacock Case

Some states continue to recognize the common law rule that witnessing a spouse in the act of adultery constitutes adequate provocation. Maryland is among the states that no longer follow this rule. The Maryland legislature eliminated spousal adultery as adequate provocation in homicide cases, and the Kenneth Peacock case spurred this change in the law.

In February 1994, Kenneth Peacock was driving from Pennsylvania to Florida when he was caught in an ice storm. He called his wife to tell her that he was coming home but did not get an answer. When Peacock arrived home at midnight, he found his wife in bed with another man. He chased the man away at gunpoint, and after drinking alcohol and arguing with his wife, he shot her in the head and killed her almost four hours later.[15]

Peacock was allowed to plead guilty to manslaughter and was sentenced to eighteen months in prison by Judge Robert E. Cahill of the Baltimore County Circuit Court. At the sentencing hearing, Judge Cahill stated that he wished he did not have to send Peacock to prison at all, and said, "I seriously wonder how many men married five, four years would have the strength to walk away without inflicting some corporal punishment."[16]

The sentence and Judge Cahill's remarks set off a firestorm among women's groups, including the Women's Law Center in Baltimore, which asked the Committee on Gender Equality of the Maryland Court of Appeals to investigate the case. Sue Osthoff, the then-director of the National Clearinghouse for the Defense of Battered Women in Philadelphia, also spoke out, noting that battered women who killed their husbands are usually sentenced to very long prison terms. She said, "In the vast majority of cases where women kill their husbands, they do so because they think he is going to kill them or their children. Whatever pain this man felt at seeing his wife with someone else, he wasn't going to die."[17]

In 1995, Maryland State Delegate Joan Pitkin introduced a bill in the state legislature to remove adultery as adequate provocation to reduce murder to manslaughter. The bill did not pass that year. Delegate Pitkin introduced the bill again in 1996 and 1997, when it finally passed.[18]

Unintentional Killings ●────────────────────

Some people are surprised to learn that an individual may be charged with murder even if he unintentionally kills someone—that a person may act with malice even if he acts unintentionally. However, felony murder (discussed later in this chapter) is one of the most serious forms of murder and may be committed unintentionally. This section discusses depraved heart murder (an unintentional killing with malice that is often charged as second degree murder) and involuntary manslaughter (an unintentional killing without malice).

Depraved Heart Murder

Depraved heart murder is a killing that is committed with extreme recklessness. The actor does not intend to kill, but she knows that her actions will create a substantial and unjustifiable risk of death or serious injury. The standard is that of the "reasonable person"—a reasonable person would have known that her actions would create a substantial risk of death or serious injury. The killer knows that there is a substantial risk that her actions will cause serious bodily injury or death, but she acts anyway. She does not intend to kill, nor does she know that the person will die, but she is aware that there is a substantial risk of death—an "I don't give a damn" attitude. This person is said to act with an abandoned and malignant heart. When the act is unintentional, the malice is implied by the defendant's actions, as opposed to intentional murder cases where the malice is explicit and clear.

In the following case, the court upheld a depraved heart murder charge against a woman whose dog killed a neighbor. Did Ms. Knoller act in an extremely reckless manner? What could she have done to prevent the death of Diane Whipple?

Marjorie Knoller reacts as guilty verdicts are read in a courtroom convicting her of the second degree murder of Diane Whipple.

People v. Knoller (2007)

Supreme Court of California
41 Cal. 4th 139

In 1998, Pelican Bay State Prison inmates Paul Schneider and Dale Bretches, both members of the Aryan Brotherhood prison gang, sought to engage in a business of buying, raising, and breeding Presa Canario dogs. [The inmates were being represented by the defendants, Knoller and Noel.] A document found in defendants' apartment describes the Presa Canario as "a gripping dog . . . always used and bred for combat and guard . . . [and] used extensively for fighting. . . . "

[An acquaintance of the inmates, Ms.]Coumbs, possessed four such dogs, named Bane, Isis, Hera, and Fury. Hera and Fury broke out of their fenced yard and attacked Coumbs's sheep. Hera killed at least one of the sheep and also a cat belonging to Coumbs's daughter. Coumbs acknowledged that Bane ate his doghouse and may have joined Fury in killing a sheep. . . . Coumbs . . . turn[ed] the dogs over to defendants. Coumbs warned Knoller that the dogs had killed Coumbs's sheep, but Knoller did not seem to care.

. . . Dr. Donald Martin, a veterinarian for 49 years . . . examined and vaccinated the dogs. With his bill to Knoller, Dr. Martin included a letter, which said in part: "I would be professionally amiss [sic] if I did not mention the following, so that you can be prepared. These dogs are huge, approximately weighing in the neighborhood of 100 pounds each. They have had no training or discipline of any sort. They were a problem to even get to, let alone to vaccinate. You mentioned having a professional hauler gather them up and taking them. . . . Usually this would be done in crates, but I doubt one could get them into anything short of a livestock trailer, and if let loose they would have a battle. To add to this, these animals would be a liability in any household, reminding me of the recent attack in Tehama County to a boy by large dogs. He lost his arm and disfigured his face. The historic romance of the warrior dog, the personal guard dog, the gaming dog, etc. may sound good but hardly fits into life today." Knoller thanked Dr. Martin for the information and said she would pass it on to her client.

On April 30, 2000, defendants brought Hera to their sixth floor apartment in San Francisco. Bane arrived in September 2000. . . . A later search of defendants' apartment showed that they frequently exchanged letters with Pelican Bay inmates Schneider and Bretches. Over 100 letters were sent and received [where] defendants discussed a commercial breeding operation, considering various names such as GuerraHund Kennels, Wardog, and finally settling on Dog-O-War. Prisoners Schneider and Bretches' notes on a Web site for the business described Bane as "Wardog," and "Bringer of Death: Ruin: Destruction."

. . . [Prior to] the fatal mauling of Diane Whipple on January 26, 2001, there were about 30 incidents of the two dogs being out of control or threatening humans and other dogs. . . . When neighbors complained to defendants Noel and Knoller about the two dogs, defendants responded callously, if at all. Defendants Knoller and Noel [also] encountered Montepeque, [a dog trainer], who advised defendants to have their dogs trained and to use a choke collar. Defendants disregarded this advice. . . .

There were also instances when defendants' two dogs attacked or threatened people. David Moser, a fellow resident in the apartment building, slipped by defendants Knoller and Noel in the hallway only to have their dog Hera bite him on the "rear end." When he exclaimed, "Your dog just bit me," Noel replied, "Um, interesting." Neither defendant apologized to Moser or reprimanded the dog. . . .

One time, codefendant Noel himself suffered a severe injury to his finger when Bane bit him during a fight with another dog. The wound required surgery, and Noel had to wear a splint on his arm and have two steel pins placed in his hand for eight to 10 weeks.

Mauling victim Diane Whipple and her partner Sharon Smith lived in a sixth-floor apartment across a lobby from defendants. In early December 2000, Whipple called Smith at work to say . . . that one of the dogs had bitten her. Whipple had come upon codefendant Noel in the lobby with one of the dogs, which lunged at her and bit her in the hand. Whipple did not seek medical treatment for three deep, red indentations on one hand. Whipple made every effort to avoid defendants' dogs, checking the hallway before she went out and becoming anxious while waiting for the elevator for fear the dogs would be inside. . . .

On January 26, 2001. . . . [a]t 4:00 p.m., Esther Birkmaier, a neighbor who lived across the hall from Whipple, heard dogs barking and a woman's "panic-stricken" voice calling, "Help me, help me." Birkmaier saw Whipple lying face-down on the floor just over the threshold of her apartment

(Continued)

(Continued)

with what appeared to be a dog on top of her. Birkmaier saw no one else in the hallway. Afraid to open the door, Birkmaier called 911. . . .

. . . San Francisco Police Officers arrived in response [and] saw Whipple's body in the hallway; her clothing had been completely ripped off, her entire body was covered with wounds, and she was bleeding profusely. Defendant Knoller and the two dogs were not in sight.

The officers called for an ambulance. Shortly thereafter, defendant Knoller emerged from her apartment. She did not ask about Whipple's condition but merely told the officers she was looking for her keys, which she found just inside the door to Whipple's apartment.

[Whipple] died shortly after reaching the hospital. . . . An autopsy revealed over 77 discrete injuries covering Whipple's body "from head to toe." The most significant were lacerations damaging her jugular vein and her carotid artery and crushing her larynx, injuries typically inflicted by predatory animals to kill their prey. Plaster molds of the two dogs' teeth showed that the bite injuries to Whipple's neck were consistent with Bane's teeth.

[An] animal control officer asked defendant Knoller to sign over custody of the dogs for euthanasia. Knoller agreed to sign over Bane, but she refused to sign over Hera . . . and she refused to help the animal control officers with the animals, saying she was "unable to handle the dogs." . . .

[At trial, Knoller was] asked whether she denied responsibility for the attack on Whipple. [She] gave this reply: "I said in an interview that I wasn't responsible but it wasn't for the—it wasn't in regard to what Bane had done, it was in regard to knowing whether he would do that or not. And I had no idea that he would ever do anything like that to anybody. How can you anticipate something like that? It's a totally bizarre event. I mean how could you anticipate that a dog that you know that is gentle and loving and affectionate would do something so horrible and brutal and disgusting and gruesome to anybody? How could you imagine that happening?"

Defendant Knoller was convicted of second degree murder as a result of the killing of Diane Whipple by defendant's dog, Bane. Second degree murder is the unlawful killing of a human being with malice aforethought but without the additional elements, such as willfulness, premeditation, and deliberation, that would support a conviction of first degree murder. (See §§ 187, subd. (a), 189.)Section 188 provides: "[M]alice may be either express or implied. It is express when there is manifested a deliberate intention to take away the life of a fellow creature. It is implied, when no considerable provocation appears, or when the circumstances attending the killing show an abandoned and malignant heart."

. . . [T]he great majority of this court's decisions establish that a killer acts with implied malice only when acting with an awareness of *endangering human life*. This principle has been well settled for many years, and it is embodied in the standard jury instruction given in murder cases, including this one. The Court of Appeal here, however, held that a second degree murder conviction, based on a theory of implied malice, can be based simply on a defendant's awareness of the risk of causing *serious bodily injury* to another.

We conclude that a conviction for second degree murder, based on a theory of implied malice, requires proof that a defendant acted with conscious disregard of the danger to human life.

[T]he Court of Appeal erred, . . . mistakenly reasoning that implied malice required only a showing that the defendant appreciated the risk of serious bodily injury.

Questions

1. How does the court define second degree murder based on a theory of implied malice?

2. Using the court's definition, what facts presented at trial supported a conviction of second degree murder?

3. If you were on Ms. Knoller's jury, would you have voted to convict her of second degree murder? Why or why not?

The following section explains the less serious form of unintentional homicide involving gross negligence rather than extreme recklessness.

Involuntary Manslaughter

Involuntary manslaughter is an unintentional killing committed with gross negligence. The killer does not intend to cause death or even know that his or her actions would cause death, but he or she acts with gross negligence because he or she should have known. The standard is whether his or her behavior was a deviation from the standard of care of a reasonable person. Would a reasonable person in his situation have known that his or her actions might cause death? Involuntary manslaughter is often a lesser included offense in cases where the defendant is charged with depraved heart murder. If the jury finds that the defendant is not guilty of second degree depraved heart murder because he or she did not act with extreme recklessness, it might go on to consider whether the defendant acted with gross negligence and is thus guilty of involuntary manslaughter—a less serious form of homicide.

Involuntary manslaughter is often charged when the death almost seems accidental. The person who caused the death clearly did not intend to do so and is often remorseful or even devastated. Consider the following hypotheticals:

- Mary and John Brown are Christian Scientists. Their five-year-old child Sara contracted strep throat, eventually became very ill, and ultimately died of pneumonia. Mary and John never took Sara to a doctor or to the emergency room when it was clear that Sara might die. It was later determined that Sara would have lived if her parents had taken her to the hospital. Mary and John did not intend to harm Sara. They prayed for her recovery rather than take her to the hospital, consistent with their religious beliefs. They were heartbroken when Sara died.
- Ted was at a party at the home of his boss. He drank three glasses of wine at the party. Ted left the party at around midnight. As he was driving home, he fell asleep at the wheel, and crashed headfirst into a car, instantly killing the driver of the other car. Ted did not intend to cause the driver's death and was very sorry that he accidentally fell asleep.

Should the Browns and Ted be charged with involuntary manslaughter? Parents who fail to take a sick child to the hospital and drunk drivers who hit and kill another motorist are sometimes charged with involuntary manslaughter. If the person who causes the death was acting under the standard of care of a reasonable person, he or she would not be acting negligently and thus would not be guilty of a crime. So if a sober driver who is obeying the traffic laws accidentally hits and kills someone, he or she has not committed involuntary manslaughter. But if a person drives a car while intoxicated, then he or she is acting negligently. If that person drinks an exorbitant amount of alcohol, insists on driving after being told that he or she should not, drives well over the speed limit, and then hits and kills someone, he or she may be acting with the extreme recklessness required for second degree murder.

The Trial of Dr. Conrad Murray

The news of Michael Jackson's death on June 25, 2009, shocked the world. Dubbed "The King of Pop," Michael Jackson was probably one of the most recognized faces in the world. His success as an entertainer was unparalleled. His 1982 album Thriller was the best-selling album of all time, and he won countless awards—more than any other musician in the history of popular music. Despite his success, Jackson's life was surrounded by controversy, including repeated allegations of child sexual abuse. A civil lawsuit was settled out of court in 1993, and in 2005, he faced criminal charges for similar allegations, but was acquitted after a jury trial.

Jackson's image had been tarnished, but in 2009, at the age of fifty, he was determined to revive his career with a

(Continued)

(Continued)

ROBYN BECK/AFP/Getty Images/Newscom

Keir Whitaker

Dr. Conrad Murray and pop star Michael Jackson.

criminal charges were brought against Murray for the death of Michael Jackson.

Murray was charged with involuntary manslaughter. The felony complaint filed against Dr. Murray stated as follows:

> On or about June 25, 2009, in the County of Los Angeles, the crime of INVOLUNTARY MANSLAUGHTER, in violation of PENAL CODE SECTION 192(b), a Felony, was committed by CONRAD ROBERT MURRAY, who did unlawfully, and without malice, kill MICHAEL JOSEPH JACKSON, a human being, in the commission of an unlawful act, not amounting to a felony; and in the commission of a lawful act which might have produced death, in an unlawful manner, and without due caution and circumspection.[19]

Murray went to trial and was ultimately convicted of involuntary manslaughter. The prosecutor called numerous witnesses to prove that Murray acted with gross negligence in administering Propofol to Jackson and that his behavior deviated from the standard of care expected of a physician in his situation. He presented evidence that Murray had large quantities of Propofol and other prescription drugs shipped to his girlfriend's apartment during the time he was treating Jackson. The prosecutor also presented the testimony of several doctors who gave their expert opinions about the use of Propofol. They all testified that they would never, under any circumstances, administer the drug in a patient's bedroom because of the risk that it could lead to death. The experts also testified that Propofol is never used to treat insomnia—the condition for which Murray was treating Jackson. The prosecutor also presented evidence that Murray did not call 911 until at least twenty minutes after Jackson stopped breathing and removed evidence of his wrongdoing from Jackson's bedroom during that period of time.

Dr. Murray admitted that he had been administering doses of Propofol and other drugs to Jackson for his chronic insomnia. However, Dr. Murray denied administering the fatal dose to Jackson on June 25th, instead claiming that Jackson administered the drug to himself. Murray claimed that Jackson was having a particularly difficult time sleeping the night before he died and that he refused to give Jackson more than a "safe" dose of Propofol, despite Jackson's constant begging for more drugs.

The jury found Murray guilty and he was sentenced to the maximum period of four years in prison.

worldwide tour called "This Is It." Jackson participated in a strenuous schedule of rehearsals at the Staples Center in Los Angeles, where the tour was scheduled to begin in July 2009. It was in 2009 that Jackson hired Dr. Conrad Murray to be his personal physician at a salary of $150,000 per month.

After Jackson's death, an autopsy was performed, and the medical examiner determined that he died from an overdose of Propofol. Propofol is an anesthetic drug that is normally administered only in a hospital setting, and the amount found in Jackson's body was typically given to patients about to undergo heavy surgery. The circumstances surrounding Jackson's death were suspicious from the beginning. This finding caused prosecutors to focus on Dr. Murray. After an extensive investigation,

Questions

1. Should Dr. Murray have been charged with Michael Jackson's death? Why or why not?

2. What facts presented at trial supported the verdict in this case?

3. If you were the judge, would you have sentenced Dr. Murray to the maximum penalty of four years?

Felony Murder

Felony murder is a killing that occurs during the course of, and in furtherance of, an inherently dangerous felony. A felony murder may be intentional or unintentional. It can even be totally accidental, as long as it occurs during the commission of a dangerous felony. Felony murder statutes list the felonies that are considered inherently dangerous, and they vary from state to state, but most include robbery, rape, burglary, arson, and kidnapping.

The felony murder doctrine is one of the most controversial in the criminal law, primarily because it permits criminal liability and harsh punishment for accidental killings. Proponents of the rule use a number of theories to justify its existence. The basic idea is that individuals who intentionally participate in dangerous felonies should be held responsible for the foreseeable consequences of their actions. For example, it is foreseeable that a loaded gun might go off accidentally during an armed robbery. Therefore, those who participate in that robbery should be held liable for the accidental death of the victim even if they did not intend to kill anyone.

The United States is the only country in the Western world that still honors the felony murder rule. Although most states have a felony murder rule, some have abolished it and others have amended their criminal codes to reduce it to second degree murder. Most states, however, punish felony murder at the highest level, as first degree murder. As will be discussed later in this chapter, states that permit the death penalty recognize felony murder as one of the aggravating circumstances that permit a death sentence.

Another controversial aspect of the felony murder rule is the fact that felons who kill—accidentally or otherwise—after the felony is apparently over, may still be held liable for the death, as long as the felon has not reached his destination—also called a "point of safety." For example, if an armed robber is speeding away from the scene of the robbery and accidentally hits and kills someone on his or her way home (the "point of safety"), he may be charged with felony murder.

If more than one individual is involved in the commission of the felony, they are held liable for each other's actions. For example, if two people commit an armed robbery and one of them shoots the victim (accidentally or otherwise), both will be charged with felony murder. However, if someone other than the felon commits the homicide, most states will not hold the felon liable for the death. For example, if a cashier at a convenience store pulls his own gun with the intention of shooting an armed robber, but accidentally shoots and kills a store customer, the armed robber will not be charged with felony murder in most states because the cashier was not acting as the agent of the felon. However, some states permit an exception to this rule in circumstances where the felon took some specific action that caused the death, such as when the felon uses the decedent as a human shield or is involved in a shootout that results in the death of an innocent person. With each of these exceptions, the felon has taken some action that directly causes the death of a bystander.

The Model Penal Code does not use the terms "felony murder," but has an analogous provision that creates a "rebuttable presumption of extreme indifference" during the commission of, or an attempt to commit, certain crimes.[20] These crimes are robbery, rape or deviate sexual intercourse by force or threat of force, arson, burglary, kidnapping, and felonious escape.[21] However, unlike the common law, a defendant in a MPC jurisdiction can contest the presumption of extreme indifference—meaning that under the MPC the death is not automatically attributed to the defendant as a murder if it occurs during one of the above-mentioned crimes. As a result, the MPC is not quite as harsh as the common law with respect to felony murder, but the rebuttable presumption of extreme indifference is not necessarily easy to overcome and will vary with the circumstances of each crime.

The George Huguely Case—The Felony Murder Charge

In *Commonwealth v. Huguely* (2012), in addition to the first degree premeditated murder charge, the jury also considered charges of felony murder, robbery, burglary, entering a house with intent to commit a felony, and grand larceny. The prosecutor argued that Huguely committed the inherently dangerous felonies of robbery and burglary and that the killing occurred during the commission of those felonies. His closing argument focused more on trying to prove felony murder than premeditated murder, perhaps because the evidence of premeditation was scant. The prosecutor presented evidence that Huguely took Yeardley Love's computer, and he argued that this taking constituted a robbery, namely that he took the computer by force or the threat of force. He also argued that Huguely committed a burglary—that he broke and entered Love's apartment with the intent of committing a felony. As mentioned earlier in the chapter, the jury quickly rejected both forms of first degree murder. If the jury had found that Huguely committed either a robbery or a burglary, he may also have been convicted of felony murder.

Questions

1. Should the felony murder rule be abolished? Why or why not?

2. Should felony murder be punished as seriously as first degree premeditated murder? Why or why not?

3. Is there a justification for punishing unintentional felony murder less seriously than intentional felony murder?

Capital Punishment

Capital punishment, also known as the death penalty, permits the state to put a person to death as punishment for the commission of certain crimes. Although used almost exclusively as punishment for murder, the federal government and several states have laws that permit the death penalty for crimes other than murder, such as treason and aggravated kidnapping.[22]

Few subjects are more controversial and emotional than the death penalty. Opponents of the death penalty argue that it is cruel and unusual punishment and that it does not act as a deterrent. Death penalty proponents argue that it does deter and that it is the only appropriate punishment for the most heinous crimes. Capital punishment is a very political issue and is frequently seen as a litmus test for Supreme Court nominees and presidential candidates alike.

Thirty-two states and the federal government permit the death penalty, primarily for the most serious murders. Certain states, such as Virginia and Texas, utilize the death penalty more frequently than others. The United States is the only country in the Western world that still permits the death penalty.

The Constitutionality of the Death Penalty

With the exception of a brief four-year period between 1972 and 1976, the U.S. Supreme Court consistently has upheld the constitutionality of the death penalty. The court has not acted consistently on death penalty issues and has reversed itself on a number of occasions. For example, the court abolished the death penalty in 1972 and restored it four years later. The court upheld the constitutionality of the death penalty for juveniles before reversing itself on this issue in 2005. Similarly the court permitted the execution of the mentally retarded before forbidding such executions in 2002. Although the court has placed some limitations on the implementation of the death penalty, for over thirty years, the court has affirmed death sentences in a variety of contexts.

Table 8.2 summarizes some of the important Supreme Court cases that considered the constitutionality of the death penalty.

Table 8.2 **Important Supreme Court Death Penalty Cases**

Death Penalty Timeline[23]	Year
Furman v. Georgia, 408 U.S. 238: effectively outlawing the death penalty	1972
Revision of death penalty statutes in thirty-seven states, including the elimination of those statutes which mandated imposition of the death penalty upon conviction of a certain crime	1972–1976
Gregg v. Georgia, 428 U.S. 153: establishing the three-part process for applying the death penalty: Trial—guilt phase to determine whether defendant committed the crime Sentencing—penalty phase including mitigating and aggravating factors Appellate Review—automatic review by highest court in the state to ensure the death penalty was not applied arbitrarily	1976
Atkins v. Virginia, 536 U.S. 304: holding that executing the mentally retarded violates the Eighth Amendment prohibition against cruel and unusual punishment	2002
Roper v. Simmons, 543 U.S. 551: outlawing the execution of persons under 18 years old at the time of the murder	2005
Kennedy v. Louisiana, 554 U.S. 407: abolishing the death penalty for the rape of a child where no death occurred	2008

In *Furman v. Georgia* (1972),[24] the Supreme Court held that the death penalty was unconstitutional. The opinion was very complicated, with each of the nine justices writing his own opinion. The effect of the decision was to end all executions because the death penalty was being implemented arbitrarily and capriciously. Jurors in capital cases were given no guidance about how to decide whether a particular case warranted the death penalty. Thus, there was a greater chance that it was being implemented in a discriminatory manner.

After *Furman*, death penalty states passed new statutes that were based on the Model Penal Code, Section 210.6. This model purported to give jurors specific guidance on whether the facts and circumstances of a particular case warranted a punishment of death. The Supreme Court upheld the constitutionality of this model in *Gregg v. Georgia* (1976),[25] effectively reinstating the death penalty. This model remains in effect in death penalty states today. It provides for a two-part, bifurcated trial. In the first part of the trial, the jury decides whether or not the defendant committed the murder (the "guilt" phase). During the second part of the trial (the "penalty" phase), the same jury decides whether the defendant should receive the death penalty. The guilt phase is conducted the same as a jury trial in any criminal case. In the penalty phase, the prosecutor is required to prove the existence of one or more aggravating factors while the defense is permitted to provide evidence of one or more mitigating factors. If the aggravating factor(s) outweigh the mitigating factor(s), the jury may vote for the death penalty. If the mitigating factor(s) outweigh the aggravating factor(s), the jury votes against the death penalty.

The statutes specifically set forth the aggravating factors, one or more of which the prosecutor must prove beyond a reasonable doubt. Most death penalty statutes include aggravating factors similar to those in the following excerpt from the Georgia death penalty statute:

Georgia's Death Penalty Statute

(1) The offense of murder, rape, armed robbery, or kidnapping was committed by a person with a prior record of conviction for a capital felony;

(2) The offense of murder, rape, armed robbery, or kidnapping was committed while the offender was engaged in the commission of another capital felony or aggravated battery, or the offense of murder was committed while the offender was engaged in the commission of burglary in any degree or arson in the first degree;

(3) The offender, by his act of murder, armed robbery, or kidnapping, knowingly created a great risk of death to more than one person in a public place by means of a weapon or device which would normally be hazardous to the lives of more than one person;

(4) The offender committed the offense of murder for himself or another, for the purpose of receiving money or any other thing of monetary value;

(5) The murder of a judicial officer, former judicial officer, district attorney or solicitor-general, or former district attorney, solicitor, or solicitor-general was committed during or because of the exercise of his or her official duties;

(6) The offender caused or directed another to commit murder or committed murder as an agent or employee of another person;

(7) The offense of murder, rape, armed robbery, or kidnapping was outrageously or wantonly vile, horrible, or inhuman in that it involved torture, depravity of mind, or an aggravated battery to the victim;

(8) The offense of murder was committed against any peace officer, corrections employee, or firefighter while engaged in the performance of his official duties;

(9) The offense of murder was committed by a person in, or who has escaped from, the lawful custody of a peace officer or place of lawful confinement;

(10) The murder was committed for the purpose of avoiding, interfering with, or preventing a lawful arrest or custody in a place of lawful confinement, of himself or another; or

(11) The offense of murder, rape, or kidnapping was committed by a person previously convicted of rape, aggravated sodomy, aggravated child molestation, or aggravated sexual battery.[26]

After the prosecutor presents evidence of one or more aggravating factors, the defendant may present evidence of mitigating factors. These factors may include evidence of anything about the defendant's background or record that he or she and his or her lawyer believe will persuade the jury to decide that he or she does not deserve to be executed. Typically, a defense attorney will present evidence about the defendant's background, such as evidence that he or she was abused as a child or that he or she suffers from emotional problems or learning disabilities. The defense will also present evidence of any facts and circumstances in the case that mitigate the defendant's involvement in the crime.

The jury may only sentence the defendant to the death penalty if it finds that the aggravating circumstances outweigh the mitigating circumstances. It is not a mathematical calculation. The jury is allowed to place whatever value it deems appropriate on each aggravating and mitigating circumstance. It is possible for the jury to find that one mitigating circumstance outweighs five aggravating circumstances. Thus juries still exercise a great deal of discretion in death penalty cases, but the discretion is guided by rules and a process.

Race and the Death Penalty

One of the most controversial and heavily criticized decisions in the Supreme Court's jurisprudence is a case dealing with race and the implementation of the death penalty. In *McCleskey v. Kemp* (1987),[27] the court rejected Mr. McCleskey's claim that the death penalty was implemented in a racially discriminatory manner in violation of the Eighth and Fourteenth Amendments to the U.S. Constitution.

Mr. McCleskey, who was African American, was convicted of the murder of a White police officer during a robbery. The jury found that the prosecutor proved two statutory aggravating factors (that the killing occurred during the commission of a robbery and that the victim was a police officer). Mr. McCleskey filed a petition for habeas corpus in federal court. In support of his claim, he presented a statistical study performed by Professors David Baldus, Charles Pulaski, and George Woodworth. These professors examined over two thousand murder cases in Georgia during the 1970s and used a complicated statistical formula (multiple regression analysis) to show that defendants charged with killing White defendants were 4.3 times more likely to receive the death penalty as defendants charged with killing Blacks. The Baldus study also revealed other evidence of race discrimination in the implementation of the death penalty, ultimately concluding that Blacks who killed Whites had the greatest likelihood of receiving the death penalty. The Supreme Court accepted the legitimacy of the study, but ultimately rejected McCleskey's constitutional challenge because he did not prove purposeful discrimination on the part of the decision makers in his case. In other words, he needed to prove that the prosecutors *in his case* intended to discriminate against him because of his race. The court explained that "discretion is essential to the criminal justice process; [therefore] exceptionally clear proof is required before this Court will infer that the discretion has been abused."[28] Further, McCleskey would have to "prove that the Georgia Legislature enacted or maintained the death penalty statute *because of* an anticipated racially discriminatory effect"[29] before he could prevail. Since he failed to prove any purposeful intent, the court held that McCleskey's conviction must stand.

Since *McCleskey*, a number of states and the federal government have conducted studies to examine the effect of race on the implementation of the death penalty. In 96 percent of these studies, there was a pattern of discrimination based on the race of the victim, the defendant, or both. A North Carolina study found that individuals who killed Whites were 3.5 times more likely to receive a death sentence.[30] The Maryland

Figure 8.1 Race of Defendants Executed in the United States Since 1976[33]

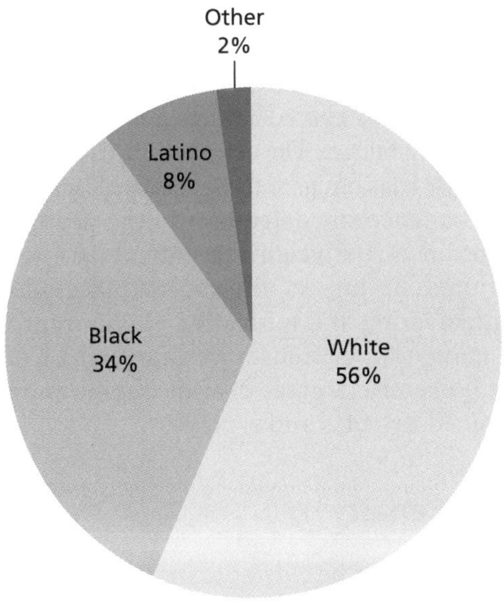

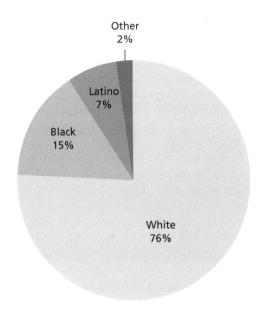

Source: Death Penalty Information Center, National Statistics on the Death Penalty and Race, available at http://deathpenaltyinfo.org/race-death-row-inmates-executed-1976#defend (last accessed July 4, 2014).

Figure 8.2 Race of Victims Since 1976

Source: Death Penalty Information Center, National Statistics on the Death Penalty and Race, available at http://deathpenaltyinfo.org/race-death-row-inmates-executed-1976#defend (last accessed July 4, 2014).

study, released in 2003, examined the implementation of the death penalty from 1978 to 1999 and found that Blacks who killed Whites were much more likely to face the death penalty than Blacks who killed Blacks or Whites who killed either Blacks or Whites.[31] The 2005 California study found that individuals who killed Whites were over three times more likely to receive a death sentence than those who killed Blacks and over four times more likely than those who killed Latinos.[32] See Figure 8.1 and Figure 8.2 on page 212 with more recent statistics on the disparity between the race of defendants and victims in the application of the death penalty.

Questions

1. Is the Supreme Court correct that a defendant should have to prove that the legislature, prosecutor, or jury intended to discriminate against him based on his race or the race of the victim?

2. How would a defendant prove intentional discrimination in a death penalty case?

3. Is discrimination always intentional?

Judicial Override

One of the most controversial procedures in the implementation of the death penalty is a practice called judicial override. This practice permits the judge to override the sentencing decision of the jury in capital cases. For example, if the jury returns a verdict of life without parole, the judge may override their verdict and impose a death sentence. The judge may also override a jury's verdict to impose a death sentence and impose a sentence of life without parole.

Only three states permit judicial override: Alabama, Florida, and Delaware. Delaware and Florida have strict standards for override and rarely use the practice. However, Alabama judges use the practice routinely, and in 91 percent of the cases involving overrides, judges have overturned jury decisions of life without parole and imposed the death penalty.[34] About 20 percent of the people on death row in Alabama were sentenced by judicial override.[35]

The judicial override section of the Alabama statute easily permits judges to overrule the decision of the jury:

Alabama's Judicial Override Statute

Ala. Code § 13A-5–47:

(e) In deciding upon the sentence, the trial court shall determine whether the aggravating circumstances it finds to exist outweigh the mitigating circumstances it finds to exist, and in doing so the trial court shall consider the recommendation of the jury contained in its advisory verdict. . . . While the jury's recommendation concerning sentence shall be given consideration, it is not binding upon the court

The statute is clear that although the judge must consider the jury's recommendation, he or she is not required to follow it.

Limitations on the Death Penalty

The Supreme Court has placed some substantive limitations on the death penalty and how it may be implemented. In *Ring v. Arizona* (2002),[36] the court held that juries rather than judges must determine the existence of one or more aggravating circumstances that make the defendant eligible for a death sentence. That same year, in *Atkins v. Virginia* (2002),[37] the court held that it is unconstitutional to execute defendants suffering from mental retardation. The court placed yet another significant limitation on the implementation of the death penalty when it decided *Roper v. Simmons* (2005).[38] In *Roper*, the court barred the execution of individuals who were under the age of eighteen at the time of the homicide. *Kennedy v. Louisiana* (2008)[39] outlawed the death penalty for the rape of a child in cases where no death occurred. Currently, thirty-two states permit the death penalty. Eighteen states and the District of Columbia have abolished it.

Concluding Note

Criminal homicide is the most serious criminal offense in our society and is punished more severely than any other crime. With very few exceptions, it is the only crime that may be punished with the death penalty. However, we have learned that there are many different forms of criminal homicide, and some are considered more serious than others. Killings that are committed with malice, such as first degree premeditated murder, second degree intentional murder and depraved heart murder, are punished more severely than killings without malice, such as voluntary and involuntary manslaughter. Felony murder, which can be either intentional or unintentional, is usually punished at the highest levels and turns entirely on whether the defendant was committing a dangerous felony when the killing occurred.

Juries are often presented with a number of options when an individual is charged with criminal homicide. If a person is charged with first degree premeditated murder, there is usually also evidence of second degree intentional murder and sometimes voluntary manslaughter. In such cases, the jury will be asked to consider those lesser included offenses and must make a factual determination about which level of criminal homicide has been proven beyond a reasonable doubt. Likewise, when the charge is depraved heart murder, there is usually also evidence of involuntary manslaughter. The jury's verdict will depend upon the strength of the evidence presented.

In Chapters 9 and 10, we will examine defenses to criminal homicide and other offenses. Now test yourself on the material we have covered in Chapter 8. Good luck with the Issue Spotter exercise.

IssueSpotter

Read the hypothetical and spot the issues discussed in this chapter.

Here Kitty Kitty!

Sally Siegfried worked as an assistant to the lion tamers at the Ring Circus. She became very attached to one of the new tiger cubs. Sally named the cub Kitty Cat and played with him all the time. When Sally left the circus, she decided to take Kitty Cat with her.

Sally moved to the state of Grace. When Sally first arrived in Grace, Kitty Cat was just a cub of three months and weighed only six pounds. She treated Kitty just like a pet—feeding her milk from a bottle and taking Kitty with her whenever she left the house. Everyone was fascinated with Kitty when she was just a little cub. Sally encouraged onlookers to pet her, and Kitty would purr just like a cat. When Kitty started eating solid food, Sally fed her cat food. But as time went on, Kitty's appetite grew. Sally fed her steaks, and she got bigger and bigger. Soon Sally was unable to carry Kitty, so she started walking her with a leash. Most of the people in the town grew accustomed to the sight of Sally walking Kitty and continued to pet her and play with her. On one occasion, Kitty Cat scratched a little boy, but he was not seriously injured.

Sally lived in a house with a big back yard. When Kitty was two years old and almost two hundred pounds, Sally decided to put up a fence so Kitty could roam around the yard. The fence was six feet tall. One day, Sally came outside and found Kitty almost halfway up her twenty foot oak tree. She was quite surprised because Kitty had never climbed a tree before. After coaxing her down, Sally scolded Kitty for her bad behavior, and to Sally's knowledge, Kitty never climbed the tree again.

About six months after the tree incident, Homer and Marge Sanders moved into the house next door. When Marge first saw Kitty roaming around in Sally's backyard, she ran screaming into her house. She called Sally, and Sally assured her that Kitty was a pet and would never harm her or anyone else. Sally also assured Marge that she always kept Kitty inside the fenced-in backyard. Nonetheless Marge was not reassured. She told Sally that tigers were wild animals that could kill humans and that she believed Kitty might jump over that fence one day. Sally told Marge that Kitty was different and that she did not have to worry. Marge bought several books about tiger behavior, wrapped them in a box, and left them on Sally's doorstep. She also emailed Sally a YouTube video showing a tiger jumping fifteen feet high.

One day Sally decided to go shopping. She planned to get home by 5 p.m. to feed Kitty, but there was a sale at Bloomingdale's, and she did not leave the store until 6 p.m. Kitty woke up from her afternoon nap in the backyard at around 5 p.m. She was hungry and started looking for food. As luck would have it, the Sanders decided to grill some steaks in their backyard that day. When Kitty smelled the steaks, she jumped the fence and headed toward the grill. Homer stood in front of the grill, and said, "Go away Kitty! I paid fifty bucks for those steaks!" Kitty lunged at Homer, killed him, and then devoured the steaks.

Police officers searched Sally's home and found an unopened package from Marge. They opened it and found several books about tiger behavior, including one titled *Tigers Can Jump Fences* and another titled *Tigers Eat People*.

1. What charge or charges might a prosecutor bring against Sally?

2. What are the strengths and weaknesses of the prosecutor's case?

Key Terms and Cases ●———————

Notes ●━━━━━━━━━━━━━━━━

1. Keith Schneider, "Dr. Jack Kevorkian Dies at 83: A Doctor Who Helped End Lives," *New York Times*, June 3, 2011, http://www.nytimes.com/2011/06/04/us/04kevorkian.html?pagewanted=all

2. U.S. Census Bureau. "Homicide Trends: 1980 to 2008" (Washington, DC: U.S. Census Bureau, Statistical Abstract of the United States, 2012), http://www.census.gov/compendia/statab/2012/tables/12s0313.pdf

3. Erica L. Smith and Alexia Cooper, "Homicide in the U.S. Known to Law Enforcement, 2011," NCJ 243035 (Washington, DC: U.S. Department of Justice, 2013), http://www.bjs.gov/content/pub/pdf/hus11.pdf

4. Alexia Cooper and Erica L. Smith, "Homicide Trends in the United States, 1980–2008," NCJ 236018 (Washington, DC: U.S. Department of Justice, Bureau of Justice Statistics, 2011), 13, http://www.bjs.gov/content/pub/pdf/htus8008.pdf

5. Ibid. at 14.

6. Erica L. Smith and Alexia Cooper, "Homicide in the U.S. Known to Law Enforcement, 2011," NCJ 243035 (Washington, DC: U.S. Department of Justice, 2013), http://www.bjs.gov/content/pub/pdf/hus11.pdf

7. National Conference of Commissioners of Uniform State Laws, *Uniform Definition of Death Act,* (Chicago: Author,1980), 3, http://pnth.org/wordpress/wp-content/uploads/Uniform-Determination-of-Death-1980_5c.pdf

8. Model Penal Code § 210.0(1).

9. California Penal Code Section 187.

10. Mary Pat Flaherty and Jenna Johnson, "Prosecutors: George Huguely Email to Yeardley Love Said, 'I Should Have Killed You,'"*Washington Post*, February 8, 2012, http://articles.washingtonpost.com/2012–02–08/local/35445952_1_caitlin-whiteley-yeardley-love-first-degree-murder

11. Ibid.

12. Samantha Koon, "Jurors Discuss Deciding Huguely's Fate," *The Daily Progress*, Feb. 25, 2012, http://www.dailyprogress.com/starexponent/news/local_news/jurors-discuss-deciding-huguely-s-fate/article_22082caf-0a6a-5177-8897-30de00260a32.html?mode=jqm

13. Ibid.

14. Ibid.

15. Tamar Lewin, "What Penalty for a Killing in Passion," *New York Times*, October 21, 1994, A18, http://www.nytimes.com/1994/10/21/us/what-penalty-for-a-killing-in-passion.html?pagewanted=all&src=pm

16. Ibid.

17. Ibid.

18. Kimberly Wilmot-Weidman, "After A 3-year Fight, Murder is Finally Murder in Maryland," *Chicago Tribune*, November 23, 1997, http://articles.chicagotribune.com/1997-11-23/features/9711230114_1_spousal-maryland-law-deadly-rage

19. Complaint at 1, *People v. Murray*, No.SA073164 (L.A. Cnty.Supp. Ct., Feb. 8, 2010), http://ww2.lasuperiorcourt.org/hp/d5kq3s45qb1fwl45pn53z5yl/1381114021.pdf

20. Model Penal Code § 210.2(1)(b).

21. Ibid.

22. Death Penalty Information Center, "Death Penalty for Offenses Other than Murder," http://www.deathpenaltyinfo.org/death-penalty-offenses-other-murder

23. See Death Penalty Information Center, "Part I: History of the Death Penalty," http://www .deathpenaltyinfo.org/part-i-history-death-penalty#EarlyandMid-TwentiethCentury, accessed July 4, 2014.

24. *Furman v. Georgia*, 408 U.S. 238 (1972).

25. *Gregg v. Georgia*, 428 U.S. 153 (1976).

26. Ga. Code Ann., § 17–10–30.

27. *McCleskey v. Kemp* 481 U.S. 279 (1987).

28. Ibid.

29. Ibid. at 298.

30. Death Penalty Information Center, "Race and the Death Penalty in North Carolina," http:// www.deathpenaltyinfo.org/race-and-death-penalty-north-carolina#factsheets

31. Death Penalty Information Center, "Maryland Race Study Author Finds Death Penalty Practices 'Disturbing,'" http://www.deathpenaltyinfo.org/race-news-and-developments-2005, accessed July 17, 2014.

32. Death Penalty Focus, "Racial Disparities in California Death Sentencing," http://www.death penalty.org/article.php?id=54, accessed July 17, 2014.

33. Death Penalty Information Center, "National Statistics on the Death Penalty and Race," http:// deathpenaltyinfo.org/race-death-row-inmates-executed-1976#defend, accessed July 4, 2014.

34. "Judge Override," Equal Justice Initiative, http://www.eji.org/deathpenalty/override, accessed August 5, 2014.

35. Ibid.

36. *Ring v. Arizona*, 536 U.S. 584 (2002).

37. *Atkins v. Virginia*, 536 US. 304 (2002).

38. *Roper v. Simmons*, 543 U.S. 551 (2005).

39. *Kennedy v. Louisiana*, 554 U.S. 407 (2008).

Chapter 9

George Zimmerman shot and killed an unarmed African American teenager named Trayvon Martin on February 26, 2012, in Sanford, Florida. Martin was walking to his father's home at around 7 p.m. after a trip to a nearby convenience store. Zimmerman was driving through the neighborhood and saw Martin walking. He called the police and reported that a suspicious guy was "walking around looking about."[1] Zimmerman got out of his car, followed Martin, and eventually confronted him. The confrontation ended with Zimmerman shooting Martin, who died on the scene. Zimmerman was taken into custody and gave a statement to the police claiming he had acted in self-defense. He was neither charged nor arrested, prompting widespread criticism of the Sanford Police Department and Florida's "stand your ground law." Zimmerman was ultimately charged with second degree murder on April 11, 2012. The Zimmerman case sparked a national discussion about the law of self-defense, racial profiling, gun violence, and the use of deadly force against young African American men. Self-defense is one of the defenses we will discuss in this chapter.

The Trayvon Martin case incited protests around the country and led to a national discussion about race, prejudice, self-defense, and the criminal justice system.

Justification Defenses

Learning Objectives

After reading and studying this chapter, you should be able to

➤ Explain the difference between an affirmative defense and an "elements" defense

➤ Provide examples of justification and excuse defenses

➤ Define self-defense

➤ Explain duty to retreat

➤ Define battered woman syndrome

➤ Know the difference between the alter ego and reasonable belief rules

➤ Differentiate between defense of property and defense of habitation

➤ List and explain the different types of defense of habitation laws

➤ Explain the castle doctrine

➤ Define the law enforcement defense

➤ Know the difference between duress and necessity

Introduction

If an individual is charged with a crime and chooses to exercise his constitutional right to a trial, he may not be convicted unless and until the state proves each element of the crime beyond a reasonable doubt. The reasonable doubt standard is the highest burden of proof in the law. It is reserved for cases involving the potential loss of liberty (incarceration) or even life (the death penalty). A person charged with a crime is presumed to be innocent unless and until the state meets that very heavy burden. An individual may always choose to plead guilty, but if he decides to go to trial, he is presumed innocent from the moment he is charged with a crime. That presumption of innocence remains throughout the trial unless and until the jury or judge finds him guilty.

Because the burden of proof rests entirely on the state, the defendant is not required to testify or present a single witness or shred of evidence. If the state is unable to prove his guilt, he will be found not guilty. Even though the burden of proof is on the state, the defendant may nonetheless choose to present a defense. There are a number of legal defenses to crimes that will be discussed in this chapter and in Chapter 10. In this chapter, we will explore the law of defensive force and the circumstances under which an individual may use force to defend himself, other people, his property, and his home. The chapter will also include a discussion of the defenses of necessity and duress.

Types of Defenses

Elements Versus Affirmative Defenses

If criminal defendants decide to exercise their rights to a trial and fight the charges against them, they may do so in several ways—by presenting an elements defense, an affirmative defense, or both. The defendant who presents an elements defense is saying to the jury, "I am presumed innocent, and I will remain innocent unless the state proves all of the elements of the offense beyond a reasonable doubt." The defendant who takes this approach is not really "presenting" a defense. Since the state has the burden of proof, it must present evidence—testimony, physical evidence, or both. The defendant then has the constitutional right to question through cross-examination any witnesses in an attempt to show they are not credible and should not be believed.[2] A criminal defendant may choose to cross examine the state's witnesses and simply argue to the judge or jury that the government has not met its heavy burden of proving each element of the offense beyond a reasonable doubt. If the jury agrees, the defendant is found not guilty.

For example, if a defendant is charged with first degree premeditated murder, the prosecutor must prove that he or she killed another human being with premeditation and deliberation. If the prosecutor fails to prove the element of premeditation beyond a reasonable doubt, the jury will find the defendant not guilty of first degree murder. He or she will be acquitted without having to present evidence of any type of defense simply because the government did not prove its case. The elements defense is always available to the defendant, whether or not he or she asserts it, but the defendant may also decide to present an affirmative defense. In such cases, after the government presents its case, the defendant then presents evidence in support of his or her defense. Even in cases where the defendant presents an affirmative defense, he or she may also argue that the government has not met its burden of proof.

When presenting an affirmative defense, the defendant has the burden of production. In other words, she must produce at least a minimal amount of credible evidence before the judge will allow the jury to consider the defense. In some jurisdictions, the defendant also has the burden of persuasion. In these jurisdictions, the defendant must prove the defense, usually by a lower standard such as the preponderance of the evidence. This burden in no way affects the government's burden of proving the elements of the offense beyond a reasonable doubt. In other jurisdictions, even when the defendant presents evidence of a defense, he or she does not take on the burden of proving it. For example, in the District of Columbia, when the defendant presents the justification defense of self-defense, the government has the burden of proving that the defendant did not act in self-defense.[3]

Excuse Versus Justification Defenses

Some defenses are called excuse defenses. Defendants who present excuse defenses do not claim that they were justified in their actions. Instead, the claim is that they should not be held responsible for their actions because of some circumstance that prevented them from acting lawfully. The insanity defense is a classic excuse defense. The defendant does not claim that she was justified in killing the decedent, but instead claims that she should be "excused" because she was suffering from a mental disease or defect that prevented her from conforming her actions to the requirements of the law.

Other defenses are called justification defenses. The defendant who presents a justification defense claims that his behavior was legally justified. Self-defense is a justification defense. The defendant who presents this defense to a murder charge claims that he was legally justified in taking another person's life because at the time he did so, he was in fear of imminent serious bodily injury or death.

The justification and excuse labels generate interesting discussions among legal scholars but have little practical significance. Whether a defense is labeled a justification or an excuse, the result is the same: If the defense is successful, the defendant is not guilty. This chapter will discuss the justification defenses, and the excuse defenses are explored in Chapter 10.

Defensive Force

Self-Defense

The killing of a human being with malice aforethought is murder. But what if the person who kills believes that he or she is about to be killed by that person? The law does not require a person who is in reasonable fear of imminent serious bodily injury or death to risk losing her life. According to the law of self-defense, that person may use a reasonable amount of force, even deadly force, to protect herself. The law of self-defense requires the following elements:

1. Reasonable fear,

2. An imminent attack, and

3. A proportionate amount of force.

General Principles

Even if an individual is in reasonable fear of an imminent attack and uses a proportionate amount of force to defend himself, he may not be successful in claiming self-defense if he was the aggressor in the altercation. The following case illustrates this rule.

U.S. v. Peterson (1973)
United States Court of Appeals, DC Circuit
483 F.2d 1222

The events immediately preceding the homicide are not seriously in dispute. The version presented by the Government's evidence follows. Charles Keitt, the deceased, and two friends drove in Keitt's car to the alley in the rear of Peterson's house to remove the windshield wipers from the latter's wrecked car. While Keitt was doing so, Peterson came out of the house into the backyard to protest. After a verbal exchange, Peterson went back into the house, obtained a pistol, and returned to the yard. In the meantime, Keitt had reseated himself in his car, and he and his companions were about to leave.

Upon his reappearance in the yard, Peterson paused briefly to load the pistol. "If you move," he shouted to Keitt, "I will shoot." He walked to a point in the yard slightly inside a gate in the rear fence and, pistol in hand, said, "If you come in here, I will kill you." Keitt alighted from his car, took a few steps toward Peterson and exclaimed, "What the hell do you think you are going to do with that?" Keitt then made an about-face, walked back to his car and got a lug wrench. With the wrench in a raised position, Keitt advanced toward Peterson, who stood with the pistol pointed toward him. Peterson warned Keitt not to "take another step" and, when Keitt continued onward shot him in the face from a distance of about ten feet. Death was apparently instantaneous. Shortly thereafter, Peterson left home and was apprehended 20-odd blocks away.

(Continued)

(Continued)

The trial judge's charge authorized the jury, as it might be persuaded, to convict Peterson of second-degree murder or manslaughter, or to acquit by reason of self-defense. On the latter phase of the case, the judge instructed that with evidence of self-defense present, the Government bore the burden of proving beyond a reasonable doubt that Peterson did not act in self-defense; and that if the jury had a reasonable doubt as to whether Peterson acted in self-defense, the verdict must be "not guilty." The judge further instructed that the circumstances under which Peterson acted, however, must have been such as to produce a reasonable belief that Keitt was then about to kill him or do him serious bodily harm, and that deadly force was necessary to repel him. In determining whether Peterson used excessive force in defending himself, the judge said, the jury could consider all of the circumstances under which he acted.

These features of the charge met Peterson's approval, and we are not summoned to pass on them. There were, however, two other aspects of the charge to which Peterson objected, and which are now the subject of vigorous controversy. The first of Peterson's complaints centers upon an instruction that the right to use deadly force in self-defense is not ordinarily available to one who provokes a conflict or is the aggressor in it. Mere words, the judge explained, do not constitute provocation or aggression; and if Peterson precipitated the altercation but thereafter withdrew from it in good faith and so informed Keitt by words or acts, he was justified in using deadly force to save himself from imminent danger or death or grave bodily harm. And, the judge added, even if Keitt was the aggressor and Peterson was justified in defending himself, he was not entitled to use any greater force than he had reasonable ground to believe and actually believed to be necessary for that purpose. Peterson contends that there was no evidence that he either caused or contributed to the conflict, and that the instructions on that topic could only misled (sic) the jury.

It has long been accepted that one cannot support a claim of self-defense by a self-generated necessity to kill. The right of homicidal self-defense is granted only to those free from fault in the difficulty; it is denied to slayers who incite the fatal attack, encourage the fatal quarrel or otherwise promote the necessitous occasion for taking life. The fact that the deceased struck the first blow, fired the first shot, or made the first menacing gesture does not legalize the self-defense claim if in fact the claimant was the actual provoker. In sum, one who is the aggressor in a conflict culminating in death cannot invoke the necessities of self-preservation. Only in the event that he communicates to his adversary his intent to withdraw and in good faith attempts to do so is he restored to his right of self-defense.

It was not until Peterson fetched his pistol and returned to his back yard that his confrontation with Keitt took on a deadly cast. Prior to his trip into the house for the gun, there was, by the Government's evidence, no threat, no display of weapons, no combat. There was an exchange of verbal aspersions and a misdemeanor against Peterson's property. It was in progress but, at this juncture, nothing more. Even if Peterson's post-arrest version of the initial encounter were accepted—his claim that Keitt went for the lug wrench before he armed himself—the events which followed bore heavily on the question as to who the real aggressor was.

The evidence is uncontradicted that when Peterson reappeared in the yard with his pistol, Keitt was about to depart the scene. Richard Hilliard testified that after the first argument, Keitt reentered his car and said, "Let's go." This statement was verified by Ricky Gray, who testified that Keitt "got in the car and . . . they were getting ready to go"; he, too, heard Keitt give the direction to start the car. The uncontroverted fact that Keitt was leaving shows plainly that so far as he was concerned the confrontation was ended. It demonstrates just as plainly that even if he had previously been the aggressor, he no longer was.

Not so with Peterson, however, as the undisputed evidence made clear. Emerging from the house with the pistol, he paused in the yard to load it, and to command Keitt not to move. He then walked through the yard to the rear gate and, displaying his pistol, dared Keitt to come in, and threatened to kill him if he did. While there appears to be no fixed rule on the subject, the cases hold, and we agree, that an affirmative unlawful act reasonably calculated to produce an affray foreboding injurious or fatal consequences is an aggression which, unless renounced, nullifies the right of homicidal self-defense. We cannot escape the abiding conviction that the jury could readily find Peterson's challenge to be a transgression of that character.

The second aspect of the trial judge's charge as to which Peterson asserts error concerned the undisputed fact that at no time did Peterson endeavor to retreat from Keitt's approach with the lug wrench. The judge instructed the jury that if Peterson had reasonable grounds to believe and did believe that he was in imminent danger of death or serious injury, and that deadly force was necessary to repel the danger, he was required neither to retreat nor to consider whether he could safely retreat. Rather, said the judge, Peterson was entitled to stand his ground and use such force as was reasonably necessary under the circumstances to save his life and his person from pernicious bodily harm. But, the judge continued, if Peterson could have safely retreated but did not do so, that failure was a circumstance which the jury might consider, together with all others, in determining whether he went further in repelling the danger, real or apparent, than he was justified in going.

Peterson contends that this imputation of an obligation to retreat was error, even if he could safely have done so. He points out that at the time of the shooting he was standing in his own yard, and argues he was under no duty to move. We are persuaded to the conclusion that in the circumstances presented here, the trial judge did not err in giving the instruction challenged. . . . In a majority of American jurisdictions, contrarily to the common law rule, one may stand his ground and use deadly force whenever it seems reasonably necessary to save himself. While the law of the District of Columbia on this point is not entirely clear, it seems allied with the strong minority adhering to the common law. In 1856, the District of Columbia Criminal Court ruled that a participant in an affray "must endeavor to retreat, . . . that is, he is obliged to retreat, if he can safely." . . .

Peterson [also] invokes . . . the so-called "castle" doctrine. It is well settled that one who through no fault of his own is attacked in his home is under no duty to retreat therefrom. The oft-repeated expression that "a man's home is his castle" reflected the belief in olden days that there were few if any safer sanctuaries than the home. The "castle" exception, moreover, has been extended by some courts to encompass the occupant's presence within the curtilage outside his dwelling. Peterson reminds us that when he shot to halt Keitt's advance, he was standing in his yard and so, he argues, he had no duty to endeavor to retreat.

Despite the practically universal acceptance of the "castle" doctrine in American jurisdictions wherein the point has been raised, its status in the District of Columbia has never been squarely decided. But whatever the fate of the doctrine in the District law of the future, it is clear that in absolute form it was inapplicable here. The right of self-defense, we have said, cannot be claimed by the aggressor in an affray so long as he retains that unmitigated role. It logically follows that any rule of no-retreat which may protect an innocent victim of the affray would, like other incidents of a forfeited right of self-defense, be unavailable to the party who provokes or stimulates the conflict. Accordingly, the law is well settled that the "castle" doctrine can be invoked only by one who is without fault in bringing the conflict on. That, we think, is the critical consideration here.

We need not repeat our previous discussion of Peterson's contribution to the altercation which culminated in Keitt's death. It suffices to point out that by no interpretation of the evidence could it be said that Peterson was blameless in the affair. And while, of course, it was for the jury to assess the degree of fault, the evidence well nigh dictated the conclusion that it was substantial.

The judgment of conviction appealed from is accordingly.

Affirmed.

Questions

1. What are the three issues that Mr. Peterson raised on appeal?

2. How did the court rule on each of the issues?

3. If Keitt had killed Peterson with the lug wrench before Peterson fired his gun, would Keitt have had a valid claim of self-defense? Why or why not?

Self-defense is a law of necessity. A person may only use the amount of force necessary to repel unlawful force against him or someone else. The person who uses more force than necessary (excessive force) may not claim self-defense. The amount of force used by a person who is defending himself must be proportionate to the force that is used against him. If a person is in imminent fear of serious bodily injury or death, he may use deadly force to defend himself. But if a person is attacked with non-deadly force, he may only use non-deadly force to defend himself. The amount of force used must be proportionate.

Consider the following hypothetical:

Rob and Kwame were construction workers on a lunch break. They got into a heated argument when Rob accused Kwame of hitting and damaging his car in the parking lot. Kwame denied hitting Rob's car, and Rob threatened to slash the tires on Kwame's car if he didn't pay for the repairs on his car. At that point, Kwame picked up a nearby hammer, raised it in the air, and charged at Rob. When Kwame was within three feet of Rob, Rob pulled a pistol out of his pocket and shot Kwame in the chest, killing him instantly.

Does Rob have a valid claim of self-defense? He probably does. Proportionality does not require that the same weapon be used in response to the threat, as long as deadly force is only used against deadly force. If Kwame had hit Rob in the head with the hammer, he could have killed or seriously injured him. The law of self-defense does not require a person in imminent danger of death or serious bodily injury to search for the same weapon as his assailant. By that time, he could be dead.

The Duty to Retreat

The Peterson case discusses the duty to retreat doctrine. Twenty-six states impose a duty to retreat before using deadly force. In these states, a person has a duty to retreat and must avoid using force, especially deadly force, but only if he or she can do so safely. For example, if John is walking in a dark alley and is approached by Bob who points a gun at him, John would not have a duty to retreat because if he turned his back and ran away, he would likely be shot in the back and killed. But if John was in his car with the motor running and Bob came toward him wielding a knife, John could easily and safely drive away and would have a duty to retreat if he were in a state that imposes such a duty.

Slightly less than half the states do NOT impose a duty to retreat and permit an individual to stand his ground and defend himself with a proportionate amount of force. These stand your ground laws were placed in the spotlight following Trayvon Martin's killing (discussed at the beginning of this chapter and in the next section). Many claimed that Zimmerman was not arrested immediately after the killing because of Florida's stand your ground law, provided below:

Florida's Stand Your Ground Statute

776.012 Use of force in defense of person.—A person is justified in using force, except deadly force, against another when and to the extent that the person reasonably believes that such conduct is necessary to defend himself or herself or another against the other's imminent use of unlawful force. However, a person is justified in the use of deadly force and does not have a duty to retreat if:

(1) He or she reasonably believes that such force is necessary to prevent imminent death or great bodily harm to himself or herself or another or to prevent the imminent commission of a forcible felony;

776.032 Immunity from criminal prosecution and civil action for justifiable use of force.—

(1) A person who uses force as permitted in s. 776.012 . . . is justified in using such force and is immune from criminal prosecution and civil action for the use of such force, unless the person against whom force was used is a law enforcement officer. . . . As used in this subsection, the term "criminal prosecution" includes arresting, detaining in custody, and charging or prosecuting the defendant.

(2) A law enforcement agency may use standard procedures for investigating the use of force as described in subsection (1), but the agency may not arrest the person for using force unless it determines that there is probable cause that the force that was used was unlawful.

Figure 9.1 **States With Stand Your Ground Laws**[5]

'Shoot first' laws, also known as 'stand your ground' laws, vary from state to state.

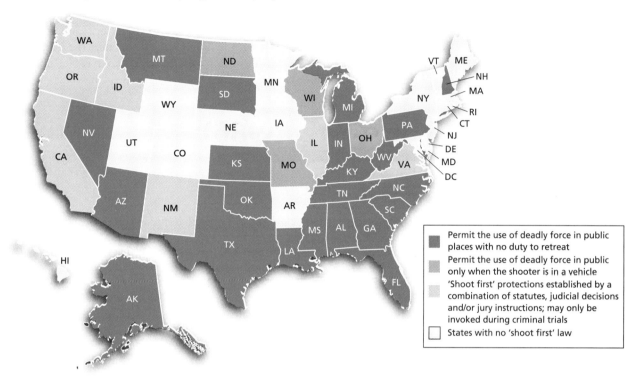

- ■ Permit the use of deadly force in public places with no duty to retreat
- ▨ Permit the use of deadly force in public only when the shooter is in a vehicle
- ▨ 'Shoot first' protections established by a combination of statutes, judicial decisions and/or jury instructions; may only be invoked during criminal trials
- ☐ States with no 'shoot first' law

Source: Law Center to Prevent Gun Violence. S. Culp, 19/02/2014.

Although many states have stand your ground laws (see Figure 9.1 above), not many of these states include provisions like Section 776.032 above, which prohibits the prosecution, or even arrest, of an individual who acts in self-defense. This section is controversial, primarily because it permits a police officer, and ultimately a judge (rather than a jury), to decide whether an individual acted in a self-defense. Florida law provides that if an individual who claims self-defense is arrested and charged, a judge must hold a pretrial hearing and decide whether the individual acted in self-defense. At this hearing, the defendant must prove, by a preponderance of the evidence, that he or she acted in self-defense. If the judge finds that the defendant acted in self-defense, he or she may dismiss the case at that point.[4] In states that do not have immunity from prosecution provisions, the defendant must present his or her defense at trial, and the jury decides whether or not he or she is guilty of the offense, as is the case with all other criminal offenses.

Bernhard Goetz with New York detectives after he turned himself in and admitted to shooting four youths on a New York subway train.

AP Photo/BERNARD GOETZ

*The "Reasonable Belief" Requirement and
the Role of Race in Self-Defense Cases*

The Bernhard Goetz Case. Few criminal cases garnered more attention and created more controversy in the 1980s than the Bernhard Goetz case. Street crime was at an all-time high in New York City when a White man shot and critically injured four Black youths on a subway car. As the headline above illustrates, the crime and the outcome of the trial produced strong and diverging views that broke down along racial lines, not only in New York City, but also throughout the nation.

People v. Goetz (1986)

Court of Appeals of New York

68 N.Y.2d 96

A Grand Jury has indicted defendant on attempted murder, assault, and other charges for having shot and wounded four youths on a New York City subway train after one or two of the youths approached him and asked for $5. The lower courts, concluding that the prosecutor's charge to the Grand Jury on the defense of justification was erroneous, have dismissed the attempted murder, assault and weapons possession charges. We now reverse and reinstate all counts of the indictment.

On Saturday afternoon, December 22, 1984, Troy Canty, Darryl Cabey, James Ramseur, and Barry Allen boarded an IRT express subway train in The Bronx and headed south toward lower Manhattan. The four youths rode together in the rear portion of the seventh car of the train. Two of the four, Ramseur and Cabey, had screwdrivers inside their coats, which they said were to be used to break into the coin boxes of video machines.

Defendant Bernhard Goetz boarded this subway train at 14th Street in Manhattan and sat down on a bench towards the rear section of the same car occupied by the four youths. Goetz was carrying an unlicensed .38 caliber pistol loaded with five rounds of ammunition in a waistband holster. The train left the 14th Street station and headed towards Chambers Street.

It appears from the evidence before the Grand Jury that Canty approached Goetz, possibly with Allen beside him, and stated "give me five dollars." Neither Canty nor any of the other youths displayed a weapon. Goetz responded by standing up, pulling out his handgun and firing four shots in rapid succession. The first shot hit Canty in the chest; the second struck Allen in the back; the third went through Ramseur's arm and into his left side; the fourth was fired at Cabey, who apparently was then standing in the corner

of the car, but missed, deflecting instead off of a wall of the conductor's cab. After Goetz briefly surveyed the scene around him, he fired another shot at Cabey, who then was sitting on the end bench of the car. The bullet entered the rear of Cabey's side and severed his spinal cord.

All but two of the other passengers fled the car when, or immediately after, the shots were fired. The conductor, who had been in the next car, heard the shots and instructed the motorman to radio for emergency assistance. The conductor then went into the car where the shooting occurred and saw Goetz sitting on a bench, the injured youths lying on the floor or slumped against a seat, and two women who had apparently taken cover, also lying on the floor. Goetz told the conductor that the four youths had tried to rob him.

While the conductor was aiding the youths, Goetz headed towards the front of the car. The train had stopped just before the Chambers Street station and Goetz went between two of the cars, jumped onto the tracks and fled. Police and ambulance crews arrived at the scene shortly thereafter. Ramseur and Canty, initially listed in critical condition, have fully recovered. Cabey remains paralyzed, and has suffered some degree of brain damage.

On December 31, 1984, Goetz surrendered to police in Concord, New Hampshire, identifying himself as the gunman being sought for the subway shootings in New York nine days earlier. Later that day, after receiving *Miranda* warnings, he made two lengthy statements, both of which were tape recorded with his permission. In the statements, which are substantially similar, Goetz admitted that he had been illegally carrying a handgun in New York City for three years. He stated that he had first purchased a gun in 1981 after he had been injured in a mugging. Goetz also revealed that twice between 1981 and 1984 he had successfully warded off assailants simply by displaying the pistol.

According to Goetz's statement, the first contact he had with the four youths came when Canty, sitting or lying on the bench across from him, asked "how are you," to which he replied "fine." Shortly thereafter, Canty, followed by one of the other youths, walked over to the defendant and stood to his left, while the other two youths remained to his right, in the corner of the subway car. Canty then said "give me five dollars." Goetz stated that he knew from the smile on Canty's face that they wanted to "play with me." Although he was certain that none of the youths had a gun, he had a fear, based on prior experiences, of being "maimed."

Goetz then established "a pattern of fire," deciding specifically to fire from left to right. His stated intention at that point was to "murder [the four youths], to hurt them, to make them suffer as much as possible." When Canty again requested money, Goetz stood up, drew his weapon, and began firing, aiming for the center of the body of each of the four. Goetz recalled that the first two he shot "tried to run through the crowd [but] they had nowhere to run." Goetz then turned to his right to "go after the other two." One of these two "tried to run through the wall of the train, but * * * he had nowhere to go." The other youth (Cabey) "tried pretending that he wasn't with [the others]" by standing still, holding on to one of the subway hand straps, and not looking at Goetz. Goetz nonetheless fired his fourth shot at him. He then ran back to the first two youths to make sure they had been "taken care of." Seeing that they had both been shot, he spun back to check on the latter two. Goetz noticed that the youth who had been standing still was now sitting on a bench and seemed unhurt. As Goetz told the police, "I said '[y]ou seem to be all right, here's another,'" and he then fired the shot which severed Cabey's spinal cord. Goetz added that "if I was a little more under self-control * * * I would have put the barrel against his forehead and fired." He also admitted that "if I had had more [bullets], I would have shot them again, and again, and again."

After waiving extradition, Goetz was brought back to New York and arraigned on a felony complaint charging him with attempted murder and criminal possession of a weapon.

On March 27, 1985, the . . . Grand Jury filed a 10-count indictment, containing four charges of attempted murder . . . , four charges of assault in the first degree . . . , one charge of reckless endangerment in the first degree . . . , and one charge of criminal possession of a weapon in the second degree . . . [possession of loaded firearm with intent to use it unlawfully against another]. Goetz was arraigned on this indictment on March 28, 1985, and it was consolidated with the earlier three-count indictment.

On October 14, 1985, Goetz moved to dismiss the charges contained in the second indictment alleging, among other things, that the evidence before the second Grand Jury was not legally sufficient to establish the offenses charged . . . and that the prosecutor's instructions to that Grand Jury on the defense of justification were erroneous. . . .

[The trial court] granted Goetz's motion. . . . On appeal by the People, a divided Appellate Division affirmed Criminal Term's dismissal of the charges.

Penal Law article 35 recognizes the defense of justification, which "permits the use of force under certain circumstances . . . " One such set of circumstances pertains to the use of force in defense of a person, encompassing both self-defense and defense of a third person (Penal Law § 35.15). Penal Law § 35.15 (1) sets forth the general principles governing all such uses of force: "[a] person may * * * use physical force upon another person when and to the extent he *reasonably believes* such to be necessary to defend himself or a third person from what he *reasonably believes* to be the use or imminent use of unlawful physical force by such other person." (emphasis added).

Section 35.15 (2) sets forth further limitations on these general principles with respect to the use of "deadly physical force": "A person may not use deadly physical force upon another person under circumstances specified in subdivision one unless (a) He *reasonably believes* that such other person is using or about to use deadly physical force * * * or (b) He *reasonably believes* that such other person is committing or attempting to commit a kidnapping, forcible rape, forcible sodomy or robbery." (emphasis added).

Thus, consistent with most justification provisions, Penal Law § 35.15 permits the use of deadly physical force only where requirements as to triggering conditions and the necessity of a particular response are met. (*see*, Robinson, Criminal Law Defenses § 121 [a], at 2). As to the triggering conditions, the statute requires that the actor "reasonably believes" that another person either is using or about to use deadly physical force or is

(Continued)

(Continued)

committing or attempting to commit one of certain enumerated felonies, including robbery. As to the need for the use of deadly physical force as a response, the statute requires that the actor "reasonably believes" that such force is necessary to avert the perceived threat.

When the prosecutor had completed his charge, one of the grand jurors asked for clarification of the term "reasonably believes." The prosecutor responded by instructing the grand jurors that they were to consider the circumstances of the incident and determine "whether the defendant's conduct was that of a reasonable man in the defendant's situation." It is this response by the prosecutor—and specifically his use of "a reasonable man"—which is the basis for the dismissal of the charges by the lower courts. As expressed repeatedly in the Appellate Division's plurality opinion, because section 35.15 uses the term "*he* reasonably believes," the appropriate test, according to that court, is whether a defendant's beliefs and reactions were "reasonable *to him.*" Under that reading of the statute, a jury which believed a defendant's testimony that he felt that his own actions were warranted and were reasonable would have to acquit him, regardless of what anyone else in defendant's situation might have concluded. Such an interpretation defies the ordinary meaning and significance of the term "reasonably" in a statute, and misconstrues the clear intent of the Legislature, in enacting section 35.15, to retain an objective element as part of any provision authorizing the use of deadly physical force.

We cannot lightly impute to the Legislature an intent to fundamentally alter the principles of justification to allow the perpetrator of a serious crime to go free simply because that person believed his actions were reasonable and necessary to prevent some perceived harm. To completely exonerate such an individual, no matter how aberrational or bizarre his thought patterns, would allow citizens to set their own standards for the permissible use of force. It would also allow a legally competent defendant suffering from delusions to kill or perform acts of violence with impunity, contrary to fundamental principles of justice and criminal law.

We can only conclude that the Legislature retained a reasonableness requirement to avoid giving a license for such actions.

Goetz also argues that the introduction of an objective element will preclude a jury from considering factors such as the prior experiences of a given actor and thus, require it to make a determination of "reasonableness" without regard to the actual circumstances of a particular incident. This argument, however, falsely presupposes that an objective standard means that the background and other relevant characteristics of a particular actor must be ignored. To the contrary, we have frequently noted that a determination of reasonableness must be based on the "circumstances" facing a defendant or his "situation." . . . Such terms encompass more than the physical movements of the potential assailant. As just discussed, these terms include any relevant knowledge the defendant had about that person. They also necessarily bring in the physical attributes of all persons involved, including the defendant. Furthermore, the defendant's circumstances encompass any prior experiences he had, which could provide a reasonable basis for a belief that another person's intentions were to injure or rob him or that the use of deadly force was necessary under the circumstances.

Accordingly, a jury should be instructed to consider this type of evidence in weighing the defendant's actions. The jury must first determine whether the defendant had the requisite beliefs under section 35.15, that is, whether he believed deadly force was necessary to avert the imminent use of deadly force or the commission of one of the felonies enumerated therein. If the People do not prove beyond a reasonable doubt that he did not have such beliefs, then the jury must also consider whether these beliefs were reasonable. The jury would have to determine, in light of all the "circumstances," as explicated above, if a reasonable person could have had these beliefs.

Accordingly, the order of the Appellate Division should be reversed, and the dismissed counts of the indictment reinstated.

Questions

1. Goetz argued that the prosecutor gave incorrect instructions to the grand jury on the law of self-defense. What was Goetz's argument?

2. What was the court's rationale in rejecting Goetz's argument?

3. After the indictment was reinstated, Goetz went to trial and was found not guilty of all charges except for possession of a concealed weapon. How could the jury have found that he acted in self-defense? Examine Section 35.12(2)(b) of the New York statute (referenced in the case).

In the *Goetz* case, the court discussed the "objective" aspect of New York's law of self-defense. Self-defense laws in most states, including New York, are both subjective and objective. As the court explained, the jury must first determine if the defendant himself believed that he was in imminent danger of serious bodily injury or death (the subjective part). If it decides that he did have that belief, the jury must then go on to determine if a reasonable person in the same circumstances as the defendant would have had that belief (the objective part). The jury may find that the defendant acted in self-defense only if it finds that the belief was both subjectively and objectively reasonable.

Suppose the defendant made a mistake—he believes that he or she is in danger of serious bodily injury or death, but he is not. Consider the following hypothetical:

> Tom is approached by Dick, and Dick takes out what appears to be a .32 caliber pistol and points it at Tom. Tom, believing he is about to be killed, takes out his pistol and fires first, killing Dick. Tom later discovers that Dick's pistol was only a toy gun and that Dick was just trying to scare him.

May Tom successfully claim self-defense? In most jurisdictions, he may, as long as his belief was a reasonable one. If the toy gun looked real, and any reasonable person would have believed that it was real, he may have a valid self-defense claim. On the other hand, if a reasonable person would have known that the gun was a toy, Tom's claim of self-defense would not be successful.

There was much discussion in the media about whether race played a role in Goetz's decision to shoot the four youths, not only because of his actions and the statements he made to the police, but also because there was evidence that he had used racial slurs at a community association meeting.[6]

Consider the following excerpt from *Murder and the Reasonable Man* by law professor Cynthia Lee.

"Murder and the Reasonable Man" by Cynthia Lee

Stereotypes are correlational constructs based on an individual's membership in an identifiable group, such as the idea that most Blacks are good athletes, most Mexicans are poor, and most Asians are smart. All of us are influenced by stereotypes, even the most egalitarian-minded of us.

In self-defense cases, racial stereotypes can influence the reasonableness determination in a myriad of ways. If the victim belongs to a racial group whose members are perceived as violent or hot-blooded, jurors may perceive ambiguous actions by the victim as more hostile than they actually are. Conversely, if the defendant belongs to a racial group whose members are perceived as violent and dangerous but the victim belongs to a racial group whose members are not marked by stereotypes of violence and dangerousness, jurors may be less willing to believe the defendant's claim of self-defense.

Race norms can also affect the reasonableness determination in other, less obvious, ways. According to social cognition theory, people tend to emphasize the positive attributes of those who are perceived to be like them and the negative traits of those who are perceived to be different or other. We have all seen examples of this in real life. If you meet a person for the first time, you are more likely to think positively of that person if you find you have common interests and mutual friends. In a homicide case in which the victim belongs to a racial or ethnic minority group whose members are perceived as foreigners or immigrants, jurors may subconsciously minimize the harm suffered by the victim and be more willing to view the defendant's use of force as reasonable.[7]

George Zimmerman was acquitted of the murder of Trayvon Martin.

The jury in the Goetz criminal trial consisted of ten Whites and two African Americans. In 1996, Darrell Cabey filed a civil lawsuit against Bernard Goetz. In this trial, Goetz admitted to prior use of racist slurs. A jury of four African Americans and two Latinos awarded Cabey $43 million in damages. Goetz filed for bankruptcy soon after the trial and never paid any money toward the judgment.

Trayvon Martin and the George Zimmerman Case. As noted at the beginning of this chapter, the killing of Trayvon Martin in 2012 sparked a national discussion about the law of self-defense. As more states adopt laws like Florida's "stand your ground" statute, discussed earlier in this chapter, there has been heated opposition to these laws, with many blaming them for tragedies like Trayvon Martin's death.

The killing of Trayvon Martin also revived a national discussion about race and its role in the criminal justice system. Some suggested that George Zimmerman was engaged in racial profiling—that his belief that Trayvon Martin looked "suspicious" was based on the type of stereotypical views described in the excerpt from Professor Cynthia Lee's excerpt above. Zimmerman denied these claims and argued that he was just trying to protect the neighborhood.

Zimmerman's trial began in June, 2013. A jury of six women (five White and one Latina)[8] was selected. The case was televised and received extraordinary publicity nationally and internationally. The jury found Zimmerman not guilty on July 13, 2013. There were protests in cities throughout the country,[9] and organizations such as the National Association for the Advancement of Colored People (NAACP) and the National Action Network called for the Justice Department to bring civil rights charges against Zimmerman.[10]

The Zimmerman verdict received so much attention nationwide that President Barack Obama decided to make a statement about it. His comments, which were unscripted and made during a surprise appearance at his press secretary's regularly scheduled White House briefing on July 19, 2013, were praised by some and criticized by others. The following is an excerpt from the president's remarks:

You know, when Trayvon Martin was first shot, I said that this could have been my son. Another way of saying that is Trayvon Martin could have been me 35 years ago. And when you think about why, in the African-American community at least, there's a lot of pain around what happened here, I think it's important to recognize that the African-American community is looking at this issue through a set of experiences and a history that—that doesn't go away.

There are very few African-American men in this country who haven't had the experience of being followed when they were shopping in a department store. That includes me. And there are very few African-American men who haven't had the experience of walking across the street and hearing the locks click on the doors of cars. That happens to me, at least before I was a senator. There are very few African-Americans who haven't had the experience of getting on an elevator and a woman clutching her purse nervously and holding her breath until she had a chance to get off. That happens often.

And you know, I don't want to exaggerate this, but those sets of experiences inform how the African-American community interprets what happened one night in Florida. And it's inescapable for people to bring those experiences to bear. The African-American community is also knowledgeable that there is a history of racial disparities in the application of our criminal laws, everything from the death penalty to enforcement of our drug laws. And that ends up having an impact in terms of how people interpret the case.

I know that there's been commentary about the fact that the stand your ground laws in Florida were not used as a defense in the case. . . . [F]or those who resist that idea that we should think about something like these "stand your ground" laws, I just ask people to consider if Trayvon Martin was of age and armed, could he have stood his ground on that sidewalk? And do we actually think that he would have been justified in shooting Mr. Zimmerman, who had followed him in a car, because he felt threatened? And if the answer to that question is at least ambiguous, it seems to me that we might want to examine those kinds of laws.[11]

Compare Professor Cynthia Lee's commentary on racial stereotypes to the president's remarks about the Zimmerman verdict. Is there a common theme? Might Professor Lee's explanation of racial stereotypes in self-defense cases be applied to the Zimmerman case?

Battered Woman Syndrome and the Law of Self-Defense

The law of self-defense permits the use of force only if an individual is in imminent danger of bodily harm. It is also a law of necessity. In some instances imminence and necessity are at odds with each other. Might it be *necessary* to use force even if the potential harm to oneself is not *imminent*? Women in abusive relationships who kill their partners under circumstances that do not involve an imminent threat often make this claim. Many of these women have been diagnosed with a condition called battered woman syndrome (BWS).

Psychologist Lenore Walker coined the term "battered woman syndrome" to describe a condition suffered by many women who are in abusive relationships. Women who suffer from BWS are beaten by their partners, but nonetheless remain in the relationship. After enduring repeated, unpredictable beatings, these women develop what Dr. Walker calls "learned helplessness"—a belief that it would be hopeless to try to escape their situation.

Battered woman syndrome was discussed widely in the media in 2014 as a result of several high profile instances of alleged domestic violence involving professional football players and other celebrities. These cases prompted numerous women across the nation to reveal their own stories on social media, using the hashtags "WhyIStayed" and "WhyILeft" on Twitter. These stories revealed that this type of abuse occurs at all levels of society and crosses all racial, socioeconomic and social lines.

The defendant in the following case presented evidence of BWS in support of her claim of self-defense:

State v. Norman (1988)
Court of Appeals of North Carolina
89 N.C. App. 384

[D]efendant was convicted by jury . . . of voluntary manslaughter, and she appealed.

At trial the judge instructed on first-degree murder, second-degree murder, and voluntary manslaughter. The primary issue presented on this appeal is whether the trial court erred in failing to instruct on self-defense. We answer in the affirmative and grant a new trial.

At trial the State presented the testimony of a deputy sheriff of the Rutherford County Sheriff's Department who testified that on 12 June 1985, at approximately 7:30 p.m.,

(Continued)

(Continued)

he was dispatched to the Norman residence. There, in one of the bedrooms, he found decedent, John Thomas "J.T." Norman (herein decedent or Norman) dead, lying on his left side on a bed. The State presented an autopsy report, stipulated to by both parties, concluding that Norman had died from two gunshot wounds to the head. The deputy sheriff also testified that later that evening, after being advised of her rights, defendant told the officer that decedent, her husband, had been beating her all day, that she went to her mother's house nearby and got a .25 automatic pistol, that she returned to her house and loaded the gun, and that she shot her husband. The officer noted at the time that there were burns and bruises on defendant's body.

Defendant's evidence, presented through several different witnesses, disclosed a long history of verbal and physical abuse leveled by decedent against defendant. Defendant and Norman had been married twenty-five years at the time of Norman's death. Norman was an alcoholic. He had begun to drink and to beat defendant five years after they were married. The couple had five children, four of whom are still living. When defendant was pregnant with her youngest child, Norman beat her and kicked her down a flight of steps, causing the baby to be born prematurely the next day.

Norman, himself, had worked one day a few months prior to his death; but aside from that one day, witnesses could not remember his ever working. Over the years and up to the time of his death, Norman forced defendant to prostitute herself every day in order to support him. If she begged him not to make her go, he slapped her. Norman required defendant to make a minimum of one hundred dollars per day; if she failed to make this minimum, he would beat her.

Norman commonly called defendant "Dogs," "Bitches," and "Whores," and referred to her as a dog. Norman beat defendant "most every day," especially when he was drunk and when other people were around, to "show off." He would beat defendant with whatever was handy—his fist, a fly swatter, a baseball bat, his shoe, or a bottle; he put out cigarettes on defendant's skin; he threw food and drink in her face and refused to let her eat for days at a time; and he threw glasses, ashtrays, and beer bottles at her and once smashed a glass in her face. Defendant exhibited to the jury scars on her face from these incidents. Norman would often make defendant bark like a dog, and if she refused, he would beat her. He often forced defendant to sleep on the concrete floor of their home and on several occasions forced her to eat dog or cat food out of the dog or cat bowl.

Norman often stated both to defendant and to others that he would kill defendant. He also threatened to cut her heart out. Witnesses for the defense also testified to the events in the thirty-six hours prior to Norman's death. On or about the morning of 10 June 1985, Norman forced defendant to go to a truck stop or rest stop on Interstate 85 in order to prostitute to make some money. Defendant's daughter and defendant's daughter's boyfriend accompanied defendant. Some time later that day, Norman went to the truck stop, apparently drunk, and began hitting defendant in the face with his fist and slamming the car door into her. He also threw hot coffee on defendant. On the way home, Norman's car was stopped by police, and he was arrested for driving under the influence.

When Norman was released from jail the next morning, on 11 June 1985, he was extremely angry and beat defendant. Defendant's mother said defendant acted nervous and scared. Defendant testified that during the entire day, when she was near him, her husband slapped her, and when she was away from him, he threw glasses, ashtrays, and beer bottles at her. Norman asked defendant to make him a sandwich; when defendant brought it to him, he threw it on the floor and told her to make him another. Defendant made him a second sandwich and brought it to him; Norman again threw it on the floor, telling her to put something on her hands because he did not want her to touch the bread. Defendant made a third sandwich using a paper towel to handle the bread. Norman took the third sandwich and smeared it in defendant's face.

On the evening of 11 June 1985, at about 8:00 or 8:30 p.m., a domestic quarrel was reported at the Norman residence. The officer responding to the call testified that defendant was bruised and crying and that she stated her husband had been beating her all day and she could not take it any longer. The officer advised defendant to take out a warrant on her husband, but defendant responded that if she did so, he would kill her. A short time later, the officer was again dispatched to the Norman residence. There he learned that defendant had taken an overdose of "nerve pills," and that Norman was interfering with emergency personnel who were trying to treat defendant. Norman was drunk and was making statements such as, "'If you want to die, you deserve to die. I'll give you more pills,'" and "'Let the bitch die. . . . She ain't nothing but a dog. She don't deserve to live.'" Norman also threatened to kill defendant, defendant's mother, and defendant's grandmother. The law enforcement officer reached for his flashlight or blackjack and chased Norman into the house. Defendant was taken to Rutherford Hospital.

The therapist on call at the hospital that night stated that defendant was angry and depressed and that she felt her situation was hopeless. On the advice of the therapist, defendant did not return home that night, but spent the night at her grandmother's house.

The next day, 12 June 1985, the day of Norman's death, Norman was angrier and more violent with defendant than usual. According to witnesses, Norman beat defendant all day long. Sometime during the day, Lemuel Splawn, Norman's best friend, called Norman and asked Norman to drive with him to Spartanburg, where Splawn worked, to pick up Splawn's paycheck. Norman arrived at Splawn's house some time later. Defendant was driving. During the ride to Spartanburg, Norman slapped defendant for following a truck too closely and poured a beer on her head. Norman kicked defendant in the side of the head while she was driving and told her he would "cut her breast off and shove it up her rear end."

Later that day, one of the Normans' daughters, Loretta, reported to defendant's mother that her father was beating her mother again. Defendant's mother called the sheriff's department, but no help arrived at that time. Witnesses stated that back at the Norman residence, Norman threatened to cut defendant's throat, threatened to kill her, and threatened to cut off her breast. Norman also smashed a doughnut on defendant's face and put out a cigarette on her chest.

In the late afternoon, Norman wanted to take a nap. He lay down on the larger of the two beds in the bedroom. Defendant started to lie down on the smaller bed, but Norman said, "'No bitch . . . Dogs don't sleep on beds, they sleep in [sic] the floor.'" Soon after, one of the Normans' daughters, Phyllis, came into the room and asked if defendant could look after her baby. Norman assented. When the baby began to cry, defendant took the child to her mother's house, fearful that the baby would disturb Norman. At her mother's house, defendant found a gun. She took it back to her home and shot Norman.

Defendant testified that things at home were so bad she could no longer stand it. She explained that she could not leave Norman because he would kill her. She stated that she had left him before on several occasions and that each time he found her, took her home, and beat her. She said that she was afraid to take out a warrant on her husband because he had said that if she ever had him locked up, he would kill her when he got out. She stated she did not have him committed because he told her he would see the authorities coming for him and before they got to him he would cut defendant's throat. Defendant also testified that when he threatened to kill her, she believed he would kill her if he had the chance.

The defense presented the testimony of two expert witnesses in the field of forensic psychology, Dr. William Tyson and Dr. Robert Rollins. Based on an examination of defendant and an investigation of the matter, Dr. Tyson concluded that defendant "fits and exceeds the profile, of an abused or battered spouse." . . . Dr. Tyson . . . stated, "Mrs. Norman didn't leave because she believed, fully believed that escape was totally impossible. . . . She fully believed that [Norman] was invulnerable to the law and to all social agencies that were available; that nobody could withstand his power. As a result, there was no such thing as escape." . . .

When asked if it appeared to defendant reasonably necessary to kill her husband, Dr. Tyson responded, "I think Judy Norman felt that she had no choice, both in the protection of herself and her family, but to engage, exhibit deadly force against Mr. Norman, and that in so doing, she was sacrificing herself, both for herself and for her family."

Dr. Rollins was defendant's attending physician at Dorothea Dix Hospital where she was sent for a psychiatric evaluation after her arrest. Based on an examination of defendant, laboratory studies, psychological tests, interviews, and background investigation, Dr. Rollins testified that defendant suffered from "abused spouse syndrome." Dr. Rollins defined the syndrome in the following way: The "abused spouse syndrome" refers to situations where one spouse has achieved almost complete control and submission of the other by both psychological and physical domination. . . . When asked, in his opinion, whether it appeared reasonably necessary that defendant take the life of J.T. Norman, Dr. Rollins responded, "In my opinion, that course of action did appear necessary to Mrs. Norman." . . .

In North Carolina, a defendant is entitled to an instruction on perfect self-defense as justification for homicide where, viewed in the light most favorable to the defendant, there is evidence tending to show that at the time of the killing:

(1) it appeared to defendant and he believed it to be necessary to kill the deceased in order to save himself from death or great bodily harm; and

(2) defendant's belief was reasonable in that the circumstances as they appeared to him at the time were sufficient to create such a belief in the mind of a person of ordinary firmness; and

(3) defendant was not the aggressor in bringing on the affray, i.e., he did not aggressively and willingly enter into the fight without legal excuse or provocation; and

(4) defendant did not use excessive force, i.e., did not use more force than was necessary or reasonably appeared to him to be necessary under the circumstances to protect himself from death or great bodily harm. . . .

(Continued)

(Continued)

The State . . . argues that defendant was not entitled to an instruction on self-defense. The State contends that since decedent was asleep at the time of the shooting, defendant's belief in the necessity to kill decedent was, as a matter of law, unreasonable. The State further contends that even assuming *arguendo* that the evidence satisfied the requirement that defendant's belief be reasonable, defendant, being the aggressor, cannot satisfy the third requirement of perfect self-defense. . . .

The question then arising on the facts in this case is whether the victim's passiveness at the moment the unlawful act occurred precludes defendant from asserting perfect self-defense.

Applying the criteria of perfect self-defense to the facts of this case, we hold that the evidence was sufficient to submit an issue of perfect self-defense to the jury. An examination of the elements of perfect self-defense reveals that both subjective and objective standards are to be applied in making the crucial determinations. The first requirement that it appear to defendant and that defendant believe it necessary to kill the deceased in order to save herself from death or great bodily harm calls for a subjective evaluation. This evaluation inquires as to what the defendant herself perceived at the time of the shooting. The trial was replete with testimony of forced prostitution, beatings, and threats on defendant's life. The defendant testified that she believed the decedent would kill her, and the evidence showed that on the occasions when she had made an effort to get away from Norman, he had come after her and beat her. Indeed, within twenty-four hours prior to the shooting, defendant had attempted to escape by taking her own life and throughout the day on 12 June 1985 had been subjected to beatings and other physical abuse, verbal abuse, and threats on her life up to the time when decedent went to sleep. Both experts testified that in their opinion, defendant believed killing the victim was necessary to avoid being killed. This evidence would permit a finding by a jury that defendant believed it necessary to kill the victim to save herself from death or serious bodily harm.

Unlike the first requirement, the second element of self-defense—that defendant's belief be reasonable in that the circumstances as they appeared to defendant would be sufficient to create such a belief in the mind of a person of ordinary firmness—is measured by the objective standard of the person of ordinary firmness under the same circumstances. Again, the record is replete with sufficient evidence to permit but not compel a juror, representing the person of ordinary firmness, to infer that defendant's belief was reasonable under the circumstances in which she found herself. . . .

To satisfy the third requirement, defendant must not have aggressively and willingly entered into the fight without legal excuse or provocation. . . .

Mindful that the law should never casually permit an otherwise unlawful killing of another human being to be justified or excused, this Court is of the opinion that with the battered spouse there can be, under certain circumstances, an unlawful killing of a passive victim that does not preclude the defense of perfect self-defense. Given the characteristics of battered spouse syndrome, we do not believe that a battered person must wait until a deadly attack occurs or that the victim must in all cases be actually attacking or threatening to attack at the very moment defendant commits the unlawful act for the battered person to act in self-defense. Such a standard, in our view, would ignore the realities of the condition. . . .

[A] jury, in our view, could find that decedent's sleep was but a momentary hiatus in a continuous reign of terror by the decedent, that defendant merely took advantage of her first opportunity to protect herself, and that defendant's act was not without the provocation required for perfect self-defense.

Based on the foregoing analysis, we are of the opinion that, in addition to the instruction on voluntary manslaughter, defendant was entitled to an instruction on perfect self-defense.

A year after the above ruling of the Court of Appeals, the Supreme Court of North Carolina reversed the decision, finding that

The term "imminent," as used to describe such perceived threats of death or great bodily harm as will justify a homicide by reason of perfect self-defense, has been defined as "immediate danger, such as must be instantly met, such as cannot be guarded against by calling for the assistance of others or the protection of the law."(citations omitted). . . . The evidence in this case did not tend to show that the defendant reasonably believed that she was confronted by a threat of imminent death or great bodily harm. The evidence tended to show that no harm was "imminent" or about to happen to the defendant when she shot her husband.[12]

Judy Norman was sentenced to six years in prison, but two months after she started serving her prison term, the Governor of North Carolina commuted her sentence. She was freed from prison, but her conviction for voluntary manslaughter was not expunged.

Questions

1. What was the court of appeals' rationale in holding that Ms. Norman should have been able to present a defense of self-defense?

2. What was the rationale of the North Carolina Supreme Court in reversing the decision of the court of appeals?

3. Self-defense is a law of necessity. Might it be argued that it was necessary for Judy Norman to kill her husband even though she was not in imminent danger of being killed while he was sleeping? Why or why not?

Recall that Judy Norman was charged with first degree murder. The judge also instructed the jury on the lesser included offenses of second degree murder and manslaughter (as discussed in Chapter 8). The jury found Ms. Norman guilty of voluntary manslaughter. This verdict may very well have been a result of the jury finding that Judy Norman's self-defense claim was imperfect. The term imperfect self-defense is often used to describe cases in which the defendant's behavior does not quite fall within the definition of self-defense. For example, if the defendant uses more force than is necessary under the circumstances (excessive force) or if she was not quite in imminent danger of harm but was reasonably in fear, she did not legally act in self-defense. In such cases, if the defendant was charged with murder, the jury may find her not guilty of murder, but guilty of the lesser included offense of manslaughter. Such a verdict is consistent with the definition of manslaughter in a case where it is clear that the defendant acted in the heat of passion after adequate provocation.

Defense of Others

The law of defensive force permits an individual to lawfully use force in defense of another person. The following case explains the rules for when force may be used to defend another person.

State v. Beeley (1995)

Supreme Court of Rhode Island

653 A.2d 722

This case comes before us on appeal by the defendant, James Beeley (Beeley), from a Superior Court jury conviction of breaking and entering . . . and simple assault . . . In this appeal Beeley avers that the trial justice erred in denying his motions requesting judgment of acquittal and a new trial. We sustain the appeal.

At the outset we shall set out the basic facts of record that led to Beeley's convictions. The record reveals that on Sunday, May 19, 1991, Beeley was working as a bartender at a social club in East Providence. Beeley's friend and codefendant in the Superior Court trial, John Perry (John), was a patron at the club that evening. After the club closed,

(Continued)

(Continued)

Beeley and John went to a friend's house to play cards until approximately two-thirty on the morning of Monday, May 20, 1991. Beeley drove John to 80 Evergreen Drive in East Providence where, John testified, he lived in an apartment with his wife, Julie Perry (Julie). By then it was approximately four o'clock in the morning. John invited Beeley to spend the night at the apartment since it was so late. Beeley dropped off John at the entrance to the apartment building and then went to park his car.

The testimony in the record is contradictory as to what occurred next. John testified that he used his key to gain entry into the apartment through the front door, which was locked. Upon entering the apartment, John walked toward the bedroom and came face-to-face with his wife, Julie, in the hallway. Julie turned on the hallway light and John observed a man sleeping in the bed. John began screaming at Julie and asked her, "Who was in the bed?" Julie responded, "You know who it is." John recognized the man as Robert Harding (Harding). Harding was not wearing any clothes. The two men began wrestling and moved toward the door of the apartment. Harding attempted to force John out of the apartment through the door. John yelled out to Beeley who was waiting outside the apartment. Beeley entered through the doorway and pulled John out of the apartment. John testified that he waited outside of the apartment with Beeley for the police to arrive who had been called by Julie. John then went around to the window of the apartment, opened it, yelled to Julie, "How could you do this to me?" and threw a plant on the ground.

Julie and Harding offered a different version of the events. Julie testified that on May 20, 1991, Harding was sleeping on the couch in the living room of the apartment. At approximately four o'clock in the morning she was awakened by "noise." From her bedroom she observed John standing in the hallway. Julie testified that she was sure that John had gained entry into the apartment through a living-room window because plant pots located on the window sill were broken. Julie and John began arguing and Harding woke up. John kicked Harding in the face several times as he sat on the couch. As the two men struggled, Julie called the police. John hollered to Beeley, "somebody is in here" and then unlocked the door. Beeley entered the apartment, punched Harding in the face, and then left with John.

Harding corroborated Julie's testimony and indicated that as he was locked in combat with John, both tried to open the door. Harding testified that as he attempted to

push John out the door, John unlocked the door. Initially Harding testified that John had opened the door, but later on cross-examination he recalled that he opened the door after John had unlocked it. John then called out to Beeley and Beeley entered and hit Harding in the face. Harding indicated that this was the first time he had ever met Beeley. . . .

Beeley testified that as he waited outside the apartment, he could hear John and Julie yelling. He walked to the door and banged on it but did not attempt to open it. The door opened and then slammed shut. When the door opened again Beeley could see Harding who was naked grabbing John by the waist. Beeley did not know Harding and did not know what Harding was doing in the apartment. John was crying, and he yelled to Beeley, "This is the guy." Beeley hit Harding once to break his hold on John. Beeley observed Julie on the telephone, talking to the police. He then grabbed John and pulled him out of the apartment. Beeley and John waited outside for the police to arrive.

Beeley contends that the trial justice erred in instructing the jury that one acting to defend another has only a derivative right of self-defense, and that his or her actions are not judged by the reasonableness of his or her own conduct and perceptions.

It is undisputed that Beeley hit Harding as Beeley entered the apartment. Beeley's defense to the charge of simple assault upon Harding was that when he entered the apartment, he saw John being held by a naked man (Harding) and speculated that the latter was an intruder who may have raped Julie. Beeley, in an attempt to break Harding's hold on John, executed a single punch at Harding. Beeley contends that he was therefore justified in assaulting Harding.

In instructing the jury on the charge of assault against Beeley, the trial justice stated:

"[T]he state must prove by evidence and proof beyond a reasonable doubt the following facts: One, that on May 20, 1991 James Beeley assaulted Robert Harding. Two, that at the time James Beeley was not justified in coming to the assistance of John Perry."

The trial justice later instructed the jury with respect to defense of another and explained that

"one who comes to the aid of another person must do so at his own peril and should be excused only when that other person would be justified in defending himself. Thus, if you find that Mr. Perry was not the aggressor and was justified in defending himself from the acts of Mr. Harding, then Mr. Beeley is then excused from any criminal responsibility for coming to the aid of Mr. Perry if Mr. Beeley in so doing did not use excessive force. However, if you find that Mr. Perry was in fact the aggressor and was not justified in his actions and was inflicting punches and kicks on Mr. Harding, then Mr. Beeley acted at his own peril and his actions would not be justified. In short, if Mr. Perry was justified in his actions, then so was Mr. Beeley in coming to his assistance. If Mr. Perry was not justified in his actions, then neither was Mr. Beeley. Our Supreme Court has said on repeated occasions, an intervening person stands in the shoes of the person that he is aiding."

The issue before us is whether an intervenor in an altercation between private individuals should be judged by his or her own reasonable perceptions or whether he or she stands in the shoes of the person that he or she is defending.

A review of the relevant authorities reveals that there are two rules followed by American jurisdictions. The first rule, adopted by the trial justice in the instant case, is sometimes referred to as the "alter ego" rule, and it holds that the right to defend another is coextensive with the other's right to defend himself or herself. The other view, which follows the Model Penal Code, is that as long as the defendant-intervenor reasonably believes that the other is being unlawfully attacked, he or she is justified in using reasonable force to defend him or her.

The Model Penal Code § 3.05, entitled "Use of Force for the Protection of Other Persons," provides in pertinent part as follows.

> "(1) Subject to the provisions of this Section and of Section 3.09, the use of force upon or toward the person of another is justifiable to protect a third person when:
>
> (a) the actor would be justified under Section 3.04 in using such force to protect himself against the injury he believes to be threatened to the person whom he seeks to protect; and
>
> (b) under the circumstances as the actor believes them to be, the person whom he seeks to protect would be justified in using such protective force; and
>
> (c) the actor believes that his intervention is necessary for the protection of such other person."

Model Penal Code § 3.05(1)(Adopted 1962).

Under this section in order for the defense to be raised successfully, three conditions must be met. First, the force must be such as the actor could use in defending himself or herself from the harm that he or she believes to be threatened to the third person. In other words, the actor may use the same amount of force that he or she could use to protect himself or herself. Second, the third person must be justified in using such protective force in the circumstances as the actor believes them to be . . . Finally, the actor must believe that his or her intervention is necessary for the protection of the third party.

This view, which has been adopted in the new state criminal codes, is in our opinion the better view. We favor the doctrine which judges a defendant upon his or her own reasonable perceptions as he or she comes to the aid of the apparent victim. The justification should, of course, be based upon what a reasonable person might consider to be the imminence of serious bodily harm. As one court expressed it, not only as a matter of justice should one "not be convicted of a crime if he selflessly attempts to protect the victim of an apparently unjustified assault, but how else can we encourage bystanders to go to the aid of another who is being subjected to assault?". . . Moreover, to impose liability upon the defendant-intervenor in these circumstances is to impose liability upon him or her without fault.

In sum, it seems to this court preferable to predicate the justification on the actor's own reasonable beliefs. We are of the opinion that an intervenor is justified in using reasonable force to defend another as long as the intervenor reasonably believes that the other is being unlawfully attacked. This rule is "predicated on the social desirability of encouraging people to go to the aid of third parties who are in danger of harm as a result of unlawful actions of others." . . .

The judgments of conviction are vacated. The case is remanded to the Superior Court for a new trial on the assault charge consistent with this opinion.

Questions

1. What is the difference between the alter ego and reasonable belief rules?

2. What is the court's rationale for holding that the reasonable belief rule is better than the alter ego rule?

3. What is the best argument in support of the alter ego rule?

Defense of Property and Defense of Habitation

Under what circumstances may a person defend his or her property? If someone attempts to steal your property, may you use force to stop him or her? If so, how much force and under what circumstances? The general rule is that a person may use a reasonable amount of force under the circumstances to prevent his property from being taken or even to take his property back. However, the common law rule that is still followed in most states is that a person may never use deadly force to protect property. If someone is breaking into a person's car, he may not legally take out a gun and shoot them. The idea is that human life is more important than property—even the life of a criminal.

All states allow the use of deadly force to prevent an intruder from entering a home. Laws that permit the use of deadly force to protect a home or dwelling are sometimes called defense of habitation laws. Defense of habitation laws are not the same as defense of property laws in that deadly force may be used to defend the home, but it may not be used to defend property. In fact, the purpose of defense of habitation laws is to protect persons inside the home from harm, not the physical structure of the house. Defense of habitation laws vary from state to state, but there are three general categories of these laws:

1. The broadest defense of habitation laws permit an individual to use any and all force that appears necessary, including deadly force, to prevent any invasion of the home. States with this type of law do not require the resident of the home to demonstrate that she feared for her safety or the safety of anyone in the home. As long as the individual believes that someone is about to invade her home—regardless of the invader's purpose—the resident of the home may shoot to kill.

The South Carolina law is an example of this broad type of defense of habitation law:

South Carolina's Habitation Statute

Presumption of reasonable fear of imminent peril when using deadly force against another unlawfully entering residence, occupied vehicle, or place of business.

(A) A person is presumed to have a reasonable fear of imminent peril of death or great bodily injury to himself or another person when using deadly force that is intended or likely to cause death or great bodily injury to another person if the person:

    (1) against whom the deadly force is used is in the process of unlawfully and forcibly entering, or has unlawfully and forcibly entered a dwelling, residence, or occupied vehicle, or if he removes or is attempting to remove another person against his will from the dwelling, residence, or occupied vehicle; and

    (2) who uses deadly force knows or has reason to believe that an unlawful and forcible entry or unlawful and forcible act is occurring or has occurred.

2. A more common version of the defense of habitation permits an individual to use deadly force only if there is reason to believe that the intruder will commit a felony inside the home. For example, if the intruder is wearing a burglar's mask and carrying burglar's tools, the resident of the home would have reason to believe that the intruder is going to burglarize the home.

3. The narrowest version of the defense only permits the use of deadly force to prevent entry into the home if the resident of the home has reason to believe that the intruder poses a threat to the safety of an occupant of the home. For example, if the intruder is carrying a gun or some other deadly weapon as he is entering or attempting to enter the home, the resident would be justified in using deadly force.

The Illinois statute provides for the use of deadly force in the latter two scenarios:

Illinois' Defense of Dwelling Statute

Illinois' Criminal Code § 7–2. Use of force in defense of dwelling.

(a) A person is justified in the use of force against another when and to the extent that he reasonably believes that such conduct is necessary to prevent or terminate such other's unlawful entry into or attack upon a dwelling. However, he is justified in the use of force which is intended or likely to cause death or great bodily harm only if:

(1) The entry is made or attempted in a violent, riotous, or tumultuous manner, and he reasonably believes that such force is necessary to prevent an assault upon, or offer of personal violence to, him or another then in the dwelling, or

(2) He reasonably believes that such force is necessary to prevent the commission of a felony in the dwelling.

Most states allow the use of deadly force either to prevent the commission of a felony in the home or to protect the safety of individuals inside the home. Why do you think the Illinois statute permits deadly force in both circumstances? Section 7–2(a)(1) allows deadly force to "prevent an assault . . . or offer of personal violence . . . in the dwelling." Some assaults (such as simple assault, discussed in Chapter 7) are classified as misdemeanors. An "offer of personal violence" might include a threat to kill. Thus, Section 7–2 (a)(2) alone (which only covers the prevention of a felony) would not permit the use of deadly force in such circumstances.

Some defense of habitation laws only allow the use of deadly force to prevent entry into the home. Once an intruder is already inside the home, the regular self-defense rules apply. Other rules apply to intruders who are trying to enter and to those who have already entered. Some states have expanded the defense of habitation to include occupied cars. Florida is one of those states:

Florida's Home Protection Statute

776.013 Home protection; use of deadly force; presumption of fear of death or great bodily harm.

(1) A person is presumed to have held a reasonable fear of imminent peril of death or great bodily harm to himself or herself or another when using defensive force that is intended or likely to cause death or great bodily harm to another if:

(a) The person against whom the defensive force was used was in the process of unlawfully and forcefully entering, or had unlawfully and forcibly entered, a dwelling, residence, or occupied vehicle, or if that person had removed or was attempting to remove another against that person's will from the dwelling, residence, or occupied vehicle; and

(b) The person who uses defensive force knew or had reason to believe that an unlawful and forcible entry or unlawful and forcible act was occurring or had occurred.

Allowing the use of deadly force to prevent an intruder from entering an "occupied vehicle" as well as a home may appear to violate the rule that deadly force may not be used to defend property. However, its proponents would argue that allowing deadly force to be used against an intruder of an occupied vehicle is about protecting the persons in that vehicle, not the vehicle itself.

Note that these laws do not require imminence and proportionality. If someone is entering a person's home, she does not have to wait until the intruder is about to attack her or someone else before using deadly force. Nor does she have to be sure that the intruder is armed. Both the South Carolina and Florida laws state that a person is "presumed" to be in fear of imminent death or great bodily harm if an intruder is trying to enter or has already entered his or her home. Consider the following hypothetical:

> Antonio was watching television in his upstairs bedroom when he heard a noise at his front door. He looked out his bedroom window and saw a stranger using a crowbar to try to break the lock on the door. Antonio went to his closet and retrieved his pistol. He walked downstairs and shot his pistol through the door, killing the stranger instantly.

If Antonio were charged with homicide in Illinois, would the statute provide a defense? What if he were charged in Florida? Both statutes would likely provide a complete defense. It would certainly be reasonable to believe that a person using a crowbar to break into a home is likely to commit a burglary or some other felony (under the Illinois statute), and the use of the crowbar is an unlawful and forceful entry (under the Florida statute).

Questions

1. How does defense of habitation differ from self-defense?

2. Why should an individual be given wider latitude in using deadly force to protect himself or others in his home than on the street or somewhere else?

3. Of the three types of defense of habitation laws, which is preferable and why?

Law Enforcement Defense

Police officers and private citizens are permitted to use force to prevent a crime and to arrest an individual. However, they are only permitted to use deadly force under certain circumstances. For example, deadly force is never permitted to prevent a misdemeanor or arrest someone who has committed a misdemeanor.

In 1985, the U.S. Supreme Court limited the use of force in felony cases in *Tennessee v. Garner*.[13] In that case, a police officer responded to a call about a burglary in progress. When the officer arrived on the scene, he saw a boy fleeing from the home. The officer ordered the boy to stop, but instead the boy attempted to climb a chain link fence behind the home. The officer testified that he believed the boy was about seventeen or eighteen and about five feet five inches to five feet seven inches tall. He also testified that he could see the boy's hands and knew that he was unarmed. (In fact the boy was a fifteen-year-old eighth grader who was about one hundred pounds.) As the boy began to climb the fence, the officer shot and killed him. The Tennessee statute permitted the use of deadly force to stop a fleeing felon. The boy's father filed a lawsuit against the state, and the case ultimately reached the U.S. Supreme Court. The Court held that the Tennessee law that permitted police officers to use deadly force against unarmed fleeing felons was unconstitutional as applied in this case:

> The use of deadly force to prevent the escape of all felony suspects, whatever the circumstances, is constitutionally unreasonable. It is not better that all felony suspects die than that they escape. Where the suspect poses no immediate threat to the officer and no threat to others, the harm resulting from failing to apprehend him does not justify the use of deadly force to do so. It is no doubt unfortunate when a suspect who is in sight escapes, but the fact that the police arrive a little late or are a little slower afoot does not always justify killing the suspect. A police officer may not seize an unarmed, non-dangerous suspect by shooting him dead. The Tennessee statute is unconstitutional insofar as it authorizes the use of deadly force against such fleeing suspects.
>
> It is not, however, unconstitutional on its face. Where the officer has probable cause to believe that the suspect poses a threat of serious physical harm, either to the officer or to others, it is not constitutionally unreasonable to prevent escape by using deadly force. Thus, if the suspect threatens the officer with a weapon or there is probable cause to believe that he has committed a crime involving the infliction or threatened infliction of serious physical harm, deadly force may be used if necessary to prevent escape, and if, where feasible, some warning has been given.[14]

After the Court's decision in *Tennessee v. Garner* (1985), deadly force may be used against a fleeing felon only if there is probable cause to believe that he or she poses a threat of danger to the officer or others.

Duress and Necessity ●────────────────────────

The defenses of duress and necessity are similar yet quite distinct. Both defenses involve some element of compulsion in that the defendant commits an act that would otherwise be considered a crime, but only because he or she was forced or compelled to do so. The duress defense is usually raised when an individual commits a criminal act because someone is threatening to seriously injure or kill him or her if he or she does not commit that act. The defense of necessity (also called choice of evils) is raised when an individual commits what would otherwise be considered a crime because acting lawfully under the circumstances would cause greater harm.

The following federal case discusses the defenses of duress and necessity and explains the difference between the two.

U.S. v. Contento-Pachon (1984)

United States Court of Appeals, 9th Circuit

723 F.2d 691

This case presents an appeal from a conviction for unlawful possession with intent to distribute a narcotic controlled substance in violation of 21 U.S.C. § 841(a)(1) (1976). At trial, the defendant attempted to offer evidence of duress and necessity defenses. The district court excluded this evidence on the ground that it was insufficient to support the defenses. We reverse because there was sufficient evidence of duress to present a triable issue of fact.

The defendant-appellant, Juan Manuel Contento-Pachon, is a native of Bogota, Colombia and was employed there as a taxicab driver. He asserts that one of his passengers, Jorge, offered him a job as the driver of a privately-owned car. Contento-Pachon expressed an interest in the job and agreed to meet Jorge and the owner of the car the next day.

Instead of a driving job, Jorge proposed that Contento-Pachon swallow cocaine-filled balloons and transport them to the United States. Contento-Pachon agreed to consider the proposition. He was told not to mention the proposition to anyone, otherwise he would "get into serious trouble." Contento-Pachon testified that he did not contact the police because he believes that the Bogota police are corrupt and that they are paid off by drug traffickers.

Approximately one week later, Contento-Pachon told Jorge that he would not carry the cocaine. In response, Jorge mentioned facts about Contento-Pachon's personal life, including private details which Contento-Pachon had never mentioned to Jorge. Jorge told Contento-Pachon that his failure to cooperate would result in the death of his wife and three-year-old child.

The following day the pair met again. Contento-Pachon's life and the lives of his family were again threatened. At this point, Contento-Pachon agreed to take the cocaine into the United States.

The pair met two more times. At the last meeting, Contento-Pachon swallowed 129 balloons of cocaine. He was informed that he would be watched at all times during the trip, and that if he failed to follow Jorge's instruction he and his family would be killed.

After leaving Bogota, Contento-Pachon's plane landed in Panama. Contento-Pachon asserts that he did not notify the authorities there because he felt that the Panamanian police were as corrupt as those in Bogota. Also, he felt that any such action on his part would place his family in jeopardy.

When he arrived at the customs inspection point in Los Angeles, Contento-Pachon consented to have his stomach x-rayed. The x-rays revealed a foreign substance which was later determined to be cocaine.

At Contento-Pachon's trial, the government moved to exclude the defenses of duress and necessity. The motion was granted. We reverse.

There are three elements of the duress defense: (1) an immediate threat of death or serious bodily injury, (2) a well-grounded fear that the threat will be carried out, and (3) no reasonable opportunity to escape the threatened harm . . . Sometimes a fourth element is required: the defendant must submit to proper authorities after attaining a position of safety. . . .

The trial court found Contento-Pachon's offer of proof insufficient to support a duress defense because he failed to offer proof of two elements: immediacy and inescapability. We examine the elements of duress.

Immediacy: The element of immediacy requires that there be some evidence that the threat of injury was present, immediate, or impending . . . The district court found that the initial threats were not immediate because "they were conditioned on defendant's failure to cooperate in the future and did not place defendant and his family in immediate danger."

Evidence presented on this issue indicated that the defendant was dealing with a man who was deeply involved in the exportation of illegal substances. Large sums of money were at stake and, consequently, Contento-Pachon had reason to believe that Jorge would carry out his threats. Jorge had gone to the trouble to discover that Contento-Pachon was married, that he had a child, the names of his wife and child, and the location of his residence. These were not vague threats of possible future harm. According to the defendant, if he had refused to cooperate, the consequences would have been immediate and harsh.

Contento-Pachon contends that he was being watched by one of Jorge's accomplices at all times during the airplane trip. As a consequence, the force of the threats continued to restrain him. Contento-Pachon's contention that he was operating under the threat of immediate harm was supported by sufficient evidence to present a triable issue of fact.

Escapability: The defendant must show that he had no reasonable opportunity to escape. . . . The district court found that because Contento-Pachon was not physically restrained prior to the time he swallowed the balloons, he could have sought help from the police or fled. Contento-Pachon explained that he did not report the threats because he feared that the police were corrupt. The trier of fact should decide whether one in Contento-Pachon's position might believe that some of the Bogota police were paid informants for drug traffickers and that reporting the matter to the police did not represent a reasonable opportunity of escape.

If he chose not to go to the police, Contento-Pachon's alternative was to flee. We reiterate that the opportunity to escape must be reasonable. To flee, Contento-Pachon, along with his wife and three-year-old child, would have been forced to pack his possessions, leave his job, and travel to a place beyond the reaches of the drug traffickers. A juror might find that this was not a reasonable avenue of escape. Thus, Contento-Pachon presented a triable issue on the element of escapability.

Surrender to Authorities: As noted above, the duress defense is composed of at least three elements. The government argues that the defense also requires that a defendant offer evidence that he intended to turn himself in to the authorities upon reaching a position of safety. Although it has not been expressly limited, this fourth element seems to be required only in prison escape cases. . . . In cases not involving escape from prison there seems little difference between the third basic requirement that there be no reasonable opportunity to escape the threatened harm and the obligation to turn oneself in to authorities on reaching a point of safety. Once a defendant has reached a position where he can safely turn himself in to the authorities he will likewise have a reasonable opportunity to escape the threatened harm.

That is true in this case. Contento-Pachon claims that he was being watched at all times. According to him, at the first opportunity to cooperate with authorities without alerting the observer, he consented to the x-ray. We hold that a defendant who has acted under a well-grounded fear of immediate harm with no opportunity to escape may assert the duress defense, if there is a triable issue of fact whether he took the opportunity to escape the threatened harm by submitting to authorities at the first reasonable opportunity.

The defense of necessity is available when a person is faced with a choice of two evils and must then decide whether to commit a crime or an alternative act that constitutes a greater evil . . . Contento-Pachon has attempted to justify his violation of 21 U.S.C. § 841(a)(1) by showing that the alternative, the death of his family, was a greater evil.

Traditionally, in order for the necessity defense to apply, the coercion must have had its source in the physical forces of nature. The duress defense was applicable when the defendant's acts were coerced by a human force . . . This distinction served to separate the two similar defenses. But modern courts have tended to blur the distinction between duress and necessity.

It has been suggested that, "the major difference between duress and necessity is that the former negates the existence of the requisite mens rea for the crime in question, whereas under the latter theory there is no actus reus." . . . The theory of necessity is that the defendant's free will was properly exercised to achieve the greater good and not that his free will was overcome by an outside force as with duress.

The defense of necessity is usually invoked when the defendant acted in the interest of the general welfare. For example, defendants have asserted the defense as a justification for (1) bringing laetrile into the United States for the treatment of cancer patients . . . (2) unlawfully entering a naval base to protest the Trident missile system . . . (3) burning Selective Service System records to protest United States military action. . . .

Contento-Pachon's acts were allegedly coerced by human, not physical forces. In addition, he did not act to promote the general welfare. Therefore, the necessity defense was not available to him. Contento-Pachon mischaracterized evidence of duress as evidence of necessity. The district court correctly disallowed his use of the necessity defense.

Contento-Pachon presented credible evidence that he acted under an immediate and well-grounded threat of serious bodily injury, with no opportunity to escape. Because the trier of fact should have been allowed to consider the credibility of the proffered evidence, we reverse. The district court correctly excluded Contento-Pachon's necessity defense.

REVERSED AND REMANDED.

Questions

1. What is the difference between necessity and duress?

2. What was the court's rationale in holding that the trial court erred when it prevented Mr. Contento-Pachon from presenting a duress defense?

3. Do you agree with the court's holding? Why or why not?

Concluding Note

The justification defenses in this chapter share a common theme—individuals are justified in performing certain acts for which they would otherwise be held criminally liable to protect themselves or others. They must only take such action that is absolutely necessary and no more than is necessary. The law even permits the use of deadly force under certain limited circumstances—such as when a person is in imminent danger of seriously bodily injury or death, when someone is trying to enter a dwelling and poses a danger to its inhabitants, and to prevent the escape of a fleeing felon who poses a danger to a police officer or others. Now test yourself on the material we have covered in Chapter 9. Good luck with the Issue Spotter exercise.

Issue Spotter

Read the hypothetical and spot the issues discussed in this chapter.

Bad Party Guest

John and Renee Kennedy celebrated the birth of their baby daughter Rosie by hosting a lavish shower at their mansion in Los Angeles. They invited numerous celebrities and media personalities. John didn't want to invite Lisa Loman because she was a drug addict and was on probation for stealing a necklace from a jewelry store. However, Renee thought it would be rude to exclude Lisa, so Lisa was invited.

When Lisa arrived, she mingled with the guests for a while before wandering up to the second level of the mansion. She opened the door of the master bedroom and saw little Rosie's crib in the corner and photographs of John and Renee. Lisa quickly left that bedroom and continued down the hallway. The second bedroom appeared to be a guest bedroom. Lisa noticed a beautiful diamond necklace on the bedside table, and just as she was about to walk over to take the necklace, she heard someone coming up the stairs. Lisa decided to leave the bedroom and go back downstairs to join the other guests.

The shower ended at about 9 p.m. As the guests started to leave, Lisa sneaked back upstairs to get the diamond necklace from the guest bedroom. She went into the bedroom, picked up the necklace, and was about to sneak back downstairs when she heard John and Renee walking up the stairs. Lisa ran back into the bedroom and closed the door. John and Renee went into their bedroom with little Rosie and closed the door.

Lisa decided to wait in the bedroom until everyone had gone to sleep before making her escape. After about thirty minutes, the house became very quiet. Lisa opened the door and began to tiptoe into the dark hallway. Unfortunately, Lisa did not see Rosie's stroller in the hallway and bumped into it, causing it to go crashing down the steps. When John heard the noise, he grabbed his pistol from his bedside table, ran into the hallway, and saw Lisa running down the steps. He turned on the light, and Lisa turned around just as she was shoving the diamond necklace into her jacket pocket. He aimed his pistol at her and fired, killing her instantly. The prosecutor has charged John with second degree murder.

You are his defense attorney. John tells you that he is sorry Lisa died, but he thought she was reaching for a weapon, and he had to do whatever he could to protect himself and his family.

1. What defenses might John raise at trial?

2. What are the strengths and weaknesses of each defense?

Key Terms and Cases

Notes

1. L. Song Richardson and Phillip Atiba Goff, "Self-Defense and the Suspicion Heuristic," 98 *Iowa Law Review* 98 (2012): 293, 316.

2. U.S. Const. amend. VI.

3. Barbara Bergman, "Instruction 9.500 Self Defense—General Considerations," in *Criminal Jury Instructions for the District of Columbia*, 5th ed. (Conklin, NY. Mathew Bender, 2012).

4. See *Dennis v. State*, 51 So. 3d 456, 462–63 (Fla. 2010).

5. Pamela Engle, "Look at All the States that Let People Stand Their Ground and Shoot," *Business Insider*, February 20, 2014, http://www.businessinsider.com/stand-your-ground-laws-from-state-to-state-2014-2

6. Cyntiha Kwei Yung Lee, "Race and Self-Defense: Toward A Normative Conception of Reasonableness,"*Minnesota Law Review* 81 (1996): 367, 500, (footnote noting at a community meeting, Goetz was reported to have said, "The only way we're going to clean up this street is to get rid of the spics and niggers.")

7. Cynthia Lee, *Murder and the Reasonable Man* (New York: NYU Press, 2003).

8. 22 Fla. Prac., Criminal Procedure § 17:4 (2014 ed.) (noting Florida requires a jury of twelve in death penalty cases. In all other criminal cases, only six person juries are required.)

9. Verena Dobnik, "Zimmerman Trial Protestors Aim to Keep up Momentum,"*Yahoo News*, July 15, 2013, 11:16 a.m., http://news.yahoo.com/zimmerman-trial-protesters-aim-keep-momentum-151535224.html

10. Catherine E. Shoichet and Jessica Yellin, "Zimmerman Could Still Be Held Responsible for Martin's Death," *CNN*, July 15, 2013, 10:02 a.m., http://www.cnn.com/2013/07/14/us/martin-family-legal-paths/

11. Washington Post Staff, "President Obama's Remarks on Trayvon Martin (Full Transcript),"*Washington Post*, July 19, 2013, http://www.washingtonpost.com/politics/president-obamas-remarks-on-trayvon-martin-full-transcript/2013/07/19/5e33ebea-f09a-11e2-a1f9-ea873b7e0424_story_3.html

12. *State v. Norman*, 324 N.C. 253 (1989).

13. *Tennessee v. Garner*, 471 U.S. 1 (1985).

14. Ibid. at 11–12.

Chapter 10

On March 30, 1981, a man named John Hinckley attempted to assassinate President Ronald Reagan as he was leaving a speaking engagement at the Washington Hilton Hotel in Washington, DC. Although he did not kill the president, he shot and wounded him, his press secretary, a secret service agent, and a police officer. Hinckley was charged with numerous offenses, including attempted assassination of the president of the United States and multiple counts of assault with intent to kill. He was found not guilty by reason of insanity and committed to St. Elizabeth's Hospital in Washington, DC. The outcome of Hinckley's trial sparked a national debate over the fairness of the insanity defense and resulted in numerous changes in the law in many states and in the federal system. The Hinckley case raises some of the issues we will discuss in this chapter.

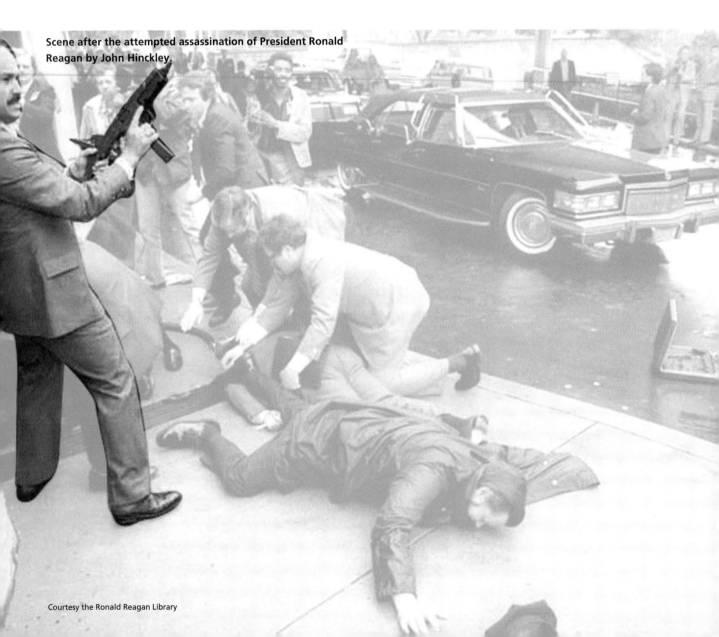

Scene after the attempted assassination of President Ronald Reagan by John Hinckley.

Excuse Defenses

Learning Objectives

After reading and studying this chapter, you should be able to

➤ Explain the difference between competency and insanity

➤ Differentiate between the M'Naghten, irresistible impulse, and product tests

➤ Define the American Law Institute Model Penal Code test

➤ Explain the bifurcated trial process

➤ Define guilty but mentally ill

➤ Know the difference between voluntary and involuntary intoxication

➤ Explain post-traumatic stress disorder

➤ Give examples of cultural defenses

Introduction

As discussed in Chapter 9, some defenses are called justification defenses and some are known as excuse defenses. With justification defenses, the actor is justified in taking action that would otherwise be deemed criminal if such action is necessary to protect himself or others from harm. Criminal defendants who present the defenses discussed in this chapter are asking the fact finder (judge or jury) to excuse them because they had a condition at the time they committed the alleged act that caused them to commit a criminal act. In some instances, these defenses only serve as partial defenses, resulting in convictions on less serious charges.

In this chapter we will discuss the insanity defense and other excuse defenses, including infancy, voluntary and involuntary intoxication, syndrome defenses, and cultural defenses. As we examine these defenses, think about how they differ from the justification defenses we discussed in Chapter 9. Also consider whether it matters that the law distinguishes between excuse and justification defenses.

Competency and Insanity

Incompetency is not a defense to criminal behavior; it describes the defendant's mental condition and ability to understand the charges against her at the time of the court proceedings. A criminal defendant presents the insanity defense when she claims that she is not responsible for the crime because of her mental state at the time the crime was committed. Over the years, a number of tests have been used to determine whether the defendant was insane at the time she committed the offense. Not all states recognize the insanity defense, and the definition of insanity varies from state to state. This section will examine competency to stand trial and the different definitions of insanity.

Competency to Stand Trial

A defendant is considered incompetent if he is suffering from a mental disability that prohibits him from understanding the proceedings or assisting in his defense.[1] If the defendant is incompetent, he may not stand trial. Competency refers to the defendant's mental condition at the time of the court proceedings, not at the time of the offense. Although competency to stand trial is often an issue in cases where the defendant raises an insanity defense, it may occur in any type of case, regardless of the defense. Anyone may raise the issue of competency at any point in the proceedings, but typically the defense attorney is the first to notice the signs of incompetency. The defendant will begin to say and do things that indicate that he is suffering from some kind of mental illness or condition that affects his ability to understand his case or work with his attorney. Once the issue is raised, the judge will order the defendant to be evaluated by a mental health professional. If the defendant is found to be incompetent, he is sent to a mental health facility for further evaluation and treatment. Treatment usually consists of prescribed medication. The Supreme Court has held that a defendant in treatment for incompetence may be forced to take medication against his will so that he may gain competence and face the charges against him.[2] When the defendant becomes competent, the court proceedings resume.

If the defendant does not become competent in a reasonable period of time and his doctors determine that there is a substantial probability that he will not become competent in the foreseeable future, he may not be held indefinitely. If the government opposes the defendant's release in these circumstances, it must institute civil commitment proceedings and prove that he is a danger to himself or others. If the government proves dangerousness, the court will order indefinite commitment to a mental institution. If the government is unable to prove dangerousness, the defendant must be released.[3]

The Jared Lee Loughner Case

http://commons.wikimedia.org/wiki/File:Jared_Loughner_USMS.jpg

Jared Lee Loughner was sentenced to serve seven consecutive life terms plus 140 years in prison without parole.

Jared Lee Loughner went to a Safeway grocery store in Tucson, Arizona, on January 8, 2011, where Congresswoman Gabrielle Giffords was hosting a meeting with constituents. He took out his 9mm Glock pistol and opened fire at close range, killing six people and critically injuring Representative Giffords and thirteen others. Giffords was shot in the head and suffered permanent damage from which she has never recovered, compelling her to eventually resign from her congressional seat.

Loughner was charged with forty-nine offenses, including the attempted assassination of Representative Giffords and numerous counts of murder and attempted murder. Soon after he was indicted, the prosecutors in his case requested that he be evaluated to determine if he was competent to stand trial, noting that some of his online writings indicated that he might be suffering from some form of mental illness.[4] Judge Larry Burns ordered a competency examination, and in May 2011, heard the testimony of a psychiatrist and psychologist who had conducted extensive examinations of Loughner. Judge Burns ruled that Loughner was incompetent to stand trial and ordered that he be sent to the psychiatric wing of a federal prison to receive treatment. The judge later ordered that he be forcibly medicated, over the objection of his lawyers. The forced medication continued for over a year, until July 2012, when he began to take the medication voluntarily.[5] In August 2012, Judge Burns heard the testimony of Loughner's treating psychologist and found him competent.

On that date, Loughner pled guilty to the offenses in exchange for the prosecutors' agreement not to seek the death penalty.[6]

The Insanity Defense

The Tests for Insanity

A person who pleads not guilty by reason of insanity (NGI) claims that she should not be held responsible for her actions because she acted as a result of a mental disease or defect. There are several tests for determining insanity.

The earliest test for insanity was established in England in 1843. Daniel M'Naghten was charged with murdering the secretary of the leader of the Tory Party. The jury acquitted him, finding him not guilty by reason of insanity. Queen Victoria was outraged by this outcome and requested that the House of Lords review the decision. The verdict was thrown out, and M'Naghten was found guilty. The judges created a new standard for evaluating an insanity defense, holding that a defendant could not be responsible for his actions if he could not tell that his actions were wrong at the time he committed them. According to the **M'Naghten test**, to establish a defense on the ground of insanity, the defendant had to prove that, at the time of the act, he was laboring under such a defect of reason, from disease of the mind, as to not know the nature and quality of the act he was doing, or if he did know it, that he did not know what he was doing was wrong.[7]

American courts adopted the M'Naghten "right-wrong" test with almost no modifications until the mid-nineteenth century. Some states began to adopt a modified M'Naghten standard that included an **irresistible impulse test** to account for defendants who could tell right from wrong but could not control their actions because of mental illness. In 1954, the U.S. Court of Appeals for the District of Columbia decided *Durham v. United States*, which established the **product test**. The court held that a defendant could not be held criminally responsible for his or her acts "if his unlawful act was the product of mental disease or defect."[8]

Less than twenty years later, the same court abandoned the *Durham* test and adopted the **American Law Institute Model Penal Code test** for the insanity defense. In the 1972 case of *United States v. Brawner*, the court held that a defendant is not criminally responsible for his acts if, at the time he committed the acts and "as a result of a mental disease or defect, he lacks substantial capacity either to appreciate the criminality of his conduct or to conform his conduct to the requirements of the law."[9] This language softened the M'Naghten requirement that the defendant have absolutely no understanding of the criminality of his acts to now requiring that the defendant only "lack substantial capacity." Further, it excluded those defendants whose only symptom of mental defect was the crime itself. Therefore, a serial killer whose only symptom of mental illness is the killing of his victims could not successfully use the insanity defense.[10]

John Hinckley was found not guilty by reason of insanity after the attempted assassination of President Ronald Reagan.

The Impact of the Hinckley Case

The jury in *United States v. Hinckley* (1982) (discussed at the beginning of this chapter) found Mr. Hinckley not guilty by reason of insanity. There was massive public outrage after the verdict, despite the fact that Hinckley was committed to a mental institution. In response to the outcry, Congress and many states began to modify the insanity defense, making it more difficult for defendants to be found not guilty by reason of insanity. The burden of proving insanity shifted to the defendant, and many states added an additional option for juries—guilty but mentally ill. With this verdict, the defendant is found criminally responsible for the crime but is given the opportunity to receive treatment for his mental illness, either in a prison setting or in a mental health facility. If the treatment is provided in a mental hospital, the defendant is transferred to a regular prison after he completes a course of treatment and serves the remainder of his sentence. A few states abolished the insanity defense altogether.

John Hinckley has been committed to St. Elizabeth's Hospital for over thirty years. He has been allowed visits to his parents' home in Williamsburg, Virginia, more recently for periods of up to ten days. Nonetheless, Hinckley remains a ward of St Elizabeth's Hospital, despite the fact that all of his doctors, including the government experts, agree that his mental disease is in full remission. At least one doctor at St. Elizabeth's testified at Hinckley's last hearing that he does not pose an imminent risk of danger to himself or others.[11]

Table 10.1 shows the number of states that recognize each of the insanity tests.

Table 10.1 States and the Insanity Defense[12]

Standard	Number of States
M'Naghten	24
With some modification	5
With "irresistible impulse" provision	4
Model Penal Code	21
Durham	1
Abolished, but retain guilty but insane defense	4

Source: http://criminal.findlaw.com/crimes/more-criminal-topics/insanity-defense/the-insanity-defense-among-the-states.html

Procedural Issues

As with most criminal laws, the insanity defense varies from state to state. Just as states are not uniform on the test for insanity, they vary on the trial process as well. Some states have a bifurcated trial process analogous to the two-part trial used in capital cases (discussed in Chapter 8).[13] The first part of the trial, called the guilt phase, is an ordinary criminal trial in which the government attempts to prove the defendant's guilt beyond a reasonable doubt through the normal process of putting witnesses on the stand who are cross-examined by the defense attorney. The defense does not put on evidence of the insanity defense during the first stage of the trial. If the government fails to prove the defendant's guilt beyond a reasonable doubt, the trial is over, and the defendant never has to present evidence of insanity.

If the jury finds the defendant guilty beyond a reasonable doubt, the second part of the trial, called the insanity phase, begins. Some states use a different jury for this phase of the trial while others use the same jury. During the insanity phase, in most states the burden of proof shifts to the defendant to prove that she is not guilty by reason of insanity by either a preponderance of the evidence or by clear and convincing evidence.[14] Whether or not the trial is bifurcated, the defendant and the government offer expert testimony from one or more mental health professionals (usually psychiatrists or psychologists) who have examined the defendant. The doctors offer their expert opinions on whether the defendant was insane at the time of the offense, in accordance with the insanity test used in that jurisdiction.

If the jury finds that the defendant is not guilty by reason of insanity, she is usually ordered to a mental hospital for further evaluation. Some states require a commitment proceeding in which the government must prove that the defendant is a danger to herself or others, while other states allow automatic commitment after a finding of not guilty by reason of insanity. The defendant may be released if she is able to prove that she is no longer a danger to herself or others. The reality is that very few individuals charged with violent offenses found not guilty by reason of insanity are released soon after their commitment,[15] and most of them are housed in very secure units of the state hospital.

Infancy

Under the common law, there was a presumption that anyone under the age of seven did not have the capacity to commit a crime because he was too young to form the criminal intent and could not appreciate the wrongfulness of his behavior. Persons between the ages of seven and fourteen were presumed incapable of committing a crime, but the state could rebut that presumption by presenting evidence to prove otherwise. Persons over the age of fourteen were presumed capable and treated as adults for purposes of the criminal law. Some states have adopted the common law rule, and others have modified it by altering the age at which a child is presumed incapable and the age at which the state may rebut that presumption.

Today, the common law rules have less relevance because all states have juvenile justice systems that handle criminal behavior by children. The juvenile justice system focuses on rehabilitation rather than punishment, and its goal is "the care and rehabilitation of the child."[16] State statutes determine the maximum age a child may be charged in juvenile court (typically sixteen or seventeen), and there is usually no minimum age. The terminology used in juvenile court is different from adult court. Children charged with crimes are called respondents rather than criminal defendants. Although they enjoy most of the procedural trial rights as adults, they do not have the right to a jury trial.[17] Cases are tried before judges, and if the judge finds beyond a reasonable doubt that the respondent committed the crime, she is found "involved" rather than "guilty." A respondent found involved is committed to a juvenile facility rather than sentenced to prison, if the judge determines she needs to be in a secure facility.

All states have laws that permit children to be tried as adults. The laws vary from state to state, and the minimum age for trying children as adults ranges from no minimum to fifteen.[18] Some statutes permit children of a specified age to be charged as adults for certain serious crimes at the discretion of the prosecutor, while others permit judges to transfer juveniles to adult court for prosecution at their discretion or if certain criteria are met.

In states that follow the common law rules, a child charged as an adult may challenge the state's decision to charge her as an adult if she is below the age of fourteen. In the following case, a twelve-year-old child was charged as an adult with the murder of his grandparents. He challenged the evidence the state used to show that he should be tried as an adult.

State v. Pittman (2007)

Supreme Court of South Carolina

373 S.C. 527

Christopher Pittman was arrested and charged with double homicide in connection with the deaths of his paternal grandparents. Pittman was twelve years old at the time of the incident. After a hearing, the family court waived jurisdiction allowing Pittman to be tried as an adult. The jury convicted Pittman of both murders and the trial judge sentenced Pittman to two concurrent terms of thirty years imprisonment. This appeal followed. We affirm.

In November of 2001, Christopher Pittman (Appellant) shot and killed his paternal grandparents, Joe Frank and Joy Pittman, at close range with a .410 shotgun. At the time of the incident, Appellant was twelve years old and had recently come from Florida, where he lived with his father, to live with his grandparents in Chester, South Carolina.

Shortly before moving to Chester with his grandparents, Appellant's relationship with his father became strained. Specifically, Appellant had attempted to run away from home, and also had threatened to harm himself with a knife. In response to this behavior, Appellant's father committed him to an inpatient facility. While at the facility, Appellant began taking the antidepressant Paxil. Soon after a short period of commitment, Appellant's father had him released from the facility and agreed to allow Appellant to live with his grandparents in Chester.

Upon moving to Chester, Appellant enrolled in school and began to actively participate in church with his grandparents. His grandmother also continued Appellant's treatment for depression by taking him to a local physician to refill his Paxil prescription. The physician did not refill the Paxil prescription, but instead offered free samples and a prescription of Zoloft.

On the day of the murders, the assistant principal of Appellant's school called Appellant's grandparents to the school in response to an incident which occurred the previous day on the school bus. During the incident in question, Appellant allegedly choked a second grade student. After leaving the school, Appellant and his grandparents attended choir practice. The church musician testified that she admonished Appellant for kicking her chair, at which time his grandfather took him outside to talk to him. Upon their return, the musician noted that Appellant had an angry expression.

According to Appellant, when they returned home, his grandparents locked him in his room and his grandfather warned him that he would paddle Appellant if he came out of the room. Later that night, Appellant came out of his room and his grandfather paddled him. After his grandparents went to bed, Appellant waited for ten minutes, loaded a shotgun, entered their bedroom, and shot his grandparents to death in their bed. Appellant then lit several candles and positioned them so that the house would catch on fire after he left. Appellant collected some money, weapons, and his dog, took the keys to his grandparents SUV, and drove away.

Early the next morning, two hunters found Appellant wandering around in the woods with a shotgun. Appellant told the hunters that he had been kidnapped by a Black man who had shot his grandparents and set their home on fire. Appellant further told the hunters that he was able to escape when the kidnapper got the SUV stuck in the woods. He further stated that the kidnapper had shot at him before throwing the vehicle's keys and running into the woods. Upon hearing this story, the hunters, who were also firemen with the Corinth Fire Department, took Appellant to the fire station where they alerted the police.

A search ensued for the Black man who allegedly committed the crimes as Appellant suggested. During this time, Chester deputy Lucinda McKellar (McKellar) arrived to speak with Appellant. Under the impression that Appellant was a victim and possible witness to the crimes, McKellar took an oral and written statement from Appellant. In the statements, Appellant related the story that he had told the hunters.

As the search for the alleged kidnapper continued, the Chester police were also conducting an investigation of the crime scene. At some point in the afternoon, McKellar's supervisor notified her that the information from the crime scene and the search of the vehicle indicated that Appellant was a possible suspect in the crimes. At that time, McKellar took Appellant to the police station.

When they arrived at the police station, McKellar took Appellant to a conference room and told him that they needed to have an "adult conversation." Pittman sat down at the table and McKellar explained the *Miranda* rights. At that time, Appellant gave the officers a third statement in which he confessed to the murders and detailed the events of the night. McKellar wrote the statement and Appellant read and signed it.

After his confession, the police arrested Appellant for double homicide and arson. The prosecution filed a motion with the family court to waive its jurisdiction, which the family court granted. After several pretrial motions, various continuances, and delays, Appellant's trial was held from January 31, 2005 to February 15, 2005. The jury convicted Appellant on both counts of murder. The trial judge sentenced Appellant to the shortest sentence possible under the mandatory minimum sentencing guidelines—two concurrent terms of thirty years imprisonment.

After unsuccessfully arguing several post-trial motions for a new trial, Appellant filed this notice of appeal.

Appellant argues that the trial court erred in failing to grant his motion for directed verdict because the prosecution failed to present sufficient evidence during its case in chief to rebut the presumption of incapacity. Specifically, Appellant argues that lay testimony is insufficient to rebut the presumption, and suggests that expert testimony is required. We disagree.

Generally, a criminal defendant is presumed to have the requisite capacity to be held responsible for the commission of a crime. . . . However, "[w]here a person is between seven and fourteen years of age, he is presumed not to have the mental capacity of committing a crime, but that is a rebuttable presumption, and it may be shown that he was mentally capable of committing a crime, although he was between the age of seven and fourteen years.". . .

Although this Court has not previously addressed whether expert testimony is required to rebut the presumption of incapacity regarding children under age fourteen, the Court has addressed similar issues relating to the capacity of adults. In *State v. Smith,* this Court held that the State could use lay testimony to rebut a criminal defendant's insanity defense. Additionally in *State v. Poindexter,* we found that the "jury was free to rely on circumstantial evidence to find [the defendant] sane even though expert testimony favored a finding that he was insane.". . .

During its case in chief, the State presented several witnesses who testified about Appellant's behavior and demeanor the day after the murders. Both of the hunters who encountered Appellant in the woods testified regarding the detail and clarity of Appellant's kidnapper story. They also testified that although Appellant seemed a little scared because he was lost, Appellant was quiet and calm, and they could understand everything that he said to them.

The State also presented the testimony of several investigators. Darryl Duncan, the initial law enforcement officer to whom Appellant spoke, testified that Appellant relayed the story about the kidnapper to him and that Appellant seemed calm and was very understandable. Additionally, Lucinda McKellar, the investigator who spent the most time with Appellant, testified that Appellant told her the kidnapper story and gave her a very detailed statement about the events that occurred the previous day. During McKellar's trial testimony, the State also admitted Appellant's confession. The confession describes the murders and the arson executed to cover up the murders.

The State did not present any expert testimony as to Appellant's capacity until its case in reply. During reply, the State offered the testimony of Dr. Pamela Crawford, a court appointed examiner. Dr. Crawford testified that, in her opinion, Appellant was competent and capable of understanding the difference between right and wrong. She further testified that Appellant admitted that what he did was wrong, but maintained that his grandparents deserved it.

The State also presented the testimony of Dr. Julian Sharman, a Department of Juvenile Justice psychiatrist. Dr. Sharman testified that Appellant admitted he sat in his room and thought of a plan to get rid of his grandfather. Dr. Sharman also testified that Appellant showed no remorse for his actions, and although upset about the murders, he felt his grandparents "asked for it."

Through the testimony presented in its case in chief, the State presented evidence which demonstrated that Appellant was able to think of a story to cover up his involvement in the crime and relate the story, with little deviation, to several different people. The State also presented

(Continued)

(Continued)

evidence to show that Appellant was calm and articulate as he repeatedly retold the story. This testimony regarding the cover-up story alone was sufficient to at least create a reasonable inference that Appellant knew right from wrong and that he had done something wrong.

Although no expert testimony was presented in the prosecution's case in chief, we hold that the lay testimony of the hunters and investigators was sufficient to at least present a question for the jury as to Appellant's capacity. Given that the State's case in chief contained such voluminous testimony about Appellant's demeanor and behavior, the trial judge correctly made the finding that there was enough evidence to rebut the presumption of incapacity and send the case to the jury.

Furthermore, if we consider the evidence presented in the State's reply case, the record contains sufficient expert testimony regarding Appellant's capacity to warrant a denial of a directed verdict on this ground. Both experts examined Appellant shortly after he was arrested for the murders and were able to observe his behavior. Both experts testified that Appellant understood that his actions were

wrong, but showed no remorse for his actions because he felt justified. We find this evidence more than adequate to rebut the presumption of incapacity and allow the jury to determine whether Appellant had the capacity to be held accountable for the murders of his grandparents.

Accordingly, the trial court did not err in denying Appellant's motion for a directed verdict. The State is not required to present expert testimony to rebut the presumption of incapacity.

Questions

1. What was the basis of Mr. Pittman's appeal?

2. What was the rationale for the court's holding?

3. The judge sentenced Christopher Pittman to the minimum period of incarceration allowed by law—thirty years for each murder, to be served concurrently (a total of thirty years). Should judges take a juvenile offender's age into account in determining the appropriate sentence, and if so, how?

Intoxication

There are two types of intoxication defenses: voluntary and involuntary. Voluntary intoxication occurs when an individual knowingly and voluntarily drinks alcohol or takes a drug that causes him or her to become intoxicated or "high." Involuntary intoxication occurs when an individual unknowingly consumes food or drink that contains alcohol or some intoxicating drug or takes a drug without the knowledge that it will cause him or her to become intoxicated.

Involuntary intoxication is a permissible defense in most states. However, voluntary intoxication is rarely a successful defense, and some states have passed laws banning the defense altogether. The rationale for banning the defense is the idea that any person who voluntarily drinks or takes some other substance that impairs his or her judgment or behavior should be held responsible for his actions. The states that do permit the defense of voluntary intoxication generally allow it as a defense to specific intent crimes only.

Consider the following hypothetical:

Carlos was in a bar drinking with his buddies. He went to the restroom and left his beer on the table. While Carlos was gone, one of his friends dropped a pill in his beer. The pill was a drug called Rohypnol, which causes dizziness, lack of inhibition, and amnesia. Carlos came back, drank the rest of his beer, and went to his car. He began to feel dizzy, so he asked one of his friends to drive him home. When Carlos' friend dropped him off at the corner near his house, Carlos stumbled past his house and went to his neighbor's house instead. When his key would not open the door, Carlos picked up a brick, broke the glass window in the door, reached in and unlocked the door from the inside. By this time, his neighbor had called the police. Carlos later told his attorney that he had no memory of breaking into his neighbor's house and did not know why he had done so. His lawyer's investigation revealed that his friend had spiked his beer with Rohypnol.

If Carlos presents evidence that his drink was spiked without his knowledge, along with evidence of the effects of Rohypnol, he could be found not guilty because of involuntary intoxication.

Montana is one state that does not permit the defense of voluntary intoxication. In the following case, the constitutionality of the Montana statute was challenged.

Montana v. Egelhoff (1996)

U. S. Supreme Court
518 U.S. 37

In July 1992, while camping out in the Yaak region of northwestern Montana to pick mushrooms, respondent made friends with Roberta Pavola and John Christenson, who were doing the same. On Sunday, July 12, the three sold the mushrooms they had collected and spent the rest of the day and evening drinking, in bars and at a private party in Troy, Montana. Some time after 9 p.m., they left the party in Christenson's 1974 Ford Galaxy station wagon. The drinking binge apparently continued, as respondent was seen buying beer at 9:20 p.m. and recalled "sitting on a hill or a bank passing a bottle of Black Velvet back and forth" with Christenson. . . .

At about midnight that night, officers of the Lincoln County, Montana, sheriff's department, responding to reports of a possible drunk driver, discovered Christenson's station wagon stuck in a ditch along U.S. Highway 2. In the front seat were Pavola and Christenson, each dead from a single gunshot to the head. In the rear of the car lay respondent, alive and yelling obscenities. His blood-alcohol content measured .36 percent over one hour later. On the floor of the car, near the brake pedal, lay respondent's .38-caliber handgun, with four loaded rounds and two empty casings; respondent had gunshot residue on his hands.

Respondent was charged with two counts of deliberate homicide, a crime defined by Montana law as "purposely" or "knowingly" causing the death of another human being. Mont.Code Ann. § 45–5-102 (1995). A portion of the jury charge, uncontested here, instructed that "[a] person acts purposely when it is his conscious object to engage in conduct of that nature or to cause such a result," and that "[a] person acts knowingly when he is aware of his conduct or when he is aware under the circumstances his conduct constitutes a

crime; or, when he is aware there exists the high probability that his conduct will cause a specific result." . . . Respondent's defense at trial was that an unidentified fourth person must have committed the murders; his own extreme intoxication, he claimed, had rendered him physically incapable of committing the murders, and accounted for his inability to recall the events of the night of July 12. Although respondent was allowed to make this use of the evidence that he was intoxicated, the jury was instructed, pursuant to Mont.Code Ann. § 45–2-203 (1995), that it could not consider respondent's "intoxicated condition . . . in determining the existence of a mental state which is an element of the offense." . . . The jury found respondent guilty on both counts, and the court sentenced him to 84 years' imprisonment.

The Supreme Court of Montana reversed. It reasoned (1) that respondent "had a due process right to present and have considered by the jury all relevant evidence to rebut the State's evidence on all elements of the offense charged," . . . that evidence of respondent's voluntary intoxication was "clear[ly] . . . relevant to the issue of whether [respondent] acted knowingly and purposely," . . . . Because § 45–2-203 prevented the jury from considering that evidence with regard to that issue, the court concluded that the State had been "relieved of part of its burden to prove beyond a reasonable doubt every fact necessary to constitute the crime charged." . . . and that respondent had therefore been denied due process. We granted certiorari.

([T]he Due Process Clause does not permit the federal courts to engage in a finely tuned review of the wisdom of state evidentiary rules). Respondent's task, then, is to establish that a defendant's right to have a jury consider evidence of his voluntary intoxication in determining

(Continued)

(Continued)

whether he possesses the requisite mental state is a "fundamental principle of justice."

Our primary guide in determining whether the principle in question is fundamental is, of course, historical practice. . . . Here that gives respondent little support. By the laws of England, wrote Hale, the intoxicated defendant "shall have no privilege by this voluntary contracted madness, but shall have the same judgment as if he were in his right senses." . . . According to Blackstone and Coke, the law's condemnation of those suffering from *dementia affectata* was harsher still: Blackstone, citing Coke, explained that the law viewed intoxication "as an aggravation of the offence, rather than as an excuse for any criminal misbehaviour." . . . This stern rejection of inebriation as a defense became a fixture of early American law as well. The American editors of the 1847 edition of Hale wrote:

> "Drunkenness, it was said in an early case, can never be received as a ground to excuse or palliate an offence: this is not merely the opinion of a speculative philosopher, the argument of counsel, or the *obiter dictum* of a single judge, but it is a sound and long established maxim of judicial policy, from which perhaps a single dissenting voice cannot be found. But if no other authority could be adduced, the uniform decisions of our own Courts from the first establishment of the government, would constitute it now a part of the common law of the land.". . .

Against this extensive evidence of a lengthy common-law tradition decidedly against him, the best argument available to respondent is the one made by his *amicus* and conceded by the State: Over the course of the 19th century, courts carved out an exception to the common law's traditional across-the-board condemnation of the drunken offender, allowing a jury to consider a defendant's intoxication when assessing whether he possessed the mental state needed to commit the crime charged, where the crime was one requiring a "specific intent."

It is not surprising that many States have held fast to or resurrected the common-law rule prohibiting consideration of voluntary intoxication in the determination of *mens rea,* because that rule has considerable justification which alone casts doubt upon the proposition that the opposite rule is a "fundamental principle." A large number of crimes, especially violent crimes, are committed by intoxicated offenders; modern studies put the numbers as high as half of all homicides, for example. . . . Disallowing consideration of voluntary intoxication has the effect of increasing the punishment for all unlawful acts committed in that state, and thereby deters drunkenness or irresponsible behavior while drunk.

The rule also serves as a specific deterrent, ensuring that those who prove incapable of controlling violent impulses while voluntarily intoxicated go to prison. And finally, the rule comports with and implements society's moral perception that one who has voluntarily impaired his own faculties should be responsible for the consequences. . . .

There is, in modern times, even more justification for laws such as § 45–2–203 than there used to be. Some recent studies suggest that the connection between drunkenness and crime is as much cultural as pharmacological—that is, that drunks are violent not simply because alcohol makes them that way, but because they are behaving in accord with their learned belief that drunks are violent. . . . This not only adds additional support to the traditional view that an intoxicated criminal is not deserving of exoneration, but it suggests that juries—who possess the same learned belief as the intoxicated offender—will be too quick to accept the claim that the defendant was biologically incapable of forming the requisite *mens rea.* Treating the matter as one of excluding misleading evidence therefore makes some sense.

In sum, not every widespread experiment with a procedural rule favorable to criminal defendants establishes a fundamental principle of justice. Although the rule allowing a jury to consider evidence of a defendant's voluntary intoxication where relevant to *mens rea* has gained considerable acceptance, it is of too recent vintage, and has not received sufficiently uniform and permanent allegiance, to qualify as fundamental, especially since it displaces a lengthy common-law tradition which remains supported by valid justifications today.

"The doctrines of *actus reus, mens rea,* insanity, mistake, justification, and duress have historically provided the tools for a constantly shifting adjustment of the tension between the evolving aims of the criminal law and changing religious, moral, philosophical, and medical views of the nature of man. This process of adjustment has always been thought to be the province of the States." . . . The people of Montana have decided to resurrect the rule of an earlier era, disallowing consideration of voluntary intoxication when a defendant's state of mind is at issue. Nothing in the Due Process Clause prevents them from doing so, and the judgment of the Supreme Court of Montana to the contrary must be reversed.

It is so ordered.

Questions

1. What was the basis of Mr. Egelhoff's claim that the Montana statute was unconstitutional?

2. What was the court's holding?

3. What are the arguments for and against allowing a defense of voluntary intoxication?

As stated earlier, involuntary intoxication is a permissible defense. If an individual is forced or tricked into taking a substance that makes him unable to control his behavior or appreciate the wrongfulness of his actions, it would be fundamentally unfair to hold him criminally liable for his behavior. In the following case, the defendant attempted to present the defense of involuntary intoxication, claiming that medication administered by medical personnel caused his criminal behavior.

Miller v. State (2001)

District Court of Appeal of Florida (2nd Circuit)
805 SO.2d 885

An admitted heroin user, Miller went to the Parental Awareness and Responsibility (PAR) clinic seeking treatment for his addiction and enrolled in a methadone program. After a number of months, Miller decided he wanted to be free of all drugs, including methadone. He attempted to get off the methadone through the PAR clinic but was unsuccessful. He then turned to Neuraad, a clinic that offered a different type of treatment called opiate detoxification. Under this program, intense doses of numerous toxic drugs are introduced into the patient's system, following which the patient is sedated with anesthesia. The patient then sleeps during the period that his or her body undergoes the physical manifestations of withdrawal, thus greatly reducing the patient's conscious awareness of the most acute symptoms of withdrawal.

Miller checked into the Neuraad clinic on a Tuesday morning. The staff administered the medications and the anesthesia. Some twenty-seven hours later he was released, still under the influence of significant amounts of medication and with prescriptions for additional medication. Within three hours of his release, Miller went to the PAR clinic. When he arrived, the clinic was closed for the day. Upset that he could not get in, Miller shot the lock off of the gate. He walked around the building, shooting into it several times. He then broke a window and climbed inside. He ultimately surrendered to the police when they entered. Miller was charged with shooting into a building, burglary with a firearm, and aggravated assault.

At trial, Miller raised the defenses of insanity and intoxication. He argued that because of the drugs that Neuraad had given him, he did not have the capacity to distinguish between right and wrong and, thus, was legally insane when he arrived at the PAR clinic. In the alternative, he argued that due to the drugs, he did not have the ability to form the specific intent to commit the offenses of armed burglary and shooting into a building. The trial

court properly found that the evidence supported instructing the jury on both defenses.

Miller's trial counsel requested, and the trial court gave, both the standard instruction on insanity and the standard instruction on voluntary intoxication. However, Miller's counsel also presented the court with two proposed instructions on involuntary intoxication. Although one of the proposed instructions was an accurate statement of law, the trial court accepted neither and chose instead to give the jury an instruction of its own design, which failed to adequately instruct the jury. Accordingly, we must reverse.

At the outset, we observe that there is a crucial distinction between the defense of insanity and that of intoxication. A successful insanity defense results in the defendant's acquittal of all charges on the theory that one cannot be held criminally responsible for acts that he or she did not know were wrong. . . . By contrast, a successful intoxication defense results in an acquittal of specific intent crimes only, not general intent crimes. . . . The rationale is that although an intoxicated defendant may know the difference between right and wrong, he or she may not be able to form the specific intent required to commit certain offenses.

The issue here is whether the intoxication defense applies where the intoxication is involuntary, but does not rise to the level of legal insanity. When intoxication is voluntary, it is considered to be a defense to specific intent crimes. However, where the intoxication is involuntary, it typically has been raised in an attempt to prove an insanity defense rather than an intoxication defense. The definition of insanity has been expanded to include those situations in which a person could not distinguish right from wrong as the result of an involuntarily-induced intoxicated state. *Brancaccio v. State,* 698 SO.2d 597 (Fla. 4th DCA 1997).

At trial, the State argued that involuntary intoxication that did not rise to the level of legal insanity was not a defense, and an instruction that allowed the jury to acquit

(Continued)

(Continued)

the defendant of specific intent crimes as the result of involuntary intoxication was an inaccurate statement of the law. In support of its position, the State cited *Brancaccio* where the Fourth District reversed the trial court for its failure to instruct the jury that involuntary intoxication could be a basis for finding insanity. In a footnote, the court indicated that the insanity instruction should have been amended to provide that a person could be found to be insane as the result of involuntary intoxication. Although *Brancaccio* enlarged the existing definition of insanity to include involuntary intoxication, it did not say, nor should it be read to say, that proving insanity was the exclusive way to apply the defense of involuntary intoxication or that the standard intoxication defense to a specific intent crime was unavailable if the intoxicants were consumed involuntarily.

Indeed, common sense dictates against such a conclusion. If one who willingly and purposely consumes intoxicants to the point that he is unable to form a specific intent is to be excused from guilt of a specific intent crime, why should one who has unknowingly consumed the intoxicant be denied the same relief? *State v. Mriglot,* 88 Wash.2d 573, 564 P.2d 784 (1977). As the Supreme Court of Washington stated in *Mriglot,* "If a defendant is so intoxicated (voluntarily or involuntarily) as to be unable to form the requisite intent, he cannot be guilty of a specific intent crime. He need not prove temporary insanity simply because the intoxication happened to be involuntary." 564 P.2d at 576. The State is required to prove the defendant's state of mind. . . . Therefore, if the defendant could not form the required state of mind

due to intoxication, it should be irrelevant whether the intoxication was voluntary or involuntary.

In this case, it is clear that the jury rejected the insanity defense and concluded that Miller knew the difference between right and wrong. However, it is not clear what the jury concluded in regard to the intoxication defense. As instructed, if the jury concluded that Miller was involuntarily intoxicated, it could not consider the intoxication defense at all; it was limited to the insanity defense. That is, it is not clear whether the jury found Miller had the requisite intent or, instead, found he lacked the requisite intent but also found his intoxication was involuntary, and, under the erroneous instruction, the intoxication defense did not apply.

Because the instruction was misleading and misinformed the jury as to the applicable law, we reverse Miller's convictions on the specific intent crimes and remand for a new trial on the charges of burglary with a firearm and shooting into a building.

Reversed and remanded.

Questions

1. What is the difference between an insanity defense and an intoxication defense?

2. Mr. Miller argued that he should have been allowed to present a defense of involuntary intoxication. Did the court agree or disagree and why?

3. Mr. Miller claimed that he was involuntarily intoxicated. Is there an argument that his intoxication was voluntary?

Syndrome "Defenses"

In addition to the traditional excuse defenses of insanity, infancy, and intoxication, there are a number of modern defenses that have emerged in recent years that are based on the same premise: The defendant should not be held criminally responsible because he was suffering from some condition that prohibited him from either controlling his behavior or forming the requisite mens rea for the specific crime. They are called syndrome defenses because the defendant claims to have been exhibiting certain symptoms at the time of the offense that are characteristic of a particular recognized condition or disease. They are not the same as traditional defenses in that the defendant does not argue that he or she should be acquitted solely because he or she was suffering from the condition, but because the condition caused him or her to lack an essential element of the crime—usually the required mens rea. Often, the defendant will be guilty of some other, lesser offense, so these defenses are sometimes referred to as partial defenses. Evidence of Battered Woman Syndrome (BWS), discussed in Chapter 9, is usually presented in connection with self-defense to explain why the defendant killed the victim in the absence of an imminent threat. But there are other syndrome defenses that are presented independent of any other defense. We will examine two of these defenses in this section: post-traumatic stress disorder (PTSD)and premenstrual syndrome (PMS).

Post-Traumatic Stress Disorder

PTSD is recognized in the American Psychiatric Association's Diagnostic and Statistical Manual of Mental Disorders, Fifth Edition (DSM-V). Persons suffering from PTSD have seen or experienced some frightening or stressful event that causes them to relive that event through flashbacks and/or bad dreams. They may experience these flashbacks because of some event that triggers the memory of the previous event and may be frightened or stressed even when they are not actually in danger. When PTSD is used as a legal defense, the defendant often claims that he or she was experiencing a flashback that prohibited him or her from forming the specific intent to commit the crime.

War veterans often suffer from PTSD as a result of traumatic experiences during combat. Some of these veterans have been charged with criminal offenses and have argued that that their behavior was caused by PTSD. One study found that over 15 percent of all Vietnam veterans were diagnosed with PTSD and about half of them had been arrested or jailed at least once (34 percent more than once).[19] Over 11 percent of them had been convicted of a felony.[20] While there are no current statistics on the number of veterans from the wars in Iraq and Afghanistan charged with crimes, criminal justice officials report increasing numbers of veterans suffering from PTSD. Nicholas Horner is one such veteran.

Horner was one of thousands of soldiers and veterans diagnosed with post-traumatic stress disorder (PTSD) after returning from fighting in Iraq or Afghanistan.

©iStockphoto.com/ArtPhaneuf

The Nicholas Horner Case

Nicholas Horner returned home to Altoona, Pennsylvania, after serving in Iraq and receiving numerous medals for his combat service. His mother and wife noticed a drastic change in his behavior after the war. Horner had been a talkative, outgoing person before the war. When he returned, he barely spoke, and his wife frequently found him in the basement of their home in tears. Horner started carrying a gun everywhere and always kept the doors in his home locked. He also suffered from panic attacks.

On April 6, 2009, Nicholas Horner went shopping with his wife after dropping their kids off at school. Horner and his wife got into an argument, and Horner stormed off, armed with his .45 caliber handgun. He went to a local bowling alley and started drinking beers. After leaving the bowling alley, he went to a Subway sandwich shop and started banging on the back door of the shop. Horner cut the electrical wiring of the shop and tried to shoot the utility box as well.

Horner then shot and killed high school senior Scott Garlick, who was working in the shop at the time. He also shot and injured another employee, Michelle Petty. Horner then left the store and walked several blocks. He saw sixty-four-year-old Raymond Williams, who had just left his home to get the mail. Horner shot and killed Williams as well.[21]

Horner was charged with two counts of capital murder. His lawyer argued that he was in the middle of a PTSD episode at the time of the killings and that he thought the subway shop was a building in Iraq. Dr. Ernest Boswell, a medical expert specializing in PTSD, testified that Horner was definitely suffering from PTSD and other mental health issues. Boswell believed that Horner was in a state of delirium at the time of the shootings as a result of medications he was taking to treat the PTSD and other conditions. It was Dr. Boswell's opinion that because of that state of delirium, Horner could not have formed the specific intent to kill.[22] The jury had to find that Horner had the specific intent to kill his victims to convict him of first degree murder. The jury rejected Horner's defense and found him guilty of both counts of murder. The jury could not agree on the death penalty, so he was sentenced to life in prison.

Premenstrual Syndrome

Premenstrual Syndrome (PMS) is a group of symptoms that some women experience one to two weeks before their menstrual cycles. The symptoms are both physical and emotional and may include bloating, headaches, exhaustion, food cravings, depression, tension, irritability, mood swings, and memory loss. The symptoms may be minor or very severe.

Women suffering from severe mental and emotional symptoms of PMS have attempted to use it as either a partial or complete defense to certain crimes. As early as the mid-1800s, English courts recognized PMS as a defense. Women charged with crimes as minor as petty theft and as serious as murder successfully claimed that they should not be held liable because they were suffering from PMS at the time of the offense.[23]

The PMS defense was used in several high profile cases in England in the mid-1980s. One such case involved a woman named Sandie Craddock, a bar maid who was charged with murder after stabbing a coworker to death. Ms. Craddock had over thirty prior convictions for theft, arson, and assault and had attempted suicide twenty-five times. It was discovered that her violent behavior and suicide attempts always occurred around the same time each month, leading a doctor to diagnose her with PMS.[24] Craddock claimed diminished capacity, alleging that "PMS turned her into a raging animal each month and forced her to act out of character."[25] Her claim of diminished capacity due to PMS resulted in a verdict of manslaughter rather than murder. Craddock was sentenced to probation and ordered to continue progesterone treatments, which seemed to control her condition.[26]

The Craddock case and several other English cases involved PMS being used successfully either as a partial defense—reducing murder to manslaughter—or as a mitigating factor at sentencing, resulting in probationary sentences rather than prison time. In the United States, the defense rarely has been successfully used as a complete defense to a crime and most often has been offered as a mitigating factor at the time of sentencing.

The Geraldine Richter Case

In at least one case in the United States, a woman was acquitted after presenting evidence that she was suffering from PMS at the time of the offense. Dr. Geraldine Richter, a forty-two-year-old orthopedic surgeon, was charged with driving while intoxicated after being stopped in Fairfax, Virginia, in November 1990. The state trooper who stopped her detailed the facts in a memorandum to his superior. He wrote that she had been driving erratically (weaving across both lanes of a two lane highway), failed a Breathalyzer test, became verbally and physically abusive, and at one point attempted to kick the trooper in the groin. The state trooper claimed that he noticed a strong odor of alcohol on Dr. Richter's breath, and when he inquired about how much she had to drink, Dr. Richter replied that "it was none of [his] damn business, and that she was not drunk."[27] He further noted that when he and an assisting officer tried to restrain Dr. Richter she exclaimed, "You son of a b___; you f___ can't do this to me; I'm a doctor. I hope you f___ get shot and come into my hospital so I can refuse to treat you, or if any other trooper gets shot, I will also refuse to treat them."[28] Once detained, Dr. Richter allegedly continued this violent and abusive behavior, cursed at the magistrate, kicked the Breathalyzer table, and initially refused to take additional tests. After being placed in restraints, Dr. Richter complied with testing, which occurred approximately an hour after she was stopped by the trooper. The results indicated that her blood-alcohol level was .13, which was above the legal limit.[29]

At trial, Dr. Richter's lawyer, David Sher, challenged the results of the Breathalyzer test and argued that PMS, not intoxication, was the cause of Dr. Richter's erratic and violent behavior. Dr. Emine Cay, a gynecologist, testified as an expert for the defense, and concluded that Dr. Richter's conduct was consistent with the symptoms of PMS. After considering the "totality of the evidence,"

including a challenge to the Breathalyzer results based on expert testimony, the observation of a witness who interacted with Dr. Richter before she left a gathering that took place moments prior to her arrest, and an evaluation of Dr. Richter's behavior that arguably could have been attributed to PMS, the judge acquitted Dr. Richter of driving while intoxicated.

The judge credited the testimony of the Breathalyzer experts who testified about the inaccuracy of the tests and problems with how it was administered in Dr. Richter's case. The judge also credited the testimony of Dr. Cay:

> That leaves us with the behavior, the outrageous behavior at the scene, and it's a real close call as to what would have caused that. Yes, it could have been caused by intoxication. We also know it could have been caused by the premenstrual-syndrome problem. And so I guess, when we're saying that it could have been caused by something or it could have been caused by something else, and if I had had this much trouble deciding what happened, there's only one solution. What I'm saying is, the defendant has marshaled sufficient resources to reactivate the presumption, if you will, of innocence.[30]

Questions

1. Should defendants be permitted to present syndrome defenses? Why or why not?

2. Should juries be permitted to acquit a defendant based on a syndrome defense?

3. Should judges permit some syndrome defenses and not others?

Cultural Defenses ●━━━━━━━━━━━━━━━

Like syndrome defenses, cultural defenses are not complete defenses to crimes. Instead, the defendant typically presents evidence of his or her cultural background or beliefs to demonstrate that he or she lacked the required mens rea for a particular offense. As Professor Alison Dundes Renteln explains in the following excerpt, the introduction of this evidence may result in the defendant being found guilty of a less serious offense, but it rarely results in a complete acquittal.

"A Justification of the Cultural Defense as Partial Excuse" by Alison Dundes Renteln[31]

The purpose of this essay is to offer arguments in favor of the establishment of an official "cultural defense." A cultural defense is a defense asserted by immigrants, refugees, and indigenous people based on their customs or customary law. A successful cultural defense would permit the reduction (and possible elimination) of a charge, with a concomitant reduction in punishment. The rationale behind such a claim is that an individual's behavior is influenced to such a large extent by his or her culture that either (i) the individual simply did not believe that his or her actions contravened any laws (cognitive case), or (ii) the individual was compelled to act the way he or she did (volitional case). In both cases the individual's culpability is lessened.

The reason for admitting a cultural defense lies not so much in a desire to be culturally sensitive, although that is surely a large part of it, but rather in a desire to ensure equal application of the law to all citizens. By equality I mean, not merely the desire to treat all culture conflict cases in a more uniform manner, but also the desire to treat all individuals in society as equals. As I shall argue, individual justice demands that the legal system focus on the actor as well as the act, on motive as well as intent. This, in turn, necessitates the introduction of cultural information into the courtroom.

Oftentimes cultural information is brought into the courtroom by defense attorneys in the context of a pre-existing defense, such as provocation or insanity. For many reasons, however, this strategy is unsatisfactory for the generic culture conflict case. The most salient drawback is that the standards against which a defendant's actions are judged are those of "the reasonable person." But it is precisely this idea of reasonableness that lies at the heart of the conflict. As I shall argue, the actions of defendants should be judged against behavioral standards that are reasonable for a person of that culture in the context of this culture. This would balance the requirements of individual justice and cultural accommodation with the competing demands of social order and the rule of law.

It must be emphasized from the outset that the consideration of cultural evidence in no way requires that it be dispositive. A common fear is that the establishment of a cultural defense may force us to condone practices which contravene the rights of historically disenfranchised groups, including women and children. The argument seems to be that, although human rights are respected in the United States, the rest of the world is still barbaric. Ignoring the culturally patronizing overtones of such an argument, I should like to point out that sometimes it is women (and children) who benefit from the existence of cultural defenses. . . .

More importantly, as I shall explain in more detail below, the sort of cultural defense I advocate is one which functions as a partial excuse. The advantage of such a formulation is that a demonstration of cultural influence is not sufficient to acquit. Juries must decide whether cultural factors were determinative in a defendant's behavior, and, if so, whether that is sufficient to warrant either a lesser charge or complete acquittal. By employing the cultural defense as a partial excuse, courts would be better able to fit the punishment to the crime, which is surely one of the goals of the criminal justice system.

Insanity and Culture

Even assuming that the facts of a cultural defense case were to make it appropriate to use the insanity defense (either the cognitive or volitional type), there are at least several disadvantages to taking this approach. Given the narrowly circumscribed meaning of "morally wrong," defendants who wish to raise a cultural defense will have difficulty trying to introduce cultural arguments through the cognitive insanity defense given existing doctrine: (a) wrong means legally wrong and (b) when wrong means morally wrong, it refers only to the delusional belief in divine commandments. Immigrants and refugees in most cultural defense cases are, in fact, perfectly sane according to the standards of their own culture, and, indeed, according to Western clinical standards. Giving them no option other than an insanity defense to present the cultural dimension of the case would require a gross falsification of the facts.

Furthermore, comparing the logic of immigrants with that of the insane is, at the very least, insulting. Just because someone has a worldview that differs from the mainstream surely does not justify suggesting that worldview is insane. Such a comparison, even if successful as a strategy for avoiding incarceration, would require the ethnocentric assessment of the perspectives of other peoples. Forcing cultural arguments into the insanity defense would symbolically denigrate the way of life of others. The logic of another culture is not "irrational" when judged from the culture's point of view. To rely on an insanity defense would require distortion of the worldview of other groups.

If the defendant were willing to misrepresent himself and his culture in order to avoid being held criminally responsible, success might not be particularly desirable. He would be subject to commitment to a mental institution for an undetermined period of time where he would be treated. But trying to "cure" someone of having been raised in a different culture is cultural genocide.

In many instances, cultural defendants can invoke only the cognitive type of insanity defense, because the M'Naghten test is found in the majority of jurisdictions. But an explanation of a culturally motivated act may require the volitional form of the insanity test. This means that it will be a matter of luck whether an immigrant happens to commit the offense in the right state, that is, in one which has the requisite type of insanity test. Such circumstances are clearly arbitrary and unfair. Moreover, even if the cultural defendant does adjudicate the claim in a jurisdiction that admits a volitional insanity test, it is notoriously difficult to establish such a claim.

There have been some cases in which the defense counsel has advanced a defense combining the mental illness and cultural considerations all in one. Under some circumstances this approach may be necessary, because the defendant suffers from some sort of mental trauma related to his or her culture. The case of *People v. Kimura* is one such example. It provides an illustration of a case in which the cognitive insanity defense was successfully employed. The other case I shall consider, *People v. Metallides*, is an illustration of the use of the volitional insanity defense.

People v. Kimura

When Fumiko Kimura, a Japanese American living in Santa Monica, California, learned of the infidelity of her husband, she attempted oyako-shinju, parent-child suicide, by wading into the Pacific Ocean with her two children. The two children died, but she survived and was charged with first-degree murder with special circumstances which could have brought the death penalty. Oyako-shinju, while illegal in Japan, is not unheard of as a means by which a family can avoid an otherwise unacceptable social predicament. The Japanese-American community gathered a petition with over 25,000 signatures appealing to the Los Angeles County district attorney not to prosecute her, arguing that her actions were based on a different worldview. According to this worldview, it is more cruel to leave the children behind with no one to look after them than it is for the mother to take them with her to the afterlife.

Six psychiatrists testified that Kimura was suffering from temporary insanity. Some based their conclusion on her failure to distinguish between her own life and the lives of her children. Through a plea bargain her homicide charge was reduced to voluntary manslaughter and she was sentenced to one year in county jail (which she had already served), five years probation, and psychiatric counseling. She was subsequently reunited with her husband(!).

Though her attorney, Mr. Klausner, claimed that his argument relied on psychiatric testimony, commentators believe that cultural factors played a role in the process. It is worth pointing out that Kimura appears to have benefitted from a cultural defense though she had resided in the United States for several years. As she had remained culturally isolated, she had not become assimilated. This suggests that assimilation often does not occur as rapidly as many believe.

Another important point is that the children's rights dimension of this case has hardly been discussed in the literature. While the court may have been correct in considering the cultural aspects of the case, it is arguable that probation was an unjustifiably light sentence to impose.

People v. Metallides

In the Miami, Florida case of *People v. Metallides* a Greek immigrant, Kostas Metallides, killed his best friend when he found out that he had raped Kostas' daughter. Metallides' attorney, a public defender, used a temporary insanity argument based on culture. Though not recognized as a defense in Florida, the attorney relied on the "irresistible impulse" test. Metallides' attorney constructed an argument around the cultural idea that the "law of the old country" is that "you do not wait for the police if your daughter has been raped." Though the jury was given temporary insanity as the official issue to decide, apparently it recognized that honor was a cultural concept. Metallides was acquitted because the jury technically found him not guilty by reason of temporary insanity, but those involved say it was because of arguments based on Greek culture. The defense attorney said

(Continued)

(Continued)

that the judge may have allowed the cultural evidence because the judge's wife was Greek.

It seems unfair that it was possible to introduce the cultural defense only surreptitiously. Had the judge been unwilling to consider the irresistible impulse test, due to the absence of statutory authorization, or to interpret the cultural evidence as relevant, Metallides would not have had the benefit of a cultural defense. Moreover, the accuracy of the claims made concerning Greek culture could have been questioned, considering that no expert witness was consulted on this point.

While it was appropriate to allow the cultural argument to be heard, it appears that the jury gave excessive weight to it. Although one can only speculate about the jury's reasoning, it may have been that the jury felt that a vote to convict would lead to an excessive punishment under the circumstances, and so the preferred option was acquittal. One of the reasons for instituting the cultural defense as a separate defense is to avoid such artificial dichotomies.

Under the current system, a defendant's fate would appear to hinge upon the attitude of the judge to the relevancy of the cultural evidence and on the availability of particular insanity tests. Although Metallides was able to escape punishment by relying on the irresistible impulse test, other defendants may not have such good fortune. Another reason for adopting a cultural defense is to achieve a greater degree of uniformity in the handling of such cases.

Questions

1. What is a cultural defense?

2. What are Professor Renteln's arguments for and against allowing defendants to present a cultural defense?

3. Did the cultural defenses presented in the *Kimura* and *Metallides* cases produce fair results?

Consider Professor Renteln's arguments as you read the following case, where the defendant attempts to introduce expert testimony about Laotian culture:

People v. Aphaylath (1986)

Court of Appeals of the State of New York
502 N.E.2d 998

Defendant, a Laotian refugee living in this country for approximately two years, was indicted and tried for the intentional murder of his Laotian wife of one month. At trial, defendant attempted to establish the affirmative defense of extreme emotional disturbance to mitigate the homicide . . . on the theory that the stresses resulting from his status of a refugee caused a significant mental trauma, affecting his mind for a substantial period of time, simmering in the unknowing subconscious and then inexplicably coming to the fore. . . . Although the immediate cause for the defendant's loss of control was his jealousy over his wife's apparent preference for an ex-boyfriend, the defense argued that under Laotian culture the conduct of the victim wife in displaying affection for another

man and receiving phone calls from an unattached man brought shame on defendant and his family sufficient to trigger defendant's loss of control.

The defense was able to present some evidence of the Laotian culture through the cross-examination of two prosecution witnesses and through the testimony of defendant himself, although he was hampered by his illiteracy in both his native tongue and English. Defendant's ability to adequately establish his defense was impermissibly curtailed by the trial court's exclusion of the proffered testimony of two expert witnesses concerning the stress and disorientation encountered by Laotian refugees in attempting to assimilate into the American culture. It appears from the record before us that the sole basis on which the court excluded the expert testimony was because "neither one * * * was going to be able to testify as to anything specifically relating to this defendant." It is unclear from this ruling whether the Trial Judge determined that she had no discretion to allow the testimony because the experts had no knowledge of this particular defendant or that she declined to exercise her discretion because of the experts' lack of knowledge of the defendant or his individual background and characteristics. Under either interpretation, however, the exclusion of this expert testimony as a matter of law was erroneous because the admissibility of expert testimony that is probative of a fact in issue does not depend on whether the witness has personal knowledge of a defendant or a defendant's particular characteristics. . . Whether or not such testimony is sufficiently relevant to have probative value is a determination to be made by the Trial Judge in the exercise of her sound discretion . . . .

Accordingly, because the court's ruling was not predicated on the appropriate standard and the defendant may have been deprived of an opportunity to put before the jury information relevant to his defense, a new trial must be ordered.

Questions

1. What was the basis of Mr. Aphaylath's appeal?

2. What was the court's holding and rationale?

3. Should juries be allowed to acquit a defendant based on a cultural defense? Why or why not?

Concluding Note

Excuse defenses have a common theme. The defendant claims that he or she committed the act because of some condition, circumstance, or disease. With some excuse defenses—as with insanity, infancy, or intoxication—the defendant may seek a total acquittal, alleging that he or she is not criminally liable at all. With others, such as the syndrome and cultural defenses, the defendant may present evidence to demonstrate that he or she did not have the requisite mens rea at the time of the offense, resulting in a partial defense and a conviction on a less serious offense (manslaughter instead of murder, for example). Overall, excuse defenses have been less successful than justification defenses. Now test yourself on the material we have covered in Chapter 10. Good luck with the Issue Spotter exercise.

Issue**Spotter**

Read the hypothetical and spot the issues discussed in this chapter.

Battle Fatigue

Before joining the army, George was a very outgoing, active, and friendly person. He was popular in school and excelled in sports. George married his childhood sweetheart Nancy and joined the army shortly after they graduated from high school. George and Nancy had three sons and enjoyed a happy marriage during the early years. George was very successful in the army and was promoted to the rank of Master Sergeant.

George was deployed to Iraq in 2005 and returned home the following year. He did not talk about his war experiences on the frontlines very much, and Nancy noticed that he was quieter and much more subdued after his return from war.

In 2007, George volunteered for a second tour of duty in Iraq. This time he stayed for two years. When George

(Continued)

(Continued)

returned home in 2009, he was very moody and appeared depressed. Nancy suggested that George get counseling, but he declined. Instead, he immediately volunteered for a third tour of duty—this time, in Afghanistan. Nancy was very upset and begged him not to go, but he insisted.

George was wounded six months after going to Afghanistan. Although George's injuries were not serious, he saw several members of his brigade killed by a suicide bomber. When George returned home, Nancy convinced him that it was time to end his army career. Nancy again urged George to get counseling, but he refused.

After this third tour of duty, George's behavior was markedly different. Not only was he moody and depressed, he also had trouble sleeping. Nancy noticed that he tossed and turned and frequently woke up in a sweat. George told her that he was having nightmares about Afghanistan. He began to carry his service weapon with him all the time and spent hours in the basement with the door locked. Nancy was worried, but she could not convince George to get help.

One day, George decided to meet some members of his old brigade for drinks. The men met at a local bar and began to drink as they talked about old times. George stayed at the bar for hours and drank six beers followed by shots of tequila. When he stood up to leave, he was unsteady on his feet and clearly intoxicated. His buddies offered him a ride home, but he refused.

George went to the parking lot and headed toward his car. It was close to midnight, and the parking lot was very dark. As he looked for his car, he heard an explosion behind him. Startled, George turned around, pulled out his service revolver, and began shooting. Unfortunately, he shot and killed two of his buddies.

George was charged with two counts of first degree murder. You are his attorney. George tells you that when he heard the explosion, he thought he was in Afghanistan and that he had a flashback to the suicide bombing he witnessed in Afghanistan. When he turned around, all he saw were the Taliban soldiers, so he started shooting. George admitted that he was intoxicated when he left the bar.

1. What defenses might George present at trial?

2. What are the strengths and weaknesses of each defense and the likely outcome at trial?

Key Terms and Cases

Notes ●━━━━━━━━━━━━━━━━━━━━━━━━━━━━

1. *Dusky v. United States*, 362 U.S. 402 (1960).

2. *Sell v. United States*, 539 U.S. 166, 179 (2003).

3. *United States v. Curry*, 410 F.2d 1372, 1374 (5th Cir. 1969).

4. Marc Lacey, "Prosecutors Want Tucson Suspect to Undergo Psychiatric Testing," *New York Times*, March 8, 2011, http://www.nytimes.com/2011/03/09/us/09loughner.html

5. Fernanda Santos, "Life Term for Gunman After Guilty Plea in Tucson Killings," *New York Times*, August 7, 2012, http://www.nytimes.com/2012/08/08/us/loughner-pleads-guilty-in-2011-tucson-shootings.html?ref=jaredleeloughner

6. Ibid.

7. M'Naughten's Case. House of Lords, Mews' Dig. i. 349; iv. 1112. S.C. 8 Scott N.R. 595; 1 C. and K. 130; 4 St. Tr. N.S. 847, May 26, June 19, 1843.

8. Durham v. United States, 214 F.2d 862, 874–75 (D.C. Cir. 1954).

9. 471 F.2d 969, 969 (D.C. Cir. 1972) (quoting § 4.01, Mental Disease or Defect Excluding Responsibility, Model Penal Code § 4.01).

10. Ira K. Packer, *Evaluation of Criminal Responsibility* (Oxford: Oxford University Press, 2009) 13.

11. James Polk, "Doctors: Reagan Shooter Is Recovering, Not a Danger," CNN.com, March 26, 2011, 9:55 p.m., http://articles.cnn.com/2011–03–26/justice/hinckley.today_1_john-hinckley-furloughs-insanity?_s=PM:CRIME

12. "The Insanity Defense Among the States," http://criminal.findlaw.com/criminal-procedure/the-insanity-defense-among-the-states.html

13. Twelve states have a bifurcated trial process. State Court Organization, "Table 38: The Defense of Insanity: Standards and Procedures" (Washington, DC: U.S. Department of Justice, Bureau of Justice Statistics, 1998), http://www.bjs.gov/content/pub/pdf/sco9805.pdf

14. Ibid. In a few states, once the defendant has put on some evidence of insanity, the government must prove that the defendant was not insane at the time of the offense.

15. "A Crime of Insanity,"*Commitment, Confinement and Release,* PBS website, http://www.pbs.org/wgbh/pages/frontline/shows/crime/trial/faqs.html#4, accessed July 12, 2011, quoted in Michael Perlin, *The Jurisprudence of the Insanity Defense* (Carolina Academic Press, 1994).

16. D.C. Code § 16–2301.02.

17. *McKeiver v. Pennsylvania*, 403 U.S. 528, 533 (1971).

18. "State Laws," *Juvenile Justice*, PBS website, http://www.pbs.org/wgbh/pages/frontline/shows/juvenile/stats/states.html, accessed August 5, 2014.

19. Chris Lawrence and Jennifer Rizzo, "Under Fire: Wartime Stress as a Defense for Murder,"CNN.com, May 11, 2012, 11:28 a.m., http://www.cnn.com/2012/05/05/justice/ptsd-murder-defense

20. Ibid.

21. Ibid.

22. "Horner Trial Day Five," WeAreCentralPA website, http://www.wearecentralpa.com/story/horner-trial-day-five/d/story/4MdwIW1A-k6qF5PsgrccYw

23. Becky L. Jacobs, "PMS HAHAcronym: Perpetuating Male Superiority," *Texas Journal of Women & Law* 14 (2004): 1, 9–10.

24. Ibid.

25. Patricia Easteal, *Premenstrual Syndrome (PMS) in the Courtroom,* Australian Institute of Criminology (1991), http://www.aic.gov.au/media_library/publications/proceedings/16/easteal2.pdf

26. Ibid.

27. Christina L. Hosp, "Has the PMS Defense Gained a Legitimate Toehold in Virginia Criminal Law? *Commonwealth v. Richter,*" *George Mason Law Review* 14 (1991): 427, 432–33.

28. Ibid.

29. Ibid. at 434.

30. Ibid. at 436.

31. Alison Dundes Renteln, "A Justification of the Cultural Defense as Partial Excuse" *Southern California Review of Law & Women's Studies* 2 (1993): 437.

Chapter 11

In 2010, Tyler Clementi, an eighteen-year-old gay college student, learned that his roommate, Dharun Ravi, had used a webcam to secretly tape his intimate encounters with a man. Ravi sent Twitter and text messages encouraging others to watch Clementi. In a text-message exchange with his friend, Michelle Huang, Ravi stated, "Yeah, keep the gays away." After Clementi discovered that Ravi had placed one of the videos on the Internet, he jumped to his death off the George Washington Bridge.

Ravi was charged and convicted on fifteen counts, including bias intimidation, invasion of privacy, lying to investigators, tampering with witnesses, and tampering with evidence.

The maximum penalty Ravi faced was ten years in prison. In 2012, the trial court judge sentenced him to thirty days in jail, three years probation, three hundred hours of community service, counseling, and ordered him to pay a ten thousand dollar fine. Following the sentencing, Ravi apologized to Tyler Clementi's family. After serving twenty days in jail, Dharun Ravi received an early release for good behavior. The Clementi case presents several of the issues involving punishment and sentencing that will be explored in this chapter, including which actions deserve punishment and what factors are important in determining the appropriate punishment.

Dharun Ravi (right) with his attorney after his release from jail, following a twenty-day sentence.

Punishment and Sentencing

Learning Objectives

After reading and studying this chapter, you should be able to

➤ Identify the rationales for criminal punishment

➤ Know the rights protected by the Eighth Amendment

➤ List three types of punishment for a criminal conviction

➤ Define invisible punishment

➤ Know the rationales for determinate sentencing and indeterminate sentencing

➤ Describe purpose of victim impact statements

➤ State the goals of mandatory minimum sentences and the federal sentencing guidelines

➤ Describe the federal crack cocaine law

➤ Provide three facts about capital punishment

➤ Define capital punishment

Introduction

On the morning of June 10, 1991, Jaycee Dugard was kidnapped from a school bus stop. She was eleven years old. Dugard was help by captors, Phillip and Nancy Garrido, for eighteen years. Dugard was subjected to multiple sexual assaults by Phillip Garrido. As a result of these rapes, she bore two children. Dugard and her daughters were forced to live in a squalid, ramshackle tent behind the Garrido's suburban California residence. In August 2009, Phillip Garrido took Dugard's daughters to the University of California, Berkeley campus. He sought permission to hold an event for the group, "God's Desire." A campus police officer, who noticed something odd about the girls, made an appointment with Garrido for the following day. Following a background check that revealed Garrido was a registered sex offender and her conversation with the two girls, the campus officer contacted Garrido's parole officer. Garrido was promptly arrested. It was later determined that he and his wife Nancy Garrido, were holding Jaycee Dugard. In 2011, following guilty pleas, the pair received lengthy prison sentences: Garrido, who had a long history as a sexual predator, was sentenced to 431 years in prison. Nancy Garrido was sentenced to thirty-six years to life behind bars.[1] The length of Phillip Garrido's sentence in particular raises questions about the goals and value of punishment.

The Eighth Amendment, which prohibits cruel and unusual punishment, establishes the boundaries for criminal sanctions. Punishment cannot be barbaric, it must be proportionate to the crime, and it may only be imposed after a criminal conviction (see Chapter 8 for a detailed discussion of the Eighth Amendment). The Garrido case poses questions at the core of criminal punishment and sentencing. This includes issues such as why society inflicts punishment, which punishments are acceptable in a civil society, and which punishments are permissible for which crimes. This chapter explores these questions and more.

Jaycee Dugard (left), Phillip Garrido (center), and Nancy Garrido (right). Was the punishment imposed upon the Garridos proportionate?

Punishment

In earlier times, barbaric punishments were commonplace. Offenders faced grave penalties for both small offenses (e.g., pig stealing, idleness, adultery) and grand offenses (e.g., murder). Punishment frequently involved a physical sanction, such as dismemberment (e.g., removal of a limb), the whipping post, or branding on the cheek or forehead. Other forms of punishment, such as placing someone in the stocks or the pillory, caused great discomfort. Some types of punishment, such as forcing a guilty person to wear a sign or parading him through town tethered to a rope, for all to see, were designed to cause humiliation and public shame. Many who were convicted of criminal wrongdoing were sentenced to serve time in a penal colony, which often included hard labor. When the punishment was death, various methods were available, including hanging, drawing and quartering, and stoning. Another hallmark of the criminal sanction during this period was the public nature of punishment. It was not uncommon for offenders to receive their punishment in the public square, where crowds of onlookers could gather to bear witness.

Today, these harsh punishments would be considered unlawful torture—unfit for civil society. Many of these punishments go centuries back. However, some are part of the United State's more recent past. The laws used against African American slaves—the slave codes—are an example. These codes imposed severe punishments against Blacks for a wide range of activities that would be lawful for Whites. For example, the slave codes made it unlawful for slaves to learn to read, to use abusive language, or to gather in small groups (unless a White person was present). Punishment for violating the slave codes included whippings, banishment, and death. These codes, the first of which were passed in Virginia in the early 1700s, were officially in operation until 1865, the end of the Civil War. In this section we will delve into the many issues raised by criminal sanctions, highlighting the various rationales for punishment. In particular, the discussion explores deterrence, rehabilitation, incapacitation, retribution, and restorative justice. This broad range in rationales for punishment push us to consider whether some are better than others for a democratic society.

Rationales for Punishment

What are the aims of criminal punishment? For centuries, philosophers, academicians, and the lay public have debated this question. Our reasons for sanctioning criminal wrongdoing are a collective statement about our social values on crime, punishment, offenders, and our community. There are four longstanding rationales for criminal punishment: deterrence, rehabilitation, incapacitation, and retribution. In recent years, restorative justice has emerged as a viable approach to punishment. As the below discussion makes clear, in some instances the rationales for punishing crime overlap or complement one another. In other instances, the rationales are in direct conflict. Following a discussion of each rationale is an application to the Garrido case.

Deterrence

> The purpose of punishment . . . is none other than to prevent the criminal from doing fresh harm to fellow citizens and to deter others from doing the same.
>
> *Cesare Beccaria*[2]

The above quote, by Eighteenth century Italian philosopher Cesare Beccaria, nicely and clearly summarizes the dual aims of deterrence philosophy. With deterrence, the threat of punishment is used as a way to discourage people from engaging in crime. This is known as "general deterrence"—since the threat is directed at the general public. Whether a particular sanction is a disincentive to commit crime is influenced by three factors: certainty, severity, and celerity. Certainty refers to the perceived likelihood that an offender will receive punishment for her wrongdoing, severity refers to the perceived harshness of the punishment that she will receive, and celerity refers to the perceived speed with which the offender will receive punishment after she commits the crime. It is hard to determine how successful deterrence is as a method of crime prevention. Deterrence is what criminologists and sociologists label a nonevent—when deterrence works a crime does not occur.

The other goal of deterrence is to prevent an offender from committing additional crimes. This is referred to as "specific deterrence" because the punishment is targeted at a specific class of offenders—repeat offenders. The sanctions for repeat offenders are harsher than those directed at people who have not been convicted of prior offenses.

Applied to the Garrido Case. The long prison sentences in the Garrido case exemplify the aims of specific deterrence. In particular, Phillip Garrido's sentence of more than four hundred years behind bars was triggered by his lengthy criminal history. Nancy Garrido received a thirty-sex-year prison sentence. The sentences in this case ensure that neither Garrido nor his wife will reoffend (see Table 11.1). In addition to sending a message to other repeat offenders, Garrido's sentence also meets the goals of general deterrence. His sentence sends a message to potential offenders that if they commit similar crimes they will receive severe punishment.

Rehabilitation

People who commit crime can learn to make different and better decisions. This is the basic premise of rehabilitation. Under a rehabilitation model of punishment, the criminal justice system assesses the causes of individual criminal behaviors and selects a remedial course of treatment. The rehabilitative umbrella covers a broad range of responses by the justice system, including drug treatment, school completion (e.g., coursework for a GED), job training, and psychological counseling.

Until the mid-1970s, rehabilitation was the popular approach to punishment. In an influential article published in 1974, sociologist Robert Martinson concluded that very few treatment programs reduce recidivism. His findings were based on evaluations of 231 criminal rehabilitation programs between 1945 and 1967.[3] These findings were used as political leverage to argue that rehabilitation and its focus on the "root causes" of crime did not work and should no longer be the basis of U.S. penal philosophy. In later decades, researchers have established that a wide array of rehabilitation programs may be successful. Today many researchers argue that our correctional institutions should implement programs that will improve the chances that former prisoners can find employment and reduce recidivism. This includes prison programs that allow offenders to learn a trade or complete college courses. Studies indicate that programs that have the greatest impact on recidivism are ones that use cognitive-behavioral therapy, such as anger management, substance abuse, interpersonal problem solving, and critical thinking. Although rehabilitation programs still exist within U.S. correctional institutions, rehabilitation remains unpopular as a primary aim of the criminal justice system.

Applied to the Garrido Case. A rehabilitative approach would not have changed the outcome of the Garrido case. Phillip Garrido would still have received a life term for the kidnapping and sexual assault of Jaycee Dugard. Likewise, Nancy Garrido would still have received a long prison term. What might have been different is the justice system's response to Phillip Garrido's prior criminal case. For instance, Garrido might have been required to have counseling or sentenced to a longer sentence for his previous kidnapping and rape convictions. A different punishment might have decreased the chances that Garrido would have kidnapped and assaulted Dugard.

Incapacitation

The rationale for incapacitation is simple. If criminals are not on the street, they cannot commit crime. According to this rationale, once offenders are removed from society, the crime rate will drop. Incapacitation is sometimes referred to as "warehousing" because its main goal is to remove offenders from society. In contrast to rehabilitation, incapacitation is less concerned with how prisoners spend their time and whether this impacts their actions after they are released.

Selective incapacitation as an approach to punishment has drawn interest and controversy. It focuses on career criminals, people with long histories of arrests and incarceration. It is estimated that high-level repeat offenders are approximately 5 to 10 percent of the criminal population. Career offenders commit upwards of 50 percent of all crime. The goal of selective incapacitation is to identify these repeat offenders and incarcerate them for lengthy prison terms. Two and three strikes legislation targets repeat offenders. These are laws that allow an offender to be punished more severely if he has previously been convicted of a crime.

Some people argue that selective incapacitation is unfair because it allows the law to treat people differently based on their criminal history. For instance, assume that both Courtney and Delonte were convicted of burglary. Also assume that Courtney had previously been convicted of assault. A selective incapacitation approach would allow a judge to give Courtney a harsher sentence since she is a prior offender. Selective incapacitation is also controversial because of the difficulty of predicting who is likely to become a repeat offender.[4]

Applied to the Garrido Case. Phillip Garrido was a repeat offender and the lengthy sentence he received provides an example of selective incapacitation at work. During his sentencing hearing, the judge expressed surprise that Garrido had served a relatively short sentence for his prior crimes of kidnapping and rape. The judge reviewed Garrido's criminal history, the prior convictions, and the crimes against Dugard and imposed a 431-year sentence. (The issue of penalty enhancement is discussed later in this chapter.)

Retribution

The basic idea of retribution is that when someone causes criminal harm, he deserves harm in return. This justification for punishment is rooted in Christian religious doctrine: "Breach for breach, eye for eye, tooth for tooth: as he hath caused a blemish in a man, so shall it be done to him again."[5] In earlier societies, these words had literal meaning. Barbaric sanctions have a long history. Dismemberment, drawing and quartering, or placing people in the stockades—once commonplace—are no longer permissible forms of punishment. Contemporary forms of retribution allow for lengthy prison terms (for serious and low-level offenses) and the denial of benefits for offenders and ex-offenders, such as the right to bear arms and the right to vote. Retribution takes a two-part approach to criminal punishment. One, it ensures that the offender receives his just desserts, which is believed to be necessary to make him whole again. Two, the punishment also enables community members, the people who have been harmed by the crime, to become whole again. However, the primary goal of retribution is to punish the offender. Today, retribution is the popular, public choice for punishment.

Applied to the Garrido Case. Phillip Garrido's 431-year prison term and Nancy Garrido's thirty six-year term reflects a focus on punishing the offender, which is the hallmark of retribution. The Garridos held Jaycee Dugard (and her daughters) for eighteen years against her will. Now both will be held behind bars, against their will, for the rest of their lives.

Restorative Justice

Because crime hurts, justice should heal.

John Braithwaite, criminologist

Restorative justice is among the newer rationales for punishment. Criminologist John Braithwaite identifies restorative justice as a way to help victims, society, and offenders recover from crime. The basic premise is that crime is more than a violation of law: it harms people and relationships. Further, criminal violations create liabilities and obligations. A restorative justice approach requires that the people most directly affected by the offense come together and decide the appropriate sanction. This is most often done through victim–offender mediation. The process allows the victim to ask the offender questions and express in detail the impact of the crime on her life. The mediation is structured to make the victim, the offender, and society whole again. The three-part focus of restorative justice—offender, victim, and society—distinguishes it from the other justifications for punishment (see Table 11.1 below). Beyond the United States, this criminal justice approach has gained popularity in Canada, England, Scotland, Japan, and Australia.

Applied to the Garrido Case. A private meeting between the Garridos and the victims would have been one possible outcome of a restorative justice approach to the case. A mediated meeting in which Jaycee Dugard, her daughters, her mother, and her father expressed their pain, rage, and disbelief at the Garridos' crimes might have led them to request certain actions by Garrido. For instance, a written apology by Phillip Garrido to the Dugard family or his consent to be interviewed by criminal justice researchers who study sexual predators.

We turn now to *People v. Mooney* (1986), a court case that uses a restorative justice model to determine punishment in a criminal case.

People v. Mooney (1986)
County Court of New York, Genesee County
506 N.Y.S.2d 991

GLENN R. MORTON, J. The defendant was originally indicted for two counts of attempted manslaughter in the first degree arising out of a single criminal transaction involving the shooting of two separate individuals. Incident thereto, the defendant, with the consent of the People, pleaded guilty to two counts of attempted assault in the first degree as lesser included offenses, and the parties stipulated to a mitigation hearing pursuant to (cite omitted) to determine whether sufficient statutory circumstances existed as would permit the imposition of an alternative community-based sentence in lieu of an indeterminate State prison sentence . . .

The public purpose of our penal philosophy is to provide an appropriate response to particular crimes, including consideration of the consequences to the victim and the community, and to ensure public safety through the deterrent influence of the sentence, rehabilitation of the offender and confinement when required in the interest of public protection (cite omitted). As such, the sentencing process requires, on an individual basis, a delicate balance of the numerous factors relating not only to the nature of the crime and the particular circumstances of the offender, but also the four principal objectives of our penal sanctions involving deterrence, rehabilitation, retribution and isolation of the offender where necessary for community safety [case cite omitted].

Essentially, the proof here is uncontroverted that the offense is serious involving the intentional shooting of two people with a .22 caliber semiautomatic rifle in the Village

of LeRoy. The nature of the offense is further aggravated here in that it was committed in a sniper-like fashion using a telescopic sight in which the victims received life threatening injuries. However, the proof reflects that the offense was committed under bizarre circumstances across from a police station with little or no rational motive. The People do not oppose the defendant's application for a community-based sentence, and I find for the following reasons that the mitigating circumstances here are sufficiently unique as to permit the imposition of an alternative local sentence instead of a State prison term.

The Grand Jury minutes reveal that the defendant also shot himself twice in the head and received similar serious injuries. The language of the indictment alleges that both counts were committed under the influence of extreme emotional disturbance . . .

. . . The defendant has no criminal history. At the time of the offense he was barely acquainted with one victim and only casually with the other. There had been no immediate contact between them and, at most, the proof would show a weak motive relating to certain misconceptions the defendant and one victim had over statements made to them by a mutual female acquaintance. The defendant was 18 years old at the time of the offense and had been a chronic abuser of a variety of drugs, mainly alcohol and marihuana, over the past five and one-half years. On the night of the offense, the defendant, with two others, consumed a quart of vodka and one ounce of marihuana during the last four hours; and immediately before, the defendant also consumed two "hits" of LSD. Based thereon, the defendant has no recollection of the actual events, and it does appear that an irrational act was involved.

The proof submitted here fails to reflect that the defendant has any psychotic mental illness and principally suffers from a personality disorder. The documentary exhibits and testimony reveal an all too familiar pattern of emotional problems developing from family and social deprivation, which have been severely aggravated by inordinate alcohol and substance abuse. Following the offense, the defendant has participated in extensive personal, social and drug counseling. The expert proof submitted reflects that the defendant has made positive gains during the pretrial period and has remained drug free since December 3, 1984. Currently the expert proof reveals that the defendant, although a polydrug dependent person, does not constitute a community threat so long as he abstains from all mood altering drugs, including alcohol.

Given the pervasive exposure to criminal activity, the Legislature, commencing in 1984, also has established certain standards for the fair treatment of crime victims, which, inter alia, include that the victim and their families be consulted and their views obtained as to the suitability of sentencing alternatives such as community supervision (cites omitted). The victim impact statement submitted here adds a certain amount of sophistication to the legislative intent and provides some objective criteria for consideration as to the effect of the offense, rather than the usual subjective evaluation of the sentencing court.

Basically it appears that through an intensive type program, contact was made with each victim shortly after the offense, and their active intervention solicited. As a result thereof, the victims agreed on January 14, 1985 to participate in a pretrial diversion program designed to monitor and evaluate the defendant's ongoing treatment for psychological problems and substance abuse for a minimum six-month period.

The victim impact statement includes here a videotape of a victim reconciliation conference conducted on August 17, 1985 approximating four hours in length. Parts one and two consist of a mediated face-to-face confrontation between the defendant and the two immediate victims involved, along with the mother of one victim. Parts three and four consist of an additional confrontation between the same parties, along with other selected representatives of the LeRoy community from law enforcement, the clergy, governmental officials and the citizenry.

The first two parts show, as borne out by the testimony of the victim assistance officer, that both victims, although harboring a great deal of anger as to what happened to them, have from their own life-styles, a large amount of empathy with the defendant's personal plight. A reconciliation was accomplished with one victim during the conference, and he is not opposed to a community-based sentence. The remaining victim continues in a state of reproachment [sic], with strong feelings of anger and revenge. However, it would appear from the probation report that the actual character of the feelings may be adaptive; and at the conference, while supportive of her son, the victim's mother expressed a less hostile attitude and was more receptive to a conciliatory process to eliminate the destructive nature of such feelings to his own future welfare.

Parts three and four relating to the community aspect fail to reveal a discernible sense of outrage; and indicate that a common community understanding exists as to a perceived correlation between the offense and drug abuse. For the most part, those participating were either directly or indirectly involved as a result of the offense in a small cohesive community, and are representative of the attitudes in the immediate area.

The victim impact statement also contains what purports to be a survey of the sentencing attitudes of some 31 other county residents based on a written poll containing a synopsis of the offense and available alternatives. The results would reflect of the 25 persons responding, 23 considered a local community-based sentence appropriate under similar circumstances. No proof as to the particular methodology utilized has been submitted in connection therewith which would permit this court to fairly access whether the survey constituted a representative sample of the extended community. However, considering that it coincides with the prosecutorial discretion exercised here, and is consistent with the narration of the events described by the proof, I find that it does represent a valid expression of community concern.

Considering such, together with the defendant's remorseful attitude, it appears that little purpose would be served here by extended confinement in a State prison for either rehabilitation purposes or to isolate the defendant from the community. Given the described circumstances and the availability of the intensive probation supervision program from the presentence report to closely monitor the defendant, these purposes would be more appropriately served by a community-type sentence. There does remain for consideration whether, for deterrence or retribution purposes, a State prison sentence is warranted. Experience in this area has established that lengthy incarceration is not cost effective to serve these specific purposes where community protection is not a controlling factor. As developed

(Continued)

(Continued)

at the two victim reconciliation conferences, the community is supportive and, in the final analysis, no amount of punishment as a practical matter could adequately undo the harm to the actual victims. Significantly, at the community portion of the conference, an expression was made that a more realistic deterrent would be achieved if the defendant served as a living example as to the dangers of drug abuse through an education process. Accordingly, it is determined here that society would be better served by a community-based sentence with more limited incarceration on the defendant's consent to perform 600 hours of community service designed to educate the public to the problems associated through drug abuse. . . .

Questions

1. The victim impact statement included information about some county members' attitudes toward sentencing. What is the court's response to this information?

2. In determining the appropriate sentence, what is the court most concerned with—the victim, the offender, or the community?

3. Does the court's decision meet the aims of restorative justice? How?

Table 11.1 offers a summary of five approaches to punishment discussed above. It includes the central focus and goal for each one and the sanctions Phillip Garrido might have received under each of these punishment schemes. Further, the table lists the five main justifications for criminal punishment: deterrence, rehabilitation, incapacitation, retribution, and restorative justice. The first column describes the key components and focal point for each rationale (criminal, victim, or society). The second column provides a practical application of each justification to the Garrido case, discussed throughout the chapter. As indicated, the rationale for punishment determines the punishments that are available for a particular offense.

Table 11.1 **Rationales for Punishment**

	Description	Applied to the Garrido case
General Deterrence	Focus: Society Goal: Send message to general public that if they commit crime, they will face criminal sanctions.	Lengthy incarceration
Specific Deterrence	Focus: Offender Goal: Punish repeat offender for additional criminal actions; deter him from further crime; send message to other repeat offenders.	Lengthy incarceration
Rehabilitation	Focus: Offender Goal: Provide offender with treatment	Incarceration; Psychological counseling
Incapacitation	Focus: Society & Offender Goal: Protect society from offender	Lengthy incarceration
Retribution	Focus: Offender & Society Goal: Punish wrongdoer	Lengthy incarceration; Chemical castration
Restorative Justice	Focus: Offender, Victim, & Society Goal: Victim healing, offender takes responsibility for harm and social repair	Lengthy incarceration; Offender apology to victim

Types of Punishment

A criminal conviction can trigger a wide range of punishments, including a fine, house arrest, banishment, deportation, community service, jail time, or prison time. An offender may receive multiple punishments for a single offense (e.g., fine, community service, and probation). Punishment is determined by numerous factors, including the type of crime (e.g., misdemeanor or felony), the applicable law (state or federal), the age of the victim (minor or adult), age of the offender, the offender's status (citizen or noncitizen), and the offender's criminal history (first time or repeat offender). Based on these variables, an offender could receive anything from a low-level fine to a sentence of death.

The prosecutor (or U.S. attorney in a federal case) has charging authority. The prosecutor decides whether to file criminal charges and if charges are appropriate, which charges to file. This decision impacts the potential punishments an offender may face if there is a conviction. Below are the main sanctions that criminal offenders face. As noted, an offender may receive a combination of sanctions. For instance, following Phillip Garrido's guilty plea, he was assessed a fine of $560 (court security), ordered to pay restitution in the amount of $76,937 (to the Victim Compensation Fund), and he was sentenced to 431 years behind bars.

Fines

An offender may be required to pay a fee for violating a criminal statute or municipal ordinance. The amount of the fine depends upon the offense. Fines associated with felonies are typically greater than those assigned to misdemeanors or municipal code infractions. A fine may be the only sanction for an offense. It is common in misdemeanor cases for a fine to be imposed in conjunction with other types of punishment. For instance, under the Oklahoma misdemeanor statute that punishes animal cruelty, a person found guilty could face a maximum five hundred dollar fine and one year behind bars. In Oklahoma, the money the state receives from criminal fines is placed in the state treasury and may be distributed to school funds in the county of the crime.[6]

Restitution

The goal of restitution is to make the victim whole again. The offender makes payments to compensate the victim for the costs associated with the crime. For instance, a burglar who stole a laptop from someone's home could be required to pay the victim restitution in the amount it would cost to replace the laptop. Under Idaho law, for instance, an offender is required to pay restitution for economic loss. This includes the value of any property taken, broken, destroyed or otherwise harmed; lost wages; and out-of-pocket costs (e.g., medical expenses).[7] Restitution differs from a fine because it is directly tied to the victim's loss.

Correctional Supervision

In 2012, it is estimated that there were approximately seven million people under correctional supervision in the United States. This figure includes people in prison, in jail, on probation, and on parole. As shown in Table 11.2, probation represents the largest category of people under correctional supervision. The next largest group is prison, followed by parole, and jail. One in thirty-five adults in the United States is under the supervision of the criminal justice system. In 2011, Blacks were 38 percent of the prison and jail population, Whites were 35 percent, and Hispanics were 21 percent.[8] These figures are underscored by the findings on the lifetime chances of going to prison by race. It is 3.4 percent for Whites, 18.6 percent for Blacks, and 10 percent for Hispanics.[9]

Table 11.2 **Persons Under Correctional Supervision in the United States, 2012**

	Total Number	Percentage Overall
Probation	3,942,800	57%
Prison	1,483,900	21%
Parole	851,200	12%
Jail	744,500	11%
Total	7,022,400	100%

Source: Lauren Glaze and Erinn Herberman "Correctional Populations in the United States, 2012," Table 2, NCJ 243936 (Washington, DC: Department of Justice, 2013).

Notably, the United States has the highest incarceration rate in the world. In the United States, there are approximately 760 prisoners per 100,000 citizens. By way of comparison, the rate for Britain is 153; South Korea, 97; France, 96; Germany, 90; and Japan, 63 per 100,000 citizens.[10]

Probation and Parole. Probation is both a stand-alone sanction and one that may be included with other punishments. Probation is the most frequently used correctional sanction. When people receive a sentence of probation, it means they have been found guilty of a crime and are subject to court supervision. As long as they do not violate the terms of their probation, they remain free from confinement. Typically, the judge will sentence the defendant to a term of imprisonment, but suspend the sentence and place him on probation for a period of years. The defendant usually has to comply with certain conditions, such as staying in school, reporting to a probation officer, or undergoing periodic drug testing. As long as the defendant complies with these conditions, he will not have to serve the sentence. However, if he violates any of the conditions, his probation may be revoked and he may be ordered to serve part or all of the sentence.

For instance, in 2007, following a conviction for driving under the influence and reckless driving, Lindsay Lohan was sentenced to three years of probation. She was also required to complete a drug rehabilitation program, an eighteen-month alcohol education program, and ten days of community service. When Lohan violated the conditions of probation, the judge sentenced her to ninety days in jail. Probation may also be added at the end of a prison sentence. For instance, in a case involving a conviction for second degree manslaughter and burglary, the offender could be sentenced to a fifteen-year prison term for manslaughter, followed by a ten-year probationary term for burglary. This is sometimes referred to as a "split sentence."

In contrast to probation, parole is not a separate sentence. It follows a prison sentence. Once an offender is released from prison, he or she is on parole. In some instances, parole refers to an early release from prison. It may be granted by a state board for good behavior during incarceration. Many states have truth-in-sentencing laws, which require that prisoners serve a minimum percentage of their sentence before they are eligible for an early release (e.g., 85 percent). Parole comes with a list of conditions, which if violated may result in the parolee's return to prison. In West Virginia, for instance, parolees are required to do the following: obtain employment, stay within a specific geographical area, submit to searches (house or person) at any time by a parole officer, and pay a forty dollar monthly supervision fee. Parolees may not possess firearms or weapons, cannot enter drinking establishments, and cannot use drugs or alcohol.[11] Under the federal system there is "supervised release," not parole. A person who has been convicted of violating a federal law must serve at least 85 percent of their sentence.

Jails and Prisons. Jails, run by cities and counties, hold three categories of inmates. In the first category are people who have been arrested and must wait to appear before a judge to have the criminal charges read to them. Unless they are able to secure a release, for instance, on their own recognizance, they must remain in jail until the hearing (pre-arraignment). In the second category are people in jail until their case is decided (by a judge or jury). These are people who have already gone before a judge who has read the criminal charges against them. They remain in jail because they are unable to post bail. If they are found guilty at trial (or plead guilty), they will return to jail until the sentencing hearing (post-arraignment). In the third category are those people who are serving a sentence in jail. Offenders convicted of misdemeanor offenses serve out their sentences in jail. As a general rule, these are sentences of one year or less.[12] As prisons reach and exceed peak capacities, some states have considered measures that would allow low-level felony offenders to serve their time in jails.

Prisons are state or federal facilities that hold people who have been convicted of crimes. A prison sentence is distinct from a jail sentence in two ways—it requires a felony conviction and one year or more behind bars. Prisons vary in security level. The level is

Louisiana State Penitentiary ("Angola"), the largest maximum security prison in the United States.

Patrick Semansky

determined by the type of offender housed at the prison facility. Maximum security prisons represent the highest, most tightly secured correctional facilities. The Louisiana State Penitentiary is the largest maximum security prison in the United States. It is known as "Angola," a reference to the city where it is located. It has over six thousand inmates, including more than eighty inmates on death row.

Alternative Sanctions. Judges have many sentencing options besides incarceration. House arrest is one alternative. This sanction is typically combined with an electronic ankle bracelet, which is used to monitor the offender's movements. House arrest can also be used prior to a conviction when the defendant is considered a flight risk—a person who might not attend future court hearings. When Dominique Strauss-Kahn, then head of the International Monetary Fund, was charged with the rape of a hotel maid, he was placed under house arrest (charges were later dropped). Other choices, beyond fines and restitution (discussed earlier), include community service, drug testing, mediation, counseling, work programs, alternative education programs, residential programs, and intensive community supervision. These sanctions are also standard conditions of probation.

Next we consider two additional punishments, public shaming and banishment. Though they are rarely imposed, these punishments are noteworthy because they revive historical forms of community sanctions.

Public Shaming. Punishment that is intended to cause embarrassment to the offender is known as public shaming. Shaming sanctions are typically imposed in low-level criminal cases. Shaming sanctions are controversial. Here are a few examples, based upon actual cases:

- Requiring a thief to hold up a sign at a busy intersection that reads, "I steal."
- Requiring someone convicted of larceny to wear a shirt that says, "I am on probation for theft."
- Requiring someone convicted of drunk driving to display a bumper sticker that reads, "Convicted of DUI."
- Requiring male prison inmates to wear pink boxer shorts.

Advocates believe that shaming is an important expression of social norms. Further, they believe shaming is a valuable punishment tool because it may deter offenders and others from future crime. In some instances, judges impose shaming sanctions to avoid the costs of sending an offender to prison. The empirical research, however, does not support the claim shaming deters crime. An alternative approach is that shaming sanctions should reintegrate rather than humiliate offenders. Some researchers, including John Braithwaite, argue for "reintegrative shaming." This process involves having family and friends of the offender confront him or her about the harms that resulted from his or her actions. Offenders are less likely to reoffend when they are aware of the specific harms their actions have caused their friends and relatives. As discussed earlier, this is a restorative justice approach to punishment. Some believe that because public shaming encourages us to view some offenses and offenders as shameful, it violates human dignity.[13]

Banishment. The requirement that an offender be forced to move from a particular geographical area as punishment for his or her offense has historic roots. Banishment was viewed as a kind of community justice and form of community protection when an offender's actions were seen as a threat to the community's ability to function as usual. Today, only a handful of states allow for banishment, either as an alternative to incarceration or as part of a sentence of probation. This sanction is used as a key tool in the punishment of sex offenders—including limits on where they can work and live. Generally speaking, banishment requires an offender to leave a town, city, or county for an established period of time. During the banishment term, he or she may not return to the area. In Georgia, an offender who violates his or her probation may be forced to move to another county. *Terry v. Hamrick* (2008), a Georgia case, offers a contemporary look at banishment as a criminal sanction.

Terry v. Hamrick (2008)
Georgia Supreme Court
284 Ga. 24

In 1994, [Gregory Mac] Terry was indicted by a Douglas County grand jury on charges of aggravated stalking, kidnapping with bodily injury, aggravated assault, reckless driving, attempting to elude a police officer, passing within 200 feet of oncoming traffic, driving with a suspended license, and criminal trespass. On August 10, 1995, Terry pled guilty to all charges but kidnapping with bodily injury, and was sentenced to serve a total of 30 years, with 20 in custody; an order of nolle prosequi was entered on the charge of kidnapping with bodily injury. In 2006, Terry filed a petition for a writ of habeas corpus, asserting that his guilty plea was not knowingly and voluntarily entered, trial counsel was ineffective, the trial court was biased against him, and that his sentence was unconstitutional in that the trial court included the condition that during the duration of probation and parole, Terry would be banished from all counties in Georgia except Toombs County . . .

. . .

Although Terry asserts that there is no logical relationship between the limitation that he remain in Toombs County during his probation and the rehabilitative scheme, the habeas court found otherwise. As the habeas court noted in its order, the trial court imposed the condition because of "the trial court's concern with the Petitioner's continued obsession with his ex-wife." And, there was more than ample basis for the trial court to have such concern. To commit his crimes, Terry violated a protective order regarding his ex-wife, and entered her home to await her arrival; he was psychologically evaluated as obsessed with her; he was "fixated on winning his family back"; and he was contemplating suicide at the time he committed the crimes, which included placing his ex-wife under his control.

At his plea hearing, Terry admitted that he threatened to stab his ex-wife with scissors, and then to use them to kill himself, expressed his jealousy about his ex-wife's supposed affair with her employer, and said that before the police chased him, he was going to go confront the employer; he also professed that he "still love[d] her today." Terry also expressed the desire that upon release, he hoped to regain some visitation with his children, despite the statement of his oldest son that he had written to Terry and asked him to stop writing to him; Terry continued to write his son, despite the request to cease. In announcing its sentence, the trial court noted that it was particularly concerned that the incident could have resulted in a murder/suicide, and that a letter from Terry to his ex-wife referred to "when I'm released, even if it's after a hundred years." The trial court found that for years Terry had followed a violent course of conduct toward his ex-wife, that he remained obsessed with her, and that she needed to be protected from that obsession.

The record clearly authorized the trial court to conclude that Terry had demonstrated a propensity for violence toward the victim that fully justified the court's concern for her safety, even after Terry's release from incarceration. . . . The trial court has broad discretion in fashioning probation conditions. The rehabilitative scheme devised promoted the victim's protection; it was Terry whose movements had to be curtailed, not hers, and a scheme that allowed her to move freely about most of the state without fear of Terry was appropriate. The requirement that Terry remain in Toombs County is properly protective of the victim, and logically related to the rehabilitative scheme. Terry contends that the trial court could have fashioned probation conditions leaving him more freedom, and notes that the trial court has

(Continued)

(Continued)

"the ability to protect the victim with appropriate orders of restraint." However, the very facts of this case show the inefficacy of such orders as applied to Terry; a restraining order was in place when he committed his crimes. Also, the habeas court determined that the ten-year period of time during which the banishment provision was effective was not unreasonable, and, given the evidence of Terry's obsession with his ex-wife, this was not error. . . .

Questions

1. What is the holding in the case?

2. Which justification for punishment does the Georgia Supreme Court use to justify banishment?

3. Is banishment an appropriate punishment? If so, for which crimes?

This section has reviewed the various punishments that may apply to people who have been convicted of a crime. The next part discusses some of the main issues related to prisoners' rights—during and post incarceration.

Prisoners' Rights

Once they are placed behind prison walls, the convicted lose the bulk of their constitutional freedoms. However, they do not lose all of them. The Eighth Amendment mandates that living conditions for prisoners must be humane and habitable. In *Brown v. Plata* (2011),[14] the U.S. Supreme Court found there was gross overcrowding in California's correctional institutions. Some facilities were operating at almost twice their intended capacity. In the majority opinion Justice Anthony Kennedy states,

> As a consequence of their own actions, prisoners may be deprived of rights that are fundamental to liberty. Yet the law and the Constitution demand recognition of certain other rights. Prisoners retain the essence of human dignity inherent in all persons. Respect for that dignity animates the Eighth Amendment prohibition against cruel and unusual punishment. "The basic concept underlying the Eighth Amendment is nothing less than the dignity of man."[15]

Post-Conviction Punishment

Jeremy Travis, the former head of the National Institute of Justice, makes the provocative argument that the end of a criminal sentence is the beginning of a large, ongoing set of what he labels invisible punishments. According to Travis, these punishments make it impossible for people who were incarcerated to reintegrate back into society. His argument is detailed in the excerpt below.

"Invisible Punishment: An Instrument of Social Exclusion" by Jeremy Travis[16]

Prisons have this virtue: They are visible embodiments of society's decision to punish criminals. As we punish more people, the number of prisons increases. We can count how many people are in prison, measure the length of the sentences they serve, determine what we spend to keep them there, and conduct empirically grounded analysis of the costs and benefits of incarceration.

Not all criminal sanctions are as visible as prisons: We punish people in other less tangible ways . . .

This [essay] focuses on a criminal sanction that is nearly invisible: namely, the punishment that is accomplished through the diminution of the rights and privileges of citizenship and legal residency in the United States . . . Because these laws operate largely beyond public view, yet have very serious, adverse consequences for the individuals affected, I refer to them, collectively as 'invisible punishment.'

. . . [T]hese punishments should be brought into open view. They should be recognized as visible players in the sentencing drama played out in courtrooms every day, with judges informing defendants that these consequences flow from a finding of guilt or a plea of guilty . . .

The idea that convicted offenders should be denied certain rights and benefits of citizenship is certainly not new . . .

What is new at the beginning of the twenty-first century is the expansive reach of these forms of punishment . . . After a thirty-year period when these indirect forms of punishment were strongly criticized by legal reformers and restricted by state legislatures, they experienced a surge in popularity beginning in the mid-1980s. And because of the significant increase in arrests and criminal convictions, they simply apply to more people. More than 47 million Americans (or a quarter of the adult population) have criminal records on file with federal or state criminal justice agencies. The proportion of felony convictions among African-American adult males is even higher. Invisible punishments reach deep into American life.

The new wave of invisible punishments . . . chip away at critical ingredients of the support systems of poor people in this country. Under these new laws, offenders can be denied public housing, welfare benefits, the mobility necessary to access jobs that require driving, child support, parental rights, the ability to obtain an education, and in the case of deportation, access to the opportunities that brought immigrants to this country . . .

Why have our policy makers embraced this category of punishment in addition to building more prisons and expanding the reach of criminal justice supervision? . . . When we consider the expanded reach of the network of invisible punishment, we detect a social impulse distinct from the robust retributivism that has fueled harsher sentencing policies over the past twenty-five years. When sex offenders are subjected to lifetime parole supervision, drug offenders are denied student loans, families are removed from public housing, and legal immigrants with decades-old convictions are deported from this country, all without judicial review, even the harshest variants of just deserts theories cannot accommodate these outcomes.

In this brave new world, punishment for the original offense is no longer enough; one's debt to society is never paid. Some . . . refer to this form of punishment as "internal exile."

. . . Congress created a web of collateral sanctions that transformed a conviction for certain state crimes into ineligibility for federal benefits. Furthermore, it used the power of the federal purse to encourage states to extend the reach of collateral sanctions. [T]he laws enacted during [the] resurgence of collateral sanctions construct substantial barriers to participation in American society . . .

Congress also enacted legislation to cut offenders off from the remnants of the welfare state. One provision of that law requires that states permanently bar individuals with drug-related felony convictions from receiving federally funded public assistance and food stamps during their lifetime . . . [I]ndividuals who violate their probation or parole conditions are "temporarily" ineligible for Temporary Assistance to Needy Families (TANF), food stamps or Social Security Income benefits, and public housing.

Congress also authorized the exclusion of certain offenders from federally supported public housing. Statutes enacted in the late 1990s permit public housing agencies and providers of Section 8 housing to deny housing to individuals who have engaged in "any drug related or violent criminal activity or other criminal activity which would adversely affect the health, safety, or right to peaceful enjoyment of the premise [by others]." For those convicted of drug crimes, they can reapply for housing after a three-year waiting period, and must show they have been rehabilitated . . .

Congress cut offenders off from other benefits as well. The Higher Education Act of 1998 suspends the eligibility for a student loan or other assistance for someone convicted of a drug-related offense. In the 2000-2001 academic year, about 9,000 students were found to be ineligible under this provision. The Adoption and Safe Families Act of 1997 . . . accelerates the termination of parental rights for children who have been in foster care for fifteen of the most recent twenty-two months.

. . .

(Continued)

(Continued)

This wave of restrictions creates a formidable set of obstacles to former offenders who want to gain a foothold in modern society. Not only is it harder to find work, drive to work, and get an education, it is harder to exercise the individual autonomy that is taken for granted by others in society[.] In the modern welfare state, these restrictions of the universe of social and welfare rights amount to a variant on the tradition of "civil death" in which the offender is defined as unworthy of the benefits of society, and is excluded from the social compact.

Question

1. More than 90 percent of all criminal cases are resolved by plea bargain. Should there be a requirement that before a person enters a guilty plea he must be informed about invisible punishments? Why or why not?

Sentencing

Determinate and Indeterminate Sentencing

There are two types of sentencing systems, determinate sentencing and indeterminate sentencing. In a determinate sentencing structure, courts are bound by a strict set of guidelines that operate at the front end of the sentencing process. The guidelines are designed to create uniformity in sentences by limiting the amount of discretion judges have in assigning sentences. For instance, many jurisdictions have passed truth-in-sentencing laws. As noted above, these laws mandate that offenders serve a legislatively mandated percentage of their sentence (e.g., 85 percent) before they are eligible for early release. The use of sentencing guidelines and the end of discretionary parole are also features of a determinate sentencing scheme. In a determinate system, the judge also considers the presentence report and his or her own observations of the defendant during the court proceedings.

By contrast, an indeterminate sentencing system utilizes a variety of factors to determine when an offender's sentence is complete. Most notably, an indeterminate system views criminal sentencing as a process—not a final decision that is made before the offender begins to serve his or her sentence. In this scheme, the offender is subject to continuing evaluations and assessments by the judicial system. Assessments may include presentence reports, victim impact statements, behavior records kept by correctional staff, and evaluations by the parole board.

There is a long-standing debate about the value and impact of these two sentencing frameworks. Some commentators argue that determinate sentencing works best because it reduces discretion by judges and parole boards. They also argue that it will reduce crime because it sends a message to would-be offenders about the punishment they will face if they commit crime. Determinate sentencing systems emphasize the front-end of the justice system (legislation).

Supporters of indeterminate sentencing argue that it is preferable because it allows input from the criminal justice officials who have direct contact with offenders. These officials, who sometimes participate at the back-end of the system—e.g., probation and parole officers—are in the best position to determine when an offender should be released back into society. This structure encourages judges and other justice system officers to work within the system to impose just and uniform sentences.[17] By design, indeterminate sentencing supports a rehabilitative model of criminal justice. States vary as to how they approach sentencing. Approximately one-half employ determinate sentencing and the other-half use indeterminate sentencing.

Sentencing Guidelines

Sentencing guidelines, passed by state legislatures and Congress, identify the many factors that are part of the sentencing calculus. Each jurisdiction has its own guidelines. For instance, Florida uses its Criminal Punishment Code to determine sentences for all felonies (except capital felonies). The code includes a score sheet, which is prepared by a state attorney, reviewed by defense counsel, and signed by the judge. The scoring process involves a complex set of factors. Foremost is the crime itself. Under the punishment code, offenses are graded by degree from one to three. Then they are assigned a level of offense seriousness, from one to ten. Table 11.3 offers some examples:

Table 11.3 Florida Criminal Punishment Code, Offenses and Level of Offense Seriousness

Low Level (3rd degree)		Mid Level (2nd degree)		Upper Level (1st degree)	
Tampering with lottery ticket	[1]	Tampering with bid	[7]	Homicide	[10]
Bigamy	[1]	Lewd exhibition, by adult	[5]	Aggravated white collar crime	[9]
Rely on prostitute's earnings	[3]	Insurance fraud ($20,000 to $50,000)	[5]	Aircraft piracy	[8]
Forgery	[2]	Abuse of dead body	[7]	Robbery with weapon	[8]
Felony BUI*	[3]	Retail theft over $3,000	[6]	Treason against state	[10]

Source: Florida Dept. of Corrections & Office of the State Courts Administration.
*BUI—Boating Under the Influence.

An offender's punishment score rises with the severity of the crime. Other factors may aggravate or mitigate the punishment tally. Under the Criminal Punishment Code, factors that aggravate a sentence include whether the offender has a prior record, whether a firearm was used, and the nature of the victim's injury. In some cases, judges conclude that the sentenced mandated by the code is not appropriate in a particular case. In this instance, the code permits a judge to depart from the guidelines and impose a less severe sentence. Various reasons may be used to justify a departure in Florida, including the fact that an offender entered a plea bargain, was under duress at the time of the crime, has shown remorse, had a minor role in the crime, or was a youthful offender at the time of the offense.

Some states mandate racial impact statements. These statements, modeled after environmental and fiscal impact statements, are utilized during the legislative process to identify how the law would impact racial disparity. In 2008, Iowa became the first state to require racial impact statements. At the time, it had the nation's highest rate of racial disparities in prison population (13:1 Black to White ratio).

A judge may also consider a victim impact statement. This is a statement read at the sentencing hearing by a crime victim. The victim impact statement allows crime victims to express their opinion about the crime, the offender, and tell the court what sentence the offender should receive. Here is the statement read by Terry Probyn, Jaycee Dugard's mother, at the sentencing hearing for Phillip and Nancy Garrido:

I am Terry Probyn, and my oldest daughter is Jaycee Lee Dugard. On May 3rd, 1980, at 10:52 at night, Jaycee was born, my precious little baby daughter: healthy and happy to be here, a true miracle and certainly a gift from God . . . And then, on June, 10th, 1991, my world went dark. My sunshine was taken away. I asked God, 'What did I do wrong? Why am I being punished? How could anyone with a heart or a conscience or a soul for that matter, take an innocent child away from its mother? How could someone take away the one person in this world that I loved so deeply? Where is she? Is she cold, is she hungry, is she hurt?" . . .

I could hear her crying, not with my ears but with my heart. I could feel her pain, not with my body but again with my heart, completely unbearable and debilitating. For eighteen excruciating years, I endured a huge gaping hole in my heart that some evil being had put their hand into and had ripped out. For eighteen agonizing years, I guarded what little I had left and lived in hell on this earth . . .

It was you, Nancy Garrido, and you, Phillip Garrido, that broke my heart. You took something that didn't belong to you. You hurt my baby . . .

I hate you both for the torment and anguish you put my daughter, myself, and my family through. I am nauseous at the thought of the sexual exploitation and the brutal abuse she endured at your uncaring hand. I am sickened by the reality that she had to suffer your cruel and heartless imprisonment for so long. You are the epitome of disgust, and no amount of jail time or even death will cleanse your corrupt souls. You do not deserve to live or die or even exist.

I am expecting that all I have to say today will fall on deaf ears, but this testimony is not for you. It is for me. It is for every mother and father out there that have experienced my pain. It is for every child and their siblings that have suffered at the hands of a predator. It is for those here today. My nightmare has finally ended, thank God. But my battle against abduction has just begun, and I plan to win just as I've done here today.[18]

Federal Sentencing Guidelines

The federal sentencing guidelines have been a point of contention for many years. Opponents believe they are harsh and deny judges the ability to use their discretion and legal expertise to determine the appropriate sentence in a particular case. Like the Florida guidelines discussed above, the federal sentencing guidelines assign a certain number of points to various factors. Prior to 2005, it was believed that judges had to impose the sentences set forth in the guidelines. However, in 2005, in *U.S. v. Booker* (2005),[19] the Supreme Court held that the federal sentencing guidelines are advisory only, not mandatory. In a later case, *Kimbrough v. U.S.* (2007),[20] the Supreme Court reiterated that the guidelines are "effectively advisory" and "now serve as one factor among several courts must consider in determining an appropriate sentence." Further, the courts are to impose a sentence that is "sufficient but not greater than necessary" to achieve sentencing goals. Derrick Kimbrough had been charged with conspiracy to distribute cocaine and possession with intent to distribute cocaine (powder and crack). The court upheld the lower court's decision to impose a sentence that was four and one-half years less than the minimum required by the guidelines.

Mandatory Minimums

Mandatory minimum sentences require that judges operate within the boundaries of legislatively determined sentencing ranges. As the name indicates, mandatory minimums dictate a base sentence that must be imposed by the judge if the offender is found guilty. The judge has no discretion to sentence the defendant to less time than mandated by the law, even if she believes that a lower sentence would be fair under the circumstances. Mandatory minimums exist at both the federal and state levels. They are different from sentencing guidelines in at least one important way—judges are not permitted to issue a departure from mandatory minimum sentence. In response to this limitation, many people argue that mandatory minimums place an unfair bar on judicial discretion. The concern is that they result in a kind of rough justice—where less serious offenses receive sanctions that should be reserved for more serious crimes.

The harshness of mandatory minimums is highlighted by the Kemba Smith case. Smith was a college sophomore when she became romantically involved with Peter Hall, known around campus for wearing flashy clothes and driving fancy cars. Early on in the relationship, Smith was unaware that Hall was a well-known and longtime drug dealer—who ran a four million dollar crack cocaine ring. Over time, their relationship became physically and emotionally abusive. Smith became aware of Hall's activities and tried unsuccessfully to leave him. At Hall's insistence, Smith became involved in his drug ring as a mule and gofer. In 1994, Smith, who was seven months pregnant, pled guilty to three federal crimes: participating in a drug trafficking conspiracy, money laundering, and making false statements to Federal Bureau of Investigation (FBI) officials. Smith, a first time offender, was sentenced to the mandatory minimum, 294 months in prison. The case caused an international stir. In 2000, after serving six and one-half years of her sentence, Smith was granted clemency by President Bill Clinton.

Judges have been among the most outspoken critics of mandatory minimums. A few have resigned from their lifetime judicial appointments to protest against the confinements of the mandatory minimums. More than one U.S. Supreme Court Justice has expressed reservations about mandatory minimums. Chief Justice William Rehnquist said they exemplify the law of unintended consequences. Justice Anthony Kennedy labeled them as an "unwise and unjust mechanism for sentencing." Justice Stephen Breyer stated that the mandatory minimums "are fundamentally inconsistent with Congress' simultaneous effort to create a fair, honest, and rational sentencing system."[21]

The Genarlow Wilson case, excerpted below, placed mandatory minimums under the national spotlight. The case brought renewed attention to the question of whether mandatory minimums result in unfair and disproportionate sentences.

Humphrey v. Wilson (2007)
Georgia Supreme Court
282 Ga. 520

In February 2005, [Genarlow] Wilson was found guilty in Douglas County [Georgia] for the aggravated child molestation of T.C. Wilson was seventeen years old at the time of the crime, and the victim was fifteen years old. The sexual act involved the victim willingly performing oral sex on Wilson. At the time of Wilson's trial, the minimum sentence for a

(Continued)

(Continued)

conviction of aggravated child molestation was ten years in prison with no possibility of probation or parole; the maximum sentence was thirty years in prison. The trial court sentenced Wilson to eleven years, ten to serve and one year on probation. In addition to the foregoing punishment, Wilson was also subject to registration as a sex offender. In this regard, under OCGA § 42-1-12, Wilson would be required, before his release from prison, to provide prison officials with, among other things, his new address, his fingerprints, his social security number, his date of birth, and his photograph. Prison officials would have to forward this information to the sheriff of Wilson's intended county of residence, and Wilson, within seventy-two hours of his release, would have to register with that sheriff, and he would be required to update the information each year for the rest of his life. Moreover, upon Wilson's release from prison, information regarding Wilson's residence, his photograph, and his offense would be posted in numerous public places in the county in which he lives and on the internet. Significantly, Wilson could not live or work within 1,000 feet of any child care facility, church, or area where minors congregate.

. . .

[Court's response to Wilson's Eighth Amendment claim]

Under the Eighth Amendment to the United States Constitution and under Art.I, Sec. I, Par. XVII to the Georgia Constitution, a sentence is cruel and unusual if it "is grossly out of proportion to the severity of the crime." Moreover, whether "a particular punishment is cruel and unusual is not a static concept, but instead changes in recognition of the "evolving standards of decency that mark the progress of a maturing society." Legislative enactments are the clearest and best evidence of a society's evolving standard of decency and of how contemporary society views a particular punishment.

In determining whether a sentence set by the legislature is cruel and unusual, this Court has cited with approval Justice Kennedy's concurrence in *Harmelin v. Michigan*. Under Justice Kennedy's concurrence in Harmelin, as further developed in *Ewing v. California*, in order to determine if a sentence is grossly disproportionate, a court must first examine the "gravity of the offense compared to the harshness of the penalty" and determine whether a threshold inference of gross disproportionality is raised. In making this determination, courts must bear in mind the primacy of the legislature in setting punishment and

seek to determine whether the sentence furthers a "legitimate penological goal" considering the offense and the offender in question. If a sentence does not further a legitimate penological goal, it does not "reflect . . . a rational legislative judgment, entitled to deference," and a threshold showing of disproportionality has been made. If this threshold analysis reveals an inference of gross disproportionality, a court must proceed to the second step and determine whether the initial judgment of disproportionality is confirmed by a comparison of the defendant's sentence to sentences imposed for other crimes within the jurisdiction and for the same crime in other jurisdictions.

. . .

Although society has a significant interest in protecting children from premature sexual activity, we must acknowledge that Wilson's crime does not rise to the level of culpability of adults who prey on children and that, for the law to punish Wilson as it would an adult, with the extraordinarily harsh punishment of ten years in prison without the possibility of probation or parole, appears to be grossly disproportionate to his crime. . . .

Authors' Note

While Wilson's case was on appeal to the Georgia Supreme Court, the governor signed a bill that amended the law that Wilson had been charged with violating. Under the new subsections, the sexual conduct Wilson engaged in is a misdemeanor and does not require registration as a sex offender (OCGA Sect 16–65; 42–1–12). The law took effect in July 2006 and was not retroactive.

Questions

1. What is the holding in the case?

2. Which rationale for punishment could be used to justify a mandatory minimum term of ten to thirty years for aggravated child molestation under the facts in the Wilson case?

3. How do you think the court would have decided the case if the victim had been twelve years old at the time of the crime?

The Federal Crack Cocaine Law

On June 17, 1986, college basketball star Len Bias was selected as the National Basketball Association's (NBA) number two draft pick. The University of Maryland standout forward was chosen by the Boston Celtics. On June 19, two days later, Len

Bias was dead. He was found unconscious in his dorm room and later died of cardiac arrhythmia—apparently the result of a drug overdose. It was widely reported that Bias had overdosed on crack cocaine. It was later discovered that Bias had ingested a fatal dose of powder cocaine, not crack cocaine. At the time of his death, there were widespread media reports about the rising crack epidemic. There were searing images of its ravages within America's inner cities, reports about its extraordinary potency, cautionary tales about its powers of addiction and its likelihood to create a generation of "crack babies," and the drug's potential to cause its users to commit random acts of violence.

1986 NBA draft pick Len Bias died from an overdose of powder cocaine.

The Anti-Drug Abuse Act of 1986 was quickly introduced to Congress, and hearings were held. The bill included the provision that later became known as the federal crack cocaine law. During the congressional hearings, arguments were made about the necessity of sentencing crack cocaine users to longer terms than powder cocaine users. Some politicians suggested a twenty to one disparity would be appropriate, others argued for fifty to one. The language in the bill, which allowed for a one hundred to one disparity between crack cocaine and powder cocaine, was overwhelmingly passed in September 1986. Under the federal law, the punishment for possession of five grams of crack cocaine was equal to the punishment for possession of five hundred grams of powder cocaine. As a result, it was labeled the "100:1" federal crack cocaine law. Table 11.4 below highlights this law.

The federal crack cocaine law was on the books for almost twenty-five years. More than seventy-five thousand people were sentenced under the federal crack law.[22] In 2010, in response to decades of criticism from judges and other criminal justice professionals, studies indicating that the law had a disproportionately unfair impact on African Americans, and empirical research that raised doubts about the value of the stiff sentences, the Sentencing Commission reduced the disparity to 18:1. The new law was made retroactive—thus the sentences for the people convicted under the previous law were adjusted downward. Further, in 2012, the Supreme Court held that offenders who committed crack offenses before the new law was passed but who were sentenced after the new law took effect, should be sentenced under the newer, less harsh law.[23] In 2014, the U.S. Senate Judiciary Committee voted in favor of the Smarter Sentencing Act. If passed, the act would reduce and eliminate mandatory minimum sentences in drug cases. Today, several states have laws that punish crack cocaine possession more severely than the possession of powder cocaine.

Table 11.4 Mandatory Minimum for First Time Offense Under Federal Crack Law

	Crack Cocaine	Powder Cocaine
5-year sentence	5 grams	500 grams
10-year sentence	50 grams	5000 grams

Repeat Offender Laws

Consider the following hypothetical:

Westminster robbed a grocery store. He walked into the store and pointed a gun at one of the clerks. He told her to place all the cash in her register into his reusable grocery bag. The clerk put $1,001 in marked bills into the bag. A bank teller notified the authorities when Westminster attempted to deposit some of the marked money into his savings account. Westminster is later arrested and charged with armed robbery.

If Westminster is found guilty of armed robbery, the severity of his punishment will depend upon several factors. If Westminster is in a state where the maximum punishment for armed robbery is seven to ten years in prison, it will fall somewhere within that range. However, if Westminster was previously convicted of a crime, such as passing bad checks or impersonating a police officer, this will impact the length of his sentence. Westminster's term of incarceration would increase under the state's habitual offender statute. These are also known as repeat offender or "two strike" laws. These laws permit the state to impose increased punishment against an offender who has a prior offense history. The rationale for these laws is specific deterrence—to punish and hopefully deter future offending by someone who has previously engaged in crime.

In some instances, repeat offender laws focus on a specific crime, such as drunk driving. Someone convicted of a second and third driving under the influence (DUI) offense might receive a harsher sentence than someone convicted of a first DUI offense. Other repeat offender laws punish an offender for committing a second or third crime. In *Lockyer v. Andrade* (2003),[24] the Supreme Court upheld a fifty-year sentence for an offender charged with stealing $150 in videotapes. Leandro Andrade, who was charged under a California three-strikes law, had previously been convicted of several offenses, including petty theft, transportation of marijuana, and residential burglary. Some federal laws include repeat offender provisions.

Applied to the Garrido Case. Phillip Garrido pled guilty to several crimes, including six counts of engaging in a forcible lewd act upon a child and two counts of forcible rape. California law allows a penalty enhancement of five years for each count of a forcible lewd act upon a child and each count of forcible rape. For these two offenses alone, the court added forty years to Garrido's prison sentence.

Bias Crimes and Penalty Enhancement Statutes

Hate crimes, also known as bias offenses, are punishable under state and federal law. Under many state laws, bias crimes include a penalty enhancement provision. This means the offender may be sentenced to serve additional time because his or her offense was motivated by bias. Penalty enhancement provisions for bias crimes are controversial, and opponents argue that they violate the First Amendment. Not surprisingly, these issues have made their way to the U.S. Supreme Court.

Wisconsin v. Mitchell (1993)

U.S. Supreme Court
508 U.S. 476

CHIEF JUSTICE REHNQUIST delivered the opinion of the Court.

Respondent Todd Mitchell's sentence for aggravated battery was enhanced because he intentionally selected his victim on account of the victim's race. The question presented in this case is whether this penalty enhancement is prohibited by the First and Fourteenth Amendments. We hold that it is not.

On the evening of October 7, 1989, a group of young Black men and boys, including Mitchell, gathered at an apartment complex in Kenosha, Wisconsin. Several members of the group discussed a scene from the motion picture "Mississippi Burning" in which a white man beat a young Black boy who was praying. The group moved outside and Mitchell asked them: "'Do you all feel hyped up to move on some white people?'" Shortly thereafter, a young white boy approached the group on the opposite side of the street where they were standing. As the boy walked by, Mitchell said: "'You all want to fuck somebody up? There goes a White boy; go get him.'" Mitchell counted to three and pointed in the boy's direction. The group ran toward the boy, beat him severely, and stole his tennis shoes. The boy was rendered unconscious and remained in a coma for four days.

After a jury trial in the Circuit Court for Kenosha County, Mitchell was convicted of aggravated battery. Wis. Stat. 939.05 and 940.19(1m) (1989–1990). That offense ordinarily carries a maximum sentence of two years' imprisonment. 940.19(1m) and 939.50(3)(e). But because the jury found that Mitchell had intentionally selected his victim because of the boy's race, the maximum sentence for Mitchell's offense was increased to seven years under 939.645. That provision enhances the maximum penalty for an offense whenever the defendant "[i]ntentionally selects the person against whom the crime . . . is committed . . . because of the race, religion, color, disability, sexual orientation, national origin or ancestry of that person . . . " 939.645(1)(b). The Circuit Court sentenced Mitchell to four years' imprisonment for the aggravated battery.

Mitchell unsuccessfully sought postconviction relief in the Circuit Court. Then he appealed his conviction and sentence, challenging the constitutionality of Wisconsin's penalty-enhancement provision on First Amendment grounds. The Wisconsin Court of Appeals rejected Mitchell's challenge, . . . but the Wisconsin Supreme Court reversed. The Supreme Court held that the statute "violates the First Amendment directly by punishing what the legislature has deemed to be offensive thought." 169 Wis.2d 153, 163, (1992). It rejected the State's contention "that the statute punishes only the 'conduct' of intentional selection of a victim." Id. at 164. According to the court, "[t]he statute punishes the 'because of' aspect of the defendant's selection, the reason the defendant selected the victim, the motive behind the selection." Ibid . . .

The Supreme Court also held that the penalty-enhancement statute was unconstitutionally overbroad. It reasoned that, in order to prove that a defendant intentionally selected his victim because of the victim's protected status, the State would often have to introduce evidence of the defendant's prior speech, such as racial epithets he may have uttered before the commission of the offense. This evidentiary use of protected speech, the court thought, would have a "chilling effect" on those who feared the possibility of prosecution for offenses subject to penalty enhancement. See id. at 174. Finally, the court distinguished antidiscrimination laws, which have long been held constitutional, on the ground that the Wisconsin statute punishes the "subjective mental process" of selecting a victim because of his protected status, whereas antidiscrimination laws prohibit "objective acts of discrimination." Id. at 176.

We granted certiorari because of the importance of the question presented and the existence of a conflict of authority among state high courts on the constitutionality of statutes similar to Wisconsin's penalty-enhancement provision. We reverse.

Mitchell argues that we are bound by the Wisconsin Supreme Court's conclusion that the statute punishes bigoted thought, and not conduct. There is no doubt that we are bound by a state court's construction of a state statute. R. A. V., supra, at 381; *New York v. Ferber*, 458 U.S. 747, 769, n. 24 (1982); *Terminiello v. Chicago*, 337 U.S. 1, 4 (1949). In *Terminiello*, for example, the Illinois courts had defined the term "'breach of the peace,'" in a city ordinance prohibiting disorderly conduct, to include "'stirs the

(Continued)

(Continued)

public to anger . . . or creates a disturbance.'" Id. at 4. We held this construction to be binding on us. But here the Wisconsin Supreme Court did not, strictly speaking, construe the Wisconsin statute in the sense of defining the meaning of a particular statutory word or phrase. Rather, it merely characterized the "practical effect" of the statute for First Amendment purposes. See 169 Wis.2d at 166–167, ("Merely because the statute refers in a literal sense to the intentional 'conduct' of selecting, does not mean the court must turn a blind eye to the intent and practical effect of the law—punishment of motive or thought"). This assessment does not bind us. Once any ambiguities as to the meaning of the statute are resolved, we may form our own judgment as to its operative effect.

The State argues that the statute does not punish bigoted thought, as the Supreme Court of Wisconsin said, but instead punishes only conduct. While this argument is literally correct, it does not dispose of Mitchell's First Amendment challenge. To be sure, our cases reject the "view that an apparently limitless variety of conduct can be labeled 'speech' whenever the person engaging in the conduct intends thereby to express an idea." . . . Thus, a physical assault is not, by any stretch of the imagination, expressive conduct protected by the First Amendment. See *Roberts v. United States Jaycees*, 468 U.S. 609, 628 (1984) ("[V]iolence or other types of potentially expressive activities that produce special harms distinct from their communicative impact . . . are entitled to no constitutional protection"); *NAACP v. Claiborne Hardware Co.*, 458 U.S. 886, 916 (1982) ("The First Amendment does not protect violence").

But the fact remains that, under the Wisconsin statute, the same criminal conduct may be more heavily punished if the victim is selected because of his race or other protected status than if no such motive obtained. Thus, although the statute punishes criminal conduct, it enhances the maximum penalty for conduct motivated by a discriminatory point of view more severely than the same conduct engaged in for some other reason or for no reason at all. Because the only reason for the enhancement is the defendant's discriminatory motive for selecting his victim, Mitchell argues (and the Wisconsin Supreme Court held) that the statute violates the First Amendment by punishing offenders' bigoted beliefs. . . .

. . . [I]t is equally true that a defendant's abstract beliefs, however obnoxious to most people, may not be taken into consideration by a sentencing judge. *Dawson v. Delaware*, 503 U.S. 159 (1992). In Dawson, the State introduced evidence at a capital sentencing hearing that the defendant was a member of a White supremacist prison gang. Because "the evidence proved nothing more than [the defendant's] abstract beliefs," we held that its admission violated the defendant's First Amendment rights. Id. at 167. In so holding, however, we emphasized that "the Constitution does not erect a per se barrier to the admission of evidence concerning one's beliefs and associations at sentencing simply because those beliefs and associations are protected by the First Amendment." Id. at 165. Thus, in *Barclay v. Florida*, 463 U.S. 939 (1983), we allowed the sentencing judge to take into account the defendant's racial animus towards his victim. The evidence in that case showed that the defendant's membership in the Black Liberation Army and desire to provoke a "race war" were related to the murder of a White man for which he was convicted. See id. at 942–944. Because "the elements of racial hatred in [the] murder" were relevant to several aggravating factors, we held that the trial judge permissibly took this evidence into account in sentencing the defendant to death. Id. at 949, and n. 7. . . .

Moreover, the Wisconsin statute singles out for enhancement bias-inspired conduct because this conduct is thought to inflict greater individual and societal harm. For example, according to the State and its amici, bias-motivated crimes are more likely to provoke retaliatory crimes, inflict distinct emotional harms on their victims, and incite community unrest. . . . The State's desire to redress these perceived harms provides an adequate explanation for its penalty-enhancement provision over and above mere disagreement with offenders' beliefs or biases. As Blackstone said long ago, "it is but reasonable that, among crimes of different natures, those should be most severely punished which are the most destructive of the public safety and happiness." 4 W. Blackstone, Commentaries 16.

. . .

The First Amendment, moreover, does not prohibit the evidentiary use of speech to establish the elements of a crime or to prove motive or intent. Evidence of a defendant's previous declarations or statements is commonly admitted in criminal trials subject to evidentiary rules dealing with relevancy, reliability, and the like. Nearly half a century ago, in *Haupt v. United States*, 330 U.S. 631 (1947), we rejected a contention similar to that advanced by Mitchell here. Haupt was tried for the offense of treason, which, as defined by the Constitution (Art. III, 3), may depend very much on proof of motive. To prove that the acts in question were committed out of "adherence to the enemy" rather than "parental solicitude," *id.*at 641, the Government introduced evidence of conversations that had taken place long prior to the indictment, some of which consisted of statements showing Haupt's sympathy with Germany and Hitler and hostility towards the United States. We rejected Haupt's argument that this evidence was improperly admitted. While "[s]uch testimony is to be scrutinized with care to be certain the statements are not expressions of mere lawful and permissible difference of opinion with our own government or quite proper appreciation of the land of birth", we held that "these statements . . . clearly were admissible on the question of intent and adherence to the enemy." Id. at 642. . . .

For the foregoing reasons, we hold that Mitchell's First Amendment rights were not violated by the application of the Wisconsin penalty-enhancement provision in sentencing him. The judgment of the Supreme Court of Wisconsin is therefore reversed, and the case is remanded for further proceedings not inconsistent with this opinion.

It is so ordered.

Questions

1. What is the defendant's argument that he should not have received a four-year sentence for the crime of aggravated battery?

2. What reasons does the court give for upholding laws that allow an offender to receive greater punishment if he singled out his victim on the basis of race?

3. Do penalty enhancement laws support any of the rationales for punishment (discussed earlier in the chapter)? If so, which one(s)?

Capital Punishment

The use of the death penalty as a form of punishment raises many issues. These include whether state-sanctioned death is moral, whether capital punishment deters violent crime, and whether the death penalty should only apply to murder cases. Table 11.5 provides some current death penalty statistics.

In 1972, the Supreme Court struck down Georgia's death penalty statute as unconstitutional under the Eighth Amendment. The court, in a lengthy opinion that included multiple concurring opinions and dissents, found that the Georgia sentencing scheme allowed for arbitrary and discriminatory outcomes. One major consequence of the *Furman v. Georgia* (1972)[25] case was that over six hundred offenders, who were then on death row, had their sentences commuted to life without parole. Another outcome of the landmark decision was that Georgia, as well as legislatures in more than thirty-five other states, revamped their death penalty statutes to meet the capital sentencing requirements outlined by the *Furman* majority. Four years later, in *Gregg v. Georgia* (1976),[26] the Georgia death penalty was challenged again. This time the justices upheld the new Georgia, statute as constitutional. The court based its decision on three components of the statute: its requirement that the jury consider both aggravating and mitigating circumstances before voting for death, the fact that the sentence (life without parole or death) was decided after a determination of guilt (bifurcation), and the implementation of appellate review. It has been more than thirty-five years since the Supreme Court upheld capital punishment as constitutional under the Eighth Amendment. However, there remain a number of constitutional challenges to the death penalty (see Chapter 8 for a detailed discussion of the legal challenges to capital punishment statutes).

Why do we kill people who kill people to show that killing people is wrong?

This expression was popular on bumper stickers and buttons in the 1960s and 1970s.

Table 11.5 **Death Penalty Statistics for 2013**

Number of People on Death Row	3,070
Percentage of Men on Death Row	98%
Percentage of Whites v. Blacks on Death Row	43% v. 42%
Number of Jurisdictions with Capital Punishment	34*
States with Largest Death Row Populations	California (742); Florida (410); Texas (278)
Number of Executions in 2013	39
Total Number of Executions since 1976	1,359
Death Row Exonerations (since 1973)	144 (18 based on DNA evidence)
Methods of Execution	Electrocution; Lethal injection; Gas chamber; Hanging; Firing Squad

Source: **Death Penalty Information Center, "Death Row USA," (New York: NAACP LDF, Winter 2014).**
*This includes the U.S. military and the U.S. government.

Methods of Execution

As highlighted in Table 11.5, states use various methods to carry out capital punishment. The gas chamber, electrocution, and lethal injection are the most common. The gas chamber and electrocution have been challenged as forms of cruel and unusual punishment, in violation of the Eighth Amendment. To avoid this concern, most states with the death penalty use lethal injection as the primary method of execution. Hanging has also been used as a method of death.

In rare cases, a firing squad has been used for an execution. In 1985, Ronnie Lee Gardner was convicted of capital murder for the killing of Michael Burdell, a Utah attorney. Gardner killed Burdell in an attempt to escape from custody at a court hearing (for a previously committed murder). In Utah, death row inmates whose crimes were committed prior to 2004, have a choice between death by lethal injection or by a firing squad. Gardner opted for the firing squad, and in 2010, he was executed by a five-man shooting squad. In 1977, Gary Gilmore was the first person executed after the Supreme Court reinstituted capital punishment in *Gregg v. Georgia* (1976). Gilmore chose to die by a firing squad.

Concluding Note

Society's approach to punishment and sentencing reflects our underlying beliefs about right and wrong. As the above discussion indicates, there is room for debate about which rationales for punishment are best and which approaches to sentencing benefit society as a whole. The issues addressed in this chapter provide additional grounding for the earlier discussions of specific criminal offenses and their elements.Now test yourself on the material we have covered in Chapter 11. Good luck with the Issue Spotter exercise.

IssueSpotter

Read the hypothetical, based on an actual case, and spot the issues discussed in this chapter.

Escape From Punishment?

Aloysius and Millicent Ford were involved in a fraudulent mortgage scheme. In the 1990s, they used their company, Houses R Us, to purchase residential property and sell it at highly inflated prices. As part of their scheme, they gave lenders false information about the buyer's finances and the sources of the down payments. The married pair carried out thirty-five separate fraudulent transactions. This resulted in losses for several lenders—to the tune of more than $650,000.

Eventually, the mortgage scheme fell apart and the Fords declared bankruptcy. They were never charged with any crimes.

The pair stayed on the straight side of the law. Millicent worked as a nurse at a local hospital, and Aloysius worked as a lawn technician and cable installer. They raised their four children and became involved in numerous community activities, including their neighborhood watch association. They both coached sports at their local Boys and Girls Club and YMCA. They did not commit any crimes from 1999 to 2002.

One day before the ten-year statute of limitations would have expired for their crimes, the Fords were charged with one count of wire fraud and two counts of bank fraud. They each pled guilty to one count of wire fraud. Relying on the U.S. Sentencing Guidelines, the federal district court sentenced Millicent to forty-one months in prison and Aloysius to sixty-three months in prison. They were also ordered to repay $650,000 in restitution.[27]

You are the judge. Write a short opinion in which you decide whether to reverse or affirm the decision by the federal district court. Your opinion should address (1) the rationale(s) for criminal punishment that support finding the Fords guilty (and rationale that do not), (2) any relevant constitutional issue(s) related to their sentence and amount of restitution, and (3) whether you believe there should be a departure from the U.S. Sentencing Guidelines.

Key Terms and Cases

Notes ●━━━━━━━━━━━━━━━━━━━━━━━━━━━━━━

1. See, *People v. Garrido,* Case No. P10CRF0364, (Cal. Sup. Ct. El Dorado Cnty.2011), http://www.eldoradocourt.org/garrido/pgdocuments.aspx

2. Cesare Beccaria, *On Crimes and Punishments,* ed. Aaron Thomas and Jeremy Parzen (Toronto: University of Toronto Press, 2008) 26.

3. See Robert Martinson, "What Works?—Questions and Answers About Prison Reform." *The Public Interest* 35 (1974): 22–54; Francis Cullen and Paul Gendreau, "Assessing Correctional Rehabilitation: Policy, Practice, and Prospects," *Criminal Justice* 3(2000): 109-175.

4. See, e.g., Kathleen Auerhahn, "Selective Incapacitation and the Problem of Prediction," *Criminology* 37(1999): 703–734.

5. King James, Leviticus 24:20.

6. See, Oklahoma Stat. 21 §§ 1692, 141 (2014).

7. Idaho Code, §19–5304(1)(a) (1999).

8. Department of Justice, "U.S. Prison Population Declined for Third Consecutive Year During 2012" (Press Release, July 25, 2013).

9. Thomas Bonczar "Prevalence of Imprisonment in the U.S. Population, 1974–2001," Table 9, NCJ 197976 (Washington, DC: Bureau of Justice Statistics, 2003) 8.

10. Fareed Zakaria, "Zakaria: Incarceration nation," March 22, 2012, http://globalpublicsquare.blogs.cnn.com/2012/03/22/zakaria-incarceration-nation

11. West Virginia Division of Corrections, Standard Conditions of Parole, http://www.wvdoc.com/wvdoc/ParoleServicesResources/StandardConditionsofParole/tabid/143/Default.aspx

12. Texas and some other states have created "state jail felonies." These offenses, typically technical violations of probation, may carry a sentence up to two years.

13. See, e.g., Martha Nussbaum, *Hiding from Humanity* (Princeton: Princeton University Press, 2004).

14. *Brown v. Plata*, 563 U.S. ___ ; 131 S.Ct. 1910 (2011).

15. Ibid. at 1928 (citations omitted).

16. Jeremy Travis, "Invisible Punishment: An Instrument of Social Exclusion," in *Invisible Punishment: The Collateral Consequences of Mass Imprisonment*, ed. Marc Mauer and Meda Chesney-Lind (New York: The New Press, 2002) 15–36. [PE: Awaiting cost for permission from The New Press].

17. See, e.g., Dhammika Dharmapala, Nuno Garoupa, and Joanna M. Shepard, "Legislatures, Judges, Parole Boards: The Allocation of Discretion Under Determinate Sentencing" *Florida Law Review* 62 (2009): 1037; William Sabol, Katherine Rosich, Kamala Kane, David Kirk, and Glenn Dubin "Influences of Truth-in-Sentencing Reforms on Changes in States' Sentencing Practices and Prison Populations, Executive Summary," NCJ 195163 (Washington, DC: Urban Institute, U.S. Department of Justice, National Institute of Justice, 2002).

18. See full transcript, Statement of Jaycee Dugard's mother at the Garrido sentencing, June 2, 2011, http://www.mercurynews.com/jaycee-dugard/ci_18192031?nclick_check=1

19. *U.S. v. Booker,* 543 U.S. 220 (2005).

20. *Kimbrough v. U.S.,* 552 U.S. 85 (2007).

21. "Mandatory Sentencing Is Criticized by Justice," March 10, 1994, *New York Times*, http://www.nytimes.com/1994/03/10/us/mandatory-sentencing-is-criticized-by-justice.html; Rachel Barkow, "Institutional Design and the Policing of Prosecutors: Lessons from Administrative Law," *Stanford Law Review* 61 (2009): 869, 872.

22. U.S. Sentencing Commission, "Report to Congress: Cocaine and Federal Sentencing Policy," Fig. 2–1 "Trend in Number of Powder and Cocaine Crack Cocaine Offenders," FY 1992-FY 2006 (Washington, DC: U.S. Sentencing Commission, 2007).

23. *Dorsey v. U.S.,* 132 S.Ct. 2321 (2012), 11–5683; *Hill v. U.S.,* 132 S.Ct. 759 (2012), 11–5721.

24. *Lockyer v. Andrade,* 538 U.S. 63 (2003).

25. *Furman v. Georgia,* 408 U.S. 238 (1972).

26. *Gregg v. Georgia,* 428 U.S. 153 (1976).

27. This hypothetical is based upon *U.S. v Robertson,* 662 F.3d 871 (7th Cir. 2011).

Chapter 12

On March 8, 1971, members of the Citizens' Commission to Investigate the FBI, used a crowbar to break into a FBI office in Media, Pennsylvania. They removed over 1,000 classified documents. Members spent ten days reviewing the documents at another location.

The documents revealed that the FBI was conducting surveillance on numerous civil rights and anti-war organizations. The documents revealed that the government was engage in widespread surveillance of Black student groups on college campuses. They also revealed that the FBI operated a counter-intelligence program—"COINTELPRO." This program was designed to spy on political organizers, civil rights leaders, and others suspected of having ties to the Communist Party. As part of these efforts, the FBI tried to get Dr. Martin Luther King Jr., before he received the Nobel Prize, to commit suicide. They sent Dr. King an anonymous letter with taped evidence of his marital indiscretions, indicating they would expose the evidence unless King killed himself: "King, there is one thing left for you to do. You know what it is."[1]

The Citizens' Commission leaked documents to newspapers, including the *Los Angeles Times*, *New York Times*, and the *Washington Post*, and also to select members of Congress.

The FBI was never able to locate the burglars, and the statute of limitations—the time period within which criminal charges must be filed—elapsed. In 2014, forty-three years after the burglary, some members of the Citizens' Commission identified themselves and told their story. After breaking their silence, some members voiced support for another person who had stolen and released government documents—Edward Snowden.

The Citizens' Commission case raises many of the issues explored in this chapter, including how crimes committed against the state and crimes committed by public officers are defined and the different social harms caused by both types of offenses.

FBI building in Media, Pennsylvania, that was broken into in 1971 by members of the Citizens' Commission to Investigate the FBI.

Smallbones

State-Involved Crimes

Introduction

State-involved crimes are those offenses that involve the government—as either the victim or the offender. There are two broad categories of state-involved crimes. The first group—crimes against the state—involves crimes that are perpetrated against the state. These are crimes that undermine the functioning of the government. Espionage, treason, and terrorism are a few examples. However, this category also includes lower-level offenses, such as perjury, obstruction of justice, and official misconduct. Individuals who engage in actions that intentionally undermine and threaten the government's ability to operate typically encounter stiff criminal penalties. However, actions against the state are not always easy to prove. The country's founders, who had fled an oppressive government regime, desired to both encourage loyalty to the new government and to protect dissent.

The second category consists of crimes that involve public officials. The focus is on offenses that are perpetrated by government representatives against individuals or groups. These offenses involve people who work as state or federal government officials, such as judges, elected officials, and police officers. A police officer who is caught on video beating a homeless man, a police officer who helps a fellow officer cover up an unlawful shooting death, or a state worker who fraudulently diverts millions dollars in funds from individual retirement accounts to her own bank account all fit in this category.

Crimes against the state have not always been included as part of the core of criminal law studies. However, as terrorist incidents have become increasingly prominent—most notably the September 11, 2001, attacks against the United States—the focus on state-based assaults has moved from the margins to the center. The realities of contemporary terrorism have altered the way Americans go about their daily lives. Enhanced security and surveillance in public spaces are commonplace today. The realities of terrorism have also shifted public perceptions about the likelihood of future terrorist assaults in the United States. Today, many Americans fear future attacks.

Bonnie and John Raines, members of the Citizens Commission who broke into the FBI building. Bonnie is holding an FBI drawing done of her in 1971 after the break-in.

Crimes against the government are the primary focus of this chapter. These are offenses designed to disrupt and dismantle government operations. The chapter also examines crimes committed by public officials, how they are defined, how they compare with crimes against the state, and why they are subject to criminal punishment.

Crimes Against the State ●——————

This section examines a range of crimes against the state including-espionage, treason, sedition, terrorism, perjury, obstruction of justice, and bribery. Conviction for some of these offenses, such as espionage and treason, can result in a death sentence. However, the thread that ties these crimes together is that they cause fear and distrust and disrupt essential government functions.

Espionage

Et tu, Brute?

Julius Caesar, *William Shakespeare*

Espionage is the betrayal of one's country. It is a federal crime that is punishable by death. When spying involves a country's political or military secrets, it places lives at risk and threatens the political stability and security of the country. Whether carried out by a high ranking government official or a common man, people who gather classified U.S. secrets and share them with enemy nations can be charged with espionage. The motivation for this crime varies. In some instances, the spying is done for

Ethel and Julius Rosenberg separated by heavy wire screen, following convictions for espionage. Do you think their death sentences were just?

pecuniary gain. In others, it is done to upend a political regime or wreck political havoc. The 1917 Espionage Act was passed during World War I, while Woodrow Wilson was president. President Wilson looked for ways to sanction disloyalty, what some referred to as "warfare by propaganda."[2]

In 1951, Julius and Ethel Rosenberg, who were both members of the Communist Party, were accused of providing secret intelligence about the atomic bomb to the Soviet Union. They were charged with conspiracy under the Federal Espionage Act. The 1917 law was designed to punish actions considered disloyal to the country. The Espionage Act made it unlawful to gather or deliver national defense information that could harm the United States or benefit a foreign nation. The Rosenbergs went to trial, and a jury found them both guilty of conspiracy to commit wartime espionage.

The judge said their crimes were "worse than murder."[3] The penalty for violating the Federal Espionage Act ranged from twenty years imprisonment to death, and the Rosenbergs received the maximum sentence. They were executed in 1952 and were the first U.S. citizens put to death under the Espionage

Act. Their case remains highly controversial. Many believe Ethel Rosenberg was sentenced to death not for her crimes, but for those committed by her husband. Some also believed that the pursuit of the Rosenbergs was partly driven by their Jewish ancestry. Many have argued that their prosecutions were motivated by the couple's involvement in the Communist Party combined with Cold War era fears of Soviet dominance. FBI Director, J. Edgar Hoover, referred to the Rosenbergs' case as the "crime of the century."[4] The Rosenbergs were prosecuted at the height of the hearings held by the House Un-American Activities Committee (HUAC), led by Senator Joe McCarthy. The HUAC investigated and subpoenaed thousands of people—private citizens, public employees, and celebrities—who were alleged to be disloyal citizens because of their ties to Communist organizations.

Wen Ho Lee, former Los Alamos nuclear scientist wrongly accused of espionage.

The prosecution of the Rosenbergs highlights the thin line between protecting national security and protecting the constitutional right to freedom of expression. After World War II, Congress enacted another espionage statute. Today, espionage is punished under several federal statutes. The U.S. Code punishes the gathering and passing of data and information about the U.S. military during wartime. It is also a federal offense to gather defense intelligence to "advantage" a foreign nation or cause injury to the country. Whether the spying takes place during wartime or peacetime, it is punishable by death.[5]

Espionage cases continue to attract national and international headlines. In 1987, Jonathan Pollard was found guilty of selling classified information to Israel. Pollard, an American Naval Intelligence analyst, was sentenced to life in prison for espionage. In another case, Aldrich Ames, once head of the Central Intelligence Agency's (CIA) Soviet Counterintelligence Division, was convicted of espionage. Ames's 1994 conviction was based on a finding that he had shared information on covert operations with Russia. This included intelligence about U.S. listening devices that were installed near Moscow's space facility. Ames also gave details about a newly developed device that could count Soviet nuclear warheads. He received more than $2.7 million for selling U.S. secrets. Ames later confessed that his motives for spying were "personal, banal, and amounted . . . to greed and folly."[6] He is currently serving a life sentence. More recently, Robert Hanssen, who was a top-ranked FBI counterintelligence officer, was convicted of espionage and conspiracy. In 2002, he was sentenced to life imprisonment for selling classified U.S. national security data to Russia and the former Soviet Union.

A person may be wrongly accused of spying against the state, as the case of Wen Ho Lee illustrates. Dr. Lee, a Taiwanese-born physicist, worked at the Los Alamos National Laboratory, in California. In 1999, allegations of espionage surfaced against Dr. Lee. It was widely reported that he had supplied the Chinese government with secret information about the U.S. arsenal. The case made international headlines. Dr. Lee was indicted on fifty-nine counts under the Federal Espionage Act and the Federal Atomic Energy Act. He spent nearly one year in solitary confinement prior to any finding of guilt by a court. Dr. Lee pled guilty to one count of improper downloading of secure files. Prior to his release from prison, the judge apologized to Dr. Lee for the treatment he received by the court system.[7]

U.S. v. Edward Snowden

Some cases prompt a serious consideration of where to draw the line between actions that constitute an offense against the government and actions that are in

The United States filing of criminal charges against Edward Snowden. Should Snowden be prosecuted for these offenses?

the public interest. An example is the Citizens' Commission case discussed at the beginning of this chapter. The Citizens' Committee's burglary of an FBI office and their theft of over one thousand documents were violations of the criminal law. Many people believed that the perpetrators should face stiff penalties for their antigovernment activities. However, today many people view the members of the Citizens' Committee as whistle-blowers and consider their release of FBI documents as not only informative, but also critical in altering the government's surveillance practices. The Edward Snowden case, which raises similar issues, also pushes us to consider whether spying on the government is justified to uncover mass surveillance by the government.

In 2013, the case of Edward Snowden dominated the headlines. Snowden, a contractor with the National Security Agency (NSA), worked as an infrastructural analyst. He released thousands of classified files to media outlets. The documents revealed that the NSA was conducting numerous widespread surveillance programs. The records also showed that the U.S. government can intercept data from fiber-optic cables and can gain warrantless access to private, personal information stored by major technology companies.

Snowden's actions have been widely condemned as jeopardizing U.S. security and giving aid to U.S. political enemies. Snowden left the country and has received asylum in Russia. The United States has filed criminal charges against Snowden (see criminal complaint above) for theft of government property, unauthorized communication of national defense information, and willful communication of classified communications intelligence information to an unauthorized person.

Some have praised Snowden for risking his life to reveal the activities of the NSA. Others believe he has placed the country at risk.[8]

Treason

There is no crime which can more excite and agitate the passions of men than treason.

Ex parte Bollman (1807)[9]

It is no compliment to refer to someone as a Benedict Arnold. It suggests that the person did something to dishonor the United States, something only a traitor would do. The term refers to Benedict Arnold, a general in the American Revolutionary War. Upset that he had not received the credit he believed he had earned for his military maneuvers, Arnold decided to hand over West Point, New York, to the British. Arnold later defected to the British Army and became a brigadier general. His actions were considered treasonous.

The drafters of the U.S. Constitution believed that loyalty to the country was essential to the establishment of a successful republic. Loyalty to

Edward Snowden in Moscow, Russia, where he has received temporary asylum.

the government was considered to be so important that treason has the unique distinction of being the only crime explicitly defined in the U.S. Constitution. Article III, Section 3 states,

> Treason against the United States, shall consist only in levying War against them, or in adhering to their Enemies, giving them Aid and Comfort. No Person shall be convicted of Treason unless on the Testimony of two Witnesses to the same overt Act, or on Confession in open Court.

Treason has two core elements—adherence to the enemy and providing the enemy with aid and comfort. Under the federal code, sanctions for treason range from a ten thousand dollar fine and five years imprisonment to death. A person who is convicted of treason cannot hold political office. At common law, treason was assigned the harshest of all punishments. At a time when all felonies were subject to death, a person convicted of treason faced death by public hanging, followed by one's head being cut off and a drawing and quartering of the body.

A treason conviction requires a confession or the testimony of two witnesses. This imposes a high bar for conviction. The drafters of the Constitution did this so that the treason clause would not be used to punish people with unpopular opinions or to hamper legitimate, nonviolent opposition to the government. In *Cramer v. United States,* a 1945 case, the Supreme Court overturned a conviction for treason. The Court made clear that treason requires a two-part finding: adherence to the enemy and actions that provide the enemy with aid and comfort:

Abolitionist John Brown led a raid on Harper's Ferry in 1859.

http://en.wikipedia.org/wiki/File:John_Brown_portrait,_1859.jpg

> A citizen intellectually or emotionally may favor the enemy and harbor sympathies or convictions disloyal to this country's policy or interest, but so long as he commits no act of aid and comfort to the enemy, there is no treason. On the other hand, a citizen may take actions, which do aid and comfort the enemy—making a speech critical of the government or opposing its measures, profiteering, striking in defense plants or essential work, and the hundred other things which impair our cohesion and diminish our strength—but if there is no adherence to the enemy in this, if there is no intent to betray, there is no treason . . . [T]houghts and attitudes alone cannot make a treason.[10]

In later cases, the Supreme Court has noted that a conviction for treason is "difficult but not impossible."[11] The U.S. government has prosecuted less than fifty treason cases. States as well punish treason, either within their constitutions or by statute.

The Case of John Brown

On October 16, 1859, John Brown, an abolitionist, launched a raid on a federal arsenal at Harper's Ferry, Virginia. Brown and his armed followers, Black and White men, took control of the arsenal but were later captured by the local militia. Brown's plan was to seize the weapons and redistribute them to slaves who would then demand their freedom. Virginia charged Brown with treason, murder, and slave insurrection. Following a swift trial, Brown was convicted. John Brown was hanged on December 2, 1859.

Sedition

Antigovernment advocacy is the hallmark of sedition. Sedition laws punish people whose words, spoken or written, are used to advocate for the overthrow of the government. Proof that someone has taken specific actions to actually disrupt the government is not required for sedition—which distinguishes it from treason. Sedition was a misdemeanor offense at common law and conviction required proof of the defendant's specific intent to create contempt and disloyalty toward the state. Sedition was prosecuted in various forms, including seditious libel, seditious words and rumors, and seditious conspiracies.

In 1798, the Alien and Sedition Acts were passed. These laws were designed to punish outspoken critics of the government. In the 1800s, state sedition laws were primarily directed at abolitionists. For instance, under Georgia law, it was unlawful to circulate any pamphlet or paper "for the purposes of exciting to insurrection, conspiracy or resistance among the slaves, negroes or free persons of colour [sic]."[12]

While many states enacted sedition laws, most did not impose a specific intent requirement. As a result, it was much easier to convict someone of sedition and punish their advocacy as if it were a more serious offense (e.g., anarchism or criminal syndicalism). Many states imposed stiff sanctions for sedition. *State v. Boloff* (1932)[13] provides an example. In this 1931 Oregon case, an unemployed sewer digger was arrested for vagrancy. Following Mr. Boloff's arrest, police found a Communist Party membership card in his possession. Boloff was charged with sedition, convicted, and sentenced to ten years in prison. In general, defendants convicted under state sedition laws received lengthier sentences than defendants found guilty under federal statutes.[14]

In 1940, Congress passed the Alien Registration Act—known as the Smith Act (named after Congressman Howard Smith who proposed the bill).[15] It was signed into law by President Franklin Roosevelt. Here is an excerpt:

> Whoever knowingly or willfully advocates, abets, advises, or teaches the duty, necessity, desirability, or propriety of overthrowing or destroying the government of the United States or the government of any State, Territory, District or Possession thereof, or the government of any political subdivision therein, by force or violence, or by the assassination of any officer of any such government; or
>
> Whoever, with intent to cause the overthrow or destruction of any such government, prints, publishes, edits, issues, circulates, sells, distributes, or publicly displays any written or printed matter advocating, advising, or teaching the duty, necessity, desirability, or propriety of overthrowing or destroying any government in the United States by force or violence, or attempts to do so; or
>
> Whoever organizes or helps or attempts to organize any society, group, or assembly of persons who teach, advocate, or encourage the overthrow or destruction of any such government by force or violence; or becomes or is a member of, or affiliates with, any such society, group, or assembly of persons.[16]

The maximum punishment for violating the Smith Act is twenty years in prison, and any person convicted under the act is barred from working for the federal government for five years. The Smith Act was initially designed to target and prosecute immigrants who were believed to be working in collaboration with U.S. enemies. Over time, sedition laws were increasingly used as a tool to punish U.S. citizens who were associated with Communism, no matter how remote the connection. The Smith Act and other laws passed following World War II were part of what some labeled the Red Scare—the belief that Communists and Fascists would overtake the U.S. government and that the Soviet Union would initiate nuclear attacks. The case of *Dennis v. U.S.* (1951) offers an example.

In *Dennis*,[17] the Supreme Court reviewed the convictions of eleven leaders of the national Communist Party. The members had been charged with violating the Smith Act, which made it a federal crime to advocate the overthrow of the U.S. government by force (or to be a member of an organization that promotes such advocacy). The Court upheld the convictions. The defendants argued that they did not advocate violence and that their speech was protected under the First Amendment. The Court found that the Smith Act distinguished between the mere teaching of Communism and the active advocacy of Communism. Further, the Court stated that the defendants had conspired to organize the Communist Party and to teach and advocate for the overthrow of the U.S. government by force. The Court said the convictions were justified because the defendants' "conspiracy to organize the Communist Party and to teach and advocate the overthrow the Government by force and violence" created a "clear and present danger."[18] In the years since *Dennis* was decided, the Supreme Court has placed an increased value on protecting free speech. (See Chapter 2 for a discussion of *Brandenburg v. Ohio*, 1969).

In 1949, leaders of the U.S. Communist Party were tried for violating the Smith Act.

Terrorism

There is no single definition of terrorism. It is more useful to think of terrorist actions—specific steps taken to carry out a terrorist objective. This includes an expansive range of activities that threaten to destabilize or upend a political or social system (federal, state, or local). Notably, a criminal incident could involve more than one crime against the state (e.g., espionage antiterrorist acts). A few examples are mailing a letter threatening a judge with physical harm; purchasing bomb-making equipment with the intent to detonate a car; sending a deadly substance through the mail, with the intent to harm the addressee; boarding a plane with the ingredients necessary to ignite a fire; and taping homemade videos that detail plans for a deadly rampage at a high school. As a general rule, terrorism is not a crime of happenstance committed by an accidental terrorist.[19] In most cases, acts of terror are intentional—the perpetrators intend their actions to wreak havoc, mayhem, and disorder.[20]

The threat of terrorism poses a unique problem for a democratic society. The challenge, as noted by one legal scholar, is how to "prevent and punish ideologically-motivated violence without infringing on political freedoms and civil liberties."[21]

The building of fallout shelters was encouraged during World War II and the Cold War as a protection against an air raid or a nuclear attack.

This is one of the core questions raised by the September 11, 2001, attacks. On that day, nineteen members of al-Qaeda, an Islamic extremist group, hijacked four commercial U.S. airplanes. The planes were used as suicide bombs to attack the U.S. Pentagon in Virginia and the World Trade Center Towers in New York. An airplane was flown into the Pentagon building and each of the Twin Towers. A fourth airplane crashed in a rural Pennsylvania field after crew members and passengers thwarted the hijackers' attempts to fly the plane into the U.S. Capitol Building.[22] Approximately three thousand people were killed in the airplane-to-building assaults. Thousands more were injured. The 2001 attacks were designed to strike at the heart of U.S. international business commerce and foreign relations intelligence.

Today, Americans live with heightened levels of fear of foreign assaults. Surveys show that most people believe that future terrorist attacks are imminent.[23] This widespread fear of terrorism has been referred to as the new normal. The September 11 strikes have been met with sweeping changes in the political and social landscape of the United States. These include the establishment of the Department of Homeland Security, a cabinet-level department; tightened airport security, including color-coded threat alerts; increased documentation required to obtain official identification (e.g., drivers' licenses and passports); enhanced border security; and the passage of the Uniting and Strengthening America by Providing Appropriate Tools Required to Intercept and Obstruct Terrorism Act (USA Patriot Act). Since the September 11, 2001, attacks, more than 120,000 people around the world have been arrested for terror-related offenses and more than thirty-five thousand have been convicted of terror-related crimes.

Numerous terrorism cases have made front-page news in recent years. Cases include the "Christmas Day" bomber. On December 25, 2009, Umar Farouk Abdulmutallab, a Nigerian-born member of al-Qaeda, attempted to ignite a bomb on a commercial international flight from Amsterdam to Detroit, Michigan. He boarded the plane with explosives in his underpants. Abdulmutallab was restrained by fellow passengers. In 2010, in another high-profile incident, Faisal Shahzad, a Muslim and naturalized U.S. citizen from Pakistan, attempted to ignite a car bomb in Times Square. As a result of these cases and others, the debate about terrorism has focused on how to stem the growth of Islamists in the United States, who some view as a threat to U.S. security. The vitriol over the plan to build an Islamic Center a few blocks away from the ruins of the World Trade Center, exemplifies this debate. In 2010, in response to plans for the Islamic Center, Congress held a hearing to examine the "radicalization" of American Muslims. In protest against the planned location of the Islamic Center, a Florida pastor burned the Koran. In the international protests that followed, twelve Afghans were killed.

The September 11 attacks were among the first terrorist assaults against the United States in the twentieth-first century. However, violent aggression, by forces outside the United States, is not new. The December 7, 1941, attack on Pearl Harbor, sixty years earlier, was an indelible act of terrorism that launched a U.S. war. The Japanese military strike against Pearl Harbor, Hawaii, resulted in more than two thousand fatalities. The next day, the United States declared war on Japan. During World War II, shelters were built to provide people with a safe harbor in the event of an air attack. Across the country, schools and businesses held air raid drills to prepare for future assaults. The army's air raid drills were initiated by shrill sirens; local air raid wardens moved from house to house to ensure that all lights, kerosene lamps, and candles had been extinguished.

Federal Law

Terrorist acts are punishable under a wide body of federal law. The U.S. Code identifies specific crimes as terrorism and defines it as a federal offense that is designed to "influence or affect the conduct of the government by intimidation or coercion, or to retaliate against government conduct."[24] Federal statutes distinguish between international terrorism and domestic terrorism. In both instances, however, the actions are intended to harm or intimidate U.S. officials. Offenses labeled international terrorism take place beyond U.S. borders. The federal code defines international terrorism as acts of violence or life-threatening actions, which are intended to:

1. Intimidate or coerce a civilian group,

2. Influence state policy by intimidation, or

3. Effect government through mass upheaval or physical harm.[25]

Domestic terrorism involves actions that take place primarily on U.S. soil. It addresses harms similar to those defined as international terrorism. Federal law identifies several offenses as acts of terrorism. These are offenses designed to coerce, intimidate, or retaliate against government actions. Determining when an act goes from being protected under the First Amendment to being punished as an act of terrorism is the subject of heated legal debate. The federal offense of providing material support to terrorists (which highlights the free speech versus national security tensions) is discussed in the next section. This is followed by an examination of the federal offense of using weapons of mass destruction.[26]

Material Support for Terrorists

The passage of both the Patriot Act and the Anti-Terrorism and Effective Death Penalty Act (AEDPA) greatly expanded the U.S. government's power to combat terrorism. Congress passed the Patriot Act six weeks after the September 11 attacks on the World Trade Center and the Pentagon. It allows for enhanced surveillance of suspected terrorists, increased intelligence-gathering, tightened border security, and restricted donations to terrorist groups. It enables the government to monitor whether groups or individuals are providing material support to terrorists. There was heated opposition to enactment of the Patriot Act. Opponents argue that the Act, reauthorized in 2006, encroaches on the fundamental constitutional guarantees of free speech and freedom of association. Proponents state that it is an essential legal tool to fight terrorism and protect national security.

In *Holder v. Humanitarian Law Project* (2010),[27] the Supreme Court addressed the tension between the individual right to free speech and the state's interest in combating terrorism. In this case, several groups and individuals sought to provide aid to two organizations involved in humanitarian efforts. However, both of these organizations—Kurdistan Workers' Party (PKK) and the Liberation Tigers of Tamil Eelam (LTTE)—had been designated as foreign terrorist organizations by the U.S. government. Specifically, the plaintiffs said they wanted to assist these groups with their lawful, nonviolent goals (including instructing them on how to peacefully resolve disputes using international and humanitarian law). Under 18 U.S.C. §2339B, it is a federal crime to "knowingly provide[e] material support or resources to a foreign terrorist organization." The PKK and LTTE engage in humanitarian and political activities, as well as terrorist activities. The Court found that it is permissible for the government to prohibit speech and advocacy of foreign organizations labeled as terrorist—even when the speech is aimed at supporting an organization's legal and peaceful activities. The Court observed that both the legislative and executive branches concluded that support provided to the legitimate work of the named terrorist organizations would be used to support their terrorist activities. The Supreme Court concluded, "The material support statute is on its face, a preventative measure—it criminalizes not terrorist attacks themselves, but aid that makes the attacks more likely to occur."[28]

Weapons of Mass Destruction. Terrorist acts can be committed with relatively simple tools, such as matches and lighter fluid. However, devices and implements that cause wide scale harm raise the greatest concern. These are weapons of mass destruction (WMDs). Under the U.S. Code, there are several federal statutes that punish their use. These laws punish a range of activity, including:

- Use of biological agents
- Use of toxins
- Use of radiation
- Use of explosives (e.g., missiles, grenades)

Under these laws, if the WMDs cause death, the maximum penalty is life in prison or capital punishment. Faisal Shahzad, the Times Square bomber, discussed above, was charged with attempting to use a WMD. Shahzad pled guilty and was sentenced to life in prison. Umar Farouk Abdulmutallab, the Christmas Day bomber also discussed above, pled not guilty to charges of attempting to use a WMD, attempted murder, and conspiracy to commit terrorism. In 2012, on the second day of his trial, he pleaded guilty and was later sentenced to life in prison.

Domestic Terrorism

As noted above, domestic terrorism involves terrorist incidents that take place primarily within the United States. Acts of terrorism may be committed by foreigners or citizens on U.S. land. Attacks may be motivated by a general dislike of government, particular governmental actions, or foreign policy decisions. Assaults committed by U.S. citizens against national, state, or local government are referred to as domestic or "homegrown" terrorism. Regardless of the name, these attacks are not new. American history is filled with instances of domestic terrorism. The list includes the killings of millions of American Indians through forced removal from their lands and exposing them to smallpox as well as the widespread lynching of African Americans in the 1800s and 1900s. Following the Civil War, ritual killings were used as a terrorist device to control the newly freed slave population.[29] The U.S. government reports that between the 1880s and mid-1960s, there were approximately five thousand lynchings. In the 1960s, there were numerous incidents of terrorism, including the bombings of Black churches by White supremacist groups as retaliation for attempts to integrate public spaces; campus bombings by radical groups, such as the Weather Underground, as protests against the Vietnam War; and the assassinations of political leaders, including President John F. Kennedy, Senator Robert F. Kennedy, and the Reverend Martin Luther King Jr. The next section provides a summary of contemporary cases of domestic terrorism.

Alfred P. Murrah Federal Building. Domestic terror attacks are typically carried about by individuals or groups, with the goal of sending a message of anger, disenchantment, or distrust of the government. The 1995 bombing of the Alfred Murrah

Federal Building, by Timothy McVeigh and Terry Nichols, killed 168 people and injured hundreds of others. In the aftermath of the bombing, there was media speculation that the perpetrators were Middle Eastern terrorists. It was later determined that McVeigh and Nichols, young White men who met in the army, had meticulously planned the violent assaults. McVeigh and Nichols faced numerous federal counts, including use of a weapon of mass destruction. Nichols was sentenced to serve 161 life terms. McVeigh was sentenced to death and executed in 2001. Below is an excerpt from a letter Timothy McVeigh wrote in the weeks before his execution.

Timothy McVeigh Letter to Fox News, April 26, 2001[30]

I explain here why I bombed the Murrah Federal Building in Oklahoma City . . . I chose to bomb a federal building because such an action served more purposes than other options. Foremost, the bombing was a retaliatory strike; a counter attack, for the cumulative raids (and subsequent violence and damage) that federal agents had participated in over the preceding years (including, but not limited to, Waco.) From the formation of such units as the FBI's "Hostage Rescue" and other assault teams amongst federal agencies during the '80's; culminating in the Waco incident, federal actions grew increasingly militaristic and violent, to the point where at Waco, our government—like the Chinese—was deploying tanks against its own citizens.

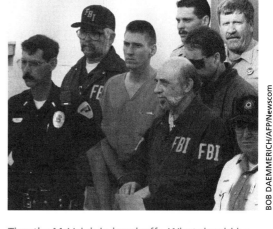

Timothy McVeigh in handcuffs. What should be the legal response to acts of domestic terrorism?

Knowledge of these multiple and ever-more aggressive raids across the country constituted an identifiable pattern of conduct within and by the federal government and amongst its various agencies . . . [F]ederal agents had become "soldiers" (using military training, tactics, techniques, equipment, language, dress, organization, and mindset) and they were escalating their behavior. The . . . bombing was also meant as a pre-emptive (or pro-active) strike against these forces and their command and control centers within the federal building. When an aggressor force continually launches attacks from a particular base of operation, it is sound military strategy to take the fight to the enemy.

Additionally, borrowing a page from U.S. foreign policy, I decided to send a message to a government that was becoming increasingly hostile, by bombing a government building and the government employees within that building who represent that government. Bombing the Murrah Federal Building was morally and strategically equivalent to the U.S. hitting a government building in Serbia, Iraq, or other nations . . . Based on observations of the policies of my own government, I viewed this action as an acceptable option. From this perspective, what occurred in Oklahoma City was no different than what Americans rain on the heads of others all the time, and subsequently, my mindset was and is one of clinical detachment. (The bombing of the Murrah building was not personal, no more than when Air Force, Army, Navy, or Marine personnel bomb or launch cruise missiles against government installations and their personnel.)
I hope that this clarification amply addresses your question.

Sincerely,
Timothy J. McVeigh

USP Terre Haute (IN)

In his letter, Timothy McVeigh offers a justification for his vigilante actions in response to what he perceived as wrongdoing by the government. Consider what weight, if any, his justifications for the bombing should have had on his punishment.

The Unabomber. Between 1978 and 1995, Ted Kaczynski, a Harvard-trained mathematician, sent sixteen anonymous letter bombs to university professors and business offices. Three people were killed. In his "Unabomber manifesto," Kaczynski stated that his terrorist actions were necessary to highlight the harms of technology and modernization. In 1995, the *New York Times* and *Washington Post* newspapers jointly published his anti-technology manifesto. Following the publication, Kaczynski's brother, David, recognized his writing and contacted law enforcement. Kaczynski pled guilty to the mail bombings and was sentenced to four life terms.

Columbine High School. In 1999, Dylan Klebold and Eric Harris, opened fire at their high school in Columbine, Colorado. Thirteen people, twelve students, and one teacher were killed in the attacks and twenty-four others were injured. Following the massacre, as they had planned, Klebold and Harris killed themselves. Police later uncovered online videos made by Klebold and Harris, who claimed they were at war with the world.

Washington Area Sniper. In 2002, there were several shootings in the Washington, DC area. Over a three-week period, ten people were shot and killed. Criminal profilers and media analysts predicted that the sniper was a White, antisocial male in his thirties. Police later discovered that the attacks had been carried out by John Allen Muhammad and his seventeen-year-old accomplice, Lee Malvo. Muhammad faced numerous charges in several states. Based on its record of securing death sentences, Virginia was selected as the state for the first trial. Muhammad was charged under both federal and state law. He faced two charges of capital murder. He also faced a charge under Virginia's antiterrorism statute (orders to kill to intimidate communities or influence governments). Muhammad was convicted of capital murder, sentenced to death, and executed in 2007. Lee Malvo was charged with two counts of capital murder, convicted, and sentenced to six life terms.

Contemporary Cases

In the last few years, there have been numerous incidents involving rampages and mass killings. These incidents include

- *2014:* Isla Vista, California. Killings near the University of California, Santa Barbara campus left seven people dead and thirteen people injured. The killer, Elliot Rodger, left behind a manifesto, "My Twisted World," which expressed his desire to punish "all of the popular kids and young couples for the crime of having a better life than me."[31]
- *2014:* Las Vegas, Nevada. Jerad Miller and Amanda Miller, a married couple, went on a shooting rampage and killed three people, including two police officers. Following the shootings, Amanda Miller killed Jerad and then herself. The pair, adherents of the Patriot Movement, expressed their hatred of the government and police authority on social media.

- *2013:* Los Angeles, California. Christopher Dorner, a former police officer, went on a two-week rampage and killed four people, took hostages, and injured four others. As police officers surrounded his cabin, he killed himself.
- *2013:* Boston, Massachusetts. During the Boston marathon, brothers Dzhokar and Tamerlan Tsarnaev set off homemade bombs. Their rampage led to five deaths (including Tamerlan's) and left 264 people with injuries. The Chechen brothers set off the explosions to create fear and terror.
- *2013:* Washington, DC. Aaron Alexis went on a shooting spree at the Washington Navy Yard and killed thirteen people and injured eight others. He was killed by police.
- *2012:* Newtown, Connecticut. Adam Lanza shot and killed twenty-eight people. Twenty were children at Sandy Hook elementary school. Prior to the school shootings, Lanza killed his mother. After the school shootings, he killed himself.
- *2012:* Oak Creek, Wisconsin. Michael Page went on a shooting rampage at a Sikh Temple. He killed six people. Page died after shooting himself and being shot by a police officer who arrived on the scene. Four people were injured during the shootings. Page, a U.S. Army veteran, had links to a White separatist group.
- *2012:* Aurora, Colorado. During a midnight premiere of *The Dark Night Rises*, James Holmes opened fire in a movie theatre. Twelve people were killed and seventy people were injured.
- *2011:* Tucson, Arizona. Jared Loughner opened fire at a Safeway store, where a "Congress on Your Corner" meeting, sponsored by Congresswoman Gabrielle Giffords, was being held. The shootings left six people dead and Giffords severely injured.

Notably, most of these killings were carried out by lone gunmen. In several of these cases, hand-written notes, video footage, or social media messages prepared by the killer revealed disdain or distrust for certain groups of people, sometimes the U.S. government (e.g., Boston marathon bombings and Las Vegas shootings). With only one exception, each of these acts of domestic terrorism was carried out by Americans. Also notable, all but one of the cases involved the use of guns. These cases turned up the national debate about the availability of firearms (see Chapter 2 for a discussion of the Second Amendment).

State Laws

In response to the September 11 attacks, more than thirty states enacted terrorism-related offenses to their criminal codes. Six days following the attacks, New York passed its "Crime of Terrorism" statute. These post-9/11 state laws impose greater penalties for crimes carried out with terrorist intent. For instance, in Florida and Ohio, a crime committed with terrorist intent may be upgraded to a more serious felony. In New York, murder in the furtherance of a terrorist act was added to its list of capital felonies.

State laws also punish threats of terrorism. For example, Ohio law makes it a felony to threaten to intimidate, influence, or affect the conduct of any government where the threat causes a reasonable expectation of fear.[32] In 2004, Rodney Roach made several calls to the Ohio Department of Jobs and Family Services. Roach sought unemployment benefits. In one of these calls, Roach stated that if he did not receive the money, he would do something that would make "9/11 look tame." Roach followed this by making gunfire sounds. He then asked the employee if he heard the noises and said, "That's someone getting hurt." Roach was charged with making a terrorist threat.[33] The *Roach* case and others ask the question whether antiterror laws impinge upon First Amendment rights to free speech. As the next section highlights, antiterror laws raise other questions about their applicability.

Antiterrorism Laws and Street Gangs. Should the law draw a line that separates violent crimes committed by street gangs from violent crimes carried out by terrorists? In at least one case, an offense committed by a member of a street gang was punished under a law originally enacted to punish terrorists. In what some have called an unanticipated application, Edgar Morales, a member of the St. James Boys, was convicted under New York's terrorism statute, passed after the September 11, 2001, attacks.[34] In 2002, following an argument outside a church christening, Morales and other gang members sought retribution. Morales' gunfire left a ten-year-old girl dead and one man paralyzed. He was convicted of first degree manslaughter, attempted murder, criminal possession of a weapon, and conspiracy. Each of these offenses was held to be a crime of terrorism, defined as an offense committed with

> [I]intent to intimidate or coerce a civilian population, influence the policy of a unit or government by intimidation or coercion, or affect the conduct of a unit of government by murder, assassination or kidnapping.[35]

Under New York law, if a crime is classified as a crime of terrorism, the penalty increases by one level. For instance, had Morales been convicted of first degree manslaughter under the standard New York law, the maximum penalty would have been twenty-five years in prison. However, under the terrorism law, the penalty is twenty-five years to life in prison. The controversial extension of terrorism laws to street criminals has been challenged as an unconstitutional and improper use of laws designed to punish international terrorism organizations.[36]

Under some state statutes, street gang activity is labeled as a form of terrorism. In California, the Street Terrorism Enforcement and Prevention Act (The STEP Act) was passed prior to September 11, 2001. Georgia and Illinois passed similar laws after September 11 terrorist attacks.[37]

The large-scale offenses of espionage, treason, and terrorism are what typically come to mind when we consider crimes against the government. However, there are a range of other offenses, typically prosecuted at the state level, that also threaten the functioning of government operations. These offenses include perjury, obstruction of justice, and bribery.

Perjury

Perjury is both a state and federal crime. Lying under oath forms the core of the offense. Perjury was an offense at common law. It was considered a serious offense, one that could be punishable by death. At common law, the offense could only be charged in limited circumstances. Today, as there are more legal forums where testimony can be given (e.g., grand juries and depositions), perjury laws now have a broader reach. The basic elements of the crime include taking an oath to tell the truth, providing testimony in a judicial case, and lying about a material fact in the case. Compare the Hawaii and South Carolina statutes, below.

Hawaii and South Carolina Perjury Statutes

Hawaii Perjury Statute[38]

1. A person commits the offense of perjury if in any official proceeding the person makes, under an oath required or authorized by law, a false statement which the person does not believe to be true.

2. No person shall be convicted under this section unless the court rules that the false statement is a "materially false statement." . . . It is not a defense that the declarant mistakenly believed the false statement to be immaterial.

3. Perjury is a class C felony.

South Carolina Perjury Statute[39]

1. It is unlawful for a person to wilfully give false, misleading, or incomplete testimony under oath in any court of record, judicial, administrative, or regulatory proceeding in this State.

2. It is unlawful for a person to wilfully give false, misleading, or incomplete information on a document, record, report, or form required by the laws of this State.

3. A person who violates the [above] provisions . . . is guilty of a felony and upon conviction, must be fined in the discretion of the court or imprisoned not more than five years, or both.

Perjury is a felony offense in Hawaii and South Carolina, as it is in many states. The South Carolina statute casts a broader net for perjury than the Hawaii statute. For instance, in Hawaii, the false statement has to be "material," or essential to the case. Under South Carolina law, materiality is not a requirement. Consider the following hypothetical:

Dolph has been called as a witness in a burglary case against his friend Sergio. When he takes the witness stand he takes and oath and is asked to state his name, address, and place of employment. He provides all the requested information. However, he gives a former house address—a place he moved out of more than three months ago. Dolph does not want his mother (who is in the courtroom) to know that he lives at his girlfriend's house. The trial ends and Sergio is convicted.

Did Dolph commit perjury? There are no facts to indicate that Dolph's home address has any relevance to the burglary. Therefore it is unlikely that he would be charged with perjury under the Hawaii law. It would be easier to charge Dolph under the South Carolina law. He was under oath and willfully gave false testimony in court.

Another difference between the two laws is the type of false statement that is punishable. The Hawaii law requires "a false statement." South Carolina law does not require an affirmative false statement. South Carolina makes it unlawful to give "misleading or incomplete testimony." Given this language, a person could be convicted of perjury in South Carolina for the failure to share information. It is also unlawful to solicit or encourage someone to commit perjury. This offense is called subornation of perjury.

Obstruction of Justice and Bribery

Obstruction of justice was a misdemeanor offense at common law. It remains unlawful today under both state and federal law. The offense punishes people who engage in activities that hinder or derail the operation of the justice system. At the state level, obstruction of justice covers a broad range of activities against the government, such as tampering with a jury, tampering with evidence, tampering with witnesses, filing a false police report, or tampering with public records.

A person may be charged under a broad "obstruction of justice" law or depending on state law, he may be charged with a more specific offense. The offense of bribery, which is punished under federal and state law, offers an example. Bribery is offering to give someone in a position of public authority, such as an elected official, something of value in exchange for an action on their part. The action by the public official could be his promise to render a vote, opinion, or decision as requested by the person making the bribe. Bribery is a type of solicitation—sometimes referred to as "corrupt solicitation," because it involves an attempt to influence a public official (see Chapter 4 for a detailed discussion of solicitation and other incomplete offenses). Under many state laws, bribery is a felony offense.

This section has presented some of the offenses that fall under the umbrella of crimes against the state. The common thread that links them together is action that is believed to pose a threat to the stability of the U.S. government. Whether the threat is domestic or international, the law punishes actions that purposefully disrupt government functions. In some instances, the criminal actions have the potential for broad harm including homicide (e.g., espionage, treason, and terrorism). In others, the harm may be relatively minor and may not involve violence (e.g., perjury cases).

Crimes Committed by Public Officials ●———————

The next section addresses another type of offense and harm to the state and the citizenry at large. These are harms that involve criminal actions carried out by federal, state, or local officers—while they are carrying out official job duties. These are crimes committed by public officers. These offenses undermine government functions and foster public disdain and distrust. If the public does not have faith in the government then it is less likely that they will respect the law. If people believe that the government is corrupt, it is less likely that they will obey the law. Psychologist Tom Tyler's research that examines why people obey laws finds that people obey the law when they believe legal authority is legitimate. "[P]eople want to believe that the government can effectively enforce laws by punishing those, *themselves* or others, who break them."[40]

In some cases, there may be an overlap between crimes against the state and crimes by public officials. One example is a case where a city commissioner (a government official) accepts money to vote in favor of a private company's bid on a construction contract (bribery). Another example is a police officer who is called to testify as an eye-witness in an vehicle theft case, who agrees to lie on the witness stand and say that she "does not remember" what the offender looked like or what he was wearing.

We now turn to consider two cases involving crimes by justice system officials. The first is a political corruption case, *U.S. v. Terry* (2013).

U.S. v. Terry (2013)

United States Court of Appeals, Sixth Circuit

707 F.3d 607

Opinion

SUTTON, Circuit Judge. "If you can't eat [lobbyists'] food, drink their booze, . . . take their money and then vote against them, you've got no business being [in politics]," said Jesse Unruh, a one-time Speaker of the California General Assembly, in the 1960s. Bill Boyarsky, Big Daddy: Jesse Unruh and the Art of Power Politics 112 (2007). That is one way of looking at it. Another way of looking at it comes courtesy of the federal anti-corruption statutes, one of which prohibits an official from accepting things of value "in return for" official acts. 18 U.S.C. § 201(b)(2). A jury found that a state court judge did just that and convicted him of several honest services fraud violations. We affirm.

I. In April 2007, Governor Ted Strickland appointed Steven Terry to fill a vacancy on the Cuyahoga County Court of Common Pleas. Soon after, Terry announced that he intended to seek reelection to retain the seat the following November. Having never run for elected office before, Terry sought the help of County Auditor Frank Russo, a presence in Cleveland politics. Russo agreed to help Terry with his reelection campaign and indeed had already helped him by recommending Terry to the Governor for the appointment and by lobbying members of the local judicial nominating committee to support him.

Terry knew that Russo was helping him behind the scenes. What Terry did not know was that the FBI was investigating Russo on corruption charges and that federal agents had tapped Russo's phones. On July 15, 2008, Russo had a phone conversation with a local attorney, Joe O'Malley, about two foreclosure cases on Terry's docket. O'Malley represented several homeowners in a lawsuit against American Home Bank, and he asked Russo to convince Terry to deny the bank's motions for summary judgment. Russo promised to call Terry and make sure Terry did what he was "supposed to do" with the cases. Gov't Ex. 116; 2 Trial Tr. 294.

Two days later, Russo and Terry spoke on the phone. Russo told Terry to deny the motions for summary judgment, and Terry said he would. In the same conversation, the two men also discussed Russo's attendance at future fundraisers for Terry's reelection campaign.

That same day, Terry contacted the magistrate judge responsible for the foreclosure cases and told her to deny the motions for summary judgment. Surprised by Terry's directive, the magistrate passed along the docket so that Terry could deny the motions himself. Terry did just that, even though he never reviewed the case files, never read the motions before denying them and never obtained a recommendation from the magistrate or anyone else (within the court system) about how to rule on the motions.

Terry's collaboration came relatively cheap. Russo's political action committee donated $500 to Terry's reelection campaign in July 2007. Russo's committee purchased around $700 worth of stationery, envelopes and car magnets for Terry's campaign in July 2007. And Russo had his official staff work for Terry's campaign during business hours and provided other political help throughout the relevant time period. In exchange for this assistance, Russo explained that he expected Terry "to answer the phone any time I called. And any time I called with a recommendation, or a problem, or a case, I would expect Steve to give it special attention" and "follow through for me." 2 Trial Tr. 290. Russo in other words expected that his political and financial patronage meant Terry "would do what I asked him to do," including "granting [] a motion so it wouldn't tie [a] case up." Id. For his part in this and like-minded arrangements with other Cleveland-area officials, Russo pled guilty to twenty-one political corruption counts of one form or another and received a 262-month prison sentence.

For his part, Terry ran into similar problems. A grand jury indicted him on five political corruption charges. Count One alleged that Terry conspired with Russo to commit mail fraud and honest services fraud. Count Two alleged that Terry committed mail fraud by denying the bank's summary judgment motions. And Counts Three, Four and Five alleged that he committed honest services fraud by "accepting gifts, payments, and other things of value from Russo and others in exchange for favorable official action." R. 24 ¶ 52. Each honest services fraud count was tied to a mailed document: Counts Three and Four stemmed from checks Russo's political action committee wrote to pay for Terry's stationery, envelopes and car magnets, while Count Five stemmed from a thank you note Terry wrote to Russo. Id. ¶ 54.

After a five-day trial, a jury convicted Terry on Counts One, Three and Four, and acquitted him on Counts Two and Five. The district court sentenced him to 63 months in prison on each count, to be served concurrently.

II. Terry presses three arguments on appeal: (1) the district court should have dismissed the indictment because

(Continued)

(Continued)

it failed to identify a crime under *Skilling v. United States* (cites omitted); (2) the district court improperly instructed the jury on the requirements for showing that Terry accepted a bribe; and (3) insufficient evidence showed that Terry accepted a bribe.

. . .

[Appeal Argument #3: Evidence of Accepting a Bribe]

Based on the [jury] instructions, the jury found that Terry accepted a bribe. We may overturn that conclusion only if, after "viewing the evidence in the light most favorable to the prosecution, [no] rational trier of fact could have found the essential elements of the crime beyond a reasonable doubt." *Jackson v. Virginia*, 443 U.S. 307, 319, 99 S.Ct. 2781, 61 L.Ed.2d 560 (1979).

A jury could find that Terry and Russo entered an agreement to fix cases. Start with the benefits, financial and otherwise, that Russo provided to Terry during the relevant time period. He gave Terry's campaign $500. He supplied Terry's campaign with approximately $700 in campaign materials. He expected his employees in the Auditor's office to engage in electioneering for Terry during office hours. And he hired a woman Terry had fired from his chambers staff to prevent Terry from suffering negative publicity.

A flow of benefits from one person to a public official, to be sure, does not by itself establish bribery. The benefits instead must be part and parcel of an agreement by the beneficiary to perform public acts for the patron. That existed as well. On one side of the bargain, Russo thought that they had a deal. In return for showering Terry with benefits, Russo expected Terry to use his official powers whenever and however Russo requested. Any time Russo called, he expected Terry to "give it special attention" and "follow through for me." 2 Trial Tr. 290. "Special attention," he clarified, meant that "whether it would be a character reference or whether it would be a case," Terry would "do what I asked him to do." Id.

So, too, on the other side of the bargain. Although Terry disclaimed at trial any agreement to fix cases in which Russo had a stake, his actions belied his words. Terry's rulings on the foreclosure cases were, at the very least, highly irregular, and the reality that a tape recording captured the Russo-Terry conversation immediately preceding these rulings did Terry no favor. No subtle winks and nods were needed. Russo straight up asked Terry to deny the bank's motions for summary judgment in the two cases, and with Terry's tape-recorded reply ("Got it." Gov't Ex. 117), Terry agreed to do just that. And he did, within hours of the conversation. Here is the timeline: Terry and Russo spoke at 11:58 a.m. on July 17; Terry called the magistrate later that afternoon, around

12:30 p.m.; and Terry called Russo at 10:31 a.m. the next morning to confirm he had denied the motions. Without reading the motions, without consulting the case files and without relying on the recommendation of anyone—within the court system—who had read the files, Terry did just what Russo asked. That is not an everyday occurrence in the judicial branch, and a jury could readily infer that Terry's unusual behavior, along with the other evidence, stemmed from an agreement to use his position as a public official to do Russo's bidding in return for Russo's financial, campaign and staff support.

In the face of this evidence, Terry claims that the record nonetheless does not establish an agreement between him and Russo to exchange campaign contributions and help for official acts. Yes and no. Yes, the government never presented a formal agreement between Russo and Terry stating that Russo's gifts would control Terry's actions. But no, there was ample evidence for the jury to infer that an agreement nonetheless existed between the two men.

Not every campaign contribution, we recognize, is a bribe in sheep's clothing. Without anything more, a jury could not reasonably infer that a campaign contribution is a bribe solely because a public official accepts a contribution and later takes an action that benefits a donor. See, e.g., McCormick, 500 U.S. at 272, 111 S.Ct. 1807. But when a public official acts as a donor's marionette—by deciding a case to a donor's benefit immediately after the donor asks him to and without reading anything about the case—a jury can reject legitimate explanations for a contribution and infer that it flowed from a bribery agreement. Here, the jury rejected any legitimate explanation for Russo's contributions in the face of strong circumstantial evidence that Terry and Russo had a corrupt bargain. Once the jury found Terry and Russo had an agreement, it could easily find that Terry accepted a bribe, violating the honest services fraud statute along the way. The same holds true for Terry's conspiracy conviction.

For these reasons, we affirm.

Questions

1. According to the prosecution, what "flow of benefits" existed between the defendant (Mr. Terry) and Mr. Russo?

2. Which evidence by the prosecution is the most persuasive that there was an agreement between the Mr. Terry and Mr. Russo?

3. Comment on Mr. Terry's sixty-three-month prison sentence. Was it adequate or too harsh? Why or why not?

Criminal trials involving politicians who have been convicted of corruption-related offenses are fairly commonplace. In 2014, C. Ray Nagin, the former mayor of New Orleans, was found guilty on twenty of twenty-one counts, including bribery and conspiracy. During the economic recovery following Hurricane Katrina, Nagin had schemed to award city projects and favors to businessmen who rewarded him with large amounts of money, trips to the Caribbean, lawn care, free shipments of granite for his countertop company, and cell phone service. Nagin was sentenced to serve ten years in prison.

Former Illinois governor Rod Blagojevich was at the center of another big political corruption case. He attempted to trade a vacant Illinois Senate seat (the one left open once Barack Obama became president) for cash and personal favors. In 2011, Blagojevich was convicted on seventeen counts of what the U.S. attorney called, "a political corruption crime spree." At trial, prosecutors introduced taped phone conversations of Blagojevich bargaining for money or other favors for himself in exchange for the Senate seat. Blagojevich was sentenced to fourteen years in prison.

We turn now to a second case involving crimes committed by justice system officials. This time the public official is a police officer. It is not uncommon for police officers to face criminal charges for violence. There have been numerous cases involving allegations of police brutality against citizens.[41] In 2014, there was widespread social unrest in Ferguson, Missouri, following the police killing of an unarmed man. In most instances, the officers are acquitted. It is rare for a prosecutor to be able to persuade a jury to convict a police officer for allegations of criminal violence. The facts have to be undeniably egregious, such as those in the next case, *U.S. v. Bartlett* (2009).

U.S. v. Bartlett (2009)

United States Court of Appeals, Seventh Circuit
567 F.3d 901

EASTERBROOK, Chief Judge. The distance between civilization and barbarity, and the time needed to pass from one state to the other, is depressingly short. Police officers in Milwaukee proved this the morning of October 24, 2004.

Andrew Spengler held a housewarming party that started on October 23 and lasted into the next morning. Spengler and many guests were police officers. Liquor flowed freely. Katie Brown and Kirsten Antonissen were among the invitees. They arrived after 2:30 AM on October 24 with Frank Jude and Lovell Harris. The quartet was immediately made to feel unwelcome because the women are White, and the men are not. (Harris describes himself as Black; Jude describes himself as bi-racial.) After five minutes, the four prepared to leave— but they were prevented when at least ten men stormed outside, surrounded Antonissen's truck, and demanded to know what the four new arrivals had done with Spengler's badge.

Spengler says that he could not find it after the quartet arrived, and he accused them of theft. The men demanded that the four get out of the truck and surrender the badge. When they stayed inside, the men threatened them ("Nigger, we can kill you") and began to vandalize the truck. Harris tried to wake the neighbors; the men responded: "Nigger, shut up, it's our world."

Eventually all four were dragged from the truck. A search did not turn up the badge. Instead of concluding that Spengler's accusation was mistaken, the men became enraged and violent. One cut Harris's face in a way that he described as "slow and demented." Harris managed to free himself and run away. Multiple men began to kick and punch Jude. Antonissen managed to call 911; she told the operator "they're beating the shit out of him." When the men saw Antonissen use the phone, they wrested it from her hand and flung her against the truck so forcefully that its metal was dented. Brown made two calls to 911 before her phone, too, was seized.

The first call was logged at 2:48, and two officers (Joseph Schabel and Nicole Martinez) arrived at 3:00. The

(Continued)

(Continued)

beating continued until their appearance. Men punched Jude's face and torso; when he fell to the ground, they kicked his head and thighs. The partygoers behaved as a mob. Not a single person in the house tried to stop the attack or even to call for aid. Jon Clausing, who had slashed Harris's face, explained his conduct as "just kind of going along with everybody." That is the way of the mob. Society has police forces to pose a counterweight to mobs, yet here the police became a mob.

Schabel and Martinez were on duty and had not been drinking, so they should have put a stop to the violence. Instead Schabel joined it, while Martinez watched. On being told that Jude had stolen Spengler's badge, Schabel called Jude a "motherfucker" and stomped on his face until others could hear bones breaking. After telling Martinez "I'm really sorry you have to see this," Daniel Masarik picked Jude off the ground and kicked him in the crotch so hard that his body left the ground. Jon Bartlett then took one of Schabel's pens and pressed it into each of Jude's ear canals, causing severe injury and excruciating pain. The men also broke two of Jude's fingers by bending them back until they snapped. Spengler put a gun to Jude's head and said: "I'm the fucking police. I can do whatever I want to do. I could kill you." Bartlett used a knife to cut off Jude's jacket and pants, leaving him naked on the street in a pool of his own blood.

The violence tapered off when additional on-duty police arrived. At 3:09 officers arrested Jude. Yes, they arrested the victim, although Jude had never fought back. (He had suffered a concussion and was unable to defend himself.) Jude was taken to an emergency room; the admitting physician took photographs because "[t]here were too many [injuries] to document" in writing. The injuries to Jude's ears could not be diagnosed because the physicians could not control the bleeding. One physician testified that she had never seen ear injuries so severe. While Jude was receiving treatment, on-duty officers recovered Jude's car. Bartlett and other men had ripped up its seats with knives and poured antifreeze over them; apparently they poured antifreeze into the gas tank too, damaging the engine. The radio had been wrecked. The men broke a headlight and tore a mirror off Antonissen's truck. Spengler's badge was not found in either the car or the truck; perhaps he had put down the badge in the house and was too soused to remember where.

Bartlett, Spengler, and Masarik were prosecuted in state court and acquitted after Schabel and others committed perjury on their behalf, while many people who had been at the party claimed to suffer memory loss. That made it impossible to show who had done what, and the judicial system (unlike a mob) demands personal responsibility.

The Civil Rights Division of the Justice Department then investigated, and federal prosecutors persuaded several witnesses to cooperate. Four men (Joseph Schabel, Ryan Lemke, Jon Clausing, and Joseph Stromei) pleaded guilty to obstruction of justice (by perjury, including false testimony before the federal grand jury), to violating Harris's and Jude's civil rights, or both. Bartlett, Spengler, and Masarik were convicted by a jury of conspiring to violate Harris's and Jude's right to be free from unreasonable searches and seizures (18 U.S.C. § 241), and of the substantive offense (18 U.S.C. § 242). (Excessive force in making an arrest violates the fourth amendment to the Constitution, applied to state police officers by the fourteenth amendment. See *Graham v. Connor*, 490 U.S. 386, 109 S.Ct. 1865, 104 L.Ed.2d 443 (1989).) Bartlett was sentenced to 208 months' imprisonment, Spengler and Masarik to 188 months apiece. All seven men have been fired by the Milwaukee Police. Two more officers were fired but later reinstated; an additional four were disciplined.

Bartlett, Spengler, and Masarik present twelve appellate issues. Only four require discussion. The rest have been considered, and we reject them without comment.

. . .

Authors' Note

In the remainder of the opinion, The Court of Appeals evaluates four of the issues raised on appeal by the defense: (1) The defendants argued that their sentences should be reduced because there is insufficient proof that they were engaged in a conspiracy; (2) Defendant Masarik said that he did not participate in the beating and was a mere bystander and cannot be guilty of misprision of felony; (3) All three defendants argued that their sentences are "unreasonably high" and disparate when compared with other cases; and (4) Defendant Bartlett argued that his sentence, exceeded the range set forth in the Sentencing Guidelines, was too harsh.

The Court rejected all four of the above arguments on appeal. It affirmed the convictions for each of the three defendants and the sentences for Spengler and Masarik. The 208-month sentence for Bartlett was upheld in a later decision.[42]

Questions

1. Comment on Bartlett's sentence of 208 months in prison. Given the facts of the case, is it appropriate or too severe? Why or why not?

2. Now compare Bartlett's sentence with the 188-month sentences given to Spengler and Masarik. Discuss whether the difference in sentence length is justifiable.

3. Judge Easterbrook's opinion makes references to the difference between a police force and a mob. What point is he making and how does this tie to the rationale for punishing crimes by public officers?

The *Bartlett* case illustrates the difficulty of holding police officers accountable for even heinous criminal actions. Note that all three officers were acquitted in state court. Federal charges were later brought by the Civil Rights Division of the U.S. Justice Department. Federal laws, which punish a variety of abuses, provide avenues of relief for victims of crime who have been denied their constitutional rights. In *Bartlett,* the officers were convicted of violating a federal statute that prohibits conspiracies that "injure, oppress, threaten, or intimidate" a person who is engaged in lawful, constitutional activity.[43] The officers were also found guilty of violating another federal law that prohibits a person who is acting "under the color of law"—such as a police officer—from depriving a person of their rights because of their race, color, or citizenship status.[44]

Concluding Note

This chapter has covered the landscape of offenses that fall under crimes against the state. These crimes punish a range of actions, from advocating the forceful overthrow of the government, to acts of terror committed to instill fear and cause state instability, to lying on the witness stand. Crimes committed by public officials pose a social detriment as well. When public officials engage in crimes, it harms the populace at large and violates the public trust. Federal and state officials—the guardians of the government—have to be held accountable for crimes they engage in as representatives of the state. If public officials could do harm without punishment, what message would that send to the rest of society? The bottom line is that both crimes against the state and crimes by public officials undermine confidence and trust in government. Now test yourself on the material we have covered in this chapter. Good luck with the Issue Spotter exercise.

IssueSpotter

Read the hypothetical and spot the issues discussed in this chapter. This hypothetical is loosely based on Professor Derrick Bell's well-known legal tale, "The Space Traders."[45]

The Mystery Trade

The year is 2050. The country of Mystery (formerly "America") has hit hard times. It is rapidly running out of oil and water. The available jobs do not match the available labor force and over the past two years, the unemployment rate has skyrocketed to 50 percent. Mystery has a racially diverse population—Whites are 51 percent, Latinos are 22 percent, Blacks are 17 percent, Asians are 7 percent, and American Indians are 3 percent.

Representatives from Shola Way, a little-known planet, have approached the government of Mystery. They have asked Mystery for the "return of their native sons and daughters." The Shola Way people want all the people of color in Mystery. In exchange for 49 percent of the population, Shola Way will provide all the resources that Mystery so desperately needs—an unrestricted supply of water, oil, and jobs for anyone who wants one. With nearly one-half

(Continued)

(Continued)

of its population gone, Mystery could return to the good old days when life was great for everyone. The Shola Way people have given Mystery until December 31, 2050, to decide.

The trade offer sends the country of Mystery into a tailspin. The following events occurred in Mystery following the visit from the Shola Way People:

- Holden Hightower, the sole member of the president's cabinet who opposed the trade, secretly released dozens of documents to the press. The papers show that the government is capable of monitoring everyone's activities through their home televisions and their smartphones. Hightower also sent out transcripts of the minutes from the cabinet meeting discussions about the trade. The documents made front page news across the country.
- A group known as the "51 percenters" threatened to blow Mystery "to smithereens" if the government did not accept the trade offer. The group, which has over one thousand charter members, has a vast stockpile of arms, explosives, and food. They hold weekly meetings where the leaders lecture their followers on what is wrong with the Mystery government and why anarchy is the solution.
- Opinion polls showed that the public, by a slight fifty-one to forty-nine margin, favors the trade. Following these poll showings, several members of Congress proposed passage of a new constitutional amendment:

  Each Mystery citizen, at the call of Congress, may be selected for special service for a period deemed necessary to protect domestic interests.

This amendment—the Twenty-Eighth Constitutional Amendment—was passed by the required two-thirds vote of the House and Senate. Under the new amendment, the government could require any one or any group of people (such as people of color) to be assigned to selective service and force them to leave the country.

- Julie Washington, a Senator from Nevada, held a news conference. She tells the world that she can no longer keep silent. She accepted twenty-five thousand dollars in exchange for her promise to vote in favor of the Twenty-Eighth Amendment (and therefore in favor of the trade). Senator Washington drops another bombshell. She knows of ten other senators who also accepted money to vote in favor of the trade. Senator Washington says that she has not yet received any money.

Anti-trade groups, with members of all races, have mobilized to fight against the trade. They hold daily rallies at city halls across the country. Maurice, a microbiologist who lives in Montana, is angry with Congress for passing the Twenty-Eighth Amendment. He has concocted a mix of chemicals (including arsenic), which can cause serious injury, even death. He sent letters laced with the deadly chemicals to each member of the Congress who voted in favor of the trade. The letters never made it to the members of Congress. They were taken by a postal worker who hid them (along with other mail) in the shed in his backyard.

On October 1, 2050, the National Guard began rounding up Mystery's people of color. On December 31, 2050, the National Guard handed them over. After the Shola Way people placed the people in state-of-the-art space ships, their leader said "Thank you," and handed a thick envelope to Mystery's president.

1. Assume that you are the research assistant for the Mystery Attorney General. What specific criminal charges will you advise her to bring based on the above scenario?

Key Terms and Cases

Notes ●━━━━━━━━━━━━━━━━━━━━━━━━━━━━━━━━━━

1. Allan M. Jalon, "A Break-in to end all break-ins," *Los Angeles Times*, March 8, 2006. http://articles.latimes.com/2006/mar/08/opinion/oe-jalon8

2. See generally, Geoffrey Stone, *Perilous Times: Free Speech in Wartime From the Sedition Act of 1798 to the War on Terrorism.* (New York: W.W. Norton & Company, 2004).

3. William R. Conklin, "Atom Spy Couple Sentenced to Die, Aide Gets 30 Years," *New York Times,* April 6, 1951, 1.

4. J. Edgar Hoover, "The Crime of the Century," *Reader's Digest*, May 1951, 167.

5. See,18 U.S.C. §§ 793, 794 (1996).

6. "Secrets, Lies, & Atomic Spies: Aldrich Hazen Ames," PBS, 2002, http://webcache.googleusercontent.com/search?rlz=1T4ADFA_enUS449US450&hl=en&q=cache:9j24W5KIhwAJ:http://www.pbs.org/wgbh/nova/venona/dece_ames.html

7. Asian Pacific American Legal Center, "Hostility Exposed: A Report on Racial Profiling and Discrimination in the National Nuclear Weapons Laboratories," 2002, http://www.wenholee.org/apology; U.S. District Judge James Parker stated,

   I am sad that I was induced in December to order your detention, since by the terms of the plea agreement that frees you today without conditions, it becomes clear that the executive branch now concedes, or should concede that it was not necessary to confine you last December or at any time before your trial . . . I sincerely apologize to you, Dr. Lee, for the unfair manner in which you were held in custody by the executive branch.

8. NBC News National Survey, Project No. 14353, 2014, http://msnbcmedia.msn.com/i/MSNBC/Sections/A_Politics/14353%20May%20NBC%20News%20National%20Survey%20Interview%20Schedule.pdf; 2014 NBC poll showed that 34 percent of those polled disagree with Snowden's actions, while 24 percent support his actions.

9. *Ex parte Bollman*, 8 U.S. 75 (1907).

10. *Cramer v. United States*, 325 U.S. 1 (1945).

11. *Haupt v. U.S.*, 330 U.S. 631, 644 (1947).

12. Ga.L. 1829, p. 170, sec. 10.

13. *State v. Boloff*, 138 Ore. 568, 4 P.2d 326 (Ore. 1932).

14. See, e.g.,"State Sedition Laws: Their Scope and Misapplication," *Indiana Law Journal,* 31 No. 2 (1956): 270, 282–283.

15. 18 U.S.C. § 2385 (1940) (amended). It was named after Virginia Congressman, Howard Smith, the lead sponsor of the bill.

16. 18 U.S.C. § 2385 (1994).

17. *Dennis v. U.S.*, 341 U.S. 494 (1951).

18. Ibid. at 517.

19. See, e.g., Associated Press, "Mexican Authorities Accuse 2 of Being Twitter-Terrorists," *Florida Times-Union*, Jacksonville.com, September 5, 2011; South American case involved a re-tweet of a hostage takeover of school. The two tweeters were arrested as terrorists because their messages caused widespread panic.

20. See generally, Gary LaFree and Gary Ackerman, "The Empirical Study of Terrorism: Social and Legal Research," *The Annual Review of Law and Social Science*, 5 (2009): 347–374; Criminologists have studied various explanations for involvement in terrorism—macro- (legitimacy, democratization, weak states, and religion) and micro-level decisions (rational choice, socialization, and group dynamics).

21. David Cole and James X. Dempsey, *Terrorism and the Constitution: Sacrificing Civil Liberties in the Name of National Security* (New York: The New Press, 2002) 1.

22. See, e.g., Jason Potteiger, "Young People Don't Fear Terrorist Attack," June 3, 2011, http://apolls teronpolling.com/2011/05/18/americans-believe-terrorist-attack-imminent; Suffolk University Poll of likely voters nationwide, finding that most (51 percent) believe there will be a terrorist attack in the United States in the next year.

23. "CNN Poll: Fear of Terrorist Attack in U.S. Rises," May 28, 2010, http://politicalticker.blogs.cnn.com/2010/05/28/cnn-poll-fear-of-terrorist-attack-in-u-s-rises

24. 18 U.S.C. § 2332(b) (2008).

25. 18 U.S.C. § 2331(1) (2001).

26. Two others offenses include terrorism transcending national boundaries, 18 U.S.C. § 2332b (2008), and Harboring or concealing terrorists, 18 U.S.C.§ 2339 (2002).

27. *Holder v. Humanitarian Law Project*, 561 U.S. _____(2010).

28. Ibid. at 30.

29. Ida B. Wells, *Southern Horrors and Other Writings* (Boston: Bedford/St. Martins Press, 1996).

30. "McVeigh's Apr. 26 Letter to Fox New," *Fox News*, April 26, 2001, http://www.foxnews.com/story/2001/04/26/mcveigh-apr-26-letter-to-fox-news

31. Elliot Rodger, "My Twisted World: The Story of Elliot Rodger," http://abclocal.go.com/three/kabc/kabc/My-Twisted-World.pdf

32. Ohio Revised Code, § 2909.23 (2002).

33. *State v. Roach*, 165 Ohio App 3d 167 (Oh. App. Ct. 2005).

34. *People v. Morales*, 924 NYS2d 62 (N.Y. App. Div. 1st Dep't, 2010). *See, also,* Timothy Williams, "Gang Member is Convicted Under Terror Law," *New York Times*, Nov. 1, 2007.

35. New York Penal Law § 490.25 (2001).

36. See generally, Louis Jim, "Overkill: The Ramifications of Applying New York's Anti Terrorism Statute Too Broadly," *Syracuse Law Review*, 60 (2010): 639.

37. CPC §186.20 (1988); OCGA §16–15–1 (1998); 740 ILCS 147 (1993).

38. Hawaii Rev. Stat. § 710–1060 (1984).

39. South Carolina Code of Laws, Ch. 9, Art.1, §16–9–10 (1993).

40. Margaret Levi, Tom Tyler, and Audrey Sacks, "The Reasons for Compliance with Law," Paper for Workshop on the Rule of Law. Yale University (Draft), 2008, http://www.yale.edu/macmillan/ruleoflaw/papers/ReasonsforCompliance.pdf (italics added).

41. Well-known cases involving allegations of police brutality or police abuse include Oscar Grant, Amadou Diallo, Rodney King, Abner Louima, David Cunningham, Eleanor Bumpers, and Michael Stewart.

42. *U.S. v. Bartlett*, 2013 WL 6271530 (E.D. Wis. 2013).

43. 18 U.S.C. § 241 (1996).

44. 18 U.S.C. § 242 (1996). See also, 18 USC §1983 ("Civil Action for Deprivation of Rights").

45. Derrick Bell, *Faces at the Bottom of the Well* (New York: Basic Books, 1992).

Appendix

U.S. Constitution, Selected Sections

PREAMBLE

WE THE PEOPLE of the United States, in Order to form a more perfect Union, establish Justice, insure domestic Tranquility, provide for the common defence, promote the general Welfare, and secure the Blessings of Liberty to ourselves and our Posterity, do ordain and establish this Constitution for the United States of America.

ARTICLES I-III & VI

Article I

Section 1 All legislative Powers herein granted shall be vested in a Congress of the United States, which shall consist of a Senate and House of Representatives.

Section 9 No bill of attainder or ex post facto Law shall be passed.

Article II

Section 1 The executive Power shall be vested in a President of the United States of America . . .

Article III

Section 1 The judicial Power of the United States shall be vested in one supreme Court, and in such inferior Courts as the Congress may from time to time ordain and establish . . .

Article VI

Section 1 (Clause 2) This Constitution, and the Laws of the United Sates which shall be made in Pursuance thereof; and all Treaties made, or which shall be made, under the Authority of the United States, shall be the supreme Law of the Land; and the Judges in every State shall be bound thereby, any Thing in the Constitution or Laws of any State to the Contrary notwithstanding . . .

AMENDMENTS 1–10 & 14

First Amendment

Congress shall make no law respecting an establishment of religion, or prohibiting the free exercise thereof; or abridging the freedom of speech, or of the press; or the right of the people peaceably to assemble, and to petition the Government for a redress of grievances.

Second Amendment

A well regulated Militia, being necessary to the security of a free State, the right of the people to keep and bear Arms, shall not be infringed.

Third Amendment

No Soldier shall, in time of peace be quartered in any house, without the consent of the Owner, nor in time of war, but in a manner to be prescribed by law.

Fourth Amendment

The right of the people to be secure in their persons, houses, papers, and effects, against unreasonable searches and seizures, shall not be violated, and no Warrants shall issue, but upon probable cause, supported by Oath or affirmation, and particularly describing the place to be searched, and the persons or things to be seized.

Fifth Amendment

No person shall be held to answer for a capital, or otherwise infamous crime, unless on a presentment or indictment of a Grand Jury, except in cases arising in the land or naval forces, or in the Militia, when in actual service in time of War or public danger; nor shall any person be subject for the same offence to be twice put in jeopardy of life or limb; nor shall be compelled in any criminal case to be a witness against himself, nor be deprived of life, liberty, or property, without due process of law; nor shall private property be taken for public use, without just compensation.

Sixth Amendment

In all criminal prosecutions, the accused shall enjoy the right to a speedy and public trial, by an impartial jury of the State and district wherein the crime shall have been committed, which district shall have been previously ascertained by law, and to be informed of the nature and cause of the accusation; to be confronted with the witnesses against him; to have compulsory process for obtaining witnesses in his favor, and to have the Assistance of Counsel for his defence.

Seventh Amendment

In Suits at common law, where the value in controversy shall exceed twenty dollars, the right of trial by jury shall be preserved, and no fact tried by a jury, shall be otherwise re-examined in any Court of the United States, than according to the rules of the common law.

Eighth Amendment

Excessive bail shall not be required, nor excessive fines imposed, nor cruel and unusual punishments inflicted.

Ninth Amendment

The enumeration in the Constitution, of certain rights, shall not be construed to deny or disparage others retained by the people.

Tenth Amendment

The powers not delegated to the United States by the Constitution, nor prohibited by it to the States, are reserved to the States respectively, or to the people.

Fourteenth Amendment

Section 1 All persons born or naturalized in the United States and subject to the jurisdiction thereof, are citizens of the United States and of the State wherein they reside. No State shall make or enforce any law which shall abridge the privileges or immunities of citizens of the United States; nor shall any State deprive any person of life, liberty, or property, without due process of law; nor deny to any person within its jurisdiction the equal protection of the laws . . .

Glossary

Abandonment: A defense to the incomplete offenses of attempt and solicitation. Requires a complete and voluntary renunciation and withdrawal from the crime.

Actus reus: A voluntary act that, when combined with other elements, constitutes a crime.

Administrative regulations: A source of criminal law, such as the regulations of the Equal Employment Opportunity Commission (and other federal or state agencies), that may subject a violator to criminal penalties.

Adultery: A common law offense that makes it a crime for a married person to have sexual relations with someone other than a spouse. It remains a misdemeanor offense in many states today.

Affirmative defense. A defense involving the defendant presenting evidence in support of a particular defense after the prosecution has rested its case.

Alcohol offenses: A category of public order offenses that involve alcohol, such as public drunkenness, open container laws, and driving under the influence. These offenses range in seriousness from misdemeanors to felonies. As a group, these laws respond to social concerns about the impact of alcohol on public behavior.

American Law Institute Model Penal Code test: The insanity test that finds a defendant not criminally responsible for his or her acts if, at the time he or she committed the acts and as a result of a mental disease or defect, he or she lacks substantial capacity either to appreciate the criminality of his or her conduct or to conform his or her conduct to the requirements of the law.

Animal cruelty: Crimes that involve harm to animals, ranging from misdemeanor to felony offenses, such as abandonment or maiming.

Arson: The intentional burning of the dwelling of another. This common law definition is modified in modern statutes that provide various degrees of arson, depending on the seriousness of the offense.

Asportation: The carrying away element of the crime of larceny.

Assault: An attempt to cause bodily injury to another, or causing such injury purposely, knowingly, or recklessly.

Attempt: An inchoate offense that requires specific intent to commit a crime and overt steps toward carrying out the crime.

Banishment: A requirement that an offender move from a particular geographical area as punishment for a crime.

Battered woman syndrome: A condition suffered by some women who are in abusive relationships. After enduring repeated, unpredictable beatings, these women develop a belief that it would be hopeless to try to escape their situation, and they remain in the relationships.

Battery: Any unlawful or unwanted touching of another. Most modern statutes use the term "assault" instead of this common law term.

Bifurcated trial: A two-part trial used in insanity cases in some states that involves a criminal trial with the government assuming the burden of proof in the first part of the trial. If the defendant is found guilty, the defendant assumes the burden of proving insanity in the second part of the trial.

Bigamy: A common law offense that makes it unlawful for someone to be married to more than one person at one time.

Bill of Rights: The first ten amendments of the U.S. Constitution, including the right to free speech, the right to bear arms, the prohibition against cruel and unusual punishment, and due process. Some of the Bill of Rights protections are made binding on the states through the Fourteenth Amendment.

Bribery: When someone attempts to persuade a public official to make a favorable decision in exchange for a gift, money, or other favor.

Burglary: Breaking and entering the dwelling of another at night with the intent to commit a felony therein. Modern statutes modify this common law definition by providing various degrees of burglary, depending on the seriousness of the offense.

"But for" causation: The actual cause of a crime—"but for" the defendant's act, the crime would not have occurred.

Capital offense: A serious crime, usually certain types of murders, for which the prosecutor may seek the death penalty.

Capital punishment: The imposition of the death penalty as punishment for the commission of certain crimes, most often for various forms of murder.

Case brief: A sheet that summarizes the central elements of a court case, including the name of the case, the legal citation, prior proceedings, facts, issues, holding, and rationales.

Common law: In the absence of codified law, over time, judges made and applied legal rules. American criminal law is based on English common law.

Competency: A term that refers to the defendant's mental condition at the time of the court proceedings, not at the time of the offense. A defendant is not competent and may not stand trial if he is suffering from a mental disability that prohibits him from understanding the proceedings or assisting in his defense.

Computer crime: Describes a wide range of criminal activity that includes using a computer to commit a crime or stealing from or destroying computer hardware or software.

Consent: A complete defense to common law rape and many forms of sexual assault. Lack of consent is an element of common law rape and some forms of sexual assault in modern statutes.

Conspiracy: An inchoate offense involving an agreement between two or more people to commit a crime. Some state laws require an agreement and an overt action taken toward commission of the crime.

Conversion: The taking element of the crime of embezzlement.

Correctional supervision: When a person who has been convicted of a crime is subject to oversight by a state or federal corrections agency, including jail, prison, probation, or parole.

Crime: An act or omission punishable by the state or federal government through the enforcement of its criminal laws.

Crimes committed by public officials: Offenses by public officials (e.g., judges, police, or elected officials), which involve a violation of the public trust. Examples include bribery, perjury, and official misconduct.

Cruel and unusual punishment: The Eighth Amendment to the U.S. Constitution prohibits punishment that is cruel and unusual. Post-conviction punishment must be proportionate to the crime and must not exceed society's norms for sanctions.

Cultural defenses: Defenses that involve the defendant presenting evidence of her cultural background or beliefs to demonstrate that she lacked the required mens rea for a particular offense. At best, these defenses usually result in a conviction on a lesser offense rather than a total acquittal.

Dangerous proximity to success: One of several tests used to determine whether the actions a person has taken toward committing a crime are punishable as an attempt crime. Using this high threshold would mean conviction only in cases where the potential offender had almost completed the target offense.

Decriminalization: Legislative changes that eliminate the criminal penalties for drug-related offenses, such as the distribution and use of marijuana.

Defense of habitation: A defense that permits the use of deadly force to protect a home or dwelling. Unlike self-defense, the threat need not be imminent or proportionate.

Defense of others: A defense that permits an individual to lawfully use force in defense of another person.

Defense of property: A defense that permits the use of a reasonable amount of force under the circumstances to prevent property from being taken or even to take property back. Deadly force may never be used to protect property.

Depraved heart murder: An unintentional killing done with extreme recklessness, also known as second degree unintentional murder. The actor does not intend to kill, but he knows that his actions will create a substantial and unjustifiable risk of death or serious injury.

Determinate sentencing: A sentencing system that applies strict guidelines to determine which sentence shall apply in a particular case, with the goal of achieving uniformity across cases.

Deterrence: A rationale for criminal punishment premised on the belief that people are discouraged from committing crime because they are punished or because they observe that other people who commit crime are punished.

Domestic terrorism: Criminal actions designed to cause widespread harm, destruction, and fear that take place primarily within the United States.

Due process clause: Constitutional guarantee in the Fifth and Fourteenth Amendments, which requires that a person not be deprived of "life, liberty or property without due process of law." It guarantees a fair process, including clear notice of which actions are unlawful.

Duress: A defense that involves a person claiming that he committed a criminal act because someone was threatening to seriously injure or kill him if he did not commit that act.

Duty to retreat: A doctrine in many states that requires a person to retreat from a threat and avoid using force, especially deadly force, if he or she can do so safely.

Eighth Amendment: U.S. constitutional prohibition against cruel and unusual punishment for someone convicted of a crime.

Elements defense: A defense that involves challenging the state's evidence through cross-examination and arguing that the state has not met its burden of proving every element beyond a reasonable doubt.

Embezzlement: The fraudulent conversion or theft of property by someone in lawful possession of the property.

Equal protection clause: U.S. constitutional guarantee protected by the Fourteenth Amendment, which provides that all persons are entitled to equal protection under the law.

Espionage: A serious federal offense involving spying against one's country.

Excuse defenses: Defenses that involve the claim that the defendant should not be held criminally responsible for her actions because of some circumstance (such as a disease or condition) that prevented her from acting lawfully.

Executive order: Legal directive that becomes federal law enacted by a sitting U.S. president, such as the Emancipation Proclamation and Order No. 9066, which mandated the internment of Japanese Americans at the start of World War II. State governors also have authority to issue executive orders.

Ex-post facto law: A law that punishes people for engaging in actions that were not unlawful at the time they were committed. This type of law is unconstitutional.

Extreme recklessness: The state of mind required for unintentional "depraved heart" murder. The actor does not intend to kill, but he knows that his actions will create a substantial and unjustifiable risk of death or serious injury. The standard is that of the reasonable person—a reasonable person would have known that his actions would create a substantial risk of death or serious injury.

Factual impossibility: A typically unsuccessful defense to the inchoate crimes of attempt, solicitation, and conspiracy. Defense arises in instances where a defendant did all he could to carry out a crime but for reasons beyond his control (e.g., the person he plans to rob moved out of state), the crime could not be completed. Because the crime would have been successful if the circumstances had been as the defendant believed them to be, the law does not allow him to benefit from the "impossibility" of which he was unaware.

False pretenses: False representation of a material past or present fact that the person making the representation knows to be false made with the intent to defraud a person into passing title to property to the wrongdoer.

Federal crack cocaine law: Law passed in 1986 punished the possession and sale of crack cocaine one hundred times more severely that the possession and sale of powder cocaine. In 2010, the U.S. Sentencing Commission reduced this disparity from 100:1 to 18:1.

Federal legislation: Laws passed by the U.S. Congress and applied within the federal court system.

Felony: A crime that is punishable by more than one year of imprisonment, may also result in a fine, and is more serious than a misdemeanor.

Felony murder: A killing that occurs during the course of, and in furtherance of, an inherently dangerous felony. The killing may be intentional, unintentional, or even accidental.

Fifth Amendment: Included within the U.S. Constitution's Bill of Rights and mandates due process of law.

Fighting Words: In *Chaplinsky v. New Hampshire* (1942), the U.S. Supreme Court defined fighting words as words, "which by their very utterance inflict injury or tend to incite an immediate breach of the peace." Fighting words are not constitutionally protected under the First Amendment.

Fines: Punishment for criminal conviction that requires an offender to pay a fee to the court.

First degree premeditated murder: An intentional murder that involves premeditation—thinking about the killing ahead of time, turning it over in one's mind, and making a choice to kill.

Force: Force or threat of force is one element of common law rape and many forms of sexual assault in modern statutes.

Fornication: A common law offense involving sexual intercourse between people who are not married to one another.

Fourteenth Amendment: Includes the constitutional guarantee of Equal Protection and Due Process. This amendment makes some of the Bill of Rights' protections applicable to state laws.

Free exercise clause: Constitutional provision within the First Amendment that permits people to practice religion without undue interference by the state.

Freedom of Speech: A right protected under the First Amendment to the U.S. Constitution, which allows people to express their opinions through speech, so long as the state does not have a compelling reason to regulate or prohibit the speech.

Good Samaritan laws: Laws that requires a bystander to provide assistance to a person who has suffered or is in danger of suffering serious physical harm.

Gross negligence: The state of mind required for involuntary manslaughter. The killer does not intend to cause death or even know that her actions would cause death, but she acts with gross negligence because she should have known. The standard is whether her behavior was a deviation from the standard of care of a reasonable person.

Guilty but mentally ill: A verdict permitted in some states after the presentation of an insanity defense. It involves the defendant being found criminally responsible for the crime but being given the opportunity to receive treatment for his or her mental illness, either in a prison setting or in a mental health facility. Treatment may be followed by a term in prison.

Hate speech: Speech used to express hatred toward an individual or group based upon specific characteristics, such as race, ethnicity, gender, sexual orientation, or religion. Hate speech alone is not criminal. However, when it is joined with conduct, it may be subject to additional criminal sanctions (e.g., penalty enhancement).

Heat of passion: One of the elements of voluntary manslaughter. The person who kills in the heat of passion loses his or her self-control after some act of provocation by the victim.

Homelessness: State of living without a home, usually outside. The lack of housing may cause some people who are homeless to spend more time outdoors, and this may result in an increased likelihood of arrest on charges of loitering or vagrancy.

Homicide: The killing of a human being by another person.

House arrest: Punishment, typically combined with electronic monitoring, that requires the offender to stay within specific geographical confines for a specified period of time.

Identity theft: The term used to describe the crime of obtaining another person's name, social security number, or other identifying information for purposes of committing fraud, theft, or some other criminal behavior.

Imminent, lawless action: Test used by the U.S. Supreme Court in *Brandenburg v. Ohio* (1969) to determine whether particular speech is constitutionally protected. Speech that is likely to cause imminent, lawless action is not protected under the First Amendment.

Incapacitation: A rationale for criminal punishment that focuses on placing offenders behind bars so that they cannot commit more crime.

Incarceration: Punishment following a conviction that requires the offender to serve time in prison or jail.

Inchoate offenses: See "incomplete crime" below.

Incomplete crime: When a person takes a step toward committing crime but the crime is not completed, he may still be held criminally liable. Examples of incomplete (or inchoate) crimes include attempt, solicitation, and conspiracy. Specific intent is required for incomplete crimes.

Incorporation: Legal doctrine that makes some parts of the Bill of Rights applicable to the states through the Fourteenth Amendment.

Indeterminate sentencing: Sentencing scheme that allows criminal justice officers to exercise discretion in determining the length of an offender's sentence.

Infancy: A common law defense that presumes persons between the ages of seven and fourteen are incapable of committing a crime, but permits the state to rebut that presumption by presenting evidence to prove otherwise.

Insanity: A defense involving the claim that the defendant should not be held responsible for his or her criminal acts because he or she acted as a result of a mental disease or defect.

International terrorism: Criminal actions designed to cause widespread harm, destruction, and fear that take place primarily outside of the United States.

Invisible punishments: Punishments, prohibitions, and limitations that are triggered by a felony conviction, but are not part of the official punishment imposed by the justice system. Examples include restrictions on voting, employment, education, and housing.

Involuntary intoxication: A defense involving the claim that the defendant should not be held criminally liable because his criminal acts were caused by his unknowing consumption of food or drink that contained alcohol or some intoxicating drug.

Involuntary manslaughter: An unintentional killing committed with gross negligence.

Irresistible impulse test: An insanity test that involves a defendant who can tell right from wrong but cannot control his or her actions because of mental illness.

Jail: A correctional facility, run by a city or county, where people are typically held following an arrest and prior to trial. It may also be used for individuals who are sentenced to relatively short periods of incarceration.

Judicial override: The practice that permits a judge to overrule or override the sentencing decision of the jury in capital cases and impose an enhanced or reduced sentence.

Justification defenses: Defenses that involve the claim that the defendant should not be held criminally liable because his or her actions were legally justified under the circumstances.

Juvenile court: A special court for juveniles that focuses on rehabilitation rather than on punishment.

Kidnapping: The forcible abduction and carrying away of a person. Modern statutes provide modifications of this common law definition, often requiring that the abduction be done with a particular purpose, such as getting a ransom.

Knowingly: The state of mind that involves awareness that one's conduct is practically certain to cause a particular result.

Larceny: The trespassory taking and carrying away of the personal property of another with the intent to permanently deprive. Modern statutes provide modifications of this common law definition.

Law enforcement defense: A defense that permits police officers and private citizens to use a reasonable amount of force under the circumstances to prevent a crime.

Legal impossibility: A defense offered by a defendant who has been charged with an inchoate offense, such as attempt, solicitation, or conspiracy. This defense is raised when the defendant's intentional actions toward committing a crime could not legally result in a crime due to circumstances she did not know about—for example, the person she planned to purchase drugs from was an undercover police officer. Under these circumstances, a legal impossibility defense would not be successful for the same reason that a factual impossibility defense would not be: If the circumstances had been as the defendant believed them to be, she would have been successful in committing a crime.

Loitering: Standing or idling in a public place may subject a person to criminal punishment under anti-loitering laws that are sometimes used to arrest members of socially-marginal groups, such as the homeless.

M'Naghten test: An insanity test in which the defendant has to prove that, at the time of the act, he was laboring under such a defect of reason, from disease of the mind, as to not know the nature and quality of the act he was doing, or if he did know it, that he did not know what he was doing was wrong.

Mala in se: Crimes that society considers inherently evil and morally wrong, such as theft, rape, and murder.

Mala prohibita: Actions that are not inherently wrong, but wrong because they violate the law, such as public intoxication, vagrancy, and laws that impose regulations on seat belt use and restrictions on hunting.

Mandatory minimums: State and federal sentencing schemes that impose a minimum length of prison time an offender is required to serve.

Manslaughter: The unlawful killing of a human being without malice.

Marijuana: A drug that comes from the dried leaves, flowers, and seeds of Cannibis sativa, a hemp plant. It is the most popular illicit drug in the United States. It is classified as a Schedule I substance by the federal government. Recreational marijuana use is legal in Washington and Colorado.

Material support for terrorists: The provision of substantial aid to terrorists, with knowledge that the support will lead to criminal violations under the Antiterrorism and Effective Death Penalty Act (AEDPA).

Mens Rea: A guilty state of mind that, when combined with other elements, constitutes a crime. Not required for strict liability crimes.

Mere preparation: Test used to determine whether a person's actions meet the actus reus requirement for the crime of attempt. Mere preparation is insufficient for an attempt conviction.

Merger doctrine: When two or more incomplete crimes are committed, the less serious offense may merge into the more serious offense. For instance, solicitation merges with attempt. When a person completes the target crime, the attempt merges with the completed offense, and a person may only be convicted of the completed offense or attempt.

Misdemeanor: Low-level criminal offense punished less severely than a felony, but more than an infraction.

Model Penal Code (MPC): Non-binding legal code designed to enhance uniformity across criminal law statutes by providing legislatures with ideal statutory language regarding definitions of crime, defenses, and excuses. The MPC was written by members of the American Law Institute—a group of judges, lawyers, and law professors.

Municipal ordinances: Criminal legislation adopted by municipalities that subject offenders to jail or fines typically for low-level offenses.

Murder: The killing of a human being with malice aforethought.

Necessity: A defense (also called choice of evils) that involves a person claiming that he or she committed what would otherwise be considered a crime because acting lawfully under the circumstances would have caused greater harm.

Negligently: A person acts negligently when she is not aware of a substantial and unjustifiable risk that harm will result from her conduct but should be aware. The failure involves a gross deviation from the standard of care that a reasonable person would observe in the actor's situation.

Obscenity: Lewd or vulgar language that is not protected under the First Amendment and may be prohibited by state law. In *Miller v. California* (1973), the U.S. Supreme outlined a three-part obscenity test: (1) whether the average person, applying contemporary community standards, would believe that the work appeals to the prurient interest; (2) whether the material describes sexual activity in a patently offensive way under state law; and (3) whether the material has literary, artistic, political, or scientific value.

Obstruction of justice: Criminal offense that involves the intentional disruption of the effective operation of the justice system. It may involve interfering with the work of law enforcement officers, prosecutors, or judicial officials.

Overt act: Action taken by someone who plans to commit a crime, such as a person who drives to the bank he or she intends to rob. An overt act is required for some inchoate offenses, such as attempt and conspiracy.

Parole: The early release of a prisoner granted by a state board for good behavior during incarceration. Prisoners granted parole remain under the supervision of state officials and must abide by certain conditions. If any conditions are violated, parole may be revoked and the offender will be returned to prison.

Partial defenses: A defense that results in a conviction on a less serious offense rather than a total acquittal.

Patriot Act: The Uniting and Strengthening America by Providing Appropriate Tools Required to Intercept and Obstruct Terrorism Act passed by Congress following the September 11, 2001, terrorist attacks. The federal statute gives law enforcement greater power to investigate terrorist organizations and individuals, including increased investigative authority, easier access to private data (e.g., phone records, library records), and greater electronic surveillance.

Perjury: The offense of lying while under oath.

Post-traumatic stress disorder: A syndrome involving the defendant having seen or experienced some frightening or stressful event that causes him to relive that event through flashbacks and/or nightmares. When used as a legal defense, the defendant often claims that he was experiencing a flashback at the time of the offense, which prohibited him from forming the specific intent to commit the crime.

Premeditation: An element of first degree premeditated murder that involves thinking about a killing ahead of time, turning it over in one's mind and making a choice to kill.

Premenstrual syndrome: A group of symptoms that some women experience one to two weeks before their menstrual cycles. When used as a defense, the defendant claims that she should not be held liable because she was suffering from PMS at the time of the offense.

Prison: A penal institution that confines individuals as punishment for a criminal conviction.

Probation: Sentence offender completes without serving time in prison or jail, often accompanied by conditions such as community service, reporting to a probation officer, and obeying the law. Offender may avoid prison so long as he or she does not violate conditions of parole.

Product test: An insanity test in which the defendant is not held criminally responsible for her acts if her unlawful acts were the product of mental disease or defect.

Prostitution: Offense of providing sexual services in exchange for money or other compensation.

Provocation: An element of voluntary manslaughter. Provocation is behavior by the victim that incites the killer, causing him or her to kill in the heat of passion.

Proximate causation: The legal cause of a crime—at issue when other acts or omissions occur after the defendant's act or omission and contribute to the resulting harm.

Public decency offenses: Actions involving consenting adults that some people consider morally offensive and other people consider victimless, such as adultery, prostitution, and drug use.

Public order crimes: A category of offenses involving actions that take place in public spaces that are believed to endanger the public and cause social disruption. Examples include public drunkenness, loitering, and weapons offenses.

Public shaming: Punishment that involves a public announcement of an offender's crime, such as requiring a thief to wear a sign that reads, "I'm a thief."

Purposely: A person acts purposely when he or she consciously chooses to engage in certain conduct or cause a certain result.

Rape: Unlawful sexual intercourse with a female by force or the threat of force and without consent. Modern statutes modify this common law definition, often referring to the crime as sexual assault, using gender neutral language, and providing various degrees of the offense.

Rape shield laws: Laws that limit the defendant's ability to introduce evidence of the complainant's prior sexual conduct at trial.

Recklessly: A person acts recklessly when he or she consciously disregards a substantial and unjustifiable risk that a certain result will occur. It involves a gross deviation from the standard of conduct that a law-abiding person would observe in the actor's situation.

Rehabilitation: Approach to punishment that seeks to identify causes of offending and implement programmatic solutions, such as counseling, job training, and education.

Renunciation: A defense to an incomplete crime, such as attempt, solicitation, or conspiracy. As a general rule, renunciation (or abandonment) will not be a successful unless the offender has done everything she can to make sure the crime she initially intended to carry out (or help another person carry out) does not take place.

Restitution: Offender payment to a crime victim to compensate her for harm that she suffered as a result of the crime. It is often part of a sentence or a condition of probation. For example, the defendant may be required to pay the victim the cost of stolen items.

Restorative justice: An approach to punishment that permits the victim to have a direct conversation with the offender and input in the case resolution, including the appropriate punishment for the crime, with an eye toward victim healing and justice.

Retribution: Rationale for punishment, premised on the belief that in order for society to heal from an offense, the offender must be punished.

Right to privacy: Not explicitly written in the Constitution but rooted in several amendments; protects privacy in areas that include contraception and family relations.

Robbery: The trespassory taking and carrying away of the personal property of another by force or threat of force with the intent to permanently deprive the owner of the property.

Second Amendment: U.S. constitutional amendment that protects the right to bear arms.

Second degree intentional murder: An intentional killing done with malice but without premeditation or deliberation.

Second degree unintentional murder: An unintentional killing done with extreme recklessness, also known as depraved heart murder. The actor does not intend to kill, but he knows that his actions will create a substantial and unjustifiable risk of death or serious injury.

Sedition: Common law offense that prohibits teaching or advocating the overthrow of government.

Self-defense: A defense that permits a person to use a reasonable amount of force, even deadly force, to protect him or herself against the threat of bodily harm. The threat must be imminent, and the amount of force used must be proportionate to the threat.

Sentencing guidelines: Federal and state rules that determine the factors that will impact the sentencing calculation.

Sexting: The sending of sexually explicit text messages.

Smith Act: Federal Act passed in 1940 that banned teaching and advocacy designed to cause the overthrow of the U.S. government.

Edward Snowden case: Case involving U.S. citizen who while employed as a contractor for the National Security Agency, downloaded and disseminated thousands of classified documents to news agencies, revealing the CIA's wide-spread surveillance of U.S. citizens.

Sodomy: An offense at common law that criminalizes certain sexual acts, including oral and anal sex.

Solicitation: Inchoate offense that involves encouraging another person to engage in a criminal act.

Stalking: A course of conduct directed at a specific person that would cause a reasonable person to fear.

Stand your ground laws: Self-defense laws that permit a person to defend herself against a threat using a proportionate amount of force without retreating, even if she could do so safely.

State legislation: Laws enacted by state legislatures that apply to offenders who commit crimes within the state.

State-involved crimes: Crimes that involve either wrongdoing by public officials (e.g., bribery) or crimes committed against the state (e.g., espionage).

Status crimes: Crimes that involve having a certain condition or status rather than doing an act with a particular state of mind.

Statutory rape: The common law term used to describe the crime of an adult having sex with a minor under the age of consent. Many modern statutes no longer use this term but define the crime as a form of sexual assault.

Strict liability: The criminalization of a particular voluntary act even when the actor does not have a guilty state of mind.

Substantial step: Test to determine whether a defendant's actions satisfy the actus reus requirement for attempt.

Symbolic speech: Speech communicated through the use of images or symbols, such flag burning.

Syndrome defenses: Defenses that involve the defendant claiming that he should not be held criminally responsible because he was suffering from some recognized condition that prohibited him from either controlling his behavior or forming the requisite mens rea for the specific crime. Syndrome defenses are usually partial defenses.

Target offense: The crime an offender takes steps toward committing and intends to carry out.

Terrorism: Intentional actions taken by an individual or group, with the objective of destabilizing a government or political action, typically through the creation of fear and violence.

Theft: The term used in modern statutes to describe larceny, embezzlement, and false pretenses. These statutes often consolidate these crimes in one theft statute.

Threats: An inchoate offense that involves promises to harm, injure, or kill with intent to place the victim in fear.

Time, place, and manner: Regulations by government entities that state when and where public speech may take place, such as regulations for a public university that list the rules for when students may hold protest rallies on campus.

Tort: A civil wrong may involve a lawsuit by someone (plaintiff) who complains that another person or entity (defendant) caused him harm. The remedy for a tort action is typically monetary compensation.

Treason: Crime of betraying one's country by providing damaging, classified government information to enemies of the country. It is the only crime explicitly referenced in the U.S. Constitution.

Treaties: Source of criminal law, when treaties impose criminal sanctions for violations.

U.S. Constitution: Founding U.S. document that encompasses rights, privileges, guarantees, immunities, and protections promised by the state to citizens.

U.S. Supreme Court: The highest court within the United States judicial system; it has nine Justices and hears cases involving matters of federal and constitutional law.

Vagrancy: Public order offense that involves idling or loitering in a public place.

Victim impact statement: A statement prepared by a crime victim that is submitted to a judge before he sentences the defendant. In this statement, the victim may share her feelings about the case, including the pain and suffering the crime caused her and her family, her anger toward the offender, and the punishment she believes the court should impose.

Victimless crime: Actions engaged in by consenting adults, such as prostitution, gambling, and drug use. Some people refer to these acts as "victimless" offenses and argue that they should not be subject to governmental regulation.

Void for vagueness: Laws that are unconstitutional under the due process clause because they are so general and unclear that they do not provide notice to the public as to which actions are criminal.

Voluntary act: An act done consciously and willingly, as opposed to actions taken while a person is unconscious (for example, a seizure or reflexive act).

Voluntary intoxication: A defense that involves the defendant voluntarily ingesting alcohol or some mind-altering drug and claiming that he or she could not formulate the required mens rea for the crime. It is rarely permitted as a defense, but states that do allow the defense permit it only in cases involving specific intent crimes.

Voluntary manslaughter: The intentional killing of a human being in the heat of passion caused by adequate provocation.

Weapon offenses: A broad category of offenses that prohibit the use of weapons. These laws prohibit the possession, sale, display, and use of certain weapons.

Weapons of mass destruction: Type of weapon that can cause substantial harm and death; may be a chemical, radiological, or nuclear weapon.

White-collar crime: The term used to describe a broad range of property crimes, including embezzlement, fraud, computer crimes, identity theft, and other nonviolent crimes involving the taking of property.

Subject Index

Case Index

⑤SAGE research**methods**

The essential online tool for researchers from the world's leading methods publisher

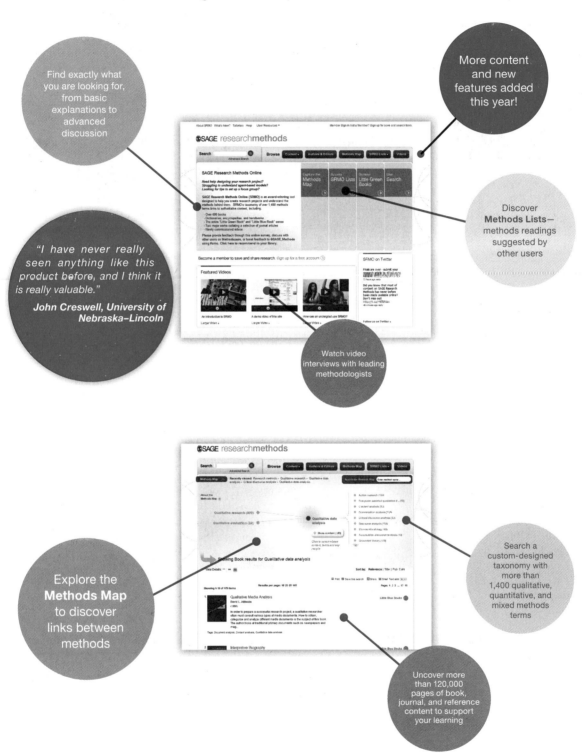

Find exactly what you are looking for, from basic explanations to advanced discussion

More content and new features added this year!

"I have never really seen anything like this product before, and I think it is really valuable."

John Creswell, University of Nebraska–Lincoln

Discover **Methods Lists**— methods readings suggested by other users

Watch video interviews with leading methodologists

Explore the **Methods Map** to discover links between methods

Search a custom-designed taxonomy with more than 1,400 qualitative, quantitative, and mixed methods terms

Uncover more than 120,000 pages of book, journal, and reference content to support your learning

Find out more at
www.sageresearchmethods.com